ISBN 978-1-397-32199-2
PIBN 11374588

1 MONTH OF
FREE
READING

at
www.ForgottenBooks.com

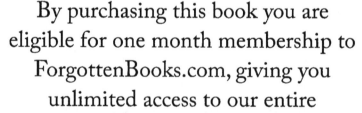

By purchasing this book you are eligible for one month membership to ForgottenBooks.com, giving you unlimited access to our entire collection of over 1,000,000 titles via our web site and mobile apps.

To claim your free month visit:
www.forgottenbooks.com/free1374588

ANNUAL REPORT

OF THE

⊰BOARD OF HEALTH⊱

OF THE

STATE OF LOUISIANA

⊰To The General Assembly,⊱

FOR THE YEAR 1880

NEW ORLEANS:

J. S. RIVERS, STATIONER AND PRINTER, 74 CAMP STREET,

1881.

MEMBERS OF THE BOARD OF HEALTH.

JOSEPH JONES, M. D., PRESIDENT.

DR. F. FORMENTO,
DR. F. LOEBER,
ROBERT BREWSTER, ESQ.,
E. HERNANDEZ, ESQ,

EDWIN BOOTH, ESQ.,*
J. N. MARKS, ESQ.,
DR. J. C. BEARD,
DR. E. T. SHEPARD.

STANDING COMMITTEES OF THE BOARD.

Finance Committee,
MESSRS. MARKS, HERNANDEZ AND SHEPARD.

Committee of Conference with Auxiliary Sanitary Association,
MESSRS. BEARD, LOEBER, MARKS, FORMENTO AND BOOTH.

Committee on Monthly Reports,
MESSRS. FORMENTO, BOOTH AND SHEPARD.

Committee on Street-Cleaning,
DR. FORMENTO.

Committee on Apparatus of Vidangeurs,
MESSRS. BEARD, SHEPARD AND BREWSTER.

Committee on Sewerage,
MESSRS. BOOTH, MARKS AND FORMENTO.

Secretary and Treasurer,
S. S. HERRICK, M. D.

Attorney,
H. L. O'DONNELL, ESQ.

Clerks of Registration,
MR. H. PERALTA,   MR. P. H. LANAUZE.

Clerk and Book-keeper of the Board,
MR. JAMES S. ZACHARIE.

Collector and Messenger,
MR B. B HOWARD,

Coal Oil Inspectors,
MR. EUGENE LeGARDEUR,   MR. C. F. HUMBRECHT,

Vice J. P. Davidson, M. D., *Resigned,*

SANITARY INSPECTORS.

First District - - - - - - JOSEPH HOLT, M. D.
Second District - - - - - W. R. MANDEVILLE, M. D.
Third District - - - - - - W. H. WATKINS, M. D.
Fourth District - - - - - R. A. BAYLEY, M. D.
Fifth District - - - - - E. J. MIOTON, M. D.
Sixth and Seventh District - - - W. H. CARSON, M. D.

SANITARY POLICE OFFICERS.

First District,
HENRY KOHLHAASE.   T. J. KELLEHER.

Second District,
L. C. WILTZ.   D. MAYRONNE.

Third District,
T. C. WILL.

Fourth District,
CHARLES CURTIS.   E. LUSSAN.

Fifth District,
H. LABARRE.

Sixth District,
H. F. EVANS.

Seventh District,
H. F. DAVIS.

For Inspection of Shipping in Port,
HENRY DUCATEL.

CONTENTS.

Contents.

ILLUSTRATIONS OF PRESIDENT'S REPORT.

REPORT OF

JOSEPH JONES, M. D.,

PRESIDENT OF THE

╼BOARD OF HEALTH╾

OF THE

STATE OF LOUISIANA.

FOR THE YEAR 1880.

INTRODUCTION.

To His Excellency, Louis A. Wiltz, Governor of Louisiana:

SIR :—The Board of Health of the State of Louisiana, have the honor to submit, through your Excellency, to the General Assembly of Louisiana, the annual report for the year eighteen hundred and eighty.

Louisiana has been free from epidemics of contagious and infectious diseases during the year 1880.

The remarkable exemption of New Orleans from contagious and infectious diseases, as well as its undoubted healthfulness during the past year, are clearly demonstrated by the following comparative tables of the mortality from the various forms of fever, diarrhœal diseases, congestion of the brain, convulsions, phthisis pulmonalis, and from all causes, in the individual months during the past twelve years —1869 to 1880.

COMPARATIVE TABLE OF THE MORTALITY IN THE CITY OF NEW ORLEANS DURING THE MONTH OF

JANUARY

DURING THE YEARS 1869 TO 1830 INCLUSIVE. SHOWING DEATHS BY SOME OF THE PRINCIPAL DISEASES. TOTAL NUMBER OF DEATHS AND DEATH RATE PER 1000 INHABITANTS PER ANNUM.

	1869.	1870.	1871.	1872.	1873.	1874.	1875.	1876.	1877.	1878.	1879.	1880.	Total deaths for 12 years.
Yellow Fever........	....	....	....	....	....	....	....	....	....	....	....	....	....
Malarial Fever......	13	15	7	15	17	11	10	15	22	10	5	10	150
Typhoid Fever......	6	4	7	3	9	3	2	3	4	2	2	6	51
Scarlet Fever........	....	3	1	....	....	....	1	19	1	....	....	1	26
Measles..............	....	....	....	1	....	....	....	....	....	....	....	....	1
Small Pox...........	3	69	....	....	64	87	32	8	126	13	....	....	402
Diphtheria..........	2	3	....	4	7	8	1	4	7	3	7	5	51
Diarrhœal Diseases ..	21	22	26	24	20	24	48	18	23	16	23	29	294
Cong. of the Brain..	11	7	6	14	17	12	8	8	7	2	15	6	113
Convulsions.........	16	28	21	23	23	15	26	14	17	15	7	15	220
Phthisis Pulmonalis..	42	56	55	56	90	81	80	76	74	65	76	67	818
Total number deaths	328	471	443	447	642	583	572	434	571	403	574	446	5914
Death-rate per 1000..	20.83	29.59	27.83	28.08	40.33	33.31	32 68	24.80	32.62	23.02	32.80	24.77	29.24

FEBRUARY.

	1869.	1870.	1871.	1872.	1873.	1874.	1875.	1876.	1877.	1878.	1879.	1880.	Total deaths for 12 years
Yellow Fever........	....	....	....	....	....	....	....	....	....	....	....	....	....
Malarial Fever......	8	9	11	20	14	12	8	14	20	7	3	13	139
Typhoid Fever.......	4	5	5	5	9	1	5	6	8	2	1	4	55
Scarlet Fever........	2	5	....	....	....	1	1	29	....	....	1		39
Measles.............	2	....	....	9	1	....	....	....	....	....	....	1	13
Small Pox...........	1	56	2	2	83	82	44	25	191	20	....	....	506
Diphtheria...........	....	....	2	5	1	4	6	5	2	4	4	4	37
Diarrhœal Diseases..	8	10	16	35	27	18	16	14	9	15	13	15	196
Congestion of Brain..	9	7	8	22	7	14	3	11	7	6	4	7	105
Convulsions.........	13	19	16	21	18	23	16	6	12	11	10	6	171
Phthisis Pulmonalis.	43	52	54	81	58	64	84	60	81	55	73	69	774
Total number deaths	292	429	347	630	556	481	454	460	529	511	360	438	5546
Death-rate per 1000..	18.34	26.95	21 80	30.58	34.93	27.42	23.94	26 28	33 63	29 20	20.57	24.33	27.38
Population..........			191000				210000				216000	Av.pop. 202500(x)	

4   *Louisiana Board of Health.*

COMPARATIVE TABLE OF THE MORTALITY IN THE CITY OF NEW ORLEANS DURING
THE MONTH OF

MARCH.

OF THE YEARS 1869 TO 1880 INCLUSIVE, SHOWING DEATHS BY SOME OF THE PRINCI-
PAL DISEASES, TOTAL NUMBER OF DEATHS AND DEATH RATE PER 1000 INHABI-
TANTS PER ANNUM.

	1869.	1870.	1871.	1872.	1873.	1874.	1875.	1876.	1877.	1878.	1879.	1880.	Total deaths for 12 years.
Yellow Fever........	....	....	....	....	....	....	....	....	....	....	....	....	....
Malarial Fever......	13	20	15	20	20	12	14	13	12	16	11	18	184
Typhoid Fever......	2	14	8	5	3	2	4	5	5	1	1	4	54
Scarlet Fever.......	....	....	....	....	....	....	2	27	3	1	....	6	39
Measles..............	22	2	....	2	6	....	....	9	7	....	....	4	52
Small Pox...........	1	121	....	5	79	88	94	22	260	52	....	....	722
Diphtheria...........	1	....	....	3	....	6	10	2	4	4	3	5	38
Diarrhœal Diseases..	21	11	31	14	34	14	11	21	21	15	17	17	227
Congestion of Brain.	6	7	8	15	15	13	6	15	5	12	12	7	121
Convulsions.........	24	16	16	8	16	13	15	14	16	15	4	11	168
Phthisis Pulmonalis..	48	81	84	58	66	52	67	94	86	77	77	85	432
Total number deaths	408	600	491	430	603	452	461	553	788	437	376	402	6007
Death rate per 1000..	25.63	37.69	30.84	27.01	37.88	23.92	26 34	31.94	45.02	24.97	21.48	22.34	29.66

APRIL.

	1869.	1870.	1871.	1872.	1873.	1874.	1875.	1876.	1877.	1878.	1879.	1880.	Total deaths for 12 years.
Yellow Fever........	....	....	....	....	....	....	....	....	....	....	....	....	....
Malarial Fever......	16	20	15	14	17	16	19	19	23	23	8	14	204
Typhoid Fever......	5	2	9	3	3	1	5	2	6	2	3	4	45
Scarlet Fever.......	2	7	....	1	1	....	2	18	4	....	....	3	38
Measles..............	45	2	....	2	10	6	....	....	30	2	1	20	118
Small Pox...........	2	123	....	....	5	67	94	62	25	157	31	....	565
Diphtheria..........	4	1	1	2	2	9	4	2	3	10	4	2	44
Diarrhœal Diseases..	35	19	64	24	108	24	18	17	32	32	28	20	421
Congestion of Brain.	10	7	5	13	10	15	12	11	8	10	4	7	122
Convulsions.........	52	17	19	14	15	16	12	21	14	14	16	16	226
Phthisis Pulmonalis.	72	74	56	49	68	79	65	58	57	66	74	68	786
Total number deaths	559	545	440	418	600	609	522	447	555	475	369	461	6000
Death rate per 1000..	35.12	34.24	27.64	26.26	37 69	34.80	29 82	25.54	31 71	27.14	21.03	25 61	29.82

MAY.

	1869.	1870.	1871	1872.	1873.	1874.	1875.	1876.	1877.	1878.	1879.	1880.	Total deaths for 12 years.
Yellow Fever........	....	....	....	....	....	....	....	....	....	....	....	....	....
Malarial Fever......	22	31	11	31	30	24	15	20	18	16	13	26	257
Typhoid Fever......	7	7	4	5	4	4	4	3	5	7	3	3	56
Scarlet Fever........	2	5	2	3	....	1	2	13	....	....	1	5	34
Measles.............	74	5	1	22	21	....	....	72	....	....	....	39	234
Small Pox...........	....	78	....	4	71	79	26	11	105	12	....	1	387
Diphtheria..........	1	4	....	6	2	6	6	4	3	3	2	4	41
Diarrhœal Diseases..	48	61	38	68	238	66	38	47	54	55	42	45	800
Con. of Brain.......	19	9	5	22	21	12	14	14	12	6	10	12	156
Convulsions.........	25	22	16	35	30	19	13	21	9	16	13	26	245
Phthisis Pulmonalis..	59	53	59	79	73	67	52	70	71	68	71	69	791
Total number deaths.	602	621	411	713	930	548	403	601	738	535	509	581	7192
Death rate per 1000...	37.82	39.01	25.82	44.79	57.90	31.31	23.02	34.34	42.17	30.57	29.08	32.27	35.51
Population..........	191,000						210.000					216000	Av. pop. 202,500

COMPARATIVE TABLE OF THE MORTALITY IN THE CITY OF NEW ORLEANS DURING THE MONTH OF

JUNE.

OF THE YEARS 1869 TO 1880 INCLUSIVE, SHOWING DEATHS BY SOME OF THE PRINCIPAL DISEASES, TOTAL NUMBER OF DEATHS AND DEATH RATE PER 1000 INHABITANTS PER ANNUM.

	1869.	1870.	1871.	1872.	1873.	1874.	1875.	1876.	1877.	1878.	1879.	1880.	Total deaths for 12 years.
Yellow Fever.........	....	1	....	....	....	....	....	....	....	....	....	....	1
Malarial Fever.......	19	50	35	18	25	24	26	23	47	26	16	32	341
Typhoid Fever.......	4	7	7	4	2	13	5	3	7	3	3	5	63
Scarlet Fever.......	2	8	....	....	....	....	8	6	1	....	....	6	31
Measles.............	51	9	....	17	13	....	....	63	1	....	...	23	177
Small Pox...........	3	59	....	1	35	73	30	10	137	18	....	....	366
Diphtheria..........	2	2	....	....	1	10	....	5	5	6	5	9	45
Diarrhœal Diseases..	55	81	67	41	56	33	81	62	10?	52	53	56	738
Con. of Brain........	9	4	20	12	19	10	15	6	22	9	9	15	150
Convulsions.........	34	28	26	39	27	18	24	27	19	16	17	14	289
Phthisis Pulmonalis..	62	64	74	66	58	58	59	64	92	108	37	70	812
Total number deaths.	525	673	535	572	562	517	551	605	633	427	402	573	6985
Death rate per 1000 ..	32.98	42.28	33.61	35.90	35.30	29.54	31.48	35.14	36.31	24.40	22.97	31.83	34.48

JULY.

	1869.	1870.	1871.	1872.	1873.	1874.	1875.	1876.	1877.	1878.	1879.	1880.	Total deaths for 12 years.
Yellow Fever........	1	....	....	....	3	....	...	....	....	26	3	1	34
Malarial Fever.......	47	43	40	34	62	67	39	55	41	47	33	26	534
Typhoid Fever	6	5	7	7	4	17	5	9	9	3	6	7	85
Scarlet Fever........	2	5	2	1	1	....	20	5	....	....	....	11	47
Measles.............	20	3	6	10	16	....	....	20	1	....	....	9	85
Small Pox	....	14	....	....	11	41	24	17	56	5	....	....	168
Diphtheria..........	6	....	1	3	3	13	7	4	1	5	2	6	51
Diarrhœal Diseases..	54	42	46	30	71	52	62	54	49	39	57	32	588
Con. of Brain........	15	8	17	17	20	22	16	19	9	11	8	11	173
Convulsions.........	33	20	26	12	45	21	31	19	17	18	10	14	266
Phthisis Pulmonalis..	67	66	58	66	83	63	77	82	70	69	98	67	866
Total number deaths.	551	497	488	483	773	700	622	635	504	492	422	422	6589
Death rate per 1000..	34.61	31.22	30.65	30.34	48.56	40.00	35.54	36.28	28.80	28.11	23.63	23.44	32.53

AUGUST.

	1869.	1870.	1871.	1872.	1873.	1874.	1875.	1876.	1877.	1878.	1879.	1880.	Total deaths for 12 years.
Yellow Fever	....	3	2	1	19	....	5	1	....	1025	4	....	1060
Malarial Fever.......	60	46	64	46	55	125	63	38	61	177	30	30	795
Typhoid Fever.......	9	8	8	6	7	18	8	5	5	10	1	4	89
Scarlet Fever........	....	2	....	....	1	1	21	3	....	....	....	4	32
Measles.............	1	....	1	3	3	....	....	10	....	1	....	1	20
Small Pox	1	4	....	....	2	10	14	6	22	....	....	...	59
Diphtheria..........	2	1	1	....	4	6	11	3	2	4	9	7	50
Diarrhœal Diseases ..	36	37	39	39	30	42	26	27	37	57	21	26	417
Con. of Brain	7	14	21	26	14	76	3	24	....	33	7	9	234
Convulsions.........	16	11	22	29	29	19	27	5	9	43	16	21	247
Phthisis Pulmonalis..	59	48	63	76	64	69	62	63	57	88	47	54	750
Total number deaths.	421	480	551	569	498	708	447	403	516	1784	422	407	7506
Death rate per 1000...	26.45	30.15	34.61	35.74	31.28	40.45	25.54	23.02	29.47	101.94	24.11	22.61	37.06 Av. pop.
Population...........	191,000					210,000					216000		202,500

COMPARATIVE TABLE OF THE MORTALITY IN THE CITY OF NEW ORLEANS DURING THE MONTH OF

SEPTEMBER

OF THE YEARS 1869 TO 1880, INCLUSIVE, SHOWING DEATHS BY SOME OF THE PRINCIPAL DISEASES, TOTAL NUMBER OF DEATHS AND DEATH RATE PER 1000 INHABITANTS PER ANNUM.

	1869.	1870.	1871.	1872.	1873.	1874.	1875.	1876.	1877.	1878.	1879.	1880.	Total deaths for 12 years.
Yellow Fever	....	231	9	5	108	2	24	20	....	1,780	7	.	2,186
Malarial Fever	61	90	65	38	91	50	100	83	79	229	19	79	984
Typhoid Fever	1	12	3	10	6	9	7	7	3	10	5	3	76
Scarlet Fever	....	2	....	....	....	....	28	1	1	....	....	1	33
Measles	....	....	....	1	....	....	....	4	3	1	....	....	9
Small-Pox	1	3	...	....	7	6	4	4	16	....	....	....	41
Diphtheria	....	1	1	5	6	6	8	1	2	5	4	3	42
Diarrhœal Diseases	35	41	27	29	30	36	38	37	32	29	21	23	378
Congestion of Brain	7	13	12	12	15	14	13	30	12	29	4	19	180
Convulsions	25	22	9	21	23	10	25	11	12	49	8	16	231
Phthisis Pulmonalis	51	71	63	57	67	51	87	88	83	89	54	65	826
Total number deaths	422	858	451	425	624	440	675	596	439	2,55?	324	450	8,262
Death rate per 1000	26.51	53.91	28.33	26.70	39.20	25.14	38.57	34 05	25.08	146.17	18.51	25.00	40.80

OCTOBER.

	1869.	1870.	1871.	1872.	1873.	1874.	1875.	1876.	1877.	1878.	1879.	1880.	Total deaths for 12 years.
Yellow Fever	2	242	22	24	79	6	20	15	....	1,065	5	1	1,481
Malarial Fever	35	48	45	32	79	79	55	56	40	163	32	39	703
Typhoid Fever	10	6	7	6	3	16	1	2	7	...	2	7	67
Scarlet Fever	....	2	....	....	1	....	19	....	....	....	....	2	24
Measles	....	2	1	....	2	....	....	5	1	....	....	...	11
Small-Pox	5	....	....	1	8	2	4	5	13	....	....	....	38
Diphtheria	1	1	2	5	7	7	7	....	1	2	10	13	56
Diarrhœal Diseases	30	28	27	26	34	46	20	35	27	24	26	25	348
Congestion of Brain	5	4	8	18	23	17	8	10	6	27	10	12	148
Convulsions	30	16	23	16	30	16	20	11	10	29	15	15	231
Phthisis Pulmonalis	60	55	66	79	89	81	58	66	63	59	101	60	837
Total number deaths	474	681	441	532	713	636	473	439	417	1,845	492	466	7,609
Death rate per 1000	29.78	42.78	27.70	33 42	44.79	36.34	27.00	25 08	23 83	105 42	28.11	25.88	37.57

NOVEMBER.

	1869.	1870.	1871.	1872.	1873.	1874.	1875.	1876.	1877.	1878.	1879.	1880.	Total deaths for 12 years.
Yellow Fever	....	106	19	7	17	2	9	4	1	147	....	....	......
Malarial Fever	27	46	26	11	25	36	18	41	29	55	20	....	......
Typhoid Fever	3	4	4	4	5	7	7	6	5	4	3	....	......
Scarlet Fever	1	1	...	4	1	....	20	1	....	....	....	....	......
Measles	2	....	....	1	1	....	1	9	....	...	....	....	......
Small-Pox	32	1	....	....	26	10	1	30	7	....	....	....	......
Diphtheria	....	4	5	5	8	14	3	6	1	7	7	....	......
Diarrhœal Diseases	44	45	45	31	45	38	20	29	44	27	22	....	......
Congestion of Brain	2	12	16	6	16	6	9	20	9	6	8	....	......
Convulsions	20	21	22	15	16	28	19	12	11	22	9	....	......
Phthisis Pulmonalis	60	53	88	68	57	66	52	92	83	89	54	....	......
Total number deaths	452	465	568	430	500	527	443	587	543	492	400	....	......
Death rate per 1000	28.39	29.22	35.68	27 01	31.41	30 20	25.31	33.54	31.03	28.11	23 28	....	......
Population	191,000					210,000						216000	Av. pop. 202,500

COMPARATIVE TABLE OF THE MORTALITY IN THE CITY OF NEW ORLEANS DURING THE MONTH OF

DECEMBER

OF THE YEARS 1869 TO 1880, INCLUSIVE, SHOWING DEATHS BY SOME OF THE PRINCIPAL DISEASES, TOTAL NUMBER OF DEATHS AND DEATH RATE PER 1000 INHABITANTS PER ANNUM.

	1869.	1870.	1871.	1872.	1873.	1874.	1875.	1876.	1877.	1878.	1879.	1880.	Total deaths for 12 years.
Yellow Fever........	....	5	2	2	....	1	3	1	....	3	....	....	......
Malarial Fever......	21	17	14	12	11	32	16	24	17	8	12	....	......
Typhoid Fever	6	6	2	9	2	4	4	5	5	....	3	....	......
Scarlet Fever	2	4	....	....	....	1	21	2	....	....	....	....	......
Measles..............	...	...	1	....	....	....	....	2	....	....	....	....	......
Small-Pox..........	88	1	....	11	52	15	7	69	69	....	....	....	......
Diphtheria..........	...	2	1	1	5	13	6	6	2	6	7	....	......
Diarrhœal Diseases ..	35	35	26	29	31	36	21	25	20	24	22	....	......
Congestion of Brain..	9	7	15	9	15	3	10	16	9	4	4	....	......
Convulsions.........	21	26	8	15	10	24	27	8	9	15	12	....	......
Phthisis Pulmonalis	60	84	60	59	72	74	56	69	71	47	61	....	......
Total number deaths	563	572	429	473	504	597	494	560	415	359	459	....	......
Death rate per 1000 ..	35.37	35.93	26.95	29 71	31.66	34.11	28.23	32.00	23.71	20.51	26.23	....	Av.Pop.
Population.........			191,000					210,000				210000	202,500

It is worthy of note, that in this great city, with its 216,000 inhabitants, extending twelve miles along the banks of the Mississippi River, during the year 1880, only two deaths were reported by the physicians of New Orleans, as due to yellow fever; and one of these was an imported case from the bark Excelsior.

During the entire year 1880 less than one dozen cases of fever were reported by the entire medical profession of New Orleans, in which a consultation was requested with the President of the Board; and in each and every case submitted to the Board of Health the malarious nature of the fever was recognized. Under the proper division of this report, a comprehensive statement of these cases will be given.

The annual death-rate per 1,000 inhabitants was far less for the ten individual months of 1880, recorded in the preceding tables, than for the similar months during the twelve years—1869-1880, inclusive—as will be manifest from the following comparison:

DEATH RATE PER 1,000 INHABITANTS.

	1880.	Average 12 years. 1869-1880.
January	24.77	29.24
February	24.33	27.38
March	22.34	29.66
April	25.61	29.82
May	32.27	35.51
June	31.83	34.48
July	23.44	32.53
August	22.61	37.06
September	25.00	40.80
October	25.88	37.57

The National Board of Health and its agents and employees have asserted through the columns of the daily press, through the pages of the Bulletin of this National Board of Health, and of the New Orleans Medical and Surgical Journal edited by one of this organization, that yellow fever was propagated by the bark Excelsior and that an indefinite number of cases occurred in and around New Orleans.

If the statements of the members, agents and employees of the National Board of Health be true, the mortuary records of the city of New Orleans should manifest the havoc created by this disease, the Board of Health and the entire medical profession of Louisiana, to the contrary notwithstanding.

A critical examination of the mortuary records of New Orleans shows: that the annual mortality per 1000 inhabitants was greater in the month of June, 1880, than in the corresponding month in 1874, 1875, 1878 and 1879, 32 deaths were caused by the various forms of malarial fever, 5 by typhoid, 6 by scarlet fever, 23 by measles; in July the death rate fell to 23.44, against 31.83 in the preceeding month, and was lower than in any similar month during the preceeding twelve years, 1869–1880; the death rate was even lower in August, being only 22.61, and lower than in the same month during the period embraced from 1869 to 1880; in September the death-rate was only 25.00, and was less than that of any similar month, with exception of September, 1879; and in October, when a death from Yellow Fever was reported, the death-rate was only 25.88, and was lower than the similar month, with the exception of 1876 and 1877, in both of which years the mortality in October was slightly less.

During the year 1880, the monthly rate of mortality in New Orleans compared favorably with those of all large cities in America and Europe, and an illustration of an important fact was offered, that in the absence of epidemic diseases, the death-rate of New Orleans may be actually lower in the hot months than in the colder months of the year.

Had Yellow Fever been present in New Orleans during the past summer and autumn, instead of a progressive decline of mortality in the months of September and October, there would on the other hand have been a progressive increase, especially during the month of September, as will be clearly seen from the following statistics, illustrating the date of appearance and mortality from Yellow Fever during a period of 32 years:

YELLOW FEVER FROM 1847 TO 1878—NEW ORLEANS.
MONTHLY DEATHS BY YELLOW FEVER DURING A PERIOD OF THIRTY-TWO YEARS.

Year.	May.	June.	July.	August.	September.	October.	November.	December.	Total Deaths by Yellow Fever.	Date of First Case.
1847	..	..	74	965	1,100	198	33	.....	2,359	July 6.
1848	..	4	33	200	467	226	20	.....	759	June 21.
1849	..	..	1	17	214	416	112	9	769	July 28.
1850	1	..	4	62	33	4	....	.....	107	1 death January, 2 March, 1 May.
1851	..	..	....	8	6	2	1	.....	17	
1852	..	..	2	8	91	198	105	11	415	July.
1853	2	31	1,521	5,133	982	147	28	4	7,849	May 22.
1854	..	2	29	532	1,234	490	131	7	2,425	First death June 12.
1855	..	5	382	1,286	874	97	19	7	2,670	June 19.
1856	..	..	....	14	40	16	4	7	74	June 28.
10 years.	3	42	2,046	8,225	5,041	1,796	453	38	17,444	
1857	..	1	1	8	98	82	8		200	1 death reported in January.
1858	..	2	132	1,140	2,204	1,137	224	5	4,845	1 death reported January 10.
1859	..	..	......	1	59	28	3		91	June.
1860	..	..	3	7	5				15	
1861										
1862	..	..	1		1				2	
1863	..	..	....		2				2	About 100 cases in U. S. S. River Fleet.
1864	..	..	....			4	1	1	6	⎰ About 200 cases and 57 deaths, U. S. Gun-
1865	..	..	....	1					1	⎱ boats and River Fleet.
1866	..	..	....	5	56	89	81	4	185	1 death August 10.
10 years.	..	3	137	1,154	2,277	1,387	339	21	5,347	
1867	..	3	11	255	1,637	1,072	103	26	3,107	1 case died June 10.
1868	..	..	......			5			5	October 5, died in Charity Hospital.
1869	..	..	1		2				3	July 17.
1870	..	1	....	3	231	242	106	5	588	May 26.
1871	..	..	....	2	9	22	19	2	54	July 30.
1872	..	..	....	1	5	24	7	2	39	August 28.
1873	..	..	3	19	108	79	17	.....	226	July 9.
1874	..	..	......		2	6	2	1	11	August 19.
1875	..	..	....	5	24	20	9	3	61	August 8.
1876	..	..	....	1	19	17	4	1	42	August 11.
10 years.	..	4	15	288	2,037	1,484	267	39	4,136	
1877	..	..	......				1	.....	1	November.
1878	2	..	50	974	1,893	1,044	90	3	4,056	May 22.
2 years.	2	..	50	974	1,893	1,044	91	3	4,057	
32 years.	5	49	2,248	10,641	11,158	5,711	1,150	101	30,984	

From the preceding table it is evident that as a general rule the great epidemics, as those of 1847, 1848, 1849, 1853, 1854, 1855, 1858, 1867 and 1878, commenced early in the hot months—May, June and July—and attained their maximum intensity in August and September. Thus, during the entire period of thirty-two years the deaths from Yellow Fever in New Orleans were as follows : January, 6; February, 0; March, 2; April, 0; May, 5; June, 49; July, 2248; August, 10,641; September, 11,158; October, 5711; November, 1150; December, 101. The curve of Yellow Fever, therefore, corresponds to a certain extent with the curve of temperature. Thus, from the records of thirty-eight years, which have been consolidated and calculated from the most reliable data, the mean temperature of New Orleans is as follows: January, 56.28; February, 58.03; March, 64.27; April, 69.41; May, 75.00, June, 81.35; July, 83.21; August, 83.14; September, 79.64; October, 70.27; November, 62.30; December, 56.43. Spring, 69.56; summer, 82.53; autumn, 70.75; winter, 56.91. Year, 69.51 F.

The exemption of New Orleans from epidemics of contagious and infectious diseases, and especially from *Yellow Fever*, during 1880, was due to several causes, amongst which may be mentioned as of importance.

2

1. CLIMATIC CAUSES.

Under this head are included the low temperature and abundant rains of the past summer.

2. RIGID AND EFFECTIVE QUARANTINE MEASURES.

That the system of fumigation by means of sulphurous acid gas, was effective in destroying the cause of Yellow Fever in the holds and cargoes of ships, appeared to find confirmation in the histories of the ships from Rio, and especially in that of the only one brought prominently before the public. So thorough and effective was the disinfection of the cargo of the ship Excelsior, that although discharged in the heart of this great city, not a case of disease has been traced to this source.

The prompt action of the Board of Health in removing the bark Excelsior back to Quarantine, certainly freed the city of New Orleans from the infected crew, and in the opinion of a portion at least of the medical profession, preserved the citizens from an epidemic.

3. THE RIGID EXECUTION OF THE SANITARY LAWS OF THE BOARD OF HEALTH.

Under the direction and by the orders of the Board of Health a system of inspection by the sanitary inspectors and police has been carried on, and thousands of foul privies have been disinfected, and their contents poured into the Mississippi river.

Nearly one hundred thousand pounds of copperas have been gratuitously distributed by the officers of the Board of Health, and this powerful disinfectant and deodorizer has removed vast volumes of the most noxious of all gases, namely, sulphuretted hydrogen, from the atmosphere of this city.

The garbage, as well as the fœcal matters of the city, have been systematically and daily removed, and large sections of the city have been benefited by the labors of the New Orleans Auxiliary Sanitary Association in flushing the gutters.

The preceding statistics and facts expose fully the nature of the attempt on the part of the members and employees of the National Board of Health, and more especially of the resident member of the National Board of Health, to create the impression upon the minds of the civil and health authorities of surrounding States, who have not daily access to the mortuary records of New Orleans, and who are not brought in contact with the learned and honorable practitioners of medicine of this great city, that an indefinite number of cases of Yellow Fever have occurred within the confines of New Orleans during the year 1880, and that said cases were concealed by the profession and Board of Health, and more especially by the president.

It is worthy of note that although the resident member of the National Board of Health has resorted to the daily press and to his Medical Journal, (New Orleans Medical and Surgical Journal) and to the pages of the Bulletin of the National Board of Health, for the deliverance of his attacks upon the Board of Health of the State of Louisiana, at the same time *no member or employe of the National Board of Health has officially reported a case of Yellow Fever within the confines of the city of New Orleans, in accordance with the laws of the State of Louisiana, during the year 1880.*

If Yellow Fever was present in New Orleans, and if the President and Board of Health concealed its existence, and if the entire medical profession of New Orleans, were banded together to delude the surrounding States; how did it happen that the resident member of the National Board of Health and his employees, did not officially report cases, according to the laws of the city and State, which impose a severe fine upon any physician who fails to report a case of Yellow Fever within twenty-four hours of its occurrence?

The falsity of the charge that the Board of Health of the State of Louisiana, had misrepresented the sanitary condition of New Orleans during the year 1880, and that cases of Yellow Fever had been concealed, is shown by the statements of the most eminent practitioners of medicine of New Orleans and by the fact that the weekly mortality classified absolutely according to the death certificates of the physicians of New Orleans, were regularly sent to the National Board of Health and to all surrounding Boards of Health. The Board of Health at its regular weekly meetings, has published a larger number of carefully prepared statistics, and has given fuller reports of all diseases, than any other board of health in the United States. Every meeting of the Board of Health has been open to the representatives of the press, not only of New Orleans, but of New York, St. Louis, Cincinnati and Galveston.

The Board of Health of the State of Louisiana, by its candid statements, by the weekly publication and dissemination of the mortuary reports, and by the frank and open manner in which it has thrown open everything relating to the sanitary affairs of the city and state to the honorable representatives of sister states, has preserved the city and state from panic and senseless quarantine.

The National Board of Health, after pursuing a hostile course towards the Board of Health of the State of Louisiana, has seen fit to bring its complaints before the public through the daily press and through its Bulletin, and before the President, and Congress of the United States. In view of these facts its course will be unfolded under the divisions of this report, in which it may be necessary to illustrate the official acts and sanitary labors of the Board of Health of the State of Louisiana.

At the regular meeting of the Board of Health of the State of Louisiana, held in the State House on the 28th of October, 1880, the following resolution offered by Mr. I. N. Marks, was unanimously adopted:

" Resolved that the President of the Board of Health, be requested at the earliest practicable moment, to embody and publish in the annual report of the Board of Health, all matters of importance relating to the quarantine and sanitary legislation of the state authorities,, of Louisiana with the official correspondence of the Board of Health, with State and Federal authorities; and the official investigations concerning certain diseases, with the illustrations thereof."

In accordance with the preceding resolution, the President of the Board of Health respectfully submits the following outline of the acts, labors and correspondence of the Board of Health of the State of Louisiana, classified and consolidated under the following general divisions;

(*a*). Mississippi Quarantine Station.

(*b*). Atchafalaya Quarantine Station.

(*c*). Rigolets Quarantine Station.

(*d*). Port Eads and Pilot Town and Passes of the Mississippi River.

II. Relations of National and State Boards of Health to the constituted authorities of the State of Louisiana:

(*e*). Ship Island Quarantine of the National Board of Health, established by the central national authority at Washington, District of Columbia.

(*f*). Inter-State or domestic quarantines.

III. Diseases demanding investigation as to their causes and prevention :

(*g*). Yellow Fever.

(*h*). Malarial Fever.

(*i*). Leprosy.

IV. Sanitary measures executed by the Board of Health of the State of Louisiana during the year 1880 :

(*j*). Disinfection of vaults and privies.

(*k*). Privy system, and excavation of privy vaults.

(*l*). Disposal of night-soil and garbage.

V. Legislation of the General Assembly and Board of Health of Louisiana and Council of New Orleans, relating to quarantine and domestic hygiene and sanitation :

(*m*). Classification, consolidation and publication of the acts of the Legislature of Louisiana establishing and regulating quarantine; also rules and regulations of the Board of Health of the State of Louisiana, and health ordinances of the city of New Orleans.

(*n*). General outline of the history of the quarantine and sanitary legislation of Louisiana.

VI. Vital statistics and mortuary records of New Orleans during 1880 :

(*o*). Population classified according to districts and wards.

(*p*). Births and marriages.

(*q*). Mortality.

DO NOT
SCAN

ε

t

I

.

a:
h

lε
r·
o:

ti

QUARANTINE.

QUARANTINE STATIONS OF THE STATE OF LOUISIANA.

In accordance with section 4 of "An Act to Establish Quarantine for the Protection of the State," approved March 15, 1855, the President, as early as practicable after the organization of the present Board of Health, inspected the Quarantine Stations of the State of Louisiana, and the following observations embody the main results of said inspections.

MISSISSIPPI QUARANTINE STATION

The Mississippi Quarantine Station is located upon the eastern bank of the Mississippi River, about seventy-five miles below New Orleans and thirty-five miles from the Gulf of Mexico. The grounds, immediately on the Mississippi River, are inclosed by a levee of moderate height and strength, which needs repair in several places and elevation throughout its entire extent. The levee, running parallel with the Mississippi River, is about 1700 feet in length; and the opposite, or back levee, about 1600 feet; the upper levee, which runs perpendicularly from the Mississippi River, is about 730 feet in length. The entire arena, inclosed by this levee, within the lines of which are situated the Quarantine Hospitals, physicians' residence and United States warehouse, is about 1.113,750 square feet.

The grounds slope back gently to Quarantine Bay—an arm of the Gulf of Mexico—about one mile distant.

By reference to the map of Louisiana, by the late Col. T. S. Hardee, Chief Engineer of the State of Louisiana, it will be seen that from a point about midway between New Orleans and the Gulf of Mexico, the eastern portion of the alluvial delta, through which the Misssissippi River flows, is narrowed to a mere strip of land, ranging from one to two miles in width. This entire strip of land, therefore, is subjected to peculiar climatic conditions. On the one side flows the Mississippi River, bearing its cool waters from the Alleghanys in the east, and the Rocky Mountains in the west; on the other open the waters of the broad Gulf of Mexico. Located thus between the

Mississippi River and an estuary of the Gulf of Mexico, the atmosphere is agitated by sea breezes, and the climate is purer and more stimulating than that of New Orleans.

Careful inquiry revealed the facts that whilst this narrow strip of land, is elevated only a few feet above the level of the Gulf of Mexico, at the same time from the close proximity of the atmosphere of the salt water of the Gulf, the type of malarial fever in these localities where rice is not cultivated, is mild, and many diseases of more elevated regions, as typhoid fever, inflammatory rheumatism, pneumonia, pleuritis, and phthisis are almost unknown. Under moderate circumstances, and when removed from the vicinity of rice fields, the inhabitants of this portion of Louisiana, enjoy as long lives as in the most famed regions of the tropical and semi-tropical and temperate regions of the earth; whilst at the same time the soil is of unexampled fertility, and the earth rewards the labors of the husbandman with abundant fruits and harvests. The orange attains perfection, and the sugar-cane has been known to tassel in this portion of the delta, whilst the surrounding waters abound with fish, shell fish, crabs and shrimp, and in the winter season teem with ducks and geese.

The Mississippi River at the Quarantine Station, as well as in the harbor of New Orleans, (which in depth and safety is unsurpassed by any other on this globe), affords an anchorage for ships of all sizes.

It is evident therefore from the preceding facts, that the location of the Mississippi Quarantine Station was well chosen, both for the protection of the Mississippi Valley from foreign pestilence and for the welfare and protection of shipping during the performance of Quarantine.

This Quarantine Station commands the mouths of the Mississippi River, and can be superceded by no other Quarantine removed from the banks of this river.

Quarantine establishments may be located either at the mouths of the Mississippi River, or at the head of the Passes, or further up beyond the present location, nearer the city, as was the case in former times at the English Turn. But the protection of the Mississippi Valley from the introduction of foreign pestilence, demands the existence of a thoroughly equipped and efficiently officered Quarantine establishment on the banks of the Mississippi River, between New Orleans and the Gulf of Mexico.

No one at all conversant with the topography of the coast of Louisiana, Texas, Mississippi and Alabama would for a moment conceive that the commerce of this great Valley could be forced by the way of Ship Island or any other point beyond the borders of the Mississippi River.

However and whenever detained and quarantined on the Coast of the Gulf of Mexico, ships must again undergo thorough inspection, and be subjected to rigid quarantine regulations, when they enter the gateway of the valley of the Mississippi.

Drainage canals are located on the water side of the upper and lower levee, and communicate with Quarantine Bay, and the grounds are intersected with ditches at regular intervals. The levees are covered with grass, and at the upper bank and lower lines are in better condition than on the river front.

Upon the area surrounded by the levee, the following buildings are located and in this examination we will proceed from the upper portion of the quarantine grounds downwards.

1st. *Fever Hospital.* The Hospital devoted to the treatment of fever, and more especially Yellow Fever, is a two-story frame building, situated about 230 feet from the line of the upper levee, and one hundred and fifty feet back of the levee fronting the river: 125 feet long, 33 feet wide and 35 feet high;

upper and lower galleries, 9 feet wide and 125 feet long, run along the front of the Hospital. This building contains nine rooms, on the lower floor, and four rooms on the upper; in all thirteen rooms. Halls divide the lower floor at right angles. The upper floor is divided into four capacious, well ventilated wards. The rooms and halls are plastered and the ventilation is excellent. The entire building is well adapted to the treatment of fever patients.

The following table gives the dimensions of the rooms and wards of the Fever Hospital.

Floor.	No. of Floor.	Length. Feet.	Breadth. Feet.	Height. Feet.	Capacity, Cubic feet.
First	Room, Ward No. 1	28	10	11	3080
"	Room, Ward No. 2	28	10	11	3080
"	Room, Ward No. 3	15	10	11	1650
"	Room, Ward No. 4	12	10	11	1320
"	Room, Ward No. 5	15	10	11	1650
"	Room, Ward No. 6	12	10	11	1320
"	Room, Ward No. 7	27	10	11	2970
"	Room, Ward No. 8	27	10	11	2970
"	Room, Ward No. 9	28	24	11	7392
"	Long Hall........	93	4	11	4092
"	Middle Hall... ..	24	7	11	1848
Second ...	Room, Ward No. 1	28	24	11	7392
"	Room, Ward No. 2	28	24	11	7392
	Room, Ward No. 3	28	24	11	7392
	Room, Ward No. 4	28	24	11	7392
	Cross Hall.......	24	7	11	1848
	Total capacity..	....	....	....	63,818

The wards are supplied with windows, at regular intervals in front and rear, and thorough ventilation can at all times be secured.

The cubic capacity of the wards and rooms of the Fever Hospital is 55,030 feet; of the halls and corridors 8788 cubic feet, giving a total cubic capacity, exclusive of the galleries, of 63,818 cubic feet.

If 1100 cubic feet of air be allowed to each patient, this hospital is capable of accommodating about sixty patients.

In the rear of this hospital, or connected with it by a platform 20x4 feet, is a kitchen with two room 14x14 feet and 10 feet in hight, with gallery 28x 8x14 feet.

The graveyard of the Quarantine Station is located about 200 feet to the rear of the Fever Hospital, and is surrounded by a rude fence and covers about three-fourths of an acre. Marks of about one hundred graves can be discerned in the inclosure, which are thickly covered with tall grass, brambles and shrubs.

There is only a solitary marble monument, which bears the following inscription:

"A la memoire de Trente Marins, faisant partie de l'équipage de l'avito a vaisseau de la Marine Imperiale le Tonnerre, décédés a la Quarantine de la Nouvelle Orleans en Aût, 1857. Erigé par l'odre de S. E. l'Admiral Hamelin, Ministre de la Marine de l'Empereur Napoleon III."

BOATMEN'S QUARTERS AND QUARANTINE LIGHT.

This wooden structure is situated 320 feet from the center of the Fever Hospital, immediately in front of the Levee; 31 by 21 feet, divided into six rooms. The Quarantine Light is connected with the Boatmen's quarters by a gangway 126 feet long and five feet wide, projecting into the Mississippi River. The lower portion of the Quarantine Light has been used as a boat-house until the formation of a sandbar rendered it useless for this purpose. The Quarantine Light is a wooden structure 33 by 21 feet. A large bell, which is tolled in foggy weather, is attached to the Quarantine Light. Immediately to the rear of the Boatsmen's quarters (forty feet within the line of the Levee) stands a small frame house, thirty feet square, which is used as a storehouse for disinfectants.

RESIDENCE OF QUARANTINE PHYSICIAN.

The residence of the Quarantine Physician and his assistant occupies very nearly the centre of the front of the Quarantine grounds, about 314 feet from the Boatsmen's house and 100 feet back of the levee. This small wooden building contains four rooms, a hall, gallery and kitchen. A small house, 12 by 16 feet occupies the upper angle of the small enclosure, surrounding the Resident Physician's quarters.

SMALL POX HOSPITAL.

The Small Pox Hospital, situated 500 feet from the Physician's residence and 106 feet from the front levee, has two stories, each of which has four rooms or wards, 18 feet wide, 20 feet long and 11 feet high, giving a cubic capacity of each ward of 3,960 feet, and for the entire Hospital, eight wards, 31,860 cubic feet. There is on each floor a cross-hall, 20 feet long by 7 feet wide and 11 feet high; cubic capacity of each hall, 1590 cubic feet, and of both halls, 3080 cubic feet.

Total capacity of Small Pox Hospital, (80 feet in length, 20 feet wide, 11 feet high) 34,760 cubic feet.

If 1100 cubic feet of air be allowed to each patient this Hospital would accommodate about thirty patients. Galleries run the length of the front of the Hospital, above and below, and are each 80 feet in length, 9 feet in width and 11 feet in height. There is a small building in the rear, designed as a kitchen, 14 by 14 by 10 feet.

UNITED STATES WAREHOUSE.

The government grounds commence about seventy feet from the small-pox hospital, and extend to the lower levee. The government warehouses is a substantial fire-proof brick building, situated about 125 feet from the centre of the small-pox hospital, and consists of a main hall and two wings, and is two stories in height. The upper story is supported by brick and iron arches. No wood is used in the construction of the building.

The two main halls, in the first and second floors, are each 140 feet in length by 23 feet in width, and 12 feet in height, giving a cubic capacity of 38,640 cubic feet; total 77,280 cubic feet. The two wings are each 54 feet in length and 25 feet in width, and 12 feet in height, each floor giving a capacity of 16,200 cubic feet for each wing; total capacity of wings 64,800 cubic feet; total capacity of Government Warehouse, 142,080 cubic feet.

The United States wharf is substantially built, with boat-house attached. The main wharf is 100 feet long by 30 feet, and the depth of water immediately at the river front is 22 feet. The gang-way leading from the wharf to the warehouse, is substantially built, and is 239 feet long by 20 feet wide, with wooden railway extending from the wharf to the warehouse.

HISTORY OF THE ERECTION, AND AMOUNTS EXPENDED
UPON THE MISSISSIPPI QUARANTINE STATION.

On the 15th of March, 1855, the Legislature of Louisiana, appropriated the sum of $50,000 for the erection at the Quarantine Station on the Mississippi river, of two separate buildings, as hospitals for the sick, of a small house as residence for the officers appointed under this act, and of a well ventilated store for the reception of the freights of such infected vessels as the Resident Physician may deem necessary to cause to be unloaded.

By the first section of act of Congress entitled "An Act making appropriation for certain civil expenses of the government for the year ending the 30th of June, 1858," approved 3d of March, 1857, the sum of $50,000 was appropriated for the construction of warehouses at Quarantine Station, on the Mississippi River, below New Orleans.

On the 8th of February, 1858, it was enacted by the Senate and House of Representatives of the State of Louisiana, in General Assembly convened, " That the State of Louisiana does cede to the United States jurisdiction over the cite of such warehouses as shall be constructed under the act of Congress, approved the 3d of March, 1857, aforesaid, at Quarantine Station on the Mississippi River, below New Orleans, and does hereby further grant to the United States the use of so much land as may be necessary for the construction of such warehouses, with water front, and privilege of the wharf now built or hereafter to be built on said Station."

It was further enacted "that the Board of Health of the State of Louisiana be and they are hereby authorized and required to designate so much land to said Quarantine Station as may be necessary for the construction of the warehouses aforesaid."

On the eighteenth of March, 1858, it was enacted by the Senate and House of Representatives of the State of Louisiana in General Assembly convened, " That the property at the Quarantine Station, on the Mississippi River, located in this State, the use and jurisdiction over which has been granted by the State of Louisiana to the United States for the purpose of constructing Government warehouses, together with the improvements and buildings which the Government of the United States may erect thereupon, shall be and is hereby exonerated from all taxation and assessments by the State, or by any authorities acting under the State, so long as said property is in possession of the United States."

CONDITION OF THE MISSISSIPPI QUARANTINE STATION AT THE TIME OF THE INAUGURATION OF THE PRESENT QUARANTINE PHYSICIAN, APPOINTED BY GOV. WILTZ.

The hospitals were almost absolutely bare of furniture, beds, bedding and utensils, and without the necessary facilities for the treatment of even a limited number of sick; the grounds were open and roamed over by cattle, the drainage ditches were in many places choked up, and the building needed cleansing, painting and thorough repair.

After thorough inspection of the Mississippi Quarantine Station, the following conclusions were urged upon the consideration of the Board of Health of the State of Louisiana, and were accompanied by detailed statements of all the repairs and articles of furniture and the medicines needed.

3

GENERAL CONCLUSIONS AND RECOMMENDATIONS SUBMITTED TO THE BOARD OF HEALTH, WITH REGARD TO THE MISSISSIPPI QUARANTINE STATION, BY THE PRESIDENT, ON THE 12TH OF JUNE, 1880.

1. *(a).* The location of the Quarantine grounds and buildings is excellent, and the service is energetic.

(b). The Mississippi Quarantine contains a considerable amount of valuable property. The United States Warehouse alone cost $50,000, and is well adapted to the reception of the cargoes of ships. The entire value of the buildings cannot be less than $75,000.

(c). The immediate wants of this Quarantine Station are : 1. Medical stores for hospitals. 2. Bedding, linen, and utensils for hospitals. 3. Fumigating apparatus. 4. One launch boat. 5. A competent man, who shall be placed in charge of the hospital stores and furniture. 6. One or more laborers, whose duty it shall be to open the drains, repair and build the fences, whitewash the houses and wards and keep the buildings and grounds in good sanitary condition.

(d). The position of this Quarantine Station, at the mouth of this great river, which has over 20,000 miles of navigable streams, tributary to the great valley with its 20,000,000 of inhabitants is of vast importance.

(e). It is is the solemn duty of the Board of Health of the State of Louisiana to place the Mississippi Quarantine Station in the best and most effective condition, to fulfill its important mission of protecting this great valley from the importation of foreign pestilence, and at the same time affording a safe retreat, where sick seamen may receive kind and humane nursing and skillful medical treatment.

2. *(f).* While protecting this valley rigidly from the introduction of foreign pestilence, at the same time the commerce and prosperity of the valley should be promoted by the perfection and enlarged application of all reliable means for disinfection, fumigation and sanitation.

PROCESS OF DISINFECTION.

The process of disinfection now employed consits of burning sulphur in iron pots. These pots are placed in tubs containing water. This method is liable to the grave objection that there is in many cases, and especially during rough weather, danger of firing the ship.

FUMIGATING APPARATUS.

Properly constructed fumigating apparatus should at once be procured by the Board of Health for the Mississippi Quarantine Station. The following is an estimate of the cost of such apparatus as has been devised by the President of the Board of Health :

Blower	$50 00
Furnace	30 00
Forty feet hose ($2.30 per foot)	92 00
Fittings for same	15 00
Couplings	32 00
Two sets of wheels	30 00
Total cost	$249 00

3. (*g*). The Mississippi Quarantine Station, notwithstanding the absence of certain hospital furniture and supplies, is administered by the Quarantine Physician and his assistant with intelligence and energy.

(*h*). The laws of the State of Louisiana, and the rules and regulations of the Board of Health, are rigidly executed.

(*i*). All vessels arriving from infected ports, or from ports in which Yellow Fever usually prevails at certain seasons of the year, are detained and thoroughly cleansed and fumigated.

(*j*). All vessels arriving at Quarantine Station are carefully inspected.

(*k*) All vessels from infected ports, even though they may bring clean bills of health, are detained not less than seventy-two hours for inspection, observation, purification, disinfection and fumigation.

(*l*). The length of detention depends upon the nature of the bill of health, the condition of the port from whence the vessel sails, the history of the vessel while in port and during the voyage, and the actual condition of the crew, cargo and vessel at the time of arrival at the Quarantine Station.

This is the case with the ships from Rio de Janeiro, a badly infected port. Every effort is made for their thorough purification. The cargo is removed from the hold and thoroughly ventilated; the hold fumigated at intervals with sulphurous acid gas; the sides and floors of the ship and decks are scraped and washed with antiseptic disinfectants; the bilge water is removed and replaced by a solution of copperas and carbolic acid. In such cases the detention is not less than ten days, and often varies from fifteen to twenty days.

4. (*m*). In order to secure thorough inspection and observation, the shipping is again inspected in the harbor of New Orleans; and the cargo of ships from badly infected ports again subjected to fumigation and disinfection.

(*n*). The vigilance exercised over our shipping is also extended to the city of New Orleans, and the members and officers of the Board of Health stand ready to investigate all cases which may arise in the future, and will use all known useful means for the abatement, circumvention and eradication of infectious diseases.

5. (*o*). In conclusion the President of the Board of Health respectfully urges that the Board of Health confer upon him the power to make, at the earliest practicable moment, the following appointments and the following appropriations for the Mississippi Quarantine Station:

One hospital steward and druggist.

One laborer.

One hospital nurse.

Amount for disinfecting apparatus	$250
Hospital furniture, beds and bedding	250
Hospital utensils	150
Drugs, medicines and medical apparatus	100
Hospital and quarantine tools, spades, axes, hatchets, saws, planes, hoes, nails, whitewash brushes, etc	75
Repair of boats	59
Removal and repair of boat-house	150
Disinfectants	100
Total	$1,125

In the above estimate I have included only those expenditures which are immediately demanded to give efficiency to the Mississippi Quarantine Station, and to provide for the actual wants and treatment of the sick.

The thorough repair of the buildings and the thorough ditching **and** fencing of the grounds, together with the erection of a suitable frame building for the well passengers, will require further consideration and liberal appropriations.

At this moment the Board of Health of the State of Louisiana is not in a position to advance the necessary amounts.

But with economy, energy and perseverance, it is the hope of the board that the Mississippi Quarantine Station may be placed in the most effective condition for the protection of the State from the importation of foreign pestilence and for the protection of commerce and the relief of sick and suffering humanity.

The relations of the actual resources and the necessary expenses of the Mississippi Quarantine Station, are shown by the following tables:

RECEIPTS OF THE BOARD OF HEALTH FROM MISSISSIPPI QUARANTINE STATION.

1869	$23,960 00
1870	20,995 00
1871	23,624 00
1872	18,803 50
1873	18,336 69
1874	19,280 60
1875	13,801 59
1877	15,121 60
1878	19,931 00
1879	18,114 75

ANNUAL EXPENSES FOR SALARIES.

Resident Physician	$ 5,000
Assistant	2,000
One watchman	540
One coxswain	540
Four boatmen	1,920
Total annual expenses for salaries of officers and boatmen	10,000

NECESSARY EXPENSES FOR THE EFFICIENT CONDUCT OF THE MISSISSIPPI QUARANTINE STATION.

1 Druggist and hospital steward, at $75 per month—12 months	$900
2 Hospital Nurses, at $50 per month—12 months	1,200
1 Hospital cook, at $30 per month—12 months	360
2 Laborers and keepers of hospital grounds, at $30 per month each,	720
Medicines and hospital supplies, furniture, bedding, etc.	1,000
Repair of boats	200
Disinfectants and disinfecting apparatus	1,500
Repair of buildings, painting, whitewashing, etc., per annum	5,000
Food and stimulants for the sick	1,000
Ship Chandler supplies	500
	$12,380

According to the organic law of the State the salaries of the President, and of the Secretary and Treasurer, should be included in the above estimate; which at the present rates per annum would bring the total amount necessary for the proper conduct of the Mississippi Quarantine Station during the year 1880, up to at least $26,780, a sum considerably in excess of the receipts of any one year, since the recent civil war."

The report was received and adopted, and $2100 appropriated by the

Board of Health, to be applied by the President and Finance Committee for the necessary supplies of medicines, disinfectants and disinfecting apparatus for the Quarantine Station.

Hospital furniture, beds, bedding, mosquito bars, blankets, pillows and pillow cases, and medicines sufficient for the efficient treatment of about twenty patients, together with cooking stove and kitchen furniture, and disinfecting apparatus, paints, tools, etc., were purchased at the earliest practicable moment, and shipped to the Mississippi Quarantine Station.

The report of the Resident Quarantine Physician will exhibit the number of vessels inspected, disinfected and detained at the Mississippi Quarantine Station; also, the total number of cases of disease treated in Hospital during the year 1880.

At the meeting of the Board of Health on the 19th of November, an additional sum of five thousand dollars ($5000) was appropriated to the repair of the Mississippi Quarantine Station.

ATCHAFALAYA QUARANTINE STATION.

By the seventh section of the act of 1855, " To establish quarantine for the protection of the State," it is ordained that there shall be a quarantine "on the Atchafalayla River, two miles below Pilot's Station, at the mouth of Wax Bayou." It is also enacted that " There shall be no permanent building erected at Pilot's Station, on the Atchafalaya River, but the Board of Health shall use as an hospital for the reception of the sick, hulls and cabins of steamboats." In the twenty-fifth section of the same act it is further stated that "At the Atchafalaya Station a good shade shall be provided for the freights of vessels to be unloaded. The Board of Health shall receive the transfer of such lands as may be necessary at the Atchafalaya River, in the same manner and under the same conditions as are required by section one, and all plans, specifications and contracts for the above buildings, shall be submitted to and approved by the Governor of the State ; provided that the cost of said buildings shall in no case exceed the amount hereinafter appropriated."

In accordance with the acts of the General Assembly and the proclamation of the Governor of Louisiana, a quarantine strictly governed by the rules and regulations of the Board of Health, was maintained on the Atchafalaya River until the first of November. During the entire period of the maintenance of the quarantine no infected vessel arrived at the station, and Morgan City remained free of contagious and infectious diseases.

RIGOLETS QUARANTINE STATION.

An efficient quarantine was maintained up to the 1st of November at this important station, and it will be seen from the report of the intelligent and active Resident Physician, Dr. Daniel W. Adams, that a large number (1170) vessels were inspected.

The recommendation of Dr. Adams, as to the selection of Grassy Island in the adjacent channel, as a proper objective point for Quarantine operations, as well as to the necessity of reducing the Quarantine fees at this station, are worthy of the consideration of this Honorable body and of the General Assembly.

The relations of the Rigolets Quarantine Station to the Ship Island Quarantine Station of the National Board of Health will be considered hereafter.

APPOINTMENT OF QUARANTINE AND SANITARY INSPECTOR

FOR THE MOUTH AND PASSES OF THE MISSISSIPPI RIVER.

In accordance with the resolution of the Board of Health, empowering the President to appoint a Quarantine and Sanitary Inspector for the mouth and passes of the Mississippi River, with headquarters at Port Eads ; Dr. B. F. Taylor, formerly Secretary and Treasurer of the Board, was commissioned in August, and the following letter of instructions will illustrate the nature of the duties required :

OFFICE BOARD OF HEALTH, STATE-HOUSE, STATE OF LOUISIANA. }
New Orleans, August 21, 1880. }

Dr. B. F. Taylor, of New Orleans, is hereby appointed Quarantine and Sanitary Inspector for the mouth of the Mississippi River, with especial supervision over the Jetties, Port Eads, Pilot Town and Southwest Pass.

Dr. Taylor will allow no communication between the shore by unauthorized persons with vessels subject to quarantine; he will regulate the mode of towing infected vessels, and he will report promptly to the Board of Health, through its Executive Officer, all infractions of the Quarantine laws and of the rules and regulations of the Board of Health of the State of Louisiana.

Dr. Taylor will also direct the sanitary affairs of the Jetties, Port Eads and Pilot Town, and report promptly the occurrence of contagious or infections diseases to the President of the Board of Health.   JOSEPH JONES, M. D.,
President Board of Health, State of Louisiana.

In addition to the performance of the duties indicated in the preceding commission, Dr. Taylor was ordered by the President to investigate the nature of the fever prevailing in and around, above and below Point Michel on the Mississippi River, and was empowered to co-operate with the local practitioners, and to render all necessary aid, at the expense of the Board of Health.

As the nature of the fever which prevailed during the summer and autumn of 1880 in the parish of Plaquemine will form a subject of special inquiry, the report of Dr. Taylor will be found under the special division relating to this subject.

GENERAL RESULTS OF THE QUARANTINE OPERA-TIONS OF THE BOARD OF HEALTH OF THE STATE OF LOUISIANA, DURING THE YEAR 1880.

In order to supplement the operations of the Mississippi Quarantine and of the Rigolets and in order to secure the highest attainable sanitary condition, in the shipping in the harbor along the river front, and within the basins lying within the heart of this great city, the President drew up a code of sanitary rules and regulations, which were unanimously adopted and promulgated, by the Board of Health on the 22nd of April.

In accordance with section III of the Sanitary Rules of the Board of Health of the State of Louisiana, regulating shipping in the Port of New Orleans, the President commissioned the Sanitary Inspectors of the several districts and appointed an assistant deputy inspector, and empowered them in accordance with the acts of the Board of Health, to carefully inspect the shipping and to use such measures as were in accordance with the regulations.

From the following table it will be seen that during the months of May, June, July, August, September and October, 462 vessels were inspected in the Harbor of New Orleans, exclusive of the vessels inspected in the old and new basins.

TABLES SHOWING THE NUMBER, CLASS AND NATIONALITY OF VESSELS ARRIVED IN THE PORT OF NEW ORLEANS DURING THE SIX MONTHS, ENDING OCTOBER 31, 1880, WHICH WERE INSPECTED BY THE SANITARY INSPECTORS OF THE BOARD OF HEALTH, STATE OF LOUISIANA:

Months.	Steamships.	Ships.	Barks.	Brigs.	Schooners	Total.
May..	33	15	25	5	18	96
June..	35	2	17	1	11	66
July	40	2	18	1	6	67
August..	38	3	11	....	4	56
September.......................................	53	13	3	....	4	73
October..	67	7	25	....	5	104
Total...................................	266	42	99	7	48	462

Nationality.	Steamships.	Ships.	Barks.	Brigs.	Schooners	Total.
American	103	27	21	2	42	195
British..	134	9	26	1	....	170
Spanish....................................	26	....	14	1	....	41
Norwegian.......................................	....	....	10	1	....	11
Swedish......	....	....	3	1	....	4
German...	3	3	3	....	....	9
Italian..	....	....	7	1	....	8
French..	....	3	8	....	1	12
Austrian..	....	....	6	....	....	6
Mexican......	....	....	....	....	5	5
Danish..	....	....	1	....	... .	1
Total	266	42	99	7	48	462

Sanitary rules were also recommended by the Board of Health of the State of Louisiana, to be observed by vessels during their stay in the port of New Orleans, and in other ports and on their passage to and from New Orleans. The co-operation of the State and Federal authorities, and of the various Foreign Consuls was urged. Four thousand copies of these sanitary rules were printed, and they have been systematically and continuously distributed by the Sanitary Inspectors of the Board of Health, and by the various quarantine officers at the Mississippi, Atchafalaya and Rigolets Quarantine Stations to the captains, masters and agents of all vessels entering the waters of Louisiana.

BRITISH CONSULATE, New Orleans, May 7.

Dear Sir:—In the Picayune's report of your last meeting it is stated that you had called on all the Conuls of Foreign Nations, except the British Consul, and that they had all promised co-operation with the Board of Health, in accordance with Circular No. 3.

This would give the public to believe that I am not in accordance with the Board upon this subject, whereas the very contrary is the fact, for within the same hour in which I had the pleasure of receiving your visit I issued the enclosed Circular Notice. I am, dear sir,

Yours faithfully,   A. DE FONBLANQUE.

Dr. Joseph Jones:

[Notice to Masters of British Ships.]

The attention of masters of British ships is called to Circular No. 3, issued by the Board of Health, for the State of Louisiana (a copy of which has been delivered on board your ship), and especially to the second article thereof.

It is most important that all such cases of disease as are therein mentioned should be reported without delay.

The Sanitary Rules which conclude the Circular in question are also strongly recommended for your adoption.   A. DE FONBLANQUE. Consul.

New Orleans May 5, 1880.   ———

OFFICE BOARD OF HEALTH, STATE-HOUSE, STATE OF LOUISIANA. }
New Orleans, May 8, 1880.   }

Hon. A. de Fonblanque, British Consul, British Consulate, New Orleans, La.:

DEAR SIR—I have the honor to acknowledge receipt of your favor of the 7th inst., and in reply would state that the mistake with reference to the British Consul was accidentally made by the reporter, and was not entered upon the official minutes of the Board of Health.

It gives the Executive Officer of the Board of Health of the State of Louisiana great pleasure to correct this error, especially as he recalls with gratification his interview with the accomplished and zealous representative of the first commercial power of the globe.

I desire to express the thanks of the Board of Health for the prompt and energetic manner in which the representative of the commercial interests of the British Government has been pleased to indorse the efforts to preserve the health of the seamen and protect the Mississippi Valley from the introduction of foreign pestilence.

With high esteem, respectfully yours,   JOSEPH JONES, M. D.,
President Board of Health, State of Louisiana.

On May 24, 1880, the rules and regulations for the government of quarantine officers and stations, and for the enforcement of the acts of the Legislature of Louisiana, "establising and regulating quarantine for the protection of the State,"* were submitted by the President, and unanimously adopted by the Board of Health, and four thousand copies have been printed and distributed by the Board of Health to the local boards in the United States, to Foreign Consuls, captains, masters and agents of vessels.

On the nineteenth of August additional rules and regulations governing the Mississippi Quarantine Station were prepared by a committee composed of Dr. J. C. Beard, J. P. Davidson and F. Loeber, and were adopted by the Board of Health.

In noting the fact that New Orleans escaped an epidemic of Yellow Fever, and was also free from other contagious and infectious diseases, the history of the quarantine of 1880 would not be complete without the consideration of the cases of the Vanguard and Excelsior.

---

*Acts of the Legislature of Louisiana establishing and regulating Quarantine for the protection of the State; Organizing and defining the powers of the Board of Health, and regulating the pactice of Medicine, Midwifery, Dentistry and Pharmacy; also rules and regulations of the Board of Health of the State of Louisiana and Health Ordinances of the City of New Orleans, by Joseph Jones, M. D. New Orleans, 1880, pp. 36–51.

RESISTANCE OF THE QUARANTINE AUTHORI-TIES BY THE BRITISH STEAMSHIP VANGUARD.

At the regular meeting of the Board of Health on the twenty-fourth of May the President presented the facts relating to the violation of the quar. antine laws of the State of Louisiana by W. J. Gell, Master of the British steamship Vanguard, and laid before the Board the following letter to the Attorney General advising prompt and decisive action:

OFFICE BOARD OF HEALTH,
 State House, May 24, 1880.

Hon. J. C. Egan, Attorney General, State of Louisiana:

DEAR SIR—The attention of the Attorney General is respectfully directed to the follow. ing telegram:

MISSISSIPPI QUARANTINE STATION, May 23, 1880—To Dr. Joseph Jones, President Board of Health: Steamer Vanguard passed Quarantine at 12 m, to-day from Colon. Captain refused to anchor for disinfection, and proceeded to the city without permit. This case should be laid before Attorney General for prosecution and the vessel sent back to station.
J. F. FINNEY, M., D.,
Resident Physician.

The latter portion of the 13th and the 16th Sections of *"An Act to establish Quarantine for the protection of the State;"* reads thus:

"SECTION 13. Every master of a vessel subject to a quarantine or a visitation, arriving in the port of New Orleans, who shall refuse or neglect either. First: To proceed with and anchor his vessel at the place designated for quarantine at the time of his arrival. Second: To submit his vessel, cargo and passengers to the examination of the physician, and to furnish all necessary information to enable that officer to determine what quarantine shall be fixed for his vessel. Third: To remain with his vessel at the Quarantine ground dur. ing the period assigned for her quarantine, and while there to comply with the directions and regulations prescribed by this "Act" or by the Board of Health, or with such directions prescribed for his vessel, crew, cargo and passengers, by the Resident Physician, shall be guilty of a misdemeanor, and be punished by a fine not exceeding two thousand dollars ($2,000), or by imprisonment not exceeding twelve months, or by both, at the discretion of the court. * * *

SECTION 16. Be it further enacted that the Resident Physician report to the Attorney General, all violations of this "Act," and it shall be his duty to prosecute all person or per. sons thus offending; to collect the fines and remit the amount thereof to the Secretary of the Board of Health, whose duty it shall be to keep a separate book for fines collected, to be approved of every three months by the Attorney General, who shall receive such com. pensation as the Board may fix for his services. The latter portion of an "Act" to amend an "Act" entitled an "Act to establish Quarantine for the protection of the State," ap. proved March 16, 1870, appears about to be applicable to the case of the "Vanguard," now under consideration. "The Board of Health shall have power to define the duties of offi. cers employed by them, and impose additional duties on officers appointed under this "Act," to issue warrnts to any constable, police officer or sheriff in the State to apprehend and retain such person or persons as cannot be otherwise subjected to the provisions of this "Act," or who shall have violated the same, or whenever it shall be necessary so to do, to issue their warrant to the sheriff of the city or parish where any vessel may be having violated the provisions of this "Act," commanding him to remove said vessel to the Quaran. tine ground, and arrest the officer thereof; all which warrant shall be executed by the of. ficer to whom the same shall be directed, who shall possess the like power in the execu. tion thereof, and be entitled to the same compensation as if the same had been issued out of any court of the State."

I would most respectfully and earnestly urge the Attorney General to take prompt and energetic action in the vindication of the Quarantine laws of the State which have been violated by the Captain of the Vanguard.

Respectfully, your obedient servant,
JOSEPH JONES, M. D.,
President Board of Health State of Louisiana.

P. S.—I have directed the Attorney of the Board, H. L. O'Donnell, Esq , to render such assistance in this case as the Attorney General may deem necessary.
JOSEPH JONES, M. D.

4

BOARD OF HEALTH, ⎱
State-House, May 24, 1880. ⎰

Mr. H. L. O'Donnell, Attorney Board of Health:

DEAR SIR—Enclosed please find letter of President Board of Health to the Attorney General with reference to the Steamship Vanguard.

The case is an important one and should be dealt with at once and in a determined manner.

I would respectfully suggest that the Attorney of the Board, render all necessary assistance to the Attorney General.

Respectfully, your obedient servant,

JOSEPH JONES, M. D.,
President Board of Health, State of Louisiana.

———

The Attorney General replied to the above communication, that it was the duty of the District Attorney to attend to such matters.

After considering the opinions of the District Attorney and of the Attorney of the Board, the Board of Health authorized the President to take such further action in the vindication of the quarantine laws of the State of Louisiana, as he might deem best.

It was manifest that the protection of the State of Louisiana and of the entire Mississippi valley from the introduction of foreign pestilence depended upon the vindication and the rigid execution of the quarantine laws. The fact was appreciated that the prevention of inland quarantines and the commerce of New Orleans as well as that of the greater portion of the Mississippi Valley, depended upon such an administration of the quarantine at the mouth of the Mississippi river, as would secure the confidence of the authorities and citizens in the surrounding States. After an examination of the various legal processes by which the public safety might be assured, the following appeared to offer the most direct and speedy solution of the questions involved in the case of the master of the S. S. Vanguard.

By the acts of the Legislature relative to quarantine passed in 1855, and re-enacted in 1870, the Board of Health is empowered " Whenever it shall be necessary so to do, to issue their warrant to the sheriff of the city or parish where any vessel may be, having violated the provisions of this act, commanding him to remove said vessel to the quarantine ground, and arrest the officers thereof, all which warrants shall be executed by the officer, to whom the same shall be directed, who shall possess the like powers in the execution thereof and be entitled to the same compensation as if the same had been duly issued out of any court of this State."

By this same act, it is made "the duty of the President of the Board of Health to reside in New Orleans, and superintend the different quarantine stations of the State." It is also enacted that " he shall have the power to issue during the adjournment to constables or sheriff's, all orders and warrants provided by the provisions of this act."

Upon careful examination, the President found the following decision of the Supreme Court bearing upon the question at issue.

"The arrival of a vessel at New Orleans after refusing to obey the orders to remain in quaratine at the Quarantine Station, in the parish of Plaquemines, is an offense commited in the parish of Orleans, and triable in the First District Court of New Orleans." [Session Acts of 1855 ; p. 316, sec. 6.]

Immediately after the adjournment of the Board on the twenty-fourth of May, the President, after due consultation with the District Attorney and the Attorney of the Board, issued the following warrant to the Sheriff of Orelans:

THE STATE OF LOUISIANA.

To the Civil Sheriff of the Parish of Orleans—Greeting:

Whereas, due and sufficient proof has been adduced before the "Board of Health of the State of Louisiana" that on the twenty-third day of May, A. D. 1880, one W. J. Gell, commander of the steamship "Vanguard," and being subject under the laws of Louisiana to detention, inspection and fumigation, at the Mississippi River Quarantine Station, has caused said steamship to come to and arrive at the City of New Orleans without undergoing the necessary inspection, fumigation and detention at said Quarantine Station.

Now, therefore, this is to command you to remove forthwith said steamship "Vanguard" from the City of New Orleans to the Mississippi River Quarantine Station, and there retain said steamship until inspected, fumigated and detained in accordance with the laws of the State of Louisiana in reference to Quarantine; and for so doing this shall be your warrant.

Given under my hand and the official seal of the Board of Health of the State of Louisiana, in the City of New Orleans, this twenty-fifth day of May, A. D. 1880.

JOSEPH JONES, M. D.,
President Board of Health, State of Louisiana.

After the seizure of the vessel by the Sheriff, the British Consul called upon the President of the Board of Health, and urged the necessity of considering certain possible international complications and suits for heavy damages which might grow out of the execution of this summary process.

When the law under which the process was issued was fully unfolded, the British Consul frankly admitted that the Master of the Vanguard had violated the Quarantine laws of the State of Louisiana; but at the same time he requested that the President should lay his statement before the Board of Health, and request an arrest or modification of its action.

Whilst holding that it was his manifest duty to execute rigidly and fearlessly the laws for the protection of the State against the introduction of foreign pestilence, the President nevertheless laid the statement of the British Consul before the members of the Board. The unanimous response was that the resolution of the Board of Health and the mandate of its Executive Officer should be maintained.

The Vanguard was accordingly returned by the Sheriff back to the Mississippi Quarantine Station, and was subjected to thorough inspection, disinfection and fumigation.

The following communication was received from the British Consul on the twenty-ninth of May:

BRITISH CONSULATE, New Orleans, May 29, 1880.

Dr. Joseph Jones, President of the Board of Health:

Sir:—I much regret to find in the Times of this day, an article, apparently inspired by Capt. Gell, of the British steamship "Vanguard," in which an attempt is made to justify his action in disobeying the orders of the Quarantine Physician, and bringing his ship to New Orleans without a permit.

If Capt. Gell has read the laws relating to quarantine, he has proved himself incapable of understanding them; yet they are very clear.

Having stood by while his agents and his consul admitted his mistake, and obtained a remission of penalties by frankly apologizing for it, he now puts forth a foolish plea in justification.

As this might lead to an impression that I have not been acting conscientiously in this matter, I beg to assure you that I do not agree with Capt. Gell's pretensions, or approve his conduct.

I have the honor to be, sir, your obedient servant,

A. DE FONBLANQUE, British Consul.

To this communication the following reply was given:

OFFICE BOARD OF HEALTH, May 29, 1880.

Hon. A. de Fonblanque, British Consul, New Orleans:

Sir:—I have the honor to acknowledge the communication of the British Consul of the 29th inst., and shall lay the same before the Board of Health at the next regular meeting, June 3.

As President of the Board of Health, I desire to express my thanks for your prompt action in this matter relating to the steamship "Vanguard."

Respectfully, your obedient servant,

JOSEPH JONES, M. D.,
President of the Board of Health.

In the New Orleans Times of the 30th of May, the following card appeared, signed by the master of the Vanguard:

A CARD.

NEW ORLEANS, May 29, 1880.

To the Editor of the New Orleans Times:

    SIR—Referring to a conversation published in your issue of to-day, in which I am reported to have said that the Vanguard (steamship) was not subject to Quarantine—

    Having to-day been presented with a copy of the laws on the subject (the first I have seen since coming to this port), I am convinced that every vessel, without exception, on entering the Mississippi River, is subject to inspection, and for the purpose of inspection the law is explicit in requiring that the vessel shall be anchored, no matter where she comes from, or how many clear bills of health she may have.

    Yours faithfully,   W. J. GELL, Master Steamship Vanguard.

As the quarantine laws of the State of Louisiana had been promptly vindicated, the President of the Board of Health took no further action in the case of the master of the British steamship Vanguard.

In order to enforce the prompt detection of any violation of the quarantine laws, the following communication was addressed to the

HARBOR MASTERS.

OFFICE BOARD OF HEALTH, STATE OF LOUISIANA, STATE-HOUSE, }
New Orleans, May 29, 1880. }

Harbor-Master, District Port of New Orleans:

    Sir:—Your attention is hereby called to sections 17 and 18, of "An Act to establish quarantine for the protection of the State," approved March, 1855, p. 7, which reads thus:

    SECTION 17. Be it further enacted, etc., That it shall be the duty of the Harbor-Masters, in their respective districts, to demand of the captain of every vessel arriving from sea to New Orleans, the permit of the Resident Physician, and to report to the Secretary of the Board of Health, all vessels having entered the port without such permit.

    SEC. 18. Be it further enacted, etc., That from the first of May to the first of November, all towboats plying from the mouth of the river to New Orleans, shall be liable to inspection and quarantine, and it shall be the duty of the different Harbor-Masters to require from the captains of said towboats the certificate of the Resident Physician, as provided by section 8, which certificate shall not be granted before a detention of at least five days; provided nothing herein contained shall be so construed as to apply to towboats plying between New Orleans and the Quarantine ground and no farther.

    The protection of this city from the importation of foreign pestilence necessitates the rigid enforcement of the preceding rules by the Harbor-Masters.

    Respectfully,   JOSEPH JONES, M. D.,
                                  President of the Board of Health.

The prompt action of the Board of Health in the case of the British steamship Vanguard, was followed by no similar breach of the Quarantine laws.

QUARANTINE OF VESSELS

FROM THE INFECTED PORT OF RIO DE JANEIRO—CASE OF THE BARK EXCELSIOR.

The prevalence of Yellow Fever in the City of Rio de Janeiro received the prompt and earnest attention of the Board of Health immediately after its reorganization on the eighth of April, 1880.

The various vessels arriving with coffee from this port were detained at the Quarantine Station for periods ranging from twelve to twenty days.; the Resident Quarantine Physician was ordered to shift the cargoes by acclimated laborers (that is by men who had suffered with the Yellow Fever), natives of New Orleans.

The [general [measures instituted with the ships from this infected port are indicated briefly in the following official telegrams and correspondence:

[Telegram.]

MISSISSIPPI QUARANTINE STATION, April 26, 1880.—To Joseph Jones, M. D., President Board of Health : Brig Hildegard left Rio 24th February, several cases off vessel sick on shore in Rio only one case at sea, taken 4th March, and recovered. Vessel fumigated and disinfected yesterday, now undergoing heavy fumigation with 4000 sacks of coffee in hold.

P. S. CARRINGTON, Resident Physician.

[Telegram.]

To DR. CARRINGTON, MISSISSIPPI QUARANTINE STATION, April 26th, 1880.—Detain Brig "Hildegard." Discharge cargo from hold. Fumigate and ventilate cargo and ship. Pump out bilge water, and replace with strong solution of copperas and carbolic acid. Have decks and hold washed with same Continue fumigation.
[Signed.]   JOSEPH JONES, M. D., President Board of Health.

[Telegram.]

April 27th 1880.—You will please write me fully with reference to Brig "Hildegard" from Rio. The cargo should be discharged, ventilated and fumigated, and the bilge water pumped out and replaced with a solution of copperas and carbolic acid. The enclosed circular will give formula : of course the amount should be proportionate to the space occupied by the bilge water. The decks and hold should be washed with the same solution The fumigations with sulphurous acid gas should be frequent and thorough. Hold the ship and crew under observation until further advice.
[Signed]   JOSEPH JONES, M. D., President Board of Health.

[Telegram.]

April 28th, 1880,—Transfer the sacks of coffee from the hold to the open deck so as to allow of free ventilation. Subject the hold and all parts of the vessel to the fullest extent of fumigation. It will be necessary to take the cargo from different section of the vessel at diferent times. Ventilate every part at least two days and fumigate each vacant space from which the sacks of coffee have been removed. Upon completion of these processes, subject the entire cargo and vessel, lockers, cabins and closets, bunks, bedding and clothing, crew etc., to thorough disinfection and fumigation.
[Signed]   JOESPH JONES, M. D., President Board of Health.

QUARANTINE STATION, MISSISSIPPI RIVER, May 1, 1880.

Joseph Jones, M. D., President Board of Health:

Dear Sir—In response to yours of the 27th ult., received on yesterday, I would state that the brig Hildegard. from Sundwall, Sweden, with a cargo of deals, arrived at Rio on the 26th of December last. There were eleven persons on board, consisting (inclusive of Captain) of ten in crew and one passenger, who was the wife of the Captain. During the time the vessel was at Rio every one of these people were taken sick, but it is not clear that every case was Yellow Fever.

On January 14, Karl W—— was taken sick, removed to hospital, and returned on board vessel the 3d of February.

On the 28th of January Capt. Johansson was sick and went ashore. but, from his statement, was so slightly affected as to be scarcely kept in bed for it

His wife, who was on shore with him. returned to the vessel. and on the night of the same day was taken sick, was carried on shore the next morning (that of the 29th) and died on the 2d of February.

The second mate taken on the 29th, was placed in hospital, and died on the 3d of February.

John Lonquist sickened the 3d and returned to the vessel the 13th of February.

The cook was taken on the 4th and returned on board the 27th of February.

E. Pesterling sickened on the 5th and died on shore the 9th of February.

G. Peterson sick on the 8th, returned to the brig the 24th of February.

S. P. Johansson, because of a bite from a fish was taken on shore, and while in hospital became sick. He was left in Rio.

In the place of two of the crew who died and one left on shore three new members were shipped at Rio.

Having discharged cargo the brig anchored near one-half mile from shore. where it took on cargo. With a cargo of coffee and some rock ballast taken at Rio the Hildegard left for New Orleans on the 29th of February.

On the 4th of March Michael ——, one of the crew shipped at Rio was taken sick. His was probably a case of Yellow Fever. which terminated in recovery. No other case occurred during the voyage.

On the 25th of April the brig arrived here with all well on board. The same day the hold of the vessel. cabin, forecastle, bedding and clothing were fumigated and bilge disinfected with carbolic acid and sulp. of iron. The next day heavy fumigation and carbolic acid in the bilge. besides had mattress and pillow of sailor sick at sea brought on shore and burned. The cargo, now in process of removal from hold to the deck, and vacant spaces fumigated in detail.

In the preceding I neglected to enumerate the carpenter being sick on the 11th, and returned on board the 27th of February.

Very respectfully,
P. S. CARRINGTON, M. D., Resident Physician.

[Telegram.]

MISSISSIPPI QUARANTINE STATION, May 8, 1880.—Joseph Jones, M. D.. President Board of Health. care of Westfeldt Bros.: Last coffee to be ærated from hold of brig Hildegard. on deck since yesterday, will be in readiness for release to-morrow.   P. S. CARRINGTON, M. D., Resident Physician.

[Telegram.]

NEW ORLEANS, May 8th, 1880.—Dr. Carrington, Resident Physician, Mississippi Quarantine Station : If no case of fever has occurred among the officers, crew or passengers of the Brig Hildegard. since the arrival at the Mississippi Quarantine Station, and if the instructions of the Board of Health, with reference to removal, ventilation and fumigation, of her cargo have been fully carried out, and if you deem it entirely safe, release the vessel and allow her to come up to the city.

JOSEPH JONES, M. D. President Board of Health.

Immediately upon the arrival of the bark Hildegard at her wharf in the First District, Dr. Joseph Holt, the Sanitary Inspector of this District, received written instructions as to her thorough inspection, disinfection and fumigation. Orders were also issued for the thorough fumigation of the warehouse in which the coffee was stored, with sulphurous acid gas.

The following are the results of the inspection and sanitary measures instituted by Dr. Holt:

[Questions Propounded by the President, Quarantine Officers and Deputy Inspectors of the Board of Health of the State of Louisiana to the Masters, Captains and Medical Officers, of Vessels at the Port of New Orleans and Quarantine Stations of Louisiana.]

NEW ORLEANS, May 13, 1880.

1. Name of Vessel ? Hildegard.
2. Name of Captain or Master ? Erick Gustave Johansson.
3. Tonnage or Class of Vessel ? 256.42.
4. From whence is the vessel you Command ? Rio de Janerio.
5. How many days have you been on passage ? 54 days.
6. At what port or ports have you touched ? None.
7. Were any Contagious or Infectious Diseases prevailing at the port from whence your vessel sailed ? Yes.
8. If so, name the Diseases. Yellow Fever.
9. Were any Contagious or Infectious Diseases prevailing at the port or ports at which you touched ? None.
10. If so, name the Diseases. None.
11. Was any freight or passengers received at the ports at which your vessel touched ? None.
12. If so, give particulars. None.
13. Have you any Bills of Health ? Yes.
14. If so, produce them Did produce them.
15. During the course of your Cruise or Passage, what cases of disease have occurred on board ? One case of fever.
16. At what dates ? March 4th.
17. Have any deaths taken place on board your vessel since you left the last port ? None.
18. If so, at what dates and from what causes ? None.
19. Are there any sick on your vessel at this time ? None.
20. Has Yellow Fever, Small Pox, Cholera or Plague ever existed on this ship ? Yes.
21. If so, when ? At Rio de Janerio, just previous to leaving port.
22. What is the number of Officers ? Three.
23. What is the number of the Crew ? Seven.
24. What is the number of Passengers ? None.
25. What is your cargo ? Coffee and Mats.
26. To whom is the cargo consigned ? Westfeldt Bros.
27. What is the present sanitary condition of the vessel, cargo, crew and passengers ? Good.
28. Have you a Medical officer ? None.
29. Give the name of the Medical officer. None.
30. Produce the Reports of the Medical officer. None.

E. G. JOHNASSON, Master.

Subscribed to before me, JOSEPH HOLT, M. D., Sanitary Inspector, First District.

SPECIAL REPORT—BRIG HILDEGARD, WITH CARGO OF COFFEE, FIFTY-FOUR DAYS FROM RIO; SIXTEEN DAYS AT MISSISSIPPI QUARANTINE STATION; ARRIVED AT NEW ORLEANS, HEAD OF CALLIOPE STREET, MORNING OF MAY 12, 1880—BY JOSEPH HOLT, M. D., SANITARY INSPECTOR, FIRST DISTRICT, NEW ORLEANS, MAY 13, 1880.

OFFICE SANITARY INSPECTOR, FIRST DISTRICT, }
New Orleans, May 13, 1880. }

Joseph Jones, M. D., President Board of Health:

Sir:—I have the honor to report having executed your orders in relation to the brig Hildegard, and present with this list of questions definitely answered. I have disinfected the bilge-water, and have had it emptied and the hold washed and the vessel thoroughly fumigated with burning sulphur; also cargo in warehouse.

While in the port of Rio de Janeiro, during the month of February, 1880, eleven persons sickened with Yellow Fever, and were sent as soon as falling ill, to hospital. This number included all on board. The captain's wife and two sailors died.

The bill of health, signed by United States Consul General Thomas Adamson, February 26, 4 o'clock P. M., certifies to 132 deaths from Yellow Fever in Rio de Janeiro, for the week ending February 24, 1880.

JOSEPH HOLT, M. D.,
Sanitary Inspector, First District.

The measures just described were applied to each and every vessel arriving from Rio up to the middle of October, 1880. The following correspondence was elicited by an erroneous report published in one of the daily newspapers:

NATIONAL BOARD OF HEALTH, }
No. 113].   River Inspection Service, Office of the Director, }
Memphis, Tenn., June 1, 1880. }

My dear Doctor—Not having yet received the blank forms from you, I have ordered a supply printed here, and enclose you a copy for comparison, that you may note one or two inaccuracies of the printer (in those furnished you by Graham).

Both the Mississippi and Tennessee State Boards of Health express solicitude concerning railroad freight from New Orleans, and I have had repeated inquiries as to when the inspector of such freight would be put on duty. You are, of course, the judge of the necessity, and, also, I know realize the importance o some concession to the State and local Boards.

I noticed in the New Orleans Times of the 25th of May, the arrival of the Swedish bark Robert, from Rio, with 4000 sacks of coffee, coupled with the statement in the same paper that this vessel had lost her captain and all of her crew but two of Yellow Fever while loading. As a matter of interest I wish you would advise me what treatment this vessel and her cargo were subjected to by the Louisiana State Board.
Very truly yours,

R. W. MITCHELL,
Member National Board of Health, Director River Inspection Service.
To Dr. S. M. Bemiss, Member National Board of Health, New Orleans, La.

This communication was endorsed as follows:

Respectfully referred to President State Board of Health for his information and for suggestion con. cerning railroad inspections. He will please return this with suggestions at earliest convenient hour. Attention is respectfully called to remarks concerning bark Robert. S. M. BEMISS, M. N. B. H.

OFFICE BOARD OF HEALTH, STATE-HOUSE, STATE OF LOUISIANA,
New Orleans, June 1, 1880.

Prof. S. M. Bemiss, M. D., Member National Board of Health:

SIR—That portion of the communication of Dr. Mitchell relating to inspection of railroad freights in this city, will be referred to the State Board of Health at the meeting to-morrow evening, June 3. * *

Full information has been communicated to Dr. Mitchell with reference to the bark Robert, from Rio, and also as to the rigid measures instituted by the Board of Health with all vessels from Rio. Respectfully,

JOSEPH JONES, M. D.,
President Board of Health, State or Louisiana.

OFFICE BOARD OF HEALTH, STATE OF LOUISIANA,
New Orleans, June 1, 1880.

R. W. Mitchell, M. D., Member National Board of Health, Director River Inspection Service:

SIR—In reply to your inquiry addressed to Prof. Saml. M. Bemiss, M. D., of the National Board of Health, with reference to the "treatment" which the bark Robert, from Rio, was subjected to by the Louisiana State Board: I have to state that said vessel was detained at the Mississippi Quarontine Station about fifteen days; the coffee was removed from the hold and thoroughly ventilated, and the hold and entire ship fumigated and disinfected. Only two (2)of her crew were taken sick in Rio, and were transferred to the hospital during the voyage from Rio to Mississippi Quarantine Station, occupying over sixty days no case of disease af any description occurred. This observation applies also to the crew whilst at Quarantine Station and at this port.

The Board of Health has instituted rigid measures with all vessels from Rio, not only detaining them for observation, but also causing breaking of bulk and thorough fumigation, disinfection and cleansing, also thorough ventilation of cargo.

The statement which you quote from the New Orleans Times of the 25th of May, to the effect that this vessel had lost her captain and all her crew but two, of Yellow Fever, while loading in Rio, evidently conveyed an erroneous impression. Respectfully,

JOSEPH JONES, M. D.,
President Board of Health.

The following is the report of Dr. Joseph Holt, Sanitary Inspector of the First District, concerning bark Robert:

NEW ORLEANS, May 29, 1880.

1. Name of Vessel? Robert.
2. Name of Captain or Master? G. W. Erlandson.
3. Tonnage or Class of Vessel? 346.
4. From whence is the vessel you Command? Rio Janeiro.
5. How many days have you been on the the passage? 62 days.
6. At what port or ports have you touched? None.
7. Were any Contagious or Infectious Diseases prevailing at the port from whence your vessel sailed? Yellow Fever.
9.. Were any Contagious or Infectious Diseases prevailing at the port or ports at which you touched? No.
11. Was any freight or passengers received at the ports at which your vessel touched? No.
13. Have you any Bills of Health? Yes; but in possession of Quarantine Health Officer.
15. During the course of your Cruise or Passage what cases of disease have occurred on board? None.
17. Have any deaths taken place on board your vessel since you left the last port? No.
19. Are there any sick on your vessel at this time? No.

20. Has Yellow Fever, Small Pox, Cholera or Plague ever existed on this ship? Yes, at Rio. Yellow Fever.
21. If so, when? February, 1880.
22. What is the number of Officers. Two.
23. What is the number of the Crew? Eight.
24. What is the number of Passengers. None.
25. What is your cargo? Coffee.
26. To whom is the cargo consigned? G. L. Phipps.
27. What;is the present sanitary condition of the vessel, cargo, crew and passengers? Good.

G. W. ERLANDSON, Master.

Subscribed to before me, JOSEPH HOLT, M. D., Sanitary Inspector of First District.

The following replies were returned by Dr. R. M. Mitchell, Member of the National Board ot Health, residing in Memphis, Tennessee:

No. 121.]   NATIONAL BOARD OF HEALTH,
                          River Inspection Service—Office of the Director.
                                          Memphis, Tenn., June 3, 1880.

Prof. Joseph Jones, M. D., President Louisiana State Board of Health:

My Dear Doctor:—I have to thank you for your prompt and satisfactory response to my query ad dressed to Dr. Bemiss, concerning the treatment of the coffee ship "Robert."

The details of the thorough measures adopted and enforced at the Mississippi Quarantine Station, as set forth in your letter of the first instant, are very reassuring, and I beg again to thank you tor your courtesy, pressed, as I know you must be. for time in which to discharge all the onerous duties of your position.

Believe me, my dear doctor, very sincerely yours,

R. M. MITCHELL,
Member N. B. H. Director River Inspection Service.

No. 125.]   NATIONAL BOARD OF HEALTH,
                          River Inspection Service—Office of the Director.
                                          Memphis, Tenn., June 5, 1880.

Prof. Joseph Jones, M. D., President Louisiana State Board of Health, New Orleans, La.:

Sir:—I beg to acknowledge receipt of a copy of the Rules and Regulations of the Board of Health, State of Louisiana, concerning quarantine, together with your letter accompanying the same, tor both of which please accept my thanks.   Very respectfully, your obedient servant,

R. M. MITCHELL,
Member N. B. H. Director River Inspection Service.

The following data extracted from the inspection records of the Board of Health of the State of Louisiana, will serve still further to illustrate the continued reinspection of vessels from Rio, in the harbor of New Orleans. The cargoes of all these vessels were subjected to fumigation by sulphurous acid in the warehouses in which they were deposited.

NEW ORLEANS, June 10, 1880.

1. Name of Vessel? Stella.
2. Name of Captain or Master? M. Johnson.
3. Tonnage or Class of Vessel? 190.
4. From whence is the vessel you command? Rio de Janeiro.
5. How many days have you been on the passage? Sixty days.
6. At what port or ports have you touched? None.
7. Were any Contagious or Infectious Diseases prevailing at the port from whence your vessel sailed? Yellow Fever.
13. Have you any Bills of Health? Yes.
15. During the course of your Cruise or Passage, what cases of disease have occurred on board? None.
17. Have any deaths taken place on board your vessel since you left the last port? No.
19. Are there any sick on your vessel at this time? No.
20. Has Yellow Fever, Small-Pox, Cholera or Plague ever existed on this ship? No.
22. What is the number of officers? Two.
23. What is the number of the Crew? Five.
24. What is the number of Passengers? None.
25. What is your cargo? Coffee.
26. To whom the cargo consigned? Mississippi Warehouse.
27. What is the present sanitary condition of the vessel. cargo, crew and passengers? Good.
28. Have you a Medical Officer? No.

M. JOHNSON, Master.
Per F. ELLINGSEN.

Inspected by JOSEPH HOLT, M. D.

NEW ORLEANS, June 17th, 1880.

1. Name of Vessel? Leopold et Maire.
2. Name of Captain or Master? Lescalles.
3. Tonnage or Class of Vessel? 400.
4. From whence is the vessel you command? Rio de Janerio.
5. How many days have you been on the passage? Fifty-five.
6. At what port or ports have you touched? None.
7. Were any Contagious or Infectious Diseases prevailing at the port from whence your vessel sailed? Yes.
   If so, name the Diseases. Yellow Fever.
18. Have you any Bills of Health? Yes.

15. During the course of your Cruise or Passage, what cases of disease have occured on board? Two deaths ; one consumption, other with symptoms of Yellow Fever.
17. Have any deaths taken place on board your vessel since you left the last port? Two.
18. If so, at what dates and from what causes? Twenty-eighth and twenty-ninth April.
20. Has Yellow Fever, Small Pox, Cholera or Plague ever existed on this ship? Above instance only.
21. If so, when ? From 22nd to 29th April, 1880.
22. What is the number of Officers? Two.
23. What is the number of the Crew ? Seven.
24. What is the number of Passengers? None
25. What is your Cargo ? Coffee.
26. To whom is the cargo consigned? Smith, Rea & Co
27. What is the present sanitary condition of the vessel. cargo, crew and passengers? Good.
28. Have you a Medical officer? No.
29. Give the name of the Medical officer, None.

M. BLANCHEMEIN, Pour le Capitaine.
Subscribed to before me, JOSEPH HOLT, M. D. Sanitary Inspector First District.

NEW ORLEANS, June 21, 1880.

1. Name of Vessel? Eastern Chief.
2. Name of Captain or Master? Young.
3. Tonnage or Class of Vessel? 401.
4. From whence is the vessel you Command? Rio de Janerio.
5. How many days have you been on the passage? Sixty-six.
6. At what port or ports have you touched? None.
7. Were any Contagious or Infectious Diseases prevailing at the port from whence your vessel sailed ? Yes.
8. If so, name the Diseases. Yellow Fever.
15. During the course of your Cruise or Passage, what cases of disease have occurred on board? Two cases of fever.
16. At what dates ? Taken one on 13th, other on 16th April.
17. Have any deaths taken place on board your vessel since you left the last port? No.
19. Are there any sick on your vessel at this time? No.
20. Has Yellow Fever, Small Pox, Cholera or Plague, ever existed on this ship ? Yellow Fever.
21. If so, when? While in Rio. Three sent to hospital.
22. What is the number of Officers ? Three.
23. What is the number of the Crew? Eight.
24. What is the number of Passengers? None.
25. What is your cargo ? Coffee.
26. To whom is the cargo consigned ? Johnson, Gordon & Co.
27. What is the present sanitary condition of the vessel, cargo, crew and passengers? Good.

YOUNG, Per pro. EDWARDS, Mate.
Subscribed to before me, JOSEPH HOLT, Sanitary Inspector First District.

As a general rule the coffee ships from Rió discharge their cargoes in the First District of New Orleans, in which are located the large coffee ware-houses.

The following facts with reference to the prevalence of Yellow Fever, and other diseases in Rio de Janerio, were communicated monthly to the Board of Health by the Consul General Thomas Adamson.

In Rio de Janeiro there occurred in the month of November, 1879, total deaths from all causes 850, Yellow Fever 9; small-pox 11; enteric or typhoid fever 20; pernicious fever 22; month of December, 1879, total deaths 915; Yellow Fever 18; small-pox 9; enteric or typhoid fever 13: pernicious fever 43; consumption 153; month of January, 1880, total deaths 1062; Yellow Fever 133; small-pox 2; enteric or typhoid fever 14; scarlet fever 5; pernicious fever 54; consumption 166; month of February, 1880, total deaths 1352; Yellow Fever 484; small-pox 1; typhus fever 1; typhoid or enteric fever 19; scarlet fever 1; pernicious fever 76; consumption 140. Present estimated population of Rio de Janeiro 330,000. March total deaths 1389; Yellow Fever 468; typhus fever 3; enteric or typhoid fever 17; pernicious fever 60; consumption 153; month of April, 1880, total deaths 1008; Yellow Fever 274; typhus fever 2; enteric or typhoid fever 15; pernicious fever 40; consumption 150; month of May, 1880, total deaths 914; Yellow Fever 105; typhoid fever 14; pernicious fever 28; consumption 148; month of June, 1880, total deaths 812; Yellow Fever 55; typhus fever 1; typhoid fever 8; pernicious fever 24; consumption 143.

BARK EXCELSIOR,

It is important that the essential facts relating to the occurrence of Yellow Fever on the Swedish bark Excelsior, as well as the measures instituted by the Board of Health for the exclusion of this disease from the City of New Orleans and the Mississippi Valley, should be placed on record ; not only as a contribution to the history of quarantine in the United States, but also because this occurrence has been the occasion of unjustifiable insinuations against, and attacks upon the Board of Health of the State of Louisiana by certain representatives of the National Board of Health.

While such instances have not been rare in the history of this and other great American cities, it is nevertheless true that never before in the history of this country have such efforts been made to create alarm in surrounding States.

The Board of Health of the State of Louisiana was assembled on Monday, the twelfth of July, and the occurrence of Yellow Fever on board the bark Excelsior, as well as the seizure of the ship by the Civil Sheriff, on the night of the tenth of July, and its return to the Mississippi Quarantine Station, by order of the President, was laid before this body, and after the consideration of all facts in the case, the action of the President was on motion of Dr. J. C. Beard unanimously sustained.

On motion, the President was empowered to give all the essential facts to the public press. In compliance with the last resolution, the press were furnished with the full report of the proceedings of the Board of Health, and the morning papers of the thirteenth instant contained a statement essentially the same as that embodied in the letter of the President to the Acting Governor of Louisiana.

OFFICE BOARD OF HEALTH, New Orleans, July 13, 1880.

Hon. S. D. McEnery, Lieutenant Governor of the State of Louisiana :

DEAR SIR—I have the honor to submit to the Governor of the State of Louisiana the following record of my official acts as President of the Board of Health, in the case of the Swedish bark Excelsior.

On the tenth of July, 1880, in company with Dr. F. Loeber, I visited a patient, James Kenney, at the Touro Infirmary.

The said James Kenney had been brought from the Swedish bark Excelsior, Saturday morning at 10 o'clock. The patient presented the symptoms of Yellow Fever.*

---

*Note—On the 7th inst., (Wednesday) at 8½ o'clock, p. m., complained of being sick; was visited by Dr. Victor C. Frogue on the 8th and 9th, and on Saturday morning 10th inst at 10½ o'clock, a m. was transferred to the Touro Infirmary.

On the 10th of July, 1880, at 1 p. m., Dr. F. Loeber, Member of the Board of Health of the State of Louisiana, informed me that there was a suspicious case of fever at the Touro Infirmary. In company with Dr. Loeber I repaired immediately to the Touro Infirmary and found the patient in a ward on the left side of the building on the second floor—John Kinney, age 22, native of England; fair; florid complexion; light, brown hair, blue eyes. full developed muscular system; seaman from Sweedish bark Excelsior from Rio de Janeiro; skin hot, eyes injected, epestaxis, stupor, jaundice, capillarie of surface injected, urine loaded with albumen and granular casts of tubuli urinifii. light orange colored; gums spongy. At 1:15 o'clock p m., hæmorrhage from nose. At 1:45 p. m. threw up black vomit in large quantities. Microscopical examination of urine revealed numerous cells from pelvis and urinary tubes of kidney; also numerous yellow granular casts. Microscopical examination of black vomit: colored blood corpuscles; mucus corpuscles and cells of torula (torula cereviae.)

Early Sunday morning I repaired to the Touro Infirmary and found that the man had died at 11:30 o'clock p m., a little over twelve hours after entering the hospital. Black vomit and hemorrhage from the bowels had been profuse. Dr. Loeber drew off by the catheter about six fluid ounces of urine when the patient first entered, and although the catheter was introduced several times, no farther urine was excreted. There was therefore urinary suppression during the last twelve hours of life. I examined the corpse and found the features blotched and discolored, and the entire surface of the body yellowish, with deep purplish ecchymoses. The capillary congestion and discoloration was great in the most dependent portions of the body. Black vomit issued from the corners of the mouth and ran down along the face and shoulders and neck. The sheets were smeared with black vomit from stomach and bloody discharges of bowels. These facts, as well as careful drawings of the urinary deposits and black vomit were submitted to the Board of Health.

The bark Excelsior, lying at the foot of Calliope street, Post 13, First District, was carefully inspected, the crew mustered on deck and ordered to remain on board.

The bark Excelsior, Capt. J. L. Bjorkgren, sailed from London, February 17, 1880, and arrived at Rio de Janeiro April 13; left Rio on the tenth of May, and arrived at the Mississippi Quarantine Station June 24, having been on the voyage about fifty-six days. Her crew consisted of three officers and nine seamen.

No case of sickness occurred either at Rio or on the voyage to the Mississippi Quarantine Station.

In accordance with orders issued by the President of the Board of Health, the Excelsior was detained at the Mississippi Quarantine Station for twelve days. During this time the coffee, 3600 sacks, constituting the entire cargo, the ballast being of granite rock, was shifted, aired and subjected to repeated fumigations with sulphurous acid gas; the ship was cleaned and the bilge water pumped out and replaced with a solution of copperas and carbolic acid.

Arrived at New Orleans on the fifth of July, commenced discharging cargo, which was consigned to Messrs. Johnston & Gordon, No. 138 Gravier street, and the coffee (3600 sacks) was deposited in the Montgomery Warehouse, on Fulton, between St. Joseph and Julia streets.

The following orders were immediately issued:

OFFICE BOARD OF HEALTH, July 10, 1880.

Capt. Thos. McLellan, N. O. Towboat Line:

DEAR SIR—You are hereby authorized and commanded to return the Swedish bark Excelsior, now lying at the foot of Calliope street, to the Mississippi River Quarantine Station at the earliest practicable moment.

Respectfully, JOSEPH JONES, M. D.,
President Board of Health, State of Louisiana.

OFFICE BOARD OF HEALTH, July 10, 1880.

Capt. S. L. Bjorkgren, Bark Excelsior:

DEAR SIR—In behalf of the public safety, and in obedience to the Acts of the Senate and House of Representatives, in General Assembly convened, establishing and regulating quarantine for the protection of the State against the importation of foreign pestilence, you are hereby commanded to return your vessel, the bark "Excelsior," to the Mississippi Quarantine Station. In case of the absence of the master, the officer next in command will execute this order. I have authorized Capt. Thos. McLellan, of the New Orleans Towboat Line, to execute this order.

Respectfully, JOSEPH JONES, M. D.,
President Board of Health, State of Louisiana.

In the absence of the captain, the second officer refused to leave the wharf on the ground that the vessel was not properly ballasted, and would capsize if towed into the stream.

An order was then issued to the Civil Sheriff of the parish of Orleans, commanding him, in the name of the State of Louisiana and of the Board of Health, to remove the bark Excelsior forthwith to the Quarantine Station.

BOARD OF HEALTH, July 11, 1880.

Joseph Holt, M. D., Sanitary Inspector, First District:

Dear Sir—I have ordered the bark "Excelsior," lying at the foot of Calliope street, First District, back to Quarantine Station. She is at this moment in the hands of the Civil Sheriff of the parish of Orleans. I desire that you shall at once execute the following important offices:

1. Assist the authorities (if necessary), in having the vessel properly ballasted and speedily towed off.

2. Communicate all facts in your possession with reference to the fumigation of this vessel, and of the coffee in the warehouse; also full record of your inspections whilst in the harbor of New Orleans.*

*NEW ORLEANS, July 6, 1880.

1. Name of Vessel? Excelsior.
2. Name of Captain or Master? S. L. Bjorkgren.
3. Tonnage or Class of Vessel? 450.
4. From whence is the vessel you command? Rio de Janerio.
5. How many days have you been on the passage? Fifty-eight to New Orleans.
6. At what port or ports have you touched? None
7. Were any Contagious or Infectious Diseases prevailing at the port from whence your vessel sailed? Yellow Fever.
13. Have you any Bills of Health? Yes.
15. During the course of your Cruise or Passage, what cases of disease have occurred on board? None.

   3. Ascertain the names and address and residence of all persons who visited the vessel up to date, and hold them under careful observation.

   Report at once to the Board of Health any cases of disease which may in future occur among the people.*

   17. Have any deaths taken place on board your vessel since you left the last port? No.
   19. Are there any sick on your vessel at this time? No.
   20. Has Yellow Fever, Small Pox, Cholera or Plague ever existed on this ship? No.
   22. What is the number of Officers? Three.
   23. What is the number of the Crew? Nine.
   24. What is the number of Passengers? None.
   25. What is your cargo? Coffee.
   26. To whom is the cargo consigned? Johnston, Gordon & Co.
   27. What is the present sanitary condition of the vessel, cargo, crew and passengers? Good.
   28. Have you a Medical officer? No.

S. L. BJORKGREN, Master.
H. G. F. MIKSTROM.

Subscribed to before me, JOSEPH HOLT, M. D., Sanitary Inspector First District.

---

   *Special report of discharge of cargo of Excelsior, by Joseph Holt, M. D., Sanitary Inspector, First District.

Joseph Jones, M. D. President Board of Health :

   SIR—Accompanying this, I present you a complete list of persons employed in discharging the cargo of the ship Excelsior, twenty in number. eighteen of whom are colored and two whites, and all of them of long residence in this city. The warehousemen handling the cargo are colored, and also of long residence. The gentlemen engaged in supervising the work and as book-keepers, etc , are likewise fully acclimated.

   One hundred and thirty-one bags of this coffee which had been sent to Mobile railroad depot for shipment was returned to warehouse, together with eighty bags from the Mississippi warehouse which had come in contact with it. No sickness on vessels or in houses in vicinity of where the Excelsior was moored.

Respectfully submitted,
JOSEPH HOLT, M. D..,
Sanitary Inspector, First District.

NAMES OF PERSONS EMPLOYED IN DISCHARGING CARGO OF BARK EXCELSIOR, JULY 7TH, 1880.

Duncan McNeill, Stevedore, residence, 57 Orange street.
   Jno. Foley, Foreman. Robin, between Peters and Tchoupitoulas.

Daniel Webster, colored.	Chas. Crosby. colored.	Silas Smith, colored.	Alex. Payne, colored.
George Butler, "	D. W. Daniels, "	Wm. Adams, "	Peter Robinson, "
Joe Harris, "	Jessy Hall, "	Chas. Irvine, "	Abraham Shields, "
Alex. Harris, "	Joshua Jones, "	A. Larceno, "	Dan Smith, "
Tom Smith, "	Frank Ray, "		

LIST OF NAMES OF PERSONS WHO HANDLED COFFEE IN WAREHOUSE, FROM BARK EXCELSIOR, 7TH TO 12TH OF JULY, 1880, BY JOSEPH HOLT, SANITARY INSPECTOR, FIRST DISTRICT.

Chas. Dittman, Proprietor.   J. F. Jourdan, Clerk.   H. Wight, Warehouseman.

LABORERS.

—— Charbonet, white.	A. Barbe, colored.	Jack Wilson, colored.	Jack Leonard. colored.
—— Torregosa, white.	Ed. Vincent, colored.	Ed. Boon. colored.	Chas. Jefferson. colored.
P. Seguin, white.	Gab. Bernard, colored.	Poland John, colored	A Joseph, colored.
L. Davis, colored.	—— Casimere, colored.	Alex. Robinson, colored.	Robt. Fillmore, colored.
—— Godfrey, colored.	Thos. Briscoe, colored.	P. Jones, colored.	Fred. Domingo, colored.
A. Nibert, colored.	H. Hunt, colored.	Jack Rogers. colored.	John Pierre, colored.
T. Venerable, colored.	Mose Darson, colored.	Jos. Reville, colored.	Chas. Wright, colored.
—— Palmer, colored.	Jos. Auguste, colored.	Wm. Walker, colored.	—— Hardie, colored.
Pierre Regis, colored.	Baptiste Dalbi, colored.	Louis Emile, colored.	Clem. James, colored.
Chas. James, colored.	Joe Valdez, colored	Joe Williams, colored.	

NAMES OF PERSONS EMPLOYED IN HANDLING COFFEE (EX. BARK EXCELSIOR) IN MONTGOMERY WAREHOUSE AFTER ITS FUMIGATION, JULY 8TH TO 12TH, 1880.

Mr. Chas. Dittman, Proprietor.   Mr. J. F. Jourdan, Clerk.   Mr. H. Wight, Warehouseman.

LABORERS.

*Paul Seguin, white.	Dick Miller, white.	Mark Thompson. colored.	—— Nicholas, colored.
—— Goldsmith, white.	—— Heins, white.	Joe Baptiste, colored.	Joe Cherre colored.
Louis Landry, white.	—— Ibos, white.	*Wm. Walker, colored.	*Pierre Regisse, colored.
Paul Jordan, white.	—— Sancier, white.	*—— Palmer, colored.	*Joe Willams, colored.
George Schumberg, white.	*Fred. Domingo, colored.	*——Hardie, colored.	*Joe Valdez, colored.
H. Schumberg, white.	*A. Nibert, colored.	John Edwards, colored.	*—— Gabi colored.
O. Schumberg, white.	*T. Venerable, colored.	*Louis Davis, colored.	*Chas. Wright, colored.
*—— Charbonet white.	*Jack Rogers, colored.	*—— Godfrey, colored.	*Alf. Barbe, colored.
A. Giraud, white.	*Chas. James, colored.	Dan McCray, colored.	*Edw. Vincent, colored.
Joe Prudhomme, white.	—— Hegano, colored.	Chas. Day, colored.	

   N. B.—Those marked * were also employed before the fumigation of the coffee took place.

RECORD RAILROAD INSPECTION FOR JULY 12, 1880, BY J. M. WATKINS, M. D., INSPECTOR.

NEW ORLEANS, July 13, 1880.

To Dr. Joseph Jones, President Board of Health :
   Dear Sir—Since my last report I have inspected freight and waybills of Trains Nos. 10 and 12, at the

4. The public safety demands that the warehouse in which the coffee has been stored shall be immediately and sufficiently fumigated with sulphurous acid gas. I am aware of the fact that you have already fumigated the cargo of the "Excelsior." both in the vessel and in the warehouse, but it is necessary that the process should be repeated. These measure are directed by the fact that one of the crew died at the Touro Infirmary with the symptoms of Yellow Fever." Respectfully,

JOSEPH JONES, M. D.,
President Board of Health.

These measures were fully executed, and the Civil Sheriff returned the bark "Excelsior" to the Mississippi Quarantine Station on the morning of th- 11th inst.

Under the direction of Dr. Loeber, surgeon in charge of the Touro Infirmary, all the necessary measures of fumigation and disinfection have been executed.

———

BOARD OF HEALTH, July 12, 1880.

Messrs. Johnston, Gordon & Co., 138 Gravier street.

Gentlemen—The Board of Health regard it to be inexpedient to ship any of the cargo of the Bark "Excelsior" until such time as shall be indicated.†

Respectfully,   JOSEPH JONES, M. D.,
President Board of Health, State of Louisiana.

———

The representative of the National Board of Health in New Orleans was also notified on the 10th inst. of the existence of a case of Yellow Fever at the Touro Infirmary.

It is worthy of note that neither at Rio nor at the Quarantine Station during a period of fifty-eight days, did any sickness occur on board the "Excelsior," and the case of the seaman, James Kenney, was not developed until the vessel had been not exceeding sixty hours at her wharf at New Orleans.

The Swedish Consul has notified me that he will protest officially against the action of the President of the Board of Health, and lay the whole matter before his Government. I

depot of the New Orleans, Mobile and Texas Railroad. The following shipments of coffee were refused a certificate, and in consequence the railroad authorities declined taking it:

E. P. Cottraux to M. Forcheimer & Co., at Mobile, 131 bags.
E. P. Cottraux to M. Forcheimer & Co.. at Mobile, 90 bags.
H. T. Cottam to Greenwood, Shubuta, at Miss , 10 bags.
Zuburbeir & Behan. to Green & Co., at Blackwater, Fla., 8 bags.
Pohlman to L. M. Davis at Pensacola, Fla., 3 bags
Pohlman to J. Ollinger, at Milton, Fla., 5 bags.
Bailey to A. E. B. W., at Biloxi, Miss, 1 bag.

The shipment by E. P. Cottraux included 100 bags of the cargo of the Excelsior from Rio, and it is now in car No. 246 at the depot of the New Orleans, Mobile and Texas Railroad.

The following shipment was allowed to go through on a guarantee by the shipper that it had been in store six months and received from Mexico.

Smith Bros. & Co., to Johnson, Fewman & Co., at Louisville, Ky., 50 bales.
• Smith Bros. & Co., to Pearson. Roberts & Co., Lexington, Ky., 25 bales.

Respectfully,   J. M. WATKINS, M. D., Inspector.

*It having been rumored, and also asserted by an agent of the National Board of Health, that two men had deserted from the bark Excelsior. I made inquiry of the Royal Vice Consul of Sweden and Norway, and of the agents of the ship, and also directed the police of New Orleans to investigate and arrest the men, and in addition commissioned Dr. Holt to make a thorough investigation. I found the statement to be false. No seamen deserted from the bark Excelsior.

The following is the special report of Dr. Joseph Holt, Sanitary Inspector, First District:

[Special report on two men, said to have deserted from the bark Excelsior, by Joseph Holt, M D., Sanitary Inspector, First District.]

Joseph Jones, M. D., President Board of Health:

Sir:—After diligent inquiry in all of the known sailor boarding-houses, it is impossible to discover the whereabouts of the two sailors said to have left the Excelsior while in this port.

If it were possible to furnish their names and nationality it would be of advantage in prosecuting the search. Respectfully submitted, JOSEPH HOLT. M. D.,
Sanitary Inspector, First District.

The Royal Vice Consul of Sweden and Denmark affirmed that no men had deserted from the bark Excelsior, and stated that such an event was impossible without the knowledge of the Royal Vice Consul.

† Previous to the issuance of this order, about 600 bags of coffee had been shipped from the cargo of the Excelsior to several points, and a portion of this to Houston Texas.

‡OFFICE BOARD OF HEALTH, STATE-HOUSE. STATE OF LOUISIANA, }
New Orleans, July 10, 1880. }

S. M. Bemis, M. D., Member National Board of Health, New Orleans, Louisiana:

Sir—Case presenting symptoms of Yellow Fever, carried this day from bark Excelsior to Touro Infirmary.

I have ordered bark Excelsior back to Mississippi Quarantine Station, and have take all necessary precautions.

Will furnish any further information desired. Respectfully,

JOSEPH JONES, M. D.,
President Board of Health, State of Louisiana.

have advised him to take time and consider, and to consult me fully in any steps which he may take, as it mav be possible. by friendly advice, to prevent any litigation, especially as in the capacity of Executive Officer of the Board of Health, my action was dictated solely with regard to the public safety and welfare.

With great respect, I have the honor to be your obedient servant,

JOSEPH JONES, M. D ,

President Board of Health, State of Louisiana.

The following is the reply of his Excellency, S. D. McEnery, Acting Governor:

STATE OF LOUISIANA, EXECUTIVE DEPARTMENT, }
New Orleans, July 14, 1880. }

Dr. Joseph Jones, President Louisiana Board of Health:

SIR—I have received and read with pleasure, your reply of the action of the Board of Health. in the matter of the Swedish bark "Excelsior."

That action has m y approval in every particular, as entirely necessary and strictly legal.

I especially approve the return of the "Excelsior" to the Quarantine Station, as a measure of necessary precaution wholly in accordance with law.

I have the honor to be your obedient servant,

S. D. McENERY, Acting Governor.

———

[Telegram.]

NEW ORLEANS, July 10, 1880—Dr. Wilkinson, Mississippi Quarantine Station: I have ordered the bark Excelsior back to Quarantine Station. Retain her until further orders.

(Signed)   JOSEPH JONES, M. D.

———

July 13, 1880—Dr. Wilkinson, Mississippi Quarantine Station: Telegraph condition of crew bark Excelsior. Render the sick all possible assistance.

———   (Signed)   JOSEPH JONES. M, D.

Telegrams and also written instructions were dispatched by the President of the Board of Health of the State of Louisiana to the Resident and Assistant Resident Physicians at the Mississippi Quarantine Station, giving the facts relating to the occurrence of a case of fever and the return of the vessel to Quarantine; and stringent orders were issued to keep the vessel and crew in close quarantine, separated from all other vessels, allowing no communication with the shore on either side, or with the city of New Orleans, or with the settlements at the Jetties and Pilot Town.

[Telegram.]

MISSISSIPPI QUARANTINE STATION. July 11, 1880.—To Joseph Jones, M. D., President Board of Health: This is to certify that Capt Bovle, Deputy Sheriff, brought to anchor Swedish bark Excelsior at Mississippi River Quarantine Station on July 11, at 10 o'clock P. M.   C. P. WILKINSON.
Assistant Resident Physician.

[Extract from letters of instructions to Resident Quarantine Physician.]

The accident to the Resident Quarantine Physician, and the unfortunate occurrence of Yellow Fever upon the bark Excelsior necessitating her immediate return to Quarantine; has necessarily thrown much additional labor upon the Assistant Quarantine Physician, employ acclimated nurses for the sick; supplies, including brandy, coffee, tea, sugar and flour, have been shipped for the use of the sick in hospital.

Accurate and full information is required by the Board of Health concerning the following matters:

(*a*). Detail accurately the process of disinfection and fumigation to which the bark Excelsior was subjected during the detention of twelve days at Quarantine. State the mode of shifting and ventilating cargo, and the amount of sulphur used in each fumigation. Give an accurate transcript of the Quarantine Record relating to this vessel. State the condition of the bilge water, the hold, keelson, forecastle, cabin bunks, etc , and all facts relating to the cleansing of the vessel.

(*b*). Give an accurate account of the vessel after her arrival at Quarantine, with full history of crew.

(*c*). Give an accurate outline of each case treated in hospital, including name, age, nativity. general condition, temperature, pulse, respiration, treatment and result.

(*d*). Anchor the Excelsior in an isolated situation, at least 1000 yards from other vessels. and allow no communication between this and other vessels, or with the city or the settlements along the Mississippi River.

(*e*). In the event of the arrival of another ship from Rio, telegraph the facts at once to the President of the Board of Health, and await orders as to disposition of ship and cargo.

(*f*). The Board of Health of the State of Louisiana demand that every law of the State now in force relating to the protection of the State from the introduction of foreign pestilence, shall be rigidly executed; and that under no circumstances shall the Quarantine Physician or his assistant assume any authority as to the modification of the execution of said laws.

* * * * *

(*g*). Isolate all ships, by as great a space at the Quarantine Station, as may be practicable.

(*h*). The bark Excelsior should be again subjected to repeated and thorough fumigations and cleansings. The bilge water should be replaced several times with copperas and carbolic acid solution. The decks, hold and all woodwork should be thoroughly scrubbed and washed with carbolic or copperas solution, indicated in the rules and regulations of this Board of Health.

* * * * *

JOSEPH JONES, M. D.,
President Board of Health, State of Louisiana.

The following protests were received from the Royal Vice Consulate of Sweden and Norway:

ROYAL VICE-CONSULATE OF SWEDEN AND NORWAY, }
New Orleans, July 15, 1880. }

To the Hon. Joseph Jones, M. D., President Board of Health, City of New Orleans:

Sir—I have the honor to hand you herewith enclosed the protest of the Captain of the Sweedish bark Excelsior against the action of your honorable Board of returning the vessel to Qurantine Station.

From the evening papers I learn that Acting Mayor Isaacson has suggested to you to remove the Excelsior to Ship Island, or some other isolated place. I do not believe that you or your honorable Board will entertain any such suggestion, but nevertheless I, George Gerdes, Vice-Consul of Sweden and Norway, herewith do most solemnly protest against removing the Swedish bark Excelsior from Quarantine Station to any other place than back to this city.

I have the honor to sign myself your most obedient servant,
GEORGE GERDES, Royal Vice-Consul of Sweden and Norway.

STATE OF LOUISIANA, Port of New Orleans, July 13, 1880.

To the Honorable Joseph Jones Esq., M. D., President Board of Health, and members thereof:

Gentlemen.—Your orders for the removal of my vessel, the Swedish Bark "Excelsior" from her wharf at the foot of Calliope street, and returning her to the Quarantine station having been executed, I now respectfully submit this, my solemn protest against said action of your honorable Board; and urgently request a reconsideration of your action in the premises on the following grounds set forth by me, all of which are submitted with truth to your honorable Board, and relief asked for at your earliest convenience, to-wit:

1st. That no cause for such removal existed or at this moment exists, for the detention of said Bark "Excelsior," on account of any violation of law or custom, whereby maritime Nations are allowed the right or freedom of your port, having submitted myself, crew and vessel, to all and every restriction required necessary and assisted thereto, with all means at my command, to entitle me to those rights in the premises which when once granted, are by all nations considered inviolable·

2nd. That any case of sickness that have occurred on board of my vessel the "Excelsior," since her arrival at this port, or what may hereafter occur, are traceable only to local causes met with and encountered in this city and port, and the consequences thereof can not be attributable to any cause or causes previously taken place on board of said vessel as the entire facts relating to my present voyage, and hereafter explained, will set forth, viz:

That myself and crew arrived in this port in a perfect state of health, having performed a long and tedious voyage of one hundred and forty days since leaving London on the 17th of February last, after fifty-seven days passage to Rio de Janerio remaining in that port twenty-six days, and was forty-six days at sea, before reaching your quarantine station, where we remained twelve days, enduring the trying ordeal of fumigation, and during all this time not one of my crew had been sick or in any way ailing. After remaining two days at the wharf of Calliope street, where my crew had full liberty for the first time since leaving London, to indulge themselves in Fruit, Liquors, and a total change of diet, two of my crew were taken sick, and I employed a regular city physician to attend them, and one of them immediately recovered under his treatment, while the other grew worse, was sent to the Touro Infirmary where he died; of what disease I do not know; but most solemnly believe was caused by above mentioned change and indulgences, no doubt aggravated by the excessive heat in the day and cool nights, bringing on inflammation and sickness, which terminated fatally in the case of John McKenna.

That my vessel has been kept in a perfect state of cleanliness during said voyage, and was particularly so upon her arrival at this port, which fact you can ascertain from your Inspector, and by whose testimony I rest this matter.

That myself, crew, vessel and cargo, having once performed the rigorous quarantine, established according to the theories of your National and Local Board of Health, and when practiced by your authorities, guaranteed to the world to be sufficient safeguard against all infectious diseases, and having during twelve days endured said rigorous measures, during which time all my crew remained in their former good state of health and that only after your authorities were convinced of the safety of my vessel and crew passing through this ordeal, was a *release* granted, which according to maritime rules, should be sufficient safeguard to entitle myself, crew and vessel from further detention, and grant me the same privileges enjoyed by other maritime nations visiting your port.

That resting my convictions on the facts of above mentioned principle, I have chartered my vessel to perform another voyage from this port, to a port in France, binding myself by a contract, which will be violated should you much longer detain my vessel; and myself and vessel, and all parties interested therein be damaged.

Having thus presented all the points as they truly are, I respectfully request your reconsideration of the vessels removal and that you will order her release at first practical opportunity, so that I may be able to fulfil my obligations into which my vessel is legally bound, but now entirely prevented by your actions in the premises.

Hoping your favorable reply, I remain yours truly.

　　　　　　　　　　　　　　S. L. BJÖRKGREN, Master Swedish Bark "Excelsior."

OFFICE BOARD OF HEALTH, STATE-HOUSE, STATE OF LOUISIANA. }
　　　　　　　　　　　　　New Orleans, July 19, 1880. }

Hon. George Gordes, Royal Vice-Consul of Sweden and Norway :

Sir—Your communication of the 15th inst. was duly laid before the Board of Health. The bark Excelsior will not be removed from the Mississippi Quarantine Station.

By telegram received from Quarantine S ation, yesterday, two deaths had occurred among the three men in Hospital. The other two of the crew are reported as doing well. Shall be pleased to have a personal interview with the Royal V ce-Consul of Sweden.

　　　Respectfully, your obedient servant,　　　JOSEPH JONE , M. D.,
　　　　　　　　　　　. President Board of Health, State of Louisiana.

The following is an extract from the report of the Assistant Quarantine Physician, Dr. C. P. Wilkinson, with reference to bark Excelsior, in reply to inquiries of President Board of Nealth :

　　　　　　　MISSISSIPPI RIVER QUARANTINE STATION, July 21, 1880.

To Dr. Joseph Jones, President Board of Health, New Orleans, La. :

Dear Sir—The Swedish bark Excelsior arrived at this station on June 25, 1880, from Rio, forty-five days out, loaded with 3600 bags of coffee and some few tons of rock ballast, twelve men all told, being on board. Had never had any sickness on board since leaving London, in the month of February, and had never had, to the knowledge of the present captain.

The vessel was capable of carrying about twelve thousand bags of coffee, and consequently had only about one-third of cargo.

On June 26 the vessel was fumigated, hold, cabin and forecastle—say twenty pounds of sulphur burned in iron pots in hold, ten pounds in cabin and ten pounds in forecastle.

June 27 being Sunday, the bark was not disturbed, as the men on board the bark were not disposed to shift cargo.

The bilge pumps of the vessel were worked by the crew of the vessel, and foul bilge water was discharged. Carbolic acid and copperas were put into the pumps every day, and the bilge water was made clean and smelled only of carbolic acid Cargo was shifted sack by sack from amidships, both forward and aft. Under my personal supervision, acting under Dr. Finney, two fumigations were given to the bark. During my absence two more fumigations were given, making in all four.　　*　　*

Since the return of the bark Excelsior I have, in my opinion, thoroughly disinfected the bark with one continuous fumigation. burning not less than one hundred pounds of sulphur in her various compartments.

One man on board was removed to Hospital at 6 a. m., July 12.

The second at 7:30 a. m., July 13.

The third at 7 p. m., July 14.

The two last died, respectively, at 2 a. m., 17th inst., and 3 a. m., 18th inst.

**There are present on board the said bark seven men, which fills her complement—so none have deserted; the rumor, therefore, is false.　　*　　　*　　　*　　　*　　　*

Very respectfully, your obedient servant,　　　　　　C. P. WILKINSON,
　　　　　　　　　　　　　　　　　　　　　　Assistant Resident Physician.

At the regular meeting of the Board of Health, on the 15th of July, 1880, a committee of three consisting of Dr. J. C. Beard, Dr. J. P. Davidson and Dr. F. Loeber, were appointed to visit the Mississippi Quarantine Station and to investigate matters relating to its conduct, and more especially all facts relating to the Bark Excelsior.

Acting Governor of the State, Hon. S. D. McEnery, was invited to accompany the committee.

Dr. Rutherford, Health Officer of Texas, who on the solicitation of *the member of the National Board of Health residing in New Orleans,* had been sent by the Governor of Texas to *investigate the sanitary condition of New Orleans, and the case of the Excelsior,* was also invited to accompany the members of the Board of Health.

The following is the report of the committee :

OFFICE BOARD OF HEALTH, STATE-HOUSE, STATE OF LOUISIANA, }
　　　　　　　　　　　　　New Orleans, July 22, 1880. }

To the Board of Health, State of Louisiana :

Sirs—We, the undersigned committee, appointed by your honorable body to inspect and investigate the workings of the Mississippi Quarantine Station, would most respectfully report that they proceeded to the above-named station on W dnesday, July 12, 1880, accompanied by Gov. S. D. McEnery, Dr. R. Rutherford, of Houston, Texas, Drs. E. T. Shepard and F. Formento, and gentlemen of the press. We investigated as regards all vessels that have been at Quarantine Station during our administration, but more especially as regards the Swedish bark Excelsior, and elicited the following testimony:

TESTIMONY REGARDING BARK EXCELSIOR.

C. Henry Merritt, Assistant Boarding Officer, U. S. Warehouse—Boarded Excelsior and unsealed her hatches on the day of her arrival, June 25, 1880, and sealed them on her departure, July 5, 1880; knows she was fumigated; no one sick on board to his knowledge; while at Quarantine boarded Excelsior several times and each time smelled sulphur burning very strongly; this vessel appeared cleaner than the average vessel.

R. H. Taylor, U. S. Warehouse Boatman—Boarded Excelsior on morning of July 5, 1880, to assist in sealing hatches; smelled sulphur burning; no one on board sick to his knowledge.

G. T Wilkstrom, Mate of bark Excelsior—Arrived at Quarantine June 25, 1880; left July 5, 1880; no one sick at Rio; no one sick at sea; crew all went ashore at Rio twice; crew comprised twelve men, captain, two mates, nine seamen; crew went below decks seven or eight times while at sea; Excelsior was twenty-nine days at Rio; was at sea fifty six days; whole crew assisted in shifting cargo at Quarantine; crew obliged to sleep on deck while at Quarantine on account of sulphur fumes; Excelsior was fumigated four times at Quarantine; bilge water pumped out and renewed; very foul at first, less so afterwards; no one was sick while at Quarantine June 25 to July 5, 1880; present crew consists of seven men, all well, and one man in hospital convalescing.

James Daly, Coxswain Quarantine Boat—Boarded Excelsior; assisted in fumigating her; used each time five pots, each containing from fifteen to twenty pounds of sulphur; no one sick on board vessel; was fumigated twice to his knowledge; left for city before the completion of fumigation.

Henry Car., Boatman Quarantine Station—Boarded Excelsior; assisted four times in fumigating her; used five pots; amount of sulphur used each time in each pot about fifteen to twenty pounds.

Frank Richmond, Boatman Quarantine Station—Boarded Excelsior; assisted in her fumigation four times; cargo was shifted; bilge water was pumped out and replaced by solution of copperas and carbolic acid; used five pots in fumigation, each pot contained each time fifteen to twenty pounds of sulphur; positive that whole vessel was saturated with fumes of sulphur; crew all well while at Quarantine; no one except crew allowed on vessel while at Quarantine; no intercourse allowed between vessels lying at Quarantine.

Joseph Swan, Boatman Quarantine Station—Assisted four times in the fumigation of Excelsior; used each time five pots, each containing fifteen to twenty pounds of sulphur; no one sick on board; bilge water pumped out and replaced by solution of copperas and carbolic acid

Dr. J. F. Finney, Resident Physician, Quarantine Station—Excelsior's condition was about the average for sailing vessels in point of cleanliness; no sickness on board while at Quarantine; fumigated vessel repeatedly used at each fumigation sixty to seventy pounds of sulphur; bilge water pumped out and replaced by solution of copperas and carbolic acid, (this is done to all vessels); all vessels are inspected and cleaned thoroughly even though they may not come from an infected port.

Dr. Wilkinson, Assistant Quarantine Physician—Corroborates Dr. Finney's statement, and adds that the bilge water was pumped out and renewed several times and replaced by solution, copperas and carbolic acid; the Excelsior was fumigated to his certain knowledge four times; crew all well while at Quarantine; one of the crew is now in the hospital convalescing; no one else sick; there is no sickness in the neighborhood of Quarantine Station, either on this or the other side of the river; no communication is allowed between vessels while at Quarantine, the cargo of Excelsior was shifted from one part of the hold to the other and thoroughly fumigated; the hold of the vessel was ventilated as well as fumigated; the crew of the Quarantine boat are all acclimated persons.

The Committee most respectfully request further time for the completion of the report on the Buildings, etc., at the Mississippi Quarantine Station.
J. C. BEARD,
W. DAVIDSON.
F. LOEBEB.

The Board of Health retained the Excelsior at the Quarantine Station for over one month after the removal of the last case from the vessel on the fourteenth of July.

The man removed on the twelfth to Quarantine Hospital, and who recovered, was released on the twenty-fifth from the hospital as entirely convalescent.

The President of the Board of Health advocated the release of the vessel one month after the removal of the last case to the hospital, on condition that she be retained at some point below the city, on the opposite side of the River, there receiving her cargo. It was held that it was not advisable for the vessel to come up into the harbor among the shipping.

The opinion of the Resident Quarantine Physician was also to the same effect, as will be seen from the following letter:

MISSISSIPPI QUARANTINE, August 4, 1880.

Dr. Joseph Jones, President of Board of Health, New Orleans, La.:

Sir—Knowing of considerable discussion arising as to the detention of the Swedish bark Excelsior at this station, I beg leave to state:

That it having been abundantly proved that the vessel and cargo were thoroughly fumigated at this station, and the Yellow Fever contracted by members of the crew was contracted whilst the crew were engaged in the then unfumigated portion of the cargo, which they were shifting preparatory to fumigation; and, that the first case of Yellow Fever occurring on said bark in New Orleans, appeared on eighth day of July, without further spread of the disease.

6

That the second, third and fourth cases appeared at this station respectively, the eleventh, thirteenth and fourteenth of the same month. That the two last died respectively on the seventeenth and eighteenth of same month, all their effects brought on shore, consisting of a shirt, pair of pants, shoes, socks and a quilt, were buried with them. That the first case occurring here has recovered and is now on board the bark, being returned there 31st of July, having first thoroughly washed himself, a clean suit of clothes given him, and those with which he came on shore having been thoroughly boiled and washed. That the vessel has again been subjected to a thorough disinfection with sulphurous acid gas, copperas and carbolic acid. That no further cases of illness or disease at any time having occurred on board since the vessel has been at this station, I suggest that after another fumigation, and should no further cases of illness occur on board within thirty days after the last, that the vessel be allowed to proceed to New Orleans, and to satisfy public uneasiness, be made to anchor in mid stream; receive her supplies and cargo there, and be allowed to proceed to sea.

In my opinion, the best manner of proceeding in reference to the repairs necessary at this station, would be to request one of the State Board of Engineers to proceed to this station, make a thorough examination and report plans and specifications upon the same; upon which report the Board of Health could advertise for sealed proposals for the work.

Respectfully, your obedient servant,

JAS. F. FINNEY, Resident Physician.

———

[Telegram.]

NEW ORLEANS, August 16, 1880.—Dr. Finney, Mississippi Quarantine: Board directs release of Excelsior thirty days from transferring last case of fever to hospital, July 14.

Fumigate ship, clothing, etc. Sprinkle ballast with fifty gallons copperas and carbolic acid solution.

JOSEPH JONES, M. D.,
President Board of Health. State of Louisiana.

———

The Bark Excelsior was released from quarantine on the eighteenth of August, and was allowed to come up to Wood's Powder Wharf, on the opposite side of the Mississippi River, below Algiers, across from the United States Barracks.

The President of the Board of Health placed the vessel in the charge of Dr. Mioton, Sanitary Inspector of Fifth District. A policeman was detailed to remain on board to prevent communication with shore or city. The vessel was sealed by acclimated carpenters, and loaded with grain, the floating grain elevator being towed down.

Every effort was made to protect the State of Louisiana and Valley of Mississippi from the introduction of Yellow Fever from this vessel; and the effort of the Board of Health was crowned with success, as no case of Yellow Fever was propogated from the bark Excelsior.

The following is the report of the Sanitary Inspector of the Fifth District, in whose charge the Excelsior was placed:

OFFICE BOARD OF HEALTH, STATE-HOUSE, STATE OF LOUISIANA. }
New Orleans, November 15, 1880. }

Joseph Jones, M. D., President Board of Health:

Sir—I most respectfully furnish you with the following informations concerning the Swedish bark Excelsior, Capt. Bjorkgren, and its sojourn at Wallace Wood's Powder Wharf, at Tunisburg, Fifth District:

The Excelsior on its return from Quarantine Station landed at the above named place, on the sixteenth day of August, 1880, at about half-past 2 o'clock p m Having been informed of her arrival I immediately took charge of the vessel, placed one of my officers, Mr. James Norvell, on board, strictly forbidding any person to come on board without a written permit from the President of the Board of Health; and also not to allow any of the inmates of said bark to go on land. These instructions were strictly carried out, and none but those employed in loading the bark were admitted, not before, however, having been carefully examined by me as to whether they were fully acclimated or not. The Excelsior remained twenty-nine days at the Powder Wharf, and left for Bayonne, France, on the thirteenth day of September, 1880, loaded with grain.

I visited the bark twice, daily, morning and evening as I was instructed to do, my officer remaining on board from 5½ o'clock a. m. to 8 o'clock p. m. Two cases of dengue occurred on board during her stay in port, which I reported personally to the President of the Board of Health. Quinine and a light purgative were administered, the fever readily subsided, and patients got well.

All of which is respectfully submitted. Your most obedient servant,

EUG. J. MIOTON, M. D., Sanitary Inspector, Fifth District.

———

OFFICE BOARD OF HEALTH, STATE-HOUSE, STATE OF LOUISIANA. }
New Orleans, November 15, 1880. }

Carpenter's force on board of Excelsior:

George Anderson, fifty-seven years in city, 505 Craps street.
Chas. Boutiller, twenty years in city, 51 Kerlerec street.
N. Rigamier, life in city, Dorgenois, near St. Bernard street.
Aug. Sandrock, life in city, 51 Kerlerec street.
A. Donatort, life in city 166 St. Anthony street.
H. D. Gross, twenty-eight years in city. 29 Spain street.
W. Lowe, thirty-five years in city, 517 Dauphine street.
E. S. Taylor, life in city, 167 Constance street.
C. Anderson, four-and-a-half years in city 298 Old Levee street.
F. Fisher, fifteen years in city, Seventh street, between Fulton and Tchoupitoulas.

EUG. J. MIOTON, M. D., Sanitary Inspector, Fifth District

The preceding official records illustrate the prompt action of the Board of Health of the State of Louisiana, in the cases of the Vanguard and Excelsior, and the efforts to cleanse and disinfect vessels from Rio de Janerio, and other infected ports, regardless of the time necessary to accomplish these results. The resident member of the National Board of Health, under the guise of an editorial letter, headed " a card of explanation to my professional friends," published almost simultaneously in the New Orleans Medical and Surgical Journal* and New Orleans Democrat, uses the following language :

" There are three heresies regarding quarantine, which are each held to a limi'ed extent in this city ; 1st. Persons who have had Yellow Fever will not have it again, don't fear it, and have very little patience with those who do; 2nd. It originates *de novo* here and elsewhere, consequently quarantines are futile and should be abolished ; 3rd. Quarantines obstruct trade and it is right to keep them off, if even by the concealment or misrepresentation of facts. The President of the State Board, expresse ! himself very decidedly in favor of the indigenous origin of the first Excelsior case. Certainly his conduct would indicate that the third mentioned heresy has had its influence over him. While I shall not accuse the daily papers of this city with having adopted either one of these heresies, in all probability they were persuaded that it was their duty to advocate any policy which governed the conduct of the State Board."

The calumnies with reference to the "indigenous origin of the first Excelsior case," and with reference to the keeping off the quarantines by the *"concealment and misrepresentation* of facts," were first published in the daily papers of Memphis, Tenn. without the name of the fabricator.

---

* November 1880. Vol. VIII, No. 5, p. 476, edited by S. M. Bemiss, M. D., W. H. Watkins, M. D. and S. S. Herrick, M. D.

RELATIONS

OF

NATIONAL & STATE BOARDS OF HEALTH

TO THE

LEGAL AUTHORITIES OF THE STATE OF LOUISIANA.

SHIP ISLAND QUARANTINE

OF THE

NATIONAL·BOARD OF HEALTH, ESTABLISHED BY THE CEN-
TRAL NATIONAL AUTHORITY AT WASHINGTON.

INTER-STATE AND DOMESTIC QUARANTINES.

NATIONAL BOARD OF HEALTH.

It is not our intention to enter into any account of the differences which
arose between the National Board of Health and the State Board in 1879; it
is well known, however, that the relations were not of the most amicable nature; and it was thought by many that New Orleans would form the objective point of operations in 1880.

The attitude of the National Board of Health to the Board of Health of
the State of Louisiana at the opening of the year 1880 was forcibly stated
by Surgeon, John S. Billings, M. D., of the United States Army, and Vice
President of the National Board of Health, in his popular article on Yellow
Fever, published in the International Review, January, 1880, pp. 29–49.

The learned Dr. Billings thus alludes, in complimentary terms, to the merchants and physicians of New Orleans:

"The first is the difficulty of obtaining information as to the existence of
the earlier cases in time to prevent communication with, or from them. It is
to the interest of many wealthy business men to prevent the announcement

of the existence of such cases, as the matter now stand; for the announcement of the existence of a case of fever in New Orleans or Mobile results in the establishment of local quarantines at once against those cities. Were such quarantines established only when really necessary, and on uniform and reasonable plan, such concealment would be far less necessary and the motives to it would be much less powerful.

"On the other hand, if the inland towns in more immediate commercial intercourse with New Orleans could feel that they had reliable information as to the disease in the latter city, they would be much less fearful and much more judicious in their efforts to protect themselves than they now are. The concealment of the few cases of the fever which occurred in Morgan City last August, and the resulting epidemic which could have been easily prevented had timely warning been given, illustrate one side of the question; while on the other may be placed the local quarantine against New Orleans during the greater part of the summer, although there was no necessity for such quarantine for more than three weeks of the time, had it been possible to obtain reliable information as to the actual condition of the city. This is by no means generally understood, and New Orleans in particular has, prior to last summer, pursued what we consider to be a mistaken policy in this respect. Just as our ports establish quarantine during the summer against all vessels coming from West Indian ports regardless of the bills of health they may have, on the ground that no reliable information can be obtained as to the freedom of these ports from Yellow Fever, so a tendency to a similar action against New Orleans is being developed on the part of interior towns, and for the same reason.

* * "But no amount of assurance to this effect given by citizens, physicians or sanitarians of New Orleans will at present, nor for some time to come, give complete confidence to the interior towns. *The policy of concealment has been pursued so long and so uniformly, and its results have several times in the past proved so disastrous, that we can scarcely blame Pensacola or Galveston, Vicksburg or Memphis, for quarantining against New Orleans during the summer months.* There is but one remedy for this; and that is, to secure the fullest publicity; and to do this through persons whose competence and disinterestedness will not be doubted."*

Of course, the Vice President of the National Board of Health, having described the business men and physicians of New Orleans, as neither competent nor disinterested, and charged them with uniformly persuing the policy of concealment: There was no agency left for the salvation of the country from the dreaded epidemics of Yellow Fever, but the competent and disinterested members and agents of the National Board of Health.

Of the competency and disinterestedness of the members and employees of the National Board of Health, the citizens of New Orleans, have had ample opportunities of judging during the past summer and autumn.

---

*International Review, January, 1880, Yellow Fever by John S. Billings, M.D., pp. 29, 49. The italics are ours.

SHIP ISLAND QUARANTINE,

ESTABLISHED BY THE NATIONAL BOARD OF HEALTH.

The Board of Health of the State of Louisiana, was re-organized on the eighth of April, 1880, and on the following day, the member of the National Board of Health residing in New Orleans, presented certain propositions with reference to the Ship Island Quarantine, which are fully set forth in the following correspondence:

OFFICE BOARD OF HEALTH, STATE OF LOUISIANA, }
New Orleans, April 12, 1880. }

Hon. J. C. Egan, Attorney General, State of Louisiana:

Sir—As President of the Board of Health of the State of Louisiana, I have the honor respectfully to submit to the Attorney General the following extracts from the proceedings of the Board of Health of the State of Louisiana, on the eleventh of April, 1880, containing the official communication of Prof. S. M. Bemiss, M. D., member of the National Board of Health, relative to the establishment and regulation of the Quarantine Station on Ship Island:

NATIONAL BOARD OF HEALTH, }
New Orleans, April 10th, 1880. }

Professor Joseph Jones, President State Board of Health:

Sir—I wish respectfully to lay before the State Board, the following points of information regarding the Ship Island quarantine.

The precise rules and regulations for the government of Ship Island quarantine, will not be promulgated, until the meeting of the National Board of Health, on the second of May. They will not vary essentially from the following schedule of main points.

1st The intentions of the Station at Ship Island, are (a) to diminish the danger of importation of infectious and epidemic diseases, by detaining and disinfecting infected vessels, at a distance sufficiently remote from the coast to prevent communication of disease from those quarantined; (b) to provide for passengers and crews of infected vessels good hospital accommodations and treatment for the sick, and comfortable and well isolated accommodations for the well, who may be detained for observation; (c) to provide suitable warehouses for storing cargo, while vessels are being fumigated, in order that goods, clothing, etc., shall be disinfected promptly and thoroughly.

2nd. Vessels which will be required to stop at Ship Island Quarantine Station are, (a) those which actually have infectious diseases among their passengers or crew; (b) those which have had such diseases on board during the voyage or their stay in a foreign port; (c) those which sail from ports dangerously infected with epidemic diseases or touch at such ports; (d) those vessels which will be required by the quarantine regulations of Louisiana, Mississippi or Alabama, to stop at Ship Island Station.

3rd. Vessels not included in the above enumerated classes, are not required to stop at Ship Island Quarantine.

4th. The station at Ship Island does not supersede or in any manner interfere with any state regulations now in force or hereafter to be enforced.

5th. It is not to deprive local boards of health of any revenues or pecuniary profits which would otherwise accrue to them.

The Quarantine Station at Ship Island, is intended to be entirely co-operative with those sanitary organizations engaged in the same important work of protecting from pestilential diseases, and their concurrence and co-operation are absolute necessities to its success. Therefore. the member of the National Board of Health to whose supervision this work is entrusted, respectfully asks an immediate reply to the following inquiries:

1st. Will the State Board of Health of Louisiana co-operate with the National Board, in enforcing such rules for the government of Ship Island Quarantine, as to not conflict with the above schedule?

2nd. Will the State Board of Health order vessels back to this port in contravention to these rules, except under any peculiar circumstances where the State Board and the undersigned, acting for the National Board, might concur in opinion that it was safe and proper to direct otherwise?

Will the State Board order its quarantine inspectors to accept bills of health and certificates of disinfection from the chief medical officer at Ship Island, and not subject vessels provided with them to further quarantine restrictions?

(Signed)   SAMUEL M. BEMISS, M. D., Member National Board of Health.

The President stated that Dr. Bemiss requested immediate action by the Board of Health of the State of Louisiana on the propositions contained in his communication, as the Quarantine buildings were not yet commenced at Ship Island; and that his action as a member of the National Board of Health would be influenced to a certain extent by the response given to his propositions by the Board of Health of the State of Louisiana.

The President had replied to the author of the above communication by suggesting that it would be impossible to respond immediately and categorically to those propositions which related to the assumption of certain powers by the Board of Health of the State of Louisiana over the commerce of the Mississippi Valley, as they involved questions of civil and commercial law. Without entering into an exhaustive analysis of the communication from the member of the National Board of Health, the President directed the attention of the Board of Health of the State of Louisiana to the second proposition, namely, "Will the State Board of Health order vessels back to Ship Island which attempt to come to this port in contravention to these rules, except under any peculiar circumstances where the State Board, and the undersigned, acting for the National Board, might concur in opinion, that it was safe and proper to direct otherwise."

The Board of Health of the State of Louisiana possesses no powers except those conferred by the acts of the Legislature of Louisiana, and such powers can only be exercised in accordance with the laws of the State and the laws of the United States, regulating the foreign and domestic commerce of the entire country. The several acts establishing "Quarantine for the protection of the State of Louisiana," passed by the Legislature of Louisiana March 15, 1855, February 8, 1858, March 18, 1858, March 16, 1870, March 24, 1876, and April 20, 1877, confer no power upon the Board of Health to order vessels out of the waters of Louisiana to any foreign or domestic port, or to any island or quarantine station under the jurisdiction of the United States.

A critical examination of the acts of Congress constituting the National Board of Health, approved March 3, 1879, and entitled "An Act to prevent the introduction of infectious and contagious diseases into the United States, and to establish a National Board of Health," and the subsequent "Acts to prevent the introduction of contagious and infectious diseases into the United States," approved June 2, 1879, confer no power either upon the National Board of Health or upon local Boards of Health to control foreign and domestic commerce to the extent of ordering ships from the ports of their destination to points beyond the jurisdiction of local State Boards. As the Board of Health of the State of Louisiana possesses no such power, and as the National Board of Health is incompetent to confer uch power, the negative reply to the second proposition cannot be adduced as evidence that the Board of Health of the State of Louisiana is unwilling to co-operate with the National Board of Health in legal sanitary or quarantine measures.

While the State of Louisiana possess-s quarantine buildings on the Mississippi River which have already cost more than sixty thousand dollars ($60,000), the buildings and appliances for the Ship Island Quarantine have not yet been erected, and the efficiency or value of the Ship Island Quarantine has yet to be demonstrated.

It is manifest that should the Board of Health assume absolute control of the commerce of the Mississippi River from the northern confines of Louisiana to the Gulf of Mexico, the mere ordering of vessels back to Ship Island "which attempt to come to this port in contravention to their rules," might result in driving the commerce of the Mississippi Valley to other great commercial centres as Boston, New York, Baltimore, Norfolk, Charleston and Savannah.

In view of the legal questions involved in the communication of the member of the National Board of Health, the President of the Board of Health of the State of Louisiana urged the reference of the paper to the Attorney General of the State.

On motion of Mr. I. N. Marks, the Board empowered the President to refer the communication of the member of the National Board of Health to the Attorney General of the State of Louisiana, with the request that his legal opinion be furnished at the earliest practicable moment. .

. In obedience to the preceding resolution I have the honor to place in the hands of the Attorney General the communication of Samuel M. Bemis, M. D., together with certain manuscript and printed documents relating to the Ship Island Quarantine, and the Acts of Congress constituting and defining the powers of the National Board of Health.

Very respectfully, your obedient servant,   JOSEPH JONES, M. D.,
President Board of Health, State of Louisiana.

ATTORNEY-GENERAL'S OFFICE, STATE OF LOUISIANA. }
New Orleans, April 15, 1880. }

Joseph Jones, M. D., President of the Board of Health.

Dear Sir—Your communication, of the 12th inst., has been received; but as the questions propounded are ones of great importance. I would prefer to have until next week in which to give my opinion on them, as other official duties have precluded me from giving them the attention they deserve in time for your meeting this evening.

Very respectfully,   J. C. EGAN, Attorney-General.

ATTORNEY GENERAL'S OFFICE, STATE OF LOUISIANA, }
New Orleans, La., April 22, 1880. }

Dr. Joseph Jones, President Board of Health :

Dear Sir—Your communication referring to me the letter of the National Board of Health has been received. I consider that for the purposes of quarantine it would be in the power of your board to order ships coming to this port, back to Ship Island as a condition to their entry, if in your opinion, such a measure would tend to the better security of the State from infectious diseases. But as there is no absolute requirement, and as quarantine is in restraint of free commerce, it is, in my opinion, within the discretion of the Board to adopt such prudential measures as will protect the State from the importation of disease, and which will the most lightly affect the trade of our port.

- While the law confides largely in the discretion of the Board, I think the trust reposed was not intended to be delegated, and no matter how high the character of the National Board may be, I think the law contemplates the personal service of the State Board in the prevention of pestilence. I am of the opinion, therefore, that bills of health and certificates of disinfection from the Chief Medical Officer at Ship Island should not be conclusively satisfactory to the State Board of Health. It is useless for me to advise your Board to a spirit of the fullest and most cordial co-operation with the National Board of Health compatible with your view of a sound system of prevention of epidemic diseases.

Very respectfully, J. C. EGAN, Attorney General.

OFFICE BOARD OF HEALTH, STATE-HOUSE, STATE OF LOUISIANA, }
New Orleans, April 23, 1880. }

Professor S. M. Bemis, M. D., Member National Board of Health, New Orleans, La.:

Sir—In reply to your communication of April 10, relating to the Ship Island Quarantine, I beg leave respectfully to submit the following :

On the 12th inst., on motion of Mr. I. N. Marks, the Board empowered the President to refer the communication of the member of the National Board of Health to the Attorney General of the State of Louisiana, with the request that his legal opinion be furnished at the earliest practical moment.

The reply of Attorney General J. C. Egan, was received on the 22d, and laid before the Board of Health at its meeting on the evening of the same date, at 7½ o'clock, p. m.

Upon reading the report Mr. I. N. Marks offered the following resolutions :

"Whereas, Dr. Bemis, of the National Board of Health, in a communication addressed to this Board, propounded certain interrogatories growing out of the proposed National Quarantine at Ship Island ; and

"Whereas, the said communication was referred to the Attorney General of the State, in order to ascertain how far this Board possessed the legal power to carry out the desires of the National Board ; and

"Whereas, the Attorney General holds the opinion that this Board can not delegate its power, and must, therefore, (under the laws of the State) perform its own functions;

"Be it therefore resolved, That the President of this Board be, and is hereby requested to reply to the communication of Dr. Bemiss, conveying to him in substance the opinion of the Attorney General."

In obedience with this resolution I herewith enclose the following copy of the letter of the Attorney General. Respectfully, your obedient servant,

JOSEPH JONES, M. D.,
President Board of Health, State of Louisiana.

NATIONAL BOARD OF HEALTH, Washington, May 10, 1880.

Dr. Joseph Jones, President State Board of Health of Louisiana, New Orleans, La.:

Dear Sir—I am directed by the National Board of Health to acknowledge the receipt of your communication of April 22, addressed to Dr. S. Bemiss, the representative of the Board in New Orleans, and transmitting an opinion of the Attorney-General of the State on certain questions relative to the quarantine to be established under the auspices of the National Board at Ship Island, in aid of the State and municipal authorities in preventing the introduction of contagious and infectious diseases into the Gulf ports.

I am instructed to say that this Board is much gratified and obliged by your polite note and by the tenor of the opinion of the Attorney-General, which has been read with attention and entire concurrence in its conclusions. No specific practical conclusion is announced in your communication, but this Board understands that whilst the State Board of Health of Louisiana does not intend to, and does not in fact, delegate any one of the powers entrusted to it by law, and will not hold any bill of health or certificate of disinfection from the Chief Medical Officer at Ship Island "conclusively satisfactory" to the State authorities, they will nevertheless order infected ships cruising to the port of New Orleans back to the Quarantine Station established by the National Board at Ship Island as a condition to their entry into that port.

I am very respectfully and truly yours,

J. L. CABELL, President National Board of Health.

OFFICE BOARD OF HEALTH, STATE-HOUSE, STATE OF LOUISIANA, }
New Orleans, May 15, 1880. }

Prof. J. L. Cabell, M. D., L.L. D., President National Board of Health, Washington, D. C. :

Sir—In reply to the communication of the President of the National Board of Health, of the tenth instant, relating to Ship Island Quarantine ; the State Board of Health, at the

last regular meeting on the tenth instant, held that there was nothing in the official communication to the National Board of Health which warranted the assertion that "they will
order infected ships coming to the port of New Orleans back to Quarantine Station, established by the National Board at Ship Island, as a condition of their entry into that port."

Enclosed please find copy of resolution offered by Mr. Marks on the twenty-second of
April.

The Board of Health of the State of Louisiana cannot delegate its quarantine powers
to any other organization, whether created by Congress or by individual States.

Respectfully, your obedient servant,   JOSEPH JONES, M D.,
President Board of Health, State of Louisiana.

The action of the Board of Health of the State of Louisiana in declining
to order vessels from infected ports back to Ship Island, in accordance with
the demands of the National Board of Health, excited the animosity of the
latter body, and gave it a pretext, during the entire summer, to refuse all ap-
peals for aid for the repair and equipment of the Quarantine Stations of the
State. Notwithstanding the most pressing needs of the health authorities of
Louisiana, every appeal was meet .on the part of the National Board of
Health by pointing to the Ship Island Quarantine as an ample protection to
the State against the introduction of foreign pestilence. On the other hand,
when no aid was asked, and after the State Board had successfully conducted
the quarantine and sanitary affairs of Louisiana to that period of the year
in which it was improbable that Yellow Fever, even if it had been present,
could make progress, the representative of the National Board of Health·
thrust his advice, and his offers of help before the Board of Health, based
upon the report of one of the agents and employes of the National Board,
which was at variance with all the facts in the case, and with the official
enunciations of the Local Board.

The hostile attitude assumed by the National Board of Health, after the
rejection of the Ship Island scheme, is shown by the following official correspondence of the Governor of Louisiana with the President of the United
States and with the President of the National Board of Health :

STATE OF LOUISIANA, EXECUTIVE DEPARTMENT. }
New Orleans, May 14, 1880. }

His Excellency, R. B. Hayes, President United States of America, Washington, D. C.:

Sir—The Chief Executive of the State of Louisiana respectfully submits, for the information of the President of the United States, the enclosed copy of official correspondence with the National Board of Health, with the view of avoiding inhar-
monious action between this body and the legally commissioned Board of Health of the
State of Louisiana. Respectfully,

(Signed)   LOUIS A. WILTZ. Governor State of Louisiana.

NATIONAL BOARD OF HEALTH, Washington , D. C., May 8, 1880.

His Excellency, Louis A. Wiltz, Governor of Louisiana, New Orleans, La.

Sir—I am directed by the National Board of Health; to transmit to your Excellency. the enclosed pre
amble and iresolution adopted at a meeting of the Board of Health held this afternoon, and respectfully to
request your immediate attention to the same.

Very Respectfully your obedient servant,
(Signed)   J. L. CABELL, President National Board of Health.

Whereas, the attention of the National Board of Health has been called to an official proclamation issued
by his Excellency the Governor of Louisiana under date of May 4, 1880, declaring that all vessels arriving from
and after the tenth of May, 1880, from the following ports, known to be infected with Yellow Fever, viz:
Havana, Vera Cruz and Rio de Janeiro, and the officers and crews, passengers and cargoes arriving from the
above named and infected places, or having touched or stopped at any of them, shall be subject to such detention and quarantine as the Board of Health may direct; and

Whereas, it may be inferred from the proclamation that vessels arriving from other'West Indian, Central
American or South American ports than those mentioned in said proclamation are not to be subject to quarantine; and

Whereas, if the proclamation be thus interpreted and the quarantine at New Orleans enforced accordingly, it is the opinion of the National Board of Health that there will be great danger of the introduction of Yellow Fever into the United States; and

Whereas, Under the provisions of sections 3 of the Act, approved June 28, 1879, entitled an "Act to prevent the introduction of Contagious and Infectious diseases into the United States," it is made the duty of the

National Board of Health to co-operate with and so far as it lawfully may aid State and Municipal boards of health, in the execution and enforcement of the rules and regulations of such boards, to prevent the introduction of contagious and infectious diseases into the United States, from foreign countries * * * and at such ports and places within the United States, where quarantine regulations may exist under the authority of the State, which in the opinion of the National Board of Health, are not sufficient to prevent the introduction of such diseases into the United States, or into one State from another, the National Board of Health shall report the facts to the President of the United States, who shall, if in his judgment, it is necessary and proper, order said Board of Health to make such additional rules and regulations as are necessary to prevent the introduction of such diseases into the United States from foreign countries, * * * which when so made and approved by the President shall be promulgated by the National Board of Health, and enforced by the sanitary authorities of the states. * * * Therefore,

Resolved, That the President be directed to communicate at once with the Governor of Louisiana, inviting his attention to the preliminary report of the Havana Yellow Fever Commission as to the annual prevalence of Yellow Fever in all Cuban ports, and requesting that he will at once inform the Board as to the precise sense in which this proclamation is to be interpreted as regards vessels coming from the Cuban ports other than Havana, or the Central American and South American ports other than Vera Cruz and Rio de Janeiro.

STATE OF LOUISIANA, EXECUTIVE DEPARTMENT, }
New Orleans, May 13, 1880. }

J. L. Cabell, President National Board of Health, Washington, D. C.:

Sir—The Governor of the State of Louisiana directs the attention of the National Board of Health to the following information relating to his proclamation of the 4th inst.:

1. The proclamation of the Governor of Louisiana has been issued in accordance with sections seven and thirteen of "An Act to establish Quarantine for the protection of the State, approved March 13, 1855."

2. In accordance with the aforesaid "Act" the Board of Health will notify the Governor from time to time of the existence of Yellow Fever, or other contagious diseases, in such localities as may become infected, and the proclamation will be extended so as to embrace such localities.

3. A rigid system of inspection, disinfection and quarantine is perpetually maintained at the Mississippi Quarantine Station throughout the entire year, and at the other Stations from the first of May to the first of November. Such quarantine regulations are independent of the official proclamations. Every vessel from an infected port, and every vessel with a foul bill of health, or with sickness on board, has been and will be subjected to a rigid system of inspection, disinfection and quarantine.

4. The length of quarantine is fixed by the several Acts of the Legislature, approved respectively, March 15, 1855, March 18, 1858, and March 24, 1876.

5. It should be observed that section four of "An Act, supplementary to an Act, entitled, an Act relative to quarantine, approved March 18, 1858, enacts, "That in cases of emergencies the Board of Health shall have power to issue proclamation of quarantine without reference to the Governor, and to enact all needful regulations for the enforcement of the same."

6. It should be still further noted that by the provisions of the "Act approved March 24, 1876," the Board of Health of the State of Louisiana "be and is hereby authorized and empowered, at its discretion, at any time, to cause the detention at Quarantine Station for purposes of disinfection and purification, and to disinfect, fumigate and purify any and all vessels from ports in which Yellow Fever usually prevails, or from ports where other contagious or infectious diseases are reported to exist." * * *

7. Not only does the Board of Health of the State of Louisiana maintain a rigid quarantine, according to the laws enacted by the Legislature, but also a rigid system of inspection of all vessels in the harbor of New Orleans has been established during the past twenty-one days, as is manifested by Circular No. 3, issued by the State Board of Health, and furnished to all masters, captains and medical officers of vessels, and to all ship owners, agents and foreign Consuls.

8. From the preceding facts, it is evident that there is no foundation for the following statements of the National Board of Health, which have been couched in the formal and official language of "Preamble and Resolution."

"Whereas, it may be inferred from this proclamation that vessels arriving from other West Indian, Central American or South American ports than those mentioned in said proclamation, are not to be subject to quarantine; and

"Whereas, if the proclamation be thus interpreted, and the quarantine at New Orleans be enforced accordingly, it is the opinion of the National Board of Health that there will be great danger of the introduction of Yellow Fever into the United States."

9. The resolutions of the National Board of Health, adopted on the eighth of May, and forwarded by the President, J. L. Cabell, to the Chief Executive of the State of Louisiana, appear to have been conceived in the absence of accurate information as to the quarantine and sanitary regulations and operations of the Board of Health of the State of Louisiana.

Respectfully,   L. A. WILTZ,
                                           -   Governor State of Louisiana.

The resolutions of the National Board of Health, communicated by Professor J. L. Cabell, M. D., LL. D., to his Excellency, Louis A. Wiltz, Governor of Louisiana, on the eighth of May, 1880, were submitted to the President of the Board of Health, and the reply of the Governor, received the unanimous approval of the Board of Health.

The resolutions of the National Board of Health appeared to have been hostile in their conception and expression; and their promulgation either by that organization, or through the agency of the President of the United States, would have tended to destroy public confidence in the wisdom of the Chief Executive of the State of Louisiana, and in the efficiency of the Board of Health, which he had created and commissioned. These resolutions were supplemental to the effort to exact such concessions from the Board of Health of the State of Louisiana with reference to the proposed Ship Island Quarantine Station, as would render the Mississippi Quarantine Station subordinate to the central authorities at Washington. The resolutions of the National Board of Health appeared to be of the nature of a threat, to the effect that if the Governor of the State of Louisiana did not conform to the mandates of the National Board of Health, the power of the President of the United States would be invoked for the subordination of the quarantine regulations, and commerce of the State of Louisiana, to the rules and regulations of the National Board of Health in Washington.

The haste with which these resolutions were passed by the National Board of Health, four days after the issuance of the quarantine proclamation of the Governor of Louisiana, indicated a settled aggressive policy against the State Board of Health.

On the other hand, the State Board of Health had pursued a dignified, but respectful and conciliatory course towards the National Board of Health, as will be manifest from the following reports, which, in addition to their intrinsic merit, serve to illustrate the question now under consideration.

NATIONAL BOARD OF HEALTH, University of Virginia, April 15, 1880

Dr. Joseph Jones, President State Board of Health of Louisiana.

Dear Doctor—If you will have the kindness to refer to Nos. 34 and 35 of the National Board of Health Bulletin, you will see that this Board proposes to hold two conferences on the 5th and 6th of May next. The object of the first conference to be held on the 5th of May, with such of the quarantine authorities of the several States as may attend, is to consider the propriety of amending the rules and regulations prepared by the Board last year, and recommended by it to State and municipal quarantine authorities for adoption.

The object of the second conference to be held on the 6th of May, is to consider the best methods for the collection and publication of vital statistics, and it is earnestly desired that all interested in this subject and especially those who are charged with the duties of State and municipal registration, will meet with the Board in Washington at that time

On behalf of the Board, I respectfully solicit your attendance at these conferences, and request that you will make known to the other quarantine authorities of your State, the desire of this Board to have the benefit of their aid and council.

Very Respectfully yours,

J. L. CABELL, President National Board of Health.

OFFICE BOARD OF HEALTH, STATE-HOUSE, STATE OF LOUISIANA, {
New Orleans, April 20, 1880. }

Prof. J. L. Cabell, M. D., LLD., President National Board of Health, Washington, D. C:

Dear Sir—I have the honor to acknowledge receipt of your valued favor of the 15th inst., containing an invitation from the Executive Committee of the National Board of Health "to visit and engage in a convention of vital statisticians to be held in Washington, May 6, ensuing," also in a "convention of persons interested in the securing of a uniform system of quarantine"

Allow me to say, that whilst desiring to engage actively and personally in the discussion of the important questions embraced in the official communication of the National Board of Health, which accompanied the invitations to these conventions, my duties connected with the quarantine stations and city of New Orleans, will confine me closely to this State during the hot months. It is my purpose to inspect the various quarantine stations, at my earliest convenience, and draw up rules and regulations for the same, as well as for the shipping in the port of New Orleans. These laws, as well as those connected with the sanitation of the city, will necessarily involve much time. I shall lay the communication of the National Board of Health, before the Board of Health of the State of Louisiana, at the next meeting on Thursday, April 22.

Respectfully, your obedient servant,

JOSEPH JONES, M. D.,
President Board of Health State of Louisiana.

The communications of the National Board of Health were laid before the State Board of Health on the 22d of April, and on motion of Dr. Loeber they were referred to a committee for consideration and report. The President appointed on this committee, Dr. F. Loeber, Dr. J. P. Davidson and Dr. J. C. Beard, who drew up the following report:

OFFICE BOARD OF HEALTH, STATE OF LOUISIANA, {
New Orleans, La., April 29, 1880. }

Dr. Joseph Jones, President Board of Health, State of Louisiana:.

Sir—Your committee to whom were referred certain interrogatories from the National Board of Health, designed to elicit suggestions for, additions to, or alterations in their rules and regulations, beg leave to report as follows:

1. Our attention is specifically directed to the "desire of the Board to make a distinction between the terms *suspected, infected* and *dangerously infected,* as applied to ports and places or to vessels," with the request that suggestions be offered as to the sense in which these words should be used. In reply we would remark that, in our opinion, the term *suspected* is objectionable for the reason that it is indefinite and liable to misconstruction, inasmuch as its use and application in any one case may act prejudiciously on public sentiment against either the officers or the vessels to which the term is applied. We would therefore suggest that the term *liable to have incurred infection* be substituted for the word *suspected.* The term liable to have incurred infection" we would apply to any vessel coming from a port where Yellow Fever exists, but having no such sickness aboard, either at the port of departure or during the voyage.

2. We would apply the term *infected* to any vessel which had Yellow Fever on board during her voyage, or on which a case occurred in port, though removed immediately and treated in hospital.

3. We would apply the term *dangerously infected* to any vessel on which cases of Yellow Fever occurred in port, whether treated aboard or sent to hospital, and on which other cases occurred during the voyage.

4. The application of the term *infected* to localities and communities should be restricted, in our opinion, to those in which several undoubted cases of the disease in question have occurred, originating in the locality, with a tendency to spread; and it should be understood that infection may be limited to a portion of a city or town, or to a single building, square or number of squares, without involving other portions. Positive evidence of these facts should be obtained through the agency of State or Local Boards of Health. The term *infected* does not strictly apply to localities or communities into which a case or cases of Yellow Fever have been introduced.

5. The term *dangerously infected* is properly used when applied to ports, localities and communities where Yellow Fever prevails endemically or epidemically.

6. Relative to the rules necessary to be enforced in regard to vessels infected with other diseases than Yellow Fever, as small-pox, cholera, plague, typhus fever, we are of the opinion that to vessels dangerously infected the same rules should apply as in case of Yellow Fever; that is to say, isolation, removal of cargo, thorough cleansing and disinfection.

7. In reply to the interrogatory, "as to the propriety and possibility of exempting from detention and observation, on account of Yellow Fever, passengers or other persons who present satisfactory evidence that they have had the fever, or that they are natives of one of the West India Islands," we are of the opinion that such persons should be exempt from the restrictions imposed on the unprotected; but that they shall. in all cases of an infected vessel, be detained until after proper disinfection of their apparel and effects. Only persons born in seaport towns where Yellow Fever is endemic, should be regarded as exempt from Yellow Fever.

8. "*Satisfactory evidence* of their acclimation," should be an affidavit, setting forth their nativity or their having had Yellow Fever, and made before the American consul at the port of departure. In the absence of such affidavit, the quarantine official should be required to ascertain under oath, that the affiant is acclimated.

9. "As to the circumstances which would render it necessary or expedient to remove the cargo from a ship and have her thoroughly cleansed and disinfected, and the cargo aired before either is allowed to pass from the quarantine grounds," we consider that it would only be necessary or expedient to remove the cargo from a ship when she was *dangerously infected,* as before set forth. In the case of a vessel *liable to have been infected,* or of an *infected vessel,* we think it unnecessary to disturb the cargo; but the vessel should be detained at quarantine, at the discretion of the quarantine officer, to be thoroughly cleansed and disinfected.

(Signed)　　　　　　　　　　　　F. LOEBER, M. D.
　　　　　　　　　　　　　　　　J. P. DAVIDSON. M. D.
　　　　　　　　　　　　　　　　J. C. BEARD, M. D.

The preceding report was promptly forwarded to the Executive Committee of the National Board of Health, in Washington, but no acknowledgment of its reception was received.

At the regular meeting of the Board of Health, on the third of June, Dr. J. C. Beard, chairman of the committee appointed by the President to examine "the rules and regulations for the conduct of the Mississippi River inspection service; rules and regulations of railway travel and traffic in regions exposed to or infected by Yellow Fever, and rules and regulations to be enforced when Yellow Fever exists at or in the vicinity of any port or place on the Mississippi River, as suggested or advised by the National Board of Health," submitted the following report, which was adopted:

REPORT OF COMMITTEE OF THE BOARD OF HEALTH OF THE STATE OF LOUISIANA AP-
POINTED TO EXAMINE THE RULES OF THE NATIONAL BOARD OF HEALTH.

[Copy.]

To the President and Members of the Louisiana State Board of Health:

Gentlemen—Your committee appointed to consider the rules and regulations for the conduct of the Mississippi River Inspection Service; rules and regulations of railway travel and traffic in regions exposed or infected
by Yellow Fever, and rules and regulations to be enforced when Yellow Fever exists at or in the vicinity of any
port or place on the Mississippi River, as suggested or advised by the National Board of Health, beg leave re
spectfully to submit the following report:

Impressed with the great importance of these rules and regulations, and actuated by the earnest desire to
co-operate with other Boards of Health in the Mississippi Valley to carry out all reasonable suggestions of the
National Board of Health to prevent the introduction of contagions or infectious diseases into the United States
from foreign countries, and into one State from another; and realizing full well the necessity that the rules and
regulations of the several State or Municipal Boards of Health should be uniform, as far as possible, to secure
the desired result, we earnestly recommend their adoption by this Board, and would request the President of
the Louisiana State Board of Health to appoint inspectors immediately, as recommended in the above rules
and regulations. Your committee is unanimously in favor of giving to the National Board of Health their approval and support, and of placing themselves in accord with it by adopting further rules and regulations.

Desiring to make known their precise attitude towards the National Board of Health and the grounds of
delay in putting themselves into co-operation and harmonious action with it, beg leave to represent that from
the organization of the present State Board of Health to the present time, they have been ready and willing to
place themselves in harmonious action with the National Board of Health, but have taken no action in this respect, from the fact that no official communication has ever been laid before them emanating from the National
Board of Health, other than one relating to a Quarantine Station at Ship Island; that no copy of the rules and
regulations of the National Board of Health, or publication of any character, have ever been officially presented
to their consideration, except certain interrogatios forwarded by the Secretary of the Board relative to the
sense in which certain terms named in the rules and regulations should be used, which interrogations were respectfully answered by a committee appointed by the State Board of Health and forwarded to Washington.

Your committee, while expressing their desire of co-operation and harmonious action, would, therefore,
respectfully call the attention of the National Board of Health to section 3 of an act to prevent the introduction of contagious and infectious diseases into the United States, approved June 2, 1879.

(Signed)   J. C. BEARD, M. D.
                                                                     F. FORMENTO. M. D.
                                                                     J. P. DAVIDSON, M. D.
                                                                     F. LOEBER, M. D.

OFFICE BOARD OF HEALTH, STATE HOUSE, STATE OF LOUISIANA, }
New Orleans, June 5 1880. }

Professor J. L. Cabell, M. D. LLD., President National Board of Health, University of Virginia, Charlotsville, Va.

Sir—I have the honor to forward to the President of the National Board of Health,
report of committee appointed by the President of the State Board of Health of Louisiana,
on rules and regulations of the National Board of Health. For the information of the President of the National Board of Health, I also forward copy of my letter to Professor
Samuel M. Bemiss, member of the National Board of Health.

Not being informed as to the number of Inspectors which will be approved by the
National Board of Health, I have named those physicians which I believe to be available.
As President of the Board of Health of the State of Louisiana, I respectfully request a
prompt and full answer from the President of the National Board of Health.

Respectfully your obedient servant,

JOSEPH JONES, M. D., President Board of Health State of Louisiana.

NATIONAL BOARD OF HEALTH, University of Virginia, June 9, 1880.

Dr. Joseph Jones, President State Board of Health of Louisiana:

Sir—I have the honor to acknowledge the receipt of your two communications of June 3 and June 5 re.
spectively, the former transmitting the "Rules and Regulations of the Board of Health of the State of Louis.
iana," relative to quarantine, the latter enclosing "Report of the committee appointed by the President of the
State Board of Health of Louisiana on the rules and regulations of the National Board of Health" together with
a copy of a letter addressed by yourself to Dr. S. M. Bemiss of this Board on the 4th of June.

Both these communications will be forwarded this day to the central office of the National Board in Wash.
ington, and will doubtless, receive early attention on the part of the Executive Committee.

I am very respectfully, your obedient servant,

J. L. CABELL, President National Board of Health.

At a subsequent meeting of the Board of Health, held on the twenty-
fourth of June, on motion of Mr. Marks, it was resolved that the President
of the Board be, and is hereby authorized to make an estimate of such an
amount of money as may be deemed necessary in the event of any emergency arising for its use, and to submit the same to the National Board of
Health.

The President was also authorized to apply to the National Board of
Health for the necessary amount of money to put the quarantine stations of
the State in an effective condition.

In accordance with these resolutions a communication was addressed to the President of the National Board of Health, setting forth the wishes of the Board of Health, and the quarantine and sanitary needs of the State, and urging an appropriation of the funds of the National Board of Health to the following extent and for the purposes specified :

To repairs of Mississippi Quarantine Station, about................$4000
To Rigolet's Quarantine.. 2000
To Atchafalaya Quarantine... 2000
To two steam launches for use of Mississippi Quarantine Station and
   in the harbor of New Orleans and in the Inspection service....... 2000

It was also requested that an additional sum of ten thousand dollars be placed subject to the orders of the State Board of Health, in case of an outbreak of Yellow Fever.

The letter of the President, containing estimates and asking an appropriation from the National Board of Health for the urgent necessities of the Quarantine Stations, was forwarded to Professor Cabell, on the 25th of June but it did not receive an official answer until July 14. Notwithstanding that the case of fever on the Excelsior had been announced. and the entire valley was in a state of excitement, the urgent appeal of the Board of Health of the State of Louisiana, for such pecuniary help as they deemed the act constituting the National Board of Health, not merely allowed but commanded, was not only unanswered for nineteen days, but as will be seen from the following letter of the President of the National Board of Health, was completely ignored on the ground, that the National Board of Health had afforded ample facilities for the protection of Louisiana, by the establishment of the Ship Island Quarantine.

It should be observed in order to give full force to the action of the National Board of Health, in thus denying aid to the State Board, on the ground that ample protection was afforded by Ship Island Quarantine, that this establishment was scarcely commenced, when the subject was intruded upon the attention of the Board of Health on the 9th of April, and at this date of the following letters, June 14, it was incomplete and in process of erection.

————

NATIONAL BOARD OF HEALTH, New Orleans, July 10, 1880.
Prof. Joseph Jones, President State Board of Health :
   Dear Sir—A communication from you, dated June 25th, addressed to the President of the National Board of Health, has been referred to me for report and recommendation. About the 15th inst., Dr. Smith and Dr. Mitchell, of the National Board, are expected to reach this city. I respectfully suggest that upon their arrival a conference be held between the members of the National Board and yourself, upon the matter of appropriations asked for in the above-instanced letter, as well as other subjects, which it may be found profitable to discuss.
   Very respectfully, &c.,   S. M. BEMISS, M. N. B. H.

————

NATIONAL BOARD OF HEALTH, Washington, D. C., July 14, 1880.
Dr. Joseph Jones, President State Board of Health, New Orleans, La. :
   Sir—I have the honor to inform you that your communication of June 25th, relative to railroad inspections and estimates of funds needed for quarantine stations at New Orleans, &c., has been laid before the Executive Committee, and that I am directed to reply as follows:
   1. The railroad inspections have been ordered to be continued for the time being, and Drs. Stephen Smith and R. W. Mitchell, of this Board, will visit New Orleans to confer with Dr. Bemiss and yourself upon the necessity for keeping up such inspections when Yellow Fever is not present. In this matter the committee desire to do everything that is necessary to secure confidence on the part of the surrounding communities.
   2. As to furnishing funds for construction or repair of buildings at the Mississippi River, Rigolet's and Atchafalaya Stations, after careful consideration this Board heretofore came to the conclusion that the cost of furnishing aid to construct hospital buildings, etc., at each maritime port of the Southern and Gulf coast requiring such aid, would be so great in comparison with the results to be obtained, as not to be justifiable ; and that the necessities of the case could be equally well met by fitting up certain complete refuge or hospital quarantine stations, where all the apparatus needed for dealing with an infected ship might be placed, and where such infected ships could be sent for treatment.
   Therefore, after consultation with the principal shippers and merchants of New Orleans, the National Board made arrangements to establish such a station at Ship Island, for ships known to be infected and bound for Mississippi and Louisiana ports.

In view of this action the committee does not deem itself justified in expending more money upon hospital accommodations, etc., for the Atchafalaya, Rigolet's or Mississippi River Stations of New Orleans.

In addition to this the committee are of opinion that it would not be justified, unless under very exceptional circumstances, in expending the funds under its control for repairs to buildings of a *permanent character* not being the property of the United States.

3. In case of the occurrence of Yellow Fever at New Orleans, this Board will promptly give to the State Board all aid within its power necessary for preventing the spread of the disease, and for this purpose will pay for a certain number of inspectors, sanitary policemen, etc., being guided in this respect by the recommendations of its resident member, Dr. Bemiss. to whom instructions will be given upon this point   In this connection it may not be either superfluous or premature to suggest that any work to be paid for by the Board should be confined to the immediate vicinity of the infected locality; that is, for instance, the Board can not undertake to meet the expense of cleansing and disinfecting a large section of the city because of the existence of Yellow Fever, say, upon a *single square*.

Very respectfully, &c.,   J. L. CABELL, President National Board of Health.

OFFICE BOARD OF HEALTH, STATE HOUSE, STATE OF LOUISIANA, }
                                New Orleans, July 18, 1880. }

J. L. Cabell, M. D. LLD., President National Board of Health, University of Virginia.

Sir—I have the honor to acknowledge the communication of the President of the National Board of Health, in answer to the application of the Board of Health of the State of Louisiana, for aid from the National Board in accordance with the law requiring said Board to aid local boards in the establishment and maintenance of Quarantines etc. The communication of the National Board, will be laid before the State Board of Health, and also before the Governor, Senators and Representatives of Louisiana.

Respectfully your obedient servant,

JOSEPH JONES, M. D., President Board of Health.

Drs. Stephen Smith and R. W. Mitchell, arrived in New Orleans on or about the 15th of July, and in company with the member of the National Board of Health residing in New Orleans, held a conference with the President and several members of said Board.

The necessities of the various quarantine establishments of the State, as well as the sanitary needs of New Orleans, were fully unfolded to these members of the National Board of Health, and they were urged to act promptly.

The gentlemen left the city and visited Ship Island and the Mississippi Quarantine Station, and during their absence the quarantines established against New Orleans by Tennessee and Mississippi were promulgated.

The result of this application like that to the President of the National Board of Health was productive of no result; in fact these representatives of the National Board of Health failed to give any reply either verbal or written to the respectful and earnest appeal of the State Board of Health, at a time of great anxiety, of universal peril and danger to New Orleans, and we may say to the entire Mississippi Valley.

Towards the close of August the President of the National Board of Health visited New Orleans in person, but he came not to afford support or comfort to her citizens, or to speak words of encouragement and wisdom to the State Board, but he came solely as a champion of the Ship Island Quarantine.

As usual with the members of the National Board of Health, he communicated his views not to the constituted health authorities of the State of Louisiana, but held conference with the New Orleans Auxillary Sanitary Association and the Cotton Exchange.

These statements are well illustrated by Dr. Cabell himself, in his letter addressed to the New Orleans Democrat, dated August 24, and published in the paper of the 31st.

[New Orleans Democrat, Tuesday, August 31, 1880.]

THE QUESTION OF QUARANTINE.—The Democrat has received the following letter from the President of the National Board of Health:

NATIONAL BOARD OF HEALTH, Washington, August 24, 1880.

Editor of the New Orleans Democrat:

. I have just seen your account in your daily issue of the twentieth instant of the conference in which I was invited to take a part at the New Orleans Cotton Exchange on the preceding day. While acknowledging with thanks the friendly and flattering terms in which you refer to me, I am constrained to ask your correction .

of a single sentence which is open to misconstruction and places me in a false position of inconsistency with my repeated utterances while in the city.

You state that in my remarks to the meeting I referred to Dr. Jones "in most complimentary terms." I have no recollection of having mentioned his name or having referred to him individually at all, but I desire to say that while my personal and social relations with him have always been of the most friendly character, and I have availed myself of this fact in order to assure him in a private leter of the sincerity of my disclaimer in official communications of any purpose or wish on the part of the National Board of Health to exercise in Louisiana any powers not conferred upon it by law, or in any degree to invade the prerogatives of the Board over which he presides, some of his recent official acts have been such as to compel me to refer to them in other than approving terms.

I have had occasion to say to him in substance that the National Board had been advised that no Quarantine arrangements in the lower Mississippi could furnish adequate protection to the city and the country above, and that the conviction of this truth was so deeply rooted in the minds of the people of the entire valley as that they would never be content nor cease to impose restrictions upon the commerce of the city until some other provision was made. I further stated that this Board was prepared to aid the State Board by the offer of quarantine facilities at Ship Island which would meet all the requirements of the case in the detention and disinfction of all infected vessels, or vessels from infected ports cruising to New Orleans. The persistent refusal of Dr. Jones to act in accord with the National Board in respect to this offer, and his seeming readiness to seize upon any pretext in order to excite prejudice against the Board by imputing to it attempts to exercise "illegal and unconstitutional" powers, are not specially calculated to induce me to go out of my way to refer to him in "highly complimentary terms" in such a connection.

Very respecttully yours,   J. L. CABELL.

The statement contained in the letter of Dr. Cabell addressed to the editor of the New Orleans Democrat, to the effect that "the National Board had been advised that no Quarantine arrangements in the lower Mississippi could furnish adequate protection to the city and country above and that the conviction of this truth was so deeply rooted in the minds of the people of the entire valley as that they would never be content nor cease to impose restrictions upon the commerce of the city, until some other provision was made," had been substantially enunciated in the Memphis papers, and has recently been reiterated with certain remarkable additions in the Bulletin of the National Board of Health, Vol. 2, No. 18, Supplement No. 8.

Professor J. L. Cabell, M. D. LLD., President of the National Board of Health, says in his statement to the Hon. John Sherman, Secretary of the Treasury, of the expenditures and operations of the National Board of Health, for the quarter ending September 30, 1880: "The municipalities most immediately concerned recognize the great value of these National Quarantines, and earnestly desire that the machinery which will secure them against the introduction of infections from abroad, and thus against the risk ot becoming the means of transmitting infection to other parts of the United States, shall be perfected and perpetuated. There is a partial exception to this remark in the case of New Orleans, where, although all the leading representatives of its commercial interests are known to be extremely desirous that infected vessels shall be required to proceed to the National Quarantine at Ship Island, instead of coming up the river to the Mississippi Quarantine, to the great jeopardy of the population of the surrounding country on both side of the river, the wishes of the community have been thwarted by the action of the State Board of Health, which has hitherto repelled all offers of aid on the part of the National Board looking to the reception and treatment at Ship Island of infected vessels bound for the Port of New Orleans. This action of the State Board of Health of Louisiana, has caused great dissatisfaction and alarm on the part of the people of the Mississippi Valley, who believe that there can be no adequate guarantee of the protection of the public health throughout the valley as long as infected vessels are permitted to euter the Mississippi River. This belief and the consequent distrust of New Orleans, entertained by the health authorities of the States bordering on the river and tributaries, has been expressed in firm but temperate language in numerous articles of the daily press, and in official ordinances of the State and municipal Boards of Health." Attention is specially invited to two articles from the Memphis Appeal of August 1, one respectively, under the caption "Quarantine in New Orleans," and to an

8

"open letter to his Excellency, the Chief Executive of the State of Louisiana," addressed to that officer August 14, 1880, by G. B. Thornton, M. D. and John Johnson, members of the State Board of Health of Tennessee; copies of these several papers, marked B, and hereto annexed.

We would remark in passing that the "open letter" of G. B. Thornton, M. D., and John Johnson, of the State Board of Health of Tennessee, contains no allusion to Ship Island Quarantine, while the other articles were mere newspaper effusions, and *not official* communications, although they have b.en incorporated in the official statements of the United States National Board of Health.

The President of the National Board of Health, proceeds still farther to arraign the State Board of Health: "While the State Board of Health of Louisiana has thus in defiance of the demands of the health authorities of the neighboring States, whose interests are so vitally concerned, declined to accept the offer of the National Board to receive and disinfect vessels clearing for New Orleans from infected ports, the authorities of all the ports between that city and Cedar Keys, have signified their purpose to direct all infected vessels to report to the National Quarantine at Ship Island, before proceeding to their ports of destination."

Such statements certainly demand examination on the ground that they are made by the President of the National Board of Health, to the Secretary of the Treasury, and through this high functionary to the President and Congress of the United States.

Dr. Cabell asserts, 1st. That " all the leading representatives of the commercial interests of New Orleans, are known to be extremely desirous that infected vessels shall be required to proceed to the National Quarantine at Ship Island."

2nd. The State Board of Health of Louisiana has in *defiance* of the demands of the health authorities of the neighboring States, declined to accept the offer of the National Board of Health to receive and disinfect vessels clearing for New Orleans from infected ports.

In reply to the above declarations, it may be stated, that the President of the National Board of Health, does not name substantially a single representative of the commercial interests of New Orleans. If the reports of the daily papers are correct, his address before the Cotton Exchange in favor of the Ship Island Quarantine was met by decided and unanswerable argument. As President of the Board of Health, I affirm that not one of the leading representatives of the commercial interests of New Orleans, has even, up to the present moment, addressed any communication either verbal or written to the Board of Health, either for or against the Ship Island Quarantine, with the exception of the following:

ROYAL VICE CONSULATE OF SWEDEN AND NORWAY, New Orleans, April 21, 1880.

To Dr. Joseph Jones, President of the Board of Health of the city of New Orleans, present:

Sir—Referring to the personal interview I had with you this morning I beg to draw your attention and that of the honorable Board of Health to the fact that, the export trade of our city, which our whole population is depending upon, can only be continued during the summer months, if your honorable body adopts such rules for quarantine which will allow ships to come here under the guaranty that they are no longer detained by quarantine than is absolutely necessary in the interest of the health of our city and consistent with the heavy responsibility which has been entrusted to you.

It is well known to the export merchants of New Orleans, that the ships of the United Kingdom of Sweden and Norway, which I have the honor to represent, have of late become large carriers for the products of the Mississippi Valley, but nevertheless not a single vessel of those two countries arrived here last year from the third of June to the eighteenth of September, owing to the very stringent quarantine regulations adopted by your predecessor.

Judging from communications received, ship owners will defer from sending their ships during the summer months to this port or to ports of call in the West India islands, from where they can easily reach our port, unless they are assured beforehand that a fair, just and liberal policy regarding quarantine is adopted, and that they are not liable to unnecessary expenses and delay; I therefore beg to express my sincere hope that you and the honorable body over which you preside will give this matter your most earnest consideration.

I beg further to state for the information of the honorable Board of Health, that a large part of the mercantile fleet of Sweden and Norway, and also of other nations is going out in ballast to St. Thomas or sometimes to Martinique for orders, which means to say that they proceed from these stations to such a port of the United States or the West India islands which offers the best freights to them. As such vessels never take any freight nor passengers at these ports of call nor actually enter the ports, but only lay at anchor outside, the captain alone generally coming into contact with the island. I beg to recommend to your honorable body, that such vessels, upon proper proof to that effect, from the United States consul residing at ports of call, be allowed to proceed to this city without any detention at the Quarantine Station, except in cases of sickness on board of the vessel.

Should the honorable Board of Health adopt such a rule I have no doubt that the business community would highly appreciate the liberal spirit of your honorable body, who, notwithstanding watching with all energy over the health of our good city, does at the same time throw no more impediment upon commerce than is absolutely necessary.

I respectfully ask you to communicate to me as soon as convenient the quarantine regulations which will be adopted by your Board and which I shall forward to my government as soon as received.

I have the honor to sign myself, your most obedient servant,

GEORGE GERDES, Royal Vice Consul of Sweden and Norway.

NEW ORLEANS, April 21, 1880.

To Dr. Joseph Jones, President Board of Health:

We, the undersigned merchants and ship and steamship brokers, doing business in this city, do herewith most respectfully beg leave to submit to your kind notice and attention the following requests regarding the Quarantine regulations of this port. While being fully aware of the imperative necessity of an efficient Quarantine whereby the health of the city may be as far as possible assured. We hope in framing the Quarantine regulations for the coming season you may find it consistent in your rulings to permit ve-sels or steamers which may have called at West Indian or other ports (within the Fever Zone) for orders, and while these not having taken on board cargo, passengers, coal or ballast, and not having on board on arrival here signs of disease or infection.

That they may be permitted, after inspection at Quarantine, to pass up to city.

Serious loss to the commerce of our port resulted during the past season in consequence of vessels having called at St. Thomas and adjacent ports for orders, and, while there, although having little or no intercourse with the shore, were debarred from coming here to load cargo, in consequence of the stringent regulations then governing Quarantine.

A large export trade was thus lost to our city and the West, these vessels being obliged to go to the Atlantic ports seeking business.

We would also respectfully state that Ship Island Pass does not afford sufficient water for deep draft vessels. This alone would be a great drawback, to say nothing of the distance from the mouth of the Mississippi River; and as much calm weather prevails during summer months, sailing vessels especially would suffer seriously. We mention this as we have learned that it is contemplated to make Ship Island a Quarantine Station.

Hoping you will pardon the liberty we have taken, and trusting for the favorable consideration of your honorable body, we are very respectfully yours,

A. K. MILLER & CO., Ship and Steamship Brokers.
ALF. MOULTON. Agent Cromwell Steamship Line.
NORTON & BELL, Ship Brokers.
SILAS WEEKS & CO.
FORSTALL, FOSS & CLAYTON, Ship Brokers.
HALL & VAUGHAN, Ship Brokers.
LOVELL & BAILEY, Ship Brokers.
LANG & CO
F. L. FORWOOD.
JOHN J. MITCHELL.
ED. F. STOCKMEYER, Agents North German Lloyd.

It may be further stated that during the existence of the present Board of Health not a single verbal or written communication of an official character has been received by the Board of Health, from the health authorities of the neighboring States, relating to Ship Island Quarantine.

It is not true that the State Board of Health of Louisiana acted in defiance of the demands of the health authorities of the neighboring States; but it is true that the Board of Health of Louisiana exerted every agency at its command for the protection of the Valley of the Mississippi from the introduction of foreign pestilence, and conformed its every action to the organic laws of the State from which it derived its existence and powers, and at the same time upon every occasion respected and obeyed the laws of the United States governing foreign and domestic commerce.

In protesting against the quarantines established by the Boards of Health of Tennessee and Mississippi, in the absence of all contagious and infectious diseases in the City of New Orleans, the State Board of Health was actuated solely by that sense of justice which they believed should actuate and control the relations and intercourse of the surrounding Southern States.

In conclusion we will briefly present some facts illustrating the actual value of Ship Island Quarantine to the port of New Orleans, as illustrated by the experience of the time embraced in the labors of this Board, as at present constituted.

If the coast of Louisiana, Mississippi and Alabama be carefully examined, and the positions of New Orleans and the ports of Mississippi and Alabama be compared with that of the Quarantine Station of the National Board of Health on Ship Island, it will be observed that Ship Island occupies a position on the gulf coast nearly opposite the centre of the State of Mississippi to which it belongs. The Quarantine Station on Ship Island is capable of rendering assistance to the coast of Mississippi, and more especially to the shipping and settlements at Pascagoula, Biloxi, Mississippi City, Pass Christian, Bay St. Louis and Shieldsboro.

structures of the National Board of Health; and some fair conception may

The relationship of Ship Island Quarantine to New Orleans is still further illustrated by the following table of distances:

New Orleans to Mississippi Quarantine Station, 75 miles.

New Orleans to Eadsport, 116 miles.

New Orleans to Ship Island, 211 miles.

New Orleans to Rigolets via Mississippi River, 255 miles.

New Orleans to Rigolets via Ship Island, 267 miles.

New Orleans to Rigolets via Bayou St. John and Lake Pontchartrain, 35 miles.

Ship Island to Rigolets, 52 miles.

Rigolets to New Orleans via Lake Pontchartrain and Bayou St. John, 35 miles.

Ship Island to New Orleans via Rigolets, Lake Pontchartrain and Bayou St. John, 87 miles.

Ship Island to Biloxi, 12½ miles.

Mississippi Quarantine Station to Ship Island, 130 miles.

Port Eads to Ship Island Quarantine Station, 95 miles.

The intolerable burden which the scheme of the late Dr. Woodworth, Surgeon General of the Marine Hospital Service, and founder of the National Board of Health, which, was urged by the latter organization, would entail upon the commerce of the Mississippi River and Valley, is demonstrated by the fact, that if a vessel was stopped at Port Eads and ordered to Ship Island, it would have an additional voyage of nine-five miles to perform before reaching Ship Island; if ordered back from the Mississippi Quarantine Station, 130 miles; if from the Port of New Orleans, 211 miles. No vessel drawing over six feet of water can reach New Orleans via Rigolet's and Bayou St. John, therefore the cargo, if sent by lighters, must traverse an additional eighty-seven miles before reaching its destination.

If the ship, after detention and discharge of cargo and disinfection, was returned to New Orleans, then the distance above-mentioned from the various points must be doubled.

In addition to this add the loss of time occasioned by calms and the destruction of shipping by the storms which often prevail along this dangerous coast, and the danger of fire in storing valuable cargoes in the wooden

be formed of the dangers attending the execution of the scheme by the National Board of Health, and a demonstration of the absolute absurdity of comparing this experiment with the magnificent quarantine establishment and system of the harbor of New York.

Granting for purposes of argument, that the Board of Health of the State of Louisiana, had absolute jurisdiction over the waters of the Gulf of Mexico, to the exclusion of the rights of all States and nations; that it had control of Ship Island, which is the property of the State of Mississippi, and also of the entire coast of Mississippi; even then the ordering of vessels from the mouths of the Mississippi River to Ship Island would entail such enormous expense, in towage, loss of time, and in various accidents by storm and fire, as would effectually drive foreign commerce from the Mississippi River, annually during the months of May, June, July, August, September and October.

Another fact of great moment in the consideration of the Ship Island Quarantine of the National Board of Health, is, that the experience of the past summer has shown that it affords an imperfect protection to the coast of Mississippi.

The port of entry for the State of Mississippi is located at Shieldsboro, where the Collector of Customs resides.

A careful inspection of the records of the Custom-House, shows that during the past ten years, the imports have been largely exceeded by the exports, the latter consisting chiefly of lumber.

Vessels have no difficulty in flanking the Ship Island Quarantine by running through Cat Island Pass, which is some twenty miles wide, and reporting at Shieldsboro, Bay St. Louis and Pass Christian, where they are boarded by the Custom-House and Quarantine Officers who reside in these thickly populated summer resorts.

The following communications to the Board of Health will illustrate the preceding statement:

CONSULADO DE ESPANA EN NUEVA ORLEANS, August 21, 1880.

Sir—I have just received a letter from the masters of the Spanish vessels Tomasita and Elisa, arrived respectively to Ship Island from the Island of Cuba on the twelfth and eighth instants, complaining of delays and vexations caused by the authorities of that Quarantine Station, and asking my advice under the circumstances.

As this is the first notice I have received on the subject, I shall feel obliged by your informing me why the Eliza has been detained so long and what foundation there is for the complaint of these two Spanish captains.

Hoping you will favor me with this information I remain, sir, your very obedient servant,
JOSE BAZAN.

To Dr. Joseph Jones, President Board of Health.

OFFICE BOARD OF HEALTH, STATE-HOUSE, New Orleans, August 23, 1880.

Jose Bazan, Esq., Spanish Consul at New Orleans:

Sir—In reply to your inquiry respecting delays at the Ship Island Quarantine, I have to say that this establishment is out of the jurisdiction of this Board, being under the direction of the National Board of Health.

For information on the subject I would refer you to Dr. S M. Bemiss, resident member of that Board, whose office is at the University, corner of Baronne and Common streets.

Respectfully, your obedient servant,
JOSEPH JONES, M. D., President Board of Health.

MISSISSIPPI—BAY ST. LOUIS.

THE BLOCKADE RUNNER THERESA G.—PARTICULARS OF WHAT HAPPENED TO HER AFTER PASSING THROUGH CAT ISLAND PASS.

Special Telegram to the N. O. Times:

BAY ST. LOUIS, August 19, 1880.

The Times correspondent called on Dr. Latham, the Sanitary Inspector of the National Board of Health, and in answer to interrogatories propounded to him, obtained the following statement regarding the schooner Theresa G. and the alleged cases of Yellow Fever on board of her:

" " The Theresa G. arrived in this port yesterday having left Havana on the fourteenth instant. She had one man taken sick in Havana with Yellow Fever, who was left there so the captain informed me. I boarded her on her arrival and found no one sick. As for the patient you speak of, I know nothing of him.

" I ordered the schooner to Ship Island, or to anchor in the channel and wait for the Day Dream to tow her to Ship Island. I did not search the vessel thoroughly, but simply looked through it, and the captain informed me that he had no sickness aboard. I would have made a thorough search, but did not think it necessary, as she was compelled anyhow to go to Ship Island.

" I never heard anything about the man dying abroad, consequently, cannot give any name, and as for the patient you speak of, if any, he must have been taken sick after leaving here on the eighteenth instant, at 9 o'clock a. m., for I saw all the crew, and one passenger, and all looked to be in good health."

THE CITY—THE BLOCKADE RUNNER.

**RUNNING THE BLOCKADE—MORE PARTICULARS OF THE SHIP THAT EVADED QUARAN-
TINE AND CAME INTO BAY ST. LOUIS.**

The Times of yesterday morning contained a report of the appearance of a vessel at Bay St. Louis, which had given the quarantine officials considerable trouble and anxiety.

The Collector of the port received information yesterday afternoon that the vessel, the Theresa G., had two cases of Yellow Fever on board, one proving fatal, and the other now on the vessel No particulars save the above were obtained by Collector Badger.

A reporter called on Dr. Bemiss. of the National Board of Health, yesterday evening, to learn further particulars of the matter, and found that gentleman willing to give the Times all the information at his command.

"The schooner alluded to is the Theresa G., an old offender against quarantine laws, and one, too, that we have had our eyes upon for a long time. For the past two or three years she has been running the blockade through Cat Island Pass. We had trouble with her in 1879."

"Had you been warned of her coming?"

"Oh, yes; an official telegram was sent here stating that there was a case of yellow fever on board of her, which probably occurred in Havana, as the man either died on board of the schooner or got well while she was yet in that port. She came into Bay St. Louis with a clean bill of health."

"Who is to blame for this fact?"

"I don't know; I am not informed whether the bill of health was given by our resident consul, Hall, or by the authorities at Havana. It is more probable, however, that she obtained the bill from the latter, as it appears that Mr. Hall telegraphed the fact of her having fever on board. She left Havana on the 14th and arrived at Bay St. Louis on the 18th. Previous to her arrival, I was informed that she was on the way, and immeditely telegraphed to the inspectors of the National Board to stop her wherever she was found

"Dr. Latham the inspector at the Bay, boarded her on her arrival there and sent her back to Ship Island where she is undergoing cleaning and disinfection. I instructed Dr. Martin not to spare soap or muscle to get her clean. I believe more in the efficacy of soap than of sulphur for such purposes."

"How did the schooner get to Bay St. Louis?"

"She went through Cat Island Pass, and by the way, there ought certainly to be some means of imposing and collecting heavy fines from water-crafts that run the blockade in this manner. The Theresa G., is a small boat, of about one hundred tons carrying capacity.

"Have you been informed of any other cases of fever on board of the schooner?"

"No; Dr. Latham, after examining her, telegraphed that he found everybody on board well

"Did you tell any member of the State Board of Health what you have stated?"

"I told Dr. Herrick, the Secretary of the Board."

"Do you think that proper precautions are taken against the possibilities of such occurrences as the one under discussion?"

"Oh yes; there are sanitary inspectors of the National Board at Pearlington, Bay St. Louis, Pass Christian and Biloxi. Dr. Griffin is the health officer and inspector at Pascagoula."

Dr. Bemiss said he had instructed Dr. Martin to keep the Theresa G. at Ship Island until she was considered entirely safe, and to provdie food and suitable accommodations for her crew during her term of detention.

There being nothing further to glean on this subject, the interview was terminated.

RIGOLETS QUARANTINE STATION, August 21, 1880.

Dr. Joseph Jones, President of the Board of Health:

Sir—In reply to your telegram of this date, I will say: Schooner Annette arrived at this Station August 9, after twenty-three days' voyage from Havana.

I detained her three days, disinfected and fumigated her thoroughly, and gave a permit to proceed to New Orleans.

Two of the crew were missing, the captain said deserted before he left Havana and after he had taken out his papers. He stated that there had been no sickness during the voyage and had a clean bill of health from Dr. D. M. Burgess, representative of the National Board of Health at Havana, which affirmed the vessel had been fumigated and disinfected. On examination I found the disinfection had been very imperfect and removed considerable filth and rotten wood from around the kelson and forecastle.

The customs papers were made out for Shieldsborough, though I think she was entered at the port of New Orleans. After I released her from quarantine, she lay a day or more opposite the customs station, awaiting her clearance papers from New Orleans, and intending to go up Pearl River.

The captain replied to my question why he did not come to Ship Island, that it was thirty-five miles out of his way, and therefore more convenient to come here.

I sent you a duplicate of the questions, and herewith enclose another. This is about all I know of the schooner Annette, except that she has for some time been in the lumber trade, and I have passed her here several times before this season

Very respectfully, DANIEL W. ADAMS, M. D., Resident Physician.

P. S.—Schooner Annette is now at Pearlington, on Pearl River, Miss., loading with lumber for Havana, Cuba. The Ship Island Station does not afford the least protection to the Pearl River country.

The Annette arrived at this station at 3:35 o'clock, p. m., August 9, and was released August 10, at 10:45 a. m., though she did not sail till after two o'clock that evening. She had no cargo, not even ballast. The fact of two men being missing from the crew list looks a little suspicious; but I have known the captain some time and consider him a man of veracity. Respectfully, D. W. ADAMS, M. D.

RIGOLETS, QUARANTINE STATION, August 21, 1880.

Dr. Joseph Jones, President, etc.:

Sir—I mentioned Ship Island Quarantine in my other communication, and will here state what the captains of the schooners Norma and Mary A. Rushing said about that station, and desire you to give me the necessary information relative to the questions asked by those captains and others.

Captain Barso of the schooner Norma, who was quarantined here in June, said he went a day's travel out of his way to go by Ship Island and lay there a day with his flag hoisted before he could attract the attention of any one, and when the officer came aboard he simply instructed him to proceed to the Rigolets Station where the Louisiana State officer would quarantine his vessel.

The captain was then caught in a calm and was several days getting here, where he had to remain the usual time of detention. Hence he was considerably delayed on his voyage. The Norma was from Tabasco, Mexico.

Capt. Cook, of the Mary Rushing, from Tuxpan, Mexico, who was quarantined here the first of this month, said he went out of his way to go to Ship Island and on his arrival there was told that he would have to go to Biloxi to find the Boarding Officer. Without seeing the officer at all, he came on here, and was detained, as above stated.

Their questions were: Is it required of them to go by Ship Island ? If they were quarantined, disinfected, etc., and had a permit from the officer there, would they be allowed to proceed to New Orleans without further inspection and detention at the Station ?

Ship Island is thirty-five miles from Cat Island Pass, the regular course of commerce. A vessel in going to or coming from Ship Island would have to travel about seventy miles out of her way.

Very respectfully, etc.,   DANIEL W. ADAMS, M. D.

———

The commerce of New Orleans depends upon the deep water secured by Capt. Eads, and ships comes to us from the Ports of Europe to receive the cotton, corn, wheat, and sugar and cattle of the Mississippi Valley, because after entering the passes they are in the safe harbor of the great inland sea, and can run up to the wharves of New Orleans and receive their cargoes in the shortest possible time. The foreign nations, supporting the commerce of the Mississippi Valley, England, France, Holland, Spain, Norway, Sweden and Denmark, all have their Islands and Ports in the West Indies, and their ships are compelled to communicate with the representatives of their government in Cuba, Jamaica, Barbadoes, St. Thomas, and other West Indian Islands. According to the Havana Yellow Fever Commission and the National Board of Health, the Yellow Fever prevails annually and is indigenous in the Antilles, hence all ships communicating with with those ports, must be regarded as coming from infected ports. In like manner all European ships touching or communicating with Central and South American ports within certain latitudes, must be regarded as coming from infected ports and in like manner subject to the restrictions of the Ship Island Quarantine.

Had the propositions of the National Board of Health, with reference to the Ship Island Quarantine, been accepted by the Board of Health of the State of Louisiana, the commerce of New Orleans would have been destroyed, whilst the city would not have been protected, as the Ship Island Quarantine was scarcely capable of protecting the coast of Mississippi.

The Board of Health of the State of Louisiana has protected the commerce of the Mississippi Valley, and at the same time has excluded foreign pestilence, by confining itself to the exercise of the powers conferred upon it by the State and Federal Governments, by respecting the rights of commerce and health of sister States, and by the rejection of the preposterous schemes of the National Board of Health.

YELLOW FEVER ALARMS.

False reports with reference to the existence of Yellow Fever in New Orleans, were scattered broadcast over the country, a few days after the organization of the present Board of Health, and simultaneously with the development of the Ship Island scheme.

Whoever originated these *false reports in New Orleans*, used other agen cies than the daily press, and more especially the electric telegraph for their dissemination to distant parts of the United States.

The mortuary records of the Board of Health have been at all times open to the public and Medical Profession, and lists have been daily published in the papers, of the names of the dead, and in addition to this the weekly mortuary has been officially promulgated by the Board of Health in printed classified forms to the Boards of Health and Quarantine officers throughout the United States.

The following correspondence is submitted with the simple remark that the recurrence of similar alarms during the spring and summer, necessitated the constant weekly and monthly publication of the statistics of the past twelve years, and the constant communication by letter and telegraph of the real sanitary condition of New Orleans.

NEW ORLEANS, April 13 1880.

Surgeon J. T. Turner, M. D., Secretary National Board of Health, Washington, D. C.

Sir—In the New Orleans "Times of this instant the following telegram appears:"

WASHINGTON, April 12.—Official advices of the National Board of Health show, that during the four weeks ending March 27, there had been eleven deaths from Malignant Yellow Fever in New Orleans, and two in Memphis.

The Board of Health of Louisiana requests to be informed, from whence the National Board of Health obtained its official advices in this instance.

Up to the present moment *no case* of Yellow Fever has been reported to the Board of Health, and no physician has had a case of Yellow Fever during the present year.

The telegraphic report purporting to come from the Natioual Board of Health is without foundation, JOSEPH JONES, M. D.
President Board of Health, State of Louisiana.

OFFICE BOARD OF HEALTH, STATE OF LOUISIANA. ⎱
New Orleans, April 14, 1880. ⎰

Hon. L. A. Wiltz, Governor State of Louisiana:

Dear Sir—I have the honor to submit to your Excellency the following reply from the Secretary of the National Board of Health, which will explain the mode in which the erroneous statement, telegraphed through the Associate Press, originated:

WASHINGTON, D. C., April 14, 1880.—Prof. Joseph Jones, M. D., President Board of Health, State of Louisiana: Telegram received. The Associated Press telegraph operator is responsible for inserting yellow after the word malignant. The only official advices received so far from New Orleans are the published weekly reports of the Board of Health and the mortality cards furnished by this office. No case of Yellow Fever appears in these reports. TURNER.

Upon reference to the printed weekly statements of mortality by the Board of Health, I find the following deaths from fever during the time embraced in the original dispatch which purported to come from the National Board of Health:

Week ending March 6.—Malarial fever, unclassified, 1; during this week the total deaths from all causes were 82.

Week ending March 14.—Scarlatina 1, typhoid fever 1, malarial intermittent fever 1, remittent 1; total deaths 78

Week ending March 21—Measles 2, scarlati a 1, typhoid 1; total deaths 85.

9

Week ending March 28.—Measles 1, scarlatina 1, typhoid fever 1, malarial intermittent fever 1, malarial congestive fever 8; total deaths 109.

The total deaths from all causes during the four weeks, was 354; and the total deaths from measles, 3; scarlatina, 3; typhoid fever, 3; malarial fevers (intermittent, remittent congestive), 12.

By comparison with the following statistics, ambracing the total deaths from all causes and from fevers during the past twelve years, it will be seen that with two exception, the present month has been remarkably healthy and free from deaths caused by fevers.

TOTAL DEATHS FROM ALL CAUSES AND FROM FEVERS IN NEW ORLEANS DURING THE MONTHS OF MARCH, DURING THE PAST THIRTEEN YEARS.

Year.	Total Deaths.	Malarial Fevers.	Typhoid Fever.	Yellow Fever.
1868	345	16	4	. . . .
1869	435	12	2	
1870	525	15	8	
1871	634	20	14	
1872	430	20	5	
1873	603	22	3	
1874	452	12	2	
1875	461	14	4	
1876	559	21	5	
1877	788	12	5	
1878	544	18	1	
1879	376	11	1	
1880	354	12	3	. . . .

It will be manifest from the preceding statistics that at the present moment New Orleans is in a condition of more than usual good health.

The number of deaths from the various forms of malarial fever being for the month of March, below the average of those years which have been free from epidemic Yellow Fever.   Respectfully, your obedient servant,

JOSEPH JONES, M. D.,

President Board of Health, State of Louisiana.

———

NATIONAL BOARD OF HEALTH, Washington, D. C., April 15, 1880.

Dr. Joseph Jones, President State Board of Health of Louisiana, New Orleans, La.:

My Dear Doctor—Your telegram of the 13th inst., was received and acknowledged. I am directed by the Executive Committee of the Board to give you the history of the matter concerned in your telegram. A mistake was made by the telegraph operator of the Associated Press in interpolating the word "yellow" between the words malignant and fever. This mistake was corrected inside of twelve hours of the issue of the first dispatch, and due publicity has been given of such correction. The extraordinary amount of attention given to this matter illustrates the importance attached to any report from New Orleans, and it would inspire confidence in every direction if the State Board of Health of Louisiana would furnish the particulars of all cases reported as malignant fever or other fevers which might be mistaken for Yellow Fever. Such particulars will be published in the bulletin, if furnished.

I am, Doctor, very respectfully, &c.,   T. J. TURNER, Secretary National Board of Health.

———

OFFICE BOARD OF HEALTH STATE OF LOUISIANA, }
New Orleans, April 19, 1880. }

Surgeon T. J. Turner, M. D., Secretary National Board of Health, Washington, D. C.

Dear Sir—I have the honor to acknowledge receipt of your letter of the fifteenth instant, in which by direction of the Executive Committee of the National Board of Health the Secretary was directed to give the history of the matter concerned in the telegram of the thirteenth instant, and in reply beg leave respectfully to submit the following :

1. "The mistake made by the Telegraph Operator of the Associated Press in interpolating the word " Yellow " between the words malignant and fever, created intense excitement in this City and State, and in those States which are intimately associated with Louisiana by Geographical position and commercial relations.

2. Upon thorough investigation, I find that no case of fever bearing any resemblance to Yellow Fever, has occurred in New Orleans during the present year.

3. It will be perceived that in the weekly mortuary reports of the State Board of Health, that under the head of malarial fevers the terms *congestive or malignant* are used as designating one of the well known forms of paroxysmal or paludal fevers common to all parts of the Valley of the Mississippi and to all Towns and Cities situated upon or near those river courses emptying into the Atlantic Ocean.

4. The term of congestive or malignant malarial fever, is evidently used on the Death Report of the Louisiana State Board of Health as synonymous with pernicious malarial fever. The so-called congestive, malignant or pernicious fever of the Mississippi Valley,

occur at all times, and have been known by various names, as cold plague etc. This class of fevers differs in no essential symptom or pathological alteration from the common intermittent and remittent fevers of all parts of the United States.

5. It is well known that any one of the varied forms of malarial, paroxysmal or marsh fever, may suddenly assume the so-called congestive or pernicious type.

6. It is evident, therefore, from the preceding facts that a gross error was committed, not merely by the telegraph operator by the insertion of the word yellow, after the word malignant, but by the authority furnishing the information to the Associated Press, that during the four weeks ending March 27 there had been eleven deaths from malignant (Yellow) Fever in New Orleans.

The correct statement would have referred the deaths to malarial, conjestive or malignant fever. The grave error consists in the exclusion of the terms malarial, congestive, which could have conveyed a definite idea as to the true nature of the disease in question, and would have created no alarm in the minds of those who are capable of controlling public opinion in such matters

7. In connection with this subject it is due to the City of New Orleans that the following facts be laid before the National Board of Health.

Upon reference to the printed weekly statements of mortality of the Board of Health, I find the following deaths occurred from fevers, during the time embraced in the original dispatch which purported to come from the National Board of Health. (The table presented in a communication to Governor Wiltz was here presented.)

It will be manifest, from the preceeding statement, that at the present moment New Orleans is in a condition of more than usual health.

The number of deaths for the month of March, 1880, from the various forms of malarial fevers, is below the average of those years which have been free from Epidemic Yellow Fever.

By reference to the National Board of Health Bulletin for the week ending March 27, 1880, I find the total number of deaths in New York to be 543; of which malarial fevers caused 13, enteric 8.

The percentage representing an annual death rate per 1000 in New York during the week ending March 27 was 25.8, while that of New Orleans is placed a trifle higher, namely, 27.1.

8. I cannot fully subscribe to the following statement contained in your letter of April 13:

"The extraordinary amount of attention given to this matter illustrates the importance attached to any report from New Orleans and it would inspire confidence in every direction if the State Board of Health of Louisiana would furnish the particulars of all cases reported as malignant fevers, or other fevers which might be mistaken for Yellow Fever. Such particulars will be published in the Bulletin, if furnished."

The entire valley of the Mississippi is subject at all times to the various forms of malarial fevers, varying in form and intensity according to the season, etc.; and these have been described upon various occasions by numerous able Western and Southern medical writers, and I can see no good to accrue to this city and to this section of the country by a continual agitation of the public mind by the publication of cases of well-known fevers in the Bulletin of the National Board of Health, which holds a medium ground between the daily newspapers and the regular medical journals published in almost every city.

In conclusion, allow me to say that the officers and members of the Board of Health of the State of Louisiana repose implicit confidence in the intelligence, integrity and patriotism of the medical profession of New Orleans and of the State of Louisiana, and it is their determination to deal candidly and truthfully with all questions relating to the health and sanitation of the city of New Orleans and of the shipping in the Mississippi River.

Respectfully, your obedient servant,   JOSEPH JONES, M. D.,
President Board of Health, State of Louisiana.

ALARM CREATED BY THE OCCURRENCE OF THE CASE OF YELLOW FEVER ON THE BARK EXCELSIOR AND INVESTIGATIONS RESULTING THEREFROM.

The Tennessee State Board of Health issued a quarantine circular against New Orleans, on the 14th of July, predicated upon the following erroneous statements:

" Whereas, one death from Yellow Fever, and two other cases, have occurred in New Orleans among the crew of the coffee ship *Excelsior,* from Rio de Janerio; and

Whereas, the history of said ship, as recited at a meeting of the Louisiana State Board of Health, held in the city of New Orleans, on the 12th instant, conclusively shows that the vessel and her cargo are infected with Yellow Fever; that her infected cargo is now stored in a warehouse in that city; and that her captain, some members of her crew, and a large number of visitors, as well as persons (seventy-five or more) who were engaged in and about said infected vessel in breaking out cargo, and in handling, draying and storing her infected merchandise, are scattered throughout said city," etc.

The full report from which the Louisiana Board puports to have drawn these facts, stated that but *one case* had occurred on board the Bark Excelsior, and that said Bark had been removed to the Quarantine Station.

No allusion whatever was made in this quarantine proclamation to the prompt and efficient measures instituted by the National Board of Health for the disinfection of the cargo and for the isolation of the Excelsior by forcibly seizing her and remanding her back to the Mississippi Quarantine Station, some seventy-five miles down the Mississippi River. Neither was it true " that her captain" and "some members of her crew" were scattered throughout New Orleans.

Immediately upon the arrival of the bark Excelsior the captain went up up on the Jackson Railroad, some seventy-five miles, and did not return for some time, and was entirely ignorant of the fate of his ship, until informed by telegraph.

Not one of the crew was left behind in New Orleans.

The State Board of Mississippi issued its quarantine circular on the sixteenth of July.

The National Board of Health bulletin of July 17, contains the following:

YELLOW FEVER REPORTS.

NEW ORLEANS, La.—A dispatch from Dr S. M. Bemiss, member of the National Board of Health, dated July 11. reports one case of Yellow Fever on board the Excelsior from Rio Janeiro. The case was at once removed to hospital, and the city is reported as healty.—National Board of Health Bulletin, vol. 2, No: 3, pp. 447.

The quarantine circulars of the Tennessee and Mississippi Boards of Health were published in the National Board of Health Bulletin, Vol. 2. No. 4, dated Washington, D. C., Saturday, July 24, 1880, and this issue of the official organ of the National Board of Health contained the following account of the bark Excelsior;

YELLOW FEVER CASE AT NEW ORLEANS

On Saturday, the tenth of July, 1880, at 10 a. m., James Kenney, aged 19, a native of Scotland, was admitted to the Touro Infirmary, from the Swedish bark Excelsior, presenting symptoms of Yellow Fever.

The bark Excelsior was then lying at the foot of Calliope streeet, post 13, First District.

This vessel, 450 tons, S L. Bjorkgren, master, sailed from London the seventeenth of February, 1880, and arrived at Rio de Janeiro, April 13, 1880 ; left Rio the tenth of May, and arrived at Mississippi Quarantine Station June 24, having been on the voyage abont forty-six days. The crew consisted of three officers and nine seaman   No case of sickness occurred at Rio or on the voyage to the Mississippi Quarantine Station. The vessel was detained at the Quarantine twelve days. The cargo consisted of 3600 sacks of coffee ; ballast of granite rock. She left the Quarantine and arrived at New Orleans on the morning of the fifth of July, and commenced discharging cargo, which was deposited in the Montgomery Warehouse, on Fulton, between Julia and St. Joseph streets.

The case of Yellow Fever was not developed until the vessel had been for sixty-two hours at the wharf at New Orleans.—National Board of Health Bulletin, July 29, 1880, vol. 2, No. 4, p. 458.

It will be observed that not the slightest allusion was made (or has ever been made, as far as our information extends) by the National Board of Health Bulletin to the means instituted by the Board of Health of the State of Louisiana in the removal and isolation of the infected vessel.

The publication of the two quarantine circulars of the Tennessee and Mississippi Boards of Health in almost juxtaposition with the " Yellow Fever case at New Orleans," without giving any particulars, was calculated to excite alarm and distrust throughout the Mississippi Valley.

We have some evidence of what was really the action of one, at least, of the agents of the National Board of Health in the following account published in the Natchez Democrat.

Dr. John C. Inge, City Health Officer, and Dr. T. S. Sharpe, Health Officer for the county, visited the steamer Benner, in the service of the National Board of Health, on its passage up the river yesterday, and had an interesting interview with Dr. Reilly, the member of the National Board having charge of this district. Dr. Reilly has just returned from New Orleans, and does not seem to be satisfied with the course of the Louisiana State Board of Health.   He went to the warehouse where the coffee from the infected ship Excelsior was stored, and upon counting the sacks found that there were one thousand sacks less than the number stated to have been stored there.   The fumigation which the vessel is said to have undergone at Quarantine was not such, in the opinion of Dr. Reilly as to be effective.

Dr. Reilly advises strongly that Natchez put itself for the present *en rapport* with the National Board of Health, and thinks such action would be beneficial to our city.   The plan proposed for health certificates is very rigid, and with proper co-operation of all points on the river would probably be effective. Dr. Reilly stated that Texas would probably to-day quarantine against New Orleans.—[Natchez Democrat, July 21.

Official communications were addressed by the executive officer of the Board of Health to Dr. John C. Inge and Dr. T. S. Sharpe, directing their attention to the inaccuracies in the statements of Dr. Reilly, of the National Board of Health, and exposing their mischievous tendencies.

A protest against the quarantines established against New Orleans by the Boards of Health of Mississippi and Tennessee was addressed to the Acting Governor of the State of Louisiana, from which we extract the following :

OFFICE BOARD OF HEALTH, July 21, 1880.

Lieutenant Governor S. D. McEnery, Acting Governor State of Louisiana.

Sir—I have the honor to submit the following facts relative to the Quarantine established against the city of New Orleans and State of Louisiana, by the State Board of Health of Tennessee on the 14th instant, and by the Mississippi State Board of Health on the 16th instant.

The proclamation of the Mississippi State Board of Health, is officially approved by the Governor of the State, his Excellency J. M. Stone ; on the other hand the Tennessee decree is signed by the President and Secretary of the State Board of Health.

The said Quarantine proclamations are made upon the supposition, that in some undefined and unknown way, contagion may be communicated to the States of Mississippi and Tennessee, by the crew and cargo of the Swedish Bark " Excelsior," which reached this harbor on the 5th of July.

The entire facts of the case have been presented to your Excellency, and have been officially announced and published to the world by the Board of Health of the State of Louisiana, and it is unnecessary to recount the circumstances attending the prompt removal of the vessel, and the thorough disinfection and isolation of the cargo, twelve days ago.

The important facts to be considered, are

1.   The occurrence of an imported case of Yellow Fever in a foreign ship from a foreign port does not constitute the port in which such case occurs, "an infected port."

2. The only case of Yellow Fever which has occurred within the limits of New Orleans up to this moment, 2 p. m., July 21, 1880, originated on board the bark Excelsior, fifty-two (52) days after leaving Rio, on the seventh day of July.

Fourteen days have elapsed since the occurrence of this case, and eleven days since the death and burial of the patient, and the prompt removal of the vessel and crew to the Mississippi Quarantine Station, seventy-five miles below the city.

This period is twice as long as that specified by the National Board of Health as constituting the period of incubation of the Yellow Fever poison.

3. Notwithstanding the erroneous statements embodied in the quarantine proclamations of Tennessee and Mississippi, the official statement of the Sanitary Inspector of the First District, who was charged with the execution of the order of the President of the Board of Health, shows that only eighteen colored men and two white men were employed in the discharge of the cargo of the Excelsior.

Careful watch has been kept with reference to these men, as well as those employed in the Montgomery Warehouse, which received the cargo of the Excelsior, and up to the present moment not a single case of fever of any description has occurred within the limits of the City of New Orleans.

4. A careful inspection of the Charity Hospital, Hotel Dieu, and other charitable institutions reveals the absence of all forms of fever.

5. A careful inspection of the shipping in the harbor of New Orleans, reveals the important fact that not a case of fever exists among the seamen.

6. As will be seen by the enclosed weekly statement of mortality of New Orleans, embodied from the State records on file at the State-House, the total deaths for New Orleans during the past week was only 100, giving a death-rate of about 23 in 1000 per annum. Of this number, only six were caused by the various fevers of malarial or swamp forms, which prevail at all times and in all seasons in the valley of the Mississippi.

7. The mortuary records of New Orleans establish beyond controversey the facts that

(a.) New Orleans is absolutely free from Yellow Fever;

(b.) New Orleans at the present time has as low a death-rate as any city of the same or smaller or larger size within the bounds of the United States.

(c.) Not a case of sunstroke occurred during the past week in New Orleans, whilst numerous cases have been reported in New York, Philadelphia, St. Louis and other cities.

8. In view of these facts, the quarantine established against the city of New Orleans and the State of Louisiana, by the physicians of Tennessee and Mississippi, must be regarded as unnecessary, unwise, ungenerous and unconstitutional. * * *

With great respect, I have the honor to remain your obedient servant.

JOSEPH JONES, M. D.,
President Board of Health, State of Louisiana.

INVESTIGATION INTO THE SANITARY CONDITION OF NEW ORLEANS

AND THE NATURE OF THE QUARANTINE REGULATIONS BY THE BOARD OF HEALTH OF THE STATE OF LOU-ISIANA, INSTITUTED BY THE GOV-ERNOR OF TEXAS.

Dr. R. Rutherford, formerly of Columbus, Georgia (but at the time of this investigation instituted by Gov. Roberts, of Texas, a resident of Houston, Texas), arrived in New Orleans on the twenty-first of July, and announced himself as the *Health Officer of Texas*, under instructions from his Excellency, C. M. Roberts, Governor of Texas, to inquire into the sanitary condition of New Orleans, and more especially into the facts connected with the bark Excelsior.

Said investigation was suggested to the Governor of Texas by S. M. Bemiss, M. D., resident member of the National Board of Health.

The President of the Board of Health of the State of Louisiana afforded every facility to the agent of the Governor of Texas for a thorough investigation of the sanitary condition of New Orleans, and more especially for all facts connected with the bark Excelsior.

All the records of the Board of Health were thrown open for his inspection and examination. He was conducted to the wharf at which the Excelsior lay, to the warehouse in which the coffee was stored, the Charity Hospital and the Hotel Dieu.

The Sanitary Inspector of the First District, who had fumigated the coffee of the bark Excelsior was instructed to furnish all facts and information, and also to muster all men engaged in the handling of the coffee of the Excelsior in the presence of the Health Officer of Texas.

A steam tugboat was also chartered for the conveyance of his Excellency, Lieut. Gov. McEnery, Acting Governor of the State of Louisiana, and a committee of the Board of Health to visit the Quarantine Station, and in order to afford the Health Officer of Texas an opportunity to make a truthful report to the Chief Executive of his State.

The following is the report of this visit as taken from the daily Picayune:

A TRIP TO QUARANTINE STATION.

VISIT OF A COMMITTEE OF THE BOARD OF HEALTH AND DR. RUTHERFORD OF TENSAS—CONDITION OF THE STATION AND ITS SURROUNDINGS.

On Wednesday morning the committee appointed by Dr. Joseph Jones, President of the Louisiana State Board of Health, to inspect the Mississippi Quarantine Station, consisting of Dr. J. C. Beard, chairman, and Drs. J. P. Davidson and F. Loeber, proceeded to Quarantine Station on the tugboat Charlie Wood. The committee was accompanied by Acting Governor McEnery, Dr. R. Rutherford and wife, Drs. F. Formento and E. T. Shepard, of the State Board of Health, Stanhope Jones, and the members of the press. Dr. J. F. Finney, Resident Physician of the station also formed one of the party.

"Nothing worthy of special mention transpired until the vessels lying off the quarantine grounds were sighted. These proved to be the bark Excelsior and three steamships. The four were ranged in a line with each other, and were all within about the space of a mile. First appeared the bark looking remarkably trim and neat, her masts and yards resembling those of a newly built vessel, being very clean and orderly. The steamships Margaret, from Havana, Author from Colon, and Australia from Vera Cruz, followed in the order as named."

"At the Quarantine wharf the party disembarked, Dr. Finney proceeding at once to his residence, this being his first visit to the station since the accident he met with two weeks ago by falling twenty-three feet, in stepping at night through the open hatchway of an iron steamship. That he was not either instantly killed or fatally injured is surprising, as nothing intervened to break the fall, and there was no cargo whatever in that part of the hold. Beyond cutting his face and forehead, bruising his body and crushing together the bones of the foot which struck the hold, he received no further injury and is rapidly recovering from the effects of the fall, although he will probably continue on crutches two or three weeks longer, the foot being still very painful and much swollen.

"It having been reported from Texas that the bark Execlsior was improperly and not sufficiently fumigated after her arrival at Quarantine Station from Rio Janeiro, a careful and thorough ivnestigatian was made by the committee in presence of Dr. Rutherford, the State Quarantine Officer of Texas, and the members of the press.

"Capt. Chas. H. Merritt, Chief Custom-house Inspector, at the Quarantine Station, reports that he boarded the bark Excelsior on her arrival from Rio, on the 25th day of June, unsealed her hatches, and resealed the same on the 5th day of July. Capt. Merritt states that he can assert that the vessel was fumigated, and that no one was sick on board to his knowledge, while the bark was at Quarantine Station during the eleven days of her detention ; that he boarded the Excelsior a number of times during her detention at quarantine, and smelled sulphur on board several times, thus showing that she was either undergoing the process of fumigation or had just been fumigated previous to his going on board.

"Dr. J. F. Finney, Quarantine Physician, states that the condition of the Excelsior as regards cleanliness was about the same as the average of sailing vessels. No sickness on board while at the Quarantine Station. The Excelsior was fumigated repeatedly. At each fumigation between sixty and seventy pounds of sulphur were used. The bilge water was pumped out and replaced by a solution of copperas and carbolic acid. This, Dr. Finney states is done to all vessels quarantined, they being inspected and thoroughly cleansed, although not coming from infected ports.

"Dr. C. P. Wilkinson, Assistant Resident Physician at the Quarantine Station, and all the boatmen, corroborate the statements of Capt. Merritt and Dr. Finney. Since the return of the bark to Quarantine Station, Dr. Wilkinson states that two of the crew have died of Yellow Fever, and a third is convalescing. No other person is sick on the four vessels lying at the Station or at the Quarantine grounds or neighborhood on either side of the river to his knowledge. No communication is allowed between vessels while undergoing quarantine. The bark Excelsior had only about one-third of a cargo. This was shifted from one part of the hold to the other and thoroughly fumigated. The hold was well ventilated. The crew of the Quarantine Physician's boat are all acclimated.

"G. T. Wilkstrom, mate of the bark Excelsior, stated in answer to the question of Dr. Beard, that the vessel arrived and departed from the Mississippi Quarantine Station as stated above. No one was sick at sea or at Rio de Janeiro. The crew went ashore at Rio twice during the stay of the vessel off that port. Upon arriving at the Mississippi Quarantine Station the vessel was fumigated four times. So dense were the fumes arising therefrom that the crew were obliged to sleep on deck and even the cabin was so impregnated with the sulphur, as to render it impossible for the officers to sleep there during the nights when the vessel had been fumigated.

"The officers consisted at that time of the captain, two mates and a crew of nine men. The bark Excelsior was twenty-nine days at Rio. The crew went below seven or eight times while at sea. The voyage from Rio to New Orleans occupied fifty-six days. At the Mississippi Quarantine Station the whole crew assisted in shifting the cargo preparatory to fumigation. The bilge water was pumped out. At first it was very foul, but gradually became less so. No one on board the vessel was sick at sea or at the Quarantine Station."

Dr. Rutherford was also invited to attend the regular meeting of the Board of Health of the State of Louisiana, held for the purpose of considering the Report of the Committee.

The following is an extract from the minutes of the Board of Health, held Thursday evening, July 22, 1880, in the State Capitol:

Dr. Rutherford, after being introduced to the Board of Health by the President, stated "that as he would have to return to Texas, before another meeting of the Board would be held, he desired to thank the President and members of the Louisiana State Board of Health, for the courtesies shown and facilities rendered him in prosecuting to completion the duties that called him to New Orleans, Dr. Rutherford then said, that it afforded him great pleasure and satisfaction to state that from his own personal investigation he was able to confirm every statement made to Texas, by the Louisiana State Board, relative to the bark Excelsior, and the true sanitary condition of the city of New Orleans."

The following is the official Report of Dr. Rutherford, as published in the papers of Texas and Louisiana:

[The Galveston News, August 3, 1880.]
RUTHERFORD'S REPORT—AN INEFFECTIVE QUARANTINE.

The report made by Dr. Rutherford, State Health Officer, after his return from his investigating trip to New Orleans, and forwarded to the Governor, was sent to the Board of Health by request and received yesterday. The document received appears to be the original and was accompanied by no note or comment from the Governor. The following is what Dr. Rutherford says:

HOUSTON, TEX., July 27, 1880.—To His Excellency O. M. Roberts, Governor of Texas: My Dear Sir—Your letter of instruction, dated July 16, 1880, reached my hand the morning of the eighteenth, and upon the morning of the nineteenth I left Houston for New Orleans, stopping at Galveston and apprising Dr. Watts and his Board of your orders, which orders met their unanimous approval. Arrived in New Orleans evening of the twenty-first, was met by Dr. Joseph Jones, President of the Board of Health, and arranged for routine of investigation upon the twenty-second. I divided my work into four parts, beginning first with the ship, her location, as to probable infection of localities or persons in New Orleans, and found that she had occupied, fortunately, a place at a wharf that was a thousand yards removed from the nearest dwellings, among which buildings was the Touro Infirmary, to which place the only case of Yellow Fever that occurred during the ship's stay at New Orleans was taken. The ship herself was removed to Quarantine at Mississippi Station, seventy-five miles below the city, with the remainder of the crew on board. The ship had been retained upon her first arrival ten days at Quarantine, and was fumigated three times during that period. Upon her arrival at the wharf she was again subjected to fumes of burning sulphur and then her cargo was removed to Montgomery warehouse, on Calliope street.

Second—The disposition of this cargo and its location as to infection. There were 3600 bags of this coffee, and upon examination of the warehouse books found that only 3006 remained upon the twenty-third instant, so here was 594 bags of coffee to be found. This at first nobody seemed willing to tell me; but by a series of pumping I did find out the destination of every bag, which was as follows: 379 to St. Louis, 180 to Houston, Texas., 15 to Shreveport, La , all of which had been shipped out before fever was discovered on the vessel.

Third—The hands employed in unloading the ship, draymen and warehousemen who received it, and after two days' work got them together and found them all well, upon the morning of the twenty-fourth instant, seventeen days after their connection with the ship and her cargo, which pleased me not a little.

Fourth—The hospital and general sanitary condition of the city, which after visiting all of them I found that the city was exceptionally clear of all infectious diseases for the present. I also under this head will report unfavorably of the manner in which the quarantine is performed at Mississippi Station, below New Orleans, vessels from Vera Cruz and Havana only being detained seventy-two hours at Quarantine before being allowed to come up to the wharves at the city, which would only make them five days from wharf to wharf respectively at Havana and New Orleans; and also inclose you copy of cipher, given me by Dr. Bemiss, of which I retain a copy, the doctor promising most positively to send by wire even suspicious cases, and this I consider the only safeguard against the careless quarantine now enforced. I very much hope that the merchants' voice will reach the Board of Health in time to make them more careful in the near future. The former are almost univiversally in favor of more stringent quarantine. I shall try to visit Austin in the next three days, and will have more that I can tell you which should not properly be spoken of in this report.

Respectfully, your obedient servant,   R. RUTHERFORD, M. D. and S. H. O.

It is not material that the testimony of Dr. R. Rutherford should be examined in detail, as the testimony of the Honorable Dr. McClanahan and of the Honorable N. N. John of Galveston, Texas, will be recorded in full upon the same points ; but it is material that the following statement should be considered: Dr. Rutherford, Health Officer of Texas, and representing the Governor of Texas, after according to his own statement being afforded by the President and members of the Board of Health of the State of Louisiana, every facility for the thorough investigation of the sanitary condition of the city and of the facts connected with the bark Excelsior, and the conduct of the Mississippi Quarantine Station, reports*to the Chief Executive of Texas:

" The hospital and general sanitary condition of the city, which after visiting all of them, I found that the city was exceptionally clear of all infectious diseases for the present."

"I also under this head, will report unfavorably of the manner in which the quarantine is performed at Mississippi Station, below New Orleans, vessels from Vera Cruz and Havana only, being detained seventy-two hours at Quarantine, before being allowed to come up to the wharves at the city, which would only make them five days from wharf to wharf, respectively at Havana and New Orleans : *And also inclose you copy of cipher, given me by Dr. Bemiss, of which I retain a copy, the doctor promising most positively to send by wire even suspicious cases, and this I consider the only safeguard against the careless quarantine now enforced.*"

10

S. M. Bemiss, M. D., member of the National Board of Health, residing in New Orleans, and accredited by the National Government, as representing the sanitary interests of Louisiana, did not communicate *his cipher* to the Board of Health of the State of Louisiana, and this Board would have been profoundly ignorant of the secret measures adopted by the National Board of Health, if the communication of Dr. Rutherford had not found its way into the columns of the daily press.

The investigations of the Health officer of Texas, and his conference with the member of the National Board of Health in New Orleans, resulted in the determination to protect the great state of Texas by a cipher.

INVESTIGATION OF THE SANITARY CONDI-
TION OF NEW ORLEANS,

AND THE CONDUCT OF THE QUARANTINE OF THE STATE BOARD BY THE DELEGATION OF THE GAL-
VESTON BOARD OF HEALTH.

The investigation instituted by the Governor of Texas, not being entirely satisfactory to the health authorities of Galveston, telegraphic communications was sent to the President of the Louisiana Board, inquiring if a commission would be received.

The following statement embodies the results of this correspondence, and the conclusions arrived at by the members of the Galveston Board of Health:

[Telegram.]

GALVESTON, July 30.—To Dr. Jones and Dr. Bemiss, New Orleans: Telegram received. The detention at your quarantine not satisfactory. Will send two members of the Board of Health to your city for conference, if your reply gives encouragement to do so.
　　　　　　　　　　　　　　　　　　　W. D. KELLEY, M. D.
　　　　　　　　　　　　　　　　　　　CHAS. FOWLER.

[Telegram.]

BOARD OF HEALTH, New Orleans, July 30, 1880.
To Dr. W. D. Kelly, Galveston Board of Health:

Send member of your Board of Health.
Detention of vessel at Quarantine, according to rules of National Board of Health.
New Orleans in good sanitary condition and free from epidemic fevers of every description.
Telegraph condition of Galveston and direct your committee to bring official reports.
　　　　　　　　　　　　　　　　　　　JOSEPH JONES, M. D.

The resident member of the National Board of Health was requested to affix his signature to this telegram. The following is his reply:

NATIONAL BOARD OF HEALTH, New Orleans, July 31, 1880.
Dr. Joseph Jones, President State Board of Health:

Dear Sir—I have respectfully to state that I did not think it proper to affix my signature to your telegram in answer to that of the Galveston Board of Health, brought to me last night, but sent by the same messengers the following over my own signature: "National Board states minimum for detention, but does not prescribe limits for local Boards. Hope committee will be sent. City free from sickness. Signed, Bemiss."
　　Very respectfully, etc.,
　　　　　　　　　　　　　　S. M. BEMISS, Member National Board of Health.

BOARD OF HEALTH, New Orleans, July 31, 1880.—To Dr. W. D. Kelley, Galveston Board of Health: Hope that you will come with committee from Galveston Board of Health. Will give committee every facility for investigation, and will endeavor to make all quarantine matters satisfactory.
　　City in state of remarkable health. Death-rate continually decreasing; only fifty-three deaths from all causes during the past six days. City absolutely free from all contagious and infectious diseases.
　　　　　　　　　　　　　　　　　　　JOSEPH JONES, M. D.

[Telegram.]

HOUSTON, Texas, July 31, 1880.

Dr. Joseph Jones, President Louisiana State Board:

I have this morning been informed by Chas. Fowler that Galveston will quarantine your city, unless your quarantine regulations are made more stringent at once. I do this as your friend, that you may defend yourself and not officially.   R. RUTHERFORD.

The committee appointed by the Galveston Board of Health, consisting of Mr. Thomas McClanahan and Mr N. N. John, arrived in New Orleans on the evening of the fourth of August.

Every facility was afforded to these gentlemen by the President of the Louisiana State Board for a thorough investigation of the sanitary condition of the city, and the quarantine regulations, and a meeting of the Board of Health was called to meet the committee.

[The Daily Picayune, Tuesday morning, Aug. 19, 1880.]

THE GALVESTON DELEGATION—THEY FIND THE HEALTH AND SANITARY CONDITION OF NEW ORLEANS VERY GOOD, AND WILL SO REPORT TO THE GALVESTON BOARD.

A special meeting of the Louisiana State Board of Health was held last evening, Dr. Joseph Jones, President, in the chair.

Present—Drs Davidson, Loeber, Shepherd, and Messrs. Marks and Brewster.

Dr. Jones said the special meeting was called to receive the delegation from Galveston, Dr. Thos. McClanahan and N. N. John, Esq., of the Galveston Board of Health, who were present. Dr. Jones then requested the gentlemen to address the Board on the questions that called them to New Orleans.

Dr. McClanahan said the purpose of the visit was one of pacification, and that he was chosen by the Galveston Board one of the committee to visit New Orleans because he held conservative views relative to quarantine.

The Board of Health of Galveston were under the impression that in all cases where vessels come from infected ports there was only a detention at quarantine of seventy-two hours. This was not considered to be sufficient for security by the Galveston Board.

Just previous to leaving Galveston Dr. McClanahan said a resolution was written out to be offered at the special meeting of the board, which proposed immediate quarantine against New Orleans on this account. The result, however, was that more conservative counsel prevailed, which finally terminated in the appointment of the committee.

Dr. McClanahan said he was perfectly satisfied of the good health ot the city of New Orleans.

At Quarantine Station, he said, everything was evidently being done and had been done to prevent the introduction of infections or contagions diseases to the city. There were, however, some of the members of the Galveston board who could not be prevailed upon to believe that seventy-two hours detention of vessels was sufficient.

If again, Dr. McClanahan remarked, a resolution should be offered to quarantine New Orleans, he would certainly vote against it. The reporting of every case of Yellow Fever, attending to the sanitary condition of the shipping and of the city of New Orleans would have considerable effect in averting quarantine, but a longer detention of vessels—say tén days—from Havana, Rio Janeiro and Vera Cruz, he believed would keep up commercial relations between New Orleans and Galveston all summer.

At Galveston, it must be remembered, Dr. McClanahan continued, there were no hospitals, quarantine station, or buildings which necessitated therefore perfect non-intercourse in case of threatened danger of yellow fever.

Dr. McClanahan had no suggestions to make. He had seen what the Louisiana State Board of Health as well as the Auxiliary Sanitary Association had done. The present free intercourse might be continued as in the past, but he said he could not answer for the action of the Galveston Board if another case of Yellow Fever should appear in New Orleans with only the seventy-two hours detention at the Mississippi Quarantine Station.

Mr. N. N. John said he was no speaker, and was unable to do the subject full justice. Applications had been made to the National Board of Health and the State of Texas for aid in the construction of proper quarantine buildings, which had been refused.

The City of Galveston had appropriated only the sum of five hundred dollars for the use of the Board.

Mr. John said he was an ultra strong non-intercourse member of the Board whenever there was any danger of Yellow Fever being brought from New Orleans. It was life or death to from fifteen to twenty thousand people in Galveston alone. He was not, however, alarmed sufficiently by one case of Yellow Fever in New Orleans to establish quarantine against her for that reason alone.

Seventy-two hours will not answer, he said, for detentions of vessels from infected ports.

Mr. John then touched upon the circumstance of the resolution to quarantine against New Orleans, the postponement of action and the appointment of the committee to visit New Orleans.

Mr. John observed that when the papers, like the New Orleans Times of this morning, said the intention of Galveston, in establishing a quarantine against New Orleans was mercenary, the same was false and malicious.

Relative to the Mississippi Quarantine Station, Mr. John said he would make some changes relative to the buildings there, but taken altogether, the whole investigation might be said to be most satisfactory to both of them.

When he and Dr. McClanahan went home and made their report it would be satisfactorily received. Make the concession they asked for—ten days from dock to dock from Havana and Vera Cruz—and he believed with Dr. McClanahan that there would be no quarantine against New Orleans this summer.

Mr. Marks stated he had listened with a great deal of interest and attention to the remarks of the two gentlemen, and he believed the other members were satisfied that they were earnest and true in everything they had said in the desire expressed to preserve the commercial relations between the two cities.

Having called upon the parties having steamships running to Havana and Vera Cruz, Mr. Marks said that they were all willing to extend the time to ten days from dock to dock from these ports to the wharf at New Orleans, in order that commercial relations may continue with this city without interruption, all business men in this city agreeing that quarantining against New Orleans just as the railroad connecting Louisiana with Texas was about to be completed would be most disastrous.

The committee from Galveston found that seventy-two hours was the minimum time of detention at the Mississippi Quarantine Station, and that vessels had been detained eight, nine, ten, twelve or fifteen days, for no other reason than because it was deemed imprudent for them to come to the city in less time. When a vessel with Yellow Fever arrived at the Quarantine Station she was detained there as long as the Board deemed proper. While the lives of the people of the whole Mississippi Valley and Texas were considered, the lives also of thousands of unacclimated persons in this city had to be protected.

Dr. Davidson desired to thank Dr. McClanahan and Mr. John for the manly expressions uttered by them as well as for their candor and moderate views The Galveston Board had acted most wisely in sending a delegation to New Orleans, as their report would be calculated to allay panic. If similar action was taken by other neighboring Boards of Health, a spirit of amity, professional zeal and devotion to conservative medicine and the general good of the public health would result thereby and avert many of the dire evils that otherwise come upon us.

When Dr. Davidson had concluded his remarks, Mr. John said: "Thank you—Dr. McClanahan and John won't go back on what they've said."

Dr. Jones referred to the great work accomplished by the establishment of a thorough system of inspection. Under the old plan the case of the bark Excelsior might have been overlooked. Coffee shipped from Rio Janeiro had especially been the cause of anxiety. The thorough disinfection of coffee in warehouses was evidenced in the case of the cargo of the bark Excelsior. Although 3600 bags were landed, not a single case occurred therefrom.

Dr. McClanaham expressed himself as entirely satisfied with what had been done, and said he found the sanitary arrangements here far in advance of anything known to him before, and was satisfied with the strict enforcement of the act of 1876 on quarantine.

Dr. Jones referred to the kind spirit shown by the representatives of the Galveston Board, and thanked them for their courteous attention.

Dr. Davidson moved that the Board go into executive session.

The motion was carried.

Dr. Formento entered the room at this time, having been detained on professional business, while Dr. Beard, who had been holding an autopsy, did not arrive until after executive session.

When the doors were opened, the following resolutions, offered by Dr. Davidson, were given to the press, having been adopted while the board was in executive session :

Resolved, That from the promulgation of this action of the Board of Health of the State of Louisiana, all vessels arriving from infected ports in the West Indies and Mexico, and elsewhere, the quarantine *pratique* shall embrace the period of ten days from wharf to wharf seventy-two hours of which shall be at the Mississippi Quarantine Station for disinfection, fumigation and observation.

Resolved, That the Board of Health of the State of Louisiana hereby extend to the Board of Health of Galveston their deep sense of the amicable spirit animating them in considering a question of a quarantine against New Orleans, and that they recognize in the appointment of gentlemen representing different shades of opinion in the Board of Health, as delegates to this board, the highest evidence of their determination to preserve, if possible, the mutually beneficial commercial relations of the two cities.

Resolved, That this board cordially reciprocates a spirit of kindness and good feeling on the part of the Galveston Board of Health.

[The Galveston News, Thursday, August 12, 1880.]

PERFECTLY SATISFIED.

RETURN OF DR. McCLANAHAN, OF THE BOARD OF HEALTH, FROM NEW ORLEANS – HOW THE QUARANTINE IS CONDUCTED THERE—WORK OF THE SANITARY ASSOCIATION, ETC.

Dr. Thos. McClanahan, who, in conjunction with Mr. N. N. John, was appointed by the Board of Health to proceed to New Orleans for the purpose of investigating the mode and manner in which the quarantine at the mouth of the Mississippi was conducted, and also to confer with the New Orleans Board of Health in regard to quarantine, returned by the Morgan line yesterday. A News reporter called upon the Doctor at his office yesterday,' for the purpose of ascertaining the condition of sanitary affairs in New Orleans, and to obtain an idea of the work accomplished by the committee. Dr. McClanahan stated that the committee reached New Orleans on the fourth, and had a short consultation with with Dr. Jones, President of the Board of Health. An invitation was then received from Dr. Bemiss, Superintendent of the National Quarantine, to visit the Quarantine Station near the mouth of the Mississippi, and also the National Quarantine Buildings at Ship Island. The committee left New Orleans on the morning of the fifth, in company with Dr. Bemiss, Drs. Holliday and Watkins, of New Orleans, and Mr. Fenner, President of the Auxiliary Sanitary Association of that city, on the steam yacht Day Dream. They reached the Quarantine Station on the river at 2 p. m., examined the warehouse set apart for the fumigation of ship cargoes and disinfection, and had a consultation with Dr. Finney, Quarantine Officer at that point, who generously gave them all the information in his possession as to the manner in which the quarantine was conducted, which went to prove to the committee that the quarantine was much more effective than they believed when they left Galveston. The following certificates, obtained from Dr. Finney, show how the reports are made:

MISSISSIPPI QUARANTINE STATION, August 5.—Bark Mary Durkee, thirty-nine days from Rio Janeiro to Quarantine Station, in rock ballast No sickness whatever. Detention of same nine days this day at this Station and no immediate prospect of departure.

Bark Maria Carolina, thirteen days from Havana to this Quarantine Station. Has no sickness on board nor any at sea. Information reached here of three cases transferred from vessel to hospital in Havana. To-day the ninth day of detention. No immediate prospect of departure. I certify the above to be correct.

J. T. FINNEY, Quarantine Physician.

These certificates go to show that all sailing vessels arriving from infected ports are quarantined from ten days to an unlimited period, or until the Quarantine officers are entirely satisfied with their sanitary condition. After bidding the courteous Quarantine officers at the Station adieu the committee steamed down to the Jetties, where they remained all night. The next morning they steamed for Ship Island, situated some seventy or eighty miles to the north and east of the mouth of the river, where the buildings of the National Quarantine are located, and arrived there on the afternoon of the same day. They first landed and inspected the warehouse proper, built for the purpose of fumigating cargoes, as well as the wharf which is in process of construction. The warehouse is 60 or 80 by 150 feet, strongly built of wood, and of sufficient capacity to admit of the disinfecting of all freight that may be received for that purpose. The committee then returned to the Day Dream and steamed some six miles eastward along the Island, landing at the house built for the accommodation of well persons who are to be kept under surveillance, which is a large two-story frame building, capable of accommodating 250 persons, and is all complete with the exception of the walks surrounding it. A mile and a half further up the Island, east of the house, is the hospital proper, and separated from the building designed for well persons by a lagoon or bayou which runs through the Island. All these buildings were found to be under the supervision of Dr. Bemiss, of the National Board of Health, and under the immediate superintendence of Dr. Martin, who is the Resident Physician. After inspecting the buildings and ascertaining the mode and manner of inspecting vessels the committee left on Sunday morning for Biloxi, and from thence took the train for New Orleans, meeting the Board of Health of that city at 6 o'clock, by special invitation from the entire Board. Dr. McClanahan says the honest zeal displayed by the New Orleans Board to afford the committee every facility to pursue their investigations was proof conclusive that they were desirous, not only of protecting their own port, but every other portion of the South, from the ravages of Yellow Fever. After seeing so much zeal and fairness on the part of the Board of Health, the committee had no request to make of them, except to suggest that a lengthening of the quarantine at their station to ten days from port to port would give our people more confidence in the same, to which suggestion the New Orleans Board acquiesced in to the fullest extent. Dr. McClanahan further stated that the investigation made at the request and under the auspices of Mr. Fenner, President of the Auxiliary Sanitary Association of New Orleans, gave the committee every proof of the powerful effort made, and the grand success achieved by this Association in reclaiming low lands and the filling in of water-holes which had been used for years as a repository for garbage. A stream of clear Mississippi River water is being run through the gutters in two-thirds of the streets of the city. A pump with the capacity of 8,500,000 gallons daily, is kept at work night and day. With time, and the continuous efforts of the Sanitary Association, Dr. McClanahan thinks the sanitary condition of New Orleans will be rendered as good as that of any city on the globe.

BOARD OF HEALTH.

REPORT OF DR. McCLANAHAN AND N. N. JOHN.

In deference to Dr. Rutherford, who had come down by instructions of the Governor to hear the report of the committee just returned from New Orleans, and who desired to return by the 3 p. m. train, the regular meeting of the Board of Health was held at 1 p. m. yesterday, instead of 6 p. m., as originally designed. There were present Dr. Watts, President ; Dr. Campbell, Secretary ; Drs. Kelley and McClanahan, and Messrs. Focke, John, McLean, Noble, Vidor and Mott.

Dr. Kelley moved that the first business be the report of the committee sent to New Orleans.

Dr. McClanahan said : The committee has as yet made no written report. He was willing to report verbally, if acceptable.

Mr. John—If it is necessary to have a written report, you will have to defer the matter for at least a week.

Dr. Kelley moved that the committee be allowed to make a verbal report, with the privilege of supplementing it with a regular report.

The motion was adopted, and Dr. McClanahan proceeded : Being appointed with Mr. John, to visit New Orleans for the purpose, as I understood it, of inquiring into the nature of the quarantine of that city, as well as its sanitary condition, but more especially its quarantine, we arrived in New Orleans on the evening of the fourth. After a short consultation with Dr. Jones, President of the New Orleans Board of Health, and receiving his statements as to the condition of the city, we had an invitation from Dr. Bemiss, superintendent of the National Board of Health, to make a trip of inspection in his steamer to Ship Island, he proposing, in doing so, to land us at the quarantine station, and suggested that we make our inspection there. Together with several prominent physicians of New Orleans, we went down the river, reaching the Quarantine Station perchance at 2 o'clock. We went ashore and received from the quarantine officer at that place his assistance in making the investigation, which proved perfectly satisfactory to me, and I suppose to Mr. John. It convinced me that quarantine at that port was more satisfactory than I expected to find it when I left home. I found that all sailing vessels from infected, ports whether with cargo or in ballast—I believe save the Excelsior, none of them arrived with cargo—were detained from nine to thirty days for the purpose of inspection, fumigation, disinfection, etc. The mode of disinfecting sail vessels, as Dr. Fenner stated to me, was to burn 100 pounds of sulphur in the hold, care being taken to rip up the dunnage boards and pump out the bilge water. The dunnage boards as I understand it, fit under the knees of the vessel.

Mr. John—The skin of the boat.

Dr. McClanahan—the doctor said he took up other planks and used disinfectants, continuing to use them several times until he felt satisfied that they were entirely free from suspicion. There are four steamers plying between New Orleans and Havana—two of the Morgan line and two belonging to private parties. They have been detained at the quarantine station seventy-two hours for the purpose of inspection, surveillance and fumigation. These vessels, I was told at the Quarantine Station, as well as by the city authorities that I consulted with, were loaded solely with sugar and cigars, the sugar in tran-itu for the refinery at St. Louis, and the cigars, I presume, for the market in New Orleans and elsewhere.

Dr. Kelley—Do they not submit to the rules of disinfection suggested by the Board of Health in Havana.

Dr McClanahan—They are all disinfected and fumigated before leaving the port of Havana.

At the Quarantine Station on the Mississippi river there is a large brick warehouse, now being used for purposes of disinfection, to which the quarantine authorities can transfer the cargo of any vessel and there disinfect it to their satisfaction. I understand that the cargoes of steamers are disinfected in the steamers, but they have every facility and every convenience for protecting the city from any danger of infection The zeal manifested by every health officer, every doctor and every citizen that you meet in regard to the danger of a scourge ought to convince any man beyond a doubt that every effort is used to prevent its introduction.

Dr. McClanahan—We left the Quarantine Station, and I must say that after the examination we made there, and the assertions of the quarantine officers, I left there much better pleased than I expected to be before my visit. I must also say that I am entirely satisfied with the mode and manner of quarantine at the station.

The city is inspected by inspectors such as we have here, and then by doctors, of whom there are eight, all good physicians. The privy vaults of the city have been cleansed three times this year under the supervision of these physicians. At 6 o'clock in the evening we met the Board of Health of New Orleans, and after seeing as much as I had I was absolutely ashamed to ask anything at their hands. I told them I had no request to make, no demands, no wishes; but if they would lengthen their time of quarantine I thought it would enable some of the ultra members of our Board to rest easier.

Dr. Jones followed me with some remarks as to the nature of our visit, after which the Board went into secret session, and in a very few moments they extended the term to ten days from port to port, but with seventy-two hours at the Quarantine Station for the purpose of fumigation and disinfection.

Mr. John said : We left here on Tuesday, under your broad seal, to visit the Board of Health at New Orleans. We arrived in New Orleans next evening and were met by Mr. Pandely and Dr. Fenner. We went and got our dinner and came back to the hotel. There we met Dr. Jones, President of the New Orleans Board of Health, with other gentlemen. We appointed 7 o'clock next morning for a meeting with Dr. Jones. While we were at dinner, Dr. Bemiss came in and gave us a very cordial invitation to go to Ship Island. After going back to the hotel we were interviewed by some reporters, the full report of which was given in the New Orleans Times, a paper which I have no use for. Dr. McClanahan and I had a conversation with Dr. Jones next morning, and he satisfied us that he was full master of the situation. I undertake now to say here that he is full master of the situation, and the city of New Orleans is fortunate in having him at the head of its Board of Health, I told him I had quoted him in Galveston as a full-blooded non-quarantine man, but I took it all back. After examining the Quarantine Station thoroughly, I told Dr. Jones I thought that the buildings were too close, and that I thought the brick building was too large for thorough disinfection. He said the brick building was in charge of the customhouse. It is true, he said, that the buildings might be a little too close, but, if necessity required it, that might be remedied. Our visit to Ship Island Dr. McClanahan has described. We returned from Biloxi on Sunday night, and were met next morning by the Sanitary Association. We went to the Board of Health office, and the books there were thrown open to us. I believe I am bookkeeper enough to know what a book means. I examined them thoroughly, and I must say that I became doubly satisfied that Dr. Jones and the Board of Health generally were the proper men for their positions I told Dr. Jones of the conviction I had labored under that the New Orleans Board of Health could not be relied on ; that they never did give us a correct report ; that when we telegraphed to them about the case of the Excelsior, they telegraphed us that such was the fact and promised to furnish us full particulars by mail, which they never did After getting an explanation from Dr. Jones I could excuse him. That officer is overworked. We went into details pretty generally. Dr. Jones took me to the Charity Hospital, and I found that nineteen out of every twenty of the cots in that institution are unoccupied—a fact that goes far to show the healthfulness of the city. There are more people under the knife in the surgical department than all the balance together. I believe that is about as far as it is necessary for me to go further than to say that to Dr Jones and his board, I am willing to entrust the city of Galveston. That is a large admission for me to make, but when I have seen for myself, there is no going back on the evidence of my senses.

Mr. John, after speaking in the line of Dr. McClanahan's address to some length, concluded by saying : I assert that there is no danger from Yellow Fever from New Orleans as it stands now. The facilities are effective. Vessels have to remain seventy-two hours in quarantine, and then if there is the least sign of danger, they remain until the quarantine officers are satisfied that all is well. The coffee of the Excelsior is still in the warehouse, and likely to stay there.

Mr. Noble offered the following resolution which was adopted :

Resolved, That the reports of Dr. McClanahan and Mr. John be received and approved, and that the thanks of this Board are tendered them for the very efficient discharge of their duties, as the representatives of this Board, in their recent mission to New Orleans.

Dr. Kelley—I am peculiarly happy, first at the wisdom of our course in sending a deletion to New Orleans, for in it I see that we may have an understanding with that city, which is likely to result in great good to both, and that we may have our own views much more liberal than we have been sometimes inclined to make them. I am happy we are convinced that New Orleans is doing everything that is proper to be done, not only for its own protection, but for that of Galveston and of all Texas. I am peculiarly happy that these gentlemen have visited New Orleans and become personally acquainted with those of New Orleans in the line of their inquiry, some of whom I know myself. I am convinced from the high character of Drs. Bemiss, Jones, and others, that no man can go to New Orleans and listen to them with candor without coming away believing that they are acting in the interest not only of the people of New Orleans, but of our own people, and I hope that the excellent report of these gentlemen will be received and endorsed unanimously.

Dr. Rutherford read the following letter from Governor Roberts, pursuant to the instructions in which he had come before the Board :

AUSTIN, Texas.—Dr. Rutherford : You will please go to Galveston, and when Mr. John and Dr. McClanahan return, if the information is not satisfactory in regard to the safety of quarantine at New Orleans, both to you and the Board at Galveston, and if you believe general quarantine should be established, telegraph to me at Dallas, and I will issue orders at once for general safety of the State. I hope these gentlemen will report safe quarantine. If they do not, however much I may regret it, I must now act. If quarantine is determined on, telegraph for me to all the coast stations, letting them know what is determined on.

O. M. ROBERTS, Governor.

Dr. Kelley asked Dr Rutherford if he would not indorse the resolutions of Mr Noble. The Doctor did not wish to engage in the proceedings of the Board further than to conform to the instructions of the Governor, and declined to give an opinion. Upon motion, the Board adjourned.

[The Galveston News, Tuesday, August 17, 1880.]

THE NEW ORLEANS QUARANTINE MATTER.

DR. McCLANAHAN AND MR. JOHN EXPRESS THEIR VIEWS.

GALVESTON, Aug. 16, 1880.—As to the letter of certain members of the Board of Health, published in your report of the proceedings of the Board, in your issue of the thirteenth instant, shows some dissention in the Board, and to some extent reflects on the committee sent to New Orleans, the members of that committee desire to place the subject before the public through the columns of your paper, and to invite from the people of our State full inquiry into their action, which was had with a grave sense of the responsibility and a desire to perform fully their duty in the premises.

At a called meeting of the Board of Health of Galveston, held August 3, we were appointed a committee to visit the city of New Orleans to inquire into and examine the efficiency of their quarantine against infected ports. When we left Galveston we were impressed with the idea that their quarantine was not sufficient to protect the city of New Orleans, and that our own city and its proximity and continuous intercourse with New Orleans, was thereby endangered. With this impression we had intimated that we would support quarantine upon the basis of the inefficiency of the quarantine against infected ports by that city.

We reached the City of New Orleans on the fourth, and conferred with the President of the New Orleans Board of Health, Dr. Jones. who, with the assistance of Dr. S. M. Bemiss, Superintendent of the National Quarantine Station, at Ship Island, extended to us every facility for examination into the operation of the quarantine system and of visiting the station below the city, so that we might see for ourselves. At the station we found Dr. Finney in charge, who displayed a ready willingness to answer all questions and to give data as to arrival and departure of vessels. We found that the cargoes of all vessels from infected ports were removed, placed in warehouse for that purpose and thoroughly fumigated ; that the vessels were thoroughly cleansed, and all bilge water pumped out and replaced with solution of carbolic acid and sulphate of iron, and the vessels with hatches closed, were also subject to the fumes of burning sulphur, on repeated occasions, about one hundred pounds each time, and all clothing and everything belonging to the vessels treated in like manner. The vessels being in every instance detained for a period not less than ten days, or longer, until the Quarantine Officer is entirely satisfied with their sanitary condition. This rule is applied to all sail vessels alike, except in the case of the Excelsior. where the cargo was not removed to the warehouse, because the vessel was only partially freighted, her capacity being twelve thousand sacks of coffee, while there was on board only thirty-six hundred. It was thought that her freight could be more efficiently fumigated in her hold, and after this was done, one-third of the coffee was hoisted on deck and the balance disinfected and the vessel cleansed. The subsequent appearance of a case of Yellow Fever on. this vessel after reaching New Orleans being so unprecedented that Dr. Bemiss, of the National Board of Health, solicited Governor Roberts to send the State Health Officer to New

Orleans to make a full investigation thereof, which was done and report made to the Governor and published.

The four steamers which ply between New Orleans and Havana are managed under the strictest surveillance. The officers and crews are all acclimated. The vessels are thoroughly fumigated and disinfected at the ports where they are freighted, under the supervision of the Agent of the National Board of Health, and ten days' time must elapse from port to port; seventy-two hours of this time they are held at Quarantine for further disinfection. Their cargoes consist of sugar in transit to St Louis, and cigars. No passengers or fruit are taken, and in fact this trade is conducted.with such care and honest attention to duty on the part both of the owners of the vessels and the health authorities of New Orleans, that the danger of importing disease is certainly reduced to a minimum if not rendered impossible. We can not conceive of any right that we have to object to the trade carried on by New Orleans under these restrictions, when our own authorities carry on a trade, as at Indianola, where the only protection is fumigation and disinfection.

At the request of our Board we made the visit to New Orleans with no little inconvenience to ourselves and to friends on whom we were compelled to impose our business while absent, our sole aim being to make a faithful investigation as to the sanitary condition and the quarantine regulations of New Orleans. And we were very much surprised upon our return, and even before our report was made, to learn that some of the members of our Board had already prepared their ultimatum in regard to further communication with New Orleans. Having made a searching investigation both as to quarantine and as to the sanitary condition of New Orleans, we are satisfied that in both respects they have done everything that could be asked of them, and we can see no cause, except that of morbid fear, to warrant a quarantine against that city.   THOS. McCLANAHAN, M. D.
N. N. JOHN.

It is evident from the preceding facts that the Hon. Thomas McClanahan and the Hon. N. N. John, who so faithfully and nobly represented the city of Galveston, were largely instrumental in preventing the institution of a quartine against the State of Louisiana.

It is impossible to estimate the damage which a quarantine on the part of Texas against Louisiana, would have inflicted.

The subsequent history of the sanitary affairs of Louisiana have justified to the fullest extent the statements of Dr. McClanahan and Mr. John. Galveston and the great State of Texas remained free from all contagious and infectious diseases, and remained as free from the much-dreaded Yellow Fever, as the State of Louisiana and the city of New Orleans.

Louisiana is indebted to these truthful and upright representatives of of Texas, for an impartial, unprejudiced. honest and manly statement to the entire country, of the true sanitary condition of this State.

ILLEGAL AND UNCONSTITUTIONAL ASSUMPTION OF POWER BY THE NATIONAL BOARD OF HEALTH.

The following letters to the Acting Governor of Louisiana, will give a sufficient explanation of the charge implied in the preceding heading:

OFFICE BOARD OF HEALTH, STATE OF LOUISIANA, }
New Orleans, July 30, 1880. }

Lieutenant Governor S. D. McEnery, Acting Governor, State of Louisiana

Sir—The attention of your Excellency is respectfully directed to the following communication published in the Picayune of this date, purporting under authority of the National Board of Health, to prohibit "the shipment of any and all coffee" from the Port of New Orleans to Mobile, "from and after this date until further orders." Signed by C. A. Rice, M. D., Supervisor of Inspectors, National Board of Health.

11

OFFICE SUPERVISING INSPECTOR, Port of New Orleans, La., July 29, 1880.

Dr. J. M. Watkins, Sanitary Inspector:

Dear Sir—The Mobile Board of Health instructed me "not to allow the shipment of any coffee from New Orleans to Mobile until after they are satisfied that it is not a part of the cargo of the bark Excelsior, and they so inform you. You will therefore stop the shipment of any and all coffee to Mobile from and after this date, until further orders.

This I do not understand to apply to coffee going to other portions of Alabama in sealed cars.

Respectfully,   C. A. RICE, M. D., Supervisor of Inspectors, National Board of Health.

OFFICE SUPERVISOR OF INSPECTORS, Port of New Orleans, July 29, 1880,

To Dr. J. M. Watkins, Sanitary Inspector:

Dear Sir—The State Board of Health of Mississippi having revoked the ordinance requiring personal certificates of passengers coming from New Orleans, La., into the State of Mississippi, you will inform all persons so applying. The same Board having passed an ordinance on this the twenty-ninth July, 1880:

"That no part of the cargo of coffee from bark Excelsior will be permitted to come into the State of Mississippi, and that no coffee received at this port subsequent to this date from an infected port, will be permitted to come into the State of Mississippi." You will act accordingly. All other coffee now in the city will be permitted to come into the State of Mississippi.

Respectfully,   C. A. RICE, M. D., Supervisor of Inspectors, National Board of Health.

It will be observed that the latter portion of the preceding communication assumes to control the shipment of coffee from New Orleans to the entire State of Mississippi. In his individual capacity C. A. Rice, M. D., has no power to issue an order of any character, with reference to any matter relating to the commerce of the City of New Orleans, and State of Louisiana, and as an individual he is undoubtedly subject to the laws of the United States and of Louisiana, and liable to prosecution for damages by all parties who may be injured by his attempt to interfere with the commerce of this Port. From the title appended to his name, C. A. Rice, M. D., claims to be acting under the authority of the National Board of Health. The Act of Congress by which the National Board of Health was constituted, approved March 3, 1879, entitled "An Act to prevent the introduction of infectious and contagious diseases into the United States, and to establish a National Board of Health" provides in the second section, that, "The duties of the National Board of Health shall be to obtain information upon all matters affecting the public health, to advise the several departments of the General Government, *The Executives of the several states*, and the Commissioner of the District of Columbia, on all questions submitted by them or whenever in the opinion of this Board such advice may tend to the preservation and improvement of the Public Health."

Section 3, of "Act to prevent the introduction of contagious and infectious disease into the United States," approved June 2, 1879, reads thus:

"That the National Board of Health shall co-operate with and as far as it lawfully may aid the State and Municipal Boards of Health in the execution and enforcement of the rules and regulations of such boards, to prevent the introduction of contagious and infectious diseases from foreign countries into the United States, and into one State from another, and at such ports and places within the United States as have no quarantine regulations under State authority, where such regulations are, in the opinion of the National Board of Health, necessary to prevent the introduction of contagious and infectious diseases into the United States from foreign countries, or into one State from another, and at such ports and places within the United States where quarantine regulations exist under the authority of the State, which, in the opinion of the National Board of Health, are not sufficient to prevent the introduction of such diseases into the United States, or from one State into another. The National Board of Health shall report the facts to the President of the United States, who shall, if in his judgment it is necessary and proper, order said Board of Health to make such additional rules and regulations as are necessary to prevent the introduction of such diseases into the United States from foreign countries; or from one State into another, which, when so made and approved by the President shall be promulgated by the National Board of Health and enforced by the sanitary authorities of the States, where the State authorities will undertake to execute and enforce them; but if the State authorities shall fail or refuse to enforce said rules and regulations the President shall detail an officer or appoint a proper person for that purpose." Therefore, by the Acts approved March 3, 1879, and June 2, 1879, organizing and defining the powers of the National Board of Health, it is evident that this creation of President Hays and the Congress of the United States of America is charged with the important duty of *co-operating with and aiding State and Municipal Boards of Health in the execution and enforcement of the rules and regulations of such Boards, to prevent the introduction of contagious and infectious diseases into the United States from foreign countries or from one State into another.*

The Board of Health of the State of Louisiana has adopted the rules and regulations of the National Board of Health, in addition to its own full and explicit sanitary and quarantine ordinances.

The Board of Health of the State of Louisiana has given full and explicit and accurate reports of the sanitary condition of the city of New Orleans and of the various Quarantine establishments under its direction and control; has freely and fully published to the world its proceedings, and furnished full and complete reports of its mortuary statistics, and have endeavored to establish true and friendly relations with local and State Boards of Health and with the National Board of Health.

New Orleans is not an infected port.

New Orleans has been, throughout the entire year 1880, up to the present moment, exempt from infectious and contagious diseases; and, with the exception of the single case of Yellow Fever on the bark Excelsior, no case of Yellow Fever has occurred within her bounds. The bark Excelsior was promptly removed beyond the bounds of New Orleans, to the Quarantine Station, seventy miles below New Orleans, and efficient measures have been executed for the ventilation, purification and fumigation and disinfection of said ship and cargo by the Board of Health of the State of Louisiana. Three weeks have elapsed since such measures have been instituted, and no case of Yellow Fever has occurred among the citizens of New Orleans.

According to the testimony of Dr. Smith, of the National Board of Health, Rio de Janerio is not regarded at this time as an infected port; occurrences similar to that of the Excelsior, are by no means infrequent in the port of New York, and no restrictions have been attempted to be forced upon the coffee trade of New York by the National Board of Health.

The National Board of Health has made no official communication or suggestion to the Chief Executive of the State of Louisiana, nor through the Board of Health of Louisiana, with reference to the cargo and crew of the bark Excelsior, nor with reference to the Sanitary and Qarantine measures and regulations adopted by the State Board of Health.

In view of the preceding facts, it is the opinion of the Executive Officer and members of the Board of Health of the State of Louisiana, that the action of the National Board of Health in issuing the orders cited in the first part of this communication, without the advice or co-operation of the lawful authorities to whom are confided by legislative enactment the conduct of the Sanitary and Quarantine affairs of the State of Louisiana, is illegal, unconstitutional and destructive of the commercial relations of the individual States, which form integral parts of the United States.

With great respect and high esteem, I have the honor to remain your obedient servant,

JOSEPH JONES, M. D.,

President Board of Health, State or Louisiana.

In connection with the preceding protest of the Board of Health of the State of Louisiana, the following facts should be stated:

When the inspection service was established in New Orleans, one of the rooms of the Board of Health in the State capital was offered to Dr. C. A. Rice, Superintendent of River and Railroad Inspections, by the President, in order that free consultation might be had and all unnecessary complications avoided.

Dr. Rice saw fit to establish his headquarters at a distance, above Canal street, near the levee, and neither did he or his inspectors report in person daily at the Board of Health—the inspectors reported daily in writing.

It has been shown in the preceding pages of this report, that the Board of Health of the State of Louisiana had issued stringent orders to the merchants to whom this cargo of the Excelsior had been consigned, forbidding the shipment of this coffee, or its removal from the warehouse. The railroad and steamboat inspectors conformed to this order.

The complaint against the National Board of Health was, that orders which were dictated by the health authorities of other States, were promulgated in New Orleans, without the knowledge or concurence of the lawful authorities, to whom theS tate of Louisiana had confided the execution of her sanitary and quarantine laws.

The principle involved in this protest of the State Board against a lflagrant violation of its rights, was clear to all disinterested citizens, and cou d in no manner be construed as *an attempt to force infected goods* upon surrounding cities and States.

The State Board claimed to be the legal authority, to whom the requests of the sanitary authorities of surrounding States and cities should be conveyed, and from whom the necessary orders should issue within the confines of Louisiana.

If this right does not exist according to the Constitution of the United States in all State Boards of Health, the existence of such organizations, since the passage of the act creating the National Board of Health, is ephemeral and liable to destruction at any moment, in accordance with the will of the central authority.

If this right does exist according to the Constitution in all State Boards, then the act of Congress establishing the National Board of Health is *unconstitutional*, in that it establishes a central power capable of controlling the commerce and business relations of cities and States.

This view of the case was not met by the President of the National Board of Health, in his reply to the President of the State Board of Health, dated Washington, August 10, 1880, and published in supplement No. 8 National Board of Health Bulletin, as an appendix (marked c), to his report to the Honorable John Sherman, Secretary of the Treasury.

Thus Professor J. L. Cabell says : " With reference to the last sentence of your letter, in which you complain of the action of Dr. Rice, on the ground that it was taken without the advice or co-operation of the lawful authorities to whom are confided by legislative enactment the conduct of the Sanitary and Quarantine affairs of the State of Louisiana, I have again to repeat the statement in my letter of June 15, that the whole of this river and railroad inspection service is intended for the protection of other States than your own, and is in the aid of their health authorities. Incidentally, indeed, it was designed and has proved to be of great advantage to the commerce of New Orleans, since on the bare suspicion of a single case of Yellow Fever existing there, the health authorities of the Mississippi Valley, and of other places in the South having commercial relations with that city, have declared that they will maintain a strict quarantine against it unless the inter-State commerce be carried on in accordance with the rules of the inspection service. Those authorities have the power to protect their towns by a very simple and effective machinery.

" This Board has induced them to forego the use of such machinery and to consent to an arrangement which has proved highly advantageous to the commercial interests ef New Orleans, and yet it encounters at the hands of the health authorities of Louisiana constant opposition and detraction.

" It is needless to say that it will continue to discharge its duties in aid of the health authorities of other States and municipalities, notwithstanding the present opposition of the State Board of Health of Louisiana.

" I will add, that owing to a delay in completing the arrangements at Ship Island, which has been due to causes beyond the control of the National Board, the time for extending aid to the health authorities of New Orleans with regard to the prevention of the introduction of contagious and infectious diseases through that port into the United States from foreign countries has not yet arrived. A recent official report to this Board by a committee, consisting of three of its members, satisfies the Executive Committee that the sanitary interests of New Orleans and the surrounding country will be best subserved by requiring infected vessels, and all vessels from infected ports, to undergo quarantine inspection and treatment at the proposed station on Ship Island. In this way aid will be offered to the State Board of Health of Louisiana for the protection of New Orleans and all places in direct communication with it."

During the year 1880 the entire Mississippi Valley was free from foreign and domestic pestilence, and the existence of this expensive and cumbrous system of River and Railroad Inspection Service was justified on the part of the National Board of Health by the fear of suspicious cases in New Or.

leans. The danger of shot-gun quarantines, formed a perpetual argument for the continued and lavish expenditure of the public funds.

If a firm opposition to the destructive scheme of the Ship Island Quarantine, and if the maintenance of the rights of the Board of Health of Louisiana against unjust exactions, constituted opposition to and detraction of the National Board of Health, then the charges of the President of the National Board of Health must be accepted as succint statements of the differences between the State and National Boards of Health.

It is worthy of note that while the arrangements at Ship Island were not completed on the tenth day of August, 1880, and at this late date the President of the National Board of Health refers to it as "the proposed Station at Ship Island," the demand to send inspected vessels from the mouth of the Mississippi was made as early as the ninth of April, and the Board of Health of the State of Louisiana was arraigned in his report to the Secretary of the Treasury for acting in defiance of the demands of the health authorities of the neighboring States, in not sending vessels to a "proposed quarantine."

DO NOT
SCAN

DISEASES
DEMANDING INVESTIGATION,

AS TO THEIR CAUSES AND PREVENTION.

YELLOW· FEVER.

The entire profession of New Orleans, during the year 1880, reported to the Board ot Health of the State of Louisiana, only *two deaths as caused by Yellow Fever*.

Those reports were as follows :

1. James Kenney, 19 years of age, native of Scotland, from bark Excelsior, died on the 10th of July, 1880, at the Touro Infirmary; cause of death, Yellow Fever; attending physician, F. Loeber, M. D.

2. Frederick A. Singer, 18 years of age. native of New Orleans, died on the 4th of October, 1880, at No. 409 Liberty street; cause of death, Yellow Fever; attending physicians; Drs. W. H. Watkins and J. P. Davidson.

The first case originated on the Swedish Bark Excelsior, and the history has been fully detailed, in that section of the report. which related to the action of the Board of Health with reference to this vessel.

The second case will be noticed, in a subsequent part of this report, in its regular chronological order.

To understand fully the import of the preceding facts, representing the testimony of the medical profession of New Orleans with reference to the occurrence of only two deaths from Yellow Fever in the city during the year 1880, the following subjects should be considered :

(a) The actual population of New Orleans.

(b) The laws devised and enforced by the Board of Health of the State of Louisiana with reference to the prevention of the introduction of foreign pestilence.

(c) The laws governing the City of New Orleans with reference to the report of contagious and infectious diseases by the captains, masters of ships, keepers of boarding houses and hotels, the heads of asylums, hospitals and private families and the medical profession of New Orleans.

(d) The laws governing the Sanitary Inspectors and Sanitary Police of New Orleans.

By the statement of such facts the Board of Health of the State of Louisiana believe that the malignant attempt to array the sister States of the Mississippi Valley against the medical profession and citizens of New Orleans will be summarily defeated.

(a) POPULATION OF NEW ORLEANS.

NEW ORLEANS, August 16, 1820.

Dr. Joseph Jones, M. D., President Board of Health, State of Louisiana:

Sir—Enclosed please find a condensed statement of the number of inhabitants, races, and sex embraced within the limits of the city of New Orleans, divided into wards and districts.

Hoping such information will prove of some value to your honorable Board, I remain, very respectfully,
L. E. LEMARIE, Supervisor of Census.

POPULATION OF THE CITY OF NEW ORLEANS, CENSUS OF 1880.

	White Males.	White Females	Black Males.	Black Females.	Total by Wards.	Total by Districts.
FIRST DISTRICT.						
First Ward............................	5,225	6,318	1,123	1,769	14.435	
Second Ward........................	6,167	7,060	1,460	2,132	16,819	
Third Ward..........................	9,310	9,239	3,372	4,270	26,191—	57,445
SECOND DISTRICT.						
Fourth Ward.........................	4,077	4,991	1,547	2,102	12'717	
Fifth Ward...........................	6,380	6,676	2.706	3,504	19,266	
Sixth Ward..........................	4,349	4,895	1,502	1,940	12,686—	44,669
THIRD DISTRICT.						
Seventh Ward.......................	5,989	6,451	3,373	4,317	20,130	
Eighth Ward.........................	3,925	4,274	774	905	9,878	
Ninth Ward..........................	6,190	6,903	1,197	1,290	15,580—	45,588
FOURTH DISTRICT.						
Tenth Ward..........................	6,878	9,047	1,332	1,934	19,192	
Eleventh Ward......................	6,793	7,906	1,497	2,147	18,343—	37,535
SIXTH DISTRICT.						
Twelfth Ward........................	3 202	3 407	806	890	8,305	
Thirteenth Ward....................	1,647	2,004	781	973	5,405	
Fourteenth Ward....................	790	901	300	328	2,319—	16 029
FIFTH DISTRICT.						
Fifteenth Ward......................	2,382	2,640	1,650	2,185	8,856—	8,856
SEVENTE DISTRICT.						
Sixteenth Ward......	580	604	903	1,029	3,116	
Seventeenth Ward..................	944	984	598	595	3,121—	6,237
	74,848	4.580	24,921	32,310		216,359

L. E. LEMARIE, Supervisor of Census, First District of Louisiana.

According to the returns of the united census of 1880, the population of New Orleans is stated to be 216,359.

It is certainly a fact worthy of consideration, that the members of the medical profession of this great city, situated in the delta of the Mississippi River, only one hundred and ten miles from the Gulf of Mexico, should report only *two deaths from Yellow Fever* during the year 1880, when this disease prevailed in Rio de Janeiro and Havana, Cuba.

The Board of Health appoints six Sanitary Inspectors, namely, for the First, Second, Third, Fourth and Fifth Districts, respectively, and one for the Sixth and Seventh Districts. The preceding census of the respective districts, therefore, gives some idea of the nature and amount of the labors confided to the Sanitary Inspectors.

The duties of the Sanitary Inspectors will be fully unfolded by the record of the rules and regulations of the Board of Health of the State of Louisiana; but it may be noted in this connection that they are especially charged with the report of all contagious and infectious diseases occurring in their respective districts.

It should be noted that, although the entire city of New Orleans during the year 1880, *under the daily supervision and inspection of six medical men, assisted by an additional corps of twelve sanitary policemen, but one death from Yellow Fever was reported as originating and occurring within the confines of the city.*

(b). The laws designed and enforced by the Board of Health of the State of Louisiana, with reference to the prevention of the introduction of foreign pestilence.

The Quarantine and Sanitary laws of the State and city were collected and published by the President of the Board of Health, and distributed gratuitously to the officers of the State, the members, officers and employes of the Board of Health, physicians, druggists, merchants, shippers and foreign consuls of New Orleans, and to the captains, masters and agents of vessels of every description in the port of New Orleans, to the Governors of the several States, and the mayors of the principal cities, and to all State Boards of Health and Quarantine Officers.

The efforts of the Board of Health of the State of Louisiana to protect the State of Louisiana, and the entire Mississippi Valley, from the introduction of foreign pestilence, will be sustained by the following record :

BULES AND REGULATIONS OF THE BOARD OF HEALTH OF THE STATE OF LOUISIANA FOR THE GOVERNMENT OF QUARANTINE OFFICERS AND STATIONS, AND FOR THE ENFORCEMENT OF THE ACTS OF THE LEGISLATURE OF LOUISIANA. "ESTABLISHING AND REGULATING QUARANTINE FOR THE PROTECTION OF THE STATE."

At a meeting of the Board of Health of the State of Louisiana, held on the 24th of May, 1880, in the State-House, the President, Dr. Joseph Jones, submitted the following Rules and Regulations relative to Quarantine, which were unanimously adopted.

The President was authorized to cause the publication and distribution of said rules :

OFFICE BOARD OF HEALTH, STATE OF LOUISIANA, STATE-HOUSE, New Orleans, May 24, 1880.

Legislative acts establishing and defining the powers of the Board of Health, State of Louisiana, relative to Quarantine.

SECTION 1. The Board of Health of the State of Louisiana establishes the following rules and regulations relative to Quarantine in virtue of the powers conferred by the several Acts of the Legislature of Louisiana, " establishing and regulating Quarantine for the protection of the State," viz : "An Act to establish Quarantine for the protection of the State," approved March 15, 1855. "An Act supplementary to an Act, entitled ' An Act relative to Quarantine,' " approved March 18, 1858. "An Act to amend an Act entitled 'An Act to establish Quarantine for the protection of the State, approved March 16, 1870. " An Act to authorize and empower the Board of Health of the State of Louisiana to detain and disinfect, and to pass after disinfection, vessels from infected ports, at and from Quarantine Stations, in lieu of a time of quarantine detention in certain cases, and to repeal conflicting laws," approved March 24, 1876. "An Act to reorganize and render more efficient the Board of Health of the State of Louisiana; to define its powers and prescribe its duties and those of Quarantine and other officers under its control; to provide for its expenses, and for the recording of births, deaths and marriages in the Parish of Orleans, and to provide for the enforcement of this Act and penalties for violation of the same, and for the ordinances and orders made in pursuance thereof," approved April 27, 1877.

Powers of Board of Health Relative to Quarantine.

SEC. 2. In accordance with the said acts of the Legislature of the State of Louisiana, the Board of Health has power to fix the number of days of quarantine for vessels liable to it; to determine how said quarantine shall be performed, and to make any and all legal regulations not contrary to said acts, necessary to carry out a proper system of quarantine and to enforce the same ; to make rules and regulations for preserving good order and police within the limits of the Quarantine grounds, and to impose penalties for the breach thereof; to contract for the necessary buildings at Quarantine grounds ; to establish rules and regulations for the guidance of the Quarantine physicians, assistants and employes ; to employ nurses and assistants to attend the sick, and such other persons as may be necessary to carry out proper quarantine regulations and to fix their compensation.

12

Power of Board of Health to Issue Proclamation of Quarantine.

Sec. 3. In cases of emergency the Board of Health shall have power to issue proclamation of quarantine without reference to the Governor, and to enact all needful regulations for the enforcement of the same.

Visitation and Inspection of Vessels by Quarantine Physicians.

Sec. 4. Vessels arrriving at Quarantine Station shall immediately proceed to the Boarding Station, and shall be visited by the Quarantine Physician, between sunrise and sunset, as soon as possible after such arrival. The Quarantine officer shall inspect the ship, and require of the captain or master answers in duplicate to the following questions:

Questions

to be propounded by the President, Quarantine Officers and Deputy Inspectors of the Board of Health of the State of Louisiana to the masters, captains and medical officers of vessels at the port of New Orleans and Quarantine Stations of Louisiana.

Port or Station ———

Date of Inspection ———

1. Name of Vessel?
2. Name of Captain or Master?
3. Tonnage or Class of Vessel?
4. From whence is the Vessel you Command?
5. How many days have you been on the passage?
6. At what port or ports have you touched?
7. Were any Contagious or Infectious Diseases prevailing at the port from whence your vessel sailed?
8. If so, name the Diseases.
9. Were any Contagious or Infectious Diseases prevailing at the port or ports at which you touched?
10. If so, name the Diseases.
11. Was any freight or passengers received at the ports at which your vessel touched?
12. If so, give particulars.
13. Have you any Bills of Health?
14. If so, produce them.
15. During the course of your Cruise or Passage, what cases of disease have occurred on board?
16. At what dates?
17. Have any deaths taken place on board your veesel since you left the last port?
18. If so, at what dates, and from what causes?
19. Are there any sick on your vessel at this time?
20. Has Yellow Fever, Small-Pox, Cholera or Plague ever existed on this ship?
21. If so, when?
22. What is the number of Officers?
23. What is the number of the Crew?
24. What is the number of Passengers?
25. What is your cargo?
26. To whom is the cargo consigned?
27. What is the present sanitary condition of the vessel, cargo, crew and passengers?
28. Have you a medical officer?
29. Give the name of the Medical Officer.
30. Produce the Reports of the Medical Officer.

Signature of Master or Captain————

Subscribed to before me,———

Witness:

The preceding questions and answers shall be signed in duplicate, one copy to be retained at the Quarantine Station and the other to be transmitted to the President of the Board of Health.

Disinfection, Fumigation and Purification of Vessels from Ports in which Yellow Fever Usually Prevails.

Sec. 5. All vessels from ports in which Yellow Fever usually prevails, or from ports where other contagious or infectious diseases are reported to exist, shall be detained at Quarantine Stations, for purpose of disinfection, fumigation and purification, and shall be disinfected, fumigated and purified.

Vessels from Infected Ports to be Detained at Quarantine Stations Not Less than Seventy-two Hours.

SEC. 6. All vessels from ports in which Yellow Fever usually prevails, or from ports where other contagious or infectious diseases are reported to exist, shall be detained at Quarantine Stations, for observation, disinfection, purification and fumigation, not less than *seventy two hours;* or for such length of time as the Board of Health may determine.

SEC. 7. In case Yellow Fever, cholera, or plague, or small-pox, or typhus fever, prevails in epidemic form at the port from which the vessel sailed, or at any port at which she has touched during the voyage, or on any vessel with which she has come in contact during the voyage, the detention shall not be less than suffient to complete the full period of five days from the date of exposure to such infection.

Vessels Coming from Healthy Ports South of Latitude 26° N., to be Given Free Pratique After Thorough Inspection, Fumigation and Disinfection.

SEC. 8. In case the condition of the vessel is satisfactory, and neither Yellow Fever, nor cholera, nor plague, nor small-pox; nor typhus fever, in epidemic form, existed at the port from which she sailed, or at any intermediate ports at which she may have touched, or on any vessel with which she has come in contact during the voyage, although said vessel may come from ports south of 26° north latitude, the Quarantine officer, after thorough inspection, fumigation and disinfection, may give free pratique, and the vessel may proceed to the usual wharf or landing in the harbor of New Orleans, or other points where quarantine may be established by the Board of Health.

Infected Vessels—Rules and Regulations Governing Infected Vessels at Quarantine Stations.

SEC. 9. In case Yellow Fever, cholera, small-pox, typhus fever, plague, or any other infectious or contagious disease, has attacked whilst in port, or during the voyage, or whilst lying at the Quarantine Station, one or more of the crew or passengers of the vessel, she shall be subject to the following rules and regulations:

(*a*). The crew and passengers shall be inspected by the Quarantine Physician, and if any are sick they shall be removed to the proper hopsital.

(*b*). The clothing, baggage, bedding and equipage of the crew and passengers, both sick and well, shall be exposed to the air, and shall be ventilated, purified, disinfected and fumigated.

(*c*). The hatches shall be opened and the vessel as far as possible ventilated; the hold and cabin of the vessel and all closets and clothing, linen, carpets, curtains and fabrics of every description, shall be thoroughly fumigated with sulphurous acid gas; baggage-rooms, cabins, lockers, water-closets, and all parts of the vessel to be thoroughly ventilated, fumigated, disinfected and cleansed.

(*d*). The bilge-water shall be pumped out, and washed out with fresh water, until the bilge-water shall be clear and odorless. The following solution of sulphate of iron (copperas) and Calvert's Carbolic Acid, No. 5, shall be introduced and allowed to remain.

Disinfectant to replace bilge-water and also for cleansing water-closets and washing decayed or foul wood on shipboard.

Sulphate of iron (copperas).............................fifty (50) pounds;
Carbolic Acid (Calvert's No. 5).........................two (2) gallons;
Water ....fifty (50) gallons..

This disinfectant is readily prepared by suspending 50 pounds of copperas in a straw basket, in the upper portion of a water-tight barrel or cask, and pouring water upon the copperas, until the barrel is nearly full, and then adding two (2) gallons of Carbolic Acid (Calvert's No. 5). The copperas will be dissolved during the filling of the barrel. This disinfecting, deodorizing and antiseptic fluid may be extemporaneously prepared at any time on shipboard in the course of half an hour.

This solution should be used in the cleansing and purification of all unpainted woodwork in the hold, between decks, in the forecastle, cabins, lockers and water-closets.

(*e*). The amount of sulphur consumed during the fumigation of a vessel should be regulated by the size and capacity of the craft, nature of cargo, and general hygenic condition.

When sulphur is burned in iron pots, or pans, the fumigation should be continued until the sulphur is extinguished in the consumption of the oxygen of the air and the liberation of the sulphurous acid gas. At least two pounds of sulphur should be burned for every 1000 cubic feet of space in the vessel. The number of fumigations will in like manner depend upon the condition of the vessel, crew, passengers and cargo.

(*f*). If in the judgment of the Board of Health, a vessel require it, the Quarantine Physician may order the following sanitary measures: Baths, or other bodily care for the person ; washing, or other disinfecting means for clothing ; displacement of merchandise on board, or complete breaking out; subjection to high steam, incineration, or submersion at a distance below the surface of the water, for infected articles; the destruction of tainted or spoiled food, or beverages; the complete ejection of water; thorough cleansing of the hold, and the disinfection of the well.   In short, the complete purification of the vessel in all her parts, by the use of steam, fumigation, force-pumps, wind-blasts, scrubbing or scraping, and finally, detention at Quarantine anchorage until these means are perfected.

(*g*). All articles which have been in contact with persons sick with contagious or infectious diseases, should be burned, or treated with a boiling hot solution of sulphate of zinc and common salt, dissolved together in water, in the proportion of four ounces of sulphate of zinc and two ounces of salt to the gallon.

Discharge of Cargo and Purification of Infected Vessels.

SEC. 10.   Whenever it shall be deemed necessary by the Board of Health, the cargo of any vessel dangerously infected shall be discharged in lighters, or transferred to the warehouse especially prepared for its reception.

After the discharge of cargo, the vessel shall be thoroughly cleansed, disinfected and ventilated; the hold, the forecastle, or sleeping apartments of the crew, and the cabins for passengers, as well as bunks, or portable berths, shall be thoroughly cleansed, disinfected and ventilated.

All decaying wood shall be scraped and disinfected with strong solutions of sulphate of iron and carbolic acid. The decks and unpainted woodwork should be treated in like manner.

Until the process of discharge of cargo and purification has been completed to the satisfaction of the Quarantine Physician, there shall be no communication between the vessel and the shore, or other vessels, except by the written permit of the Quarantine Physician.

Every person who shall go on board of any vessel while performing quarantine without the permission of the Resident Physician, or his assistants, shall forfeit the sum of fifty dollars.

Rules Governing the Sick at Quarantine Stations.

SEC. 11.   The sick shall be detained in hospital until recovery, and for such a time afterwards as will insure that they will not communicate or transport the cause of disease.

SEC. 12. Passengers under observation shall be detained at least five days from the time of the last exposure, or during the period of incubation of the disease or diseases for which the ship is detained. In case of the occurrence of other contagious or infecaious diseases, they shall be detained until, in the judgment of the Quarantine officer, they may be safely permitted to proceed to their destination.

In the case of small-pox occurring on board a ship arriving at any port, the sick shall be sent to the hospital, and all not sick shall be immediately vaccinated, unless offering evidence of previous satisfactory vaccination, or of a previous attack of small-pox.

SEC. 13.   Persons employed at Quarantine Stations, who have been brought in contact with infected vessels, shall not be permitted to leave such station until their clothing has been washed and disinfected, nor until an interval of five days since their last exposure to infection.

When Necessary, the Public Health to be Protected by Additional Measures.

SEC. 14.   It shall be the duty of the Quarantine Physician to take the responsibility of applying such additional means as may be deemed indispensable for the protection of the public health; but in all such cases the Quarantine Physician shall report immediately and fully his action to the Board of Health.

Classification of Merchandise at Quarantine Station for Sanitary Measures.

SEC. 15.   For the purpose of sanitary measures, merchandise shall be arranged in three classes.

1.   Merchandise to be submitted to an obligatory quarantine, and to purification.
2.   Merchandise subject to an optional quarantine; and
3.   Merchandise exempt from quarantine.

The first class comprises all clothing, personal baggage and dunnage, rags, paper-rags, hides, skins, feathers, hair, and all other remains of animals, cotton, hemp, woolens and coffee in bags.

The second class comprehends sugar, silks and linen, and cattle.

The third class comprehends all merchandise not enumerated in the other two classes.

With existing quarantinable disease on board, or if there be any such disease on board within the ten days last preceding, merchandise of the first class shall be landed at the quarantine warehouse.

Merchandise of the second class may be admitted to pratique immediately, or transferred to the warehouse, according to circumstances, at the option of the quarantine officer, with due regard to the sanitary condition of the port. Merchandise of the third class shall be declared free, and admitted without unnecessary delay.

Rules Governing Foul Vessels.

SEC. 16. If any vessel, though not having had during the voyage any case of quarantinable disease, yet be found in a condition which the Quarantine officer shall deem dangerous to the public health, the vessel and cargo shall be detained until the case shall have been considered; the decision of the quarantine officer, however, in all such cases, shall be rendered within twenty-four hours.

Vessels in an unhealthy and foul state, whether there has been sickness on board or not, shall not be allowed pratique until they shall have been duly cleansed and ventilated.

Penalties for Violation of Quarantine Acts, Rules and Regulations.

SEC. 17. Every master of a vessel subject to a quarantine or visitation, arriving at the port of New Orleans, who shall refuse or neglect either, first, to proceed with and anchor his vessel at the place designated for quarantine at the time of his arrival; second, to submit his vessel, cargo and passengers to the examination of the physician, and to furnish all necessary information to enable that officer to determine what quarantine shall be fixed for his vessel at the quarantine ground during the period assigned for her quarantine, and while there to comply with the directions prescribed by the acts of the Legislature of Louisiana, and the rules and regulations of the Board of Health founded thereon, or with such directions prescribed for his vessel, crew and cargo and passengers, by the Resident Physician, shall be guilty of a misdemeanor, and be punished by a fine not exceeding two thousand dollars ($2000), or by imprisonment not exceeding twelve months, or by both, at the discretion of the court.

Duty of Quarantine Physician to report to the Attorney General all Violation of Quarantine Laws.

SEC. 18. The Resident Physician shall report to the Attorney General all violations of this act; and it shall be his duty to prosecute all persons thus offending; to collect the fines and remit the amount thereof to the Secretary of the Board of Health, whose duty it shall be to keep a separate book for fines collected, to be approved of every three months by the Attorney General.

Duty of Harbor-Masters to Demand Permits of Resident Quarantine Physicians.

SEC. 19. It shall be the duty of the Harbor-Masters, in their respective districts, to demand of the captain of every vessel arriving from sea to New Orleans, the permit of the Resident Physician, and to report to the President of the Board of Health all vessels having entered the port without such permit.

Power of Board of Health to Issue Their Warrant to the Sheriff of the City or Parish Where Any Vessel May Be, Having Violated the Quarantine Laws.

SEC. 20. The Board of Health shall have power to define the duties of officers employed by them, and impose additional duties to officers appointed under the acts entitled "An Act to establish Quarantine for the protection of the State," approved March 15, 1855, and March 16, 1870, to issue warrants to any constable, police officer, or sheriff in the State, to apprehend and remove such person or persons as cannot otherwise be subjected to the provisions of this act, or who shall have violated the same; and whenever it shall be necessary so to do, to issue their warrant to the sheriff of the city or parish where any vesel may be, having violated the provisions of the "Acts establishing and regulating Quarantine for the protection of the State, commanding him to remove said vessel to the Quarantine ground, and arrest the officer thereof; all which warrant shall be executed by the officer to whom the same shall be directed, who shall possess the like power in the execution thereof, and be entitled to the same compensation as if the same had been duly issued out of any court of the State.

Rules and Regulations Governing the Captains or Masters of Towboats.

SEC. 21. From the first of May to the first of November, all towboats plying from the mouth of the river to New Orleans shall be liable to inspection and quarantine, and it shall be the duty of the different harbor-masters to require from the captains of said towboats the certificate of the Resident Physician; *provided*, nothing herein contained shall be so construed as to apply to towboats plying between New Orleans and the quarantine ground, and no further.

SEC. 22. The captain of any towboat or steamboat who shall receive on board of his boat freight, goods or passengers from a vessel liable to inspection or quarantine, or who shall receive goods or passengers from the quarantine ground, without the permission of the Resident Physician, shall be punished by a fine not exceeding two thousand dollars ($2000), and by imprisonment, at the discretion of the court; and all violations of the provisions of these quarantine laws at the quarantine station on the Mississippi River, and at the Rigolets, shall be tried by the Criminal Court of New Orleans, and all violations of this act at the station on the Atchafalaya River shall be tried by the District Court of the parish of St. Mary.

Rules and Regulations Governing Pilots.

SEC. 23. The Board of Health shall cause a sufficient number of these Rules and Regulations to be printed and delivered to the pilots to be distributed to the masters of vessels, arriving as before provided.

SEC. 24. Every pilot, or any other person acting as such, shall deliver to the master of every vessel inward bound, one copy of the printed Rules and Regulations of the Board of Health of the State of Louisiana, relative to quarantine, which shall be furnished him by the Board of Health; and any pilot refusing or neglecting so to do, or aiding or landing any person or persons, contrary to the Quarantine Acts, shall forfeit one hundred dollars for every offense.

Duties and Powers of the President of the Board of Health.

SEC. 25. It shall be the duty of the President of the Board of Health to reside in New Orleans and superintend the different quarantine stations of the State, and it shall be his duty to visit them as often as the Board of Health may deem necessary. He shall have the power to issue, during the adjournment of the Board of Health, to constables or to the sheriff, all orders and warrants provided by the provisions of the "Acts of the Legislature of Louisiana, establishing and regulating quarantine for the protection of the State;" and shall report to the Attorney General all violations of the same. Whenever it shall be necessary so to do, the President of the Board of the Board of Health shall have power to issue his warrant to the sheriff of the city or parish where any vessel may be, having violated the provisions of the "Acts establishing and regulating Quarantine for the protection of the State," commanding him to remove said vessel to the quarantine ground, and arrest the officers thereof, all which warrant shall be executed by the officer to whom the same shall be directed, who shall possess the like power in the execution thereof, and be entitled to the same compensation as if the same had been duly issued out of any court of the State.

Duties of Resident Quarantine Physicians.

SEC. 26. It shall be the duty of the Resident Physicians of the Quarantine Stations, established by the Board of Health of the State of Louisiana, to faithfully carry out at all times and under all circumstances, the provisions of the "Acts establishing and regulating Quarantine for the protection of the State," and the rules and regulations of the Board of Health, founded upon said acts.

SEC. 27. It shall be the duty of the Resident Physician of the Mississippi Quarantine Station, or his assistant, to visit and inspect every vessel coming from any port or entering the mouth of the Mississippi River.

He shall require the captain of every vessel thus inspected to pay the fees fixed by the acts of the Legislature of Louisiana; *provided*, nothing contained in this section shall apply to any vessel or craft going from New Orleans to sea and returning without having touched at any port, or at the Quarantine, towboats excepted. Vessels free from disease, not in a foul condition and not from an infected district (which shall be decided upon by the Resident Physician); shall be furnished with a certificate of health and allowed to proceed to the city. The Resident Physician shall require for every inspection and certificate thus furnished the following fees: Every sailing vessel of one thousand tons and over shall pay thirty dollars ($30); every ship of one thousand tons or less shall pay twenty dollars ($20); every bark shall pay fifteen dollars ($15); every brig shall pay ten dollars ($10); every schooner shall pay seven dollars and fifty cents ($7 50); every steamboat (towboats excepted) shall pay five dollars ($5); every steamship from Florida, Alabama, Mississippi or Texas shall pay ten dollars ($10); every steamship from other ports shall pay twenty dollars ($20). The Resident Physician shall return to the Secretary of the Board of Health a weekly list of all the vessels inspected by him as well as all the fees collected by him, which shall form a fund for the support of quarantine.

SEC. 28. The Resident Physician shall have the power, and it shall be his duty, to detain at the Quarantine ground, with their cargoes, crews and passengers, all vessels coming from an infected district, or in a foul condition, or having on board persons affected with cholera, Yellow Fever, pestilential, contagious or infectious diseases. during such time as the Board of Health may deem necessary—to compel the captain to land the sick at the Quarantine ground, to fumigate and cleanse all such vessels, and to submit to such rules and regulations as may be hereafter provided by the Board of Health, and that all costs incurred for vessels found in a foul condition, including the sum of five dollars for the support of each and every sick person landed at the Quarantine Station, shall be borne by the captain and owners, and shall be paid to the Resident Physician, before a certificate shall be issued giving free pratique.

SEC. 29. The Resident Physician shall have such other powers as may be delegated to him by the Board of Health, not contrary to the provisions of the acts of the Legislature of the State of Louisiana, necessary to carry them into effect. It shall be his duty to remain at the Quarantine ground, attend the sick, and perform all such other duties as may be required of him by the Board of Health.

SEC. 30. The Resident Physician shall have power, at his discretion, to grant permits to persons acclimated and healthy, to proceed to the city. He shall employ such means of purification, disinfection and fumigation of vessels as may be directed by the Board of Health, and shall require the captains or owners of said vessels to defray the *costs of inspection, purification, disinfection and fumigation,* and the Resident Quarantine Physician shall not release the vessel from quarantine until said costs are paid.

SEC. 31. Vessels out ten days from infected ports, presenting clean bills of health, not having, nor having had sickness on board, and which are not in foul condition, shall be permitted to pass to the city after thorough fumigation by disinfecting agents, to effect which purpose the Resident Physician shall detain said vessel as long as the Board of Health may deem necessary. The Resident Physician shall, in all such cases, require evidence under oath ; and he shall, by this act, be invested with the power to administer oaths whenever he may deem this necessary to attain the objects of quarantine.

SEC. 32. It shall be the duty of the Quarantine Physicians, at their respective stations, to enter upon suitable books, furnished by the Board of Health, the following facts with reference to the vessels inspected :

1. Name of vessel.
2. Name of captain.
3. Tonnage or class of vessel.
4. Port from whence the vessel sailed.
5. Length of passage.
6. Date of sailing.
7. Date of arrival at Quarantine Station.
8. Number of days detained.
9. Sanitary condition of vessel.
10. Number of cases of disease occurring during the voyage.
11. Number of deaths occurring during the voyage.
12. Number of cases occurring at Quarantine Station.
13. Number of deaths occurring at Quarantine Station.
14. Number and character of fumigations.
15. Sanitary measures instituted.
16. Number of officers.
17. Number of crew.
18. Number of passengers.
19. Sanitary condition of crew.
20. Sanitary condition of passengers.
21. Nature of cargo.
22. Name of consignee.

Said books to be carefully preserved at the different quarantine stations.

SEC. 33. It shall be the duty of the Resident Physicians at the different quarantine stations, to prepare for the use of the Board of Health an annual report, in which the statistics recorded in the books specified, shall be consolidated and arranged in accordance with the months of the year.

By order of the Board of Health. JOSEPH JONES, M. D.,
President Board of Health, State of Louisiana.

Sanitary Rules of the Board of Health of the State of Louisiana, Regulating Shipping in the Port of New Orleans.

At the regular meeting of the Board of Health, April 22, 1880. the President, Dr. Joseph Jones, submitted the following Sanitary Rules and Regulations for the regulation of shipping in the port of New Orleans, which were unanimously adopted.

The President was authorized by the Board of Health to cause the publication and distribution of said rules.

OFFICE BOARD OF HEALTH, STATE-HOUSE, ⎱
Corner St. Louis and Royal streets, New Orleans, April 22, 1880. ⎰

I. *Resolved by the Board of Health of the State of Louisiana,* That in order to prevent the introduction and spread of contagious and infectious diseases, therefore, the President of the Board of Health is empowered to inspect the shipping in the port of

New Orleans, either in person or through the Sanitary Inspectors, and to enforce the following rules and regulations:

II. All captains, masters or medical officers of any water craft, are hereby required to report within twenty-four hours to the President of the Board of Health, at the office of the Board of Health, all cases within their cognizance of Asiatic cholera, Yellow Fever, remittent and congestive malarial fevers, typhus or ship fever, scarlet fever, small-pox, varioloid, measles, diphtheria, plague, leprosy, or any other case that may at any time be specified by the Board of Health ; and in default or failure to so report such cases, such person so failing or in default shall be liable to a fine not to exceed fifty dollars; *provided, however,* the said Board may declare it unnecessary to report further cases, when any disease shall have been pronounced epidemic. No case of disease shall be removed from any vessel in the port of New Orleans to any house, residence or hospital in the city, without a written permit from the President of the Board of Health, under a penalty of a fine of fifty dollars for each and every offense.

III. Whenever it shall be deemed necessary to prevent the introduction and spread of contagious and infectious diseases, every vessel or water-craft arriving from a foreign port shall be visited by the President of the Board of Health, or his deputy inspectors, between sunrise and sunset, as soon as possible after such arrival; and the President or his deputy inspectors shall examine the bill of health, and inspect the ship or vessel and require of the captain or master, answers in duplicate to the following questions:

Date of Inspection, New Orleans, ——— 188

1. Name of Vessel ?
2. Name of Captain or Master ?
3. Tonnage or Class of Vessel ?
4. From whence is the Vessel you Command ?
5. How many days have you been on the passage ?
6. At what port or ports have you touched ?
7. Were any Contagious or Infectious Diseases prevailing at the port from whence your vessel sailed ?
8. If so, name the Diseases.
9. Were any Contagious or Infectious Diseases prevailing at the port or ports at which you touched ?
10. If so, name the Diseases.
11. Was any freight or passengers received at the ports at which your vessel touched ?
12. If so, give particulars.
13. Have you any Bills of Health ?
14. If so, produce them.
15. During the course of your cruise or passage what cases of disease have occurred on board ?
16. At what dates.
17. Have any deaths taken place on board your vessel since you left the last port ?
18. If so, at what dates, and from what causes ?
19. Are there any sick on your vessel at this time ?
20. Has Yellow Fever, Small-Pox, Cholera or Plague ever existed in this ship?
21. If so, when ?
22. What is the number of Officers ?
23. What is the number of the Crew ?
24. What is the number of passengers ?
25. What is your cargo ?
26. To whom is the cargo consigned ?
27. What is the present sanitary condition of the vessel, cargo, crew and passengers ?
28. Have you a Medical Officer ?
29. Give the name of the Medical Officer.
30. Produce the Reports of the Medical Officer.

Signature of Master or Captain ———

          Subscribed to before me, an officer,

Witness:

          ——— Official Title.

———

Sanitary Rules Recommended by the Board of Health of the State of Louisiana, to be Observed by Vessels During Their Stay in the Port of New Orleans, and in Other Ports, and on their Passage to and from New Orleans.

(a). Each ocean-going steamship or sailing vessel should be provided with a competent medical officer versed in the sanitation and hygiene of ships sailing in tropical or semi-tropical waters.

(*b*). Physicians attached to ships, steamships or vessels of any description should be considered as the Health Officers, and should be charged with the duty of watching their sanitary condition, and with the conduct of those operations which will promote in the highest degree the health of the officers, crew and passengers, and prevent as far as possible the introduction of contagious and infectious diseases.

(*c*). As far as possible the commerce of New Orleans, with insular, tropical and sub-tropical America, should be conducted by *acclimated* officers and crews. By the term *acclimated* is understood those who have suffered at some period of their lives with Yellow Fever.

(*d*). The attention of the captain, master or medical officer shall at all times and under all circumstances be directed to the personal cleanliness of the crew, and to their food and drinking water.

(*e*). None of the crew should be allowed to sleep on shore at night, or on deck, unless protected by an awning.

(*f*). When in tropical and semi-tropical ports, the officers and men should hold as little intercourse with the shore as possible.

(*g*). Unless when engaged in the reception or discharge of cargo, vessels should lie in the harbor as far as practicable from the shore.

(*h*). Earth, sand or soft porous rock should not be used as ballast. As far as practicable the ballast should consist of hard rock, iron and other metals.

(*i*). All vessels loading or unloading should pump out the bilge-water and wash out with fresh water, until the bilge-water shall be odorless. Then a solution of one part of carbolic acid (Calvert's No. 5) to fifty parts of water, or the following compound should be introduced, and allowed to remain :

Sulphate of iron (copperas) .... fifty (50) pounds.
Carbolic acid (Calvert's No. 5) .... two (2) gallons.
Water.. .... fifty (50) gallons.

Every five days on the passage undiluted Carbolic Acid should be poured down the pump or sounding tube, and the entire hold and between decks sprinkled with one part Carbolic Acid (Calvert's No. 5) to fifty parts of water.

When practicable it is especially recommended that the hold should be fumigated with sulphurous acid gas, or chlorine gas.

As far as practicable the hatches should be kept open, both while in port or at sea, and the largest possible amount of fresh air be introduced between and below decks, by the use of wind-sails and ventilators. Whitewashing of the unpainted woodwork below and between decks is recommended.

(*j*). At the close of each day while in tropical and sub-tropical ports, all the crew should wash their entire persons, leaving off all the clothing worn that day (for washing). and dress in clean flannels and clothing throughout.

As soon as the weather will permit after leaving port, all mattresses, bedding and similar material should be got up on deck and sunned and aired for several hours, this to be repeated every two or five days, during the passage, if the weather permits.

(*k*). All baggage and clothing of passengers should be exposed to the air and disinfected or fumigated as soon as possible after coming on board, and again before arriving at Quarantine Station and the harbor of New Orleans.

(*l*). Baggage-rooms, water-closets, dirty linen, lockers, cabins and berths should be kept thoroughly clean and disinfected.

(*m*). The quarters of the crew should be kept clean and disinfected.

The Captain and Medical Officer should direct their especial attention to the general hygiene of the crew and passengers.

By order of the Board of Health, JOSEPH JONES, M. D.,
President Board of Health, State of Louisiana.

Rules and Regulations of the Board of Health of the State of Louisiana, Governing the Mississippi Quarantine Station, Adopted August 19, 1880.

The Committee on Quarantine respectfully submit the following additional rules and regulations, defining the duties of the Resident Quarantine Physicians and the employes of of the Board of Health of Louisiana at the Mississippi Quarantine Station.

1. It shall be the duty of the Resident Quarantine Physicians at the Mississippi Station to enforce the strictest sanitary regulations in all the buildings under their charge, the grounds surrounding the same, and all other parts of the Quarantine Station.

This rule is to be construed as of daily requisition, and for its fulfillment they are instructed to employ the boatmen, or a portion of them, in rotation, for the purpose.

2. It shall be the duty of the Resident Quarantine Physician to make a monthly report to the Board of Health of the State of Louisiana of the sanitary condition of the

Quarantine Station and of the sanitary measures instituted by them, and all other facts relative to the affairs of the Station that he may deem necessary for their information.

8. It shall be the duty of the Resident Quarantine Physician, or his assistant in carrying out the requisitions of section 27 of the rules and regulations of the Board of Health of the State of Louisiana, to supervise in person the cleansing, disinfection and fumigation of all vessels detained at the Quarantine Station, under section 9 of the rules and regulations of the Board of Health.

In the case of every vessel fumigated he shall assure himself of the actual weight of the sulphur employed for the purpose, that he may comply strictly in all particulars with the requirements of section 9 of the rules and regulations.

4. It is ordered by the Board of Health of the State of Louisiana, that from the 1st of May to the 1st of November, or while any contagious or infectious diseases may exist at the Quarantine Station at other periods of the year, absolute isolation shall be enforced.

(*a*). That only the Resident Quarantine Physicians, and those persons employed under the sanction of the Board of Health, shall be allowed to reside at the Mississippi Quarantine Station.

(*b*). That while infected vessels are moored at the Quarantine Station no one shall be allowed to go on board such vessels but the Resident Physicians and the employes under them.

(*c*). That within the above prescribed time (from the first of May to the first of November), or while any contagious or infectious disease prevails at the Station, no communication will be allowed with the opposite bank of the river, or the shores adjacent to the Quarantine Station, or with any vessels passing the Station.

(*d*). That all needful supplies desired from such places or vessels shall be brought to the Station by the Quarantine boat, or boats manned by the employes of the Board of Health, without going on shore or on board the vessels.

(*e*). Until the process of discharge of cargo and purification has been completed to the satisfaction of the Quarantine Physician, there shall be no communication between the vessel and the shore or other vessels.

Every person who shall go on board of any vessel while performing quarantine without a written permit from the Resident Quarantine Physician or his assistant, shall forfeit the sum of fifty dollars.

All infractions of this rule shall be immediately reported by the Resident Physician to the President of the Board of Health.

(*f*). That no vessel, tug or other craft navigating the river shall be allowed, under any circumstances, to go alongside of any infected vessel detained at Quarantine, nor shall they be permitted to land at the Government wharf, or other parts of the Quarantine Station, while any contagious or infectious disease exists on the shore, or on board of any vessel detained at Quarantine.

(*g*). All persons embarking from the Quarantine Station when required to leave it during the prevalence of any contagious or infectious disease on shore, or who have visited any infected vessel in the discharge of quarantine duty, must embark in mid-stream, after proper fumigation of their apparel and effects, as required by section 13 of the rules and regulations of the Board of Health.

(Signed)   J. C. BEARD, M. D.
(Signed)   J. P. DAVIDSON, M. D.
(Signed)   F. LOEBER, M. D.

(c). THE LAWS GOVERNING THE CITY OF NEW ORLEANS, WITH REFERENCE TO THE REPORT OF CONTAGIOUS AND INFECTIOUS DISEASES.

[Extract from Health Ordinances of the City of New Orleans, State of Louisiana.]

The majority of the Health Ordinances of the city of New Orleans have been framed and passed by the Board of Health and recommended to the City Council and been received and indorsed by this representative of the popular will. These enactments, therefore, should be regarded as the joint product of the Board of Health and City Council.

SANITARY ORDINANCES, ADOPTED BY THE CITY COUNCIL OF NEW ORLEANS JUNE 25, 1879.

[*Official.*]

MAYORALITY OF NEW ORLEANS, City Hall, June 25, 1879.

[No. 6022—Administration Series.]

AN ORDINANCE *for the better protection and preservation of the public health.*

SECTION 1. *Be it ordained by the Council of the City of New Orleans,* That no person shal bring or cause to be brought into the limits of the city of New Orleans any hides, bones, peltry, rags or other articles whatsoever which may tend to produce infection, or in any way to injure or endanger health.

SEC. 2. No person shall sell, or offer or expose for sale in public or private any blown, stale, decaying, putrid, rotten or unwholesome provisions, vegetables, fruits or tainted meats or fish or any impure or unsound food, or any drink liable to be injurious to health, or the flesh of any animal that has died of disease, or which was diseased when killed.

* * * * * *

SEC. 8. The Administrator of Police shall upon complaint of the Board of Health, remove or cause to be removed any foul or offensive matters whatever, to such place or places as may be selected by said Board, at the expense of the owner of said matter, or the occupant or owner of the premises where the same may be.

* * * * * *

SEC. 13. The Board of Health may, in its discretion, for the protection of life and health, declare any structure or place unhealthy, and may order such structure or place forthwith to be vacated and closed; and the same shall not again be occupied until it shall appear to have been so cleansed or repaired as to be fit for human habitation, and permission shall have been granted accordingly by the Board of Health.

* * * * * *

SEC. 24. No tomb, grave or vault containing any dead body shall be opened without permission, in writing, from the proper officers of the Board of Health, and no human body or remains thereof, within the jurisdiction of said Board, shall be disinterred or disentombed without its written authority, or be removed from or brought within the limits of the city of New Orleans without such authority first obtained.

* * * * * *

SEC. 25. Every sexton or other person having charge of any cemetery, graveyard or burying ground shall, on Monday of each week, before the hour of 9 A. M., make a written report and hand the same into the office of the Board of Health; which said report shall contain the full name of each and every person buried in such cemetery, yard or ground during the seven days next preceding 6 o'clock P. M. of the last Sunday before making such report, together with a statement of the color, sex, age, nativity, the cause of death of such person, occupation, place of death, social condition and birth place of parents; also what interments were made in the ground and what interments in vaults or tombs, together with the numbers and owners of said vaults or tombs and such other information as the Board of Health may from time to time require.

SEC. 26. The Board of Health may remove or cause to be removed to hospital or other place of treatment any person or persons suffering from small-pox whenever such removal shall, in the discretion of said board, be deemed necessary for the proper treatment of such person or persons for the prevention or spread of said disease.

SEC. 27. All practitioners of medicine, masters of any water-craft, hotel, boarding or lodging-house keepers, principals or masters of any public or private school, the chief officers or persons in charge of any public institution of charity or of punishment, and heads of families are hereby required to report, within twenty-four hours, to the office of the Board of Health all cases within their cognizance of Asiatic cholera, leprosy, Yellow Fever, typhus or ship fever, diptheria, malignant scarlet fever, small-pox, varioloid, trichiniasis, or any other case that may at any time be specified by the Board of Health.

SEC. 28. Parents shall inform principals of schools attended by their children of any contagious disease occurring in their families.

SEC. 29. All animals sick with any contagious or infectious disease shall be removed at once beyond the limits of the city of New Orleans by the person or persons owning or having charge of said animals, and in default of such action said animals may be removed by the Board of Health at the expense of such person or persons.

* * * * * * *

SEC. 33. All citizens are hereby authorized to lodge complaints at the office of the Board of Health, or with the sanitary inspectors, or with the sanitary police officers, of any violation of this ordinance; and in order to facilitate such complaints, books of complaint shall be kept at the office of the Board of Health, and at the office of each sanitary inspector, and said books shall be at all times open for entering therein any complaint or wrong.

SEC. 34. No person shall willfully obstruct, hinder or resist any officer or person, duly authorized by the Board of Health, in the execution or enforcement of any sanitary ordinance or order of said board, or in entering into or upon any premises for the purpose of examining the same.

SEC. 35. The penalty for violation of any section or portion of this ordinance shall be a fine not exceeding twenty-five dollars, recoverable before the recorder of the district wherein the offense was committed; or in default of payment of the fine, imprisonment not exceeding thirty days for each and every offense.

* * * * , * * *

SEC. 37. That the members of the Board of Health and its agents, officers and employes, and the members of the Crescent City Police and the Recorders of the several districts of this city are specially charged with the enforcement of the provisions of this ordinance.

SEC. 38. All ordinances or parts of ordinances in conflict with this ordinance are hereby repealed in so far as they may conflict, and this ordinance shall take effect from and after its passage.

Adopted by the Council of the city of New Orleans, June 24, 1879.

Yeas—Glynn, Houston, Isaacson, Marks, Mealey.

I. W. PATTON, Mayor.

A true copy:
ROBT. C. WOOD, Secretary.

[No. 14—Administration Series.]

AN ORDINANCE *granting additional authority to the Board of Health to protect the health of the city.*

WHEREAS, that loathsome and infectious disease, small-pox, is on the increase; and, whereas, energetic and effective measures ought to be made use of to secure the disappearance of said disease.

SECTION 1. *Be it ordained,* That the Board of Health shall have authority to remove to hospital or other place for treatment, any person or persons suffering from small-pox, whenever such removal shall, in the discretion of said Board, be deemed necessary for the proper treatment of such person or persons, or for the prevention of the spread of said disease.

SEC. 2. That the Board of Health shall have authority, at its discretion, to prevent access to or egress from, or cause to be vacated, any infected building, place or locality, and to fumigate, or otherwise disinfect any such building, place, or locality, whenever, in the discretion of said board such action shall be deemed necessary to prevent the spread of said disease.

SEC. 3. That the Board of Health shall have authority to disinfect or destroy, by burning or otherwise, any infected clothing, bedding, or any substance or material, whenever in the discretion of said board such action shall be deemed necessary to prevent the spread of said disease.

SEC. 4. That the expenses incurred in the necessary performance of any of the duties named in this ordinance shall, after their approval by the Board of Health, be borne by the city of New Orleans: *provided,* that no contract fixing the price for the future keeping, maintenance and attendance upon small-pox patients shall be valid, without the previous approval of the Administrator of Police and the Mayor.

SEC. 5. *Be it further ordained, etc.,* That all ordinances and parts of ordinances in conflict herewith be repealed, so far as they may so conflict, and this ordinance shall take effect from and after its passage.

Adopted by the Council of the city of New Orleans, April 14, 1870.

BENJ. F. FLANDERS, Mayor.

A true copy:
A. CONQUEST CLARKE, Secretary.

ORDINANCE CONFERRING POWER UPON BOARD OF HEALTH TO CIRCUMSCRIBE INFECTIOUS AND CONTAGIOUS DISEASES.

MAYORALTY OF NEW ORLEANS, City Hall, July 9, 1879

[No. 6046—Administration Series.]

AN ORDINANCE *for the further protection and preservation of the public health*

Be it ordained, etc., That the Board of Health may, at its discretion, regulate or prevent access to or egress from, or cause to be vacated, any infected building, water-craft, place or locality, or cause to be fumigated or otherwise disinfected, any infected building or water-craft whenever, in the opinion of said board, such action shall be deemed necessary to prevent the spread of any dangerous and infectious diseases ; and

Be it further ordained, etc, That the Board of Health may disinfect any infected clothing, bedding or other substances whenever, in the discretion of said Board, such action shall be deemed necessary to prevent the spread of disease.

Adopted by the Council of New Orleans, July 8, 1879.

Yeas—Houston, Issacson, Marks, Mealey.

I. W. PATTON, Mayor.

A true copy :

ROBT. C. WOOD, Secretary.

———

AN ORDINANCE RELATING TO CONTAGIOUS AND INFECTIOUS DISEASES.

MAYORATY OF NEW ORLEANS, City Hall, February 18, 1879.

[No. 4916—Administration Series.]

AN ORDINANCE *amending section* 21 *of Ordinance No.* 235, *new series, approved August* 2, 1866 (*article* 435 *of Leovy and Luzenberg's Digest of the Laws and General Ordinances of the city of New Orleans, edition of* 1870).

ARTICLE 455 (21). The coroner or coroners, or his or their deputies, masters of any water-craft, boarding or lodging house keepers, principals or masters of any boarding-school or seminary and all practitioners of medicine, surgeons, obstetricians or physicians, apothecaries, chemists, druggists, midwives and all persons who use or pretend to use medical, obstetrical or surgical means for the treatment of disease, disorder or lesion, are hereby required, each, any, or all of them, as the case may be, to report to the Board of Health of the State of Louisiana, all cases of contagious, infectious. epidemological diseases, especially cho'era, yellow fever, trichiniasis, typhus or ship fever, small-pox, diphtheria or any of the grades of such diseases, or any others that may be specified by the Board of Health, or may be generally adjudged contagious or infectious, within twenty-four hours after the same may come under their treatment, cognizance or supervision. And the penalty for offending against this section, or any portion thereof, shall not be less than twenty-five dollars for each and every offense, and in default of payment thereof, the offender shall suffer imprisonment not to exceed thirty days.

Adopted by the Council of the city of New Orleans, February 18, 1879.

Yeas—Behan, Glynn, Isaacson, Marks, Mealey.

I. W. PATTON, Mayor.

———

CEMETERIES AND INTERMENTS.

ARTICLE 159 (1). [Page 76 of Leovy & Luzenberg's Revised Ordinances of 1870.] That no keeper of any burial ground within the limits of the city shall receive or bury any corpse unless the bearers or carriers of the same shall deliver to him the certificate of a licensed physician, or of a magistrate, or of the coroner, containing a statement, specifying as nearly as possible, the death, name, age, birthplace, sex and color, and setting forth the location of the house or place from whence said corpse was taken for burial, giving the name of the owner or lessee of said house or place, and the number and street where said house is situated ; and if there is no number, as close a description of the situation of said house as possible ; and should any keeper of any burial ground refuse or neglect to perform any of the duties required by this article, he shall be fined the sum of fifty dollars for each and every violation.

ART. 160 (2). Whenever the keeper of any of the said burial grounds shall discover that the formalities required by this ordinance cannot be complied with by the bearers or the carriers of said corpse, or by any person or persons bringing the same for burial, he shall immediately inform the coroner thereof, in order that said officers may proceed to ascertain whether any crime has been committed ; and for any neglect to comply with this provision the said keeper shall be fined as provided for in the preceding section.

ART. 161 (3). All tombs must be built of the best kind of brick or stone, laid in mortar, with the proper proportion of the best cement and sharp sand, and covered with bitumen on the ground floor of each tomb, with walls not less than nine inches in thickness and plastered. All the tombs must be kept in good order, and it shall be the duty of the sexton to notify the owners thereof to have them repaired, otherwise it shall be done by the city at the expense of the owners, who shall be fined in a sum not exceeding fifty dollars.

ART. 165 (7). All sextons shall enter, within the shortest possible delay, all deceased persons who may be conveyed to the their respective cemeteries, in graves to be dug not less than four feet in depth, and to be at a distance of at least three feet from each other, according to such limitations as shall be described by the City Surveyor, and in pursuance of such directions as they may receive from the Mayor; and it shall be the duty of each of said sextons to keep a book, in which they shall insert, according to their dates, the name, sex, age, business and birthplace of each and every person they shall bury in the ground, or deposit in the tombs; and the said keeper shall be fined not less than ten, nor more than fifty dollars, for each and every violation of the foregoing provisions.

ART. 169 (11). No burial shall be permitted in any churchyard in this city, except the pastors of their churches, under a penalty of a fine of one hundred dollars.

ART. 172 (14). It shall be the duty of every person at whose domicile any person shall have died to cause the same to be buried within forty-eight hours after his death; and any person offending against this section of this ordinance, shall pay a fine not exceeding one hundred dollars for each offense.

ART. 180 (22). After the passage of this ordinance there shall not be established within the limits of this city any cemetery or depository of the dead, without first having obtained permission from the Common Council, under a penalty of twenty-five dollars per day for each and every day such establishment shall exist.

ART. 183 (2). Every burial certificate shall bear the indorsement of the Recorder of Births and Deaths of the parish of Orleans that such requirements of existing State laws have been fully complied with.

Board of Health Certificate of Vaccination.

New Orleans,——188
I hereby certify that on the——day——188 , I vaccinated (examined) ——of number——street, —— aged——years——months——weeks, and that the evidence of successful vaccination are satisfactory.   —— ——M. D.
Residence——

FREE VACCINATION

Every Wednesday and Saturday, from 1 to 2 o'clock, at the office of the Sanitary Inspectors of each District.

School children furnished gratuitously with certificates of vaccination by Sanitary Inspectors every Wednesday and Saturday from 1 to 2 o'clock.   •

New Orleans,——188
To the Board of Health:
I hereby report a case of——at number——street. Name——age——nativity——color——; date of attack——; length of time in the city——
Address——   —— ——M. D.

Certificate of Death.

Name—— cause of death——date of death——place of death—-color or race—— sex——occupation——place of birth——time in this city——age——year-—month——days. Condition: Single——married—widow—-birth place of father—— birth place of mother—— Remarks:——

I certify that I attended the person above named, who died of the disease stated, on the day named.

—— ——M. D.

Address ——

No——— Street, New Orleans, La.

Physicians are reminded of the importance of filling out these certificates with accuracy, as they are the basis of the vital statistics of the city.

OFFICE BOARD OF HEALTH, STATE OF LOUISIANA, {
New Orleans,————188— }

————————, *M. D. Dear Sir:*—Your attention is invited to the following Ordinance,
May 18, 1870:

SECTION 28. All practitioners of medicine, masters of any water craft, hotel, boarding
or lodging house keepers, principals or masters of any boarding school or seminary, the
chief officers or persons in charge of any public institution of charity or asylum, or otherwise, are hereby required to report within twenty-four hours, to the office of the Board of
Health, all cases within their cognizance of Asiatic cholera, Yellow Fever, typhus or ship
fever, malignant scarlet fever, small-pox, varioloid, trichiniasis, or any other case that may
at any time be specified by the Board of Health, and in default or failure to so report such
cases, such person so failing or in default shall be liable to a fine not to exceed fifty dollars;
provided, however, that said Board may declare it unnecessary to report further cases, when
any disease shall have been pronounced epidemic.

In addition to the list of diseases named above, the Board of Health desire cases of
diptheria to be reported in like manner, and trust that you will never neglect to give timely
information at this office, in accordance with the terms of the Ordinance.

Very respectfully,

JOSEPH JONES, M. D., *President.*

(*d*). THE LAWS GOVERNING THE SANITARY INSPECTORS AND SANITARY PO-
LICE OF NEW ORLEANS.

At the regular meeting of the Board of Health, on the thirtieth of September, 1880, Dr.
Formento submitted the following report of the special committee, which was unanimously adopted:

1. The Sanitary Inspector of each city district shall have an office located in a central
and convenient portion of his district, and which shall be open every day for the benefit of
the public from 8 o'clock a. m. to 4 o'clock p. m. Said office shall contain all the official
archives, books, papers, etc., of the district; also a special book for "complaints," in which
all complaints and notices of nuisances shall be accurately entered.

2. The Sanitary Inspector shall keep regular office hours, from 12 to 2 p. m., during
which hours he will attend personally to the transaction of his office duties.

3. He shall, once a day, report at the office of the Board of Health, either in person or
through his sanitary officer.

4. He shall strictly enforce all the rules and regulations of the Board of Health, and
see that all sanitary laws are rigorously carried out. He shall give his special attention to
sanitary measures concerning markets, public schools, prisons, hospitals, asylums and other
charitable institutions, and shall report on their condition; also on that of streets and gutters, of privies, wharves, tenement-houses, slaughter-houses, dairies, cisterns, etc.

5. He shall inspect personally all the shipping in his district on the river front, as
well as in the Old and New Basins, and report on their exact sanitary condition and health
of their crews.

6. He shall make out, in his monthly report, a complete and accurate *tableau* of the
total number of deaths, and causes of same, occurring in his district, with the age, nativity,
sex and color of each case.

7. It shall be his duty to report all cases of contagious or infectious diseases in his
district, viz: Cholera, diptheria, Yellow Fever, typhus or typhoid fever, small-pox, scarlatina, etc., and to see that the premises in which such cases have occurred be properly
cleansed, fumigated, disinfected, etc., and to see that the cases are isolated.

8. He shall vaccinate, free of charge, the poor children in his district.

9. He shall distribute gratuitously in his district the disinfectants recommended by
the Board of Health, giving necessary instructions as to the proper manner of using them.

10. He shall also distribute among the people all the printed rules and regulations and
circulars of the Board of Health, giving to those seeking them free advice and instruction on
all sanitary matters, in order to secure a more general and uniform adoption by the people
of hygienic measures.

11. All reports and communications of sanitary inspectors, whether written or verbal,
shall be addressed directly to the President of the State Board of Health, or to one of the
members of said Board, and no person outside of the President or members shall receive
any information of an official character from any of the district sanitary inspectors.
Neither shall any publication relating to the sanitary operations of the Board of Health be
made by any sanitary inspector, except by order of the Board of Health.

12. The sanitary police officers shall be assigned to their respective duties by the President of the Board of Health, and shall carry out all instructions and orders emanating
from the Board under the direction and supervision of the sanitary inspectors. It shall be
their duty to enforce all sanitary laws and regulations enacted by the city.

F. FORMENTO, M. D., Chairman Committee.

J. C. BEARD, M. D.   I. N. MARKS.
E. T. SHEPARD, M. D,   E. HERNANDEZ,
R. BREWSTER.

BOARD OF HEALTH, STATE OF LOUISIANA.

[Circular No. L]

Sanitary Measures to be Enforced by the Sanitary Inspectors of the City of New Orleans.

OFFICE BOARD OF HEALTH OF THE STATE OF LOUISIANA, }
State-House, April 22, 1880. }

1. House-to-house inspections must be pressed as rapidly as possible.
2. Order the abatement of all nuisances.
3. Order the emptying and disinfection of all foul privies.
4. Order the periodic disinfection at intervals of not less than seven days of all privies and water-closets.
5. Order the cleansing and disinfection of all foul alleys and yards.
6. Enforce the ordinance which compels all citizens to place the garbage and refuse matters of dwellings, hotels, stores, markets, manufactories and stables in boxes or barrels, or other suitable receptacles, for removal by the garbage carts.

Disinfection.

The Board of Health of the State of Louisiana deem it important that the people should be instructed with regard to the value and importance of disinfection, for the removal of foul gases and emanations, and for the destruction of the poisons of infectious and contagious diseases.

To accomplish the greatest good for the preservation of the health of the people, disinfection should be practiced at regular intervals throughout the entire year; but more fully and frequently in the city of New Orleans during the months of May, June, July, August, September and October.

By disinfection and household sanitation, the people should seek to avert or prevent pestilence, and should not delay the practice of these important measures until disease is actually developed, by the neglect and violation of sanitary laws. Each citizen, therefore, by obeying rigidly sanitary laws becomes the guardian of the health of his household.

New Orleans is without sewers, and the privies necessarily contain at all times an immense amount of fœcal matter. Even under the most energetic system of the removal of the contents of the privies, it is essential that disinfectants be used in this hot, moist climate, at regular intervals. It should be borne in mind, however, that disinfection cannot be substituted for want of cleanliness or of ventilation, but should be used for the prevention of those putrefactive processes, which result in the generation of compounds and agents deleterious to man.

In the selection of disinfectants reliable agents should be secured, which can be procured in a state of purity, and at so small a cost that they can be used in adequate quantities and at stated intervals.

Disinfectants—Disinfection of Privies and Water-Closets.

For the disinfection of privies, cess-pools water-closets and vaults, use the following:

Sulphate of Iron (green vitriol, or copperas)..............8 pounds.
Calvert's Carbolic Acid, No. 5...........................1 pint.
Water ....4 gallons.

Dissolve the green vitriol in hot water, and when cool add the carbolic acid. Add one gallon of this mixture to the privy or water closet to be disinfected, and thereafter one quart every fifth day, or oftener, if foul smell be evolved from the privy.

Lime should not be used in the disinfection of privies, as it decomposes the salts of ammonia.

This objection, however, does not apply to the sulphate of lime (Plaster of Paris), which may be used with advantage in combination with carbolic acid and copperas.

The walls of privies and all unpainted wood-work should be whitewashed.

Foul Drains, Damp Foul Yards, Stables, Cow-Houses, Markets and Slaughter-Houses.

Fresh-slacked lime, chloride of lime, plaster of Paris and sulphate of iron, should be sprinkled over damp and foul places, drains and yards. For disinfection of such places a simple solution of sulphate of iron or copperas, in proportion of one and a half pounds to the gallon, may be used. The copperas solution may be prepared in large quantities for markets, stables and slaughter-houses, foul yards, drains and gutters, by hanging a basket containing about seventy pounds of copperas in a barrel of water.

JOSEPH JONES, M. D., President Board of Health.

BOARD OF HEALTH, STATE OF LOUISIANA.

[Circular No. 2.]

Sanitary Measures to be enforced by the Sanitary Inspectors and Police of the City of New Orleans with reference to the conduct of the Nuisance Wharf and the removal and final disposition of Night Soil.

OFFICE BOARD OF HEALTH OF THE STATE OF LOUISIANA. {
State-House, August 3, 1880. }

After a careful inspection of the nuisance wharf, and after the consideration of the complaints of citizens concerning the apparatus, the mode of disinfection and manner of removal and final disposition of night soil by individuals and companies, the following regulations are established for the guidance of the Sanitary Inspectors and Police of the Board of Health of the State of Louisiana :

1. *The contents of privies are not properly and thoroughly disinfected by the various excavating companies. In order to remedy this difficulty each Sanitary Inspector should carry out the following rules, and order his police officers to compel the night soil men and excavating companies to comply fully with the specifications of this circular :

(*a*). Copperas (sulphate of iron) should be used in the preliminary disinfection of the contents of privies in the proportion of four pounds to each barrel of excrement to be removed ; one-half this amount of copperas to be used in solution twenty-four hours before the contents of the vaults are disturbed, and the remainder during the emptying of the privy. Therefore two disinfections should be practiced, namely : The first twenty-four hours before, and the second during the removal of the contents.

(*b*). In order to secure the proper and thorough disinfection of the night soil, the Sanitary Inspectors should issue special orders to the Sanitary Police, detailing them during certain days, or at certain specified periods, to superintend the labors of the vidangeurs during the disinfection and excavation of privies and privy vaults. Stringent orders should be issued by the Sanitary Inspector of each district, through his Sanitary Police, commanding the night soil men to execute the proper disinfection, and at the same time requiring full and specific reports from the police officers.

2. Grave complaints have been made against the imperfect construction and action of the apparatus (pumps, tanks, barrels, etc.), of the various excavating companies.

In order to rectify this difficulty each Sanitary Inspector will at once proceed to inspect and carefully test the apparatus for the excavation of night soil in this district, and at once report all imperfections to the Board of Health. The charges should be specific, so that the necessary legal steps may be taken.

The Sanitary Inspectors of each district should, at intervals of not more than one month, execute similar inspections as previously detailed.

3. In all cases where orders have been issued for the emptying of privies, the Sanitary Inspector should order reinspections for the verification of the execution of the sanitary order. The Sanitary Inspector of each district should also verify the execution of the sanitary ordinances relating to privies, by a comparison of the date and number of the original order, with the date and number of the permit granted by the Board of Health.

4. One or more policemen shall be detailed to superintend the execution of the law with reference to the filling, towing, emptying and cleansing of the nuisance boats. Said policemen shall be under the immediate direction of the sanitary Officer or officers of the district or districts in which the nuisance boat or boats are located.

5. With reference to the nuisance wharf and boats the following points should be observed :

(*a*). The windows of the house devoted to the reception of the night soil should be closed during the emptying of the contents of the barrels into the hold of the nuisance wharf.

(*b*). During the discharge of the excrement into the hold of the nuisance boats fresh air should be fully supplied to the house by means of bellows.

(*c*). The opening for ventilation upon the roof of the house should be sufficiently large, and should be supplied with charcoal furnaces, in which fire shall be kept burning during the discharge of the contents of the barrels.

(*d*). The furnaces covering the ventilators of the nuisance boat should be kept supplied with burning charcoal both during and after the emptying of the contents of the barrels or tanks into the hold of the nuisance wharf.

(*e*). All joints and openings on the nuisance boat should be rendered air-tight by means of canvas saturated with coal-tar.

JOSEPH JONES, M. D.,
President Board of Health State of Louisiana.

The preceding rules and regulations governing the quarantine officers and establishments of the State, and the "Sanitary Inspectors and police of the

14

city of New Orleans, were published and distributed, and were systematically and rigidly enforced by the officers and members of the Board of Health, and there is no reason to doubt for one moment the accuracy of the reports of the medical practitioners of New Orleans, who have ever been distinguished for their extensive learning, skill, philanthropy, and personal integrity.

The Coroner of the city of New Orleans, Dr. J. C. Beard, is also a member of the Board of Health, and in the execution of his arduous duties which were confined to no particular district, but embraced the entire city, has recorded not one death as caused by Yellow Fever; and yet if this disease had influenced to any extent the mortality of New Orleans, such fact could not have escaped the notice of this officer.

On the other hand, the Sanitary Inspectors were charged to take cognizance of all the cases of contagious and infectious diseases occurring in their respective districts, and to institute all necessary measures for their arrest.

In the month of January, 1880, scarlet fever caused 1 death; diptheria 5. February, scarlet fever 1; measles 1; diptheria 4. March, scarlet fever 6; measles 4; diptheria 5. April, scarlet fever 3; measles 20; diptheria 2. May, scarlet fever 5; measles 39; small-pox 1. June, scarlet fever 6; measles 23; diptheria 9. July, scarlet fever 11; measles 9; diptheria 6. August, scarlet fever 4; measles 1; diptheria 7. September, scarlet fever 1; diptheria 3. October, scarlet fever 2; diptheria 13.

It is evident from the preceding record that :

1st. Small-pox occasioned but one death in New Orleans, during the first ten months of 1880. The Secretary had standing orders to furnish all the physicians and Sanitary Inspectors, applying at the office of the Board of Health, with fresh vaccine matter.

2d. Scarlet fever occasioned forty deaths, the largest number (11), occurring in the month of July.

3d. Measles occasioned 97 deaths, the largest number (39), occurring in the month of May. The disease disappeared entirely in the months of September and October.

4th. Diptheria occasioned fifty-four deaths, the highest number (13), occurred in September.

At no time during the first ten months of the year 1880, did small-pox, scarlet fever, measles or diptheria, assume the proportions of epidemics.

In addition to the instructions contained in the preceding circulars, the Sanitary Inspectors received specific orders for the thorough disinfection and cleansing of all the houses and localities in which cases of Yellow Fever had prevailed in 1879.

Two hundred and ten (210) barrels of sulphate of iron (copperas); twelve (12) barrels of sulphur, and two hundred (200) gallons of Calvert's carbolic acid, No. 5, were gratuitously distributed by the Board of Health for the disinfection of the premises of citizens under the immediate supervision of the Sanitary Inspectors and police.

Careful watch was also kept over the mortality of the different districts, in order that local outbreaks of disease might be noted, and that all the known and recognized measures of sanitation might be employed.

The Council of New Orleans, and more especially the Administrator of Improvements (to whom is confided the repair of streets and gutters and the cleaning of the same), were constantly informed as to the sanitary condition of the different districts.

The following tables are of great value in illustrating the the relative mortality, from all causes, and from the various forms of malarial fever in the various districts of New Orleans:

COMPARATIVE TABLE OF MORTALITY OF THE DIFFERENT DISTRICTS OF THE CITY OF NEW ORLEANS DURING THE NINE MONTHS ENDING SEPTEMBER 30, 1880, TOGETHER WITH THE POPULATION, ACCORDING TO THE CENSUS OF 1880, AND THE MORTALITY PER 1000 PER ANNUM:

Months	First District Pop. 57,445 — Number of Deaths	Mortality per 1000 popula'n per annum	Second District Pop. 44,669 — Number of Deaths	Mortality per 1000 popula'n per annum	Third District Pop. 45,588 — Number of Deaths	Mortality per 1000 popula'n per annum	Fourth District Pop. 37,535 — Number of Deaths	Mortality per 1000 popula'n per annum	Fifth District Pop. 8,856 — Number of Deaths	Mortality per 1000 popula'n per annum	Sixth District Pop. 16,029 — Number of Deaths	Mortality per 1000 popula'n per annum	Seventh District Pop. 6,237 — Number of Deaths	Mortality per 1000 popula'n per annum	Number of deaths in Charity Hospital	City of New Orleans Pop. 216,359 — Number of Deaths	Mortality per 1000 popula'n per annum
January	121	25.27	74	19.87	83	21.80	52	16.62	9	9.15	30	22.45	10	19.24	67	446	24.27
February	116	24.23	94	25.47	95	25.00	50	15.99	5	6.77	23	16.59	14	26.93	51	438	24.84
March	110	22.97	78	20.95	91	23.95	53	16.94	12	16.26	12	8.35	7	13.46	39	402	22.29
April	124	25.90	80	21.49	94	24.96	46	14.70	10	13.55	25	18.72	16	30.96	66	461	25.61
May	152	31.75	109	29.28	135	35.53	75	23.97	17	23.03	39	29.19	11	21.16	43	581	32.29
June	135	28.37	119	31.96	137	36.06	81	25.89	21	28.45	29	21.71	7	13.46	44	573	31.78
July	116	24.23	82	22.05	79	20.81	51	16.30	12	16.26	26	19.46	11	21.16	45	422	23.45
August	87	18.17	82	22.05	89	23.44	55	17.58	11	14.90	28	20.96	11	21.16	44	407	22.57
September	89	18.59	110	29.55	86	22.63	63	20.14	10	13.55	33	24.24	16	30.96	43	430	24.95
Total	1050	24.37	898	24.71	899	23.99	526	18.67	107	16.14	245	20.34	103	21.96	442	4180	25.81

DEATHS FROM MALARIAL FEVER IN THE CITY OF NEW ORLEANS DURING THE NINE MONTHS ENDING SEPTEMBER 30, 1880, DISTRIBUTED TO THE DIFFERENT DISTRICTS IN WHICH THEY OCCURRED.

MONTHS	First District	Second District	Third District	Fourth District	Fifth District	Sixth District	Seventh District	Charity Hospital	City of New Orleans
January			3	2			2	1	8
February	2	3	4	2				2	13
March	3	6	1		1	1		3	15
April	4	5	3			1		3	16
May	7	8	9	2		1	1		28
June	6	5	11	8				4	34
July	7	2	10	2		2			25
August	7	4	7	3	2	3	3	5	34
September	13	18	10	13		3	4	4	68
Total	49	51	58	33	3	11	11	22	241

The first of the preceding tables, illustrating the mortality of the different districts of the City of New Orleans during the first nine months of 1880, demonstrates that the death rate of the First District, at the front of which the Excelsior lay, and in which the Touro Infirmary is situated, where the case of Yellow Fever from the Swedish bark terminated fatally, and in which district also another death from Yellow Fever was reported on the fourth of October, has been less than that of the Second and Third Districts, in which no case and no deaths from Yellow Fever were reported. The death rate in the First District was less during the months of August and September than in any preceding months of the year.

In the Fourth Districts, in which the "two so-called suspicious cases" were reported, the lowest death rate, namely, 18.67 has been found.

If the weekly mortality in New Orleans be examined just previous and subsequent to the occurrence of Yellow Fever on the bark Excelsior, it will be seen that no increase was perceptible, but on the contrary there was a remarkable stability in the weekly death rate. Thus for the week ending July 3, 1880, total deaths from all causes, 102 ; death rate for 1000 population per annum, 27.73.

Week ending July 10, deaths 99, rate 24.51.
Week ending July 17, deaths 100, rate 24.76.
Week ending July 24, deaths 93, rate 23.02.
Week ending July 31, deaths 76, rate 18.28.
Week ending August 7, deaths 89 rate 21.04.
Week ending August 14, deaths 72, rate 17.33.
Week ending August 21, deaths 107, rate 25.75.
Week ending August 28, deaths 102, rate 24.55.
Week ending September 4, deaths 102; rate 24.55.
Week ending September 11, deaths 90, rate 21.66.
Week ending September 18, deaths 125, rate 30.57.
Week ending September 25, deaths 104, rate 25.03.
Week ending October 2, deaths 103, rate 24.79.
Week ending October 9, deaths 107, rate 25.75.

It is also worthy of note, that during the past summer and autumn, the mortality was in proportion to population, much heavier amongst the colored population ; the reverse condition, being the case during the existence and prevalence of Yellow Fever.

Thus during the week ending September 11. the total deaths were 90, rate 21.66 ; colored 30.11 ; whites 18.69 ; week ending September 18, deaths 125, rate 30.57 ; whites 24.85 ; colored 46.49 ; week ending September 25, deaths 104, rate 25.03 ; whites 23.54 ; colored 29.19 ; week ending October 2, deaths 103, rate 24.79 ; whites 23.22 ; colored 29.19 ; week ending October 9, deaths 107, rate 25.75 ; whites 21.25 ; colored 38.31.

CASES REPORTED TO THE BOARD OF HEALTH BY THE PHYSICIANS OF THE CITY, WHICH DEMANDED AND RECEIVED SEARCHING INVESTIGATION.

Every case of disease reported to the President of the Board of Health, either verbally or in writing, by any member of the medical profession of New Orleans, received immediate personal attention; and whilst striving to protect the City of New Orleans and Valley of the Mississippi from pestilence, at the same time the voice of the medical profession was not only heard, but duly considered and respected.

Case 1.—On the first of June, 1880, the following case was recorded upon the mortality records of the Board of Health:

Mary E. Heath, aged 8 months; white, native of Louisiana; died on the first of June, 1880, at the residence of her parents on Jackson street, near Locust street; cause of death, scarlet fever; attending physician, C. H. Tebault, M. D.

On the seventh of June, about six days after the death of this child, Dr. Tebault gave a verbal statement to S. S. Herrick, M. D., (Secretary and Treasurer of the Board of Health, and an employe of the State Board in various capacities as Sanitary Inspector and Coal-Oil Inspector, etc., during the various Republican and Democratic administrations of the State, since the year 1872), in which he intimated that the case was of a "suspicious character." The statement of Dr. Tebault will be found in the note below :*

---

* NEW ORLEANS, June 7, 1880.

Dr. S. S. Herrick, Secretary Board of Health:

Dear Sir—The brief verbal statement left this morning at your office was all I expected necessary in connection with the case referred to. On returning home this evening I find on my slate a request for all the information in my knowledge with respect to the said case. During the latter part of April I attended a case of scarlet fever in this family (Edward Heath, Jackson, near Locust street), and reported the same to your office. This case recovered. I took all proper steps against the disease spreading to the two other children. The two living children, I will here remark, had Yellow Fever, and were treated by me during the year 1878; therefore I know this fact. The child now under consideration was, if I remember right, between eight and nine months old, and consequently this was its first summer. Last Friday, I believe, was the day this child died. Your records will show the positive date. However that may be, what facts I possess are briefly these: Some six days, or perhaps five days before the child's death, the father, Mr. Heath, came for me. I told him I could not possibly attend the child; he then asked me to call in the morning, and I again stated that I could not, for reasons then given, and not pertinent here. He begged me to try and do so. I then told him I would try, but that if I were not there (his house), by 10 in the morning that it would be an indication that my standing engagements were in the way, and that he must not expect me at all. Two days later, to my surprise, he called again; (I could not see, and had not seen the child so far), and told me the child was very sick; that he had filled my scarlet fever prescriptions employed in the case here above-mentioned, and had been using them, but that the child seemed growing worse. He again asked me to see the child. I censured him for neglecting his child in this way, and in attempting to force upon my hands when I had given such proper and ample reasons why I could not charge myself with the treatment of the case I told him that he must get another and a nearer doctor; that I could not go. The next evening he again called; told me he had gotten no one else; that the child was dying, and he wanted me just to visit his house once in order, if the child died, to give a certificate, and so avoid the necessity for the Coroner. I at once made this visit (at 6:30 p. m. of the day the child died) I found the child rejecting everything, and purging and vomiting such matter as you would expect from a Yellow Fever case; that the eyes and skin wore the peculiar appearance found in the last stages of Yellow Fever, as also the gums and lining membrane of the mouth and throat; that there had been more or less suppression of urine throughout the attack, and especially so during the last twenty-four hours; that there had been a rash, which they took for scarlet fever, and treated for such. When I saw the case the child was yet able to swallow, there being no throat difficulty, and retained what I gave with difficulty, and as long as I remained. The child lay in a semi-comatose condition, noticing no one. This child died within the next two hours.

I signed the certificate scarlet fever, but the more I have reflected over the case, the more I am impressed with its suspicious character, and with this impression upon my mind I thought it right to make the same known to you. I have written very hurriedly, but I trust intelligently.

Yours, respectfully, C. H. TEBAULT, M. D.

On or about the 8th of June, S. S. Herrick, Secretary and Treasury of the Board of Health, directed the attention of the President to the satement of Dr. Tebault.

An immediate investigation was instituted, and the following facts ascertained:

Mary E. Heath, daughter of Rosa and Charles Heath, residence 495 Jackson street, near Locust street, 4th District New Orleans.

Mr. and Mrs. Heath have had three children, namely: Henry, age 8 years, Sarah 5 years and Mary, 8 months. The two eldest children suffered with Yellow Fever in 1878, and were attended by Dr. Tebault.

Charles Heath was attacked with scarlet fever about the 1st of May 1880. Sarah was attacked with scarlet fever on or about the 15th of May. At the time of the personal inspection by the President of the Board of Health, this child was undergoing the desquamatum process and had not yet fully recovered from the effects of the scarlet fever.

The infant, Mary E. Heath, was attacked with Yellow Fever, May 22, and died June 1, 1880.

The mother stated that the scarlet fever rash was very well marked on the third day of the fever.

Two days before death, vomited dark greenish matter and also passed black matter from the bowels. The matter vomited were described as being of a dark green color.

In the light of the periods of incubation and of all the facts it was impossible to regard the case as anything but scarlet fever, and the President of the Board of Health, called personally upon Dr. Tebault and stated this decision and presented all the facts elicited by the investigation.

In order, however, to give the City of New Orleans the benefit of any difference of opinion, the efficient Sanitary Inspector of the Fourth District was directed to execute the following measures:

1st. The careful house-to-house inspection and disinfection of the premises 495 Jackson street, and of all the houses and premises within a radius of three blocks.

2d. Careful observation of this portion of the city, and immediate report of each and every case demanding investigation.

3d. Reinspection and additional disinfection of all localities of the Fourth District in which Yellow Fever had occurred in 1879.

(6). Shortly after the preceding occurrence, S. S. Herrick, M. D., informed the resident member of the National Board of Health that he had heard a rumor, that Yellow Fever had appeared at the Jetties, at the mouth of the Mississippi River.

When said statement of S. S Herrick, M. D., was communicated to the President of the State Board by the representative of the National Board telegrams were immediately dispatched to Pilot Town, Port Eads and the Mississippi Quarantine Station.

The responses showed conclusively, not only that no case of Yellow Fever had occurred at the settlements on the mouths of the Mississippi River, but that the inhabitants of these places were absolutely free from sickness of any character whatsoever.

These facts with the details of the case of Dr. Tebault, were duly laid before the Board of Health.

(2). On the thirteenth of July, the following death certificate was reported to the Board of Health:

Wilhelm W. Motts, age 5 years, native of New Orleans, died on the thirteenth of July, 1880, at 229 Customhouse street; cause of death, malarial fever. J. Borde, M. D.

On the thirteenth of July, Dr. Borde requested the President of the Board of Health to examine the corpse of this child, lying at 229 Customhouse street, stating that he had visited the patient on the evening of the twelfth, for the first time, and that the patient had died in convulsions, after a profuse hemorrhage from the stomach. Dr. Borde also kindly furnished a small bottle containing the matter ejected from the stomach. After the microscopical examination, which demonstrated the ejected matter to be blood, with no perceptible alterations of the colored blood copsules, the President accompanied Dr. Borde and inspected the corpse.

The entire face and body was pale, anaemic and bloodless; conjunctiva of eyes white; lips, tongue and gums pale.

The corpse presented no appearance of Yellow Fever.

After canvassing the symptoms with Dr. Borde, the conclusion was reached that this was a case of hæmorrhagic fever, instances of which have before occurred in the extended experience of this successful practitioner, even during the months of winter.

As the entire neighborhood was in bad sanitary condition, owing to the imperfect grading and construction of the gutters, the Sanitary Inspector of the Second District was ordered to institute a thorough house-to-house inspection and disinfection of the immediate and surrounding premises, and to hold this locality under careful observation.

No other case of hæmorrhagic malarial fever occurred in this neighborhood.

(3). On the 2nd of August, Dr. Charles Faget requested the President of the Board of Health, to visit with him a case of hæmorrhagic malarial fever, at the corner of Chartres and Hospital streets. The following facts were elicited: the patient Albert Willoz, age 18 years, native of New Orleans, had passed through the epidemics of 1867 and 1878, and had never had any connection with the shipping of New Orleans, was employed in a shoe store corner Chartres and Hospital streets. Attacked with fever July 30, at 3 p. m., quinine was freely administered, July 31, bilious vomiting, tongue coated with whitish fur, Dr. Faget visited this patient for the first time at 6 p. m., and finding the fever high, which had increased at 3 p. m., he ordered the continuance of the quinine, the patient having taken between the hours of 7 a. m., and 12 m., twenty grains of quinine. At 3 p. m., three hours before the visit of Dr. Faget, the patient had been seized with bilious vomiting, and threw up matter as yellow as gold. At this hour the fever increased, and at 9 p. m., the fever was still more intense. Vomited again after having taken 12 grains of quinine in 3 grain doses. The vomiting was bilious during the night, and the patient suffered with high fever and violent delirium and was with difficulty kept in bed.

August 1—5 a. m. to 6 a. m.—Great abatement of fever. At this time the matter ejected from the stomach commenced to present a black color, complained of ringing in the ears, pain in the side, with constipation, urine very scanty, yellow and clear; in fact, the patient had urinated but twice since the onset of the fever. Heat and nitric acid revealed the entire absence of albumen. Pulse 93; temperature 103; although to the touch the surface appeared to be cool. At night, pulse 80, temperature 102.6. August 2—Vomited three times during the night; having drank milk at 9 o'clock p. m., the first vomitting occurred at 11 p. m., and the vomited matter presented the appearance of chocolate. The second vomitting occurred at 1 o'clock p. m. and was black, so also that at 2 a. m., August 3.

August 3—Urine clear, of yellow color, and when tested was found to be entirely free from albumen; pulse 72; temperature 103; tongue coated with white fur. Pharanyx scarlet as in scarlet fever; skin natural to the touch, except near the ears where there is heat. Ringing in the ears diminished. Nine grains of quinine administered during the night. Continued to improve; convalescence rapid and no jaundice. The report of Dr. Fayet will be found in the note below. *

At the time of my visit the patient was convalescent.

The vomited matter had been preserved by Dr. Faget, and upon microscopical examination were found to contain colored blood corpuscles.

The urine was carefully tested for albumen, and also subjected to thorough microscopical examination; neither albumen nor casts were discovered.

The patient gave forth a sour smell like that of malarial fever, and did not emit the odor of Yellow Fever.

I concurred entirely with Dr. Faget, that this was a case of hemorrhagic malarial fever.

No other case of this disease occurred in this locality.

The mother of the patient stated that whenever her children had been attacked with fever they always vomited bloody matter, regardless of the season of the year, and the nature of the prevailing disease.

(4). On the 5th of August, 1880, Dr. J. D. Hunter, requested the President of the Board of Health, to visit with him two cases of fever, at the corner of Poyfarre and Annunciation streets in the old Brewery Building, Dr. Hunter regarded these cases as presenting some of the features of Yellow Fever; which request was complied with.

The patients Pat and Owen Woods, brothers were natives of New Orleans, and respectively 28 and 30 years of age.

They had each suffered with a fever of 5 days' duration, the temperature steadily declining as well as the pulse from the onset.

Both were convalescent at the time of the inspection and one was up and dressed.

Dr. Hunter informed me that in neither case was any albumen detected in the urine.

The patients were free from all evidences of jaundice, although upon the first day the temperature of Pat Woods was 104, and of Owen Woods 104.5. There was no peculiar odor, such as is characteristic of Yellow Fever, and

---

* Report of Haemontagic Malarial Fever by Dr. Charles Faget.

Albert Willoz,—né à la Nouvelle Orleans qu'il n'a jamais quittée, même pendant l'epidémies ; travaille comme comis dans un magazin de chaussures, a l'encoignure Main et Royal et habite le rez de chaussée tres humide qui fait l'encoignure Chartres et Hopital.

Vendredi 3 Juillet 1880, il a été pris de fiévre dans l'apres midi vers 3 heures ; céphalalgie, mais pas de rachialgie ; transpiration chaude énorme. On lui donne 5 grains de quinine en pilule ; 2 heures plus tard il les rejette avec du melon qu'il avait mange avant la fiévre.

Samedi matin, 31, la fiévre continuait. On lue administre de 7 heures à midi 2o grains de sulf quinine en pilules, sommeil profond ; pas de soif.

Vers 3 heures Vomissement Billieu (jaune comme de l'or.) pas de bourdonnements d'oreilles ; langue blanche comme du coton.

1ere visite du médecin, vers 6 heures du soir ; il constate une fievre ardente et se contente de conseiller la continuation de la quinine. Le redoublement de fievre avait commence vers trois heures ; vers 9 heures du soir fievre encore plus forte, vomissements, apres avoir pris 12 grains de quinine par doces de 3 grains ; les vomissements sont toujours jaunes. Pendant toute la nuit, grande fiévre, délire violent: on a de la peine à retenir le malade dans son lit.

Dimanche matin 1er Août, de 5 a 6 heures du matin la fiévre s'étant beaucoup calmé, les vomissements jaunes bilieux commencent à présenter des grumeaux noirs. Onze graines de sulfate ont été gardés dans la nuit ; bourdonnements d'oreille: pour la première fois accuse des douleurs de reins ; constipation ; urine très rare, jaune et claire , (en fait cétait pour la seconde fois qu'il urinait depuis le début de la fiévre), poul à 96 ; le thermométre donne 103, cependant au toucher la sensation perçu par la main est celle de la temperature normale.

Le soir de ce même 1er Août, le poul donne 80 et le thermométre 102,6.

Lundi 2 Août. Il y a eu trois vomissements dans la nuit ; ayant bu du lait vers 9 heures, le premier vomissement à 11 heures est la couleur chocolat ; le second, à une heure du matin est noir ; le troisième, à 2 heures est noir aussi. (Les décrire....) Une selle naturelle, moulée brune, dans la nuit on a recueilli à part la valeur de deux verres d'urine ; elle est claire, jaune, et ne décèle point d'albumine par l'acide nitrique.

Poul 72 ; thermométre 102 ; langue toujours blanche, bord rouge ; phargnx ecarlate comme dans la Scarlatine ; peau naturelle au toucher, excepté au cou, vers les oreilles, ou il y a de la chaleur ; la sudite, et les bourdonnements d'oreilles diminuent, a garde 19 grains de sulfate dans la nuit.

there had been no vomiting and no albumen in the urine. Quinine had been freely administered both internally and externally by inemation. I expressed the opinion that they were cases of malarial remittent fever and not Yellow Fever.

Dr. Hunter has since expressed the view that they were cases of *dangue fever.* The Old Brewing Building was originally the residence of a sugar planter when this section of the city was cultivated. It is probably one of the oldest buildings above Canal street in what now constitutes the First District.

The entire building and premises were in a most dilapidated and unsanitary condition, and were occupied by several families.

In accordance with the orders of the President of the Board of Health, the old brewery was disinfected and fumigated, and held under careful supervision. These measures gave rise to unfounded rumors, which found a lodgment with the New Orleans Auxiliary Sanitary Association.

The Sanitary Inspector of the First District was directed to inspect and disinfect the neighborhood.

Although some twenty people, men, women and children inhabited this dilapidated building, no other case of fever was reported.

5. On the twenty-second of August, 1880, Dr. F. S. Kennedy, Jr., made a verbal communication to the President of the Board of Health, to the effect that he had treated a case, which he regarded as Yellow Fever. The patient a young man, a native of New Orleans, was attacked on the fifth of August, *seventeen* days previous to his interview with the President of the Board of Health.

Dr. Kennedy stated that the patient was convalescent on the 16th of August, but that he had not yet informed the patient that he had suffered with Yellow Fever.

Dr. Kennedy declined giving a written report of the case, and also declined to have his patient interviewed by the President of the Board of Health.

Here was a case reported verbally to the President of the Board of Health seventeen days after its occurrence.

Instructions were immediately issued to the Sanitary Inspector of the First District to commence a rigid house-to-house inspection and disinfection, commencing at the river front of the First District and extending back to the rear of the city. He was also directed to furnish all information relating to the prevalence of any fever which had any resemblance to Yellow Fever.

After the execution of the inspections and disinfections, the Sanitary Inspector discovered no case of Yellow Fever in the First District.

6. On the seventh of September Dr. George Howe sent the President of the Board of Health a brief note, (which reached his residence about 9 o'clock at night) to the effect that he had a patient in the Parish of St. Bernard, one mile below the United States Barracks, at the place of Mr. Leon Solis, adjoining the upper side of the United States Cemetery.

Dr. Howe stated that the patient, a boy aged eight years, was a native of Louisiana, and had been brought with his mother and several other children from the Parish of Plaquemine. Was taken ill the day of his arrival, three days before the date of his note of the 7th. On the evening of the second day of illness was taken with black vomit in abundance :

The note of Dr. Howe will be found below *

---

* NEW ORLEANS, September 7, 1880.—Joseph Jones, M. D., President Board of Health, New Orleans, La. :
Dear Doctor—I have a little patient, a boy, aged about eight years, born in Louisiana; residence, parish of Plaquemines until three days' since, and now in the parish of St. Bernard, one mile from United States Barracks. Taken ill day of arrival. Suppression of urine since yesterday morning; black vomit since last even

I rose at 4 a. m. in the morning and took the car at 5 a. m., at the corner of Washington and Magazine streets, and reached the residence of Dr. Howe in the Third District, corner of Chartres and Bartholomew streets, about 6 a. m., and in company with Dr. Howe, reached the place of Mr. Leon Solis one mile from the barracks in the Parish of St. Bernard.

The patient (Anthony Anrosettæ, age 7 years, arrived from Point Michel on the 4th of September), had died during the night.

The corpse was carefully inspected. The entire surface presented a pale ex-sanguid appearance, the whites of the eyes were perfectly clear, the lips and gums pale and bloodless, rigor mortis well marked. Was shown the bed linen stained with black vomit.

The corpse presented the same general characteristics with that of the case of Dr. Borde previously reported.

The rapidity with which the profuse hæmorrhage from the stomach had occurred, namely, on the second day of the disease, as well as the absence of yellow discoloration of the skin, and whites of the eyes and the general ex-sanguined appearance of the corpse, led me to the conclusions, that this was a case of hæmorrhagic malarial fever.

These views were fully explained to Dr. Howe, who signed the death certificate hæmorrhagic malarial fever.

Another child of the same family, from the same locality, was sick with intermittent fever in the adjoining room.

I gathered from the remarks of the attending physician that the first case had not been regarded as serious until the supervention of hæmorrhage from the stomach.

The mother of these children stated that she was nearly related to Giordano, and lived only two blocks from his house, and that rice was cultivated in the rear of the settlement.

I advised the burial of the corpse upon the premises, or in the United States Cemetery, and stated that the sanitary ordinances of the Board of Health of the city prohibited the bringing of the bodies of those dying with acute diseases within the Parish of Orleans for interment.

The attending physician was advised to institute such sanitary measures as he deemed best, and in accordance with his view of the case.

The preceding facts were communicated to the Board of Health at the next meeting. The report of this meeting of the Board of Health will be given in the conclusion of this report, which treats of the malarial fever of Plaquemine Parish.

7. On Sunday evening, September 12, Dr. W. H. Watkins informed the President of the Board of Health, by a brief note, that a case of fever on Josephine street, between Liberty and Howard (Fourth District) presented symptoms worthy of investigation.

On Monday morning I called at the office of Dr. Watkins and ascertained

---

ing. Pulse from 90 to 95; temperature 104½ to 103½. Will die to night and probably be sent to the parish of Plaquemines for burial.

I hesitate to name a disease which will carry so much of terror with the announcement and do not desire my name to be associated with such publicity, but my duty requires me to make this statement to you. Four deaths in one family of a similar disease have occurred during a few days past in the parish Plaquemines, near Pointe-a-la-Hache, and the people, neighbors and relations, fled to the vicinity of New Orleans. One other child has been ill, and now convalescent from malarial fever since arrival, three days since.

I will return there to-morrow morning about eight o'clock, and if you desire any further information and would like any one to go I would be only too glad to be of service. The distance is only one mile from the Barracks, at Mr. Leon Solis, and adjoining United States Cemetery (upper side).

The black vomit is in abundance and has all the characteristics of that of 1878. I have ordered some of the clothing covered with it to be put aside for your information.

Very respectfully yours. etc.,   S. W. HOWE, M. D.,
                                             Corner Chartres and Bartholomew streets.

P. S.—If the parties should wish to bring the child in the city, what would you suggest. Also in the event of transportation to Pointe-a-la-Hache, what would you suggest.

Yours, in haste,   HOWE.

that the child had died at 7:30 p. m., the preceding night. I proceeded at once to the residence on Josephine street, between Liberty and Howard, and carefully examined the corpse.

The corpse of the child, aged three years, presented a similar appearance to that described in the cases of Drs. Borde and Howe. Surface pale and ex-sanguine; lips and gums pale and bloodless; whites of eyes perfectly clear.

The mother stated that her child (Thomas Wilkinson) had suffered with Yellow Fever in 1878. She also stated that profuse hæmorrhage had occurred from both stomach and bowels before death.

I regarded this case as one of hæmorrhagic malarial fever. The report of Dr. Watkins will be found in the note below.*

(3). On the night of the eighteenth of September, Dr. W. H. Watkins, Sanitary Inspector of the Third District, requested the President of the Board of Health to visit, on the following morning (nineteenth) a case in the Fourth District, near his residence.

On the morning of the nineteenth, I found the child (L. H., aged 11 years, white girl) with a temperature of 104°; face was flushed; whites of eyes perfectly clear, lips and tongue not specially red; gums pale and firm. Dr. Watkins' observations showed that there was a progressive rise of temperature from the first to the third day. Thus: 1st day, a. m., 103, p. m., 103.5°; 2d day, a. m., 103.5°, p. m., 104°; 3d day, a m., 104°, p. m., 105°. During this period the pulse had manifested marked oscillations, thus: 1st day, a. m., 110, p. m., 100°; 2d day, a. m., 100; 3d day. a. m., 100–120.

Weighing the symptoms and giving due weight to the absence of all delerium, and to the absence of jaundice and capillary congestion of the gums, eyes and face, and also to the total absence of all disagreeable odor, I expressed the decided opinion that this case was similar to the malarial remittent fever, prevailing in various portions of the city. In the note below will be found the statement of Dr. Watkins.†

NEW ORLEANS, La., September 15, 1880.

Joseph Jones, M. D., President Board of Health:

* Sir:—At your request I take pleasure in reporting all the facts that have been elicited in regard to the case of " congestive fever ' occurring on Josephine street, between Liberty and Howard streets Fourth District.

Thomas Wilkinson, white, a native of New Orleans, aged three years and nine months, was taken sick on Thursday, September the 9th. at 5 p. m. The symptoms present were fever and slight cough. Was seen by a physician on Friday the 10th. fever continuing. On Saturday the fever was still high and that evening the child had an action from its bowels containing blood mixed with thin watery fœcal matter. On Sunday morning the child passed several stools of black, tarry matter. Sunday evening vomiting occurred and the matter ejected was black, resembling the " black vomit" of Yellow Fever. Slight convulsions soon came on and black matter was gulped up occasionally with a slight hiccough. Death occurred Sunday, September 12, at 7.30 p. m. Would state that the secretion of urine had been free up to Sunday morning. It is not known whether any was passed subsequent to that time.

The mother of the child states that she lived in the same place in 1873, where she now resides, and that during the epidemic of 1878 the child was seriously sick with Yellow Fever.

In company with yourself, I made a careful inspection of the body early Monday morning. It presented a pale waxy appearance on the face and breast; the ears and posterior portion of the neck were mottled with purplish discolorations. The scleotic coat and conjuntivæ of eyes were remarkably clear and white. The lips were slightly blue and the gums were pale and bloodless.

The bedding and clothing of the child, soiled during sickness, were gathered together immediately after the child's death and placed in a tub. They were inspected early Monday morning and the dark stains from the vomited matter were distinctly seen. These articles were placed in water and thoroughly boiled.

The body of the child was placed in a coffin early on the morning of the 13th, (Monday) and the lid was screwed down. The funeral took place at 4 p. m. The sanitary officers of the Fourth District, as soon as the body was taken from the house, commenced the usual process of fumigation and disinfection. Sulphur was burned in the rooms and carbolic acid scattered throughout the premises, and the privy-vault disinfected with copperas and carbolic acid. I do not know the quantity of disinfecting material used. The house remained closed about four hours.

The immediate neighborhood where the child lived is healthy. No severe illness having occurred before or since this case. Dengue is prevailing to a limited extent.

Respectfully,
W. H. WATKINS, M. D.
Sanitary Inspector, Third District.

†DEAR DOCTOR—I have a case of fever (now in the fourth day of disease) that presents symptoms requiring thorough investigation. The temperature yesterday morning was 103, in the evening 105; this morning 104½, this evening 105. The pulse this morning while the temperature was 104½ was 103; this evening the pulse is 130. The urine is slightly albuminous and the vomit is full of black specks and floculi; pain

From the report of Dr. Watkins, it is evident that the fever in this case, continuing for a period of over 120 hours, with daily oscillations; that it reached its achme on the evening of the third day and then steadily declined.

The two cases reported by Dr. Watkins, were communicated by him to the Resident member of the National Board of Health, and constituted the so-called two " suspicious cases," which occurred within three squares of the fatal case on the fourth of October, at 409 Liberty street.

It is due to Dr. Watkins to state, that while being employed as Sanitary Inspector by the Board of Health, he also occupied the position of associate editor of the New Orleans Medical and Surgical Journal, with the Resident Member of the National Board of Health and S. S. Herrick, M. D.

(9). On the twentieth of September, in company with Dr. Poincy, I visited a child on Esplanade street, near corner of Royal street, who had vomitted some " black matter." Child pale and anæmic; lips and gums pale; urine abundant and free from albumen. The mother of this child was a native of the city of Mexico. The diagnosis of the attending physician, that this was a case of hæmorrhagic malarial fever, was concurred in, and the free use of quinine by external application recommended.

This case recovered and no others were reported in this section of the city.

(10). On the 25th of September, Dr. John Del Orto, requested me to visit with him an Italian who had been seized with fever at Point Michel, and had been brought to an Italian tenement house, on Bourbon, between Dumaine and St. Philip street.

The patient was very restless, and pulseless. No jaundice or vomiting of black matter; whites of the eyes clear.

The man had been harvesting rice in the fields in and around Point Michel. The following are the notes of this case as furnished by Dr. Del Orto.

"Bilious remittent fever from rice plantations."

"Augustino Latareano, a native of Italy, age 30 years 18 months in Louisiana, came to New Orleans from rice plantations below the city where he had been sick, three or four days before. I saw him on the 20th, the fever was of a remittent type and yielded to quinine. On the 22nd he was better, sleeping well and having good appetite. On the 23rd, on account of being

---

in epigastrium, and slight delirium: eyes clear and white and gums pale; tongue slightly coated and not at all red. Should you be able to see the case to-night, I am at your service. If to morrow morning suits better, call then. Your obedient servant, W. H. WATKINS, M. D.
Dr. Joseph Jones, President Board of Health, Sept. 18, 1880.

NEW ORLEANS, LA., September 23, 1880.

Dr. Joseph Jones President Board of Health:

Sir—I have the honor to report that the following case has come under my observation, and on account of conflicting rumors in regard to it, I have deemed it important to furnish you with its complete history.

Lizzie H.; native of New Orleans, white, aged 11 years. She was taken sick on Thursday, September 16, 1880, at 3 a. m. Her previous health had been good She had always lived in New Orleans, and had passed through the epidemic of Yellow Fever in 1878 without taking that disease. When seen at 9 o'clock the temperature was 103, pulse 110; great restlessness; face pale, but arms and legs congested presenting a decided rosy blush; skin hot and dry; the temperature in the morning was 103 5, pulse 100. Friday, September 17—The temperature was 103.5, pulse 100; in the morning temperature was 104. On Saturday morning, September 18, the temperature was 104, pulse 100; at 10 a. m. it had reached 104½, pulse 120. Vomiting had occurred just before observation was taken. Vomiting occurred several times during the day, and pain of a burning character was complained of in the epigastrium. The matter vomited during the day was was only the milk and seltzer water which she had taken. At night her restlessness increased and the matter vomited consisted of mucus, with a large number of black specks scattered through it. The masses of black substance were ultimately mixed with the mucus, and in some instances presented spots the diameter of a nickel. The urine at this time was examined and found to be albuminous. Tube casts were found, and epithelium from the uretra and bladder. On Sunday morning, September 19, the temperature was 104, pulse 110, at 8 a. m. temperature still the same, pulse 120; temperature at night 104. On Monday morning, September 20, temperature was 102.5; evening temperature 103 Tuesday morning, September 21, temperature normal.

At no time was there any congestion of the face The eyes were clear. Conjunctive white and glistening; the gums were firm and pale; the tongue rather large, was coated and rather red at the edges. There was no bleeding from the nose or gums.

The period of convalesence was remarkably short. There was no prostration, and to-day, September 23, she is up in the room, and except for prudential reasons, would be out of the house.
Very respectfully, W. H. WATKINS, M. D., 498 South Franklin Street.

busy, I did not see the patient, but against my advice he took a strong purgative. Since then he had several bilious vomitings and profuse evacuations and restless nights. The temperature on the evening of the 24th, was 101°. He died on the night of the 25th, with diminished secretion of urine and yellow skin. Conjunctiva was clear. No black vomit."

It is worthy of note that although this man died in a crowded Italian tenement house, and in a room occupied by four Italians, not another case of fever occurred, as I was informed by Dr. Del Orto on the twenty-fifth of November.

Two of the Giordano children were brought to the city of New Orleans from Point Michel. Both these cases were treated by Dr. H. S. Lewis, one of the most experienced, accomplished, and successful practitioners in Louisiana. One of these cases died and the other recovered.

Dr. Lewis declares, positively and unequivocally, that these were cases of the well known and often described pernicious malarial, fever and had no resemblance to Yellow Fever.

During the months of October and November, I have treated a number of cases of malarial fever from the rice fields below the city, and from the vicinity of Point Michel.

In every case and in every variety of the form, whether attended with jaundice or not, they yielded to antiperiodic remedies, and bore no resemblance to Yellow Fever.

(11), A death from Yellow Fever was reported by Drs. Watkins and Davidson, on the fourth of October, at 409 Liberty street, First District. The report of Dr. Watkins will be found in the note below.*

Dr. Watkins furnished some fragments of the liver, which upon microscopical examination did not present the accumulation of oil globules within and around the hepatic cells, usually found in the Yellow Fever liver.

As President of the Board of Health I have interrogated the most promi-

---

NEW ORLEANS, LOUISIANA, October 7, 1880.

Dr. Joseph Jones, President Board of Health.

* Sir:—I have the honor to report, herewith, the history of the case of *Yellow Fever*, occurring at No. 409 South Liberty street, terminating fatally October 4, 18-0, at 10 o'clock p. m.

Fred A. Singer aged 18 years and 9 months, white a native of New Orleans, by occupation an assistant to a fresco painter, came from McComb City, Mississippi. August 29 1880. He immediately repaired to the place where he died. and commenced work under the supervision of his uncle, Mr. Hauk. He worked last at the corner of Louisiana avenue and Chestnut streets.

He came home after he had completed his work, on the evening of Thursday September 30, and partook of a hearty supper. About 9 p. m he was seized with a chill and vomited his supper. He soon had high fever. The fever continued unabated and on Friday and Saturday, October 1 and 2 the nurse reports that h s skin was hot and dry. On Saturday October 2, his restlessness was a marked symptom. At 1.30 p. m. this day he threw up black vomit and had retention of urine Temperature 105°, pulse 100. At night his temperature was 105°, pulse 104. On Sunday morning O. tober 3, his temperature was 105°. pulse 106 Evening temperature 105°, pulse 110. On October 4. at 8 a. m., his temperature was 105°, pulse 110. At 3 p. m. temperature 104½°. pulse 110. At that time he was sweating profusely. Respiration 40 per minute, and death occurred at 10 o'clock p. m.

When seen first on the 2nd of October, his eyes were injected and skin presenting a congested appearance. His tongue was coated with edges red. Albumen was not present at that time. He threw up black vomit several times before death and the urine drawn from his bladder ten hours before death, was one-third albuminous. He was hard to arouse, was dull for the last 48 hours of his life, and had considerable delirium.

He had lived in New Orleans until three or four months ago, passed through the epidemics of 1876 and 1878, but had never had Yellow Fever.

Post mortem examination held in presence of Drs. Bemiss, Davidson, Shepard and myself, ten hours after death.

Rigor mortis well marked. Hypostatic congestion considerable. Face and breast of a light yellow color, lower extremities quite natural in color. Conjunctiva slightly yellow.

On opening the abdomen, the sub-mucous fat and cellular tissue was yellow. The liver was lighter colored than normal. The edges were olive green. The gall bladder contained ⅔ oz of bile. The spleen was very small, weighing not more than 3½ ounces, was shrivelled and firm. cutting hard

The stomach contained about 1 oz. of black vomit, was contracted and presented hæmorrhagic spots.

Kidneys not examined as tube casts and albuminous urine had been found.

I should state that hæmorrhage from the nose occurred twenty-four hours before death.

The body was buried at 10 a. m., October 5. Having been wrapped in a sheet saturated with carbolic acid.

The premises No. 409 south Liberty street were fumigated and disinfected, under the care of Dr. Joseph Holt, the efficient Sanitary Inspector of the First District.

Very Respectfully,   W. H. WATKINS, M. D.,
498 South Franklin street.

nent practitioners of medicine in the city of New Orleans with reference to the alleged existence of cases of Yellow Fever in this city during the past year, and in every case the response has been that not a case has occurred in their practice. During the past summer and autumn I have treated over one hundred cases of the various forms of malarial fever and the prevailing dengue, without a single fatal issue; and all cases yielded to the early and energetic administration of quinine. In all cases critically observed, distinct remissions could be detected*

About the middle of September I suffered with high fever and intense pains in the back and head. The temperature reached 105.5°. Quinine finally arrested the paroxysm, but the strength was prostrate for a considerable period. I suffered severely with dengue in 1873, and with Yellow Fever in 1878. Both in the malarial paroxysmal fevers and in the dengue which prevailed to so great an extent, the temperature frequently reached 105.°, and it was noticed that in many cases of dengue and remittent fever, the pulse was remarkably slow during convalescence.

The following correspondence illustrate the experience of some of the practitioners of New Orleans, and at the same time throws some light upon the so-called " suspicious cases ":

BOARD OF HEALTH, STATE-HOUSE, STATE OF LOUISIANA. }
New Orleans, October 9, 1880. }

Joseph Holt, M. D., Sanitary Inspector, First District :

Sir—Your attention is respectfully directed to the following extract from the Galveston News of October 7, 1830, with reference to the recent meeting of the Board of Health of Houston, Texas :

The Board of Health held a meeting at 3 o'clock this afternoon ; present, Mayor Baker, Aldermen Kennedy, House, Curtin and Thomas. The Mayor stated that the call was made to take action on the Yellow Fever reports from New Orleans.

Dr. Rutherford, who was present, was called on to present his views, and did so, presenting the following dispatches :

NEW ORLEANS, Oct. 6.—Rutherford : Ten (10) suspicious cases occurred within three (3) squares of last case within four weeks No known connection between them The man came from McComb City, August 29; was ignorant. No one can tell his personal history shortly before the attack. BEMISS.

During the past four weeks only two so-called suspicious cases have been reported to the Board of Health in the First and Fourth Districts, and these occurred in the practice of Dr. Wm. H. Watkins, who resides at the corner of Franklin and Josephine Streets.

The man referred to in the telegram of the member of the National Board of Health, residing in this city, died at 400 South Liberty Street, October 4, 1880.

*I extract the following cases from my note book :
Case 1 - Mr. McG., merchant, August 12, 1880, seized with high fever and intense pains in the head and back. 13th, temperature 103°, pulse 100; 14th, a. m., temperature 101 2°, pulse 86; 15th, p. m., temperature 101.8°, pulse 70; 16th, a. m., temperature 102 8, pulse 86 ; 17th, temperature 99°, pulse 70.
Case 2 - Mrs. C , age 30. October 18, a. m., temperature 105.8°, pulse 82, p. m., temperature 105°, pulse 100 ; 19th. a. m., temperature 102.3°, pulse 92, p. m., temperature 103°, pulse 96 ; 20th. a. m., temperature 102.2°, pulse 78, p. m., temperature 101.5°, pulse 84 ; 21st, temperature 96.5°, pulse 50, p. m., pulse 60, 22d, a. m., temperature 98.5°, pulse 58.
Case 3 - Mr. C., October 19 temperature 103.5°, pulse 102 ; 20th, temperature 101.9°, pulse 80.
Case 4 - B. P.; native of Ohio, age 10 years, occupation fireman on railroad. Came to New Orleans from West Virginia the latter part of October. Was taken sick with high fever, pains in his back and head a few days after his arrival and was admitted to the Charity Hospital November 1. The following is the range of his temperature and pulse, November 3, a. m.: Temperature 105 1, pulse 105, respiration 30, p. m , temperature 106, pul e 108, respiration 23. November 5th, a. m., temperature 103, pulse 102 respiration 22; p. m., pulse 94, respiration 20; 6th, a. m., temperature 104, pulse 87, respiration 23, 7th, a. m., temperature 101.3. pulse 90, 8th, a. m., temperature 103 5, pulse 83; 9th, a. m., temperature 103, pulse 92 ; 10th, a. m., temperature 101.3, pulse 102; 11th, a. m., temperature 103, pulse 98 ; 12th, a. m., temperature 101, pulse 96; 13th a. m., pulse 100, temerature 101.02 ; 14th, a. m., temperature 104, pulse 96, 15th, a. m., temperature 103 5 pulse 90 ; 16th, a. m., temperature 103, pulse 92, p. m , pulse 96; 17th, a m., temperature 101, pulse 88 p. m ; pulse 96; 18th, a. m , temperature 101 pulse 94, p. m , pulse 95 ; 19th, a m , temperature 101.5, pulse 92; 20th, a. m., temperature 101.5 pulse 88; 21st, a. m., temperature 100, pulse 90, 22d, a. m., temperature 100, pulse 88. On the 6th, belly swollen and tympanitic; eyes clear; no jaundice; bowels loose and copious bilious discharges
November 7; during the night bled very freely from the nose, and passed blood from the bowels, also vomited black matter; urine contained albumen and bile. The albumen continued for three days, when all traces disappeared. Urine abundant and orange red color throughout the attack.
Throughout the attack treated with sulphate of quinia internally and externally, and strength sustained with beef tea. Although in this case hemorrhage from the stomach and bowels occurred, and although albumen appeared, the remittent character of the disease was shown by the increase of fever on the 4th of November, and its decided decline on the 5th ; its rise again on the 7th, and marked decline on the 10th, and its elevation on the 11th, 12th, 13th and 14th, and progressive decline on the 15th, 16th and 17th.

It is important that the facts upon which the statement of Dr. Bemiss is based, that "Ten suspicious cases occurred within three (3) squares of last case within four weeks" should be thoroughly investigated by the Sanitary Inspector of the First District.

I desire that you should prepare for the Board of Health, to be submitted at its next meeting, a report based upon a thorough investigation of the following points.

1. What is the nature of the so-called suspicious cases?

The young man, Fred. Singer, who died at 409 South Liberty Street, was, according to the death certificate signed by Dr. W. H. Watkins and Dr. J. P. Davidson, afflicted with Yellow Fever.

2. Were these ten (10) suspicious cases, Yellow Fever?

3. By whom were these ten (10) suspicious cases treated?

4. Who reported the "ten suspicious cases" which "occurred within three squares of last case," to the member of the National Board of Health?

5. If these ten suspicious cases were of sufficient importance to be reported to the member of the National Board of Health, and to be telegraphed all over the country, the physician or physicians withholding such information from the Board of Health of the State of Louisiana should be known, in order that such action may be taken as may be in accordance with the importance of the questions involved.

This investigation has been entirely placed in your hands, because the case of Singer, and probably also other so-called suspicious cases, have occurred in your district.

It will be well for the perfection of this investigation that the Sanitary Inspector of the First District should not confine his inquiries to the immediate neighborhood of 409 S. Liberty street, but institute inquires amongst the prominent practitioners of medicine in the First and Fourth Districts.

You will also in your report, please state the result of your own individual experience in the treatment of the fevers of the past years. A comparative statement of the mortality by fevers in the First and Fourth Districts, as compared with that of the other districts and referred to the relative population will be of interest. Respectfully,

(Signed) JOSEPH JONES, M. D.,
President Board of Health, State of Louisiana.

OFFICE SANITARY INSPECTOR, FIRST DISTRICT, }
New Orleans, October 14, 1880. }

Joseph Jones, M. D., President of the Board of Health.

Sir:—In obedience to your order of the 9th instant, directing me to make a thorough investigation of all the facts and circumstances connected with the alleged telegram of Dr. S. M. Bemiss, Resident Member National Board of Health, to Dr. Rutherford of Houston, Texas, dated October 6, and published in the "Galveston News" of October 8, wherein the statement is made, that:

"Ten (10) suspicious cases occurred within three (3) squares of last case, within four (4) weeks;" I present you the following as the result of a most careful investigation. I will reply to the special points, upon which you desire information, in the numerical order of their statement.

(1). "What is the nature of the so-called suspicious cases?"

My investigation has led to the discovery of but two declared suspicious cases. Dr. W. H. Watkins, who was the attending physician has informed me that these were reported to you and that you saw them during their illness. It is therefore unnecessary for me to make further mention of these or of the case of Fred N. Singer, who died of Yellow Fever, October 4th instant, as certified by Drs. W. H. Watkins and J. P. Davidson.

2. Were the ten suspicious cases Yellow Fever?

3. By whom were the ten suspicious cases treated?

4. Who reported the "ten suspicious cases" which "occurred within three squares of last case" to the member of the National Board of Health residing in New Orleans.

5. If these ten suspicious cases were of sufficient importance to be reported to the member of National Board of Health, and to be telegaphed all over the country, the physician or physicians withholding such information from the Board of Health of the State of Louisiana should be known in order that such action may be taken as may be in accordance with the importance of the questions involved.

In order to reply to these interrogations it was essential that I should ascertain of Dr. Bemiss personally the facts concerning the telegram and the reported ten suspicious cases of Yellow Fever. That gentlemen, with marked courtesy, answered me that his entire knowledge of the so-called ten cases, and of every circumstance connected with them, was contained in a series of telegrams, the letter-press copies of which he submitted to me, and which I here present in the order of transmission:

NEW ORLEANS, October 5, 1880.

Turner, National Board of Health, Washington, D. C.,

Death from Yellow Fever last night, No. 409 South Liberty street, nearly a mile from commercial centres mile from harbor. Disinfection immediate burial all means to prevent spread, adopted.

F. LOEBER. M. D. Acting President Louisiana State Board of Health.
S. M. BEMISS, M. D, Resident Member National Board.

HOUSTON, TEXAS, 12 m., October 6, 1880.

S. M. Bemiss, M. D., New Orleans.

Do you consider that you have an infected district? Was the case reported, imported? Please reply before 3 o'clock, p. m.

RUTHERFORD.

———

NEW ORLEANS, October 6, 1880.

Rutherford, M D, Houston Texas.

Two suspicious cases occurred within three squares of last case within four weeks. No known connection between them. The man came from McComb City August 29. Was ignorant. No one can tell his personal history shortly before death.

BEMISS.

———

AUSTIN, TEXAS., October 6, 1880.

S. M. Bemiss, M. D., National Board of Health, New Orleans :

I rely upon you for advice and information. What should Texas do to protect us against New Orleans? What is the danger now? Advise me how and when to act, and oblige yours,

O. M. ROBERTS, Governor.

———

NEW ORLEANS, October 6, 1880.

Governor O. M. Roberts, Austin, Texas :

Telegraphed to Rutherford no danger in or from New Orleans to Texas or any other point. No centre of infection. One death over mile from harbor and business centres. No other case known.

S. M. BEMISS, Resident Member National Board of Health.

———

GALVESTON, TEXAS, October 7, 1880.

S. M. Bemiss, M. D., Member National Board of Health, New Orleans:

I see by your telegram of October 6, to Rutherford at Houston, you mention ten suspicious cases occurred within three squares of last case within four weeks. Please let me know the real condition of New Orleans, as to Yellow Fever to date.

E. H. WATTS, M. D
President Board of Health, Galveston.

———

NEW ORLEANS, October 7, 1880.

E. H. Watts M. D., Galveston, Texas :

Telegram read wrong. It should have been two suspicious cases. No Yellow Fever known to me in city now. No danger of spread here or elsewhere. Will certainly keep you advised.　S. M. BEMISS.

———

NEW ORLEANS, October 7, 1880.

Rutherford, M. D., Houston, Texas -

My telegram was written two, not "ten." There have not been as many as ten suspicious cases in the whole city this year to my knowledge or belief. Please correct.　S. M. BEMISS, M. D.

———

As requested I present with this report the certificates of several prominent physicians in the First and Fourth Districts.

In regard to my own observations, concerning the fevers of the past years, but in particular reference to the fever now prevailing, I can only state that my views coincide exactly with those of Dr. A. C. Holt. Candor demands the acknowledgment that while I have not seen a case of Yellow Fever, or one that I supposed to be other than dengue, as I have been accustomed to observe the symptoms of that disease in former times, yet I have seen this season, as formerly several cases in their features so nearly resembling Yellow Fever, that had I seen them during a time of prevalence of that disease, I would not have hesitated in pronouncing them Yellow Fever. The differential diagnosis is sufficiently established in the recovery of all my cases.

Respectfully submitted,　　　　　　　JOSEPH HOLT, M. D.,
Sanitary Inspector, First District.

———

Since 1878, I have seen no case that has resembled Yellow Fever.
[Signed]　　　　　　　　　　　　　　　ED. SCRATCHLEY, M. D.
New Orleans, October 12, 1880.

———

NEW ORLEANS, October 12, 1880.

Professor Joseph Jones, M. D., President Board of Health.

Dear Sir :—In response to your request, I have to state, that I have seen no case of Yellow Fever this entire season, nor anything in any manner approximating it.　Very respectfully yours,
[Signed]　　　　　　　　　　　　　　　B. SITLLE, M. D.

———

I hereby certify that I have not seen a case of Yellow Fever this year or anything like it.
[Signed]　　　　　　　　　　　　　　　J. CARTER, M. D.
New Orleans, October 12, 1880.

NEW ORLEANS, October 12, 1880.]

Dr. Joseph Holt:

Dear Sir—I have seen no case of Yellow Fever this season, nor have I seen one even suspicious.

I have treated over one hundred cases of the remittent fever, called "dengue," many of which presented grave symptoms such as delirium, a tendency of hemorrhages from bladder, uterus, nose and intestines; three cases of marked black vomit.

But all of the above cases occurred in persons who had unmistakable Yellow Fever in 1878; and still more significant and corroborative to the fact that they were not Yellow Fever is that, with one exception, they all recovered. Yours truly, W. C. HOLLIDAY, M. D.

———

Dr. Joseph Holt:

Dear Sir—In reply to your inquiries, I state that I have not seen a case of Yellow Fever this season.

For many weeks I have seen nothing in the way of disese, except dengue, which in all severe cases has borne its usual resemblance to Yellow Fever, viz: Continued fever of three or four days' duration with variations of temperature from 102 to 106; intense pain of head, back and limbs; injected eyes, great thirst and restlessness, frequently great gastric distress with excessive formation of gas, now and then delirium and hemorrhages from various parts; in two cases from the stomach.

The many points of resemblance to Yellow Fever has led my mind to the belief which I have held for many years, that "Dengue" is a specific disease, produced by the same cause, which produces Yellow Fever, modified in some way which I do not pretend to understand; which modification gives us a very remarkable disease, of great violence, attended with profound constitutional disturbances, but absolutely devoid of fatality.

Very Respectfully, A. C. HOLT, M. D., 107 Prytania street.

October 12, 1880.

———

I hereby certify that I have seen during the last two months, a great deal of Dengue, and intermittent malarial fever, but nothing that I thought for a moment to be Yellow Fever, nor have I seen such a case during the current year. C. J. BICKHAM, M. D.

New Orleans, October 12, 1880.

———

I hereby state that we have not seen a case of Yellow Fever, nor one that we have considered a probable case. DRS. W. J. and J. B. JOHNSON.

October 13, 1880. ———

NEW ORLEANS, October 13, 1880.

Dr. Jos. Holt:

Dear Sir—In reply to your queries communicated to me by Dr. Holliday, I will state that I have not seen a case of Yellow Fever this season, neither have I seen any case that I could regard as probable Yellow Fever.

Yours, etc., (Signed) L. F. SALAMON, M. D.

———

I hereby certify that from the first day of January of the present year, to the present date, I have not seen a case of Yellow Fever, or any disease which bears the most remote resemblance to it.

(Signed) I. L. CRAWCOUR, M. D.

October 13, 1880.

———

I hereby certify that during the present year. I have not seen a case of Yellow Fever, nor of any disease, which in the most important particulars resemble Yellow Fever. J. J. LYONS, M. D.,

New Orleans, October 13, 1880. 219 Carondelet street.

———

NEW ORLEANS, October 14, 1880.

Joseph Holt, M. D:

Dear Sir—In reply to your question, viz: Whether or not I have seen a single case of Yellow Fever during the summer of 1880, I would state that at no time during the present summer have I seen a single case of Yellow Fever. In 1878, I treated several persons having Yellow Fever, whom I have this year treated in dengue, the disease presenting symptoms closely resembling those of Yellow Fever.

Respectfully, WM. P. BREWER, M. D., 603 St. Charles street.

———

OFFICE BOARD OF HEALTH, STATE-HOUSE, STATE OF LOUISIANA, }
New Orleans, October 14, 1880. }

To His Excellency O. M. Roberts, Governor State of Texas:

Sir—S. M. Bemiss, M. D., member of the National Board of Health, having referred a copy of the letter of your Excellency, of the seventh instant, to the President of the State Board of Health, the following facts and documents are respectfully submitted for the information of the Governor of Texas:

1. Weekly statements of mortality of New Orleans, officially published by the Board of Health of the State of Louisiana, embracing the months of July, August, September and October, to date.

(*a*). An examination of these official documents of the Board of Health of the State of Louisiana will show that for week ending July 3, 1880; the total deaths from all causes were 112; death rate per 1000 per annum 27.73.

Week ending July 10, deaths 99, rate 24.51.
Week ending July 17, deaths 100, rate 24.76.
Week ending July 24, deaths 93, rate 23.02.
Week ending July 31, deaths 76, rate 18 28.
Week ending August 7, deaths 89, rate 21.04.
Week ending August 14, deaths 72, rate 17.33.
Week ending August 21, deaths 107, rate 25.75.
Week ending August 28, deaths 102, rate 24.55.
Week ending September 4, deaths 102, rate 24.55.
Week ending September 11, deaths 90, rate 21.66.

16

Whites—Death rate per annum 18.64; colored, 30.11. Week ending September 18—
Deaths, 125; rate, 30.57; whites, 24.85; colored, 46.49. Week ending September 25—Deaths,
104; rate, 25.03; whites, 23.54; colored, 29 19. Week ending October 2—Deaths, 103; rate,
24.79; whites, 23.22; colored, 29.19. Week ending October 9—Deaths, 107; rate, 25.75;
whites, 21.25; colored, 38.31.

During the past five days the deaths in the city of New Orleans (which, according to
the United States Census of 1880, contains 216,000 inhabitants), amounted to only 40, of
which number only 3 were caused by malarial fever, 1 from typhoid and 1 from common
continued fever; total deaths from fevers of all kinds, 5.

(*b.*) In the preceding statistics your Excellency has undoubted evidence of the fact that
New Orleans has, during the entire summer and fall, up to the present moment, been free
from all epidemic or contagious diseases, and has been exempt from Yellow Fever.

(*c.*) Your Excellency, as the guardian of the health of Texas, is, without doubt, familiar
with the mortality statistics of all the cities of Europe and America, and those now furnished from New Orleans, will establish, without doubt, beyond controversy, that the death
rate of New Orleans, during the past summer and autumn, will compare favorably with
that of any large city upon the face of the globe, in any latitude and under any circumstances.

2. The following table, illustrating the mortality of the different districts of the City
of New Orleans, during the entire year 1880 up to the present month, demonstrates that
the death rate of the First District, in which the reported deaths from Yellow Fever was
said to have occurred, has been less than that of the Second and Third Districts, in which
no case or death of Yellow Fever has been reported.

In the Fourth District in which two so-called suspicious cases have been reported
the Board of Health, the lowest death rate, namely, 18 67, has been found.

The death rate in the First District has been less during the months of August and
September than in any preceding months of the year.

(*d.*) Your Excellency will find in these detailed statistics a further confirmation of the
assertion that there is no evidence whatever afforded by a critical analysis of the mortality
in the different districts of any increased mortality which could be referred to hidden or
so-called "suspicious" causes. (See page 107.)

(*c.*) Your Excellency will observe that during the month of August, 1880, the mortality
was less in New Orleans than during the preceding 11 years, and during the month of September, less than in all the preceding years, with the exception of 1879.

4. In the preceding table of the Yellow Fever epidemics of New Orleans from 1847
and visitations from 1846 to 1880, it will be seen that all great epidemics commenced in
May, June and July. (See page 9.)

(*f.*) Your Excellency will perceive that no epidemic of Yellow Fever has ever commenced in the month of October.

(*g.*) New Orleans is now entirely free from Yellow Fever, and has been free of this
disease through the summer and autumn. There is therefore no ground for alarm on the
part of the Chief Executive and people of Texas, at the present time; neither is there any
probability or even possibility that at this late season of the year on the threshold of winter, any occasion will arise for the disruption of the friendly and business relations of the
great States of Texas and Louisiana.

6. Report of Dr. Joseph Holt with certificates of leading physicians.

7. Acts of the Legislature of Louisiana establishing and regulating quarantine for the
protection of the State, also rules and regulations of the Board of Health and ordinances of
the Council of New Orleans.

8. In conclusion allow me to assure your Excellency, that the Board of Health of the
State of Louisiana, when officially addressed, will at all times furnish your Excellency with
all facts and documents, which will enable the Governor of Texas to form a correct estimate of the condition of the health of New Orleans.   Respectfully,

JOSEPH JONES, M. D.,
President Board of Health, State of Louisiana.

OFFICE BOARD OF HEALTH, New Orleans, Oct. 14, 1880.

To His Excellency, O. M. Roberts, Governor of Texas, Austin, Texas:

Sir—I have the honor to furnish your Excellency with the enclosed report of Dr. Joseph
Holt, Sanitary Inspector, Fourth District, New Orleans, giving results of special investigation ordered by the President of the Louisiana State Board.

I hope that the other documents forwarded from this office will reach your Excellency
without delay.

In return the Board of Health of the State of Louisiana respectfully requests that your
Excellency will reciprocate by forwarding without delay all official information relating to
the health of Texas; also all sanitary and quarantine laws and regulations.

Respectfully, your obedient servant,   JOSEPH JONES, M. D.,
President of the Board of Health.

EXECUTIVE OFFICE, STATE OF TEXAS, Austin, November, 1880.

Dr. Joseph Jones, President Board of Health, New Orleans:

Dear Sir—I received your letter of the fourteenth of October last, and my answer has been delayed by my absence from the Capital for a few days. I thank your for the valuable inform·tion which it contains

I mail to you with this letter two pamphlets, containing the body of our Texas quarantine laws, (pages turned down), and my quarantine proclamation, from which you will get a fair view of our quarantine operations.

I hope to be able to get some of our leading quarantine officers and physicians to attend the meeting at New Orleans on the 7th to the 10th of December next.

It is of the greatest importance that there should be uniformity in the quarantine operations upon our whole Gulf coast, and especially that there should be such confidence mutually as would facilitate the operations equally in all of the States.

Such meetings may greatly aid in the accomplishments of these objects.

Respectfully yours, etc.,   O. M. ROBERTS, Governor.

Dr. Saunders, of Mississippi, visited New Orleans as a representative of the Mississippi State Board of Health.

Every facility was afforded Dr. Saunders for the thorough investigation of the sanitary condition of New Orleans, and all the records of the Board of Health were thrown open to his inspection.

This courteous and experienced physician reported to the State Board of Health of Mississippi that there was no Yellow Fever in New Orleans and that quarantine was unnecessary.

MALARIAL FEVER

OF THE DELTA OF THE

MISSISSIPPI RIVER,

AND MORE ESPECIALLY THE FORMS OF

MALARIAL PAROXYSMAL FEVER,

WHICH PREVAILED IN AND AROUND, ABOVE AND BELOW,
POINT MICHEL, IN THE PARISH OF PLAQUEMINE,
DURING THE SUMMER AND
AUTUMN OF 1880.

The Mississippi Valley comprises an area of 2,455,000 square miles, extending through thirty degrees of longitude and twenty-three degrees of latitude; and is composed of several subordinate basins, whose area and elevation are as follows: Upper Mississippi elevation above sea 1680 feet, area of basin 169,000 square miles; Missouri 6800 feet, 518,000 square miles; Ohio 1649 feet, 214,000 square miles; Arkansas 10,000 feet, 189,000 square miles; Red River 2450 feet, 97,000 square miles; Yazoo 210 feet, 13,850 square miles; St. Francis 1150 feet, 10,500 square miles; Lower Mississippi 416 feet, 1,244,000 square miles.

In such vast regions, reaching through such zones of climate and varying to such marked extent in soil and elevation; diversities must exist in the diseases of different sections: but it may be affirmed that throughout this vast Valley every form and variety of malarial paroxysmal fever prevails with greater or less intensity, according to the climate and soil, the heat, moisture, rainfall and peculiar climatic conditions associated with the annual revolutions of the seasons and the greater astronomical cycles.

It is chiefly in the Lower Mississippi that the full force at once of the waters, and the destructive and varying nature of the malarious fevers are witnessed.

The Mississippi first assumes its characteristic appearance of a turbid and boiling torrent, immense in volume and force, at the mouth of the Missouri; and from this point its waters pursue their devious way for more than 1300 miles, destroying banks and islands at one locality, reconstructing them at another, deluging with its united floods vast tracts of alluvial land, absorbing tributary after tributary, without visible increase in size, until, at length, it is in turn absorbed in the great volume of the Gulf.

The shores of the Gulf, so far as relates to the Louisiana coast, are bordered for fifty miles inland, by swamps, bayous and lakes. The swamps generally consist of an oozy mass of mud, from twenty to forty feet in depth, resting on blue clay.

When in flood, the Mississippi River extends to a width of thirty miles, and the surplus waters find their way to the ocean, through deep forests and almost interminable swamps.

AREA OF ALLUVIUM.

A wide belt of recent alluvium borders the Mississippi River from the mouth of the Ohio to the Gulf, 75 miles wide in its greatest expansion at Napoleon, and 25 miles in its greatest contraction at Natchez and Helena. The area of the alluvial tract above the Delta is 19,450 square miles. The depth of the alluvial deposits, from Cairo to New Orleans, ranges between 25 to 40 feet.

AREA OF THE DELTA.

The area of the delta, assuming that it begins where the river sends off its first branch to the sea, namely, at the mouth of Bayou Atchafalaya, is estimated at 12.300 square miles. This would be at the mouth of Red River, in latitude 31°. whilst the mouth of the Mississippi is in latitude 29°, so that the delta extends through two degrees of space.

The entire delta, is elevated but a few feet above the level of the Gulf of Mexico, and from its fertile soil and proximity to the Mississippi River and bayous is suited to the cultivation of rice. Rice culture the most unhealthy of all forms of agriculture has greatly increased of late years, and large numbers of settlements in the delta are literally situated in the midst of rice fields.

The preceding well known facts, should be carefully considered by any one, even the most profound observer of disease, before deciding upon the character of the endemics of fever which have so often prevailed in the delta of the Mississippi, which presents such uniform, geological, physical and climatic features.

EXTENSIVE PREVALENCE OF THE VARIOUS FORMS OF MALARIAL FEVER

IN THE VALLEY OF THE MISSISSIPPI DURING THE SUMMER AND AUTUMN OF 1880.

It is well known that the several grades of malarial fever, often attended with hæmorrhage from the bowels, stomach and kidneys, and jaundice, prevail at various points along the Mississippi River and its tributaries.

The rains of the spring and early portion of the summer deluged the rice fields and swamps of the delta with water, and in the months of August were succeeded by burning suns.

The several types of the remittent, intermittent and congestive fevers of the delta of the Mississippi appeared to be due to the preceding causes, and especially to the drying up of the stagnant waters of the rice fields, and the death and putrification of numerous tad-poles and small fish. Epidemics of the so-called putrid and adynamic fevers have been observed and traced to similar causes in the countries of Europe, Asia and Africa bordering on the Mediterranean Sea, from the earliest ages, and centuries before the discovery of insular and Central America, to which sections of the earth have been referred the origin of Yellow Fever.

MALARIAL FEVER OF PLAQUEMINE PARISH, . LOUISIANA, DURING THE MONTHS OF AUGUST, SEPTEMBER AND · OCTOBER, 1880.

On the third of September, Capt. C. U. Lewis, a nephew of Dr. H. S. Lewis, of New Orleans informed the President of the Board of Health, that a fatal form of fever had attacked the children of Mr. Esteve Giordano, at Point Michel, on the left bank of the Mississippi River, fifty-two miles below New Orleans. Mr. C. U. Lewis also stated that Dr. J. B. Wilkinson, of Myrtle Grove Plantation, parish of Plaquemines, had affirmed that it was the same fever as that of 1878.

Telegrams were immediately dispatched to Drs. Hays, Hebert, Wilkinson, Sr. (at Myrtle Grove), Dr. Wilkinson, Jr. (at Missisippi Quarantine Station), Dr. Finney, Quarantine Station, and to Dr. B. F. Taylor, Sanitary and Quarantine Officer of the Board of Health, at Port Eads.

The following will illustrate nature of the telegrams:

[Telegram.]

NEW ORLEANS, Sept. 3, 1880.—Dr. Wilkinson, Mississippi Quarantine Station: Mr. C. U. Lewis, nephew of Dr. Lewis, of this city, states that a fever resembling Yellow Fever, has appeared at Point Michel, in the family of Esteve Giordano. Please give me immediately by telegram all facts in your possession, and, if necessary, visit the sick in person. The Board of Health will pay all expenses incurred.
JOSEPH JONES, M. D. President Board of Health.

In addition to the preceding instructions issued to Dr. Wilkinson, Dr. B. F. Taylor was ordered to proceed at once to Point Michel and to render all necessary assistance to the sick, in co-operation with the attending physicians, in case such assistance should be required.

He was also directed to keep the President of the Board of Health constantly advised. Telegraphic communication was also opened with various residents and telegraph operators on the Lower Coast.

The following replies will illustrate the views of the physicians above named:

QUARANTINE STATION, Sept. 3, 1880.—To Dr. Jones: Have heard nothing of the case. Point Michel is too far away from here for me to neglect the Station. Dr. Hays is practicing in that locality. Telegraph to him at Pointe-a-la-Hache.
C. P. WILKINSON.

POINTE-A-LA-HACHE, Sept. 6, 1880 —To Dr. Joseph Jones, President Board of Health: Will write to you fully by to-morrow's mail.
J. B. HAYS, M. D.

PORT EADS, September 5, 1880.

Joseph Jones, M. D., President Board of Health:

Sir—I have reason to believe that there is not a particle of truth in the report.
Malarial fever in exceedingly mild form exists around and near the Passes, and all along the Coast. Will visit the family and report at the earliest date.
B. F. TAYLOR, M. D., Sanitary Inspector.

POINT MICHEL, La., September 5, 1880.

Dr. Joseph Jones, President State Board of Health, New Orleans, La.:

Dear Doctor—Your telegram of the third only came to hand after long delay, as the Station nearest to Point Michel is on the opposite side of the river, distant about nine miles, and communication is very uncertain, hence the delay in answering.

I have seen the sick children of Esteve Giordano, and called in Drs. J. P. Wilkinson and N. M. Hebert in consultation. The fever is evidently malarial, of a severe type, and yields readily to quinine. There is no albumen in the urine.

Esteve Giordano has lost three of his children from it, and that can be attributed to the great difficulty experienced in administering medicine to them. There has been no suppression of urine.

I have had thirty or forty similar cases (the total number of deaths is four), though many have been quite sick, they have recovered under the quinine and cinchonoida treatment. Just now, during the rice harvesting season, our population is always more or less liable to suffer from malaria as evidenced by records of past years, and I think it would either require a very elastic imagination or a malicious desire to create a panic to pronounce the cases referred to. Yellow Fever.

Neither Dr. Wilkinson nor Dr. Hebert, both practitioners of long experience, pronounced the disease other than a malignant malarial fever.

I have been told that Mr. C. U. Lewis removed his family to the city, actuated by fear of their falling sick; of course there is no controlling individual opinions or fears

I write by the first available mail after receipt of your telegram, as being much more satisfactory than a short telegraphic statement.

Should there be Yellow Fever down here, rest assured, I will promptly notify you.

Very truly, yours,   GEO. A B. HAYS, M. D.

P. S.—It may be of interest to state that more than three-fourths of all the sick are colored people and are all natives of the place.

MISSISSIPPI QUARANTINE STATION, Sept. 5, 1880.

Joseph Jones, M. D., President Board of Health, New Orleans, La.:

Dear Sir—I am in receipt of your telegram in reference to Yellow Fever at Point Michel (as reported by C. Uncas Lewis), and also have I seen a telegram addressed to Mr. Bernard Fasterling, Buras Postoffice (immediately opposite Quarantine Station), signed A. Baldwin & Co., asking about sickness in Buras Settlement, and whether Dr. Bemiss's presence would be advisable or not; and also know of other telegrams to other persons in various portions of the parish to the same purport.

*   *   *   *   *   *   *

I have practiced medicine two years in Buras Settlement, and a healthier place I know not of.   Since my attendance at Quarantine Station, my duties have permitted of nothing else than those appertaining immediately to the Station, but I would most certainly have known of any case of serious illness occurring in our neighborhood.

*   *   *   *   *   *   *

In my opinion, this is another endeavor to injure the quarantine system of Louisiana.

*   *   *   *   *   *   *

With respect, I am, sir, your obedient servant,

C. P. WILKINSON, Assistant Resident Physician.

_____

PORT EADS, LA., September 6, 1880.

Joseph Jones, M. D., President Board of Health :

Sir—In compliance with your instructions I have investigated the matter in reference to the report of Mr. Lewis of Yellow Fever at the Fifty-two Mile Post on the Mississippi River, and find from all the information gathered from the physicians of the neighborhood, and others, that the disease is fever of the ordinary malarial type, now prevailing all along the passes and the entire coast. I can speak confidently and personally knowingly, as I have had the disease myself The universal prevalence of the disease is due, to my mind, to a peculiar atmospheric condition, perhaps electrical, that does occur when the temperature ranges from 76° to 89° at this season of the year in this latitude.

Very respectfully,   B. F. TAYLOR, M. D.,
                                              Health Officer and Quarantine Physician, Port Eads, La.

On the sixth of September the following communication was received from the Resident Member of the National Board of Health :

NATIONAL BOARD OF HEALTH, New Orleans, September 5, 1880.

Joseph Jones, M. D., President State Board of Health :

Sir—At half-past 2 o'clock yesterday (Saturday) afternoon, Prof. Ernest Lewis brought a gentleman into my office who informed me that a very fatal form of fever was prevailing in the parish of Plaquemines, at or near Point Michel. This gentleman stated that he had given you this information about 11 o'clock Friday morning. I now respectfully ask that you give me, at the earliest moment practicable, such information as you may have received concerning this reported outbreak of serious diseases.

This request is made in the interest of public health and welfare, not only that I may exercise my influence, and, if necessary, the funds at my command in arresting the further spread of infectious disease, but also that I may aid in preventing unnecessary quarantine against this State and city.

Respectfully,   S. M. BEMISS,
                                                      Member National Board of Health.

The following reply was returned to the Resident Member of the National Board of Health :

OFFICE BOARD OF HEALTH, STATE OF LOUISIANA. }
New Orleans, September 6, 1880. }

S. M. Bemiss, M. D., Member of the National Board of Health, New Orleans, La. .

Sir—In reply to your communication of the fifth instant, I have to state that communications have been addressed by telegraph, to the officers of the Board of Health, and prominent physicians, at Mississippi Quarantine Station, Port Eads, Pointe-a-la-Hache, and other places, not only asking information as to the truth of the rumor to which you allude, but also directing a special inspection, and the institution of any sanitary precautions, should any be deemed necessary, at the expense of the Board of Health of the State of Louisiana.

Thus far it has been ascertained that two children died on the east bank of the river, about 52 miles below the city, with fever : I am momentarily expecting replies from the various physicians.

I enclose copy of the first received from Dr. Taylor, Sanitary and Quarantine Officer of the Board of Health, stationed at Port Eads, who has been ordered to proceed at once to the point from whence the report has arisen.

Respectfully,
JOSEPH JONES, M. D.,
President of the Board of Health.

Dr. Taylor during his visit to New Orleans, shortly after the preceding communication, was also directed to communicate all facts in his possession to the Resident Member of the National Board of Health.

Dr. J. B. Wilkinson who was called in consultation by Dr. Hays to see the cases at Point Michel (Rouguillo Settlement), in a letter dated Myrtle Grove Plantation, September 6, 1880, thus describes the location of the houses of Esteve Giordano and his neighbors, situated in the midst of extensive rice fields, between the Mississippi River and a low salt marsh and swamp on the borders of Grande Bayou, which empties into the Gulf of Mexico.

Dr. Wilkinson says that the houses in which the cases of fever appeared "are all low and small, surrounded completely by orange groves, which shut out the breeze which generally prevails here from the sea, and creates a still atmosphere, which in hot weather is very unpleasant, and, at this particular time, was rendered more so by an absence of rain for nearly a month, and a very elevated August temperature. These houses are much crowded by families, and they are very insufficiently provided with windows. The practice of these people is to shut up their rooms in case of sickness to prevent the sick *taking cold*. I found this to be the case particularly in the house of Esteve Giordano; and not only that, but the confinement of the sick under thick muslin bars, or mosquito nets. Immediately in the rear of these houses, approaching them within a few acres, are very extensive rice fields, now in the most favorable condition for the elimination of unhealthy exhalations, as the water has retired from the fields and the wet surface is entirely exposed to the action of the sun.

There is another phenomenon which is not usually observed here, in the rice field ditches (in fact everywhere) there are myriads of a small fish left to die and rot by the fall of water. They are about 4 inches long, the size of the little finger, and without exaggeration, can be scooped out of these ditches by the cart load. The effluvia from these fish are very offensive, and must add to the unhealthy condition of the atmosphere. The water used by almost all of these people referred to, is taken from the river, and without purification. Their food is usually meagre."

To the same effect was the testimony of Dr. D. R. Fox, of "Hygine Jesuits Bend," in reply to the inquiry of the President of the Board of Health. It may be added parenthetically, that Dr. Fox has long enjoyed the confidence of the citizens of Louisiana, as an experienced and successful practitioner of medicine.

Point Michel is about twenty-eight miles from my place. * * * * My views in regard to it (the fever prevailing at Point Michel), are that they were cases of malarial remittent fever of a severe type produced by some local cause. Point Michel is situated about fifty miles below New Orleans, and about thirty miles above the Quarantine Station. It is inhabited by Creole families owning small farms of from one to two arpents in width, and from seven to eight arpents in depth. About one or two acres of this land near the river is high enough for the cultivation of orange trees and vegetables; the balance is low prairie, which is only fit for the cultivation of rice. These rice lands are flooded at frequent intervals during the spring.

The rice is harvested in the latter part of July, August and September, and is stacked on the high land in front.

It is threshed and large piles of rice straw are usually left in heaps to rot. These piles are left rotting from year to year, and are sources of the malarial poison.

The houses are built low, and are raised but one or two feet from the ground. The orange groves surround the dwellings, and form a thick shade, which keeps the ground damp and unhealthy. A reason for its fatality amongst children is that the fever is complicated with gastro enteritis, caused by eating green oranges and pecans; also from the weak-mindedness of Creoles in not forcing their children to take the proper remedy, particularly quinine. I learn that the family in which the four children died, the medicine prescribed by the attending physician was not given.

Yours truly,
D. R. FOX.

17

Upon inquiry, the President of the Board of Health found that similar types of fever were prevalent in the delta of the Mississippi River, above New Orleans, as will be shown by the following letter, from Dr. A. C. Love, of Donaldsonville, Louisiana:

DONALDSONVILLE, LA., September 15, 1880.

Professor Joseph Jones, M. D., President Board of Health, New Oreans, La.:

Dear Sir—In answer to your inquiry as to the different types of malarial fever that have prevailed in this part of the State during the past few months, the following facts, gathered from my practice, are respectfully furnished you.

The number of cases of simple remittent fever has been much greater, and in most instances the fever has proved more tenacious than has been the case in former years. Great irritability of stomach, severe pains referrible to the loins and the lower extremities, high range of temperature and very indefinitely marked remissions have been prominent symptoms in the majority of cases.

Proportionately there has been an unusually great number of cases of pernicious remittent fever, whose temperature was as high as 107½ and 108°, without any perceptible remission for forty-eight, often seventy-two, and, in some cases, ninety-six hours. Frequently a decline in temperature marked the setting in of collapse. As a rule such patients were jaundiced; one had copious hæmorrhage from the stomach; two others, hæmaturia.

This unusual prevalence and malignity of malarial fevers must be accounted for by the full river of last spring, whose waters submerged the battures, and by the incessant rains and high temperature of the past few months. Besides, in this neighborhood hundreds of acres of land, for years uncultivated, have recently been recleared and planted in rice. About the middle of July the water was turned off from these lands for the harvesting of the crop, and during the three weeks following that time there was, in that vicinity, a notable increase in the number of cases of fever, as well as a graver malignancy in its type.

I remain very respectfully,   A. C. LOVE, M. D.

The following letter, from Dr. Hayes, dated Point Michel, September 7, still farther sustained the view expressed by this intelligent and active practitioner:

POINT MICHEL, La., September 7, 1880.

Joseph Jones, M. D., President Louisiana State Board of Health, New Orleans:

Dear Doctor—Your letter of yesterday, acknowledging the receipt of mine, has just reached me. The fever referred to is still amenable to the quinine treatment, and of some twenty patients now on hand there is not one whose condition is not satisfactory. There are two or three new cases daily, but about that number are dismissed from treatment in the same time, and there is no great variation either way in the number of patients during the last week. Some are sick three or four days, and severer cases remain ill ten or fifteen days. Since writing you, the little scare that existed here at first has about subsided, and the people are beginning to find out that patients, and especially children, who are amenable to control and will take the prescribed remedies, have a much greater prospect of recovery than those who will not. There is practical experience of that in the houses adjacent to Esteve Giordano's, which they have not failed to note. I would be glad to have been instrumental, however remote, in subduing unreasoning fears and preventing the spread of injurious, false reports.

Very truly, yours,   GEO. A. B. HAYS, M. D

N. B.—I have just received a note from Dr. Bemiss, asking for information in regard to this same matter. I have written him substantially what I told you.   H

All the facts connected with the malarial fever prevailing in and around, above and below Point Michel, were laid before the Board of Health of the State of Louisiana at the regular weekly meeting, on the ninth of September. The communications of the various physicians were also presented.

The meetings of the Board of Health of the State of Louisiana have been open to the public and to the representatives of the press, and the reporters of the daily papers, namely, the Picayune, Times, Democrat, Bee, Daily States, City Item and German Gazette, were always present and were allowed access to documents relating to the public health.

The Board of Health regarded it to be absolutely necessary, that the public should have access to all facts relating to the health of the city and State, through the intelligent and independent representatives of the daily press.

By such course it was believed, that not only Louisiana, but all the surrounding States, would be kept fully advised of the true sanitary condition of New Orleans and the delta of the Mississippi River, and it was hoped that confidence would be established and panic and useless quarantine be avoided.

In illustration of the promptness with which the Board of Health communicated to the public the facts with reference to the malarial fever of the Lower Coast, we reproduce the report of the regular weekly meeting of the ninth of September, as published in the daily Picayune of September 10, 1880:

BOARD OF HEALTH.

CONTINUED GOOD HEALTH OF THE CITY—STATEMENT BY DR. JONES.

The regular weekly meeting of the Louisiana State Board of Health was held last evening Dr. Joseph Jones, President in the chair.

Present—Drs. Formento, Davidson, Loeber and Sheppard, and Messrs. Marks and Hernandez.

The President announced the continued good health and low death rate of New Orleans. He said: "It is a fact worthy of note as showing the healthy condition of the city and the excellent condition of the public health, that the mortality for the preceding week (ending August 28) and of the week ending September 4 were precisely the same, namely 102, or for each week 24.55 per 1000 inhabitants. In the week ending August 28 the ratio for the whites was 21.25, and for the colored 33.75; for the week ending September 4, whites 20.27, colored 36.49. The mortality during the past four days has been only 30, of which 4 were from malarial fever.

The President directed the attention of the Board to the prevalence of the various forms of marsh or malarial fever, more especially in the localities of the Mississippi Valley in which rice is cultivated. Dr. Jones then gave some interesting facts concerning malarial fever, as follows :

The various forms of malarial fever prevail at all seasons of the year in the delta of the Mississippi River, as has been noted by our most accomplished and experienced physicians. While the origin and spread of Yellow Fever depends absolutely upon an elevated temperature ranging from 70° to 85° F., and its decline upon a mean temperature ranging from 65° to 56° F. On the other hand, the various forms of malarial fever are more uniformly distributed throughout the months of the year, although this class of diseases, as well as Yellow Fever, show their maximum intensity in number of cases and fatality in those months of the year in which the temperature is most favorable to the putrifaction of animal and vegetable matters, and the development of the lower and most prolific forms of animal and vegetable life, and especially those forms which are the active agents in putrifaction and fermentation, Thus the deaths caused by malarial fever in 1867 were as follows : January, 7 ; February, 7 ; March, 9 ; April, 4 ; May, 13 ; June, 31 ; July, 48 ; August, 120 ; September, 174 ; October, 153 ; November, 43 ; December, 20. During the same year the deaths from Yellow Fever were : June, 3 : July, 11 ; August, 255 ; September, 1637 ; October, 1072 ; November, 103 ; December, 26.

In like manner in 1878, the deaths caused by the various forms of malarial fever were as follows : January, 6 ; February, 3 ; March, 9 ; April, 15 , May, 12 ; June, 13 ; July, 25 ; August, 136 ; September, 146 ; October, 111 ; November, 41 ; December, 6. During the same year the deaths from Yellow Fever were : May, 2 ; July, 50 ; August, 974 ; September, 1893 ; October, 1044 ; November, 90 ; December, 3.

The mortuary report, however, gives but an imperfect view of the prevalence of the various forms of paroxysmal or malarial fever in New Orleans, from the well known fact that these diseases rarely prove fatal. The favorable results obtained in the treatment of intermittent, remittent and congestive fever, are at the present day mainly due to the prompt and free administration of quinine, by the physicians of New Orleans and other parts of the Southern country.

The records of the Charity Hospital of New Orleans furnish the best field for such inquiries, as it has justly been regarded as one of the great fever hospitals of the world.

It appears from the records of the Charity Hospital, that during a period of ten (10) years, from January 1, 1841, to January 1, 1851, there were admitted into this hospital 91,892 patients, of which number there were admitted of all the different forms of fever, 45,149, and among these last, of intermittent fevers, 25,183. Thus it will appear that nearly one-half of all the patients admitted into this hospital were for the different forms or types of fever, and that more than one-half of them were intermittents.

Then followed a statement showing the prevalence of intermittent fevers at different seasons of the year, as indicated by admissions to the Charity Hospital in the different seasons of the years from 1841 to 1849, inclusive.

He then continued:

The following statement will show the prevalence of intermittent fevers at the different seasons of the year, for the time specified:

TABLE OF ADMISSION OF CASES OF INTERMITTENT FEVER IN CHARITY HOSPITAL OF NEW ORLEANS, IN THE DIFFERENT SEASONS OF THE YEAR, 1841 TO 1849 INCLUSIVE.

Year.	Spring.	Summer.	Autumn	Winter.	All Fevers.	Yellow Fever
1841................................... ..	112	403	177	92	1991	1113
1842...................................	114	453	394	135	1758	410
1843...................................	85	208	413	137	2922	1153
1844...................................	117	469	732	231	2207	152
1845...................................	180	353	664	206	1763	1
1846	236	569	1044	218	2607	148
1847..................................	391	508	691	602	6901	2811
1848...................................	282	689	874	535	6361	1234
1849...................................	420	1701	3738	1275	7575	1060
Total	1937	5353	7728	3431	33,381	7982

Thus it will be seen that during the period specified, during spring 1937, summer 5353, autumn 7728, winter 3431, cases of intermittent fever were admitted into the Charity Hospital of New Orleans.

It is evident from this table that intermittent fever prevails in New Orleans the year round, gradually increasing from the winter up to autumn, when it begins to decline.

It is thus made evident that paroxysmal (marsh or malarial) fevers prevail every year, and in every month of the year, in New Orleans, thus presenting a marked contrast to the prevalence of Yellow Fever, which is shut up in much narrower limits.

It appears that the cause of Yellow Fever requires for its generation and propagation a higher degree of heat, and that the conditions of its existence are more narrowly defined than those of malarial fever. · The cause of the latter disease not only resists successfully a much lower temperature than that of Yellow Fever, but when once engrafted on the human system it is far more persistent and indefinite in its duration, and, in fact, in many cases produces such profound alterations in the constitution of the blood, and in certain organs as the spleen and liver, as to constitute a condition of the system which may underlie and modify supervening diseases.

EFFECTS OF RICE CULTURE UPON HEALTH OF THE POPULATION.

Dr. Jones directed the attention of the Board of Health to the important fact that during the past few years, since the close of the American civil war, (1861-1865), large areas of land in the delta of the Mississippi, above, below and around New Orleans, have been devoted to the cultivation of rice.

In the opinion of the President of the Board of Health, rice culture was one of the most unhealthy modes of agriculture, and was the prolific source of many of the severest fevers of malarial form, and, especially of that form recognized for centuries in Europe, and described by Torti. Tommasini and others, and in our own city by the learned and accomplished Dr. Charles Faget, and which has received various appellations as hemorrhagic malarial fever, malarial hematuria, hemogastric malarial fever.

Instances of the several forms of malarial fever, attended with hemorrhage from the stomach, or bowels or kidneys, and with vomiting of black matter and with jaundice, closely simulating in some of the more prominent symptoms, Yellow Fever, occur every autumn in the malarial regions of North Carolina, South Carolina, Alabama, Mississippi, Louisiana, Texas and Arkansas. So familiar are the experienced physicians of our Southern country with this severe form of malarial fever, that these occurrences occasion no alarm. As the occurrence some ten days ago of several cases of severe malarial fever in the neighborhood of rice farms. near Point Michel, occasioned some comment, an immediate investigation was instituted The President of the Board of Health had himself visited cases of this form of malarial fever in company with Dr. George Howe, in the parish of St. Bernard, and had also addressed letters of inquiry to the leading physicians of the parish of Plaquemines, and also . to the officers of the Jetties and at the Mississippi Quarantine Station.

Dr. Jones submitted the letters from the physicians referred to, who report that the cases were plainly malarial fever, and that more than three-fourths of the sick were colored people and natives of the place.

The daily papers of New Orleans also published in evidence the letters of the attending Physician Dr. Hays, and of Drs. Taylor and Fox.

The Board of Health unanimously endorsed the view of the President, as to the origin and nature of the malarial fever, prevailing upon the Rice Plantations of the lower coast.

The following reports from B. F. Taylor, were forwarded from Port Eads, after the completion of the investigation ordered by the Board of Health :

POINTE-A-LA-HACHE, LA., September 10, 1880.

Dr. Joseph Jones, President Board of Health :

Sir:—In accordance with your instructions, I proceeded to the neighborhood in which the fever was reported to exist, and found the following to be the facts connected therewith, viz :

In consultation with Dr. Hayes, the practitioner in whose practice these cases occurred, I learn that the children of the family of Giordano, were taken on the 15th August with fever, pain in the head, dry skin, tongue coated with yellow fur, very little redness, slight nausæ and continued until their death. Three of these patients died between the third and seventh day. The urine at no time gave any evidence of albumen. There was nothing resembling black vomit in either of these children There was no tinge of yellowness in the tissues, previously, or after death.

These cases are situated one and a half miles above the residence of Dr. Hayes ; right bank.

Cases have occurred in the following order of time and distance, viz :

August 16—1 case 5 miles above.
August 20—1 case 2 miles above.
August 20—1 case 7½ miles above.
August 22—2 cases 7¼ miles above.
August 23—3 cases 3 miles above.
August 23—1 case 4 miles below, opposite bank of river.
August 24—3 cases 1¼ miles above.
August 24—2 cases 6 miles below.
August 25—3 cases 1¼ miles above.
August 26—4 cases 1¼ miles below.
August 27—2 cases 1 mile above.
August 28— 1 case 1 mile above.
August 28—1 case 1 mile below.
August 29—2 cases 1 mile below.
August 30—2 cases 1¼ miles below.
August 31—1 case 1¼ miles below.
September 2—4 cases 1¼ miles above.
September 3—4 cases 1 mile above.
September 4—4 cases adjoining same.
September 5—5 cases adjoining same.
September 5—2 cases ½ mile below.
September 6—1 case 1 mile above.
September 7—1 case 7 miles above.
September 7—2 cases 2½ miles above.
September 7—2 cases 2 miles above.
September 8—1 case 1 mile above.
September 8—3 cases 1¼ miles above.
September 8—2 cases adjoining.

Total number amounting to 61 cases

Yesterday I also visited Mr. Jack Dragon's son, 17 years of age, (4) four miles above Point La Hache, left bank, a patient of Drs. Hebert and Wilkinson who had died two hours previously. The body presented a bluish motley appearance, without the least sign of any yellowish or jaundiced discoloration. This patient sickened on Saturday with the usual symptoms of fever, which continued up to the time of death. His mind remained intact. His urine was albuminous the day previously. He had no vomiting whatever, for the past two days.

In the same house were two children who had been sick two days. They had no albumen in the urine. Another child just taken. whose urine was examined, showed albumen.

In another house one mile below the Court House, the family of Pierre Hingle, four children were sick, with the usual symptoms of the epidemic. I am informed, positively and unequivocally, by Dr. Hebert, that two of these children, had in 1878, a similar fever.

Dr. Hayes informs me that quinine controlled the fever in every instance, when it could be given properly. The Giordano children were uncontrollable, and could not be induced or forced to take quinine, and he attributes their death to that circumstance.

Very Respectfully your obedient servant,

B. F. TAYLOR, M. D., Health Officer, Mississippi River.

———

PORT EADS, September 13, 1880

Joseph Jones, M. D., President Board of Health :

Dear Sir—In my report I omitted to mention that the greater number of persons sick were Creoles of mixed blood.

In most of the cases examined by myself, the temperature ranged from 101° to 104 1-5° Fahrenheit, remaining at the latter only a few hours.

Up to the time of leaving Point Michel, Saturday night, about eighty-five cases had occurred, presenting the same symptoms, though in a lighter degree.

Very respectfully, your obedient servant, . B. F. TAYLOR, M. D.

P. S —Dr. Sternberg (N. B. of H.) pronounced the cases all mild Yellow Fever. T.

———

The following communication was received from the Resident Member of the National Board of Health, on the thirteenth of September :

NEW ORLEANS, La., September 13, 1880.

Dr. Joseph Jones, President Louisiana State Board of Health :

Sir—I respectfully call your attention to the accompanying report from Dr. G . M. Sternberg, regarding the disease at this time prevailing on the Lower Coast of the Mississippi River. In my opinion the symptoms and mode of spread bear so close a resemblance to Yellow Fever, that no time should be lost in applying all possible means to prevent its further spread. With a view to the accomplishment of this end, I have to inform you that you are authorized to draw upon the National Board of Health for such sums of money as may be necessary to procure disinfectants and to pay for the services of sanitary police and sanitary inspectors, and in truth all expenses expedient for the purposes mentioned. This money cannot be drawn from the treasury except, in payment of bills of services or articles, which bills must be duly authenticated. You will therefore make requisitions from time to time, for such services, disinfectants, etc., as are in your opinion required and forward same to me. This appropriation will apply to cases of infectious diseases in this city, and in all places within the limits of the State, which have no local Boards to exercise such powers.

The organization of the work will rest with yourself subject to the approval of the National Board. You will therefore, in all cases, forward me the names of persons recommended to be employed with pay of each, and each one must take an oath of office, and have his name carefully entered upon the blank pay roll, which will be furnished you, and then no trouble will occur in regard to payments It is well to remark that the Treasury Department refuses to pay for goods or clothing destroyed to prevent spread of disease, but will pay any reasonable expenses for cleaning and disinfection.   Respectfully,

S. M. BEMISS,

The preceding communication of the Resident Member of the National Board of Health was immediately laid before the members of the Board of Health of the State of Louisiana, and the following reply was returned.

OFFICE BOARD OF HEALTH, STATE-HOUSE,
State of Louisiana, New Orleans, Sept. 13, 1880.

Prof. S. M. Bemiss, M. D. Member National Board of Health, New Orleans, Louisiana:

SIR—The communication of the Member of the National Board of Health, of this date, has been received, and its contents noted.

The Board of Health of the State of Louisiana has investigated the malarial fever, to which you refer as prevailing in the low rice lands bordering on the Mississippi River above and below Point Michel.

Such measures as the Board of Health, deem necessary, have been instituted.   Respectfully,   JOSEPH JONES, M. D.,
President Board of Health, State of Louisiana.

The measures proposed by the Resident Member of the National Board of Health were unnecessary, and their adoption and execution by the Board of Health of the State of Louisiana, would have led to the establishment of quarantines of the most rigid character against the City of New Orleans, which whilst inflicting incalculable damage and exciting panics, would have been wholly useless as a defence against an imaginary evil.

Subsequent events have demonstrated the wisdom of the course of the Board of Health of the State of Louisiana, and confirmed the view that the disease prevailing in and around, above and below Point Michel, was of purely local origin and possessed no contagious properties. It has been shown in a previous portion of this report, that cases of this disease terminated fatally in the heart of this great city, without any communication or reproduction of the disease.

Telegrams were dispatched to the leading business centres in the United States, to the effect that seventy-five cases of Yellow Fever had occurred in and around the Mississippi Quarantine Station, that the disease had been investigated by an army surgeon in the employ of the National Board of Health, and that this organization had offered ten thousand dollars to Dr. Joseph Jones, President of the State Board of Health, with which to arrest the progress of the pestilence, but this offer had been refused.

The wide dissemination of these reports led the State Board of Health to the following action at the regular meeting, held on the twenty-third of September:

[Extracts from the Minutes of the Board of Health, September 23, 1880]

Mr. Marks offered the following resolutions, which were adopted after considerable debate, being opposed by Dr. Davidson. Dr. Sheppard objected to the introductory paragraph of the preamble. The resolutions are:

Whereas, the representatives of the National Board of Health have on several occasions during the past extraordinary healthy summer, deliberately attempted through the agency of their employes to create a Yellow Fever panic against our city, and

Whereas, no case of Yellow Fever (save the imported ones on the bark Excelsior) has occurred during the present year within the domain of Louisiana; and

Whereas, the commercial interests of New Orleans are altogether too vast and important to be thus imperiled or trifled with ; and

Whereas the State Board of Health of Louisiana believing that its sworn duty in protecting and endeavoring to preserve the health of this city during the past summer has been faithfully executed, and feeling that it should give free expression to its condemnation of these repeated attempts to commercially injure and defame New Orleans, be it therefore

Resolved, That the officers of the National Board of Health at Washington be, and they are hereby respectfully requested to instruct their representatives in Louisiana to conform their conduct to the act of Congress under which they hold power, and to simply extend such aid to the State Board of Health of Louisiana as it may request, and to further prevent them interfering in any way with the duties incumbent upon and discharged by the said State Board of Health.

Resolved, That as this Board has solemnly pledged itself to promptly communicate to the country the existence within our city or State of any epidemic or contagious diseases, it requests the press of the United States not to attach any evidence to any report in relation to the public health of our city or State that does not bear the official sanction of this Board.

Resolved, That this board, through its President, will continue to keep the public thoroughly and truthfully informed as to the condition of the health of New Orleans and the surrounding country.

On the same day (September 23), there appeared in the daily Democrat an able report, signed by Drs. Bruns and Davidson, who had been requested by the Resident Member of the National Board of Health to investigate the fever of Point Michel, in company with Dr. George M. Sternberg, Surgeon in the United States army and in the employ of the National Board of Health. We reproduce this important report:

[New Orleans Democrat, Thursday, September 23, 1880.]

THE RICE FEVER.

REPORTS OF DOCTORS BRUNS AND DAVIDSON, ON THE FEVER WHICH PREVAILED IN PLAQUEMINES PARISH.

No. 142 Canal Street, New Orleans, September 18, 1880.

S. M. Bemiss, M. D. Resident Member National Board of Health :

Dear Sir—In obedience to your request of the fourteenth of September, that I should " proceed to the lower coast of the Mississippi River, to inspect and report in regard to the prevalence of any infectious or other forms of fever prevailing in that section of the State." I have the honor to report that, on the morning of the fifteenth, at 8 a. m., the committee, consisting of Dr. J. P. Davidson, of the State Board of Health; Dr. G. M. Sternberg, surgeon United States Army, and myself. with Dr. Mitchell of the National Board, who kindly accompanied us, and my son, Mr. H. D. Bruns, who volunteered to make the necessary autopsies, if opportunity offered, proceeded on the steam tug Aspinwall, directly to Myrtle Grove, the plantation of Dr. J. B. Wilkinson, the oldest and most experienced physician in the parish of Plaquemines. We there learned that the doctor had been called to visit a case of fever on the left bank of the river, seven miles below, in consultation with the resident physician, Dr. N. M. Hebert. We reached the place designated, five miles above Point-a-la-Hache, too late to meet Dr. Wilkinson, but had the good fortune to encounter Dr. Hebert, who with great courtesy, at once invited us to see his patient, a typical case, as he regarded it, of the prevailing fever. The following was his account of the case:

Paul Gravolet, white male, aged twenty-two years, had sat up for two nights with Adrian Dragou, sick of the fever, and had afterwards attended his funeral. It was the body of this A. Dragou which Dr. Sternberg had seen on his previous visit to the parish and noticed in his report. A short while after, on the afternoon of the tenth, Gravolet was taken with a chill, followed by violent headache, pain in the loins and legs, nausea, retching and fever. Dr. Hebert visited him for the first time on the twelfth instant at 8 a. m., and found him suffering from fever, with a hot, dry skin—temperature not noted. The vomiting of bile and mucous continued ; the eyes were congested, the tongue moist, streaked in centre, red at tip and edges, and was covered with a white fur ; the fur had disappeared on the fourth day, leaving the whole organ red ; the gums were red and swollen, but firm ; there was much restlessness throughout the attack ; the respiration was tranquil, without sighing; he complained of slight pain on pressure over epigastrium ; the urine had been abundant, and free from albumen ; there had been no delirium ; comp. cath. pills, followed on Monday by calc. magnes. had acted freely, and quinine, in 4 gr. doses, until 52 grains were taken—in 48 hours—had been ordered, after the action of the magnesia. The doctor could not say that he had noticed any decided remission at the period of his visits, morning and evening, but had sometimes found him perspiring. He had broken his thermometer and could not tell what the diurnal variations of temperature may have been.

At the time of our visit, 1:30 p. m., September 15, the pulse was 80 to the minute, temperature 101 1-5° F., respiration normal, tongue clean, gums pink and firm, skin pleasantly warm and soft, presenting no harshness nor pungency to the touch; the face was flushed, without capillary congestion; the body was of the natural color, and neither it nor the eyes showed the least tinge of yellowness; the *facies* was perfectly calm and the patient cheerful. He complained of some pain on pressure over stomach and abdomen. At 11 a. m. he had passed a small quantity of bright, florid blood by stool. The urine was abundant. A fresh specimen, tested on the spot, yielded, on the addition of nitric acid, a light precipitate, which cleared up perfectly on boiling. At our second visit, a little after noon the following day, we found him still convalescing. He had passed a little bright blood by stool during the night, but had slept well. The pulse was 60 to the minute, temperature 99 3-5° F. No albumen in urine.

In the same neighborhood we saw, with Dr. Hebert, Pierre Dragon, white, male, aged five years, the younger brother of the above mentioned Adrian. Three days before our visit, he had recovered from an attack of fever; but, two days after convalescence had partaken freely of sardines and chicken for breakfast, and at noon was seized with violent vomiting and purging. There had been no hemorrhage from bowels. The child was calm and cheerful; the skin soft and moist; the temperature carefully taken in axilla was 100° F. The pulse of the little patient much excited by our presence, was by first count 110 to the minute. At the close of our somewhat protracted visit, it had fallen to 92. There had been six cases of fever in this family. All had recovered but Adrian. A small specimen of the patient's urine, very dirty, full of hairs and mucus, was secured. It threw down a flaky deposit on the addition of nitric acid, not cleared by boiling. As a substitute for filtering paper a single thickness of newspaper was tried. I thought it was a clear case of failure, but if trustworthy the urine contained a trace of albumen. At our visit in the afternoon of the following day, the patient was convalescent, though still somewhat feverish.

Another patient of Dr. Hebert's visited by us in this neighborhood was Eliza Martin, white, female, aged fourteen years. She had come from New Orleans on the afternoon of the tenth, and was taken with fever three days after. She had been treated with calomel and quinine. On the second day of her fever (Tuesday) Dr. Hebert reports a well-marked remission in the morning. When seen by us on Wednesday at 3 p. m. her pulse was 120 to the minute, temperature 103 2-5 deg. F.; the tongue soft, moist, marked by the teeth, covered with light, white fur; the gums pale, pink, firm; *facies* calm; skin pleasant to touch and bedewed with slight perspiration. There was a tendency to diarrhœa and slight pain was complained of on pressure over abdomen. Urine, tested on the spot with nitric acid and heat, was free from albumen.

On the opposite side of the river, at the Franklin Rice Mill, we also visited, with Dr. Hebert, a patient of Dr. Hays's, Michael Halceran, a native of Louisiana, white, male, married, aged 33 years. He had been taken on the twelfth; at 10 a. m., with chill, violent headache and pain in the back and legs, accompanied by gastric distress and vomiting. The last continued throughout his attack; but we learned from his friends, and from his physician later, that this gastric irritability characterized him even in health. He is a confirmed dyspeptic, vomits his food frequently and is unable to retain a dose of medicine, unless it be disguised and concealed even from his suspicion. Dr. Hays informed us the next day that when he first saw Halceran, at 12 m. on Sunday—two hours after his seizure—the temperature was 103° F. Of his temperature Monday he had no record and did not recall it; but on Tuesday he found it to be 101¾° F. at his morning visit, and 102¼° F. in the afternoon. He was said to have had Yellow Fever during the epidemic of 1867.

At the time of our visit, we found him perfectly free of fever. He conversed cheerfully and readily, and his whole appearance was indicative of rapid and fine convalescence. The temperature was 100° Fahrenheit, pulse 62 to the minute, full, soft, slow; tongue clean and moist; no yellowness of conjunctiva or skin. Auscultation of heart revealed a 'soft, aortic, systolic murmer. Further inquiry afterwards confirmed by Dr. Hays, revealed the fact that the patient had suffered from more than one attack of acute rheumatic fever. The urine showed a small quantity of albumen, probably persistent.

In an adjacent town I saw Mrs. Halceran, wife of above, well advanced in convalescence from a similar attack of fever, lasting only forty-eight hours. She complained of feeling a little weak; but had a good appetite which she had been indulging for some days freely and without harm. Though we touched at this point the following day, we did not think it worth while to visit these patients again.

Moving down the right bank of the river we stopped at Dr. Geo. B. Hay's residence, Point Michel, and were immediately joined by the doctor, who came on board the tug, and took us to visit some of the more interesting cases of his own, then under treatment. The great majority of the patients he has had were well or convalescent.

Wm. Gilmore, white, male, aged 9 years, was taken at midnight Sunday with the usual light chill and pains in back and legs. Dr. Hays, at the date of his first visit, about noon on Monday, found him with high fever, hot, dry skin, frequent, quick pulse, white furred tongue, and free from nausea, or pain at epigastrium; the respiration was slightly hurried, without sighing, and there was no jactitation. His temperature was 100° F. The following forenoon it was 105° F.; in the afternoon 104½° F. On Wednesday morning it was 104½° F. At the time of our visit, 5:20 p. m., it was 103° F. Although an unusually nervous child and ministered to by a still more nervous mother, who hastened to inform him that the visit of so many doctors did not necessarily portend immediate dissolution, his expression was placid, exhibiting neither alarm nor depression. The conjunctiva were pinkish; but there was no intolerance of light, nor pain on pressure over the eyeballs. The face was slightly flushed, without capillary congestion. The color of the body was natural, and there was no yellowness of skin or eyes. To the touch the surface was dry and warm, without harshness or pungency. The pulse was 100° F. to the minute; respiration normal, no suspivia. The bowels had been freely moved, the dejections were natural, the urine copious. There was slight uneasiness manifested on pressure over epigastrium, and headache; but he made no complaint except of slight headache.

The following day we visited him again at 10 a. m. He had slept well; had two rather thin stools during the night, the last at 4 a. m.; with both had passed urine freely. The pulse was 92 deg.; temperature 101 3-5 deg. Fahrenheit. *Facies* cheerful, skin pleasant. From the excessive nervousness of the little patient, we could not secure a specimen of urine for examination at either visit.

In this locality we also visited with Dr. Hays, Millaudon Pooton, black, male, aged fourteen years, who was said to have had a relapse, succeeding a fever of four days' duration. We saw him again the following morning. At neither visit did he have any fever. The skin was rather cool, temperature normal, pulse soft and very compressible, but not frequent. The appetite was feeble, strength much exhausted, mind spiritless and dejected. He answered questions willingly, but slowly and without animation. The decubitus was lateral with the legs, semi-flexed, and we found him lying in exactly the same position, with the same air of utter indifference on our second visit as we had left him on our first. He made no complaint, and on repeated inquiry, admitted no special discomfort. His mother told us that he had been at work in the fields up to the date of his first attack; but the very great emaciation he exhibited was certainly not attributable to the brief acute attack he had experienced. He looked to me like a well advanced case of tuberculosis, and on inquiry I learned from Dr. Hays that his father had died with phthisis pulmonalis. Dr. Hays had never examined his chest, and his condition and surrounding were such as to not invite my personal auscultation of him. A specimen of his urine exhibited, on the usual tests, an abundance of albumen.

In the same room lay a younger brother of Milaudon, convalescent from a mild attack of the fever.

At the Quarantine Station, which we reached at 9 p. m., we found to our regret the Assistant Quarantine Physician, Dr. C. P. Wilkinson, down with the fever. He had been taken with the usual symptoms of chill, headache, pain in the back and legs, at 6 a. m. on Sunday, the twelfth, and when visited by us on Wednesday at 10 p. m. was, therefore, within eight hours of completing his fourth day. The Quarantine Physician, Dr. Finney, had kept an accurate record of his temperature—the sole instance in which we had the fortune to obtain it—from which it appeared that, on seizure, his temperature was 100½° F. At noon the same day it was 103 and the same in the evening.

Temp. F., deg.

Monday morning	101
Monday afternoon	104
Tuesday morning	101
Tuesday afternoon	104
Wednesday morning	101
Wednesday afternoon	104
And at 10 p. m., taken by myself	103

He had, when we saw him, a hot skin; broad, moist tongue, covered with white fur; pulse 90, full, soft, regular; no precordial nor abdominal distress nor vomiting throughout the attack. He had taken quinine in ten-grain doses three times on day of attack, but owing to the irritation it excited, had at first moderated and then discontinued its use. Wednesday he had taken two three-grain doses. He talked to us with unusual animation and energy that night, and the following morning when we visited him, a little after daybreak, we found him perfectly free from fever, in high spirits, and only anxious to resume as soon as possible the duties which he has performed with so much zeal, fidelity and intelligence.

Dr. Wilkinson is a native of Louisiana, aged thirty years. He stated that he had an attack of Yellow Fever, in common with members of his family, in 1855.

At an early hour the following morning, September 16, we crossed the river to Buras's Postoffice, which lies immediately opposite the Quarantine Station. There we had the pleasure of meeting with Dr. Westerfeld, whose practice extends for many miles above and below that point. The sum of the information gathered from him was to the effect that the fever had prevailed very extensively in that neighborhood—principally above—which he attributed to the batture, there being a caving bank, washed by the river, below. The fever had made its first appearance early in August, and about ten days thereafter had spread through the entire settlement, as many as five, six and seven cases occurring in single families, and in some of those deaths by Yellow Fever had happened in 1878. The majority of his cases had been among white children. Negroes enjoyed, seemingly, more immunity, and females still greater. The average duration of the fever was about 48 hours, he thought. It yielded readily to quinine; fevers chiefly of the remittent type, though he had seen a few intermittents. There had been no death in his practice, nor had he seen a single case in which there was jaundice, black vomit, or suppression of urine.

Dr Jones, whose area of observation and practice lies on the same bank of the river, between that of Dr. Westerfield and that of Dr. Hays, and with whom we passed some time later in the day, had treated about thirteen cases in all. There was, he thought, a well. marked remission in every case he had seen, but he had made no thermometric observations. The exacerbation took place toward night. The fever yielded readily to quinine, which he gave freely. The only difficulties he had experienced in the management of his cases arose from the tendency to undue cerebral excitement in children. He had lost none, nor had he seen any case with jaundice, black vomit or suppression of urine.

Dr. Ryan told Dr. Davidson that, at Pilot Town, the same fever had prevailed extensively. He regarded it as a malarial fever, remittent in type. It yielded readily to quinine. He had no death in his practice, nor had any of his cases been attended with yellowness of skin or eyes, or black vomit, or suppression of urine.

Visiting, with Doctors Hays, Hebert and Jones, who joined us, such cases of special interest as we had seen on the previous day, we reached Myrtle Grove about 2 p. m , and after an interesting conversation with Dr. J. B. Wilkinson—who, with two of his sons, paid us a visit on the tug—steamed directly for the city, which we reached at 6 p. m. on Thursday evening.

Through your own forethought and Dr. Mitchell's attentions we enjoyed every comfort possible on such a trip, and I take this opportunity, on the part of the whole commission, to express their deep sense of the courtesy they received from all the medical practitioners of the Coast, who, with equal candor and cordiality at just self-sacrifice, devoted a large part of two days to showing us every case of interest in their practice and giving us all the information that could possibly throw any light on the object of our mission.

From personal observation, and from the information gathered on the spot, I have no hesitation in expressing, with the utmost confidence, the conviction that the disease now and lately prevailing on the lower coast is an endemic malarial fever of remittent type, and for the most part of a mild character. Its unusual prevalence is due partly to the meteorological conditions of the past summer and partly, I believe, to the widely increased cultivation of rice. The alarm it temporarily excited was owing to its fatal results in a single family at the outset. Beyond this isolated instance it has been attended with the slightest mortality, and but for that it would scarcely excited comment except as to its prevalence and diffusion. The diagnosis obviously lies between malarial and Yellow Fever, and the reasons for assigning it to the former class seems to me patent and indisputable.

In the first place, all the practitioners in the infected district agree in the opinion, unqualifiedly expressed, that the disease is remittent fever, such as they are accustomed to treat every summer. The laity seem generally to share their views, giving the fever the trivial names, indifferently, of *la fievre du pays* or *la fievre paludienne.* Its ready amenability to quinine is, in itself, a strong proof of its miasmatic nature. If accurate records had been kept they would have been of prime assistance in arriving at certain conclusion but owing to loss or breakage of instruments, Dr. Hays was the only physician we met possessed of a thermometer, and the infrequency of his visits, from the great number of patients and the distances to be traveled, lessened the value of his observations as clinical aid to diagnosis. Nor was it possible, from the most painstaking inquiry, to extract any supplemental information from the attendants or families of the sick. For the most part untrained, ignorant, careless, incapable, alike of observing or describing the most familiar phenomena, the utmost that could be hoped from them as nurses would be to give a dose of medicine at prescribed hours. Under these circumstances the general impression of the medical attendant as to the continued or interrupted course of the fever is the only evidence that can be had, and this, as I have stated, was uniformly to the effect that in all cases diurnal remissions occurred, usually in the morning, judging from lowered pulses, diminished heat of skin, moisture, etc.

In theory and in text books a remission is a well-defined, notable abatement, at calculable intervals, of all the more prominent symptoms of the fever, lasting for many hours. But at the bedside, especially in our graver forms of autumnal fevers, a remission is too frequently an obscure, imperfect and ill-defined pause, as it were, between two prolonged exacerbations, filling up almost twice the entire round of twenty-four hours. The temporarily lowered pulse swiftly resumes its force and frequency ; the moisture, slight and transient, extending only over the forehead, face and neck, quickly dries up, and the accurate and continued observation which marks the brief return of the same phenomena at the same hour of the succeeding day can alone truly interpret its quality and meaning.

With their imperfect opportunities and means of detecting such remissions it is scarcely to be wondered at that the physicians had no charts to exhibit: But Dr. Wilkinson was suffering when we saw him with the same type of fever we had been seeing all day, and in his case the record kept by Dr. Finney supplies the missing link. It shows an access of fever, lasting all Sunday, with a well-marked remission in the morning and exacerbation in the evening of the following day. and the exact repetition of this rise and fall of temperature on two successive days thereafter, terminating at the end of the fourth day in a complete apyrexia.

Had a similar record' been kept in all the cases, I do not doubt that it would have equally exhibited their remitting character, though, doubtless, in many of them the remissions may not have been so strongly marked

So much concerning the type. Of the nature of the fever, without multiplying details, I will simply say that neither in its special features nor in their entirety could I realize a single prominent characteristic of Yellow Fever.

The broad, white, lightly furred tongue, moist in all stages, lacking the dry brown centre or fiery tip and edges; the firm gums, free from sordes or oozing, or the clear or only lightly suffused eye, not smoky or brilliant or dull, with no tinge of yellowness; the warm, pleasant skin, neither bathed in hot sweat, nor harsh, nor pungent to the touch, nor bronzed nor jaundiced nor exhibiting capillary congestion; the universal freedom from jactitation and delirium; the normal respiration, neither hurried, nor labored, nor sighing; the *facie*, free alike from terror or depression, calm, cheerful, smiling; the notable absence of any stage of calm intervening between a primary or secondary fever, or of black vomit, or any detections or suppression of the urine, or sudden cardiac syncope, render it as certain as clinical observation can, that the fever is not Yellow Fever.

And if we except the Giordano family, the extremely light mortality is no new important factor in the conclusion. Dr. Hays attributes the death of these four children of one household to their intractableness and refusal to take medicine. Now, in the graver forms of malarial fever the early and free administration of quinine often offers the sole means of saving life; but I can not help thinking that, in this instance, there coexisted some peculiarly malign local influence not made out, or special family predisposition not understood—a fact we are called on frequently ?to deplore. For of at least 150 cases that we can reckon, and doubtless a large number of others among the negroes, who neither sought nor obtained medical assistance, scattered along both banks of the river, under bad hygene conditions, crowded in close, damp, dark, ill-ventilated rooms, seen usually late and necessarily infrequently, with no nursing or worse, lifted out of bed and seated up for every occasion, in every stage of the disease, and fed or starved as fortune favored—improperly and unseasonably often, and as the waking or the whim of the nurse chanced. Out of this large number of cases, as we have said, but two deaths have occurred. Yellow Fever, whenever it prevails—so far as I know—stands high among the most fatal diseases of our horological table.

Nor is there any hint of such a march of the disease from house to house, or by personal contact, as can almost always be traced in contagious diseases breaking out among a sparse population, and never so easily traced as under such conditions as exist here, when the dwelling-houses are stretched along in one continuous and unbroken line, following the curves of the levee under which they lie.

What are the facts? Dr. Westerfield told us that his first cases occurred early in August, and by the tenth, after a pause of a few days, the whole settlement was involved. Dr. Hays gives a somewhat similar history of his section; but his first case did not occur until the fifteenth of August. Now the middle of Dr. Westerfield's line is directly opposite the Quarantine Station. Dr. Hays's practice lies many miles above. And at first sight this might seem seem to furnish a clue to to the source of the disease, if it were Yellow Fever—although we know of but one infected ship, the Excelsior, at Quarantine this summer, though of course many ships from infected ports have been detained there from time to time. The solution of the phenomenon, granting the disease to be malarial, is not far to seek. Owing to the shorter distance to the Gulf and the natural configuration of the land, drainage in the lower is much more rapid than that in the upper part of this area. Mr. F. C. Brooks, a planter of the neighborhood, informs me that, although the rice matures in both sections about the same time, the difference in time of drainage—the water being let off the field's simultaneously—is from seven to ten days, nearly. As the water is let off usually about the middle of July, the fever, as might have been anticipated, made its appearance along the river from below upwards just so soon as the hot sun of July and August could draw up from the reeking ground the miasm which, whatever its specific nature, is doubtless telluric in its origin.

Finally, the epidemic now prevailing in the parish of Plaquemines is, unhappily, not confined to the lower coast. Along both banks of the river as far up as Donaldsonville, in Jefferson, in St. John Baptist, St. Charles, St. James and Ascension. I am informed by my friends—physicians and planters—that the same or a similar fever exists. Since the latter part of June I have treated in New Orleans a fever identical with that which I found in

Plaquemines, invariably remittent, and many of them far more serious than any which I saw below. A few days only before I started on this mission I had treated for a severe remittent the clerk of the Alvin, a packet in the lower coast trade. He was seized with the fever on the coast and brought to the city with it.

And this widespread outbreak of malaria, during the present summer, is generally attributed by the residents along the river, above and below, to the increased acreage under cultivation in rice. In a letter from Dr E. Duffel, of Ascension, dated September 13, and received on my return—that most competent observer says: "I am very busy, having a great many cases of malarial fevers, at times very fatal, particularly if neglected at first. One of the worst complications is congestion of the brain, and few, if any, recover when thus affected. The extensive cultivation of rice in Louisiana will be very detrimental to the health of the people and a scourge."

A planter on the lower coast tells me that eight or nine years ago malarial fevers were comparatively infrequent and mild in that section, but have increased in numbers and severity just in proportion to the increase of the rice area. I do not doubt the truth of the statement, which is in strict accordance with all we know of the history of rice culture and its connection with miasmatic fevers elsewhere, notably in South Carolina and Georgia. In Louisiana two potent causes will contribute to the increased cultivation of this cereal. The poor man will give a natural preference to a crop which can be raised with small expenditure of labor and which needs no capital to take it off, and the wealthier sugar planter finds in it a valuable accessory to his main crop- harvested early, commanding cash readily, and furnishing, at the very season he most needs it, the large outlay required to convert his standing cane into a marketable commodity.

Whether the health of New Orleans will thus be endangered only time can show ; but that our hitherto salubrious lowland, if turned into paddy fields. will become hotbeds of malaria, hostile to the health and perhaps fatal to the presence of the white race, there is little reason to doubt.

I have the honor to be, very respectfully, your obedient servant,

J. DICKSON BRUNS, M. D.,
Chairman Committee on Fever of Lower Coast.

I concur with the above full and able report in regarding the disease prevailing on the Lower Mississippi coast as essentially a miasmatic fever of a remittent type, occasioned by the emanations from the rice fields stretched along the coast, and its diffusion over so extended an area as probably due to the peculiarities of the present season, characterized as it has been by long continued rains, followed, at harvest time of the rice, by very hot and dry weather. I saw no case of the fever which, in my judgment, could be said to present the diagnostic signs of Yellow Fever. J. P. DAVIDSON, M. D.

As Dr. Sternberg appears to have conceived himself agrieved because the daily press of New Orleans did not publish his report simultaneously with that of Drs. Bruns and Davidson, we will give this representative of the National Board of Health an opportunity to speak for himself.

Before reproducing his letter, as published in the Memphis papers, with the comments ot his friends, it should be noted that the reason assigned by the editor of the Democrat for withholding the report of Dr. Sternberg, was that its main points had already been telegraphed all over the United States, through the agency of the Associated Press, and that injury to the city and State had been produced thereby.

[The Memphis Appeal of October 7, contains the following.]

DR. STERNBERG'S

STATEMENT OF THE NUMBER AND LOCATION OF THE CASES OF YELLOW FEVER IN NEW ORLEANS AND ELSEWHERE IN LOUISIANA DURING THE MONTHS OF AUGUST AND SEPTEMBER—FACTS THAT HAVE BEEN CAREFULLY CONCEALED BY THE PRESS OF THE CRESCENT CITY AND THAT HAVE BEEN CONTRAVENED BY THE STATE AND CITY BOARDS OF HEALTH.

We make room for the following letter from Dr. Sternberg with regret, because it justifies a suspicion as to the perpetuity of Yellow Fever in New Orleans, and as to a want of sincerity in all things relating to that scourge by the health authorities of that city. It goes far, to confirm doubters as to the indifference of the scourge on the part of those in authority in New Orleans, and it will strengthen, if anything were needed to do so, the conviction that the people up here have that save through the National Board of Health, they have no guarantee that quarantine at New Orleans can or will be faithfully enforced.

DR. STERNBERG'S LETTER.

Editors Appeal—On the eighth day of September—being then engaged in the city of New Orleans in the prosecution of certain studies upon the malarial fevers, supplementary to Yellow Fever studies in Havana and elsewhere during the past two years. I was requested by Dr. S. M. Bemiss, the Louisiana representative to the National Board of Health, to proceed to Point Michel, in Plaquemine parish, about fifty miles below New Orleans, and there investigate a suspicious form of Fever, concerning which reports had reached Dr. Bemiss within the preceding forty-eight hours As a result of the report of that investigation a commission, of which I had the honor of being a member, was dispatched to the locality on the fifteenth of September, and, in company with Dr. R. W. Mitchell, of Memphis, the Tennessee representative of the National Board, proceeded to re-examine the cases. On the return of the commission to New Orleans its senior member (by appointment), a local physician of deservedly high reputation, prepared a report, which was published *in extenso* in the daily papers of that city. The gist of this report is contained in the following sentence: "Of the nature of the fever, without multiplying details, I will simply say that neither in its special features, nor in their entirety, could I realize a single prominent distinguishing characteristic of Yellow Fever"

To this extended report was appended a concurrence, signed by the member representing the Louisiana State Board of Health.

Unable to reach the same conclusion, I submitted a minority report, of which the following are the main points:

Investigations during my two visits show that the first case of this fever occurred about August 1st, directly opposite the Quarantine Station of the Louisiana State Board of Health, at which the Yellow Fever infected Bark Excelsior was anchored from June 24 to July 5, and again from July 11 to August 16. Within four or five days six more cases occurred in a family one and a half miles below the first; then seven cases in another family about the middle of August. At this time a case also appeared some distance up the river, about seven miles below Point Michel, and in this immediate neighborhood there were at least fifteen more cases. August 24, an infected locality was developed about one and a quarter miles above Point Michel, and the disease, which up to this time had been mild and tractable, assumed a more malignant character four dying out of six attacked in one family in this latter locality, and a young man in the vicinity. A family which left this neighborhood on account of sickness and moved to the vicinity of New Orleans (a short distance below Jackson barracks), lost one child with black vomit soon after its arrival. About September 4, the disease crossed the river and appeared in the Point-a-la-Hache settlement, several miles further up stream ; and at the time of my first visit I found one of the local practitioners and a large concourse of frightened people gathered around a house in which a young man had just died, and in which three children were lying sick with the fever.

It is claimed by some of the local practitioners that the fever results from malarial emanations from the rice-fields, and that it is essentially a malarial remittent fever, due to exposure in rice culture—hence the name "rice fever." That malarial remittent and intermittent fevers do prevail in the area above described is doubtless true, and they may be the result of the cause ascribed. But the claim that the cases of fever under investigation are of this character seems to me untenable from the fact that adults were the ones most exposed to these malarious rice-field emanations, while children not so exposed are the ones who have furnished the most subjects for this fever; and from the further fact that in various localities where rice is cultivated, under precisely the same conditions, this fever has not prevailed. I am informed, however, that a similar fever does prevail at Port Eads, where there are no rice-fields—and in this connection may be noted the additional point of resemblance, namely, that the origin of the fever at Port Eads, as in Plaquemine Parish, is not far to seek. At Port Eads there is a pilots' village and a customhouse station, from which there is necessarily communication with infected vessels. At the quarantine investigation of the Louisiana State Board of Health I find a little settlement within a few hundred yards of the wharf, and over which the Quarantine Physician has no control. The facilities for intercourse with infected vessels are certainly not insurmountable at this station. I find, moreover, that river packets, which make landings all along the banks of the river on their way up and down from New Orleans, are in the habit of tying up for the night at this quarantine wharf. I see no difficulty in accounting for the introduction and dissemination of a disease such as I believe this to be.

My investigations show it to be a continued fever of a single paroxysm, lasting, without perceptible remission, from one to four or five days; pulse soft and, after the first day, slow; perspiring skin, stomach irritable, intellect clear. In over 40 per cent. of the cases in which the urine was examined albumen was found in very large quantity, and, under the microscope, granular tube casts and epithelial cells from the bladder and pelves of the kidneys were found; and, finally, in a number of cases there was vomiting of a clear, acid fluid, containing dark ("coffee-grounds").

I have no hesitation in pronouncing this assemblage of symptoms one which can justify no other diagnosis than that of Yellow Fever, and that this conclusion is concurred in by Dr. Wilkerson, Sr., the oldest and most experienced practitioner in the vicinity, who has been called to see many of the cases in consultation. In the presence of the entire commission, and of Dr. Mitchell, during my second visit, Dr. Wilkerson said: "This is the same disease we had here in 1878. It was Yellow Fever then; it is Yellow Fever now."

Messrs. Editors, the report, of which the above is a summary, was furnished to the daily press of New Orleans, together with the majority report of the commission. It was furnished by Dr. Bemiss, with the express stipulation that both should be published. The New Orleans papers of September 23 contain the majority report only. Up to date the minority report has not been allowed to see the light.

In presenting the foregoing to you for publication, I assume that the season is now so far advanced that little or no harm can probably arise from the disease, and that the National Board of Health will institute such measures during the winter as will prevent any recrudescence of the contagion from these cases next summer. It is, indeed, entirely probable that the whole matter may be safely left to the board to deal with. But in the public health interests of the Mississippi Valley, and especially of your community which has made such a struggle for deliverance from epidemic pestilence by the most striking and thorough sanitary labor, it seems to me a duty to place you in possession of these facts, which you will use in your own discretion and at your own time.

GEO. M. STERNBERG,
Surgeon United States Army.

New Orleans, Sept. 30, 1880.

————

The Memphis Avalanche, which had on several occasions slandered the Board of Health of the State of Louisiana, published the letter of Surgeon George M. Sternberg, M. D., United States Army; Expert National Board of Health, under the following heading, and with the accompanying remarks:

LOUISIANA METHODS OF PRESERVING HEALTH BY SUPPRESSING THE TRUTH.

————

A STATEMENT OF FACTS BY A UNITED STATES ARMY SURGEON—THE MINORITY REPORT THAT THE NEW ORLEANS PAPERS REFUSED TO PUBLISH.

[Daily Memphis Avalanche, Thursday, October 7, 1880.]

From time to time during the past summer the Avalanche has felt called upon to animadvert upon the doings of the Board of Health of the City of New Orleans, a body styled by law "the State Board of Health of Louisiana." As is well known to those interested this Board is composed entirely of residents of New Orleans; its official head a gentleman of extensive scientific attainments, of consuming industry; and whose published labors excite alike the admiration and the incredulity of his co-workers; but who, unfortunately long ago espoused the theory of the indigenous origin of Yellow Fever in lower Louisiana, and, by consequence, became a logical, able and uncompromising opponent of quarantine or other measures looking to its exclusion by importation. Of the rest of the Board it is not necessary to speak in detail. It is cunningly made up of one or two gentlemen of respectable professional standing who are at odds with its president upon most points and of professional politicians, medical and non-medical, who know upon which side their bread is buttered—in other words, who understand the pecuniary and political advantage which arises from standing well with the advocates of an open port for New Orleans, unrestricted by any regulations or requirements conserving the public health.

This board, from its inauguration in April last, has made war not only upon every organization—beginning with the Auxiliary Sanitary Association of its own city, and including the local boards of health of Mobile, Galveston, Shreveport, Vicksburg, Memphis and Cairo, and the State Boards of Mississippi and Tennessee, and ending with the National Board of Health—but upon every individual who has ventured to express an opinion not in consonance with its methods of suppression, misrepresentation and total neglect of ordinary preventive measures. In open defiance of the expressed wish of its representative business men—outside the handful of importers, whose business lies exclusively with West

Indian and South American ports, where Yellow Fever is indigenous and perennial—this Board has opposed the Ship Island Quarantine Station for vessels from infected ports, and has allowed such vessels free access to the wharves and levees at New Orleans, in immediate contact with the steamboats plying the whole length of the river to St. Louis.

From the sixth to the tenth of July it allowed cases of Yellow Fever to lie unheeded at the levee, and only in dread of a quarantine of exclusion from points above did it finally yield an unwilling compliance with regard to the pest-stricken bark Excelsior. That this vessel was the direct source of the Yellow Fever in the Pointe-a-la-Hache Settlement, and which has finally reached New Orleans, Surgeon Sternberg's letter in another column makes clear beyond the shadow of a doubt. The dispatch published in yesterday's Avalanche, announcing a death from Yellow Fever in New Orleans, it is worthy of note, was sent upon the authority of the Acting President of the Louisiana Board of Health. Had the President in person been in New Orleans it is an open question whether this death would not have been returned as from "rice fever."

Dr. Sternberg's letter has been withheld until now, not because the Avalanche does not place the fullest reliance upon his competency to pronounce upon the question at issue, but solely in the interests of New Orleans herself. No good could have come of its publication before. No harm to the Valley above, in view of the inspection service still maintained by the National Board of Health at New Orleans and Vicksburg, could be caused by its delay. Dr. Sternberg did not need its publication for his own sake. But now that New Orleans admits, herself, that the fever has traveled from her own Quarantine Station up into the heart of the city, this straightforward, unimpassioned statement of facts, by a man whom her press was villifying and abusing only a fortnight since, possesses a value that cannot be ignored. It emphasizes, unmistakably, all that the Avalanche has had to say upon the necessity of the States and communities of the Mississippi Valley, above New Orleans, holding that city to a strict accountability in the guardianship of the outer gate. The Crescent City must shut Yellow Fever out from the Lower Mississippi, or the rest of the Valley will shut her out.

The *animus* of Dr. Sternberg and of the National Board of Health, which he represented, is fully shown in the preceding quotations from the Memphis papers. The National Board of Health has even seen fit to quote the Memphis papers, in opposition to the Louisiana State Board of Health, in their recent report, and appeal to the Congress of the United States.

The propriety, therefore, of reproducing the preceding publications from the Memphis papers, cannot be questioned.

The report of Dr. Sternberg should be regarded as cunningly devised to trace the origin of the fever, which he affirms to be Yellow Fever, to the bark Excelsior, and to account for its spread on the ground of alleged imperfections in the quarantine system and sanitary regulations of the Board of Health of the State of Louisiana.

The communications of Drs. Westerfield, Jones, Hayes and Taylor to the President subsequently, will still further illustrate the nature of Surgeon Sternberg's statement.

The Resident Member of the National Board of Health published the reports of Drs. Bruns, Davidson and of Dr. Sternberg, in the October number of the New Orleans Medical and Surgical Journal, with the following editorial remarks.

We lay before our readers the following reports in regard to a form of fever recently prevailing on the Lower Mississippi River. The circumstances which elicited these reports are as follows: The senior editor of this Journal having been informed that the oldest practitioner in the parish of Plaquemines, had pronounced a fever prevailing in that parish to be Yellow Fever, requested Dr. G. M. Sternberg, of the United States Army, now on special duty in this city, to go down and investigate the disease. The report of Dr. Sternberg, published first, will show his opinions in regard to the matter. Some question being made in respect to the correctness of Dr. Sternberg's conclusions, the writer acting in his capacity as a member of the National Board of Health, determined in the interests of science as well as in the paramount interests of public health, to order a new investigation.

To this end he requested Dr. J. Dickson Bruns and Dr. J. P. Davidson to unite themselves with Dr. Sternberg in a second visit to the seat of prevalence of the fever, and after due investigation to make a further report. Our readers will see that the result has been two reports, one, signed by Dr. Bruns and Dr. Davidson, and the other by Dr. Sternberg, alone.

The gentlemen signing the majority report are two of the most accomplished and experienced physicians in the city of New Orleans. Dr. Sternberg's reputation in the scientific world is sufficiently well-known to require no notice at our hands. In the action as above set forth, the writer was seconded and assisted by his colleague on the National Board of Health, Dr. R. W. Mitchell, who also accompanied the commission, but without participation in their discussions or reports.

It is proper also to say that the writer adopted the majority report as his rule of conduct, but by this action did not presume to adjudicate the questions at issue from a scientific standpoint. The New Orleans Medical and Surgical Journal, edited by S. M. Bemiss, M. D., W. H. Watkins, M. D., S. S. Herrick, M. D., October, 1880; p. 382.

It will be observed, that the Resident Member of the National Board of Health (Prof. S. M. Bemiss, M. D.), states distinctly and unequivocally that:

"*In the action above set forth, the writer was seconded and assisted by his colleague on the National Board of Health, Dr. R. W. Mitchell, who also accompanied the commission but without participation in their discussions or reports.*"

"*It is proper also to say that the writer adopted the majority report as his rule of conduct, but by this action did not presume to adjudicate the questions at issue from a scientific standpoint.*"

In direct opposition to the preceding statement and to the majority report of Drs. Bruns and Davidson, the *National Board of Health Bulletin, vol 2 No. 15, issued from Washington D. C.*, on *Saturday, October 9*, 1880, contains the following remarkable statement, signed by the representatives of the National Board of Health in Louisiana and Tennessee.

[National Board of Health Bulletin, Washington, D. C., October 9.]

THE FEVER ON THE LOWER MISSISSIPPI.

NEW ORLEANS, October 4, 1880.

Sir—Definite information of the existence of a suspicious form of fever in Plaquemine parish, La., on the Lower Mississippi, having been received by the member of the National Board of Health resident in New Orleans, Geo. M. Sternberg, Surgeon U. S. A., was requested to visit the locality, examine such number of cases as might be necessary to enable him to determine the nature of the fever, and report the result of his investigation to the New Orleans member. Surgeon Sternberg was selected for this duty because of his extensive and intimate acquaintance with the fevers of the Gulf coast and Spanish Main; because of the recognized skill and ability which had led to his being chosen one of the experts on the Havana Yellow Fever Commission, and to his being intrusted with the duty of preparing the article on Yellow Fever in the supplement to Ziemssen's Cyclopedia, and also because of his position as a United States Army medical officer, which, while it removed him on the one hand from the probability of having his judgment or conclusions influenced by local or personal considerations, on the other, devolved upon him the responsibility of representing an extremely sensitive professional body.

On the tenth of September, Dr. Sternberg made a detailed report, in which, after reciting the history of the sickness from the appearance of the first case, early in August, up to the date of his investigation, he positively asserted the existence of Yellow Fever of a mild type, with a low rate of mortality, except where the disease was aggravated by vicious local conditions. In the area where this prevailed, Dr. Sternberg also found a malarial fever, attributed by the local physicians to exposure in the rice harvest, and which they called rice fever.

Upon receipt of this report a telegram was sent to the Executive Committee asking that, if Dr. Sternberg's opinion was of sufficient weight, an appropriation of from five thousand to ten thousand dollars be made from the contingent fund and placed at the disposal of the Louisiana State Board of Health for use in the necessary preventive measures. The appropriation was immediately ordered, and a tender of the sum was made, as above indicated, on the 13th of September.

Recognizing only the existence of the so-called rice fever, the State Board declined the offer of the National Board and claimed to have "instuted such measures as it deemed necessary." Up to this time the action of the Louisiana member, representing the National Board of Health, had been governed by that portion of section 3 of the act of June 2, 1879, which makes it the duty of the Board to "co-operate with and, so far as it lawfully may, aid the State and municipal Boards of Health in the execution and enforcement of the rules and regulations of such boards to prevent the introduction of contagious or infectious diseases into the United States from foreign countries, and into one State from another."

The rejection of this proffer to "co-operate and aid," however, now made it incumbent upon the National Board, through its representative, to take such steps as might determine whether the contingency was grave enough to warrant action under that clause in section 3 which directs the Board to "report the facts to the President of the United States," whose duty it then is to use the Executive authority in executing and enforcing the necessary rules and regulations. With this object the member of the National Board of Health resident in Memphis was summoned to New Orleans, and, after careful consideration of all the facts, it was decided to send a commission of three medical gentlemen to the compromised locality, and to base the action of the Board upon the report of said commission. These gentlemen (selected with the approval of the Auxiliary Sanitary Association) were Dr. J. Dickson Bruns, of New Orleans, Dr. J. P. Davidson, of the Louisiana State Board of Health, and Surgeon Sternberg, U. S. A., and they were accompanied on their mission by the Tennessee member of the National Board, the Louisiana member being prevented by his only partial convalescence from the recent attack of the prevailing dengue.

Without entering upon any discussion of the two reports made, the one by Drs. Bruns and Davidson, and the other by Surgeon Sternberg, it is sufficient for the present purpose to say that it was made evident, as well by the conflicting reports of the commission as by the personal observation of the Tennessee member, that no practical benefit could now be attained from Executive interference.

Whatever danger had threatened the public health of the Mississippi Valley had either passed away—the disease having run its course—or it had been so widely scattered that preventive measures on any adequate scale were impracticable for the time being.

Considering the advanced stage of the season, the favorable health conditions of the valley, the more than doubtful utility of any steps still possible looking to isolation, disinfection, &c., and the desirability of avoiding overt action likely to create anxiety and apprehension, if not positive panic—these considerations have induced the representatives of the board to refrain from recommending further action in the premises at the present time.

They cannot, however, close this report without placing themselves on record as fully accepting and indorsing Surgeon Sternberg's conclusions, to-wit:

1. That Yellow Fever (about 100 cases) existed between August 1 and September 10 in Plaquemine Parish, Louisiana.

2. That the outbreak had its origin in the immediate vicinity of the Mississippi River Quarantine Station, the first case, August 1, occurring directly opposite the point where the infected bark Excelsior was detained from July 11 to August 16.

3. That while the type of the disease was generally mild, vicious local conditions existed which aggravated it into the most fatal form, four dying in one family out of five attacked.

The details of the investigations upon which these conclusions are based will be found in the accompanying reports of Surgeon Sternberg.

All of which is respectfully submitted,   S. M. BEMISS,
                                         Member National Board of Health, New Orleans, La.
                                                              R. W. MITCHELL,
                                         Member National Board of Health, Memphis, Tenn.
To the Secretary of the National Board of Health, Washington, D. C.

The Daily New Orleans Picayune of October 17, contained the following remarkable report of an interview with the Resident Member of National Board of Health:

THE NATIONAL BOARD OF HEALTH BULLETIN REPORTS DR. BEMISS AS SAYING THERE HAVE BEEN A HUNDRED CASES OF YELLOW FEVER IN LOUISIANA THIS FALL—DR. BEMISS DENIES EVER HAVING STATED, KNOWINGLY, ANYTHING OF THE KIND.

In the last copy of the National Board of Health Bulletin, dated Washington, D. C., October 9, is the following report signed by Drs. Bemiss and Mitchell, members of the National Board of Louisiana and Tennessee:

THE FEVER ON THE LOWER MISSISSIPPI.

* * * Here follows the full report, just published, dated New Orleans, October 4, 1880:

A reporter of the Picayune called upon Dr. Bemiss yesterday afternoon, for the purpose of ascertaing upon what facts he based the above report, when he produced the following telegrams:

                                                      NEW ORLEANS, October 11, 1880.
T. J. Turner, M. D., Secretary National Board of Health, Washington, D. C.:

Do not publish report by Mitchell and myself until letter of Saturday arrives. No fever here known to me.   S. M. BEMISS, M. D.

Dr. Turner replied as follows:

                                                      WASHINGTON, October 11, 1880.
Telegram received. Report already published in Bulletin, which comes from printer to-day. Edition now ready for delivery.   T. J. TURNER, M. D.

Dr. Bemiss then made the following statement to the representative of the Picayune: Under date of October 9, I wrote the Secretary of the National Board of Health as follows: "I respectfully state that the complaints of Dr. Sternberg, in relation to alterations in his manuscript when published in the Memphis papers, and other points connected with this so-called rice fever, do, in my opinion, make it a matter of prudence to make no official publication by the board until further developments are reached. I therefore suggest that the report over the signature of Dr. Mitchell and myself be withheld for the present."

When I signed the report, if the word "yellow" was before the word fever, it certainly escaped my observation. I have no evidence that a hundred cases of Yellow Fever have occurred in Louisiana this year. While, on the other hand, I am well satisfied from testimony furnished, that a hundred cases, or more, of fever have occurred on the lower coast, some of which were as undoubtedly Yellow Fever, as others were of a different character.

The report above referred to was prepared in the office of Dr. R. W. Mitchell, in Memphis, the Tennessee member of the National Board, who accompanied the commission to the lower coast, and from whom I will obtain, at the earliest possible moment, positive information as to the presence of the word "yellow" before fever, when I affixed my signature to the report. So far as Dr. Mitchell is concerned, his position in the matter will be determined by evidence in his own possession. He will certainly do nothing and say nothing which he does not believe to be in strict accordance with truth. The occurrence of the word "yellow" before the word fever, as published in the report of the bulletin of the National Board, under date of October 9th, was certainly a surprise to me, although I shall not positively assert that it may not have been there at the time of signing the report, and if so I hold myself guilty of very culpable inadvertence."

Comment is unnecessary.

The following communications will close the evidence with reference to the malarial nature of the fever which prevailed in the delta of the Mississippi River and are submitted without further observation or illustration:

BURAS, October 28, 1880.

Dr. Joseph Jones, President Board of Health:

Dear Sir—Yours of the twentieth instant, received, in reply I would state that no Yellow Fever exists in this locality, neither has there been one case this season in my practice, having practiced here for the last twenty-four years, and been familiar with the symptoms of Yellow Fever as it has existed along the coast and also at Quarantine Station during that period, I say positively that there has been no cases here.

We have had a mild form of 'Malarial Fever' amounting to an epidemic, prevailing since July 15, caused by heat of the sun on the battures as the waters receded, and the battures became exposed to the suns rays. The epidemic did not originate from Bark Excelsior, have not had one case of the fever where the patients had communicated with the Bark Excelsior.

As to treatment of the fever, very little is required. A few doses of Dovers' powders with simpisms of mustard, and three or four doses of quinine and followed by a mild cathartic,—I prefer castor oil—I find that treatment very successful and sufficient.

Some four hundred cases have occurred in my practice, and so far not one death from the fever, and among all those no symptoms of Yellow Fever. So mild has the disease been here that many persons have had no medical treatment whatever and permanently recovered.

Please excuse my delay in not answering sooner and believe me your friend.

Truly yours, R. WESTERFIELD, M. D.

POINT MICHEL, La., October 31, 1880.

To Dr. Joseph Jones, President of Louisiana State Board of Health:

Dear Doctor—I suppose you will be a little surprised at receiving this letter from me, dated from this place; as I am now practicing in this part of the parish, and as I see by the newspapers, that the fever lately prevailing here has created some little excitement among the people of New Orleans, and as I have seen and treated nearly as many cases of this affection as almost any other physician down here, I have ventured to think that a few lines, briefly describing my experience of the disease might not be unwelcome to you.

In the first place, I may state, it seems to me next to impossible for any educated medical man to mistake the disease for anything else than typical and well-marked cases of "bilious" remittent fever, and for an accurate and beautiful description of all the different types and phases of this malady as lately prevailing here, I would respectfully refer you to Wood's practice of medicine (volume 1; p. 264).

The fever usually begins with undefined chilly sensations, rigors or a decided chill, the tongue in the beginning is moist and broad, and covered with a white fur; sometimes it is red at the tip and edges; the gums are also hard without swelling and without sensitiveness to pressure or tendency to bleed; the pulse is mostly always at commencement soft and full without sharpness and not very frequent. Pain in the forehead, with nausea and vomiting, insatiable thirst and loathing for food, also usually attend the disease at its commencement or after it has become well developed. Cerebral congestion as denoted by heat of head, turned upsides of tongue, contracted pupils, nausea and vomiting not referable to inflammation of stomach, or tenderness in spinal column and in most of the fatal cases convulsion is oftentimes developed either as an attendant or sequel of the affection.

A distinct remission or sometimes even an entire intermission always occurs mostly in the morning.

In a few instances, fresh or clotted blood, not at all resembling black vomit has been thrown up or passed through the bowels, suppression of urine has never occurred in my practice and in only one case to be spoken of hereafter have I seen any yellowness of the skin or conjunctiva or any symptom like jaundice.

In my hands, when taken in the beginning, the fever has always been easily arrested by decided doses of quinine given only during the remission; thus treated I have seldom seen it last beyond four days, and in very few cases does it return after the first remission has taken place.

Altogether, I have treated about one hundred and fifty or one hundred and seventy-five cases of this fever, and the total number of deaths of those seen and treated by me from the beginning is only two. In these two cases the fatal terminations occurred several days after the patients had begun to convalesce, and the causes of death were altogether independent of the main disease: in the one case I ascribed it to overdoses of the fluid extract of ipecac (administered through mistake by the attending nurse for the fluid extract of digitalis) at a time when the patient was in a very weakened condition and scarcely had enough strength to recover from the effects of the fever; in the second case, to convulsions occurring three days after the fever had been arrested and brought about by worms which I found present in the alimentary canal, in large numbers, on post-mortem examination.

The first case of the disease occurring in my practice was a little colored girl named Evelina Rapp, aged nine years, first seen by me on the twenty-fifth of July last. She had had the fever several days before coming under my care: her temperature then stood at 106°, pulse sharp, soft and frequent: tongue moist, broad and indented by the teeth, covered by a light, white fur and red at the edges; gums not swollen or sensitive to pressure and without any tendency to hemorrhage. The fever, in her case, although of a decidedly remittent type, proved very intractable to quinine, and was not finally arrested until the ninth day after I had first seen her.

The last case seen by me was a mulatto girl named Juliene Phillins, aged fourteen years; had moderate fever of a remittent type, which was very easily arrested by a dose of ten grains of quinine given on the first appearance of a remission. In her case the tongue was moist, covered by a white fur and broad as usual; teeth white and clean, without sordes, and there was an absence of all the usual distressing attendants of the disease, such as pains in the head and loins, nausea, vomiting, etc.; the eyes were normal in appearance, not glistening, and the pupil was neither contracted nor dilated. About sixteen hours after the subsistence of the fever the patient was suddenly taken with violent pains in the head, incessant nausea and uncontrollable restlessness, unattended by fever, and about three days later her whole surface and conjunctiva became of a distinctly jaundiced hue. The urine at first was of a dark, heavy color, and on chemical analysis proved to consist of about seven-eighths albumen: at the time of the patient's becoming jaundiced the urine also became of a bright yellow color showing plainly the presence of bile. At about the same period the patient began to lose strength, and continued sinking notwithstanding the employment of all sorts of supporting measures until she finally died on the eleventh, after having first been seen by me. No post-mortem examination would be allowed.   *   *   *

The fever has now entirely subsided, and I have not seen nor heard of a case of the disease for more than a week.   Very truly yours,   JOHN T. JONES, M. D.

POINT MICHEL, La., October 22, 1880.

Dr. Joseph Jones, President State Board of Health of Louisiana, New Orleans, La.:

Dear Sir—Your letter of the twentieth instant, requesting further particulars in regard to the fever at Point Michel, with number of cases and total mortality, is at hand:

I willingly comply with your request and believe it a plain duty to the public to furnish a truthful statement of the character and number of cases of this much-talked of fever, more especially since the publication of the report of Dr. Sternberg, followed by that of Drs. Bemiss and Mitchell. I can speak authoritatively with regard to my own practice and that of Dr. Hebert, and as the entire number of cases of fever (with comparatively few exceptions) occurred among our patients, that should have some weight.

It appears that the first case of the fever seen by me was George Burton, native of Louisiana, white male age thirty, a resident of Union Settlement on the left bank of the Mississippi River: about fifty miles below New Orleans. I was called in consultation by Dr. Hebert, July 31. The patient died with congestion of the brain, August 2 having been sick about two weeks. The next cases were August 4, a colored woman and child at Point Michel, right bank of the river. August 8, Mrs. S., white, at Grand Prarie, left bank of river fifty-five miles below New Orleans, and a white child at Point Michel, one and a half miels below the Lightell case. August 15, one case at Petite Prairie, right bank of river fifty-eight miles below New Orleans, August 16, a case at upper limit of Point Michel, forty-seven miles below New Orleans.

I give the foregoing details to show how the first cases made their appearance almost simultaneously on different sides of the river, at localities widely separated, and in families that to my certain knowledge held no communication with each other. The fever gradually increased up to the first of September, prevailed extensively during the whole of that month, copious rains having been succeeded by nearly two months of a torrid sun and drouth and in the beginning of October a material decrease took place both in the number and severity of the cases. From July 31 to the date I find upon a careful examination of my visiting list that I have had 123 colored and 95 white patients—a total of 218 with malarial fever.

Of these 50 were white children and 59 colored children 14 years and under. Of this number there were eight deaths among the whites and five among the colored—a total of 13. Nine children died and four adults. Of the eight deaths first mentioned three occurred in one family, of children who were very intractable and who virtually had no medication, it being impossible to exercise any control over them.

As will be seen further, this statement differs materially from that of Dr. Sternberg, published in the New Orleans Medical Journal, in several particulars and I am compelled to contradict most emphatically his assertion that "it is a continued fever of a single paroxysm" and "not characterized by remissions or intermissions," as the reverse is proven to be the case. My time having been so fully occupied because of the distances to be traversed in making my daily round it was impossible to keep a thermometric record, but the observations taken show remissions in every case examined and even slight intermissions in some. Since the fever has abated somewhat I have been enabled to keep records of temperature which bear me out in that the fever was markedly of a remittent type. The following is the temperature of a typical case: Joe Stern, white, aged seventeen years, resident of Point Michel about a year, native of Poland. First visited October 10; temperature at 1 p. m., 105°; October 11, 11 a. m., 104°; 3 p. m., 102°; October 12, 11 a. m., 103°; 4 p. m., 103°; October 13, 9:30 a. m, 101½°; 7 p. m., 103½°; October 14, 4:30 p. m., 100°; October 15, 4 p. m., 100°; October 16, no fever.

Two different times in his report Dr. Sternberg says that a similar fever prevailed in 1878, "which some physicians called Yellow Fever but Dr. Hays believes it also to have been malarial fever." Presumably he refers to Point Michel and I am at a loss to know whence he derives his information, as I perfectly well remember that no other physician saw any patient of mine during the fall of 1878, either in consultation or otherwise, and consequently one could scarcely be expected to make a more accurate diagnosis than the physician actually in attendance upon the sick. In 1878, I experienced no great difficulty in recognizing a case of Yellow Fever, on the fourth of September and subsequently three other cases, and strange as it may appear to a scientific expert, did not confound the numerous cases of hæmorrhagic malarial fever with those cases, although an epidemic was prevailing at the time in New Orleans.

Dr. Sternberg is again in error when he says the fever is of "a mild type." Because he chanced upon no higher temperature than 103 1-5° like a doubting Thomas he disbelieves in its existence. The truth is that 105° and 106° was not an unusual concomitant of the disease that he characterizes as "mild," and the headache, pains in the back, joints and muscles were almost universal. Hæmorrhages were common, notwithstanding his statement to the contrary, from the nose, bowels and stomach, and hematuria was not infrequent. In not one case of the 218 was there suppression of urine, and the usual tests failed to detect albumen in more than a half dozen instances.

On the ninth of September, Dr. Taylor (representing the State Board of Health). Dr. Sternberg and myself visited the most pronounced cases in my practice and then crossed the river to Pointe-a-la-Hache and in company with Dr. Hebert, the resident physician, saw a number of his patients. The body of Andrew Dragon presented no characteristic appearances of Yellow Fever, no jaundice, no yellow conjunctival. The surface had a bluish mottled appearance. There were two little children sick in the same house who subsequently recovered under quinine treatment. The boy of twelve, referred to by Dr. Sternberg, whose urine contained the greatest quantity of albumen, and who "was dressed and sitting up," and had the "glistening eyes," mentioned in the report, never went to bed at all, and is now as well as usual I am informed by Dr. Hebert. That boy I would venture to say has albumen ever present in his urine. It was very patent to every one of the party that Dr. Sternberg came with the evident intention of finding Yellow Fever, and failing in that, his mission would not have been accomplished. It is singular that while dwelling long and lovingly upon every symptom that might be utilized in forming a Yellow Fever diagnosis he omits all mention of the fact that of three sick children in the family of Pierre Hingle at Pointe-a-la-Hache, two were sick of a similar fever in 1878, as stated by Dr. Hebert.

The same thing has occurred in my practice this season. It will doubtless be remembered that there was a sudden lowering of the temperature on the ninth of September. Before starting on our ride that morning Dr. Sternberg observed that "if the disease was Yellow Fever the change in temperature would prove disastrous to many of the sick." Our visit demonstrated that none of them were unpleasantly affected by it, yet he omits all mention of that in his report.

Had he devoted less attention to "Beranger-Ferand" and "Blair," and more to the practical observation of the fever, he doubtless would not have fallen into so unfortunate an error. He writes "I have not seen during either visit any case which alone would enable me to make a positive diagnosis of Yellow Fever, but from a consideration of all the cases seen by me during my two visits, and of the facts relating to the origin and progress of the epidemic, I cannot doubt that this fever is the mild type of Yellow Fever which has been described," etc., and then proceeds to quote "Blair." He cites Dr. Wilkinson, Sr., as having "made an unqualified diagnosis of Yellow Fever;" yet he also says: "In the practice of Dr. Wilkinson, on the west bank of the river and just above Dr. Hays no cases of the same fever has occurred."

When Dr. Wilkinson visited the Giordano children, September 1, in consultation with Dr. Hebert and myself he then coincided with us in the opinion that it was malarial fever. Thenceforward he saw no more of my patients until the twenty-sixth when he visited in consultation, a young colored man, about 18 years old in the upper part of Point Michel. That patient died the morning of the twenty-eighth, with congestion of the brain. He vomited some blood at 2 a. m. the twenty-sixth before Dr. Wilkinson saw him. He never vomited afterwards, had no suppression, no albumen. Dr. Wilkinson never told me that he thought that a case of Yellow Fever.

That was another specimen of the fever that Dr. Sternberg says "is chiefly characterized by the mildness of its course, and the absence of distressing symptoms," which, however, caused intense suffering, congestions, and finally destroyed the life of the patient just as though it had been a "high grade of malarial fever, with a tendency to local congestions and hæmorrhages."

The fever yields to quinine or cinchonidia. On his first visit Dr. Sternberg suggested that a few cases be treated experimentally without quinine, in order to see whether they too, would not recover. I told him I had already done so, involuntarily it is true, in the case of the Giordano children (who would not take or retain quinine) and that three of them had died. The fever has been restricted to natives and long residents. At the beginning of the endemic this section was overrun by tramps of every nationality, Italians, Germans, Irish Chinese, and others, seeking employment in the rice harvest. They were here temporarily, and none of them were sick.

Since the middle of September the coast has been lined with the luggers of the orange merchants who have been busily engaged gathering oranges in the yards and around the houses where lay the sick, and where people have died of the fever. All their surroundings were favorable to the development of Yellow Fever if its poison existed in the locality, and the foreign-born boatmen, many of them unacclimated, were the very material for it to feed upon, and yet none of them fell ill. When we come to consider the report published in the Picayune of the seventeenth inst. signed by Drs. Bemiss and Mitchell, it is well known that the former made no visit to the "so-called" infected locality, and it is within my own knowledge that Dr. Mitchell appeared to take but faint interest in the investigations personally.

Both those gentlemen have evidently accepted Dr. Sternberg's dictum in regard to the fever. It is a gratifying fact that my original diagnosis of malarial fever has been sustained by Dr. J. Dickson Bruns, Dr. J. P. Davidson and Dr. B. F. Taylor of New Orleans, and by Dr. D. R. Fox and Dr. N. M Hebert of this Parish. All physicians in active practice, familiar with the diseases incident to our southern climate, sufficiently accustomed to Yellow Fever as not to require fifty or sixty cases before being able to recognize the disease (as was done on Governor's Island some years ago, I am told by Dr. Sternberg, and here more recently) and can lay claim to some experience.

Very respectfully,

　　　　　　　　　　　　　　　　　　　　GEO. A. B. HAYS, M. D.

　　　　　　　　　　　　　　　　　　NEW ORLEANS, October 22. 1880.

Dr. Joseph Jones, President of Louisiana State Board of Health :

Sir—It becomes my duty, as Quarantine Officer and Sanitary Inspector at Port Eads and the Passes of the Mississippi River, to report the sanitary condition of these places during the past summer months.

In pursuance of your instructions, in August I proceeded to Port Eads and made an examination of the location in reference to its topography, hygenic and sanitary condition and found the place had been built up on either side of the river, the land having been made artificially by the deposit of ballast of various materials brought by ships from foreign ports.

In the rear of these houses, beyond the ballast fillings, there is a marsh thickly covered—so as to entirely exclude the sun—with grass and reeds ten to fifteen feet in height. The whole surface is completely submerged every twenty-four hours by salt-water from the tides of the Gulf. On the subsidence of the tides, as before mentioned, the surface of the earth is protected from the rays of the sun. The conditions, therefore, necessary for the preservation of health would seem to be all that is required, so far as is applicable to a low, level, marshy country, without forest or woody undergrowth.

The history of Port Eads, dating back from the beginning of the Jetties by its illustrious founder, Capt. James B. Eads, corroborates this view of its sanitary condition, as fevers of all intermittent types are unknown.

To malaria, therefore, as a factor in the production of fevers in this locality, can we ascribe the occurrence of the epidemic, but more philosophically, to my mind, to the high temperature, pe..uhar electric and general condition of the atmosphere, the same as prevailed all through the Southern States of this Union.

To these influences must be ascribed the fever that began at Port Eads and the vicinity of the Passes in August, continuing during the month of September and a part of October, attacking the majority of the inhabitants, without regard to exposure, age, or condition; females and children who were confined in the house, being equally subject to the disease.

In this fever, the attack came on usually with slight chilly sensations accompanied by pain in the back, loins and thighs with headache. Tongue slightly coated with a yellowish fur; no redness of consequence. The temperature, in no case that came under my observation, exceeded 103½° F. and generally 100° to 102° F. lasting but a few hours; in my own case, only three hours.

Discoloration of the conjunctiva, and the tissues generally were absent. The gums and buccal membranes were sometimes pale and flabby. The stomach was seldom disturbed, nor was there any tenderness on pressure.

In many cases the fever was of a single paroxysm, lasting from three to eight and ten hours; in others a distinct intermission in the morning. When quinine was administered upon the accession of the paroxysm, in doses sufficient to place the system under its influence, the patient recovered without any febrile disturbance, not a single death occurring.

A general disposition to constipation was observed after the subsidence of the fever, which was easily controlled by mild aperients. In no case could albumen be detected in the urine.

In a few cases there were arthritic symptoms, beginning with swelling of the joints of the fingers; followed, about the third day, by a rash on the skin, ending with a slight desquamation of the cuticle, as is seen in measles, answering to the description of dengue as given by systematic writers.

In accordance with your dispatch of the seventh of September to proceed to Point Michel, right bank, twenty miles above the Mississippi River Quarantine Station, investigate and report upon the fever reported to be prevalent in that neighborhood, I came first to the city on the 8th of September, and next day left for Point Michel.

On the steamer I met Dr. Sternberg, of the National Board of Health, who informed me that he was on a similar mission, having been requested by Professor Bemiss, member of the National Board, to investigate and report the character of the epidemic said to be prevailing at Point Michel and the lower coast.

In due time we arrived, and went to the house of Dr. Hayes, in whose practice, it was reported, those cases had occurred: particularly the four children who had died in the family of an Italian named Giordano, of symptoms of Yellow Fever

After spending the night with Dr. Hayes, and explaining the object of our mission, he very kindly invited us the next morning to visit with him every case in his practice, and investigate and examine for ourselves

Accordingly we started out early and visited quite a number of houses, perhaps twenty in all and found in a number of them as many as three cases. In that of Mr. Giordano, half a mile above, in whose family the four children died, we found one child convalescent, as well as my memory serves me.

Dr. Hays had seen these children, and stated that there were no symptoms unusually manifest, more than he was in the habit of observing in the fever that occurs every year in his practice, and their death certainly was, in consequence of his inability to make the children take any remedies that were prescribed.

We proceeded up the river ten miles, visiting patients by the way, and crossed the river at Pointe-a-la-Hache, opposite the court-house, after which our journey was continued to a point four miles above for the purpose of seeing a patient of Dr. Hebert, who was reported in a dying condition.

On our arrival we met the Doctor, and found that his patient, a young man about 17 years of age, had just died. An examination of the body, externally, revealed bluish patchide, as is usually met with in persons dying of fever. The gums were pale and flacid. No yellowness of the mucous membranes, or bronzed condition of the skin, was observed.

In this house there were two children sick in bed, and a third one not yet prostrated. Dr. Sternberg, in our presence, examined the urine of these children by subjecting it to boiling in a test tube and adding nitric acid. Not a trace of albumen was found in the urine of the children in bed. The third child, who had not yet fallen sick, had what appeared to be albumen. The deposit, however, might have been mistaken for that of lithic acid, which often presents an appearance not unlike that of albumen.

The next house visited was situated one mile below the court-house, where we found four children sick. I am not certain that the urine of these children were examined, but Dr. Hebert informed us that two of these cases had been attacked with Yellow Fever, and was treated by him, in the great epidemic of 1878

It is proper to state that the temperature in the cases examined by Dr. Sternberg was tested by a standard thermometer, and the examination of urine made by means of a test tube, and the addition of nitric acid.

In no case was the temperature found above 104° F., if my memory serves me, and in only a single case so high, nor was the urine found to be albumenious, except in the instance before-mentioned.

In the National Board of Health Bulletin, of the 9th inst., Dr. Sternberg says "that cases occurred in the practice of Dr. Westerfield, opposite the Quarantine Station, about the first of August!" It will be remembered that the infected bark Excelsior was anchored at this point for eleven days from June 24 to July 5.

"I am informed that a similar fever does prevail at Port Eads, where there are no rice fields. There is, however, in this vicinity a pilots village, and a Customhouse Station, so that it is probable that communication with infected vessels occurs before these vessels are subjected to fumigation, and I am also informed that communication between this point and the City of New Orleans, is unrestricted."

In reply to these allegations my information is to the effect that fever, as described in the preceding pages, did exist at Port Eads about the same time as at, or opposite the Quarantine Station. It was not traceable to the Bark Excelsior, however, as no communication whatever was had with that vessel, except the taking on or off the bar by river pilots, who were presumed to be acclimated, and which cannot be prevented.

In regard to unrestricted communication between Port Eads and the city by persons from infected vessels, I am not aware of any instances of the kind occurring, as I have endeavored by the strictest vigilance to guard against such communication during my official residence there.

In reference to the diagnosis of the cases at Point Michel and the adjacent coast examined by Dr. Sternberg, in the presence of Dr. Hays and myself, I stated to that gentleman at the time, that if it was a mild form of Yellow Fever, as he believed, then I had seen the same disease over and over again in an experience extending over thirty-seven years' observation of the diseases occurring in the Valley of the Mississippi and its tributaries.

In view of all the facts as presented to my mind, I am obliged to dissent from the views entertained and expressed by Dr. Sternberg, and those of the report of Dr. Mitchell and Prof. Bemiss, as made to the National Board of Health.

I concur, however, in the report of Drs. Bruns and Davidson.

Very respectfully,

B. F. TAYLOR. M. D.

Quarantine and General Inspector at the Mississippi Passes, of the Board of Health.

MALIGNANT FORMS

OF

MALARIAL PAROXYSMAL FEVER.

EXTENSIVE PREVALENCE OF MALIGNANT MALARIAL FEVER,
INCLUDING HÆMORRHAGIC FEVERS, IN THE ALLU-
VIAL REGIONS IN TROPICAL, SEMI-TROPI-
CAL AND TEMPERATE COUNTRIES
IN BOTH HEMISPHERES.

THE ENDEMIC FEVER OF THE DELTA OF THE MISSISSIPPI RIVER AS IT
PREVAILED IN 1880, ESSENTIALLY THE SAME IN ORIGIN AND
NATURE WITH THE MALARIAL FEVERS OF DIFFERENT
AND WIDELY SEPARATED COUNTRIES, AND
OF VARIOUS PERIODS OF TIME.

RELATIONS OF YELLOW AND MALARIAL FEVERS.

It is of importance to the public welfare that the Endemic Fever of 1880, in Plaquemine parish, Louisiana, should be regarded in its true relations to similar febrile diseases which have prevailed at different times and in widely separated countries.

It is admitted by disinterested observers, that the notoriety attached to the malarial fever which prevailed in the Parish of Plaquemine (and in the delta of the Mississippi and its tributaries) during the fall of 1880, was clearly due to the extraordinary statements emenating from the National Board of Health; and not to anything peculiar or different in its origin, nature and effects, from similar endemics of various times and countries, and even in remote portions of the earth, where yellow fever has been wholly unknown.

The absurd proposition was advanced that the *nature of a fever could be determined by the rate of mortality.* To state the proposition more definitely: Four children died of fever in a single family near Point Michel: Yellow Fever often proves very fatal in families; therefore the fever which destroyed these children was *Yellow Fever.*

20

As the delta of the Mississippi river, and in fact of all the rivers of the United States, have been at various times subject to the different forms of Remittent, Intermittent and Malignant Malarial Fevers, including the Hæmorrhagic variety, it is important that the profession and the public should be prepared for such endemic visitations in the future, in order that the most egregious, if not criminal blunder may not be committed of confounding an endemic malarial fever of local origin, with an infectious disease capable of transportation.

We will endeavor to illustrate the relations of the Endemic Malarial Fever of the delta of the Mississippi River during the summer and autumn of 1880, by the record of *facts relating* to the various forms of malarial fevers, under the following divisions:

1. *The wide spread and destructive effects of the Malaria of the Swamps and Rice-fields of the Southern. States, and more especially of the great State of Georgia.*

2. *The wide spread and destructive effects of the Malarial Fevers of the alluvial regions of Tropical and Semi-Tropical Africa.*

3. *Hæmorrhagic Fevers dependent upon the peculiar constitution of the Blood, as induced by salt meat, sameness of diet and the action of Febrile Poisons.*

4. *History of Hæmorrhagic Malarial Fever.*

5. *General outline of the Symptoms and Pathological Anatomy of Yellow and Malarial Fevers.*

1. WIDE SPREAD AND DESTRUCTIVE EFFECTS OF THE MALARIA OF THE SWAMPS AND RICE-FIELDS OF THE SOUTHERN STATES, AND MORE ESPECIALLY OF THE STATE OF GEORGIA.

The climate of the rich low plain, clothed with a luxuriant sub-tropical vegetation, which forms a belt along the Atlantic Ocean and Gulf of Mexico of varying width, from thirty to one hundred miles, and which is intersected with numerous swamps which discharge their waters into sluggish, muddy streams, surrounded on all sides by extensive swamps and marshes, is necessarily hostile to the white race. To the pestilential exhalations of stagnant swamps and rich river deposits, excited and disseminated by the burning rays of the sun in this hot climate during the summer and fall months, no process of acclimation has ever accustomed the white man. In the early settlement of South Carolina and Georgia, the inhabitants in most instances resided the whole year upon their rich rice and indigo plantations; many, however, soon fell victims to the climate, or dragged out a miserable existence, with constitutions broken and rendered prematurely old, by repeated attacks of climate fever. The clearing of the forests, of the swamps and rich low-lands, and the consequent exposure to the sun of the vegetable matter which had been accumulating for ages, rendered the climate so deleterious to the white race, that the planters were compelled to seek health during the summer and fall months in sea island, or in pine barren, or mountainous retreats; and with the most efficient precautions, the mortality of these regions is far greater than in the more elevated portions of the Southern States.

The following facts will illustrate the effects of the climate of the swamps, rice-fields and river bottoms, upon the mortality of the white race :

In the Midway Congregational Church, of Liberty county, Ga., (formerly St. John's parish,) the number of births from 1754 to 1804 was 600, whilst the number of deaths during this period was 628, thus showing an actual decrease during fifty years of 28. In 1817 there were 49 deaths in this congregation, which did not number more than 340 whites, showing a mortality of one in every seven of the inhabitants (14.4 per cent.;) of the 49 deaths, 34 occurred in four months (July, August, September and October,) and were in almost every case the effects of climate fever; and other years might be cited in which, if the mortality did not rise to so high a figure, it still rose to such alarming figures as from one in every ten to one in every seventeen inhabitants.

This heavy mortality was clearly referable to climate, for it is believed that no body of citizens in the Southern country excelled this congregation in intelligence and virtue, or in the careful regard for the substantial comfort and health of its families.

Before the Revolutionary war, whilst Sunbury, on the coast of Georgia, was in a highly prosperous condition, seventy emigrants came from the Bermuda Islands: of this number fifty died the first year from climate fever.

Savannah, situated on a sandy plain, terminated on the north by a turbid sluggish stream, and flanked on the east and west by extensive tide swamps, afforded during the period that these low lands were cultivated in rice a good field for the determination of the probable mortality of troops exposed to the climate of rich river-bottoms and inland swamps. The dry culture system was commenced with the lands surrounding Savannah, in 1818; we shall therefore for our present purpose, deal with the mortuary records of the city, and during the wet culture system, as far as they extend back from 1818: premising, however, that after the institution of the dry culture system the health of Savannah, excepting the years when yellow fever prevailed, has progressively improved, and will now compare favorably with cities situated in the same latitudes, and surrounded by similar alluvial deposits. After a careful examination of the records of the city, I have been able to discover no record of date earlier than 1804

The deaths of the blacks are excluded from the following statistics. The sum of the deaths of the foreigners and natives does not always correspond with the total deaths from climate fever, because, in some instances, the nativities are not given in the record.

DEATHS AMONGST THE WHITES IN SAVANNAH FROM 1804 TO 1818.

	Deaths during July, August, Septem'r and October.	Deaths from Climate Fever.	Deaths of foreigners from Climate Fever.	Deaths of Natives from Climate Fever.	Total Deaths from all cases.
1804	118	77	63	14	207
1805	141	112	78	22	238
1806	120	52	43	9	159
1807	124	80	71	9	230
1808	103	77	67	8	219
1809	98	63	52	9	183
1810	79	46	38	8	163
1811	114	87	73	13	212
1812	132	120	92	24	226
1813	109	64	45	19	214
1814	185	166	138	23	300
1815	140	130	104	18	233
1816	161	146	91	38	272
1817	283	313	236	57	461

The population of Savannah in 1800 was 5,166; of these 2,799 were whites and 2,367 slaves. In 1808 the population was 6,464; of these 3,010 were whites and 3,454 slaves. In 1810, the entire population was 5,215; in 1820, entire population 7,523.

Whilst the records of the population of Savannah at different periods are not as full and explicit as could be wished, still from the data now presented we may institute comparisons, and determine the average mortality for each year with a very close approximation to the absolute numbers : thus in 1804, the proportion of deaths in round numbers of the whites to the white population, was 1 in 13; 1805, 1 in 12; 1806, 1 in 18; 1807, 1 in 12; 1808, 1 in 13; 1809, 1 in 16; 1810, 1 in 18; 1811, 1 in 14; 1812, 1 in 13; 1813, 1 in 14; 1814, 1 in 10; 1815, 1 in 14; 1816, 1 in 13; 1817, 1 in 9.

If we compare the mortality from climate fever, of the strangers and foreigners, under which class we include the seamen, who form a large part of the transient population of Savannah, we will see that the deaths amongst this class were more than four times as numerous as the deaths of the natives. This fact illustrates still more strongly the great risks and sickness, if not heavy mortality, which must attend the transportation of troops or emigrants from Middle Georgia, and from any part of the high mountainous tracts of the Southern States to the swamps and rich rice grounds, during the months of July, August, September and October ; for without doubt the observation was made by the reader as he reviewed the preceding figures, that the rate of mortality in Savannah during the wet culture system, frequently rose to a figure which in healthy regions would have been considered as the results of pestilence ; and the correctness of this observation is placed in the clearest light, when it is known that the annual mortality in England* is one in every 45 of the living ; in France, 1 in every 42 ; in the New England States, 1 in 64 ; in the Middle States, 1 in 73 ; Coast planting States, 1 in 73 ; Northern States 1 in 80.†

Whilst we will readily grant that the improved method of medical treatment of the present day would greatly diminish the rates of mortality, we would on the other hand affirm that these improvements in practice would have little to do with the prevention of disease. We have therefore presented this view of the rates of mortality in these localities, rather to demonstrate the liability of men exposed in this climate to disease, and thus to establish the importance of the present inquiry ; for the laborers and citizens may be rendered almost as ineffective by sickness as by death.

The medical statistics of Oglethorpe Barracks during the period they were situated one mile south of the city of Savannah, just back of the present jail, illustrates still more forcibly the sickness and mortality of troops encamped in localities surrounded with rice fields and marshes. In 1828 during the months of July, August and September, there occurred 23 deaths in a command of 95 men ; and during the months of October, November and December, 18 deaths in a strength of 85 men ; the total deaths for the year was 52, besides 19 women and children—Remittent fever and dysentery were the fatal diseases which caused the high mortality. During 10 years, from 1829 to 1839, the annual ratio of mortality was $5\frac{5}{10}$ per cent. ; the annual ratio of Intermittents was 67 per cent., and that of Remittents 22 per cent.; and every man was on an average during this period, reported in a little less than every five months. So prevalent and fatal were the diseases in summer and fall seasons, that this post was finally abandoned.

The Medical statistics of the Augusta Arsenal whilst it was situated on the banks of the Savannah river, correspond with those of the Oglethorpe Barracks ; disease prevailed to so great an extent that it was necessary to abandon the post in the summer season, and encamp on the Sand Hills.

---

* Sixth Annual Report of the Registrar General of England, 1847.
† Census of United States, 1850.

These observations might be still further strengthened by the presentation of the rates of mortality of rice plantations, this subject, however, will be treated more fully hereafter, and we will merely state the result of an extended personal examination of the mortuary statistics of rice plantations; the number of births in proportion to inhabitants does not differ materially from the number in the healthiest regions, but the mortality, especially amongst the young is far greater—in fact so great that during many years instead of an increase, there is either a stationary condition, or an actual decrease.*

CASES OF MALARIAL FEVER AND OF ALL DISEASES OCCURRING DURING A PERIOD OF FIFTEEN MONTHS (OCTOBER, 1862, TO JANUARY, 1864,) IN THE COMMAND SERVING IN AND AROUND FORT JACKSON, ON THE SAVANNAH RIVER.

MONTH AND YEAR.	Congestive Fever.	Intermittent Fever Quotidian.	Intermittent Fever Tertian.	Intermittent Fever Quartan.	Remittent Fever.	Total cases of these forms of malarial fever.	Total cases for all other diseases.	Total cases of all Diseases.	Aggregate sick each month.	Mean strength of command—Officers & men.
October, 1862		262	71		12	345	126	471	583	872
November, "		67	24		5	96	44	140	218	913
December, "		128	58		11	197	118	315	350	913
January, 1863		42	88		5	135	172	307	331	1144
February, "		85	104		9	198	149	347	428	913
March, "		78	133	33	2	246	143	389	458	913
April, "		37	157		4	198	226	424	489	913
May, "		62	76		2	140	184	324	360	878
June, "		66	66		10	142	131	273	316	878
July, "		77	177		67	321	137	458	504	878
August, "		99	149		134	380	103	483	533	890
September, "		149	127		134	410	98	508	588	822
October, "		97	108		62	267	133	400	485	660
November, "	1	47	54		22	134	60	184	235	789
December, "	1	41	62		10	114	111	225	279	800
Total	2	1,335	1,444	33	489	3,313	1,935	5,248		

In an average command of 878 men, stationed at Fort Jackson and the surrounding river batteries, nearly one-half, or 410, on an average were on the sick-list each month; and the new cases of malarial fever averaged each month 220. During this period of fifteen months 3313 cases of malarial fever, in the form of congestive fevers, quotidians, tertians, quartans and

---

*The facts which have now been presented are sufficient to justify the attempt to devise some means to ward off the climate fever.

During the study of the relations of climate and soil to disease, the collection of the mortuary statistics and the investigation of the causes of diseases upon rice and cotton plantations; and during the discharge of the duties of Chemist to the Cotton Planters' Convention of Georgia, the author has necessarily been greatly exposed to the agents which produced climate fever, and the results of his experience now presented, cannot therefore be said to be wanting the test of actual experiment.

Under these exposures I have found that Sulphate of Quinia taken in from 3 to 5 grains twice during the day would, in most cases, prevent the occurrence of Malarial Fever, and if it failed to ward it off entirely, the attack would be of very slight character. I have still further observed that when the climate fever first appeared, with a sense of lassitude, headache and excitement of the pulse, with alternate flushings, it might be arrested by a dose of from five to ten grains of Sulphate of Quinia, in combination with Bicarbonate of Pottassa and Hoffman's Anodyne. From 5 to 15 grains of the Sulphate of Quinia may be given, according to the urgency of the symptoms, united with 15 grains of Bicarbonate of Potassa and two fluid drachms of Hoffman's Anodyne. From 5 to 15 grains of Gum Camphor; the whole to be dissolved in six fluid ounces of water. The feet should be placed in hot water immediately after, or before, the administration of the remedies, and the patient after this bath should be covered up in bed. so as to promote free perspiration and induce quiet sleep. I have frequently gone to bed in a feverish, restless state, with a severe headache, excited pulse, and pain in the limbs, and dry, warm skin, and under the action of these remedies, arose in the morning refreshed and able to resume active operations.

We would recommend the use of Quinia as a preventive of Climate fever, in the following manner:

    R.   Sulphate of Quinia, - - - - - - - grains, iii.
            Dilute Aromatic Sulphuric Acid, - - - - drops, v.
            Brandy, - - - - - - - - tablespoonful, 1.
            Water, - - - - - - - - wineglassfuls, ii.

Drop the diluted Aromatic Sulphuric Acid upon the Sulphate of Quinia, and then add the brandy and water. Administer twice during the day, after rising in the morning, and just before bed-time.

remittents occurred; whilst all other diseases, including also those diseases as neuralgia, which might be traced in a measure to the action of malaria, numbered 1935 cases, or only a little more than one-half the number of the cases of malarial fever.

Throughout the entire period, more than one-fourth of the command were unfit for duty; and during the fall months more than one-half of the garrison was on an average incapable of performing military duty. In case of an attack during the sickliest season of the year, the effective force of the command instead of being 878, would have been less than five hundred.

2. WIDE SPREAD AND DESTRUCTIVE EFFECTS OF THE MALARIAL FEVERS OF THE ALLUVIAL REGIONS OF TROPICAL AND SEMI-TROPICAL AFRICA.

The endemic climate fever of the coast and alluvial lands of Central Africa does not differ in any essential manner, except, perhaps, in its severity, either in its causes, symptoms or effects, from the malarial fever of North America.

The celebrated traveler, Mungo Park, suffered from two severe attacks of fever, upon his first tour through the interior of Africa, and at the conclusion of his journey the color of his skin was so altered by the disordered state of his liver induced by African fever, that he could scarcely be distinguished from a Moor; and upon his second visit to Africa, not only was he brought to the borders of the grave by climate fever, but 32 out of the 38 men who left with him the banks of the Gambia, fell victims to African fever in less than two months.

The vessel sent out in 1618, to relieve the English Explorer, Thompson, on the banks of the Gambia, lost almost the entire crew with fever and at the very outstep, failed to accomplished the desired object.

The enterprising traveler, Ledyard, who had spent his life in traveling, and had sailed around the world with Captain Cook, had lived for several years with the North American Indians, and had traveled from Stockholm, round the Gulf of Bothnia, and thence to the remotest parts of Asiatic Russia, died of African fever, in the very commencement of his journey to explore this continent.

Numerous other travelers might be mentioned, as Nicholls, Morrison, Pearce, Clapperton, and the active, athletic and temperate Frederic Horneman, who fell victims to the endemic climate fever of Africa.

The splendid expedition to the Congo, under command of Captain Tuckey, provided with a crew of fifty active individuals, and with a Botanist, Zoologist, comparative Anatomist, and a most competent Physician, melted away under the influence of the damp and burning climate, and ended with the loss of the Captain, all the officers and scientific men. A similar termination closed the expedition of Major Peddie, for the discovery of the Niger.

The average mortality amongst the better classes in Sierra Leone, according to the testimony of Dr. Nichol, Deputy Inspector of Hospitals, was formerly about one in twelve, or very nearly nine per cent.

According to Mr. Tidlie, acting Staff Surgeon at Cape Coast Castle in 1819. all the new-comers from England were seized with fever, and one-half died, more than one-third of the resident Europeans who had been there more than one year were seized with fever, and one-eighth died; in 1820 all the new-comers were seized with fever, and one-half of them died, and of the older residents one-ninth died; in 1821 all the new-comers were seized with fever, and one-third died, whilst of the older residents near one-sixth died ; thus making an average cf one death out of every two and two-thirds, of the new-comers during the first twelve months after their arrival, and one death out of every eight of the resident Europeans who had been there more than one year.

From the Report of Dr. Barry, Deputy Inspector of Hospitals in 1822, we learn that twelve white sergeants from the Isle of Wight, selected as good and healthy men of regular habits, were attacked with fever, upon their arrival upon the coast of Africa, and within a few months after their arrival, eight paid the debt of nature, and the constitutions of three of the remaining four were permanently injured, whilst the sickness and mortality amongst their wives and children were nearly in the same proportion.

According to Mr. William Ferguson, Surgeon to the Royal African Colonial Corps, in the third quarter of 1824, the mean strength of British soldiers at Sierra Leone, was 585, of this number 386 were attacked with this African climate fever ; 161 died, showing one death to 3.63 of the strength, and one death to 2.39, cases treated ; at Gambia during the same period, the strength was 108, cases of Malarial fever 92, deaths 74, giving a proportion of 1 death to 1.45 of the original strength, and 1 death to 1.24 of the cases treated ; at the Isles de Los, during the same period the mean strength was 103; cases of Malarial fever 99, deaths 23, showing one death in 4.47 of the strength and 1 death in 4.3 of the cases treated. Captain W. F. Owen of the Royal Navy, in his attempt in 1827 to found a settlement at Fernando Po, lost almost his entire colony from the Endemic fever of Africa ; and Colonel Nicholls who followed him in a similar attempt had one attack of Remittent fever, and eleven attacks of Intermittent fever, and lost twenty-five out of thirty individuals who composed the company.

Numerous other examples might be brought forward to show the dreadful effects of the climate of Africa upon foreigners, unprotected by the sulphate of quinia ; we will, however, allude to but one more—the expedition of H. B. M. ships Wilberforce, Albert and Soudan during the years 1841 and 1842, up the Niger, with the leading object of promoting the abolition of the slave trade. When the expedition entered the Nun branch of the Niger, on the thirteenth of August, its complement of men and officers consisted of— officers, including civilians and engineers, 53; white seamen, 63; marines and sappers, 29; total number of whites, 145; men of color entered in England, 25; Kroomen and liberated Africans entered on the coast, 110; blacks for model farm, 23; total black, 158; grand total, 303. The health of the expedition continued good until the ships had proceeded two hundred and fifty miles from the mouth of the river, on the fourth of September, when a most malignant fever appeared in all the vessels, and spread with great rapidity. The first death took place on the ninth; and on the seventeenth there were 69 sick, 63 of whom were whites; and seven whites had died. The expedition was now so disabled that it was deemed advisable to send two of the ships back to sea; on the nineteenth the Soudan started for the mouth of the river with forty cases of fever, and was followed by the Wilberforce, with nearly an equal number of sick, on the twenty-first. The Albert continued up the river, the officers believing that the violence of the fever was in a measure exhausted, and that the climate of the more open country, higher up the Niger, would be found more healthy. The result proved otherwise. When the ship had arrived at Egga, 340 miles from the sea, not less than twenty more of the crew had been attacked, of whom two had died; and on the third of October there remained, capable of doing any duty, only one white seaman, the sergeant and one private of marines, the geologist, the mate, one hospital attendant, and the surgeon, Dr. McWilliam. The entire enterprise was now abandoned, and the Albert steamed down the river, to Fernando Po. Of the 145 whites who entered the Niger in good health, 130 were attacked with fever and 42 died; of the 158 blacks, only 11 had the fever, and that in its mildest forms, and not one died.

The ratio of the men attacked by fever in the Albert was 1 in 1.127, the ratio of deaths in total number victualled was 1 in 2.696, and in the number of cases 1 in 2.391; the ratio of the men attacked by fever in the Wilberforce was 1 in 1.666, ratio of deaths in number victualled 1 in 8, ratio of deaths in number of cases 1 in 6.857; the entire crew of the Soudan were attacked with fever; the ratio of deaths in total number victualled was 1 in 2.7.*

* NOTE.—We will now compare these facts and rates of mortality with the health of the British squadron, employed for the suppression of the slave trade on the west coast of Africa, since the systematic employment of the sulphate of quinia as a prophylactic.

The observations which we will now present, are from the most reliable of all sources: the "Statistical Report of the Health of the Royal Navy," and we shall refer especially to the reports for 1856 and 1857, printed by the House of Commons July, 1858, and August, 1859.

In 1856, the squadron employed for the suppression of the slave trade on the west coast of Africa consisted of twenty-one vessels, with a mean force, including Kroomen and African boys, of 1630 men of all ranks and ratings. The number of men daily inefficient from wounds and sickness on the west coast of Africa averaged about 55 per 1000 of mean force.

The following summary taken from the nosological returns, will not only show that the great source of malarial fever in the squadron is exposure to effluvia or miasmata, while on shore, or in boats near the shore, or by the entrance of the cruisers into the large tidal rivers, but also that the great means of warding off the epidemic climate fever, and of moderating its violence and duration, was the daily administration of the sulphate of quinia to the men during exposure to the noxious miasmata.

The Bloodhound remained during the entire year on the northern division of the station. In March she steamed about 300 miles up the Benin river; while in the river and for fourteen days afterwards, from three to six grains of the disulphate of Quinine were given to each of the ship's company as a preventive of fever, and although they were exposed to the emanations from the mangrove swamps for twenty-seven days, only six suffered slightly from fever.

Some time afterwards they were again exposed to miasmata in the Bonny, New Calabar, and in the Sherbro, the last one of the most dangerous rivers for Europeans on the whole station; but Quinine in solution was invariably used as a prophylactic, and with good effect, as only one case occurred after the vessel had been for a week in the Sherbro, and the patient was the only person who did not take the quinine regularly. No death occurred in this vessel from fever, but one man was invalid for its sequela.

The Childers was employed almost constantly cruising, for the first six months in the year off the coast, in the Gulf of Guinea, and during the remaining months, off the coast, between Loango and Benguela. With the exception of a few unimportant cases, her crew entirely escaped fever, until three boats were sent on detached service up the Lagos River; in these there were twenty-seven white men and five officers. They remained absent for two nights, one of which was spent at anchor, off the town of Lagos. The surgeon accompanied the expedition and gave quinine-wine, which was continued after they returned on board; still notwithstanding, nine of the thirty-two persons who formed the party, were attacked with fever; two in five days after their return to the ship, one on the sixth day, one on the eighth, one on the ninth, one on the thirteenth, two on the sixteenth, and one on the seventeenth. The disease in all was the same, differing only in its degree of intensity; some were convalescent on the eighth or ninth day, and others not before the twenty-eighth; one had a jaundiced appearance. The surgeon thought the fever would have assumed a worse form, but for the quinine-wine which had been taken as a preventive. No other febrile disease of any consequence occurred in the Childers for several months subsequently, nor in fact until she had been for some time stationed on the southern division of the command, when four cases took place, after she had been eight days at anchor in the river Congo. The Firefly did not arrive on the station until August. Shortly afterwards she proceeded on a cruise off the river Pongas, while her boats armed with white men, were sent up the river. They took Quinine-wine night and morning while absent, and continued its use for ten days after they returned, and all escaped fever. Subsequently a few cases were contracted from long continued exposure to the miasmatous exhalations in the river Lagos. Eighteen cases of remitting and fourteen of intermitting fever occurred in the Hecate—the majority of the former were contracted on shore; two ended in death. The subject of one of the latter was a marine; who accidentally drifted away in the life-boat over the bar at Lagos; slept one night on shore, and was not attacked until fourteen days afterwards. In the other case, the patient, an officer, slept two nights on shore, and exposed himself to the full glare of the sun during the day time, by rowing about in a boat, without an awning, in the lagoon off Lagos; he declined taking Quinine as a preventive, and was attacked about fourteen days after he returned on board.

The Merlin arrived on the station about the middle of July, and after cruising a short while off the rivers Nunez and Congas, proceeded to the Bight of Biafra. She was then ordered on special service up the rivers Bonny, New Calabar and Brass; while thus employed, the following precautionary measures were adopted against fever. The crew were turned up at 5.30 A. M., after dressing, took half a wineglassful of quinine wine; they breakfasted at 6. The decks were washed with water (warm) from the boilers at 6.30; they took dinner at noon, and supped at 5 P. M. No white men were sent away in boats. Serge frocks and white trousers were worn during the day, and blanket dresses during the night. No water was allowed to be drawn from alongside for any purpose whatever. Quinine wine was administered to the whole crew for fourteen days after leaving the rivers, in which they remained altogther twelve days. Whether it was owing to the above measures it is impossible to state, but no sickness of any kind followed the several expeditions into these notoriously unhealthy localities. Although twenty-three cases occurred in this vessel, only one out of the whole number was of a severe character, and it was the result of intemperance and exposure on shore on the Isles of the Los. The records of the other vessels all substantiated the great value of Quinine as a prophylactic.

It thus appears, that in all these vessels, with a mean force of about 1680 men, there were only seven deaths from fever, being in the ratio of about a little more than four to the thousand, a mortality so small compared with that of former years, seems almost incredible, and might well lead to the belief that the coast, like some of the cleared portions of the North American Continent, is becoming more healthy; but, with the exception of the non-appearance of yellow fever, which does not depend on terrestrial emanations alone, the climate has undergone no salutary change.

The seemingly interminable forests which fringe the estuaries of every tidal river, are still as prolific of the fever poison as they were in times gone by, when the death-rate in the squadron was ten times greater. How then, it may be asked, are we to account for this improvement? Simply by the change which has taken place in the mode of conducting the duties of the station. By a wise and humane regulation, the deadly practice of sending boats away on detached service, to watch or intercept slaves, has been interdicted, or at all events, greatly restricted. Prize crews are no longer turned adrift to wander through the streets of Sierra Leone, when the vessels they navigate from distant parts of the station are delivered up to the authorities of the Mixed Commission Court; the orgies of the 'the barn,' which lowered the character of the white man in the eyes of the black, have long since ceased; *and last, though not least, the introduction of quinine wine as a preventive of fever has not only reduced the number of febrile attacks, but has lessened the severity of those which do occur, and thus the mortality has also been reduced to a level which does not materially exceed the death-rate from fever on some of the more healthy stations.*

There has also been a great change in the medical treatment of febrile diseases: the so-called active measures which were in vogue but a few years since have given place to others of a more rational character. Blood-letting is no longer carried to an extent which leaves the patient but little chance of recovery when the fever terminates, and the rash and empirical use of calomel in large and frequently repeated doses, to produce ptyalism, has been abandoned—not only on account of the impossibility of producing ptyalism while the fever lasts, but because mercury, given to excess in any form, has a most injurious effect on the constitution. If these changes have had no effect in reducing the mortality they, at all events, have lessened the sufferings and misery entailed on patients, who though they survived the fever, lingered long in a state of debility from the effects of blood-letting and mercury.—*Statistical Report of the Health of the Royal Navy for the year* 1856, *ordered by the House of Commons to be printed twenty-sixth July,* 1858 : *pp.* 110-116.

In 1857 there were nineteen vessels employed on the African station, with a mean force, corrected for time, of about 1620 men, including Kroomen and liberated Africans The number daily ineffective from wounds and sickness averaged 112, or in the ratio of 69.3 to the 1000 of mean force, which exceeds the ratio of the preceding year by seven. The total number of dead, exclusive of those lost by shipwreck, amounted to thirty-six—twenty-seven from disease, one from poison and eight from accidental causes; on the whole, therefore, the mortality was somewhat greater than in 1856. During the year eleven cases of endemic fever terminated in death: the ratio per 1000, 6.7; and although nearly a third greater than in 1856, it is still not greater than the mortality of some of the healthiest stations, and incomparably less than the mortality upon the African station before the use of quinine wine.

The following summary, taken from the medical journals of the squadron, affords additional proof of the usefulness of quinine as a prophylactic:

In the Trident there were forty cases of fever, but no death occurred: the greater number of these cases were contracted in the rivers which enter the sea in the Bight of Biafra. Quinine wine was freely used as a preventive. On two occasions when boats were sent up the Congo, the white men took quinine while in the river, and for fourteen days after they left it, and no fever of any consequence followed.

Fourteen cases occurred in the Sappho: they were nearly all contracted in boating expeditions up the river Congo. Quinine wine was administered to the men on these occasions, but several who did not take it regularly were attacked. Twenty men were employed off and on between the thirtieth of April and the eleventh of May on this service, watching a suspected vessel in the Congo. The medicated wine was administered carefully according to the printed circular. Only four men were attacked by fever, the disease showing itself about three weeks after they ceased taking the wine. In the Myrmidon and Pluto there were but few cases of fever, though they were employed on some of the most unhealthy places on the station; the former was laid on the beach at Sierra Leon, to be repaired, meanwhile her crew took up their abode in an old hulk which lay in the harbor. Some of the men, however, together with several of the Pluto's crew, were employed, both by day and night, as their work depended upon the tide, in patching the hull of the vessel. To these men quinine wine was administered twice daily, and the executive officers took care that they did not straggle into the town or bush, consequently no case of serious illness followed.

The gig and pinnace of the Alecto, manned by fourteen white men and six Kroomen, were sent about 150 miles up the Congo, late in December, with presents for one of the petty chiefs; they returned on the sixth of January, and between the twelfth and eighteenth every white man, with two exceptions, was attacked with fever. The same boats were again sent up the river to the same place on the fourteenth, when the two persons who had escaped fever formerly were now attacked, though one of them was not taken ill until thirty days afterwards. With the exception of these two persons the boat's crew on the second expedition were made up of Kroomen, who, as usual, entirely escaped. On these expeditions an ounce of quinine wine was given to the white men daily during their absence from the ship; but it appears to have been discontinued on their return. In January the boats of this vessel were again detached to cruise in the Congo, but did not proceed more than forty miles up the river. Quinine was given to the men during their absence and for fourteen days after their return. The same precaution was adopted after any subsequent exposure to malaria in the river, and no case of fever followed. The Bloodhound was employed in January in the river Benin, and during July in the Congo; as long as she remained within these rivers, and for ten days afterwards, four grains of quinine in a quarter of a gill of rum, was administered to every white man on board. One case only resulted from these two expeditions; and in that instance the person attacked had exposed himself in a most imprudent manner whilst shooting wild fowl amidst the slimy ooze in the mangrove thickets on the banks of the Benin; whether the patient took quinine as a preventive is not mentioned.

Three boats from the Childers went up the Congo, as far as Punto da Linha, and were absent for several days; quinine was administered to the white men, and no fever resulted.

In May, two boats were sent from the Hecla up the river Nunez, and returned on the following day. Quinine wine was issued in the usual manner, and no febrile disease followed.

In July, the same vessel entered the Sherbro, and subsequently her boats, containing fifty-six seamen and marines, with the usual number of officers ascended the river to the village Victoria—they returned the same evening and rejoined the vessel, which remained in the river for a few days longer. Quinine in rum (the quinine wine having been all used) was given to the crew while she remained in the river, and for fourteen days after she went to sea. "Eight cases of intermittent fever" the surgeon remarks, "were added to the list a few days after our departure; they were, however, all mild, and terminated favorably, after an average of seven days' treatment. To the regular and timely administration of quinine, I think our immunity from fever may be fairly ascribed; the cases that did occur were no doubt modified by the prophylactic. That this was the case, the mortality amongst the crews of the merchant shipping frequenting the river, and by whom no preventive is used, bears ample testimony."

On the 23 of May, three officers landed at Lagos from the Hecate, intending to return on board the following

21

morning; but, as frequently happens on this coast, the surf rose suddenly, and continued so long, that they could not return to the vessel until the 29th. Again, on the 2d of August, the pinnace, with seven white men in it was detached, to cruise in-shore between Little Popoe and Whydah, where she remained until the 8th. Quinine was given on both these occasions, and no fever resulted. On the evening of the 27th of November, the same boat and a gig, with nine white men on board, were left off Shark's Point, to guard the entrance to the Congo. An ounce of quinine wine was given to the men each morning. The boats remained in the same position until the morning of the 30th, when they took advantage of a sea breeze, and proceeded up the river to Punto da Linha. The gig, with one officer and two white men, returned on the 2d, and the other boat on the 5th of December. During their absence they had fine weather, and all returned apparently in good health. Quinine was now substituted for quinine wine; four grains were given daily to each person at seven in the morning; but, notwithstanding this, nine out of the eleven were attacked by remitting fever.

The Merlin, between the 1st of January and the 30th of September entered the rivers Calebar and Cameroons, in the Bight of Biafra; she also entered the Nunez several times while on the northern division of the station. During the time she was in these rivers, and for some time after she had left them, quinine wine was duly administered to the white men on board, and no febrile disease of much importance took place; but in November, after having entered the Nunez and Pongas for the purpose of communicating with the native chiefs, her crew suffered most severely from remitting fever. Quinine wine was given to the crew for some time, but the supply exhausted, quinine in rum was substituted. When the change took place is not specified; but in connection with the substitution of quinine purchased on the coast and issued in the same manner in the Hecla, the quality of the alkaloid in both instances may be doubted. The Myrmidon was employed in the River Bonny, and afterwards lay a long time in Clearance Cove, Fernando Po; during the enitire period quinine wine was given in the prescribed form; only one slight case of climatorial fever occurred. At Sierra Leone, while the vessel was under repairs, the whole crew took quinine once a day, and those who were engaged on the shore, twice; still though the latter were at work night and day, only one case of remitting fever resulted. In the same manner, the Pluto was laid on the beach at Sierra Leone early in March for repairs. The carpenters, together with the carpenters of the Hecla, and a number of blue jackets who were employed on her, took the prescribed measure of quinine wine before going to work, and on leaving off; but the men who remained on the hulk took one measure only every morning until the 28th. Two men who had not been out of the ship were subsequently attacked with fever, but so long after the vessel had gone to sea, that the disease can hardly be ascribed to miasmata from the land at Sierra Leone.

It is worthy of notice that in the preceding instances, when quinine wine was administered according to the instructions issued with it, no fever of any consequence followed exposure to land or swamp miasmata; but on two occasions, when quinine purchased on the coast was substituted, and once when the wine was suddenly discontinued after the exposure, a considerable number of men were attacked owing, it is to be supposed, to the discontinuance of the quinine wine in one instance, and to its bad quality in the other, for it is well known that, like other high priced remedies, it does not escape adulteration when it falls into the hands of dishonest traders.—*Statistical Report of the Health of the Royal Navy, for the year* 1857. *Ordered by the House of Commons to be printed,* 2d *August,* 1859, *pp.* 78-85.

3. HÆMORRHAGIC FEVERS DEPENDENT UPON THE PECULIAR CONSTITUTION OF THE BLOOD, AS INDUCED BY SALT MEAT, SAMENESS OF DIET, AND THE CONCURRENT ACTION OF FEBRILE POISONS.

The relation which may be shown between the dissolved state of the blood, and certain morbid phenomena, is one of the most important facts in medicine, a fact very carefully studied by the observers of preceding ages, and from which the exclusive Solidists doctrines of this century have diverted attention. G. Andral in a work published in 1823 (Clinique Medicale, t. 1.) admitted and described this state of the dissolution of the blood in certain cases of low fever, and pointed it out as capable of playing a part in the production of several of the symptoms of these diseases, and especially of the hæmorrhages which so often accompany them.

The investigations of M. Magendie,* threw important and additional light upon this important question of etiology.

Andral established the important fact that this state of dissolution of the blood uniformly coincided with a diminution of the quantity of fibrin, and sought to determine whether this be the ultimate alteration, we are permitted to arrrive at? Before the fibrin decreases, has there not been some other change of composition in the blood, of which the depression of the fibrin below its normal average, is itself only the consequence?

In answer to these questions, some facts may be cited: thus M. Magendie on throwing into the veins of living animals, a concentrated solution of sub-carbonate of soda, found an almost fluid blood in the bodies of these animals when dead, and that during life, their symptoms were analagous to those observed in diseases, in which the older writers admitted a state of dissolution

* Leçons sur les Phénomènes physiques de la vie, 1837.

of the blood, attended with petechiæ and hæmorrhages from the mouth, stomach, intestines and kidneys; some authors have declared that they have found an excess of alkaline matters in the imperfectly coagulated blood of persons who died of low fevers or scurvy ; and Andral in the investigation which he pursued in regard to the variations in the proportion of the inorganic constituents of the blood, found amongst other things, that the blood most highly charged with free alkali belonged to scorbutic patients. And it has been supposed with reason, that the diff-rent virulent and miasmatic substances which, on being introduced into the blood, diminish its coagulability, may then act upon the fibrin like the alkaline substances just alluded to. Thus too the venom of the viper may act, which acccording to Fontana, produces a dissolution of the blood.

Whatever may be the truth regarding the number and the nature of the causes which render the blood less coagulable, it is not the less certain that there are some diseases in which the blood shows a strong tendency to dissolution, while there are others in which the blood becomes more coagulable.

Bufalini, an Italian physician, even regarded these two states of the blood of such importance as to make use of them for dividing all diseases into two great classes: to one of these he assigns as cause what he terms the *phlogistic process*, and to the other an opposite state of the system, which he designates by the term *process of dissolution*. This division is equivalent to that established by Andral, into diseases with an excess of fibrin in the blood, and those with less than the natural quantity of this principle; for in the latter there is evidently a cause whose effect is necessarily to make the blood less coagulable.

Grant, who practiced medicine and wrote towards the close of the last century, suggested the inquiry whether the peculiar hygienic condition of the people of Europe before the eighteenth century must not have caused them to be frequently attacked with diseases, one of the principal elements, if not their starting point, being a state of dissolution of the blood ? It is certainly worthy of note, that the observers of preceding ages constantly speak of dissolved and incoagulable blood in their histories of epidemics. It is well established that certain hygienic influences, even at a period not very far distant, gave birth to and maintained in Europe these general diseases in which the alteration of the blood seems to play so important a part. Even those unfamiliar with the practice of medicine were themselves struck by it. Erasmus, the philosopher who flourished towards the close of the sixteenth century, wrote that in his day the inhabitants of London were every year, from spring to harvest, attacked by a malignant fever, which committed the greatest ravages in that city, and especially amongst the poorer classes. Erasmus gives the following details as to the causes to which he attributed the fever :

The supply of water fails the inhabitants; they have to seek it at a great distance from the city; the river water is carried upon their backs, and is so dear that the poor cannot pfocure enough of it to wash themselves and keep their houses clean. Their houses are of wood and are very cold in winter, which makes it necessary to fill the rooms with straw. But as this cannot be often renewed it becomes spoiled and very injurious.

John Huxham,* in his Essay on Fevers, published in 1757, (one hundred and twenty-four years ago), says with reference to the *Putrid, Malignant, Petechial Fevers:*

That in general they attack with much more violence than the slow nervous; the *Rigors*, if any, are greater (sometimes they are very great), the heats much sharper and permanent, yet at first sudden, transient and remittent ; the pulse more tense or hard, but commonly quick and small, though sometimes slow and seemingly regular for a time, and

---

*An Essay on Fever, London, 1757, pp. 92–97.

then fluttering and irregular. The head aches, giddiness, *Nausea* and vomiting are much more considerable, even from the very beginning, sometimes a severe fixed pain is felt in one or both temples, or over one or both eyebrows, frequently in the bottom of and orbit of the eyes. The eyes always appear very full, heavy, yellowish, and very often a little inflamed. The countenance seems bloated and more dead-colored than usual. Commonly, the temporal arteries throb much. * * The prostration of spirit, weakness and faintness are often surprisingly great and sudden, though no inordinate evacuation happens; and this too, sometimes when the pulse seems tolerably strong. The respiration is most commonly laborious, and interrupted with a kind of sighing or sobbing, and the breath is hot and offensive. Few or none of these fevers are without a sort of *lumbago*, or pain in the back and loins; always a universal weariness, a soreness is felt, and often much pain in the limbs. Sometimes a great heat, load and pain affect the pit of the stomach, with perpetual vomiting of *porraceous* or *black color*, and a most troublesome *singultus ;* the matter discharged is frequently of a very nauseous smell.

The tongue, though only white at the beginning, grows daily more dark and dry; sometimes of a shining livid color, with a kind of dark purple at the top ; sometimes exceeding black; and so continues for many days together. At the height of the disease it generally becomes vastly dry, stiff and black, or of a dark pomegranate color, hence the speech is very inarticulate, and scarce intelligible.

The thirst in the argument of this fever is commonly very great, sometimes unquenchable; and yet no kind of drink pleases, but all seem bitter and mawkish ; at other times however, one is amazed to find no thirst complained of, through the mouth and tongue are exceedingly foul and dry; this is always a dangerous symptom, and ends in a frenzy, or coma. The lips, and teeth, especially in this state, are furred up with a very black tenacious sordes.

At the outset of the fever the urine is often crude, pale and vapid, but grows much higher colored in the advance, and frequently resembles a strong *lixivium*, or *citrine urine tinged*, with a very small quantity of blood; it is without the least sediment, or even cloud, and so continues for many days together; by degrees it grows darker, like dead, and strong, high-colored beer, and smells very rank and offensive. I have frequently seen the urine, in petecchial fevers, almost black and very fœtid; particularly that of one Mr. Shirley, a sea surgeon, was almost quite black, with a sediment as black as soot; he had abundance of very black spots, *vibices*, bloody dysentery and comatose phrenzy, and died about the thirteenth day.

The stools especially near the state, or in the decline of the fever, are of the most part intolerably stinking, green, livid or black, frequently with severe gripes and blood. * * When black, livid, dun or greenish spots appear, no one doubts of the malignity; the more florid, however, the spots are, the less is to be feared. It is a good sign when the black or violet *petechiæ* become of a brighter color. The large black or livid spots are almost always attended with profuse hæmorrhages. The small dusky brown spots, like *freckles* are not much less dangerous than the livid or black ; though fluxes of blood do but seldom accompany them ; excessive, profuse, cold, clammy sweats are often concomitants, by which also they sometimes vanish, though without any advantage to the patient. The eruption of the *petechiæ* is uncertain; sometimes they appear the fourth or fifth day, sometimes not till the eleventh, or even later. The *vibices*, or large livid or dark greenish marks, seldom appear till very near the fatal period. We frequently meet with an efflorescence like the measles or malignant fever, but of a more dull and lurid hue, in which the skin, especially on the breast, appears as it were marked or variegated. This in general is an ill sympton, and I have often seen it attended with very fatal consequences.

In his fifth chapter, entitled "*Of the Dissolved and Putrid State of the Blood*," John Huxham details facts and observations which illustrate in a forcible manner the effects of salt meat and sameness of diet in the production of that state of the blood, which not only induced that peculiar state characterized as scurvy, but also established the hæmorrhagic diathesis, which underlay and affected all diseases, whether belonging to the great class of phlegmasiæ or pyrexiæ.

Thus Huxham described a state of the blood which immediately tends to dissolution and putrefaction of the blood :　.

This is evidently the case in some *scorbutics* (as they are called) when, without any considerable antecedent sensible disorder (more than perhaps a period of lassitude and langour), persons have on a sudden an eruption of violet-colored livid, or even black and blue spots, all over the body, and forthwith fall into profuse, and sometimes dangerous and even fatal *hæmorrhages*, when they have scarce thought themselves, or been thought by others, to be under any manner of disorder. Abundance of instances of this kind happen. I have seen a great many, both in children and grown persons, and frequently foretold the ensuing hæmorrhages.

When women have such eruptions, or black or blue *vibices*, or large irregular spots, like bruises, they are always subject to a vast overflow of the *catamenia*, if not to often profuse hæmorrhages. Nay, when persons of either sex are affected with these appearances, they are apt to bleed excessively from the slightest wound, and very often without any, from the gums, nose, guts or urinary passages.

The blood of such persons, when it hath been drawn, in order to prevent the further progress of the hæmorrhages, always appears a *mere gore*, as it were, not separating into *crassamentum* and *serum* as usual, but remaining in an uniform half coagulated mass, generally of a livid or darker color than usual, though sometimes it continues long very florid, but it always putrifies very soon. * * *

That I am persuaded the above mentioned hæmorrhages most commonly arise from an *acrimonious state of the humors*, which breaks the crasis of the blood and corrodes the extremities of the capillary arteries, yet they sometimes also happen from a too loose contexture of the blood globules, not sufficiently compacted by the action of the heart, arteries, etc., for want of which they become *oblate spheroids*, or irregularly formed *moleculæ*, instead of *regular spheres*, and of course of a greater diameter and a less firm *compayes* than natural. But it appears from microscopical observations (especially those made with the solar microscope) that the blood globules, in passing through the minutest ramifications of the sanguenious arteries, change their globules into a very oblong figure frequently, in order to pass through these exceeding small vessels. And it is easy to conceive how these loosely cohering globules may be broken in their passage, as their enlarged bulk makes their *transit* more difficult. Now as these broken parts are of much less diameter than the original globules, they may readily enter and even pass through some of the excretory ducts, and transude per *diapedesin*, as the ancients called it. That this is so in fact seems to appear from the bloody urine, stools and other hæmorrhages, which sometimes happen without any manner of pain, violence of motion, or the least suspicion of the rupture of any vessel. Nay, I have more than once or twice seen in malignant fever, and that too when the motion of the blood was far from being very rapid, a kind of bloody sweat from the *axillæ*, tinging the linen almost of a *Burgundy wine color.* * * *

The *Petechiæ, Vibices* or livid *stigmata* that very often attend these hæmorrhages, show that the blood globules are dissolved or broken down, and enter into the serous arteries, *vosa exhalentia*, &c., where sticking fast they form these appearances. And I have particularly noted, in some putrid, malignant fevers a kind of yellow or rather dun *Petechiæ*, vastly numerous, and of not less fatal omen than the others. Here the blood globules were broken into such small particles as to have quite lost their original color when combined. Perhaps the fuligerious sweats, and dark colored, or black urine with a lurid sediment, which sometimes happen in fevers of the malignant kind, arise from a broken corrupted state of the blood-globules. I have seen several times the urine rendered almost quite black, depositing an immense quantity of matter nearly of the color of *coffee-grounds*. And we are sometimes surprised to see the face and hands of the sick grow dirty, and sooty as it were though all imaginable care was taken to keep them clean.

Besides there are somethings that seem to destroy the *copula* of the blood globules, and greatly promote the *secession* of the *fix serous globules*, that compose them, one from another ; particularly Laurel-water, which makes the *crassamentum* vastly less dense, and exceedingly more soft and tender than natural, and turns the serum red, or of the color of *Burgundy* wine, as appears from the curious experiments of Dr. Nicholls and Dr. Zangrish

The bite of the serpent Hæmorrhous, causes such a dissolution of the blood that it breaks forth from all parts of the body, even the very *pores*, and kills by an *universal hæmorrhage*. Perhaps *profuse sweats, diarrhea, diabetes*, and spontaneous salivations, may arise from a kind of dissolution of the serous globules. A long and large use of *mercury* will turn the whole mass of blood into a mere watery *colluvies*. *Sal volatile oleosum* mixed with the blood fresh drawn, destroys or dissolves the globules in less than a minute ; spirits of Hartshorn taken in large quantities, will produce hæmorrhages ; and so will frequent and large doses of Aloetics, as I have again and again observed. Indeed, such a state of blood is commonly brought on by acrimonious diet, medicines, &c. Thus the salt and half rotten provisions of sailors, in long voyages cause such a sharpness and corruption of the humors, that they are rendered almost unfit for the common uses of life, producing great weakness, languor, wandering pains and aches, stinking breath, corroded spongy gums, black, blue and sallow spots, sordid dark, livid fungous, ulcers, gangrenes, &c., and surely *scorbutics* frequently fall into petechial fevers, bloody dysenteries, hæmorrhages, &c. What is mentioned by the Rev. Dr. Walter, in Lord Anson's voyage, is very surprising, viz: that the blood burst forth from the wound of some of these *scorbutics*, after they had been *cicatrised*, for twenty or thirty years. I have known many a ship's company set out on a cruise in high health, and yet in two or three months return vastly sickly, and eaten out with the scurvy, a third part of them being half rotten, and utterly unfit for service. About four or five weeks after they have been out, they begin to drop down one after another, and at length by dozens, till at last scarce half the *complement*, can stand to their duties, particularly I remember, some few years since, from a squadron under Admiral Martin, w ; had near 1200 men put on shore sick at one time, though they went out very healthv and returned in about twelve or thirteen weeks.

Those who accustom themselves to take largely of volatile and fixed alcalious salt, spices and aloetics, are always subjec; to these maladies. Not a few of those who took the *alcalious saponaceous hotch-potch* of Mrs. Stepheus, and the soap teas for a long time together, fell into hectical heats, a hot scurvy, hæmorrhages, dysintery, etc.

Some kinds of poison, as particularly the bite of the viper, and some other venomous animals, bring on a very sudden corruption and dissolution of the blood and turn it into a yellowish *sanies Pestilential effluvia* also soon destroy the *crasis* of the blood, and produce an universal gangrenious disposition in the humors. This is evident from the frequent and fatal hæmorrhages, excessively fœtid sweats, vomitings and stools, and the general *necrosis* that follows. which have been observed in the plague and pestilential fevers by the best authors. The hæmorrhages in particular are often vastly profuse and obstinate in the plague, and I have many times noted the same in pestilential and petechial fevers; and the blood, thus issuing, dark and coagulated, as usual. All arguments of the highest acrimony and dissolution of the blood.

The contagion of the small-pox seems to affect some constitutions much in the same manner, producing spots, putrefaction and vast effusions of blood, from several parts of the body, sometimes even at one and the same time. I have seen many instances in this disease when, within four or five dais from the seizure, pimples have appeared all over the body and hæmorrhages from several parts, in a profuse manner, particularly the uterus, urinary passages and nose, and the pustules have turned quite black, a *bloody ichor* issuing from them in abundance; and this too when no violent symptoms of any kind had preceded.—Essay on Fevers, by John Huxbam. London, 1757 : pp. 41–53.

Huxham says that it is a fatal prognostic when spots and hæmorrhages appear at the very eruption of the small-pox, and the sick seldom or never survive the ninth day of the disease; the "blood running into immediate dissolution a d putrefaction. I am persuaded, scarce one in a thousand recovers under these dreadful circumstances, especially if the spots are very livid, black and numerous."

Sarcone, in his history of the epidemic of Naples, in 1764, has spoken of the difference between the blood drawn at the commencement and that drawn towards the termination of the disease :

"The blood," says this author, "was tenacious and buffy during the first week and the first days of the second; at the end of the second week its aspect changed, and it appeared to be most distinctly altered; the clot could be easily divided—a slight pressure was sufficient to break it up. *   * Lastly, these alterations still increased in the course of the third week. and especially that tendency to dissolution which appeared at the close of the second week. The blood drawn from a vein was converted into a thin, black coagulum, swimming in a dirty and bloody serum."

The disease in which Sarcone observed this alteration of the blood was one of the last remnants of those great epidemics which continually prevailed in Europe during the middle ages, and whose incessant re appearance seemed attributable to the bad ventilation and food peculiar to those times. In those endemics which, indeed, often became epidemics, nothing was more common than to observe gangrene, hæmorrhage from various parts, extensive ecchymoses, or thousands of petechiæ covering the skin, while the general symptoms of typhus and typhoid and remittent fevers developed themselves with a high degree of intensity and the greatest rapidity. These pyrexiæ, with their assemblage of dangerous symptoms, and especially their hæmorrhagic fevers, rarely appear in these times, and when observed are usually results of penury or the hardships and privations of war. Scurvy as an endemic disease has disappeared, and it is only in great wars, like that which convulsed the North American Continent, 1861–1865, that its effects are manifested in the great increase of secondary hæmorrhage, pyæmia, foul sloughing, gangrenous wounds and ulcers, and hæmorrhagic and petechial fevers.

As these different affections are the external manifestation of the internal condition of the blood, it must be admitted that in consequence of the change in the nature of the influences, which receives before the solids the impression of the greater part of these influences, must present changes in its constitution proportioned to those undergone by the agents which operate upon it. It would appear then, that in former times a peculiar constitution of the blood engendered maladies, which in certain respects may have differed from those now observed, and may not have required the same treatment. In weighing such facts, Andral has well observed, that thus it is, that at different periods of the existence of the human race, and through the diversity of influences to which it may be subjected, diseases of very different types may arise and undergo changes in their essential nature which are revealed to the physician by the specific character of their symptoms. And this is one amongst many reasons why, according to the times, some theories may be received with peculiar favor, and explains how the development of these theories must be favored by the very nature of the facts observed.

Surgeon James Ranald Martin,* F. R. S., etc., has given in his great work on the " Influence of Tropical Climates on European Constitutions," the following valuable illustration of the change in the type of the remittent fever of Bengal, which places in an equally clear light with the observations of Huxham, Andral and others the effects of salt diet, crowding and other sanitary neglects upon the nature and effects of the malarial poison :

The remittent fever of Bengal has been long known to and carefully described by the British writers of the East. Some of the older observers termed it putrid intestinal remitting and putrid remitting marsh fever, perhaps without being sufficiently aware, that in those days, owing to the salt diet, crowding and other sanitary neglect in their long voyages, a generals corbutic taint existed amongst the newly arrived Europeans especially. Since then, under the various designations of Jungle, Hill, Terace, Bilious Remittent, Marsh Remittent, or Malarious Fever, it has been described by more modern writers: Robert Jackson terms it Gastric, or Bilious Remittent, and describes it as a fever belonging to all countries, but as endemic in the West Indies at all seasons of the year. Though common to all countries, and observed occasionally at all seasons of the year, he justly adds that it prevails more generally in warm coutries, on extensive alluvial plains, and in the autumnal season.

Remittent fevers will be found almost everywhere throughout the East Indies, varying in their intensities and in their complications, as they may occur in the deltas, along the marshy banks, or in the embouchures of rivers; in the plains extending from the basis of mountain ranges, termed teraces ; in partially inundated or irrigated lands, or in such as are traversed by percolating streams, or by canals ; in wooded districts termed jungles ; or in certain hilly districts. The seaboard, especially when there is jungle or salt marsh, and the adjacent island when of a jungly or marshy nature, are peculiarly pestilential ; and so are often found the drying up marshes, and the drying up of beds of rivers.

The British army has often been fever stricken, and occasionally destroyed, in low dry looking plains, such as those of Walcheren and of Rosendaal; in the elevated, rocky and dry-looking countries, and in the half dried water courses of Portugal; on the plains of Spain, along the courses of the Gaudiana; but everywhere, there was water to within a few inches of the surface ; the rivers were always 'half dried,' and the Guadiana itself consisted of but 'lines of detached pools.'

Whether on the coast of Kent, about Dungeness, 'during the hot summer and autumn of 1807,' or in the West India Islands, the same topographical conditions were found to exist by William Fergusson ; there was generally the presence of actual marsh, or damp ; and always the antecedents of heavy rain, or of 'flooding, in the rainy season.' 'The fevers of Cadez, Carthagena, Gibraltar, and Zealand,' says Dr. James Johnson, 'may compete in respect to virulence and fatally, with those of Batavia, Bengal, St. Domingo, and Philadelphia.'

Varying somewhat in type and in complication, each depending on locality, on constitution, and on habit of life, the essential characters of the remittent fevers are still everywhere the same ; and whether as cause or effect, this disease has much to do with almost all the derangements of health of Europeans in the East. It is also by far the most prevalent of Indian endemic diseases ; and on the right understanding of its movements, peculiar

---

* The Influence of Tropical Climates on European constitutions, including practical observations on the nature and treatment of the diseases of Europeans, on their return from tropical climates. By James Ranald Martin, F. R. S., Surgeon Bengal Army, retired, etc. New edition. London, 1856: pp. 140-145.

nature, complications, and just treatment, will always, and in a great measure depend the usefulness of the Indian medical officer.

According to a table furnished to me by Colonel Tulloch, out of an aggregate European force of 25,431 men, of her Majesty's army serving in periods of eight and ten years respectively, between 1823 and 1836, in the stations of Calcutta, Chinsurah and Buhampew, all in Bengal proper, 13,596 cases of fever, remittent, intermittent and continued, occurred. Whereas, out of the same aggregate force, 8,499 cases of dysintery and diarrhœa occurred, thus establishing the far greater prevalence of the malarious fevers over diseases of the bowels.

In the history of the remittent fever of Bengal during the last hundred years, the first observation that presents itself is the great difference as to its intensity in the present as compared to former times; and, secondly, the causes of this difference.

The earliest accounts we possess of the state of public health, and of the season of greatest mortality in Calcutta, is that of Captain Hamilton (1688–1723), wherein he mentions 460 burials out of 1,200 British inhabitants, from August to the ensuing January.

Of Major Kilpatrick's detachment of 240 men, mostly Europeans, stationed at Fultah, Ives tells us that not thirty of the whole were left alive between August and December, 1756, by one of these epidemics. He adds that the number of men buried in Bengal amounted to more than half of all who died in the several hospitals in India during the the whole term of Admiral Watson's command, a period of three years and one month.

Dr Bogue, who also served in Watson's fleet, says that out of three ships of the line and a twenty-gun ship, and these not full manned, we lost in six months upwards of two hundred men, thirty of whom died of this fever.

Dr. James Lind was surgeon of the Drake Indiaman, and writes of the fever which raged in Bengal in the year 1762, and which he terms putrid and remitting marsh fever. This fever raged more or less in different places, according as the soil was more or less swampy, and became so violent, during the rainy season especially, as to end in death during the third fit, which is generally the case. Others, he says, were exposed to the danger of dying at every fit, and when the disorder continued for any time without a change, it generally ended in death; while the weather grew hotter, it sometimes in the space of a few days from a common fever became an intermittent one, and the patient recovered, unless his liver, which was sometimes the case, happened to be affected.

Staverenas, the Dutch naval commander, speaking of "the sort of sickness or fever," which prevailed amongst the European inhabitants of Calcutta, during his visit to that city in 1766 71, says that "it generally sweeps away those who are attacked by it in the space of three days."

Dr. John Clark, who visited Calcutta between 1768 and 1771. says that 'the fever and flux were very fatal in the former year.' Of the fever, he states that 'it frequently carries off the patient in twelve hours.' * * 'During the sickly season in Bengal, the uncertainty of life is so great that it frequently happens that one may leave a friend at night in perfect health who shall not survive the following day. There have been several melancholy instances of persons who have returned home in a state of perfect health. from performing the last duties to a deceased friend, and have next day been numbered with the dead.'

The same authority records that out of 189 cases treated in ships traveling to the various ports in the East, 105 recovered and 84 died. Again "out of 876, the complement of men belonging to eight ships, 78 died in Bengal, and 55 at sea, or nearly one in six. Both the fever and flux, if obstinate have an equal tendency to terminate in abdominal obstructions, particularly in fatal swelling and suppuration of the liver." From this truthful record, and looking to the sanitary condition of the sufferers, and to the result of the treatment by bark, we are constrained to infer that the ultimate recoveries must have been few, out of all who were the subjects of the fever or flux.

Mr. Magennis states that in 1784, out of a crew of his ship the Valentine and six others stationed at Khidgeree, there died of fever and dysintery 170 men; the usual period of their stay in the Hoogley being from August to January. Curtis writes that about the same time, out of two companies of the Ninety-eighth and One Hundredth Regiments embarked in England for India, there died during a suffering and tedious passage of exactly eleven months, seventy-five men, forty of them being from fever, eighteen from dysintery and the remainder from scurvy and cachexy. It was on this occasion that the second battalion of the Forty-second Regiment alone suffered a loss by the time it landed in Calcutta, of five officers and one hundred and sixteen men, all from fevers, bowel complaints and the scurvy. It would appear that the unfortunate companies referred to by Curtis had some occasional fillings up from the other ships as the numbers decreased; but making allowance for this circumstance, the loss of life was horrible, especially when we reflect that each ship in a fleet shared a like mortality.

The ships were, in the language of Clere, crammed with soldiers, so that along with salt rations, there was crowding and consequent filth and want of ventilation, making altogether a combination of the most unfavorable circumstances to the soldiers' health.

' That a scorbutic taint was very general in these times may, I think, be admitted; and this circumstance will account for the general term putrid, as applied by the older writers to the endemic fevers and dysinterries. This unfavorable complication will go far also to account for the enormous mortality. Curtis states that in the open, well ventilated Naval Hospital at Madras, containing from four to five hundred men, the great bulk of the cases were *ulcers*; indeed, he constantly refers to the scorbutic taint, as prevalent amongst both soldiers and seamen, a fact almost entirely overlooked by modern writers when treating of the earlier results of treatment in tropical diseases.

Dr. James Lind, in his excellent treatise on Putrid and Remittent Marsh Fever of Bengal in 1762, refers expressly to the prevalence of scurvy amongst the crews of all the ships off Calcutta. So recently indeed as the beginning of the present century, James Johnson states that in the small portion of the river running between Calcutta and Khidgeree, full 300 European seamen, or more than a fourth of the ships' crews, fell annually victims to the ravages of remittent fever.

But happily we have no longer to record any such fearful ravages by endemic diseases in the capitol of the East; neither do such sweeping epidemics as that recorded by Clark in 1770, with its cold stage of twelve hours, occur, carrying off 80,000 natives and 1,500 Europeans. Such pestilences seem to have gone from us; and we find that here, as in the Western Hemisphere, the malignant fevers of former days, if they have not disappeared, are at least mitigated. Even in Jamaica, although severe epidemic fevers sometimes occur, they do not now as formerly destroy its white inhabitants once in five years.

With all the advantages of modern medical science no one could, even now, pretend to any very great success in the cure of Europeans suffering at once from the united influences of the marsh poison and of the blood depraved beforehand by a salt diet, and by crowding in ships and barracks; the seamen and soldiers were destroyed by fever and dysintery within a few hours of their admission into the hospital. Such men were in truth almost beyond any and all medical means of cure; no amount of cinchona could have cured them; but very easily devised and very obvious means of prevention MIGHT HAVE PRESERVED THEM IN HEALTH.

The causes of the present comparative improvement in public health must be of the highest interest and importance, especially to communities living within the tropics; and, with all just confidence in modern medicine, guided by the lights of an improved physiology, and those also of pathology, I cannot yet agree with those who would ascribe the *whole* of the difference here spoken of to superior modes of medical treatment, great as these confessedly are. It is not through modern improvements in the treatment of disease, as contrasted with the older modes, that public health has been so much amended, as through the great measures of prevention of disease consequent on the progress of improvement of localities, institutions of police, etc. It is to the preservative power of knowledge, to the reciprocal actions of the social state, and of political events upon each other, and upon medical science, that the advancement of public health is most indebted; and so it will continue to be, although these circumstances are not sufficiently weighed by some of us when, in our hurry to praise ourselves, we forget what is due to our predecessors of old, and that these last had frequently to treat a violent and complicated form of disease which we have never seen, and with whose fatal severity we are consequently unacquainted.

It is justly observed by a popular writer, that there were never any specifics discovered against the plague, the sweating sickness, or the leprosy; and yet the leprosy, the sweating sickness and the plague are now among the things unknown to us. They disappeared not before any marvels of medicine or any perfection of chemical science, but before the gradual amelioration of our condition through sanitary improvements.—The Influence of Tropical Climates on European Constitutions, etc. By James Ranald Martin, F. R. S., etc. London, 1856: pp. 140–145.

4. HISTORY OF HÆMORRHAGIC MALARIAL FEVER.

Malignant Intermittent and Remittent Fever, accompanied with vomiting of black bile, with petechiæ and with hæmorrhages, have from time immemorial been frequent and fatal in the warm marshy countries bordering on the Mediterranean and Black Seas. In some parts of Italy, and in other tracts of the same latitude, these fevers have appeared with such dangerous and putrid symptoms as not only to have been called pestilential, but were even confounded with the plague itself.

The more frequent reference to one form of this disease (malarial hæmaturia) by modern writers, is due rather to the employment of the microscope and chemical agents in testing the urine, than to any actual increase

22

in the number of the cases of this disease which, in certain latitudes has afflicted mankind from the earliest ages.

Although Hippocrates omits the discussion of many subjects of importance, as sphygmology* and contagion, on the other hand he made most important observations on the state of the urine in fevers, and especially at the epoch of the crisis in fevers. It is certainly remarkable that the observations of Hippocrates on the state of the urine in febrile diseases, and with reference to certain critical deposits occurring at certain definite periods or changes in diseases, should until a comparatively recent period have been lost sight of in this age when the chemical characters of the urine have been so much studied.

In section second, of constitution second, of the First Book on Epidemics, Hippocrates states that during autumn, and at the commencement of winter, of all the fevers which attacked great numbers:

The ardent fevers attacked the smallest numbers, and the patients suffered the least from them, for there were no hæmorrhages, except a few and to a small amount, nor was there delirum. * * The tertians were more numerous than the ardent fevers, and attended with more pain; but those all had four periods in regular succession from the first attack, and they had a complete crisis in seven, without a relapse in any instance. The quartans attacked many at first, in the form of regular quartans, but in no few cases a transition from other fevers and diseases into quartans took place, they were protracted, as is want with them, indeed, more so than usual. Quotidian, nocturnal, and ₌wandering fevers attacked many persons, some of who continued to keep up, and others were confined to bed. In most instances these fevers were prolonged under the Pleiades and till winter. Many persons and especially children, had convulsions from the commencement. * * *

Persons died of all these diseases, but mostly of these fevers, and especially infants just weaned, and older children, until eight or ten years of age, and those before puberty. * The only favorable symptom, and the greatest of those which occurred, and which saved most of those who were in the greatest danger, was the conversion of it to a strangury, and when in addition to this abscesses were formed. * * With regard to the strangury itself, the symptoms were protracted and painful; their urine was copious, thick, of various characters, red mixed with pus and was passed with pain. * With regard to the dangers of these cases, one must always attend to the seasonable concoction of all the evacuations, and to the favorable and critical abscesses. The concoctions indicate a speedy crisis and recovery of health; crude and undigested evacuations, and those which are converted into hard abscesses, indicate either want of crisis, or pains, or prolongation of the disease, or death or relapses; which of these it is to be determined from other circumstances.

The physician, must be able to tell the antecedents, know the present, and foretell the future—must meditate these things, and have two special objects in view with regard to diseases, namely to do good, or to do no harm. The art consists in three things—the disease, the patient and the physician. The physician is the servant of the art, and the patient must combat the disease along with the physician.

The preceding extract indicates in a clear manner the accuracy with which Hippocrates observed the changes of the urine in fevers; and the following observation recorded in the third constitution of the First Book on Epidemics, clearly relates to malignant malarial or congestive fevers, attended in certain cases with *scant black urine*, as in the malarial hæmaturia of the present day.

About the equinox, and until the season of the Pleides, and at the approach of winter, many ardent fevers set in; but great numbers at that season were seized with phrenitis, and many died; a few cases also occurred during the summer. These then made their attack at the commencement of the ardent fevers, which were attended with fatal symptoms; for immediately upon their setting in, there were acute fever and small rigors, imsomnolency, aberration, thirst, nausea, insignificant sweats about the forehead and clavicles, but no general perspiration; they had much delirious talking, fears, despondency, great coldness of the extremities, in the feet, but more especially in the hands; the paroxysms were in the even days; and in most cases on the fourth day the most violent pains set in, with

---

* Galen declares that Hippocrates paid no attention to the characters of the arterial pulse, and that the subject was not at all studied until after his time. Herophilus appears to have been the first observer that made any progress in this study. That Hippocrates should omit all allusion to the subject of contagion appears remarkable, as the contagiousness of certain diseases, as the plague, was held by his contemporary, Thucydides, and appears to have been the popular belief of his age.

sweats, generally coldish, and the extremities could not be warmed, but were livid and rather cold, and they had then no thirst; in them the urine was black, scanty, thin, and the bowels were constipated; there was an hæmorrage from the nose in no case in which these symptoms occurred, but merely a trifling epistaxis, and none of them had a relapse, but they died on the sixth day with sweats.

Hippocrates has thus given a most striking account of malarial or paroxymal fever in the warm climate of Greece, running its course unchecked by such remedies as are now known to moderns, as the preparation of Peruvian Bark.

Hippocrates records several cases of Paroxysmal fever in which the urine was black, and the following observations will sustain the view that he was not unacquainted with the so-called Malarial Hæmaturia of the present day.

"Philiscus, who lived by the Wall, took to bed on the first day of acute fever; he sweated; towards night was uneasy. On the second day all the symptoms were exacerbated; late in the evening had a proper stool from a small clyster, the night quiet. On the third day, early in the morning and until noon, he appeared to be free from fever; towards evening acute fever, with sweating, thirst, tongue parched; passed black urine; night uncomfortable, no sleep; he was delirous on all subjects. On the fourth, all the symptoms exacerbated, urine black; night more comfortable, urine of a better color. On the fifth almost mid-day, had a slight trickling of pure blood from the nose; urine varied in character, having floating in its round bodies, resembling semen, and scattered, but which did not fall to the bottom; a suppository having been applied, some scanty matter was passed; night uncomfortable, little sleep, talking incoherently; extemities alogether cold, and could not be warmed; urine black; slept a little towards day; loss of speech, cold sweats; extremities livid; about the middle of the sixth day he died. The respiration throughout like that of a person recollecting himself, was rare, and large; the spleen was swelled up in a round tumor, the sweats cold throughout, the paroxysm in the even day.

In the preceeding case the fever had regular exacerbations on the even day and slight remissions on the uneven; the spleen was enlarged, the extremities livid and covered with cold sweat, *the urine black,* and the respirations were rare or few in number, and the patient seemed like a person who forgot for a time the *besoin de respirer* and then as it were suddenly recollecting himself.

Galen, in his commentary, remarks that the fatal issue of this case might have been anticipated after the return of the fever on the third day, with a complication of bad symptoms, such as great thirst, dry tongue, *black urine,* delirium, coldness of the extremities, and so forth.

Cholera morbus and dysenteric discharges in malarial fever constituting the "*Hepatic or atrabiliary state of the malignant intermittent*" of Alibert, has been forcibly described in the epidemics of Hippocrates. Although this variety has been observed to occur in individuals of robust constitutions, who have survived its attacks, yet it is to be considered as a disease for the most part mortal, unless the ablest medical assistance be procured at its very commencement. The predominant symptom is a copious and frequent discharge from the bowels of a matter resembling the washings of raw flesh, and denominated by the ancients the *hepatic flux.* At its first onset, this disease produces apparently no great inconvenience to the patient; but in a short time it prostrates the strength to an extreme degree. The pulse becomes small and feeble; the voice is sharp, and at times is entirely suppressed. There is a remarkable coldness of the body and extremities. The patient has such a tendency to syncope that he is unable to sit erect in bed. The intellectual functions remain notwithstanding unimpared. Sometimes the matter discharged from the bowels is a blackish colored blood, liquid or solid, half coagulated, or half dissolved. If the discharge, so often spoken of by Hippocrates, and vulgarly denominated atrabiliary, be excessive, it is soon accompanied by the most alarming symptoms, such as an obliteration of the pulse, coldness and lividity of the bowels, and the *facies* hippocratica.

Aretæus, the Cappadocian, in his work on the "Causes and Symptoms of Chronic Diseases," says with reference to the kidneys, that—

Many and complicated diseases are formed, partly acute, proving fatal by hæmorrhage, fever and inflammation, but partly chronic, wearing out the patient by wasting, and although not of a fatal character, incurable and pers sting until death.

He also affirms that—

Certain persons pass bloody urine periodically; this affection resembles that from hemorroids, and the constitution of the body is alike; they are very pale, inert, sluggish, without appetite, without digestion; and if the discharge has taken place, they are languid and relaxed in their limbs, but light and agile in the head. But if the periodical evacuations do not take place, they are affected with headache; their eyes become dull, dim and rolling, hence many become epileptic; others are swollen, misty, dropsical; and others again are affected with melancholy and paralysis. These complaints are the offspring of the stoppage of a customary discharge of blood. If, then, the blood flow pure and unmixed with urine, for the most part the blood of the urine flows from the bladder. Sometimes it is discharged in great quantity from rupture of the kidneys; sometimes it is coagulated, and a thrombus is formed of extravasated blood; sometimes it is coagulated in the bladder, when dreadful ischuria comes on.

Celsus affirmed that the bilious and malignant fever is the disease of the latter part of the summer and of autumn, when the air is thickest and most foggy, and that it is most frequent in low and marshy countries.—Cels de Medicine, lib. 1, cap. x, lib. iii, cap. viii.

Cornelius Celsus, in his work on medicine, alludes to the presence of blood in the urine excreted during severe fevers as portending danger and a fatal termination. This author, as well as Aretæus and many others, clearly distinguished between hæmorrhages from the kidneys and bladder, and appear to have been fully informed as to the effects of calculi in the kidney inducing various effects, as bloody urine.

Paulus Ægineta says:

That the kidneys often getting into a relaxed state cannot retain the urine, but becoming dilated they allow the blood and other thick matters to escape from the veins. The kidneys often discharge blood periodically like hemorrhoids, and when evacuated they are relieved, in which cases we must not rashly interfere if the bleeding immediately stops; but if it continue, we must bleed in the arm, and use for hæmorrhage of the kidneys and bladder those remedies which are recommended for hemoptysis and other hæmorrhages; and more especially we must give the root of comfrey and tragicanth macerated in wine, the juice of knotgrass and plantin with oxycrate, or bitter almonds with must, or this medicine: Of fissile alum, dr. j; of tragacanth, dr. ij; of gum oboli, v; with must. And we must apply a cataplasm of raw barley meal with oxycrate or rose-oil, or that from dates, and bread of siligo acacia, or hypocistis boiled in an astringent wine or oxycrate. In hæmorrhages from the bladder, we must apply cupping instruments to the loins and ischium; and we must ascertain the part from which the blood flows by the pain in the place. and whether the blood be mixed with the urine or no, as was said with regard to pus. If there be coagulated blood in the bladder (which you may know from the flow of urine being suddenly stopped after a discharge of bloody urine, and from certain clots or bloody fluids being probably passed,) give the decoction of mugwort to drink and the seed of shrubby-everlasting, of fleabane, or of radish, or the juice of laserwort, or the cyrenaic juice, or the juice of parsely, each mixed with vinegar, or the rennet of a hare, or of a hind, or of a kid, in oxymel, or strained lye with oil, and externally sponges out of hot salt water, or strained lye, must be applied. But if they are not dissolved, we must make an incision in the perincum, as in the cases of calculus; and having removed the clots of blood accomplish the cure in the proper manner.—Book iii, section iii, xlv.

Rufus, one of the oldest writers on diseases of the kidneys, who lived according to Suidas, in the days of Trajan, so that he was prior to Galen, and perhaps to Aretaeus and Caelius Aurelianus, thus details the symptoms of inflammation of the kidneys.

Pains below the loins, so that the patient cannot stand erect nor walk, but is obliged to lie upon his back, which position affords him most relief; the pains extending to the bladder and testicles; the extremities cold, more especially the legs and feet; frequent and painful desire to make urine, which is at first thin and watery, but afterwards becomes redder

Theophilus, Actuarius, and many other ancient writers on medicine in addition to those quoted above, described with surprising minuteness the deposits in the urine, including every imaginary shade of color ; and connected these changes with the morbid conditions of the system which gave rise to them.

Rome was often afflicted with malignat malarial fevers, and Galen calls the *hemitritæ*, the epidemic of that city; and speaks of its moist air (de temperam, let ii.). In the beginning of the Republic, before the Romans seem to have been aware of the noxious effects of stagnating water, or at least before they had perfected the arrangements for draining the marshes, and stagnant pools; Rome appears to have been so sickly, that from the beginning of the State to the year U. C. 459, fifteen plagues are mentioned by Livy, which from various circumstances, appear to have been only so many malignant and destructive epidemics, occasioned by the putrid effluvia from the neighboring marshes.

When drains and common sewers were made and the Pontine marshes drained, Rome became more healthful, and then only the lower and marshy places of Latium remained sickly. When the city fell into the hands of the Goths, the drains being stopped and the acqueducts cut, the Roman territory became one continued marsh, and for a series of years malignant malarial fevers occasioned incredible destruction. Though these evils have since been partially remedied, yet still by neglecting to draw off the stagnating and corrupted water (after inundations by the Tiber, succeeded by great heats,) the malignant remitting and intermitting fevers became both general and fatal. The malignant and so-called putrid nature of these fevers has been well shown by Lancisius in his dissections and in his excellent account of these epidemics (De Nox Palud Effleo, lib. ii, epid i, cap. vi.)

Prosper Alpinus observes that the pestilential fevers are both epidemic and fatal at Alexandria in autumn after the recess of the Nile. They begin, with a *nausea*, great sickness at the stomach, extraordinary inquietude, and a vomiting of acrid bile, and many have bilious and putrid stools.

That the hæmaturia, as a symptom in certain fevers was carefully noted by the older writers, is evident from the following description of the appearance of the urine of exanthematous typhus, by Burserius (Institutes, vol. iii).

At first it is at one time thin and watery ; at another time natural, and exhibits a globular, unequal palish cloud floating in it. Sometime also, at the beginning it is whitish but copious ; shortly after it grows confused like pomegranate wine, or yellowish, thick, turpid, and deposits a sedement. It sometimes likewise grows black, as if it were mixed with soot, or turns red, being slightly tinged with blood. Sometimes during the increase and at the height of the complaint, it is nearly suppressed, which must be considered as a fatal symptom, unless it quickly comes off thick, and deposits a sediment. Trollius, in his patients, always found it proper in quantity, seldom thin and pellucid, but generally free of sediment ; sometimes of a dusky red, but never concocted or having a proper sediment. Pinaroli, however, found the urine, in the first days of the complaint, pale, clear and scanty ; during its increase, somewhat red and confused ; at its decline, turpid, and thick, but not uniformily so."

We cannot fail to recognize the *Congestive and Pernicious Fevers* in these various manifestations, with coma, convulsions, suppression of urine, congestion of various organs, as the lungs, kidneys, brain, liver and spleen, and hæmorrhages from the bowels and kidneys, in the descriptions Senac, Lancisi. Ramizzini, Lautter. Torti, Tissot, Cleghorn, Sarcone and others.

Lancisi, in his account of the malignant tertian that prevailed in many parts of Rome in the year 1695 (De Nox Palud Effluv, lib. 2,) says:

That on the fifth day the disease inclined towards a continued type ; on the seventh or eleventh the patient died; they seldom lived till the fourteenth day, unless where the disease was converted occasionally into a chronic fever or into a dysentery, which in that case continued during the whole autumn, or even during the winter. The countenances of those attacked became at first yellow ; the sick experienced a disrelish for food, and dull pains in the head ; these were followed by a severe chill and a discharge from the stomach of a watery fluid mixed with vitiated bile of different colors. Oftentimes, after two parox· ysms, accompanied by profuse sweats, the fever was marked by such a remission, that the sick considering themselves out of danger, not only rose from bed on the fourth day, but began to walk abroad. During this time, however, the urine was saffron-colored, thick and turbid. On the fifth day the fever returned, with great anxiety about the præcordia, which completely developed its malignant character; the tongue, besides, was dry and dark colored, the pulse varied ; it was oftentimes small and unequal. The limbs having become cold were agitated with convulsive motions; there were livid blotches on the skin, the face cadaverous, frequent fainting fits, delirium, abdomen tense and tumified ; stools fœtid and consisting of dark colored bile, oftentimes mixed with blood, and containing dead worms at the commencement of the disease; at length came on great drowsiness, cold sweats, limpid urine and swellings of the parotids. The patient sunk on the seventh or ninth day. Until the proper remedy for the disease was discovered they seldom survived till the twelfth day.

On opening the dead bodies Lancisi found great ravages in the viscera of the abdomen, which were almost all livid; the liver was of a very dark brown; the cystic bile was black; the intestines sphacelated in various parts, contained excrements extremely fœtid, and a great quantity of worms.

Lancisi also described a second epidemic prevalence of malignant intermittents, which lasted for several years, which put on the tertian type, were ushered in by a cold fit or a profuse sweat, accompanied with bilious vomitings, copious evacuations by stool, pain in the head and loins, cardalgia, tension of the hypocondriac regions and lower part of the abdomen. Although these fevers pursued nearly the same course, the heat increased and the sweat diminished; the debility became at length so great that the patient growing colder all over, died on the fifth or seventh day.

With these epidemic constitutions of Lancisi, may be classed that which prevailed at Turin in 1720, and of which Riche (Thom. Sydenb, op. tom. ii., fol. 38,) has given a description. Some of the sick were afflicted with excru· ciating pains in the head ; others complained of burning heats and lassitude throughout the whole body ; some were tormented by thirst, and distressed by a constant want of sleep; many were overwhelmed by a deep and unconquerable drowsiness ; an eruption of the petecchiæ made its appearance on the fourth or seventh day ; and in some cases copious stools of black grumous blood were discharged.

Ramazzini, mentions having seen at Modena, *malignant* tertian fevers, which prevailed with the greatest violence—towards the fourth or fifth paoxysm, the cold fit was so intense that the patients never became warm again ; the whole body was like ice; the pulse was incapable of expanding, and death soon closed the scene.

Lautter in describing the malignant intermittent, which prevailed in Luxumbourg in 1759 and 1760, says that the fevers of the first year, were peculiarly acute and inflammatory, and those of the second highly putrid and malignant; they all resembled each other in their most essential characteristie, that is, they were intermittent, and yielded only to the action of bark. The unfavorable symptoms which accompanied these fevers were great anxiety about the præcordia, a painful oppression of the breast, a continued and very troublesome nausea, a laborious rejection of yellow green bile, a vomiting of grumous blood, violent hysterical and convulsive motions, a vehement cardalgia, which brought on faintness and at length true syncope. All these symptoms increased and diminished with the paroxysms.

Alibert has described the malignant malarial fevers which prevailed at Pitkivius, in the department of Loiret, in the year x., and M. Boullon those which ravaged the environs of Abbeville, in the years viii, ix, x and xi, of the

French Republic. LeRoy observes that choleraic tertians were epidemic at Montpelier in the autumn of 1765 (Memoirs sur les fievres aigues), and Sydenham has also taken notice of epidemic constitutions, when intermittents with Cephalic affections predominated (Epist. at Rob. Brady); Thomas Bartholni (Hist. Anat. rar. Cent. ii; Hist. lvi,) says that the epidemic which prevailed at Copenhagen in 1652, was characterized by delirium and excruciating Cephalalgic affections, and petechial blotches which appeared during each paroxysm and disappeared during the intermission, also debilitating diarrohæ, and Sylvius de Leboe, in his account of a similar fever which raged at Lyden in 1669, makes mention of livid blotches on the skin, hæmorrhages from the nose, and hæmorrhoidal veins, and fetid urine (Prax, med. append, tract. x.) George Cleghorn, has described many of the forms assumed by paroxysmal malarial fevers, and says that the utmost danger is to be apprehended—

If black matter, like the grounds of coffee, is discharged upwards or downwards; if the urine is of a dark hue and of a strong, offensive smell; if the whole skin is tinged with a deep yellow, or anywhere discolored with livid spots or suffusions; if a cadaverous smell is perceptible about the patient's bed; if in the time of the fit he continues cold and chilly, without being able to recover heat; or if he becomes extremely hot, speechless and stupid; has frequent sighs, groans, or hiccoughs, and lies constantly on his back, with a ghastly countenance, his eyes half shut, his mouth open, his belly swelled to an enormous size, with an obstinate costiveness, or an involuntary discharge of the excrements.*

Torti is one of the first who ventured to deviate from the established custom of purging and bleeding, previously to the exhibition of the bark, and Grant judiciously remarks that every fever accompanied with paroxysms ought to be arrested in its course as soon as it manifests the smallest signs of malignity.

Lind also insisted upon this mode of practice, in consequence of having derived such important advantages from it in the destructive epidemics which prevailed in England in the years 1765, 1766 and 1767. He found from experience, in his own person and in the persons of two hundred patients, that as often as he succeeded in arresting the course of the fever by a prompt administration of the bark, its disappearance was attended by no bad consequences. But if on the contrary the use of the remedy was neglected or delayed, dropsy, jaundice, habitual headache, etc., inevitably succeeded. Lind observes that it is often necessary to administer the bark from the time of the first intermission. He speaks of some intermittents appearing with such violence in certain sickly parts of England as ottentimes to terminate fatally on the second paroxysm. Alibert also held that the most pressing indication is to arrest at once, by the free use of bark, the progress of the disease.

Jean Senac, who flourished in the reign of Louis XV, and held the position of first physician to that monarch, not only describes with force, elegance and accuracy the various forms of malignant and non-malignant intermittents, and explains the causes of the hæmorrhages characterizing these fevers, and dwells upon the deleterious effects of the bile retained in the blood, as dissolving the grosser (or red parts) of the blood and thus causing hæmorrhages and anaemia; but also thus records his observations on the characters of the urine in intermittent fever:

The change in the humors appear also from the urine itself. During the febrile action that fluid is flame colored; but as the paroxysm declines becoming thick, frothy and very red; it puts on at length a brick-dust color. This color appears in particular in the sediment, which is generally copious. This earthy sediment is apt to lodge and create a temporary obstruction in the vessels of the kidneys.

---

* Observations on the Epidemical Diseases of Minorca from the year 1744 to 1749, by George Cleghorn, M; D., with notes by Benjamin Rush, M. D. Philadelphia, 1812; p. 101.

This kind of urine belongs so peculiarly to intermitting fever, that, provided the disease be genuine, it is seldom wanting. Indeed there is no solid reason to believe that the system is free from the forms of the fever, while the urine retains its lateritious color, or is in any measure tinctured with red. This phenomenon does or can prove fallacious only in cases where the sick labor under some hepatic affection. If at any time the urine should exhibit a white matter settling copiously to the bottom of the vessel, this is to be considered as a favorable symptom, and even a sign of a crisis in the disease. I must confess however, that the phenomenon has but seldom fallen under my observation.

In some intermitting fevers the urine does not assume a lateritious color. I allude particularly to certain vernal intermittents, or to those that change into continued or remitting fevers. Even in these, however, the urine does exhibit something of a lateritious appearance during their remission. At these times, when the secretory vessels of the kidneys are suffered to relax in consequence of an abatement of the febrile spasm, the grosser and red colored particles are allowed to escape. Whence it appears, that at the commencement of the disease, if it be very severe, the urine does not depart from its natural color, but assumes a red and lateritious cast when the symptom abates.[*]

†Dr. I. L. Alibert in his treatise on Malignant Intermittents says, that:

The state of the urine in Malignant fevers demands great attention. Thus a diminution of that excretion, and its assuming a black color, are very alarming symptoms. M. Boullon, in his account of the epidemic of Abbeville, says that the sick were usually in very great danger, while their urine exhibited a membriform sediment of a mucous nature, forming a convex covering to a glairy matter placed beneath it."

Malignant and hæmorrhagic malarial fevers also prevail in Java lying between 5 and 10 degrees of south latitude, also in the southern and marshy portions of India, and in the British settlements on the Gold Coast of Guinea which are as near the line, on one side as Java is on the other. Numerous authorities might be quoted also to show that in addition to yellow fever, the severest grades of malarial fever attended with incessant vomiting of dark bile and hæmorrhages, have prevailed in the British, French, Spanish and Portuguese settlements in Insular and Continental America.

Dr. James Lind, states that Sardinia was formerly so remarkable for its unwholesome air, that the Romans used to banish their criminals thither, and that it is at present thinly peopled, owing to the mortality occasioned by autumnal fever. (Diseases incident to Europeans in hot climate. London, 1768, p. 34.)

With reference to the destructive effects of Fevers in hot climates, Dr. James Lind has recorded the following striking observations :

The recent example of the great mortality in hot climates ought to draw the attention of all the commercial nations in Europe towards the important object of preserving the health of their countrymen, whose business carries them beyond seas. It is found that sickly or unhealthy settlements require a constant supply of people, and, of course, drain their mother country of an incredible number of inhabitants, and some of these, too, its most useful individuals. Of this the Spanish dominions abroad have furnished us with striking proofs; and even at this day, many Spanish merchants, adventurers and others, who yearly take their departure from Europe, die at Porto-Bello or Carthagena, soon after their landing.

The Dutch settlements at Surinam, St. Eustatia and Curacoa, and in several places in India, have proved as fatal to the Hollanders, as the islands of Martinico, St. Domingo, and lately the climate of Cayenne, have done to the French settlers.

Great Britain itself, has its *Jamaica*, where the number of English sacrificed to the climate is hardly credible, and only to be guessed at, from the common computation, that this island burried to the amount of the whole number of its white inhabitants once in five years, until laley, that it has become more healthy.

It is now a well known and most certain truth, that of such Europeans as have fallen victims to the temperature of foreign climates, nineteen in twenty have been cut off by fevers and fluxes; these being the prevailing and most fatal maladies in unhealthy countries in all parts of the world.

In my *Essay on Preserving Seamen* (p. 49, 2d Ed.) I have said, that a malignant fever, of

---

[*]De Recondita Febrium Intermitentium tum Remittentium Natura—et de carum curatione—Geneve, 1769.

†A treatise on Malignant Intermittents, by I. L. Alibert, Physician to the Hospital of St. Louis, etc. Third Ed. Phila., 1807, p. 156.]

the remitting or intermitting kind, most frequently a double tertian, is the genuine product of heat and moisture, is the autumnal fever of all hot countries, and is the epidemic disease between the tropics. To which I may add, that it is also the disease most fatal to Europeans in all hot and unhealthy climates.—[Diseases Incident to Europeans in Hot Climates, p. 9.

With reference to the diseases of the Southern Colonies of North America, Dr. Lind adds:

In the latitude of South Carolina we find these diseases much more obstinate, acute and violent. In that colony, especially during the growth of the rice, in the month of July and August, the fevers which attrck strangers are very anomalous, not remitting or intermitting soon, but partaking of those distempers which are so fatal to the newly arrived Europeans in West Indian Climates. The same may be said of Georgia and East Florida during those two months; but in West Indian Islands.—[p. 37.

Dr. William Hillary, in his "*Treatise* on such diseases as are most frequent in, or are particular to the West India Islands, or the Torid Zone, says, with reference to the "Putrid Bilious Fever, commonly called the Yellow Fever:"

I mentioned hæmorrhages before, for the latter stage of this fever, the blood is so attenuated and dissolved, that we frequently see it flowing, not only out of the nose and mouth, but from the eyes, and even through the very pores of the skin; also great quantities of black, half baked, or half mortified blood is frequently voided, both by vomiting and by stool, with great quantities of yellow and black putrid bile, by the same ways; and the urine, which was before of a high ictericous color, is now almost black, and is frequently mixed with a quantity of half-dissolved blood.—[Phald. 1811, p. 111.

In a work published in 1845, "On the Climate and Maladies of Brazil," M. Sigaud mentions an epidemic disease attended with the discharge of bloody urine, and for which the best treatment was found to be generous diet, with a combination of iron and quinine.

Dr. R. B. Todd, in a clinical lecture, published January 19, 1849, in the *London Medical Gazette*, says:

A state of general cachexia, such as occurs in scurvy, may bring on hæmaturia; or such as results from an anguish state, brought on by the malaria of marshy districts. Nothing is more prejudicial to hæmatosis, or the healthy elaboration of the blood than the influence of the paludal poison.

In his clinical lectures Dr. R. B. Todd records three cases of hæmaturia, in one of which the hæmorrhages were accompanied with Rheumatic fever, and severe pericarditis; the second case was one of catarrhal hæmaturia, which appeared in a laborer, aged 40 years, during a depressed state of health, attended with abscesses in the axilla, and was probably induced by exposure to cold; the third case was that of a boy, who was laboring under dropsy, after scarlet fever.

That the Hæmorrhagic form of malarial fever is not unknown in the East Indies, is evident from the following statement by Dr. McLean:

Of the symptoms *nausea and vomiting* are the most constant, and the most exhausting; the vomited matters at first consist of any food that may be in the stomach, then of a watery fluid, often in a surprising quantity. Soon billious regurgitation takes place, and the rejected matters become of a greenish yellow color, then brown, and finally in extreme cases, black, resembling the vomit of yellow fever. The resemblance will be more striking if, as sometimes happens, the skin assumes a yellow tinge and hæmorrhagic tendency be evinced. I have seen two cases at Madras, both in officers of the Forest Conservdney Department, in which the hæmorrhagic range was most extensive, the patient passing blood *from the stomach, bowels and kidneys.*

Dr. McLean, states that he has notes of three other cases, in which *the urine was bloody.* He also observed cases of what the older writers describe as *putrid remittent.* These occurred on soldiers landed on the shores of Bengal, who had scurvy from protracted sea voyages, and the mortality was shocking. An entire regiment 900 strong was almost destroyed by malarial fevers and bowel complaints in a few weeks, and those who survived, bore testimony to the truthfulness of the description of putrid remittent fevers given by the older authors. Dr. McLean, also says:

That without any scorbutic taint, we may have remittent fever, presenting from the

23

commencement an adynamic character in which the skin was yellow and covered with petechiæ, the pulse exceeding 120 with a disposition to hæmorrages from nose, mouth and bowels. He was familiar with cases of this kind when serving in the immediate vicinity of Hyderabad in Decan.

Dr. Charles Faget, in his "Memoires and Letters," published in 1859, quotes Dr. Dutrouleau, former physician in chief of the French marine, to the effect that the borders of the Danube, which, with regard to its medical topography and endemic fevers, presents many analogies with those of the Mississippi, is the theatre at the end of the warm season of quotidian. double-tertian and bilious fevers, in which *jaundice and black urine* appear from the first paroxysms, with difficulty of respiration, delerium, gastric irritation and nervous and muscular prostration. The prominent anatomical lesions are enlargement of the liver and spleen. Dr. Dutrouleau terms this disease the hæmitritæa of the paludal climate of the Danubian Provinces.

Dr. Faget also quotes the following from articles of Dutrouleau, in the Archives Générales de Médicené of October and November, 1858, illustrating the nature of the hæmorrhagic malarial fever of bilious hæmorrhagic form, as it appears at Madagascar, Cayenne and in the West Indies:

1st. Madagascar.—(Here follows the description of a jaundical paroxysm at Madagascar, by Dr. Lebean.)

The scene is opened by a chill; it is followed by vomitings of the green color of arsenite of copper; to the vomitings are often added stools of the same nature; I have seen patients passing blood by this passage. Sometimes also the vomit has a black color, a color which the urine partakes of, the green tint being so deep set that it resembles ink. Reaction soon takes place, and lasts about twenty hours. When the remission takes place, an icterical suffusion is spread over the whole body, which becomes of a deep orange hue.—(p. 388.)

Anatomical lesions—Softening of the gastric mucous membranes, alteration of the color of the liver, which presents the general yellow cast of the other tissues; spleen hypertrophied.—(p. 389.)

Two other observers, Gélineau and Guilasse, insist upon the importance and danger of the passive hæmorrhages, particularly of the hæmaturia and epistaxis, which are very rebellious in these fevers.—(p. 393.)

Guilasse describes a yellow paroxysm, with intermitting type, and a yellow continuous paroxysm, one syncopal, and one soperose.—(p. 393.)

Finally, Daullé, after a long residence at Mayotte, chose as the subject of his inaugural theme in 1857, this very fever of Madagascar, which he calls pernicious icteric. "It assumes," says he, "the three paludal types of fever, oftener, however, intermittent than remittent, and seldom *continuous*."—(p. 395.)

In 1851 an occurrence took place in Guiana, bearing much analogy to what has been observed since 1853, in the parishes of Louisiana, and in the epidemic yellow fever at Cayenne in 1850.

But we must come to the end of 1851, to the transportation of European convicts in Guianna, to the increase of the European population, and its dissemination at various points of the plains or marshes of rivers, which are all intense hot-beds of paludal emenations, to observe the re-appearance of fevers of a grave type.

Here are a few extracts from the reports of the physician in chief, Dr. Laure, from 1851 to 1853: "The sick have almost invariably, from the first day, a continued fever with delerium, irregularity of pulse, *jaundice, urine scant*, yellow blood, in a word, the symptoms of the yellow disease (icteric pernicious fever of Madagascar) ignored until the present day, are a great deal more fatal than the epidemic yellow fever of 1850.

"The icterous," observed Dr. Laure, "attains its highest degree; the urine and stools contain a great quantity of black blood and yellow materials, ascertained by analysis. There exists petechiæ and sudamina."

Laure considers malarial intoxication as the first and essential cause of the disease, and, nevertheless, remarks: "the action of quinine is so doubtful that we do not know whether rational treatment is not deserving of consideration in its cure."—(p. 402.)

With regard to the intermittent fevers of the West Indies, Dutrouleau says:

In the continued form, which is also the most serious, the bilious symptoms do not appear at the onset, but only after a period of thirty-six to forty-eight hours, characterized by an inflammatory period; then the jaundice and bilious excretions becomes apparent, but less marked than in the intermittent form. The *urine is always bloody*, but in less degree than in the intermittent form; epistaxis sometimes occur, and traces of blood are found in the stool and vomit. Some observers say they have, met the *real* black vomit of yellow fever ; I have never met it. The cerebral phenomena are always prominent in this form. Sometimes we have but excitement and slight delirum, complicated with anxiety and trouble of the respiration, but sometimes also there exists ataxic symptoms of an extremely violent nature.

Such is the fever which the physicians of Point-a-Peitre, where it is more prevalent than elsewhere, have named '*Bilious hæmaturic fever*,' '*yellow fever of the acclimated and of the Creoles ;* When it is of some duration it assumes at times the mark of typhoid fever. It is subject to relapses, and ends by bringing the patient to a chacexia, p. 904.

From 1828 to 1838, a period of immunity from yellow fever, Dr. Therminier, whose name is authority at Guadaloupe, has frequently met with it in Creoles, concurrently with the other forms of pernicious fever. He also classes it among the malarial fevers, rather than with yellow fever, notwithstanding its symptoms of affinity with this last disease. (p. 405.)

Dr. Faget thus expresses the results of his investigations in New Orleans, of what he denominates the *hæmatemesic variety of hæmorrhagic malarial fever.*

At New Orleans, thin:s take quite an opposite direction. In our hæmorrhagic malar= ial fever, the hæmorrhage which I have met the most often, is that of the stomach, but in the most incontestible manner, recognizable to the naked eye, by every one, in all its shades, from the grumous of the color of chocolate to the clots of blood, sometimes yet red, some- times already blackened by the acids of the stomach, to the grumous black coffee grounds, resembling perfectly genuine black vomit of yellow fever. * * It is by such facts, pa- tiently collected without interruption for the past seventeen years, in all seasons, even in winter, in the midst as well as *outside* of epidemics of yellow fever, facts of gastric hæmor- rhage being produced in the course of fevers of all malarial types, from the larvate to the exacerbating type, in passing by the intermittent, remittent, sub-inhant and pseudo con- tinued, that I have been able to recognize the existence of the *hæmatemesic variety of hæmor- rhagic malarial fever.* New Orleans Journal of Medicine, vol. xxii, No. iv, October, 1869, pp. 768-784.

L. J. B. Berenger-Feraud, who in virtue of his position as *Medecin en Chef de la Marine,* and in virtue of the advantages for extended and critical ob- servation, which he enjoyed for many years whilst in charge of a hospital at Goree, which received annually into its wards from eleven to thirteen hun- dred patients, is entitled to consideration with reference to the pathology and treatment of that form of malignant malarial fever, which he designates " Fèivre Bilieuse Melanurique des pays chauds," regards the disease as truly malarial in its character, distinct from yellow fever, and endemic to the most malarious regions of Africa. He describes this disease for which he pro- poses a new name, (*Melanuric Bilious Fever*), as a malarial fever of variable type characterized by : 1. Persistent vomiting of bilious matter of a greenish color ; 2. Jaundice of the skin and of all tissues ; 3. A peculiar brownish color of the urine. The second and third of these characteristics he regards as the most pathognomonic, and as distinguishing this form of malarial fever from every other.

With reference to its pathological anatomy ; the color of the skin varies from a light to a dark yellow, according to the cases, and of a perfectly uni- form tint everywhere. The stomach is perfectly sound, when the patient has not formed any drunken habits ; and the pungency of the mucous matter, which has been considered pathognomic by some physicians, is positively nothing but the effect of alcoholic gastritis, entirely independent of the dis- ease. The gastric fluid is green, limpid, or contains lumps of green matter, exactly like chopped spinach—a differential sign between this disease and yellow fever. The liver is very generally increased in size, its normal weight being some 1796 grammes (57¾ ozs.), its weight in Melanuric bilious fever, being about 2196 grammes (70¾ ozs.). The congested condition of this organ is special and entirely different from the anæmic condition of the liver of yellow fever. The bile is greatly increased in quantity, thicker than in its normal state, having a black color and a consistence which gives it the exact

appearance of tár, or of *raisine*, too much colored. The spleen is decidedly hypertrophied, its normal weight being some 235 grammes (7½ ozs.); and in this disease, its average weight was about 760 grammes (24⅓ ozs.)—a positive proof of the malarial origin of this disease. In the early stages of the disease, the spleen is almost diffluent ; later it is hard. The kidneys are congested and their weight increased, but M. Berenger-Feraud does not appear to have made any carful sections and microscopical examinations of the ultimate structures of the kidneys. There is reason to believe, however, that sometimes permanent injury is done to the kidneys by the fever. The blood contains bile in sufficiently large proportion to stain linen yellow, when dipped in it.

Whilst Berenger-Feraud did not discover blood in the urine, but observed casts of albumen in some cases, and whilst he refers the peculiar dark color of the urine not to blood, but to the presence of bile ; at the same time the great fatality of the severer forms the mortality reaching more than fifty per cent.; the presence of jaundice, distressing vomiting, and the supervention of the disease after repeated attacks of malarial fever, sustain the view that this form of malarial fever as it prevails upon the coast of Africa, is closely allied with the different forms of hæmorrhagic malarial fever, and especially with the malarial hæmaturia of our Southern States.

· With reference to the first appearance of *melanuric bilious fever*, on the Senegal river, Berenger-Feraud found that the records of St. Louis Hospital show that from 1841, the *black urine* was noted, and that similarity in this instance, and in others, justify the belief that in 1839, 1830, 1825 and 1820, the disease was observed prior to the appearance of the yellow fever in Senegambia.

· The records of the ports along the Senegal furnish no additional information ; but those of the hospital at Gorée led him to think th .t what had been seen at St. Louis, was observed there also at the above-mentioned dates. Lastly, the records of the ports of the Gold-Coast and the Gaboon, show very clearly that from 1845, three years after the establishment, melanuric bilious fever was observed there. Moreover, neither Dr. Thèze, nor Di. Loupy, both of whom practiced in Senegambia about 1856, seem to have regarded it as new, since they described it among the endemic diseases of the country.[*]

The hæmorrhages that took place from the cracked fissures of the tongue, from the lips, gums and bowels, the livid petechial blotches similar to those of purpura, and the large discolorations or ecchymoses of various parts of the body, which characterized certain cases of the so-called *typho-malarial* or Chickahominy fever of the Federal army, were clearly referable to the action of the malarial and typhoid poisons on scorbutic subjects. This form of fever, which first attracted attention in 1862, as the Chickahominy fever of the Army of the Potomac, and received the name of typho-malarial fever from Dr. J. J. Woodward,[†] U. S. A., has since been common wherever the United States armies operated in malarious regions, amongst men saturated with paludal poison, exhausted by over exertion and insufficient rest, imperfectly nourished, exposed to the action of animal effluvia from the decaying bodies of both men and brutes, and drinking water impregnated with the products of common putrifaction.

---

[*]De la Fievre Bilieuse Melanurique des pays chauds comparee avec la Fievre Jaune. Etude Clinique faite au Senegal. Par L. J. B. Berenger-Feraud, Medecen-en-Chef de la Marine, etc., etc., p. 434, Paris, 1874.

[†]Outlines of the Chief Camp Diseases of the United States Armies. Phila. 1863. pp. 77-149. The Sience and Practice of Medicine, by William Aitkens, M. D.; 3d Am. Ed., Phila. 1872, vol. 1, p. 607.

These coincident causes, tending to lower the vital forces and corrupt the blood, produce a compound disorder, in which the combined action of paludal, pythogentic, and scorbutic influences are evident, and which varies in type, as one or other of the determining conditions is predominant.

As far as my experience extended, which was by no means limited, during the American Civil War 1861-1865, whilst hæmorrhages from the mucous surfaces, were not infrequent in typhoid fever and small-pox, they were comparatively rare in the various forms of malarial fever.

I witnessed however, in the Military Prisons at Richmond and Andersonville, a vast variety of diseases, in which the hæmorrhagic tendency was prominent, from the scorbutic condition of the blood.

In a number of cases of hæmorrhage from the gums, stomach and bowels which I have treated since the war, various causes appeared to have been in some of the cases, the origin of the hæmorrhagic diathasis, as the abuse of alcohol, bad diet, exposure to wet and cold, scorbutus and the prolonged action of the malarial poison.

Several of these cases, complicated with malarial fever in which large quantities of blood were vomited, and which were evidently thrown off from the mucous mebrane of the stomach, recovered under a conservative and supporting plan of treatment.

Both in the Army and Military Prisons, and in civil and hospital practice, I have found that where the hæmorrhages were clearly referable to the scorbutic state of the blood, certain well marked lesions and more especially fatty degeneration of the heart existed

In 1857, I investigated the changes of temperature, pulse, respiration and of the blood and urine in the various forms of malarial fever[*] and described cases of the so called Menanuric Bilious Fever; and it was shown both by the record of the symptoms and by pathological anatomy of the various forms of Intermittent, Remittent, Bilious and Congestive or Pernicious fevers, that they were all mere varieties of the same disease, which was radically distinct from the continued Typhus and Typhoid fevers on the one hand, and yellow fever on the other.

5. GENERAL OUTLINE OF THE SYMPTOMS AND PATHOLOGICAL ANATOMY OF YELLOW AND MALARIAL FEVERS.

YELLOW FEVER.

YELLOW FEVER SYMPTOMS AND PATHOLOGY.

DEFINITION —A pestilential fever of continuous and specific type, originally developed in tropical and insular America: confined to definite geographical limits and dependent in its origin and spread upon definite degrees of temperature, and capable of transportation and propagation in ships and in towns and cities, in those portions of North and South America, which lie between 45° N. lat. and 35° S. lat.: the disease has been limited chiefly to the coast of tropical Africa, rather from the number and position of the commercial towns, than from any climatic causes adverse to its propagation elsewhere; it has been imported from the Antilles and from the Gulf of Mexico and from tropical America, far in the interior of the Valley of the Mississippi, from New Orleans to St. Louis and along the Atlantic coast, from St Augustine to Portland, Maine, and even across the Atlantic ocean to Cadiz, Carthagena, Barcelona, Gibralta, Lisbon, St. Nazarre to Plymouth and Southampton England.

MALARIAL FEVER.

MALARIAL FEVER SYMPTOMS AND PATHOLOGY.

The general division of malarial or paroxysmal fevers into three types, namely intermittent, remittent and pernicious or congestive fever, admits of several subdivisions.

Thus the forms of malignant intermittent are numerous but all are attended with congestion of one or more vital organs, which may endanger the life of the patient, and which may pass into actual inflammation attended with effusion of plastic lymph, serum or blood. In many cases in which no structural alterations have ensued during the congestive stage, there comes on at the conclusion of the paroxysm, a perfect intermission of all the violent symptoms. The sudden disappearance of the most alarming symptoms, may lead to a false prognosis, and prevent the institution of energetic measures. It is well known that in the malarious regions of the Southern and Western States, one of those violent paroxysms, whenever occurring, even at the onset of the disease, or during the progress of an or.

---

[*]Southern Medical and Surgical Journal. 1858.
Transactions of the American Medical Association, 1859.

It presents two well-defined stages: the first characterized by intense pain in the head and back, injected eyes, rapid circulation, elevated temperature, which may extend from 24 to 160 hours, according to the severity of the disease; the second characterized by depression of the nervous and muscular forces, and of the general and capillary circulation. capillary congestion, slow and intermittent pulse, jaundice, urinary suppression, passive hæmorrhages from the stomach and bowels, nares, tongue, gums, uterus, vargina, gall bladder and anus, and in extreme cases from the eyes, ears and skin; black vomit; convulsions, delirium and coma. In its origin and propagation it is not dependon those conditions and causes which generate malarial paroxysmal fever, from which it differs essentially in symptoms and pathology. One of the prominent symptoms of the first stage, is the rapid increase of the pulse within the first few hours of the febrile excitement, and the progressive diminution of the beats of the heart, whilst the temperature progressively rises; and in like manner the slow and feeble action of the heart constitutes a prominent and striking symptom of the second stage. Yellow fever in common, with such contagious diseases as small-pox, measles and scarlet fever, occurs as a general rule but once during life, and may be propagated by contagion; it differs, however, from the exanthematous disease, in that it has never been known to propagate beyond 48° North latitude, nor below a temperature of 70° F.

I will now briefly present the general conclusions as to the nature of yellow fever which I have drawn from my original investigations during the past twenty-four years. During this period I have at various times, and in different journals, published cases sustaining the various conclusions, and I have also in my possession, in manuscript, the details of a large number of careful chemical and microspical investigations and numerous cases illustrating the symptoms and pathological anatomy of malarial and yellow fever. I hope to present the most important of these researches and cases, as well as a minute historical account of yellow fever and other fevers, in the second volume of my Medical and Surgical Memoirs, in that division of the work which relates more especially to the natural history and treatment of fevers.

GENERAL CONCLUSIONS AS TO THE NATURE OF YELLOW FEVER; AS DRAWN FROM ORIGINAL INVESTIGATIONS.

I. YELLOW FEVER is a continued pestilential fever, presenting two well-defined stages: the first characterized by active chemical change in the blood and organs, attended with elevation of temperature and aberration of nervous action, which may constitute the entire malady, and prove fatal in a manner similar to the infectious form of small-pox; and the other, a stage of depression, induced both by the sedative action of the febrile poison, and by profound changes excited in the blood, and in certain organs, viz., the heart, liver and kidneys, and by the direct sedative and poisonous action of the excrementitious matter retained in the blood, in consequence of the failure, arrest, or perversion of the functions of the liver and kidneys, and by the arrest or perversion of the digestive function, in consequence of the action of the yellow fever poison, in causing perverted nervous action, capillary congestion, and active desquamation of the secretory cells of the stomach, and in consequence of the elimination by the gastric mucous membrane of certain constituents of the blood and urine, viz., urea and carbonate of ammonia.

The various manifestations—as the intense capillary congestion, depression of the heart, delirium, coma, convulsions, vomiting, headache, urinary suppression, uræmic poisoning, jaundice and biliary poisoning—may all be referred to the action of the poison producing th edisease, and should not form the bases for the erection of distinct types of the disease.

The action of the yellow fever poison is the same in all cases, whether mild or severe; The progress and termination of the case, as well as the manifestation of the various symptoms, depending upon the extent of the action of the poison, the condition of the system

dinary mild intermittent, is the harbinger of others still more violent. If unheeded the disease may prove fatal, at the third, fourth or fifth paroxysm.

The nature and effect of the malignant paroxysm will depend upon various causes as the state of the constitution of the patients, peculiar idiosyncracies, pre-existing diseases, the effects of diet and occupation, the composition of the blood, and the organ or organs chiefly involved. If the cerebro-spinal system is chiefly affected, the paroxysm may be characterized, by delirium, coma, convulsion, and tetanic spasms, hence some writers have distinguished the *comatose*, the *delirous*, the *convulsve* and the *tetanic* varieties of the malignant intermittent.

In many cases, in which the whole force of the disease appears to fall upon the cerebro-spinal system, these symptoms indicating serious disturbances of the functions of animal life, as disorder of the mind, coma, apoplexy and paralysis catelepsy and various involuntary spasmodic movements, may disappear entirely as the paroxysm al ates, not even a trace of headache being left during the intermission; in some cases, however, effusion may take place into the ventricles, or within and around the cerebro-spinal system and lead to the establishment of permanent coma, with dilatation of the pupils general paralysis and death. In some cases the effusion consists chiefly of serum; and in others of blood with all the symptoms of hæmaplegia, paraplegia, apoplexy, and paralysis. A true inflammation of some portion of the cerebro-spinal substance may result from the congestion induced during the malignant paroxysm. Recovery is possible from such states. but convalescence is often tedious, and accompanied with paralysis of one or more sets of voluntary muscles. In many cases of malarial coma, I have observed the temperature to be elevated to a degree varying from 102° to 106° F., and such elevation may be attended either with a hot dry skin, or with a surface bathed in a hot profuse perspiration. The action of the malarial poison, is without doubt one of the causes of fatal and sudden apoplexy It is probable that the result during the paroxysm is largely determined by preceding alterations of the arteries of the brain, and spinal cord, such as fatty and calcareous degeneration.

If the lungs or pleura be primarily and chiefly involved, difficulty of breathing, syncope, capillary obstruction, and excruciating pains in the pleura, lungs and diaphragm may characterize the paroxysm. In like manner these alarming and distressing symptoms may vanish; after the disappearance of the paroxysm, or structural alterations characterized chiefly by serious effusion into the air cells, bronchial tubes, and pleural cavities, may ensue, and either destroy the patient suddenly, or lead to painful and protracted pneumonitis and pleuritis· In some cases the effusion into the air cells, consists chiefly of blood, and such pulmonic hæmorrhage must be regarded as similar, to the hæmorrhages from the stomach, small intestines and large intestines, which characterize certain forms of malignant intermittent fever.

In a third form, the heart appears to be chiefly affected, either directly or through the cerebro-spinal and sympathetic system. This, the so-called cardialgic variety, is marked by excruciating pain at the epigastrium, either continuous or intermittent, intense suffering, great anxiety of countenance, vomiting and sometimes general spasm of the muscles

In the fourth form, the abdominal viscera, the peritoneum, the stomach, the small intestines, the large intestines, the liver and the kidneys, may one and all be involved, giving rise to the so-called, peritonitic. gastric, choleraic dysenteric, hepatic and nephritic forms of malignant intermittent. The tenderness of the peritoneum, the profuse vomitings of biliary matters, and the choleraic and dysenteric and bilious discharges, may one and all disappear during the intermission.

In a fifth form known as algid fever, the cold stage is unusually protracted, there is great oppression at the chest and abdomen, restlessness, and prostration of nervous and muscular power. The attempt at the formation of the hot stage proves abortive, the skin becomes cold, pale and shrunken on the extremities, and covered with a cold clammy prespiration, while

YELLOW FEVER.

at the time of its introduction, the peculiarities of the constitution, and the supervention of other diseased states

The action of the yellow fever poison is definite, and the disease is characterized by definite manifestations. Yellow fever is a self-limited disease.

II. The changes of the blood appear to be continuous from the time of the introduction of the poison to the fatal termination ; the intensity of the changes being increased, and their character being modified, as the disease advances, not only by the direct action, upon the constituents of the blood, of the poison, but also by the addition of certain noxious substances, as bile, urea, carbonate of ammonia, sulphates, phosphates, and extractive matters, in consequence of the profound losions induced in the liver and kidneys.

Certain constituents of the blood, as the albumen and fibrine, are not only altered physically and chemically in the early stages of yellow fever, but as the disease advances, from the causes just specified, certain excrementitious matters, which in a state of health are continuously eliminated, accumulate in the circulating fluid, and by their direct action upon the elements of blood, and upon the nervous system, and by their disturbing actions upon the processes of nutrition and digestion, still further alter the physical and chemical, and vital properties of this fluid.

III. The maximum elevation of temperature is rapidly attained upon the first and second days of the disease, varying according to the severity of the attack, from 102° to 110° Farh., in the axilla, and, as a general rule, from the third to the fifth day, steadily falling and sinking down to the normal standard, and even below; in some fatal cases it rises again toward the end, rarely, however, reaching or exceeding 106° Fahr., and only in certain rare instances attaining the high degree of temperature characteristic of the stage of active febrile excitement.

In preceeding tables (see History of Epidemic of 1878 by author, published in N. O. M. and S. J.) we have recorded (case 94) a sudden rise upon the 5th day from 101.7° to 111°; (case 96) 106.8° on the 4th day; (case 97) 106.5° on 6th day ; (case 105) 105° on the 4th day; (case 122) 107.2° on 9th day; (case 133) 107° on 3rd day; (case 146) 109° on 6th day ; (case 154) 111.1° on 9th day ; (case 168) 108.2° on 9th day. The supervention of an inflammatory disease, or the occurrence of an abcess, or the access of paroxysmal malarial fever, may in like manner cause a progressive elevation of temperature, with slight evening exacerbations. The pulse at the commencement of the attack is often rapid and full; the increase in the frequency of the pulse does not, however correspond with the elevations and oscillations of temperature, as in many other febrile diseases ; and in many cases of yellow fever the remarkable phenomenon is witnessed of the pulse progressively decreasing in frequency, and even descending below the normal standard, while the temperature is maintained at an elevated degree; and on the other hand, the pulse often increases in frequency, but diminishes in force near the fatal issue; the occurrence of copious hæmorrhages from the stomach and bowels may be attended with sudden depression of temperature, and increase in frequency, but diminution in the force and fullness of the pulse.

The cause of the rapid rise and declension of the temperature in yellow fever must be sought chiefly in the changes induced in the blood and in the organs upon which the circulation and integrity of the blood depend ; neither the rapid rise nor the sudden declension of the temperature can be referred wholly to the effects of the yellow fever poison upon the nervous system.

IV. The fever of the *first state* of yellow fever, like *fever in general*, however caused, consists essentially in elevation of temperature, arising from increased chemical change in the blood and tissues, and is attended with changes in the physical and chemical constituents of the blood, and aberrated nervous action.

As long as the skin, kidneys, lungs, and gastro-intestinal canal, perform their functions, this stage is characterized, as in other fevers, by an increase in the amount of solids excreted. But this increased elimina-

MALARIAL FEVER.

on the contrary the central portion of the body and the internal organs are hot. In some cases of algid fever, I have observed the temperature of the extremities, to be 80°, whilst that of the trunk has reached 104° F , and higher. The patient complains of intense thirst, and when water is drank it is frequently rejected by vomiting, the pulse is small, frequent and almost imperceptible at the wrist, the heart beats in a tumultous irregular manner, giving a thumping sound to the ear, the number of beats to the minute sometimes reaching 180 ; the respiration is irregular, often panting, and numbering 40 and over to the minute : there is great restlessness, jactitation, impatience of bed covering, with continuous complaints of oppressive heat, not only at the chest and abdomen, but even in the cold extremities, so that the patient refuses to have them covered.

The intellect is generally undisturbed and the expression of the countenance may be quiet, even when the pulse cannot be felt, and the disorder of the circulation and temperature becomes so extreme that the heat of the trunk is reduced, and even the tongue and mouth becomes cold. The irregularity continues through the whole period of the paroxysm and it is only at the end of it, in favorable cases that the temperature and circulation are partially restored.

In algid fever, we have congestion of the internal organs, prostration of the nervous and muscular forces and marked disturbances of the circulation and calorification. As the circulation and calorification depend mostly upon the cerebro-spinal and sympathetic nervous systems, as well as upon the physical and chemical changes of the blood and organs, the algid state must be referred at least to lesions of certain ganglionic cells or tracts of the cerebro-spinal and sympathetic nervous systems ; and whilst similar phenomena, but less in degree and duration, are manifested in every true malarial chill ; it is not entirely correct to regard the algid state as simply a *prolonged chill* for in the algid state, the chill is followd by imperfect reaction, and the elevated temperature of true chill, is rarely reached in the central organs, whilst there may be an actual diminution of the heat.

When from any cause, as bad diet, excessive exposure to cold and wet, the continuous use of salt meat, or the prolonged action of the malarial poison, the constitution of the blood is altered hæmorrhages take place during the congestive stages of malignant intermittent fever, we may have a sixth variety, which has been indicated as *hæmorrhagic malarial fever*.

Without doubt in this sixth form of malignant intermittent, hæmorrhages from various organs as the stomach, lungs, kidneys and bowels, are directly due to the prolonged and potent action of the malarial poison upon the fibrin and colored corpuscles of the blood, as well as to the various alterations in the spleen and liver, characteristic of all the forms of malarial fever.

The hæmorrhagic form of malarial fever, may be attended with many of the prominent symptoms of the preceding varieties, as obstinate vomiting of biliary (grass green) acrid matters, intense thirst, restlessness, feeble rapid pulse, oscillations of temperature, oppression of breathing, coma, convulsions, and apoplexy.

In many cases of malarial hæmaturia, after the suppervention of jaundice the pulse becomes slow, falling even below the standard of health, even when the temperature of the trunk may be elevated to from 101° to 104° F. In this respect as well as in the great irritation of the gastric mucous membrane accompanied with incessant vomiting, the hæmorrhagic form of malarial resembles yellow fever. The latter disease however, differs from the former in the character of the vomited matter. Whilst in the first stages of yellow fever the vomitted matters may consist of mucous and bile, in the latter stages the black vomit is essentially altered blood. In malarial hæmaturia the dark and in some cases black vomit consist almost always of dark greenish black billiary matters, and rarely contains blood. The urine also differs essentially in the two diseases ; in grave cases of yellow fever the urine contains albumen and yellow granular casts and detached cells of the tubular uriniferi. In well marked cases

YELLOW FEVER.

tion of the products of chemical change is not, in yellow fever, a constant concomitant of the increased temperature.

Not only are large quantities of the products of oxidation formed during the hot stages of yellow fever, but, as we have shown, by numerous analyses of the blood, black-vomit, urine, brain, heart, liver, spleen, and kidneys, in this disease, they are altered to a certain extent from their characteristic state of health; the albumen of the blood, under the action of the poison, being transformed into nitrogenous and non-nitrogenous compounds, a portion of which, as the fatty matter, and altered fibrin, being arrested or accumulated in certain organs, as the heart, liver, and kidneys.

The peculiar phenomena of yellow fever, like those of acute phosphorous-poisoning, are due to the nature of the specific poison, and the character of these changes, which it is capable of exciting *primarily in the blood*, and secondly in the nervous and vascular systems, and in the nutrition of the various organs.

Neither the rapid rise nor the sudden declension of the temperature in yellow fever is necessarily referable solely to the effects of the poison upon the nervous system; because, in the first place, the changes of the blood are among the first manifestations of diseased action, and the progress and termination of each case are largely dependent upon the extent and character of the changes of the blood, and the degree of the elevation of the temperature; and, in the second place, the sudden fall of the temperature during the succeeding stage of calm may be referred to the peculiarity of the self-limited chemical changes excited by the poison, and to the structural alterations induced in the muscular tissue of the heart, and in the liver and kidneys, and the sedative action of the bile, urea, and other excrementitious products retained in the blood, upon the nervous system; and finally, in the third place, the changes of the blood and of the heart, liver, and kidneys, are of a definite physical and chemical nature, and could never be induced by a mere exaltation or depression of nervous action, and must be referred to the introduction and action of some agent or material related in a definite manner in its constitution and physical properties, to the fluids and solids in which it induces these profound physical and chemical changes.

Without doubt, the action of the yellow fever poison upon the nervous system may be of the most direct and important character; but well established facts do not justify us in locating the origin of the disease wholly in the action of the poison upon the nervous system; and, in fact, the earliest sensible manifestation of disordered nervous action, as evidenced by uneasiness, loss of appetite, and chilly sensations, may be entirely secondary to the changes in the blood, by which all parts of the nervous system are surrounded and supplied.

V. While many of the most striking phenomena of yellow fever, as chills and fever, and collapse, must necessarily be attended with disordered vascular innervation, at the same time we must look to the *blood* as the *seat* of the operations of the fever poison; and, as the nutrition of every organ and tissue depends upon the proper constitution of this fluid, its alterations must affect the entire organism, and the true commencement of yellow fever is in the alterations of the relations between the blood and tissues.

The nervous system, both cerebro-spinal and sympathetic, suffers in common with the entire system; but as the most important offices are performed by the nervous system which relates the mind to the various parts of the body, and to the exterior world, and also regulates the actions of the circulatory and respiratory systems, and co-ordinates the actions of the component members of the system, in all the phenomena which succeed the *invasion of fever* the *blood and nervous system* become *joint factors.*

VI. During the active stages of yellow fever, profound changes take place in the organs and tissues, especially in the kidneys, heart and liver; oil and granular albuminoid or fibroid matter transude through the capillaries and fill up the cells and excretory ducts, and arrest the functions of certain organs. The liver of

MALARIAL FEVER.

of yellow fever, albumen may appear as early as the first day of the disease, but most generally it appears upon the second, third or fourth day. Blood may be present in the urine of yellow fever, but it is rarely a constituent; and even when present the granular casts of the tubuli uriniferi present a yellow color. In malarial hæmaturia the urine contains albumen, but this constituent of the blood is invariably associated with blood corpuscles and hæmatin. The casts of the tubuli uriniferi in the urine of malarial hæmaturia, present a red or reddish brown color.

Suppression of urine in yellow fever appears to be due to the blocking up of the tubuli uriniferi with granular oleagenous matter and detached cells, the symptoms in malarial hæmaturia appear to be due not merely to congestion of the kidneys but to the filling of the urinary tubes with coagulated blood.

The microscopical examination of the blood also reveals marked differences in the two disease; in yellow fever the colored blood corpuscles frequently assume a crenated appearance, and in uncomplicated cases there is no accumulation of pigment particles and pigment cells, and the dark cells of an algæ, resembling enlarged colorless corpuscles filled with spores of a dark brownish red color.

In malarial hæmaturia, it is rarely the case that the colored corpuscles present any other than the normal form of the biconcave disc; whilst pigment particles, dark granular masses, and cells of a dark reddish brown hue, some of which are similar in all respects to certain pálmellæ, are often present in considerable numbers.

In malarial hæmaturia, after death, the intestines give the reaction of bile throughout their entire extent; in yellow fever we thus obtain no evidence of the presence of bile.

CHANGES OF THE BLOOD IN MALARIAL FEVER

The malarial poison is capable of altering the constitution of the solids and fluids and of modifying and altering the type, and progress and effects of various diseases, even when no symptoms of aberrated, physical, chemical, and nervous actions have been manifested sufficient to arrest the attention of the patients.

The *colored blood-corpuscles* are diminished during malarial fever; the extent and rapidity of the diminution of the colored corpuscles correspond to the severity and extent of the disease. The fixed saline constituents of the colored blood-corpuscles are often diminished in malarial fever.

The colored blood-corpuscles are destroyed both in the liver and spleen. The colored blood-corpuscle, are more uniformly and rapidly destroyed in severe cases of malarial fever, than in any other acute disease with the exception perhaps of pyæmia.

In the severe forms of malarial fever the serum presents a golden yellow color. I have shown by numerous analysis that this color in various forms of malarial fever, and even in the so-called Malarial Hæmaturia, is due to the presence of the coloring matter of the bile, and *not as has been erroneously stated upon superficial observations to the escape of the hæmatin of the colored blood-corpuscles.*

The fibrin is diminished greatly in severe cases of malarial fever; the diminution of this element of the blood is characteristic, not only of malarial fever, but of all the fevers; whilst its increase on the other hand is characteristic of the phlegmasiæ. As a general rule, the diminution of the fibrin in malarial fever as in the pyrexiæ generally corresponds with the severity of the disease, provided there be no inflammatory complication. The diminution and alteration of the physical properties of the fibrin in malarial fever to any great extent, was always accompanied by congestion of the spleen, liver and brain, and serious cerebral disturbances. The fibrin is not only diminished in malarial fever, but it is altered in its properties, and in its relation to the other elements of the blood, and to the blood-vessels, *and in severe cases, heart clots (fibrinous concretions) are frequently formed before death.*

The albumen is diminished during the active stages, but such diminution is not due to any loss of this con.

yellow fever does not present the soft, friable condition characteristic of true fatty degeneration. The jaundice resulting from the suppression or alteration of the excretory function of the liver would appear to be due to the same causes which induce the suppression of the urine, viz., to the deposits of oil and fibrinous or albuminous matter in the excretory structures of the kidney and liver.

We do not mean to say that, in the case of the liver, its secretion ceases, or is even in many cases diminished: on the contrary, it may even be increased, especially in the stage of active febrile excitement; but from the causes indicated, obstruction takes place in the stage of active febrile excitement; but from the causes indicated, obstruction takes place in the biliary tubes, and there is a rapid absortion of the bile directly into the blood-vessel system, and in this manner the delivery of the bile into the intestinal canal is impaired and sometimes arrested.

The heart in yellow fever appears to be as fully permeated with oil as the liver; in the latter organ, however, a large amount of the oil is inclosed within the cells; in the former, in addition to the deposits ot oil, there is also granular degeneration of the muscular structures.

VII. While yellow fever is characterized in common with several other diseased states by an irritation of the gastric mucous membrane, the peculiar nature of the vomitted matters does not rest entirely upon the congestion and irritation of the mucous membrane of the stomach, but is influenced to a greater or less extent by the changes of the blood, liver, kidneys, and nervous system.

The vomitings in yellow fever, may, to a certain extent be regarded as salutary, and as an effort for the elimination of certain excrementious materials from the blood. In some cases, the first effect of the black-vomit may seem to be salutary; the tongue improves in appearance, the febrile heat abates, and, if it were not for other profound changes in the blood, liver, and kidneys, lying back, as it were, of this almost universally fatal symptom, beneficial results of the most important character might flow from the relief afforded by the removal of a certain amount of excrementitious mater, as urea, and ammonia, and bile, from the blood.

Black vomit is to a certain extent an *excremtitious* product, containing *uera* and *carbonate of ammonia,* in addition to altered blood-corpuscles epithelial cells, broken capillaries, mucus, various matters received into the stomach, as food and medicine, serous exudations, and acetates, lactates, phosphates, and cholorides.

Black-vomit in yellow fever is due to several causes, as—

1. To the direct irritation and structural alteration of the gastric mucous membrane by the poison—the active agent which probably is first received into the blood, and acts in this manner or through this medium upon the gastric mucous membrane, for we find contemporaneous changes taking place in the heart, liver, and kidneys, and these changes would most probably *succeed* the gastric irritation, if the poison was received in food or drink primarily by the stomach.

2. To the structural alterations of the blood, and especially to the marked dimunition of the fibrinous element which appears to sink to a lower figure than in any other known disease.

3 To suppression of the action of the kidneys, and the retention in the blood of urea and other excrementitious products, and the elimination of urea as carbonate of ammonia by the gastro-intestinal mucous membrane.

4. To the direct irritant action of the ammonia and excrementitious materials, eliminated vicariously upon the mucous membrane of the stomach and intestines.

5. To the irritant and nauseating effects of the bile in the blood. The bile retained in the blood, without doubt, produces its characteristic effects upon the nerves supplying the stomach, inducing nausea and vomiting.

6. To the degeneration of the cells of the gastric mucous membrane, attended with or characterized by the deposit of granular fibroid or albuminoid matter

stituent of the blood in the urine. As a general rule, albumen is absent from the urine in malarial fever; and when present, as in malarial hæmaturia, it is accompanied with blood-corpuscles, and with casts of the tubuli uriniferi containing colored blood-corpuscles.

The result of my microscopical investigations upon the blood of malarial fever, pursued during the past twenty-five years, may be thus formulated.

1st. The malarial poison produces more rapid destruction of the colored blood-corpuscles than any other known febrile agent.

2d. The destruction of the colored corpuscles takes place chiefly in the spleen and liver.

3d. The black pigment resulting from this hæmatin of the blood corpuscles, is frequently observed in the blood as it circulates in the vessels and capilaries in masses of various sizes, and in the form of cellular elements.

4th. In the malarial blood we observe frequently black pigment or melanæmic corpuscles, varying from the one ten-thousandth to the one-thousandth of an inch and even less in diameter; conglomerations of these melanæmic particles, in masses of various sizes; colorless corpuscles or leucocytes which contained granular masses of black pigment; pigment cells containing ovoid bodies resembling sporules, and in all respects similar to the brownish red palmellæ obtained by passing the air of malarial regions through melting ice. Many of the particles of the melanæmic pigment are spherical, others irregular and angular, some entirely free, others incased in a hyaline mass, others incorporated with cellular elements which are more or less related to the white corpuscles of the blood and to certain forms of algæ.

5th. The black pigment particles indicate the destruction or alteration of the blood-corpuscles, and the escape of the hæmatin of the red globules.

6th. The black pigment is deposited in the capillaries of various organs and tissues, as those of the liver, medulla of the bone, brain and subcutaneous tissues.

7th. The peculiar sallow, greenish-yellow and bronzed hue, which characterizes those who have been for a length of time subjected to the prolonged action of the malarial poison, or to its powerful action in pernicious remittent fever, and in malarial hæmaturia, is due not merely to hepatic and splenic derangement, but also to the deposit of pigment particles in the subcutaneous capillaries.

8th. During the epidemic yellow fever of 1878, in New Orleans, I endeavored by the condensation of the organic and organized and inorganic and particulate matters of the air in various portions of the city to determine whether the living particles found in the air, differed in accordance with the locality whether malarious or non-malarious. After a minute examination of the solid organic organized, living inorganic and inanimate particles of the air in residences in which yellow fever was prevailing, it was observed:

a. In the well paved and well drained non-malarious portions of New Orleans, the solid matters of the air examined not only during the prevalence of the yellow fever, but also at various intervals, during a period of six to eight months, I discovered no form which could be referred to such microscopical plants, as the chloro-coccum vulgare, proto-coccus, viridis, palmella, cruenta, coccochloris, brebinonii and other confervoidæ, or unicellular algæ capable of producing chlorophyl. Certain granular cells observed in the blood of malarial fever, resembles most nearly the resting spore of bulbochæte intermedia, and the granular cells of palmella cruenta ; but no such cells were observed in the atmosphere of the houses situated in well paved and well drained sections of the city.

The forms of *non-malarial,* sick-rooms (rooms containing yellow fever patients) were referable to those most nearly connected with putrefaction and fermentation, as the bacteria and torulæ, penicillus and micrococci and cryptococae. The absence of any of the known forms of algæ in the yellow fever, air collected in the non-malarious, well drained and well paved portions of the city of New Orleans, is important, in that this class of plants is thus excluded from the consideration of the question relating to the origin and

24

and oil-globules in the secretory cells, and in the walls of the smaller blood-vessels and capillaries.

.·7. To the capillary congestion of the gastro- intestinal mucous membrane, similar in all respects to the intense capillary congestion which characterizes all the tissues in this disease, in consequence of the physical and chemical alterations of the blood, and of the morbific action of the poison and its products upon the vaso-motor system of nerves.

Black-vomit, therefore, is an *effect* or result of *preceeding* changes or actions, and is not a cause; it is an error, therefore, to search, either by chemical reagents or by microscope, for the *cause* of the disease in one of its *products*.

· VIII. The chief *causes of death* in yellow fever appear to be:

1. The direct action of the febrile poison upon the blood and nervous system, depressing and deranging the actions of the one, and rendering the other unfit for the proper nutrition of the tissues.

2. The suppression or alteration of the functions of certain organs, as the kidneys and liver, and the retention in the blood of the excrementitious matters normally eliminated by these organs.

3. The structual alterations of the heart. and consequent loss of power in this organ.

4. Profuse hæmorrhages from the stomach and bowels.

.IX. Yellow fever differs essentially in its symptoms and pathology from malarial fever

.In the latter. the constituent of the blood, which appears to suffer to the greatest and most essential degree, is the colored blood corpuscle: in the former, the constituent of the blood, which suffers to the greatest extent is the albumen.

The changes of temperature in yellow fever follow a definite course, and are never repeated· in uncomplicated cases; in malarial fever, on the other hand, they recur at regular intervals, and may be indefinitely reproduced.

· As a general rule, yellow fever attacks but once; malarial fever produces no exemption, but, on the contrary, establishes a disposition to frequent recurrence.

· Convalescence from yellow fever is comparatively rapid, and the constitution of the blood is rapidly restored; in malarial fever, the changes of the blood and organs, and especially of the liver and spleen, may be profound and long continued.

The liver in yellow fever presents various shades of yellow, and contains numerous oil-globules; the liver of malarial fever is of a dark color, most generally slate upon the exterior and bronze within, and is loaded with dark pigment-granules; the spleen is comparatively unaffected in yellow fever, while it is enlarged and softened in malarial fever, the heart and kidneys are softened and infiltrated with oil and granular albuminoid matter in yellow fever, while they are comparatively unaffected in malarial fever; the urine is almost always albuminous, and contains casts and bile in yellow fever, while in malarial fever albumen and casts are almost always absent, and the urine presents morbid periodic changes, corresponding with those of the paroxysm.

.X. Yellow fever is a self limited disease, occurring, as a general rule, but once in a lifetime. The constitution of the blood, and even of the textures of the body, is altered; the most important organs, as the heart, kidneys and liver, as well as the most important nutritive fluids, are profoundly impressed. These changes in the blood, heart, kidneys, and liver, as well as of the nervous system, may be compared to the profound changes induced in the organs, and especially in the integument, by small-pox. If this view be correct, we cannot by drugs arrest or cure yellow fever any more than we can arrest or cure small-pox, measles or scarlet fever. If drugs accomplish the effect of promoting the free and regular action of these emunctories through which the poison and the product of its action are eliminated, and if. further they tend to preserve the integrity of the blood, and to sustain the actions of the circulatory and nervous system, they will, without doubt, achieve much good, and perhaps all that we are justified in looking for, in the present state of our

causation of yellow fever.

b. The water obtained by passing the air through ice and melting ice and ice cold water, was preserved, and portions added to solutions of sugar. The water from the rooms in which yellow fever patients lay caused the development in solution of sugar. of a delicate fungus, the spores of which were distributed in regular rows, within the thallus. This plant as well as that developed in the yellow fever blood, assumed a distinct yellow color. Both penicillum and torulæ were observed in these solutions. .

CHANGES OF THE CIRCULATION, RESPIRATION AND TEMPERATURE.

INTERMITTENT FEVER.—During the cold stage (chill) there is a rapid, feeble pulse, rapid respiration, and hot trunk and cold extremities—the temperature of the extremities, is reduced far below that of the trunk, and even below the standard of health. because the circulation of the blood in the peripheral capillaries is to a great extent arrested, apparently by the contraction of the unstriped muscular tissue of the walls of the ultimate arterioles. The diminution of the capillary circulation, and the reduction of the temperature of the extremities precede the aberrated nervous and muscular phenomena denominated chill. This fact corresponds with the changes in the constituents of the blood, and indicates that the first phenomena of the cold stages are connected with derangements of the vaso-motor system of nerves. As a general rule, the higher the temperature of the trunk during the cold stage, the more rapid will be the equalization of the circulation and temperature The severity of the fever (animal temperature), which often reaches in the hot stage 107° F., is by no means an index of the character and severity of the subsequent effects. As a general rule, the higher the temperature (within of course. certain defined limits, not exceeding 102° and 107.5° F.,) the more readily does the attack yield to treatment. The changes of the temperature in intermittent, fever, are characterized by abrupt elevations and depressions, so that when the cases are projected upon a chart, they differ in the rapidity of the elevations and depressions from those furnished by yellow fever, typhus and typhoid fever and other diseases the phlegmasia, phthisis. hospital gangrene and pyæmia.

REMITTENT FEVER.—The phenomena of the cold stage preceding the hot stage of remittent fever, are similar to those of intermittent fever ; the difference is one of degree, and not of kind ; the phenomena of the cold stage of remittent fever are more protracted than those of intermittent fever : the sympathetic system does not so rapidly regain its normal action, and the circulation in the capillaries of the extremities is not so rapidly restored in remittent as in intermittent fever. The alterations of the blood are more profound in remittent than in intermittent fever, and therefore it results that the cold stage is more prolonged in remittent than in intermittent fever. The elevation of temperature corresponds more accurately with the increased action of the circulatory and respiratory system in intermittent than remittent fever. Remittent fever may be distinguished from typhoid fever by the greater and more sudden elevations and depressions of temperature.

CONGESTIVE OR PERNICIOUS FEVER.—The complete prostration of the muscular and nervous forces, the reduction of animal temperature, both in the trunk and extremities, the cold, calmmy sweat. the rapid feeble pulse, the rapid. thumping action of the heart. and the sudden intervention of the most alarming cerebral symptoms, may occur gradually or suddenly, in either intermittent or remittent fever, and may be induced by several distinct causes, acting singly or in conjunction. There is a want of coordination between the circulation, respiration and animal temeature in congestive fever. The respirations are full, accelerated, and often panting and heaving, varying from 30 to 50 per minute, the pulse beats from 120 to 160, and feels like a delicate thread, and is often so small that it cannot be counted ; the heart thumps irregularly and spasmodically and rapidly, against the walls of the chest as in some cases of narcotic poisoning ; the cir-

knowledge. By judicious treatment, by proper ventilation, diet, and rest we place the patient in that condition which is best adapted to the successful elimination of the poison and its products; but we do not arrest or cure the disease, as we certainly may do in paroxysmal malarial fever, by the proper administration of quinine.

XI. Upon a careful comparison of the main features of malarial hæmatura, with those of yellow fever, the following points may be noted:

(a) In the last stages, after the supervention of jaundice and urinary suppression, many cases of malarial hæmaturia bear a striking resemblance to yellow fever in the period of calm, depression of circulation and black vomit. The vomited matters, however, in malarial hæmaturia contain *bile*, and the dark color is due to bile rather than to blood.

(b) Important diferences are revealed by the microscope between the organic and organized elements in the urine of these diseases; in yellow fever, the casts of the tubuli uriniferi are filled with yellow granular matter and oil globules; in malarial hæmaturia, the tubuli uriniferi in many cases present a dark brownish-red color, and contain dark pigmentary matter, and altered colored corpuscles, in addition to the yellow granular matter.

(c) After death from malarial hæmaturia, the fibres of the heart present under the microscope a normal appearance, the transverse striæ being distinct, and the oil globules and yellow granular matter characteristic of yellow fever, being in most cases absent. When no preceeding lesions have existed. the heart of malarial fever, and of malarial hæmaturia, presents a firm structure, wholy different from the softened, altered and flabby yellow heart of yellow fever.

(d) There is less congestion of the mucous membrane of the stomach, and it is almost uniformly discolored by bile in malarial hæmaturia. Bile is absent from the contents of the stomach in yellow fever. Bile is universally present in the stomach of malarial hæmaturia.

(e) The heart, liver and spleen in malarial hæmaturia present the same structure, and the same microscopical and chemical characteristics, as in the various forms of paroxysmal malarial fever. In malarial fever, the spleen and liver are loaded with dark pigmentary particles; in yellow fever the former organ is without any special increment of pigmentary particles, and the latter is of a yellow color, and loaded with oil globules and yellow granular matter. When yellow fever supervenes in malarial fever, both the dark pigment particles, and the oil globules and yellow granular matter are found in the liver, and this organ presents a deeper color and more mottled appearance than in uncomplicated yellow fever. The gall bladder contains much more bile in malarial fever than in yellow fever, and this liquid is absent from the stomach and alimentary canal in yellow fever, but is universally present in malarial fever in all its forms.

(f) When in malarial hæmaturia the congestion of the kidneys is so great, and the structural alterations so profound as to cause urinary suppression, then another distinct train of phenomena is set up, which has much in common with the analogous condition in yellow fever when the function of the kidney is suspended.

CHANGES OF THE URINE IN YELLOW FEVER.

The reaction of the urine in yellow fever is acid. Even in the gravest cases, attended with suppression of the urinary excretion, jaundice and *alkaline black vomit*, the urine, however small the quantity excreted, maintains an acid reaction.

As a general rule, the specific gravity of the urine in yellow fever does not vary from that of health, and ranges from 1009 to 1028. In those specimens which gave the highest specific gravity, the increase in density was clearly referrable to the increase of *albumen;* for when this constituent was coagulated by heat, and removed by filtration, the urine was of low specific gravity.

culation in the capillaries is feeble; the temperature of the trunk, notwithstanding the full, rapid respiration, sinks below the normal standard, and the surface is covered with cold, calmny sweat.

CHANGES OF THE URINE IN MALARIAL FEVER.

INTERMITTENT FEVER.—The amount of urine excreted during the active stages of the intermission, is less than that of health, and this diminution relates to the water and not to the solid constituents. During convalescence, and especially under the action of depurants, the amount of urine is increased The color of the urine varies from light orange to deep red. During the active stages the free acid is increased, but diminishes during convalescence. The urea is increased during the active stages, above the standard of health, and especially during similar conditions of rest and starvation. The uric acid is diminished both with or without the action of the sulphate of quinia, during the active stages when the pulse is full and rapid and the respiration full and accelerated, and the temperature elevated As a general rule when the fever declines the uric acid increases above the standard of health, both with or without the action of the sulphate of quinia. In some cases the uric acid is increased to four fold the normal amont during convalescence. The urine of the intermission of malarial fever is characterized by heavy yellow deposits of urate of soda, and triple phosphates, the former in the form of granular and acicular masses, and the latter as beautiful prismatic crystals. Phosphoric acid is greatly diminished and may have entirely disappeared during the chill and first stage of the febrile excitement. The phospates are more abundant in the stage of convalescence than during the active stage. The deposits (so-called critical discharges). so common during convalescence, consist chiefly of the urates of soda. ammonia, and the phosphates, most generally in the form of triple phosphates.

The chloride of sodium is abundant during the cold and hot stages. The sulphuric as well as the phosphoric acid is increased during the height and decline of the hot stage. The urine excreted during the fever is generally deficient in uric acid, and the earthly salts, while its acidity and power of resisting decomposition is greatly increased, and it will remain for a great time without undergoing decomposition. On the other hand, during convalescence the urine rapidly undergoes change, and the deposits of the urates of soda and ammonia, and the precipitation of the tripple phosphates, by the ammonia generated during the decomposition of the urea, form the so-called critical discharges of malarial fever. Albumen is generally absent from the urine of uncomplicated malarial fever; it is present, however, in that form called malarial hæmaturia, and hæmorrhagic malarial fever characterized by intense jaundice, and congestion of the kidneys, and passive hæmorrhages. In such cases the urine contains blood corpuscles and casts of the tubuli uriniferi filled with granular matter, detached uriniferous tubes and colored blood corpuscles.

The changes of the urine in remittent fever, are the same in kind, but different in degree from those of intermittent fever. The urine is higher colored, more concentrated, and richer in urea, phosphoric acid and sulphuric acid. If the case be protracted, the chloride of sodium diminishes as in typhoid fever. When the temperature falls below the normal standard in the early stage of convalescence. the urea, as in the similar stage of intermittent fever, decreases in amount. During the period of remission and convalescence, the uric acid, which had suffered decrease in the active stages, increases above the normal standard. The formation of deposits of the urates of soda, and of ammonia, and of the triple phosphates (critical discharges) in the urine of intermittent fever, is similar in all respects, takes place at analogous periods, and is due to the same causes as in the urine of intermittent fever.

In some cases of remittent fever of a high grade approaching to the type of the continued fevers, and attended with passive hæmorrhages from the stomach,

YELLOW FEVER.

In some of the gravest cases, the specific gravity of the urine was only 1010, and presented a yellow color and was turbid from the presence of cells and casts of the excretory tubes of the kidney and granular and fibrinous matters and colorless corpuscles.

During the early stages of the disease, the urine is normal in color, clearness and quantity; as the disease proceeds, the urine becomes of a deep yellow color, from the admixture of bile, and at this stage, after the full establishment of the febrile excitement about the third, fourth or fifth day, becomes turbid from the presence of the excretory cells, tube casts and yellow granular albuminoid or fibroid matters.

The color may deepen to orange red as the disease progresses; or if the case terminates fatally from diminution and suppression of the urinary excretion, it maintains a yellow color, sometimes presenting an oily appearance and motion, and consists of but little else than albumen, bile, excretory cells and casts of the tubuli uriniferi, in a weak solution of the urinary constituents.

In some cases of suppression, although the *urea* is greatly diminished in the small amount of urine excreted, it is rarely if ever entirely absent. If the case ends in convalescence, the urine is copious and the color progressively increases in depth, and may even appear black when viewed *en masse.*

As far as my investigations extend albumen is an invariable constituent of the urine in grave cases of yellow fever, and may appear as early as the first day of the disease, but most generally it appears upon the second, third or fourth day. In yellow fever albumen may be found in the urine, as the only abnormal element, with or without other blood element, in company of abundant deposit of lithates, with or without deposits of purpurine, or other coloring matters in excess: in connection with biliary coloring matters, in connection with pyrexial states, and in connection with apyrexial states.

The constituents of bile are almost universally present in the urine, even in those cases which progress favorably and end in convalescence.

When there is no suppression of the urinary excretion, the urea is increased above the standard of health during the active stages of the disease and during the period of exhaustion or calm. I have obtained upon analysis as much as 1500 grains of urea, during 24 hours in a case of yellow fever, and that, too when no nourishment was taken. Of all known diseases, yellow fever is characterized by the earliest and most uniform appearance of albumen and casts in the urine, and by the most marked tendency to urinary suppression; when, therefore, this occurs, owing to the chemical changes excited by the febrile poison, the blood is rapidly charged with urea and coma and uremic convulsions are the result.

In yellow fever the presence of albumen in the urine is attended by desquamation, fatty degeneration and disintegration of the excretory cells of the tubuli uriniferi. The granular casts so common in yellow fever, are composed of excretory cells, oil globules, and granular fatty and albuminoid granular matter, in some cases intimately mixed with urate of ammonia.

Those who have failed to detect albumen and casts at some period of grave cases of yellow fever, are either ignorant of the ordinary chemical tests and microscopical appearances, or have been careless and superficial in their so-called researches and observations.

When the kidneys are not seriously impaired by structural alterations the amount of urea excreted both during the stage of active febrile excitement and that of calm or depression, is at least five times more abundant than the amount of this constituent which would be excreted by a patient in health or even in Bright's disease similarly situated, lying perfectly quiet in bed, and taking little or no nourishment. This facts illustrates the absurdity of comparing the effects of urinary suppression in yellow fever, with the more tardy results in chronic Bright's disease.

In yellow fever urinary suppression causes the retention of not only the greatly increased amount of urea, but also of the various products of the action of the poison, as sulphuric acid, phosphoric acid, extractive, coloring and biliary matters.

MALARIAL FEVER.

bowels, kidney and mucous membranes, generally, I have observed albumen in the urine.

I have traced the origin of albuminuria, in some cases of malarial fever, occurring in this latitude to the structural alterations of the kidney induced during the active stages of the disease.

The fever of the *first stage* of yellow fever, like *fever in general*, however caused, consists essentially in elevation of temperature, arising from chemical changes in the blood and tissues, and is attended with changes in the physical and chemical constituents of the blood and aberated nervous action. As long as the skin, *kidneys* and *lungs* and gastro-intestinal canal perform their functions, this stage is characterized as in other fevers, by an increase in the amount of the solids excreted. But this increased elimination of the products of chemical change is not, in yellow fever, a constant concomitant of the increased temperature, because, in virtue of the lesions of certain organs, as the kidneys and skin, the constituents of the urine and bile accumulate in the blood and become active agents in th production of aberrated nervous and muscular actions and even of death itself.

TABULAR VIEW OF THE PATHOLOGICAL ANATOMY OF YELLOW FEVER AND MALARIAL FEVER.

EXTERIOR.—Generally full and not reduced in flesh; features may even present a swollen, bloated aspect. Skin of face and upper portions of trunk of a golden yellow color. Dependent portions of the body of mottled purplish and yellow ecchymosed appearance. Black vomit frequently oozes from corners of the mouth, and trickles down the face and neck. When the muscles are cut a large quantity of dark blood escapes, which upon exposure to the atmosphere changes to bright scarlet hue. Putrefactive changes take place rapidly after death. In some cases of yellow fever, especially when the functions of the kidneys have been arrested for some time before death, the putrefactive changes take place with great rapidity and energy, and sometimes even appear to commence before death, the body exhaling a disagreeable order.

EXTERIOR.—The general appearance of those who die from the effects of malarial fever will depend upon the nature and length of time and the effects of the disease. When stout healthy men are suddenly destroyed by pernicious malarial fever, the body may present the fulness of health; and in such cases the superior portions of the body may, as in yellow fever, present a golden yellow color, whilst the dependent portions present a purplish and mottled apparance. The jaundice and mottling of the skin, however, is, as a general rule, present to a less degree than in yellow fever. In cases of protracted bilious fever, the body is frequently greatly emaciated. In chronic malarial poisoning, attended with enlargement of the spleen and cirrhosis of the liver, the belly and body and limbs generally are distended with dropsical effusion. The cut surface of the muscles present a purplish hue. and the change to the arterial hue. upon exposure to the atmosphere, is much slower and less perfect than in yellow fever.

CEREBRO-SPINAL NERVOUS SYSTEM—SYMPATHETIC NERVOUS SYSTEM.—The post-mortem examinations of the brain, spinal cord and sympathetic system have thus far revealed no characteristic lesions to which the aberrated nervous symptoms of yellow fever can be referred. Beyond congestion of the cappillaries of the cerebro-spinal and sympathetic systems, which congestion appeared to be referable to the same cause as that producing capillary congestion in the internal organs, I have observed no structual leesion, as fibrinous effusion, hæmorrhage, or softening of the cerebro-spinal and sympathetic nervous structurers. Chemical analysis revealed the presence of urea, bile, and leucine in the brain; and to the effects of these substances, as well as to the direct action of the yellow fever poison, must be refered the aberration of intellect, the restlessness, convulsions and coma.

The amount of the congestion of the blood-vessels of the brain will to a certain extent vary with the stage and with the conditions under which death takes place Thus, when the functions of the kidneys are greatly impaired or wholly suppressed, owing to the retention of the watery element of the blood. the vessels through the entire system are filled with blood to repletion, and the brain is especially from its soft structure and the character of its circulation, the organ most affected. In such cases, the blood is seen issuing from numberless vessels when sections of the brain are made. Under the microscope the thin sections of the brain reveal a state of great hyperæmia, the minute capillaries being filled with colored blood corpuscles.

The golden hue of the brain substance and membranes, as well as that of the tissues generrally, is due to the presence of the coloring matter of the bile and not to the escape of hæmatin from the blood vessels. When death occurs after profuse hæmorrhages from the stomach, and bowels, the cerebral structures present less evidences of congestion than when these symptoms have been absent or present to a small degree.

CEREBRO-SPINAL NERVOUS SYSTEM—SYMPATHETIC NERVOUS SYSTEM.—As far as my observations have extended in malarial fever, the dura matter was always normal; the arachnoid membrane pearl-colored, opalescent in some cases, in others perfectly transparent and normal in appearance; the blood-vessels of the pia mater congested with blood. but most generally without marks of inflammation. Subarachnoid fluid in almost all cases clear transparent, and in some cases of a golden color; the amount varied in diff rent cases, sometimes exceeding, but most generally falling short of the usual amount. Blood-vessels of the brain generally filled with blood The structures of the brain appeared in acute cases, as a general rule, to be unaltered either in structure or appearance; in chronic cases the nervous structures sometimes presented a deeper and more grayish color, from the presence of pigment granules.

The structures of the brain and spinal cord, in malarial fever, were therefore, as a general rule, altered neither in consistence nor appearance, and the same is true also with reference to the sympathetic nervous system.

The rapidity with which the symptoms of cerebral disturbance, such as coma and delirium, vanish under appropriate treatment, in many cases, render it evident that the congestion of the cerebro-spinal system is temporary and unattended with structural alterations. When death occurs in coma, the blood-vessels of the brain even to their minutest ramifications, are distended with blood, such congestions being not merely evident to the naked eye but also more fully shown under the microscope, when thin sections are made of the brain structures. The ventricles of the brain are also filled with serum, often of a golden color. The paralysis which sometimes results from a paroxysm of malarial fever, may be due to several causes, as the actual rupture of blood-vessels and the effusion of blood, the detachment of a fibrinous clot and the obstruction of some one of the arteries of the brain,

YELLOW FEVER.

It is probable that the cerebral ganglia and commissures, as well as those of the spinal cord and sympathetic nervous system are affected with the same chain of chemical reactions which result in the formation and acumulation of oil in the blood and in the heart, liver and kidneys. In this connection the recent observations of Dr. H. D. Schmidt during the yellow fever of 1878, in the Charity Hospital of New Orleans are of interest, in that they sustain the view that the accumulation of oil is not confined exclusively to the liver, heart and kidneys,

Dr. Schmidt affirms that he has observed fatty degeneration of the nuclei in the walls of the minute vessels of the pia mater venules as well as arterioles. In many vessels the nuclei have disappeared, leaving a number of fat globules in the places ; others are met with in which an increase of the mere trace of protoplasm, surrounding the nucleus in the normal condition has taken place, causing a thickening of the wall of the vessels. "With reference to the brain the most prominent observation thus far made is the existence of fatty degeneration of the blood vessels of the cortex-cerebri, similar to that observed in the vessels of the pia-mater, together with degeneration of the ganglionic bodies of the cortex."

If those observations should be confirmed by further research and especially by chemical analysis, determining the exact proportion of oil in the brain in health and various diseased states, it will thus be shown that the nervous system both the cerebro-spinal and sympathetic is involved in a similar series of changes as the other organs. The universality of these changes, point to the blood as the great medium and source of the chemical actions, and we have a confirmation of this view in the fact which I have determined by chemical analysis, that the oleagenous constituents are greatly increased in the blood of yellow fever.

That the mere presence of oil in increased amounts in certain organs, during yellow fever, is not the *cause* of the grave symptoms, is evident from the rapidity of the convalescence in many cases; and also from the well known fact that in many cases the general health is greatly improved by an attack of yellow fever.

The grave symptoms of this disease must be sought not merely in structural alterations of certain organs, but in the initial chemical changes induced by the poison, which precede the final lesions, discoverable after death.

HEART.—Pale yellow and brownish yellow, as if undergoing fatty degeneration: structures of heart flabby and somewhat softened ; numerous oil globules deposited within and around the muscular fibrillæ of the heart. Cavities of the heart, in many cases, filled with dark fluid blood ; yelow fibrinous clots sometimes present. Blood contains abnormal amounts of urea and extractive matters and ammonia. Fibrin of blood greatly diminished in amount.

I have often determined both by *chemical* analysis and microscopical examination that the heart undergoes acute fatty degeneration in yellow fever. As far as my observations have extended, the heart undergoes more rapid and extensive degeneration in yellow fever than in any acute disease. The acute fatty degeneration of the heart in yellow fever should not be confounded with similar changes observed in spirit drinkers and in certain chronic diseases, but is most probably dependent upon the same or similar chemical actions, as those leading to a similar result in phosphorous poisoning and in typhoid and typhus fevers.

In yellow fever the fat is deposited within and around the muscular fibrillæ of the heart, in the form of minute globules of various sizes There is also an alteration or degeneration of the muscular fibrillæ of the heart, leading to a disappearance of the striation. The removal of the particles of oil from the muscular structures of the heart by sulphuric ether does not restore the obliterated striæ ; neither does this agent remove all the molecular particles a portion at least being insoluble in ether, alcohol and chloroform, and having an analagous constitution to albumen and fibrin.

Fatty degeneration of the heart, therefore, is not the sole state of this organ in yellow fever ; a molecular change has taken place in the substance of the

MALARIAL FEVER.

and the impaction of the minute capillaries by pigment granules. Occasionally in cases of chronic malarial poisoning attended with a watery condition of the blood, coma, with dilated pupils, sometimes supervenes suddenly, and in such cases I have found the ventricles to be greatly distended with serous fluid, which by its pressure had caused the cerebral symptoms.

HEART.—Normal in color, presents the deep purplish red muscular appearance of the healthy heart. Muscular fibres of the heart firm and of normal appearance under the microscope. No deposits of oil in the muscular structures.

Cavities of the heart frequently distended with dark blood. Firm, laminated, fibrinous concretions very common, and in some cases of pernicious fever, the formation of these heart-clots during the cold stage, without doubt, causes death and renders unavailing the action of remedial agents.

The fibrinous concretions are not only attached to the carneæ columnæ and chordæ tendinæ and auriculo-ventricular valves, but they also frequently send forth long branches into the pulmonary arteries. The formation of these concretions is rare in yellow fever, and when formed they are much smaller and softer than in malarial fever. The blood of malarial fever contains more fibrin, fewer colored corpuscles, and changes more slowly to the arterial hue upon exposure to the atmosphere than the blood of yellow fever.

In malarial fever the heart does not, as in yellow fever, undergo fatty degeneration. We do not by any means wish to be understood as affirming that fatty degeneration of the heart is characteristic of yellow fever in contradistinction to all other diseases, but only as distinguishing this disease from the various forms of malarial, paroxysmal or paludal fever.

After careful microscopical and chemical examination of the heart, in the various forms of intermittent, remittent, congestive or pernicious malarial fever and malarial hæmaturia. I have never observed any increase in the normal amount of fat or any condition which could be designated as molecular change or acute fatty degeneration. If the heart be compared in malarial and yellow fever it will be possible to distinguish

YELLOW FEVER.

muscular fibres, and this change effects the albumenoid or nitrogenous constituents. and most probably represents one of the stages of acute fatty degeneration.

The pericardium in yellow fever presents a congested appearance. Under the microscope the minute blood-vessels appear to be injected with colored blood corpucles. Pericardial fluid of deep yellow color:

LUNGS.—Dependent portions greatly congested; otherwise normal. In some cases circumscribed effusions of blood in textures of lungs.

I have in a few instances observed pneumonia as a supervening disease in yellow fever: in such cases the sputa consisted of almost pure blood. The supervention of pneumonia causes a continuation of the febrile phenomena beyond the usual period of the uncomplicated disease.

STOMACH.—Mucous membrane of stomach in many cases intensely congested, softened, and eroded. Stomach often contains large quantities of black vomit. Reaction of black vomit often *alkaline* from the presence of *ammonia*, resulting from the decomposition of *urea*, eliminated by the gastro-intestinal mucous membrane. *Ammonia* and *urea* present in the black vomit ejected during life and also when examined almost immediately after death. The presence of ammonia in the stomach and black vomit was not the result of postmortem putrefactive changes. In many cases ammonia was present in such large amount, that when a rod, dipped in hydrochloric acid was held over the mucous membrane of the stomach, or over the black vomit, dense fumes of chloride of ammonium were formed, as if the rod had been held over a bottle containing liquor ammoniæ. Chemical analysis revealed the presence of ammonia and also of urea in the black vomit. Under the microscope the black vomit was seen to contain colored blood corpuscles, and cells of the mucous membrane of the stomach, and broken capillaries. In some cases vibriones and fungi were numerous in the black vomit; in others they were absent.

That the stomach suffers and suffers severely in yellow fever is evident from the fact, that in a great majority of cases the stomach is finely injected with blood, and exhibits even when examined immediately after death, abrasions of the tissue in pit like holes and furrows. In some cases the whole surface of the stomach is affected, in others the effusion and injection is confined to the cardiac or pyloric portion, but in some rare instances the stomach duodenum and intestines have been said to present an almost entire absence of appreciable lesions. I have not myself in post mortem examinations observed the absence of lesions in the gastro intestinal mucous membrane. The congestion of the stomach is to a certain extent due to the disturbance of the circulation in the liver, but not wholly to this cause; we must from careful chemical and microspical examinations admit the existence of irritation, desquamation and hæmorrhage.

INTESTINES.—As a general rule dark-colored and distended with gas. In some cases the reaction of the intestinal contents was strongly alkaline from the presence of ammonia.

Hæmorrhage from the intestinal mucous membrane has been observed during life. and in such cases, as well as in others in which no blood has been discharged previous to death, the intestines have been found upon post-mortem examination distended with blood. A remarkable feature in yellow fever is the frequent

MALARIAL FEVER.

by the naked eye the flabby, softened, yellowish and brownish-yellow hue of the latter from the dense, firm, dark colored heart of the former disease. All doubts are immediately removed by the chemical and microscopical examination, the malarial heart presenting no accumulation of oil and revealing a firm, normal, distinctly striated structure of the muscular fibrillæ. If acute fatty degeneration of the heart was characteristic of malarial fever, from the almost universal prevalence of this disease in the Mississippi Valley and other portions of the Southern and Western States, and from the oft recurrence of the disease in the same individual, fatty degeneration of the heart would become one of the common diseases in malarial regions. Pericardium not specially congested. In some cases pericardial fluid of clear straw color, in others, especially when jaundice has existed, the pericardial fluid is of a golden color.

LUNGS.—Dependent portions congested with blood, otherwise healthy.

Owing to the effects of the malarial poison in decreasing the fibrinous element of the blood and the colored corpuscles, pneumonia engrafted upon an individual suffering with malarial fever tends to spread by diffusive inflammation. and, in the case of pleuritis as a supervening disease, the effusion into the pleural cavity is rapid and destructive in its effects. If pneumonia, be complicated with malarial fever, the periods of congestion of the lungs, attended with oppressed breathing and increase of pulmonic inflammation, are periodic, and may be to a certain extent controlled by quinine.

STOMACH.—Mucous membrane often presents a normal appearance; sometimes ecchymosed; rarely inflamed or softened; sometimes discolored with bile; rarely contains black vomit (altered blood). Reaction of mucous membrane of stomach and intestines acid. The pathological alterations of the stomach, observed after death, do not correspond, as a general rule, with the severity of the symptoms, the vomiting and pain on pressure during the progress of the fever. The injection of the blood-vessels and the mottled, purplish-brownish red color after death appear to be indicative, not of inflammation, but rather of stagnation and accumulation of the blood in the capillaries. Consequent upon the disturbance of the relation of the blood to the capillaries. The distressing vomiting, so often a troublesome symptom in malarial fever, appears to depend upon the contact of the altered bile and the irritation of the nervous centres which supply the stomach with nervous force by the altered blood and by the malarial poison.

In cases where there has been chronic inflammation of the stomach before the appearance of the fever, and in cases of long standing where the solids and fluids were permanently altered, decided lesions of structure were found in the stomach. It may be asserted, however, that there is no constant or characteristic lesion of the stomach in malarial fever.

The vomited matters of the various forms of malarial fever, unlike those of yellow fever, contain bile. Even in that form of malarial fever which most nearly resembles yellow fever, namely, in malarial hæmaturia the dark, almost black, vomit owes its color chiefly to altered bile. It is true that, in some cases of malignant malarial fever, we may have the vomiting of dark blood and bloody matter, resembling the *vomito nigra* of yellow fever, but, as a general rule, bile is present even in these rare instances. whilst it is almost always absent from the black vomit of yellow fever. The presence of blood and its constituents occasionally in the vomit of malarial fever is due to the same causes, namely, desquamation rupture of capillaries and the transudation of the hæmoglobin of the colored corpuscles.

INTESTINES.—These remarks relating to the stomach apply also to the small intestines. The mucous membrane frequently presented a purplish, irregularly injected, mottled appearance, especially after the administration of purgatives, and it was frequently observed that the injection of the blood-vessels was greatest in the dependent portions of the intestines. In several cases Brunner's glands in the duodenum were enlarged and distinct. The solitary glands of the small intestines, appeared in many cases enlarged and

occurrence of intussusception of the small intestines. The lateprofessor John Harrison, M. D., states that intussusception of the small intestines were exceedingly common in autopsies made in 1839, in New Orleans. The quantity of intestines invaginated, sometimes exceeded a yard. The large intestines and the lower portion of the small are not so often found congested, as the stomach and duodenum yet such a condition is by no means rare. The congestion of the veins, venules, and mucous membranes generally of the intestines in yellow fever, have been referred to the anatomical distribution of the veins, which like those of the stomach, are tributaries to the portal vein. But we have been inclined in many cases to regard the congestion as active and not passive. During life the rectum in yellow fever presents an intensely red, and congested appearance, and some cases of yellow fever in 1878, were followed by irritation and fissure of the rectum.

LIVER.—Yellow color and bloodless, resembling this organ in fatty degeneration, but firmer and denser in structure. Under the microscope, textures of the liver infiltrated with oil; secretory cells of liver contain much oil. The liver of uncomplicated yellow fever, as far as my observations extend, and according to the observations of Louis and many others, is of a bright yellow color. It is probably that this color, as in the case of the malarial liver, varies with the length of the attack and the effects of previous diseases. Thus Dr. Samuel Jackson, of Philadelphia, found the livers of those who had died in the early stages engorged with blood. The decoction of the yellow fever liver is of a golden yellow color, whilst that of the malarial liver is of a brownish yellow color. The golden yellow color of the yellow fever liver can be extracted both by alcohol and water. The yellow fever liver is firmer and harder than that of malarial fever, contains much less blood, and is much less readily acted upon by liquor potassæ and acids. Liquor potassæ readily dissolves the malarial fever liver, the decoction presents the appearance of venous blood, while no such effect is produced by the action of this alkaline solution upon the yellow fever liver.

Chemical analysis reveals the presence of the urea and fat in abnormal amounts ; animal starch and grape sugar are also present in the yellow fever liver. As a general rule grape sugar is absent from the malarial liver.

In some cases the deposit of oil is confined to certain portions of the tubuli and may even differ in amount in different portions of the liver, but in the majority of cases the fatty infiltration, and fatty degeneration of the protoplasm of the hepatic cells extends throughout the whole organ. The oil is deposited both within and around the hepatic cells. Careful investigation of the relations of malaria to yellow fever, and an extended examination of the statements of various observers, have convinced me that, the apparent contradictory statements made by various observers, as to the presence or absence of the yellow color of the liver, which Louis regarded truthfully as the characteristic lesion of the disease, has arisen from two sources, namely, errors of diagnosis, and failure to detect the preceding and concurrent, and subsequent action of malaria upon this organ. In uncomplicated yellow fever, the pigment particles so uniformly present in the malarial liver are entirely absent. When yellow fever has been engrafted on malarial fever, the preceding changes wrought by the paludal poison alter and mask those developed by the yellow fever. And hence a mingling of the yellow color of acute fatty degeneration with the dark bronze and slate of the malarial liver, may produce a color very closely resembling the Spanish brown of the healthy liver. Careful sections and examinations of the organ under the microscope will reveal both the oil globules and the pigment particles.

GALL BLADDER.—The gall bladder in yellow fever is, as a general rule, contracted, flaccid, small and contains little or no bile. The amount of bile generally does not exceed 100 grains. In malarial fever, on the other hand, the gall bladder is, as a general rule, distended with dark, greenish, black bile. In yellow fever the vomiting is rarely bilious, unless in the commencement

distinct. Peyer's glands were uniformly free from any well marked morbid alteration. In some cases they were distinct and well defined in their outline, and presented a honeycomb surface dotted with dark points, but they were always free from marks of inflammation, and even of irration, and in their pale, white color contrasted strongly with the surrounding mucous membrane discolored with bile and often irregularly injected with blood.

As a general rule, bile is found in the intestinal canal of malarial fever, and in some cases in large quantities, whilst it is absent from the entire alimentary tract in fatal cases of yellow fever.

LIVER.—The weight of the liver is increased in malarial fever above the standard of health. This increase of weight is due in part to the stagnation and accumulation of blood in the capillaries and blood-vessels, and the deposit of pigment matter in the structures of the liver. This observation applies to the liver in the acute stages.

In all the different forms of malarial fever, intermittent, remittent and congestive, which had continued longer than five days, and in which there had been no previous alterations of the structures, as in cirrhosis and fatty degeneration, I found the exterior of a slate color, and the interior of a bronze color. In that form of cirrhosis of the liver which is directly induced by the prolonged action of the malarial poison, the liver is in like manner of a slate color upon the exterior, and olive green within, and loaded with dark pigment granules. The change in the color appears to be very persistent, and in several cases I have observed the liver to retain shades of light slate and light bronze several weeks, and even months, after the relief of the attack of malarial fever, the patients having been destroyed by other diseases or by violence. The liver especially in the pheripheral portions of the globules, contains pigment granules, resulting from the alteration of the colored blood-corpuscles and the hæmatin. The pigment granules are frequently distributed uniformly through both the portal and heptic systems of capillaries. There is no accumulation of oil globules, as in the yellow fever liver. If malarial fever precedes or succeeds yellow fever, the liver may contain both oil globules and pigment granules.

The peculiar color of the malarial liver can to a certain extent be extracted by boiling water. and the filtered decoction presents a brownish mahogany color, from the presence of the dark coloring matters of the pigment granules ; the decoction of the yellow fever liver, on the other hand presents a golden color. The blood issuing from the cut surface of the malarial liver presents a dark purplish hue, and does not change to a brilliant scarlet, as in the yellow fever liver. Upon chemical examination, the malarial liver contains animal starch, but no grape-sugar ; the yellow fever liver contains both substances.

Whilst, by careful analysis (quantitative), I have shown that the oil may amount to over 40 per cent. of the yellow fever liver ; I have also clearly demonstrated that there is no increase of oil in the malarial liver.

I speak of uncomplicated malarial fever , of course when this disease is engrafted upon cirrhosis or fatty liver, the effects of the malarial poison upon this organ will be masked.

GALL BLADDER. In most cases distended with more than 1000 grains of thick, greenish black bile, having frequently a specific gravity ranging from 1.030 to 1 037. The bile is more abundant in malarial fever and is of a deeper color, and frequently contains concretions of epithelial cells, from the coats of the gall bladder and biliary ducts, and casts of the biliary tubes.

YELLOW FEVER.

MALARIAL FEVER.

of the disease; and the black vomit contains little or no biliary matter.

The small intestines are rarely, if ever discolored by bile in yellow fever, whilst in malarial fever it is common to find the gastro-intestinal mucous membrane discolored by bile.

I have observed cases in which the gall bladder contained only a serous liquid coagulable by heat. In two cases, a decided hæmorrhage had taken place into the gall bladder, which was distended with black blood. The bile in yellow fever contains numerous cells from the mucous membrane of the gall bladder, and casts of the hepatic ducts.

SPLEEN.—As a general rule but slightly enlarged. In many cases normal in size and appearance. In many cases of yellow fever the spleen is neither enlarged nor softened, nor altered in appearance, either upon the exterior or within. There appears to be no special alteration or destruction of the colored corpuscles in the spleen of yellow fever as in that of malarial fever. The enlargement of the spleen in fevers does not, from these observations, depend upon the deminution of the fibrin, because this element of the blood is diminished to a much greater extent in yellow fever than in malarial fever, and at the same time the spleen is enlarged to a great and marked degree in the latter. An other fact worthy of consideration in this connection is, that in yellow fever the colored blood-corpuscles are not specially diminished in amount, whilst in malarial they are rapidly destroyed, and this destruction appears to be greatest in the liver and spleen. In malarial fever both these organs are loaded with the altered blood-corpuscles and with the pigment granules resulting from the alterations of the colored corpuscles, whilst neither the spleen nor the liver in yellow fever afford any evidence of alterations of the colored blood-corpuscles.

SUPRA-RENAL BODIES.—These bodies appear to be subjected to similar changes with the liver and heart, and oil is increased in amount in the cells of the cortical and medullary substance.

KIDNEYS.—These organs, as a general rule, present a brownish yellow color, much lighter than that of health. They, in common with the heart and liver, contain much free fat. When thin sections of the kidneys are examined under the microscope, the Malpighian corpuscles and tubuli uriniferi are found to be filled with granular albuminoid and fibroid matter, excretory cells detached, and oil globules. As far as my observation extends, these structural alterations of the kidney have escaped the notice of preceding observers. The importance of these changes in the kidneys cannot be over-estimated, for upon them apparently depends the suppression of the urinary excretion, which is an almost universally fatal symptom. The changes in the kidneys may depend upon several causes, amongst which may be mentioned as of prime importance the alterations induced in the albumen and fibrin of the blood by the febrile poison, and the congestion of the capillaries induced by derangement of the vaso-motor system of nerves and by the altered blood.

This condition of the kidneys is preceded by capillary congestion, as has been shown by the results of post-mortem examinations at different periods of the disease. The same observation applies to the liver. The fatty degeneration and structural lesions are preceded by hyperæmia; but neither in the kidneys nor in the liver and other organs, can the mere stagnation of the blood in the capillaries be regarded as the *prime cause* of the subsequent degeneration and disintegration of the textures, and more especially of the secretory cells. The chief cause is the action of the yellow fever poison on the blood and textures. The yellow fever poison excites a train of chemical changes, the final result of which is fatty degeneration and molecular disintegration. Thus in the case of the muscular fibres of the heart, there is fatty degeneration, although from the structure and action of this organ, there could be no such passive congestion, as we have in the liver and kidneys. It is probable that this fatty degeneration extends to all the unstriped muscular fibres, and may

In thin layers, and when added to water, it presents a deeper shade of green. The yellow fever bile presents a golden color in thin layers and when added to water.

Whilst hæmorrhage occasionally occurs in the gall bladder in yellow fever, I have never witnessed this remarkable condition in malarial fever; neither have I ever observed the entire absence of bile and the replacement of this secretion by an albuminous fluid in malarial fever.

SPLEEN.—Enlarged, softened and loaded with altered blood corpuscles and pigment granules; of a dark, slate color upon the exterior; the blood of the spleen does not change to the arterial hue upon exposure to the atmosphere. In many cases the spleen is so soft that it ruptures when the attempt is made to remove it from the cavity.

When the splenic mud is subjected to microscopical examination it is found to contain numerous pigment granules of various sizes and pigment cells, many of which resemble the colorless corpuscles in size, whilst others are much larger and contain oval nucleoli and resemble certain palmellæ.

SUPRA-RENAL BODIES.—Frequently discolored, of a dark brownish hue, from the deposits of melanotic or pigment particles, around the cortical and medullary cells and capillaries.

No accumulation of oil has been observed in these bodies in malarial fever.

KIDNEYS.—Normal in appearance and structure, except in malarial hæmaturia, when the textures are congested and dark colored in some cases. Occasionally slate colored spots appear upon portions of the kidneys.

I have, by careful clinical studies and by analysis of the urine at different stages of malarial hæmaturia, established the fact that many of the symptoms of the disease as well as the fatal termination, are connected with the progressive failure of the kidneys to eliminate the constituents of the urine- and of the bile.

When sections were made of the kidneys of those who had died in the acute stages of malarial hæmaturia the cortical and medullary portions presented a deep purplish red and bloody appearance. The color was deeper in some portions than others, resembling circumscribed effusions of dark blood. In many cases all portions of the kidneys were altered in appearance and the tubuli uriniferi, especially at the termination of the pyramids, could be seen resembling dark red lines of coagulated blood. Microscopical examination of sections with Valentine's knife revealed the fact that many of the tubuli uriniferi throughout their entire extent were filled with coagulated blood. The hæmorrhage appears to have taken place through the malpighian corpuscles chiefly; little or no blood was effused around the tubuli uriniferi. It would appear that during the prolonged cold stage the kidneys become in this form of malarial fever congested in a manner similar to what occurs in the spleen. During this congestion rupture of the blood-vessels and of the capsular membrane of the malpighian corpuscles occurs, such rupture being mainly due to their anatomical structure and the greater tension of the blood in this portion of the renal capillary circulation. When from any cause the blood coagulates in the tubuli uriniferi their function as excretory tubes is destroyed, and the extent of the impairment of the excretory function of the kidneys will depend upon the number of excretory tubes blocked up by coagulated blood. The grand cause of the severe, dangerous and often fatal character

25

YELLOW FEVER.   MALARIAL FEVER.

even disable the muscules of locomotion and animal life. The granules of the cells of the epithelium of the uriniferous tubes set free by the disintegration of the protoplasm, oil globules, detached cells, and albuminous matters and mucus, form opaque granular masses which block up the tubuli uriniferi.

We have in these structural alterations of the kidney which vary in kind and degree according to the stage of the disease, an explanation of the frequent occurrence of albumen casts, detached cells of the epithelium of the uriniferous tubes, and oil globules and granular matter in the urine of yellow fever.

URINARY BLADDER.—As a general rule the bladder contains little or no urine in yellow fever. The urine is of a light yellow color, without any crystalline bodies, and loaded with albumen, granular fibroid matter, urate of amonia, casts of the tubuli uriniferi, and excretory cells of the kidney. In many cases the urine is entirely suppressed for as long a period as 48 hours before death. So long as the kidneys perform their functions freely and regularly the patient may recover, even though black vomit may have appeared, but if the action of the kidneys has been arrested by structural changes, death is inevitable.

of malarial hæmaturia will be found chiefly in these structual alterations of the kidneys.

URINARY BLADDER.—Often distended, with high-colored urine, free from albumen and casts In malarial hæmaturia the urine contains casts and blood-corpuscles, and desquamated cells of the tubuli uriniferi. Casts high-colored, and often contain colored corpuscles.

PRACTICAL CONCLUSIONS.

From the preceding observations on the malignant forms of malarial paroxysmal fevers, which have prevailed in all alluvial, marshy, swampy and malarious regions in various tropical, semi-tropical and temperate regions, the following practical conclusions may be deduced:

1. The questions submitted to the Presidents of the Boards of Health in the Mississippi Valley, with reference to the nature of these diseases, require careful consideration and investigation.

2. All grave cases of fever during the fall and autumnal seasons which admit of discussion as to their nature, should be accurately reported by the attending physicians. Said reports should be promptly submitted to the Local Boards of Health.

3. The opinion of the President of the Board of Health of the State of Louisiana, and of the majority of said board, and of the local practitioners of New Orleans, and of the lower portion of the delta of the Mississippi river, that the endemic fever of the summer and fall of 1880 was of local origin, without contagious properties, and due to the cause ordinarily known as malaria of the marsh and swamp, has been fully sustained by all the succeeding events.

4. In times of danger, the inspection service upon the Mississippi river and in surrounding States, should be confided to *local practitioners*, of the highest intelligence, most enlarged experience and clear unbiassed judgment.

5. Mistakes in diagnosis tend to create unnecessary alarm, and inevitably impair the confidence of the public in the skill and judgment of the medical profession, and the effort to excite suspicion and distrust in the minds of the citizens of the several States, against the legally constituted Boards of Health, should be summarily condemned as unwise, unjust and base.

LEPROSY

IN

LOUISIANA.

The subject of leprosy has of late excited considerable interest amongst the citizens of the Southern portion of Louisiana, and a formal resolution was passed by the legislature, suggesting an inquiry as to its existence in Lafourche, as will be rendered evident by the following communication to the late Dr. Choppin:

House of Representatives, }
February 27, 1880. }

Hon. S. Choppin, M. D., President Board of Health :

Dear Sir—At the last session of the Legislature a resolution was passed suggesting an inquiry as to whether leprosy existed in Lafourche. The Board has never acted under that resolution to my knowledge. Will you be kind enough to inform me as to whether the Board will make an inquiry, at an early day, in this matter of leprosy?   *   *   *

This matter is so important that I would respectfully urge early action on the part of the Board.

I have the honor to be, sir, your most obedient servant,

JNO. S. BILLIU.

On the thirteenth of July, 1880, Major S. J. Grisamore, president of the Police Jury of the Parish of Lafourche, Louisiana, addressed an earnest communication to the President of the Board of Health of the State of Louisiana, urging an immediate investigation as to the nature of the disease called leprosy, which was reported to be prevalent more especially in the lower Lafourche.

To this communication, the following reply was given :

Office Board of Health, State House, State of Louisiana, }
New Orleans, July 26, 1880. }

Major S. J. Grisamore, President Police Jury, Thibodeaux, Parish of Lafourche :

Dear Sir—In reply to your favor of the thirteenth instant, relative to an investigation of the cases of leprosy said to exist on the Bayou Lafourche, allow me to say that the Board of Health has referred the matter to the president for investigation, and report, as soon as the occasion may offer.

Please inform me as to the position of the various cases, and also as to the best route to be pursued. At present the Sanitary and Quarantine affairs of this great city, engage fully my time and energies, and it will be probably a month or two before it will be in my power to visit the Bayou Lafourche and institute the necessary investigation.

Whenever the time arrives for the execution of the wishes of the Police Jury of Lafourche Parish, and I may add of the Legislature of the State, it will be necessary that I should be furnished with a guide thoroughly acquainted with the people and the roads of the country.

I respectfully request the P·esident of the Police Jury to write fully all particulars, and furnish all necessary information.

Respectfully your obedient servant,   JOSEPH JONES, M. D.,
President Board of Health, State of Louisiana.

The investigation indicated in the preceding correspondence was not undertaken until the 2d of October. the results of which will be detailed in a subsequent portion of this report.

In order to throw all possible light upon this important subject of leprosy, and also to fulfill in the most liberal sense, the wishes of the Legislature of Louisiana, the following results of an extended investigation of the past and present history of Leprosy and related diseases, more especially the African Yaws, are respectfully submitted for the consideration of His Excellency, Governor Wiltz, and the General Assembly of Louisiana.

YAWS AND LEPROSY IN THE DELTA OF THE MISSISSIPPI.

OBSERVATIONS ON THE AFRICAN YAWS (FRAMBŒSIA, RUBULA, PIAN, EPIAN, SYPHILIS ÆTHIOPICA, SYPHILIS VEL LUES ÆTHIOPICA, SYPHILIS AFRICANA); AND ON LEPROSY (LEPRA TUBERCULOSA, LEPRA HÆBRÆORUM, LEPRA ÆGYPTICA, LEPRA LEONTINA, LEPRA ARABIUM) IN INSULAR AND CONTINENTAL AMERICA.

· Leprosy, which is now a comparatively rare disease, was, one century ago, not an uncommon affliction in the Delta of the Mississippi River, for it is a well-established historical fact that Miro, the successor of Galvez, in 1785, founded a hospital for lepers.

Ulloa, at an earlier date in the history of Louisiana, had attempted to prevent the spread of this loathsome disease by confining the lepers at the mouth of the Mississippi River in a place known as the Balize, but this measure created great discontent and was abandoned. Upon the recommendation of Miro the Cabildo, or Council, caused a hospital to be erected for the unfortunate victims of leprosy, who congregated about New Orleans, on a ridge of land lying between the River Mississippi and the Bayou St. John, in the rear of the city.

The hospital of La Terre des Lepreux or Lepers Land appears to have had a brief existence. In the course of a few years the number of these patients gradually diminished, either by death or transportation, the disease disappeared almost entirely; the hospital went into decay, and Lepers Land remained for many years a wild looking spot, covered with brambles und palmettoes, until by the growth of the great city under the flag of the United States, it formed part of the suburbs Tremé, and was embellished with houses and the appliances of civilization.

Careful researches into the literary and medical records of the vast country then known as Louisiana, yield no exact data for the determination of the exact nature of the disease which afflicted the patients of the hospital of *La Terre des Lipreux* during the days of the Spanish domination, but it may with reason be assumed from the historical facts which we shall record, that the diseases affecting prominently the Cutaneous, Osseus and Nervous system, were in early times transplanted from Europe and Asia to Insular and Continental America. These diseases, as will be evident from the historical facts recorded, were :

1. THE AFRICAN YAWS *(Frambœsia Rubra, Pian, Epian, Syphilis Æthiopica, Syphilis vel Lues Æthiopica, Syphilis Africana).*

2. LEPROSY : THE ORIENTAL LEPROSY, OR ELEPHANTAISIS GRŒCORUM *(Lepra Tuberculosa, Lepra Hœbrœorum, Lepra Ægyptica, Lepra Leontina, Lepra Arabrium, Mediœval Leprosy).*

3. ELEPHANTIASIS ARABIUM : *(Elephants Leg, Barbadoes Leg, Buchemia ; Symphatic Hypertrophy or Varix of the Lymphatics, Scrotal Tumor).*

We desire to record in this chapter :
1. The early history of these diseases in Insular and Continental America.
2. Facts illustrating their existence at the present time.
3. Observations illustrating the gradual decline and disappearance of these diseases in the Mississippi Valley.
4. Measures for the arrest of these diseases : Hygaenic measures ; therapeutie methods ; quarantine or isolation.

1. AFRICAN YAWS.

This singular and loathsome disease was by the SLAVE TRADE, transferred at an early date in European colonization, from the shores of tropical Africa to Insula and Continental America. African slavery existed in the Antilles and Mexico and South America, long before the establishment in 1684, by La Salle, of the first French colony on the shores of the Gulf of Mexico*; and we find that in 1724, only six years after the foundation of New Orleans, the black population of Louisiana was nearly double that of the white race, the former numbering 3300, and the latter 1700 souls.

Some thirty years ago, I observed upon the cotton and sugar and rice plantations on the coast of Georgia, amongst the surviving natives of Africa, imported upon the slavers of former times, two cases of yaws and one case of oriental leprosy ; also a case closely resembling leprosy in the white race.

In the same State I observed six cases of lymphatic hypertrophy, or varix of the lymphatics. In four of these cases the foot and leg were involved, forming the so-called elephants leg. In two of the cases, the hypertrophy of the integument was confined to the scrotum, and in one the scrotal tumor was of enormous dimensions, reaching nearly to the surface of the ground, and weighing eighty pounds. The cases of *Elephantiasis Arabum* were confined to the negro race.

In Louisiana, I have observed two cases of yaws, in negroes born in the State, and a case which will be detailed, the subject of which was a native of Africa ; three cases of Elephantiasis Arabum (lymphatic hypertrophy) amongst the native whites ; one case of this disease in a native of Austria,

*NOTE.—The African slave trade was commenced by the Portuguese, fifty years before the discovery of America by Columbus. The year 1442 was distinguished by the inauguration of this infamous trade. The trade, however, was but of trifling extent till the commencement of the sixteenth century. In consequence, however, of the rapid destruction of the Indians employed in the mines of St. Domingo at Hayti. Charles V. authorized, in 1517, the introduction into the island of African slaves, from the establishments of the Portuguese on the coast of Guinea. The concurrence of the Emperor was obtained by the intercession of the celebrated Las. Casas, bishop of Chiapa, who labored to protect the Indians by enslaving the Africans. The importation of negroes into the West Indies and America having once begun, gradually increased to gigantic proportions. Sir John Hawkins was the first Englishman who engaged in it; and such was the ardor with which the English followed his example, that they exported from Africa more than 300,000 slaves between the years 1680 and 1700; and between 1700 and 1786, 610,000 Africans were imported into Jamaica only; to which adding the imports into the other islands and the Continental colonies, and those who died on their passage, the number carried from Africa will appear immense. The importations by other nations, particularly the French and Portuguese, were also very great.

and another in a native of China. ' In the case of a white woman, a native of New Orleans, the entire face and much of the trunk and upper and lower extremities were disfigured by the nodular hypertrophy of the skin. The absence of the constitutional symptoms characteristic of oriental leprosy, as well as the freedom from ulcerations of the integument and osseus system, led me to regard this latter case as one of lymphatic hypertrophy, and not oriental leprosy,

Less than twenty cases of Elephantiasis Graecorum or medieval leprosy have come under my observation in Louisiana.

At a meeting of the New Orleans Medical and Surgical Association, held October 27, 1877, I presented the following case of yaws, with accompanying observations upon the history of this disease in the West Indies and Southern States, together with certain facts, establishing the existence of leprosy in Louisiana, during the French and Spanish domination, and at the present time.*

Case of Yaws. Augustin Faiué, aged 22 years; 5 feet 7 inches in height; weighs about 150 pounds; black hair; dark eyes; copper-colored skin; in the color of the skin and his straight black hair, resembles more nearly the Mongolian race; native of the Isle of Bourbon, off the coast of Africa.

The patient states that his father was a native of France and his mother a native of Africa. Sailor by occupation. Admitted to Charity Hospital, ward 30, bed 440, October, 1877. The patient states that he contracted the disease with which he is now suffering, on the coast of Africa three months ago. He says that the ship upon which he was employed was visited by natives, several of whom were suffering with a similar disease, and he supposed that the disease was contracted from them. Had lived on the Island of Bourbon until thirteen years of age, and from that time until his admission into the charity hospital has followed the seas, and ten months ago suffered from scurvey, his gums being swollen and livid, and the surface of the body mottled with purpuric spots. He states that the yaws first made its appearance on the face in the form of two or three vesicles, about the size of a pin's head, which gradually enlarged to the size of a pea. The number of the vesicles increased, several of which united or became confluent on the face, forming irregular elevations about an inch in diameter. In ten or twelve days after their first appearance each vesicle became umbilicated and burst, discharging sanious fluid, and then drying up formed scabs, which gradually fell off. In the meantime other vesicles formed upon the face and extremities. After the eruption had continued about six weeks, any abrasion of the skin upon any part of the body would result in the formation of raw suppurating sores, upon which scabs would form. The disease attacked with greatest violence the soles of the feet, toes and fingers, causing swelling, ulceration and destruction of the joints and phalanges. The patient states that he came on a sailing ship from Havre, France, to New Orleans, and suffered severely with pains in his head, back and extremities, attended with high fever and delirium, which continued throughout the voyage. Entered the charity hospital in a prostrated and almost insensible condition.

When I first saw this patient he complained of severe pain in the head, defective vision and memory, insomnia and pains in the limbs and back. Body emits an exceedingly offensive and disgusting odor. An eruption of raised pustules of various sizes and ages, varying from the size of a pin's head to the size of a half dollar, and filled with an opaque whitish fluid, occupy various portions of the face and forehead and trunk. Marks of the successive crops of eruptions can be discerned upon the face and upon various portions of the trunk and extremities. When the pustules burst a thick viscid matter is discharged, which forms a foul, dense crust or scab upon the surface. From some of the pustules, and especially those upon portions of the body most subjected to pressure and abrasion, as the hips, elbows, knees and feet, red fungus excrescences have arisen, resembling a large mulberry, and emitting a foul, disgusting odor. On the right cheek, over the region of the malar bone, there is an aggregation, or confluent mass, of these eruptions forming an elevated fungus surface of irregular shape, varying from one to two inches in diameter. On the left side of the angle of the inferior maxillary there is another irregular mass of pustules, or fungus formation, which are covered with a scab of the dead exudation. About twenty of the pustules of various sizes occupy the forehead. The right eyelid presents a nodulated appearance and the left eyelid has three small pustules. Both elbows are occupied by oblong fungus, mulberry-like eruptions, discharging foul sanies, and a similar eruption is observed over both trochanters and both knees. Upon the left side numerous cicatrices,

---

*Observations on the American Yaws. and on Leprosy, * * etc., in Insular and Continental America. By Joseph Jones, M. D. The New Orleans Medical and Surgical Journal, Vol. 5, N. S., March 1878, No. 8—pp. 675–693,

marking the site of former eruptions, are visible. This observation applies also to other portions of the body. The scrotum and integuments of the penis much swollen and very painful. No chancres nor chancroids, nor marks of syphilitic ulcerations observable upon penis. No induration or enlargement of the lymphatics of the groin or axilla are observable.

Fungous eruptions exist upon the joints of several of the fingers, some of which have lost the first joint, and the nails are partially or entirely missing. Several of the fingers are retracted. The toes of the left foot are retracted and deformed, and several are without nails, having lost the first phalages. The external surface of the left ankle is covered by a fungus nodulated eruption. The right leg, ankle and foot is much swollen, and presents somewhat the appearance of elephantiasis; but the enlargement of the limb is clearly due to the effects of inflammatory action, in and around the bones of the instep and foot. A large corroding ulcer, discharging an offensive sanious fluid, exists on the posterior surface or palmar aspect of the right foot, about three inches in diameter. On the dorsal aspect of the foot there are several ulcers, resembling those formed over carious bones, which discharge a foul sanious fluid. These ulcerations communicate with the dead bones of the foot, and it appears that the continuous discharge is due to the presence of the dead bones, which act like foreign bodies. The outer or smallest toe, as well as the next toe, have been completely destroyed. The disease has also invaded the remaining toes, and the third toe from the exterior lost one of the phalanges, after the entrance of the patient into my wards; and upon careful examination, I could discover no erosions of the surface of the bone, as in the sequestra of diseased bones and those segments thrown off after amputation of the extremities.

The increase in the size of the left foot and leg is shown by the following measurements circumference of ankle, 13¼ inches; circumference of instep, 14 inches.*

YAWS IN THE WEST INDIES.

The existence of yaws in the West Indies was, without doubt, coeval with the importation of slaves from the coast of Africa, but the first English writer who observed and described the disease in the West Indies, was the learned physician and naturalist, Sir Hans Sloane, M.D., who, in 1687, went as physician to the Duke of Albemarle to Jamaica.

The great work of Dr. Hans Sloane, on the Natural History of Jamaica, was published in London in 1707. From that portion of the introduction which relates to the diseases which he observed in Jamaica, and the method by which he "used to cure them," we extract the following observations relating to the yaws: "A negro woman, belonging to Mr. Firwood, was brought to me. She had a great many ulcers in the extremities of the fingers and toes, and about the joints. There was also several bladders filled with serum on several of her joints, as if cantharides had been applied there to raise a blister. These bladders or *cuticula,* filled with serous matter, came on either her fingers or toes every full and new moon, and in process of time each of the bladders brought an ulcer, leaving the flesh raw, and sometimes deeper, sometimes shallower corroded, so that the longer the bladders had been raised the deeper were the ulcerations. The virulency of the humor was such, that

---

Progress of this Case, Up to this date, January 22d, 1878, the patient has presented various changes, in accordance with the phrases of the disease, but upon the whole has improved upon the plan of treatment instituted. The appearance of fresh crops of pustules has been attended with pain in the head and back, and extremities, anorexia, depression of spirits, moaning insomnia, and febrile excitement. Opium was administered to induce sleep, and iodide of potassium and tincture of iodine administered to induce some constitutional impression on the disease. After a fair trial these remedies were abandoned, and the patient placed upon bitart. of potassa two drachms, three times a day in a cup of water, and 15 drops of the tincture sesquichloride of iron three times a day in a wineglassful of water. Gentle purgation, combined with the tonic action of the tincture of iron, and daily use of warm baths, and local application of carbolic and iodine salves, yielding the best results. At this present moment all the ulcers are healed, except the large ones on the right foot, and the pustules have ceased to form, and the patient is cheerful and walks about the hospital grounds. As a local application the following was found beneficial: R.—Acidi carbolici, one drachm; acidi tannici, two drachms; tinct. iodini, three fluid drachms; tinct. oppi, two fluid drachms; cerati simplicis, two ounces; mix, apply locally to abraded surfaces with fungus growths, and to the corroding phagadenic ulcerations of the extremities This ointment was spread upon soft prepared or English lint, and applied continuously to the ulcerated surfaces. Under this treatment, conjoined with frequent ablutions in warm water, the ulcerations and fungus surfaces have healed, and the patient is able to walk about the hospital grounds. About the middle of December. one of the phalanges of of the middle toe was extracted. It presented no erosions. Since its removal, the swelling of the foot has progressively subsided. I have used the above ointment, or one of similar composition, since 1866, with satisfactory results in the treatment of gunshot wounds, and ulcerations resulting from various causes.

October 1st, 1878.—Upon resuming my wards at the Charity Hospital the patient had been transferred to one of the surgical wards. His condition was much improved.

October 1st, 1879.—During the preceeding summer the patient left the hospital and sailed for the coast of Africa.

after it had eaten into the bone, the fingers and toes would drop off, and they die, as I have been assured by those who had lost several negroes of this disease, I was assured was peculiar to blacks." *   *   *   *

" A *negro* lusty fellow was taken ill of the *yaws;* he had not been long from *Guinea,* and was all broke out into hard whitish swellings, some greater some lesser, from the bigness of a bean to that of a pin's head, of which last size there were many which appeared like the glands of the skin, swelled and white. When these tumors are large they are usually white at top, from some of the cuticula and humors, dried, lying in scales over it, and sometimes they weep out an ichor. At other times the ulcers are much larger. They likewise complained sometime of great pain in the bones, and the fellow whom I cured was broke out very much about the penis, scrotum and elbows. I fluxed him by unction in an out-house, feeding him with as much water-gruel as he could eat or drink. The flux proceeding as it was expected to do, he was quite cleared of this filthy distemper, only on his elbow he had one swelling, not quite dry, to which I applied vitriol, which made the scales fall off and heal as the rest.

" This distemper is thought to be contagious and to be communicated from one to another, from blacks to whites and from parents to children, but I couldn't observe it to be more or less contagious than the pox. There are few plantations without several of these diseased persons, who are usually cured as above. Though 'tis commonly thought that fluxing does not cure without relapse, yet I, by what I could observe, find it does, and do believe the return of this disease comes from not being thoroughly fluxed by anointing, or being kept too warm, or wrong treated afterwards, whence some remains of it staying behind in the body these dregs by degrees bring the same distemper again.   *   *   Some sorts of this distemper seem to me to be the *elephantiasis* or true *leproise* of the ancient and *Arabian* physicians. Others said to have this disease were plainly *scrofulous,* or had the king's evil, and most said to have it, had the *lues venera.* Though this disease is thought to be propagated by ordinary conversation, or trampling with the bare feet on the spittle of those affected with it, yet it is most certain that it is mostly communicated to one another by copulation, as some other contagious diseases are."*

Dr. John Hume, surgeon to the naval hospital in Jamaica, and a commissioner of the sick and hurt. drew the attention of British practictioners to the phenomena of this disease in an account of it published in the sixth volume of the Edinburg Medical Essays, in 1744. Dr. Hume pointed out the resemblance of the yaws to the disease described in the thirteenth chapter of Leviticus, as affecting the Israelites in their passage through the wilderness, and Adams has expressed his belief of their identity (Obs. on Morbid Poisons, page 206.) Dr. Hillary supposes that Haly Abbas, who lived in the tenth century, refers to the yaws under the general term *lepra,* both kinds of the Arabian leprosy having been described in a preceding chapter under the name (as it is translated) *elephantia.*—(Inquiry into the Means of Improving Medical Knowledge, by W. Hillary, M. D.) The yaws were next treated of by M. Virgile, who practised for several years in the Island of St. Domingo, and subsequently by M. Desportes, Peryrilhe, Dr. James Grainger, of St. Christophers, Dr. Hillary, of Barbadeos, Abbe Raynal. Bryan Edwards, Drs. Winterbottom, Dancer, Mosely, Ludford, Thomson, Thomas, Wright and others

---

*A Voyage to the Islands of Maderia. Barbadoes, Nieves, St. Christophers, and Jamaica, with the Natural History of the Herbs and two and four-footed Beasts, Fishes, Birds, Insects, Reptiles, etc., of the last of these Islands, etc. Illustrated with Figures of the the things described as big as Life. By Hans Sloane, M.D., Fellow of the College of Physicians and Surgeons, and Secretary of the Royal Society. 2 vols., London, 1707. Vol, 1, Introduction, cvi., cxxvi.

Some twenty-five years ago, I observed upon the cotton and sugar and rice plantations on the coast of Georgia, amongst the surviving natives of Africa imported upon the slavers of former times, two cases of yaws and one case of leprosy; also a case closely resembling leprosy in the white race. In Louisiana I have observed two cases of yaws in negroes born in the State, and the case in which the patient was a native of Africa; three cases of elephantiasis amongst the native whites, one case in a native of Austria, one case in a native of China. In the case of a white woman, a native of New Orleans, the entire face and much of the trunk and the upper and lower extremities, were disfigured by the nodular hypertrophy of the skin.

Several cases of *leprosy* have come under my observation in Louisiana.

The observations of Dr. Richard Towne, of Barbadoes, concerning the " *Joint Evil,*" evidently relate to the *African yaws,* and are as follows:

"Many of the *negroes* in the *Leeward Islands* as well natives as those imported from *Guinea,* are subject to a cutaneous distemper, which in those parts is known by the name of the *joint evil.* This malady is equally remarkable in its appearances as it is fatal in its consequences, being of so virulent a nature that it eludes the force of the most powerful *remedies* hitherto discovered.

The *description* of it is as follows : It first appears in superficial spots of a brown copper color, dispersed over several parts of the *face* but especially on the *nose,* without any unevenness, or sense of pain in the beginning. These *spots* spread by slow degrees till a great part of the body is covered with them. Then the nails curl inwards, and the extremities of the fingers and toes begin to ulcerate. These *ulcers* which never digest, but generally look dry without much foulness or fœtor, gradually creep from joint to joint, till they have invaded all the *fingers* and *toes.* The next attack this unconquerable enemy makes, is upon the *trunk* of the body, where it spreads its *patches* and at this time the distemper becomes *infectious.* The defecations of the skin never penetrate very deep into the muscular flesh, but extend themselves in circumference, and discharge on them *ichor* which insensibly dries up and emaciates the patient, sometimes in a few years, though there have been some *negroes* under these circumstances, who have protracted a miserable loathsome life for the space of ten, twelve years or longer.

Among the numerous attempts which I have known to resist this stubborn disease, *Antimonial* preparations afford the greatest relief, but I have never heard that they perfected a cure; on the other hand all preparations of mercury aggravate the *distemper,* exasperate the *ulcers,* and make them spread the faster. This is constantly true in whatever form, or with whatever intention *mercury* be given, whether as alterative, purgative, or to receive a salivation, either internally exhibited or externally applied.

The negroes, who are great pretenders to the knowledge of *specific* virtues in simples, apply several kinds of *plants* on these occasions, but I could never observe the least beneficial effect produced by them.

This being a *disease* not taken notice of, as far as I know, by any *Author,* I hope I shall be excused for giving the *description* of it, though I am forced to leave it to future industry and greater sagacity than my own to investigate the cure."

Abbe Raynal, in his *Philosophical and Political History of the Settlements and Trade of the Europeans in the East and West Indies,* vol. v., pp. 272-274, says:

"The yaws, which is the second disorder peculiar to negroes, and which accompanies them from Africa to America, is contracted in the birth, or by communication between the sexes. No age is free from it, but it more particularly attacks at the period of infancy and youth. Old people have seldom strength sufficient to support the long and virulent treatment which it requires.

"There are said to be four species of yaws: the yaws with pustules, large and small, as in the small-pox; that which resembles lentils; and lastly, the red yaws, which is the most dangerous of all.

"The yaws attack every part of the body, but more especially the face. It manifests itself in granulated red spots, resembling a raspberry. These spots degenerate into sordid ulcers, and the disorder at length affects the bones. It is not in general attended with much sensibility.

" Fevers seldom attack the persons who are affected with the yaws; they eat and drink as usual, but they have an almost insuperable aversion for every kind of motion, without which, however, no cure can be expected. The eruption lasts about three months. * *

---

*A treatise of the diseases most frequent in the West Indies, and herein more particularly of those which occur in Barbadoes. London 1726, pp. 189-192.

All the negroes, as well male as female, who come from Guinea, or are born in the islands, have the yaws once in their lives. It is a disease they must necessarily pass through; but there is no instance of any of them being attacked with it a second time after having been radically cured. The Europeans seldom or never catch this disease, notwithstanding the frequent and daily connection which they have with the negro women. These women suckle the children of the white people, but they do not give them the yaws.. How is it possible to reconcile these facts, which are incontestible, with the system which physicians seem to have adopted with regard to the nature of the yaws? Can it be allowed that the semen, the blood and the skin of the negroes are susceptible of a virus peculiar to their species? The cause of this disorder, perhaps, is the same as that which occasions their color. One difference is naturally productive of another, and there is no being or quality that exists absolutely detached from others in nature."*

Dr. William Hillary, in his treatise on the diseases of the West India Islands, or the Torrid Zone, devotes a special chapter to the *yaws*, from which we extract the following :

"That disease which the negroes in Africa, and we from them in the West Indies, call the yaws, is a native of and seems to be indigenous in Africa and Arabia, and was first brought from the former by the negroes into America and its islands. This is a distemper which has been well known for many ages in Africa, and some of the neigboring countries which are situated within the torrid zone : but I do not find that any of the Greek physicians, nor yet any of the Arabians, do mention it, except Haly Abbas, the Persian Magus. * * We are credibly told that the yaws seldom fail to attack the negroes in Africa at one time or other in their lifetime, but most frequently the children and young people ; and that they very rarely or never have it a second time, if they have been perfectly cured the first time. * * * * * * * *

"This disease generally makes its first appearance without any previous sickness or pain, and when the patient thinks himself perfectly well, in very small pimples, no bigger than the head of a small pin, and are smooth and level with the skin ; these daily increases and become protuberant pustules. Soon after the cuticle turns whitish, cracks, and rubs off, and a very small quantity of serum or clear ichor exudes out and dries, and becomes white; but neither pus nor any quantity of ichor is found in the tumor, but a pretty thick, white slough appears, and under that a red fungus flesh thrusts itself out of the skin, which gradually increases to different magnitudes, some not so large as the smallest wood strawberry, some larger ; others exceeding the size of the largest mulberry, which last they very much resemble, being red, and composed of little round knobs as they are. They appear differently on all parts of the body, but most frequently, and generally are the largest, about the groin, private parts, anus, under the arms and in the face ; and it is remarkable, that in general when the yaws are very large, there are fewer in number, and è contra, when they are more numerous they are generally smaller in size. And as the yaws are thus increasing and coming to their height, the black hairs, which grow out of the places where the yaws are, gradually turn to be perfectly white, like the hairs of an old man ; and the ichor which oozes out of the yaws, drying upon the skin, makes it appear of a whitish color, and renders the patient a disagreeable loathsome sight : and now the disease is become very infectious to those who handle or cohabit with them. * * The time from their first appearance in the before mentioned pimples to their full height or growth, is very different in different constitutions, as they are stronger or weaker, and according to the negroes being well fed or the contrary ; for when the negro is strong, lusty and of plethoric habit, and is well fed, the yaws will often arrive at their full growth, and be as large as a mulberry, in a month's time from their first appearance ; but when the negro is weak, low in flesh, and poorly fed, the yaws will be small, and often no larger than a strawberry at the end of three months.

"This disease is known to be infectious, but there is also a peculiar apitude in some constitutions to receive it more readily than others, and probably, in the same person to receive the infection more readily at one time than another."

Dr. William Hillary presents the foregoing description as relating to the disease when left entirely to nature, but he adds that when improperly treated, and interfered with in its natural course, the fungus eruptions in the yaws may in time become phagadenic ulcers, which corrode and eat away the flesh even to the bones, and then produce nodes, exostosis and carries in them, and at last totally consumes and destroy them also.

Bryan Edwards, in his *History of the British Colonies in the West Indies* (vol. ii., p. 352), says :

" Among the diseases which negroes bring with them from *Africa*, the most loathsome

---

*Philosophical and Political History of the Settlements and Trade of the Europeans in the East and West Indies, Revised, augmented and published in ten volumes, by the Abbe Raynal, M. D., London, 1787, p. 272.

are the *cacabay* and the *yaws*, and it is difficult to say which is the worst. The former is the *leprosy* of the *Arabians*, and the latter (much the most common) is supposed, by some writers, to be the leprosy mentioned in Leviticus, chap. xiii. * * Young negro children often catch the yaws, and get through it without medicine or much inconvenience. At a later period it is seldom or ever thoroughly eradicated; and, as like the small-pox, it is never had but once, the Gold Coast negroes are said to communicate the infection to these infants by inoculation. I very much doubt if medicine of any kind is of use in this disease."

Dr. James Grainger, in his *Essay on West India Diseases*, affirms that the yaws attacks the negroes but once, and is both tedious and difficult to cure, and, when repelled, infallibly ruins the constitution.

Dr. John Williamson* says that

"The yaws is a disease of such a contagious character that white people naturally feel a horror in exposing themselves to the risk of infection. It may be communicated by flies alighting from the yawy patient and penetrating in the usual manner any part of the body by which inoculation is effected, but I must acknowledge my doubts in the extent of this contagion in an equal degree to the whites as to the African or Creole negroes. White people may expose themselves with less risk than negroes. * * Some few instances came within my knowledge of white persons being infected with yaws from sexual intercourse, and it is dreadful to imagine the hard fate to which such persons are condemned, but absolute exclusion from society of their own color is necessary until a cure is completed. It is additionally unfortunate that the evil does not cease then. A white person who has had yaws, ever after has an *onus* attached to him, affecting his disposition, particularly should he feel inclined to form a connection by marriage with any reputable female of the country."

It appears that in general, if not always, the occurrence of the yaws is consequent to the application of its specific virus to an abraded surface of an individual in whom it has not previously existed; and this, although frequently by accident, is not unfrequent by design. According to Dr. Wright, the most usual circumstances under which it is contracted are, first, by sleeping in the same bed, and the ichor getting on the wounds or scratches of the uninfected; secondly, by handling the infected, and allowing the virus to touch scratches or excoriations; thirdly, by the use of the same bowl or bassin in washing their sores which had been previously used for similar purposes by the infected negroes; fourthly, and most usually, by small flies, which, having gorged themselves with the virus of the diseased, alight on the ulcers of the hitherto uninfected, its propagation being as certain by the minutest quantity as if it were ever so considerable.

The progress of the operation of the virus of yaws in the animal economy, unlike that of small-pox, is very variable in different individuals; but from the experiments of Dr. Thomson it may be inferred, that from seven to ten weeks is the usual period which elapses between the insertion of the virus and the development of the eruption. In one instance, however, for which we have the authority of Dr. Adams, the interval appears to have been ten months. It has been remarked that the blood of yaw patients does not differ in appearance from that of healthy persons, and that, when used for inoculation, it fails to communicate the disease; moreover, that the infected are as liable to other diseases as persons in a healthy condition.

NOTES ON THE HISTORY OF YAWS IN THE SOUTHERN STATES.

The first recorded observations on the yaws, as appearing amongst the negroes of Louisiana, were those of the historian, M. Le Page du Pratz, who came over with a colony of eight hundred men in 1718, when New Orleans consisted of only a few huts, and who purchased slaves upon his arrival in the colony; was a planter for sixteen years, and was likewise overseer or Di-

*Medical and Miscellaneous Observations relative to the West India Islands, vol. ii., Edinburg, 1817, pp. 141-161.

rector of the Public Plantations, both when they belonged to the West India Company and afterwards when they fell to the Crown, by which means he had the best opportunities of knowing the nature of the soil, climate and diseases of Louisiana. Du Pratz published his history of Louisiana one hundred and twenty years ago, namely, in 1758.

That the negroes of Louisiana, as early as 1718–1734, suffered with the yaws, syphilis and scurvey, is evident from the directions given by M. Le Page du Pratz as to:

" The choice of negroes; of their distempers, and the manner of curing them;"[*] from which we extract the following : "The first thing you ought to do when you purchase negroes, is to cause them to be examined by a skilful surgeon, and an honest man, to discover if they have the venereal or any other distemper. When they are viewed, both men and women are stripped naked as the hand, and are carefully examined from the crown of the head to the sole of the feet, then between the toes and between the fingers, in the mouth, in the ears, not excepting even the parte naturally concealed, though then exposed to view. You must ask your examining surgeon if he is acquainted with the distemper of the yaws, which is the virus of Guinea, and incurable by a great many French surgeons, though very skilful in the management of European distempers. Be careful not to be deceived in this point, for your surgeon may be deceived himself; therefore attend at the examination yourself, and observe carefully over all the body of the negro, whether you can discover any parts of the skin which, though black like the rest, are however, as smooth as a looking-glass, without any tumor or rising. Such spots may be easily discovered, for the skin of a person who goes naked is usually all over wrinkles. Wherefore if you see such marks, you must reject the negro, whether man or woman. There are always experienced surgeons at the sale of new negroes, who purchase them; and many of these surgeons have made fortunes by that means, but they generally keep their secret to themselves." * *

"You must never put an iron instrument into the yaw ; such an application would be certain death.

"In order to open the yaw, you take iron rust reduced to an impalpable powder, and passed through a fine search ; you afterwards mix that powder with citron juice, till it be of the consistency of an ointment, which you spread upon a linen cloth greased with hog's grease, or fresh lard without salt, for want of a better ; you lay the plaster upon the yaw, and renew it evening and morning, which will open the yaw in a very short time without any incision.

"The opening being once made, you take about the bulk of a goose egg of hog's lard without salt, in which you incorporate about an ounce of good terebinthine, after which take a quantity of powdered verdigris and soak it half a day in good vinegar, which you must then pour off gently with all the scum that floats at the top. Drop a cloth all over with the verdigris that remains, and upon that apply your last ointment. All these operations are performed without the assistance of fire. The whole ointment being well mixed with a spatula, you dress the yaw with it; after that put your negro into a copious sweat, and he will be cured. Take special care that your surgeon uses no mercurial medicine, as I have seen, for that will occasion the death of the patient."

Bernard Romans,[†] whose work on Florida was published in 1776, says :

"I have seen three or four instances of the disease called body yaws (in the islands), and in Carolina the lame distemper. This is said to proceed from hereditary venereal taints. It appears in cancerous corroding sores in the mouth and throat and spreading ulcers, together with fleshy protuberances, chiefly on the face, breast and thighs, with a swelling of the shin and knee bones, and commonly corrodes the cartilages of the nose, its first symptoms showing themselves about the throat and palate, having caused ignorant people to mistake it for the *Angina Suffocativa* before described. Mercurial medicines are used against it, afterwards diet drinks of China root, nut grass, etc.; the sores in the mouth are often to be rubbed with a feather dipped in syrup of roses, to an ounce of which two drops of sp. vit. have been added ; unctuous, salt, spiced meats and spirituous liquors are absolutely to be avoided; frequent sweats are also prescribed and a great care against catching cold."

It is evident from the statements of these authors that the yaws afflicted the Africans imported to the colonies of America. It is also well established that this disease is of comparatively rare occurrence at the present day amongst the descendants of the native Africans. These facts sustain the following propositions:

---

* History of Louisiana, vol. ii., pp. 255–240.
†Concise Natural History of East and West Florida, p. 256.

1st. The yaws is au African disease, and disappears gradually when introduced upon the North American Continent.

2d. The disease is not of a venereal nature and is not propagated and spread in the same manner as syphilis.

3d. If hereditary, the tendency to its reproduction may be lost by change of climate, habits and dress and diet. It is probable that increased cleanliness, more abundant supplies of clothing and wholesome food, may have been the chief causes of its disappearance amongst the negroes born on the soil of the Southern States.

RELATIONS OF YAWS TO SYPHLIS.

The yaws and syphilis have frequently been considered as modifications of the same disease. This view has found its most distinguished and able advocate in Dr. James Copeland,* who says :

" This distemper has existed in Africa for ages before the epidemic outbreak of syphilis in Europe at the end of the 15th century, and if not identical with, is at least a form or modification of the disease which existed in the West India Islands, when they were discovered by Columbus, and which was considered as intimately resembling, if not the same as the epidemic syphilis of the 15th and 16th centuries.

" The African syphilis, or the *yaws* as commonly termed, in all respects more closely resembles the earlier manifestations of syphilis in Europe than the modern occurrences of this distemper. Indeed, the few cases of yaws which I saw in Africa, in 1817, agreed with the early accounts of syphilis as prevalent in Europe in the 15th and 16th centuries ; not only as respected the character and severity of the distemper, but also as regarded the modes of its communication and the treatment of it found most beneficial. That the yaws in Africa is identical with the yaws or pian of the West Indies, is also undoubted ; and it is most probable that the identity existed before the discovery of America."

A comparison between the symptoms of syphilis and yaws will at once establish some important distinctions.

Whilst it is true that the yaws will affect the cartilages of the nose and palate, like syphilis, on the other hand, in primary syphilis neither eruptions nor fungi appear, as in the yaws, except in the pudenda, and then only in the form of warts. Spyhilis will never cease spontaneously like the yaws. Persons suffering from the yaws may contract syphilis, and the latter disease cannot be cured until the yaws begin to decline.

The febrile symptoms in yaws are more marked than in syphilis, and the progress of the disease depends largely upon the state of the constitution, habits and diet of the patient.

The period of incubation after inoculation varies in the two diseases ; in the case of yaws it varies from seven to ten weeks.

The eruptions or cutaneous manifestations in yaws are wholly different from those of syphilis.

LEPROSY IN THE WEST INDIES.

That leprosy was introduced into the West Indies from Africa and the South of Europe at an early day is evident from the statements of various authors. Thus Dr. Hans Sloane, whose observations were commenced in 1687, in the Island of Jamaica, records a case which he regarded as the Lepra Græcorum, and also describes the indigenous plants which were supposed to be useful in the treatment of this disease.

Dr. James Grainger, in his "*Essay on the More Common West India Diseases,*" published in Edinburgh, 1802, says that, although the white people in the West Indies are not exempted from this dreadful calamity, the negroes are most subject thereto :

."I could write a great deal upon this disorder and but little to the purpose. Like the

*Dictionary of Practical Medcine. Amer. ed., vol. iii., p. 1,473.

gout, it is the disgrace of art. I am doubtful whether it be infectious or not. The children of infected parents are not always seized with the leprosy, and I have known the wives of the leprous remain free from it for years. It is, however, the part of prudence to remove the distempered from the sound. * * I once saw a negro man whose wool grew white and whose skin put on a farinaceous appearance. He was a hideous spectacle. His appetite was gone."

Dr. William Hillary states that the leprosy of the Arabians was first brought to the West Indies by the negroes from Africa, and

"Is undoubtedly a native of that quarter of the world and Arabia, and is not originally of the western part of it; neither was it ever known here before it was brought hither by the negroes, among whom it is now too frequent here, and has made its way into several families of the white people also; and it is much to be feared that it will spread further in this warm climate, into many more both white and black families, if the legislative power do not interfere, and endeavor to prevent its spreading by some suitable, wise and effectual laws, as we see the French and Spaniards have done."*

Dr. Richard Towne, in his *"Treatise of the Diseases Most Frequent in the West Indies, and Herein More Particularly of those which Occur in Barbadoes, London,* 1726," has given the following description of the Elephantiasis (Chapter x., pp. 187–188, of the Elephantiasis):

"I shall put an end to this treatise by giving the description of two diseases to which the *blacks* are no strangers, but as far as 1 can be informed they are utterly unknown in *Europe.* I mean the *Elephantiasis.* Under the circumstances it occurs in the *West Indies,* and a distemper, called there the *Joint Evil,* and first of the *Elephantiasis.*

"This *disease,* which is no rare thing, to be met with among the negroes, bears a great affinity to the best accounts we have of the *Lepra,* of the Arabians.

"Those *blacks* are more subject to its influence, who after some acute *nervous,* long continued *intermittents,* or other odious illnesses, are either much exposed to the inclemency of rainy seasons, and the cold penetrating dew of the evenings, or are constrained to subsist upon bad diet and undigestible, unwholesome food.

"In the beginning the person is weak, cachectical, and emaciated, till the glut of vitiated *humors* subsides into the legs and feet, which are the seat of this distemper, and at this time begin to appear *oedematous,* and puffed up with water tumors as in an *anasarca,* but the swellings do not retain the mark of any pressure in the same degree, or so long as in that distemper. By degrees the leg becomes more and more tumified, and the veins are much distended with *varicose swellings,* which are very apparent from the knee down to the extremities of the toes. Then the skin begins to grow rugged and unequal, its vascular and glandulous *compages* is eularged, and a scaly substance with a sort of chops and fissures in the intestices appear upon its surface. These seeming scales do not dry up and fall off, but are daily protruded forward, and stretched in their dimensions till the leg is enlarged to an enormous bulk, so that in size, shape and all other external appearances, it minutely represents the leg of an elephant, from whence the disease receives its denomintion.

"But notwithstanding that this scaly coat appears to be harsh, callous and insensible, yet if it be touched, ever so superficially with a lancet, the blood will freely ooze out, and if the *Epidermis,* which affords this monstrous appearance, be paired off to the thickness of the scarf-skin in those parts an infinity of orifices of the blood-vessels will present themselves to the eye when assisted with a microscope.

"Tho' the *limbs* continue to proceed to this inordinate magnitude, yet the appetite of the negro remains good, his digestion strong and his secretions regular; nor is he sensible of any other inconveniency than the burthen of carrying such a *load* of *leg* along with him.

"In this condition several have been known to live twenty years, and even to a longer period, and have performed cheerfully all the duties of servitude which were consistent with such disproportionate *limbs.*

"This addition of bulk is generally confined to one *leg* at a time, but there have been several instances where it has invaded both together.

Amputation of the *diseased leg* has been performed many times, but has always failed of a cure, for the distemper constantly takes possession of the remaining *leg.*

Sometimes *white people,* whom unhappy circumstances have reduced them to hardships, but little inferior to what the *blacks* are obliged to undergo, have given us proof that this *disease* is not limited to one color, any more than the bounds in which *Lucretius* has confined it.

Est Elephas Morbus, qui propter Flubiam Nili Gignitur Egypto, in Media, neq ; prœterea usquam."

---

*A Treatise on such diseases as are most frequent in or are peculiar to the West India Islands, or the Torrid Zone.

LEPROSY IN MEXICO.

One of the forms of leprosy, would seem to be not an uncommon disease in Mexico.

Kendall, in his *Narative of the Texan Santa Fe Expedition* (vol. ii., p. 220), thus speaks of the *lazarinos* or lepers of hospital San Lazaro :

"The appearance of the unfortunate lepers is loathsome and hideous to a degree that beggars description. It makes its appearance by scaly eruptions on different parts of the face and body of the victim, and these eruptions are never perfectly healed. The limbs of many, and more especially the hands, at first appear to be drawn and twisted out of all shape. Gradually the nose and parts of the feet are carried away, while the features become distorted and hideous. The voice assumes at times a husky and unnatural tone, and again the doomed patient is unable to articulate except in a shrill, piping treble. With many when near the last stages, all powers of speech are lost, and vainly do they endeavor to make known their wants by sounds which belong not to this earth of ours. Death steps in at last to relieve the poor creatures of their sufferings ; and to them at least, it would seem that the visit of the grim tyrant must be welcome."

Mr. Kendall further states that there were some sixty males, and more than that number of females, affected with that disease in the hospital at San Lazaro, when he was there ; that he cannot say whether the disease is contagious or not ; that there is little doubt of its being constitutional and hereditary, being never entirely eradicated from the blood. He thinks that the climate has some effect in engendering and keeping alive the disease ; says that the common belief among the lower classes is, that it is communicated by contact, and expresses the opinion that the only risk a person runs of taking it is from touching the person of one afflicted with it in its worst stages. It seems that when a person is known to be a leper in Mexico, he is at once sent to the hospital, where he remains till death, for we are told that none ever recover from the horrible disease. (p. 222.)

"If all the Mexican inmates of San Lazaro," says Mr. Kendall, "were afflicted with leprosy, and we were told that such was the case, there must be three or four different species of the disease. The faces of some of the lazarinos were covered with blotches and eruptions, while their hands and feet were unmarked· Others again had complexions exceedingly fair and unblemished, yet their feet and hands were distorted or decayed. Some of the victims of the dreadful scourge were covered from head to foot with sores and ulcers hideous to look at, and then there were two or three cases where the patients presented no other marks of disease than the loss of a nose. But the most singular case of all was that of an old Spaniard, whom I have previously mentioned as continually smoking his cigarettos. His flesh appeared to be entirely gone, dried up ; his skin turned to a bluish purple, and his whole appearance was so strangely changed and distorted that he more resembled an animated mummy than aught else I can compare him to. His senses he still retained, while his actions and conversation convinced us that he was a well-informed and gentlemanly man" (p. 241).

LEPROSY IN NEW BRUNSWICK.

In the year 1844, the attention of the Canadian government was called to the existence of leprosy at Tracadie and Nequac, in the province of New Brunswick, near the Bay of Chaleur ; and a commission was accordingly appointed, consisting of Drs. Key, Skine, Tolbdarvy and Gordon, to investigate its nature and origin. The following is extracted from the report of the Canadian Parliament: " The disease is the Greek elephantiasis—the leprosy; not the elephantaisis of the Arabians, but the leprosy of the middle ages ; the lepre tuberculeur of the French, or tubercular leprosy which raged over nearly every district of Europe, from the tenth to the sixteenth century. It is the decided opinion of the gentlemen comprising the commission that the disease is contagious; and so far as they could ascertain, no person in the above districts who contracted it is ever cured. It is also their opinion that it has no affinity to scrofula; and the idea very prevalent that it is owing to the poor diet of the French settlers and their filthy habits generally, is not correct, for they found it existing in some of the cleanest dwellings and most respectable families. It has spread very rapidly during the past year. They have discovered upward of twenty cases, all of which can be traced up to one source. They have every reason to suppose that there were a greater number; but not having power to search, and the inhabitants showing a greater disposition to withhold information, or to point out the parties laboring under the disease, they could not make so minute an inquiry as they were desirous of doing." Dr. Boyle, of St. Johns, has also investigated the disease (London Medical Gazette, 1844), of which he has given an interesting account. Dr. Boyle agrees with the commission, that the disease is *tubercular elephantiasis* of modern pathologists; the juzam of the Arabians, and the *lepra Græcorum* of the middle ages; and he regards the disease as *non-contagious*, and goes into a long statement of facts to prove the position. He, however thinks the disease is hereditary, traces its existence back to 1827, numbering some twenty cases and twelve deaths since that period, although he is of opinion that it was introduced into the province much earlier. He briefly describes a case of the disease, where "the breath was extremely offensive, the face, hands and legs covered with blotches and tubercles of a livid brownish color and some of them were in a state of ulceration.'"

MORBID ANATOMY OF LEPROSY.

According to M. Danulssen, physician to St. George's Hospital at Borgen, it appears that this disease has prevailed epidemically for half a century on the coast of Norway, and that out of 200,000 inhabitants 1200 had been attacked. In the great number of autopsies the author of the memoir has had occasion to make, it was found that the skin and cellular tissues and walls of the sub-cutaneous veins were one indurated mass, yellowish and granulated. The same indication was found in the eyes, larynx, trachea, bronchial tubes, pleura, liver, spleen, intestines and uterus; the lungs alone escaped. The disease uniformly terminated fatally, however treated.

NOTES ON THE HISTORY OF LEPROSY IN THE SOUTHERN STATES.

The earliest description of leprosy in these Sonthern States, drawn from direct observations, appears to be that given by Captain Bernard Romans, in his rare and valuable " *Concise Natural History of East and West Florida*," printed in New York in 1776.

The account given by Bernard Romans of the diseases of the negroes in Western Florida, shortly after its passage into the hands of the English, and which, without doubt, also applied to Louisiana under the French and Spanish, is much more circumstantial and important than that of Du Pratz. Bernard Romans says that the chronic diseases amongst the blacks were *leprosy, elephantiasis* and *body yaws*, called in Carolina the lame distemper.

· The following description of *elephantiasis* and *leprosy*, as they prevailed in Florida more than a century ago, as given by this writer and accurate observer, will enable us to understand why, about the same time, there should have been any necessity for the foundation of a *hospital for lepers near New Orleans.*

"A loathsome disease appears sometimes among the negroes after severe acute disorders, especially if the patient has been obliged to keep his bed long, likewise after a violent exercise has brought on a surfeit; this is called the *elephantiasis,* from the swelling of the feet and legs. It is most frequently seen to affect one leg only. In the first stages of this disorder the patient becomes wretched through excessive lassitudes, which bring on an emaciation of the body; then the corrupted juices subside into the leg or legs and feet, these swell; the skin becoming distended, shines and shows the distended veins everywhere below the knee; now the skin by degrees loses its gloss and becomes unequal and sometimes scaly. After this chaps make their appearance, the glands are stretched and the scales are daily enlarged, appearing as hard and callous as the hide of an alligator, notwithstanding which, the slightest prick with a pointed instrument will cause the blood to exude. This disease affects neither the appetite nor the digestive powers of the body; on the contrary the patient in this, and cheerfulness of spirits resembles the healthiest of men, and the inconvenience of his heavy leg only prevents his ability for the more laborious part of his duty.

"No manner of cure has yet been found for this cruel disorder, but the patients often live to a very advanced age under the pressure of its yoke, even when it has been contracted in early youth. It is said that the amputation of the affected limb is no cure, for the disease will immediately attack the sound leg; this I find also affirmed by Hughes, in his Natural History of Barbadoes. * * *

"The leprosy, so-called, whether the same as was the cause of proscription to the unhappy patients under the Mosaic laws, I shall not pretend to determine. Certain it is, that it is a nauseous, loathsome and infectious disease, sometimes seen among the blacks. This appears first with the loss of beard and hair from the eyebrows, swelling of the lobes of the ears; the face begins to shine, and brown protuberances appear thereon; the lips and nose swell to a monstrous size, the fingers and toes will in the end drop off, and the body becomes at last so ulcerated as to make the poor incurable patient really a miserable object of pity."*

ESTABLISHMENT OF A HOSPITAL FOR LEPERS IN NEW ORLEANS, IN 1778.

One of the first measures of Miro's administration, which succeeded that of Galvez, in 1778, was one of a most remarkable character in its purpose, namely, the foundation of a hospital for lepers.

Judge Martin says: "There being a number of persons in the province afflicted with leprosy, the Cabildo erected an hospital for their reception, in the rear of the city, on a ridge of high land, between it and the Bayou St. John, which is probably the ridge anciently separating the waters of the Mississippi from those of Lake Pontchartrain."†

The account given by the historian Gayarre‡ is more detailed and circumstantial, and is as follows:

"It is remarkable that leprosy, which is now so rare a disease, was then not an uncommon affection in Louisiana. Those who were attacked with this loathsome infirmity generally congregated about New Orleans, where they obtained more abundant alms than in any other part of the colony. They naturally were objects of disgust and fear, and the unrestrained intercourse which they were permitted to have with the rest of the population was calculated to propagate the distemper. Ulloa had attempted to stop this evil by confining some of the lepers at the Balize, but this measure had created great discontent and had been abandoned. Miro now determined to act with more efficacy in this matter, and, in his recommendation, the Cabildo or Council caused a hospital to be erected for the reception of these unfortunate beings in the rear of the city, on a ridge of land lying between the River Mississippi and Bayou St. John. The ground they occupied was long known and distinguished under the appellation of *La Terre des Lepreux,* or *Lepers' Land.* In the course of a few years the number of these patients gradually diminished, either by death or transportation, the disease disappeared almost entirely, the hospital went into decay and Lepers' Land remained for a considerable length of time a wild-looking spot, covered with brambles, briars, woods and a luxurious growth of palmettoes. It is in our day a part of Suburb Treme, and is embellished with houses and all the appliances of civilization."

I possess no data by which to determine the precise nature of the leprosy of Louisiana, during the days of the French and Spanish domination; but it

*Concise Natural History of East and West Florida, etc., by Captain Bernard Romans, 1776, pp. 255-257.
†The History of Louisiana from the Earliest Period, by Francois Xavier Martin, vol. ii., p. 75.
‡History of Louisiana: Spanish Domination, pp. 166-167.
27

may with reason be supposed that several affections were confounded with the leprosy of the ancient Egyptians, Hebrews and Greeks, such as constitutional syphilis, elephantiasis and the yaws cf Africa.

In 1872, a case was brought from Vermillion parish, for the purpose of obtaining my medical advice and treatment. Upon examination, I concluded that the case was one of leprosy. I lost sight of this case up to October, 1877, when the following information was furnished by Dr. W. G. Kibbe, of Abbeville, Vermillion parish, Louisiana:

New Orleans, Oct. 12, 1877.

Professor Joseph Jones, New Orleans:

Dear Sir—I have been requested by Dr. W. D. White and Dr. R. Segrera, of Abbeville, in Vermillion parish, to present the following facts with reference to certain cases of leprosy. I am informed by Drs. White and Segrera that one of these cases, Felicien Ourblanc, visited New Orleans in 1872, for the purpose of obtaining your medical opinion and advice as to treatment. I am informed that your former student, Mr. Isaac Wise, of Abbeville, Vermillion parish, accompanied this patient to your office.

After a careful examination you pronounced the case one of leprosy. I have seen several of the cases, and was consulted by Joseph Drouet, fifth case.

You will oblige Drs. White and Segrera, as well as myself, by giving us all the facts in your possession upon the history of this disease and related diseases in the Southern States. Respectfully yours,

W. G. KIBBE.

LEPROSY IN VERMILLION PARISH, LOUISIANA.

The first case was an old lady, Mdm. Ourblanc. She was the daughter of Drouet (who came from the south of France many years ago). In 1866 or '7 she showed symptoms of disease. There was no physician called in. Her husband being a native of and raised in France seemed familiar with the disease, and recognizsd it to be that of leprosy, and it was useless to have her treated as it was incurable. From the time of its appearance in his wife Ourblanc separated himself from her, fearing contagion. During the year 1870 she died, I am told, from exhaustion as there was extensive ulceration.* She raised four sons and two daughters. One of the daughters died during the late war from an acute disease; was grown and married at time of her death. The second daughter is living in Vermillion Parish and is reported to have leprosy, but I have no positive proof of its correctness.

The next case was Felicien, second son of Madame Ourblanc, aged about 22 years when it made its appearance in 1871. He was clerking in a dry goods store in Abbeville at the time, and remained there about the year after, when he came to New Orleans to be examined by Professor Joseph Jones, who pronounced the disease *leprosy*. Soon after this he went to New York to be treated, and then to the Hot Springs in Arkansas; from there he went to Shreveport, La., and engaged in business, and is there at present, still suffering from the disease.†

The third and fourth cases appeared near the same time about 1872, in the oldest son, Denanceux, aged about 30 years, and the youngest son, Pierre, aged about 18 years at time

---

*Her fingers and toes had dropped off at the joints, and her body was covered with extensive fœtid sores. She was not treated by any physician." N. O. M. and S. J., June 1879.

† "It first appeared as a bright red spot on the forehead, gradually increasing in size with the opening of the skin, until it covered the whole face. As the disease progressed the bright red assumed a dusky appearance." New Orleans Medical and Surgical Journal, June 1879.

In the early part of the spring of 1878, before the great epidemic of yellow fever, an individual bearing the above name suffering with oriental leprosy, called at my office and said that the nature of his disease had become known to his neighbors and that they had ordered him to close up his store and to leave Shreveport. He attributed this result mainly to my article in the New Orleans Medical and Surgical Journal, from whence he said the neighbors had obtained their information as to the nature of his affliction. Upon my advice this patient entered the Charity Hospital.

The following notes were recorded upon the hospital register:

Case, Felix Ourblanc. (C. 136). Ward 80, bed 435, native of Fayette parish, Louisiana, age 28 years, occupation merchant. Suffered with intermittent fever before the appearance of his present disease. Has two brothers suffering with the same disease as that which now afflicts him. Disease appeared in 1870 in Vermillion parish.

Admitted to Charity Hospital June 28, 1878.

Skin on face and hands nodulated and red. Partial anæsthesia of hands. Disease leprosy.

During the eight days between June 30 and July 10 the temperature of the axilla ranged between 99° to 99.5° in the morning, and from 100° to 100.75° in the evening. He passed from 60 to 70 fluid ounces of urine daily, of sp. r. 1008 to 1010. No albumen in the urine. Patient complained of the hospital fare and was discharged at his own request, on July, 11, 1879. These notes were recorded by C. A. Bourgeois.

of its appearance. In the case of Denanceux, the disease seems to be running its course more rapidly than in the others. He is unable to do any kind of work, and much reduced in flesh and strength ; is completely disfigured, scarcely looking like a human being—his beard, eyebrows and eyelashes having all fallen out and hair is growing very thin on his head *Dr. Young, of Abbeville, informs me that there is complete anæsthesia of face and hands and toes are in state of ulceration. He also tells me that the first thing he observed in all the cases he saw was a bright red spot on forehead. The above four cases originated in the town of Abbeville.

The fifth case is that of Joseph Drouet, aged about 35 years, and lives about eight miles from Abbeville. He is the son of Baptiste Drouet, who was a brother of Mdm. Ourblanc. He applied to me during the summer of 1877 to be treated. He states he first noticed the disease in 1875—a small red spot on his face first attracted his attention. When I saw him the redness was general over the face and slightly purpled ; there were several large red spots on chest and a few yellow spots, and large dark brown spot on inner side of thigh extending nearly to knee. He said it had been bright red and gradually turned dark. His general health did not seem to be much impaired ; his eyebrows had become very white, also lashes. He has a wife and five small children. As I was not practicing I declined treating the case.

Case six was Madame Albert Guedry, daughter of a Dubois, who is of French decent, but as far as I have learned, is not related to the Ourblancs or Drouets. She has two children, and I am told the disease is making rapid progress. She was married, I think, in 1873, and Dr. Young informs me, had the disease at the time. She is supposed to have contracted the disease from nursing Madame Ourblanc during her last illness. This young girl was the only one who would remain constantly with her, except an old negro woman who attended to the room. The old negro woman says the young girl would frequently lie on the bed occupied by Madame Ourblanc.

Seventh case is of more recent occurrence. It is a young man by the name of Clemens, aged about twenty years, lived a few miles west from Abbeville, and is said not to be related to either of the families just named, and is suspected to have contracted the disease by contagion. In 1875, Pierre Ourblanc was peddling through the parish, and would frequently stop over night at the house where this young man was staying, and they slept in the same bed. In 1877, the.young man applied to a physician to be examined and treated ; the disease was recognized at once as leprosy.†

There are several other cases reported to be in the parish, but there is not sufficient evi‐ dence to justify me in stating the cases to be leprosy. The husband of the old lady who died of leprosy is now living in Abbeville, apparently in fine health.‡

The description of the preceding cases by Dr. Kibbe corresponds with my own observations on this disease in Louisiana, which presented in well marked cases discoloration of the skin, dusky red or lived tubercules of various

---

* "He was very reluctant to speak about his disease, but we succeeded in eliciting from him that, when first taken. he felt more or less eratic pains, particularly in the posterior part of the thigh and back of leg. At present he suffers no such pain, and boasts that his general health is good. His fingers are quite hard and stiff and as cold as marble. He has lost several finger nails, and the ends of one or two fingers show a tendency to ulcerate; his toes are ulcerated. His voice is quite coarse and husky, and, unless quite near, one cannot understand him when speaking. The pharynx, larynx and palate seem much ulcerated. There are several nodules on his hand ; his eyebrows and eyelashes have entirely fallen out and beard gradually becoming thin. His nose is much altered in shape, being flattened and drawn to one side, having a mashed appearance. Has the usual *lionine* expression described by writers. He says he has occasional sexual desire ; sleeps well ; does his own cooking, and performs light work at his trade. The younger brother is almost as bad as the one described, and presents much the same appearance. Has inordinate sexual desire." Reports by Drs. Young and Kibbe, N. O. M. and S. J., June, 1879.

† "Only two of these cases have been under treatment, the fourth and sixth, but without any benefit therefrom They all belong to the unæsthetic variety. It is our opinion that cold weather is better borne than warm, for the above cases all seem to suffer more in summer than winter." Drs. Young and Kibbe, N. O. M. and S. J., June, 1879.

‡ Dr. L. F. Solomon, in his Report to the Louisiana State Medical Association, April, 1879, says : " In the City of New Orleans I have learned of six cases, as follows : One in the Third District, exact residence not known at present ; one case, formerly at the corner of St. Charles and Poydras streets ; one case on Common street, near the Charity Hospital, and three cases in the Female Surgical Ward 38 of the Charity Hospital. These cases, with one exception, belong to the tubucular variety, and all present about the same history, with the exception that none are able to trace the disease to heredity. The history of one of the cases in the hospital will serve as a type of the others :

She is a white woman, aged twenty-four. About nine years ago the disease began by fleeting pains in the limbs, followed in a short time by red spots about the face, which soon became of a red color. On these spots small tubucles made their appearance and have increased in size until some of them have reached that of a *marble*. The whole cutaneous surface is of a bronze color. There are ulcerations at the ends of the fingers and toes ; sensation is almost entirely left in the hands, though this did not occur until a very short time ago. The mucous surfaces are all affected. Her voice is harsh, hearing and sight diminished to a great extent. At present she complains of no actual pain, but a burning sensation in her limbs occasionally. She menstruated before the disease developed, but has ceased to do so since the first appearance of the tubucles. She sleeps and eats well. Her face and hands are studded with nodules varying in size.

Dr. Pratt, house surgeon of the hospital, informs me that the three cases have been put under various treatments, but without beneficial results.

I will here add that I have been informed of another case, of the tubercular variety, in the person of an adult female residing on Tchoupitoulas street, between Richard and Orange, in this city, thus making fourteen cases in all, of which eleven remain in the State. There may, doubtless, be other cases which have not come under the notice of physicians." Proceedings of the Louisiana State Medical Association, at its meeting held in the city of New Orleans, April 9, 10 and 11, 1879, p. 23.

sizes on the face, ears and extremities; thickening or rugous state of the skin, a diminution of its sensibility, and falling off of the hair, excepting that of the scalp; hoarse nasal or lost voice; ozœna; foul stinking breath; loss of mobility in the fingers and toes; ulceration of the surface, and especially about the joints of the toes and fingers; extreme fætor; difficult respiration; swelling of the fingers and toes, with fissures on the integuments; muscular atrophy; the face and countenance so disfigured with tuberous knots as to appear deformed and horrid, like that of a satyr or lion.

The following cases of Oriental Leprosy have been observed by me in the Charity Hospital, and two of them have been under my treatment in ward 13:

Case 8—*Numa Kern*; age 25; native of Louisiana; Bayou Lafourche, near Labadiville. Farmer; height, 5 feet 4 inches; weight 110 pounds; parents and grandparents natives of Louisiana, Bayou Lafourche, in Lafourche parish. Brown hair, grey eyes, mild uncomplaining disposition. Cannot tell whether his ancestors came from France or Canada, to Louisiana. Gives no history of leprosy in his family. Both parents dead; mother died in confinement; father of unknown cause; two brothers died some years ago of yellow fever; one brother and sister living in good health. Affirms that he has never had any form of venereal disease. Gives no history of any constitutional disease in his family; and knows of no similar disease to that with which he suffers, amongst his neighbors. Says that he has little or no sexual appetite. Has less sexual desire now (Dec. 8, 1879.) than before the advent of the disease three years ago. Entered Charity Hospital, ward 30, July 17, 1879.

December 5, 1879, patient says that he has suffered with leprosy for three years; complexion clear and apparently healthy before the advent of the disease. At the present time the surface presents a dark, yellowish brown, bronzed and livid appearance.

Patient states that the disease commenced with some pain in the left thigh above knee joint, which was followed by a large ulcer. About the time of the appearance of this ulcer the patient states that he was attacked by an acute inflammatory affection in the feet and legs, which was swollen above the knees. This was accompanied with fever, and the physician attending called the affection erysipelas. Ulcers of the lower extremities subsequently made their appearance, and the feet presented symptoms of altered sensation; they felt benumbed.

Above the knee joints on the left thigh lower third, there is a distinct circular cicatrix about three-fourths of an inch in diameter, which the patient affirms to be the original ulcer which ushered in his disease. There is a similar scar upon the outer aspect of the left elbow which the patient affirms had no relation to the disease, but was caused by fire. Inferior portions of the lower extremities; feet an ankles deeply discolored, enlarged œdematus and extensively ulcerated. There are seven ulcers of considerable size on the left leg. The largest ulcer on the left leg, is about one and three-quarter inches, in longest diameter and a little over one inch in the short diameter, oval in form, deeply eroded with elevated edges (rounded and not everted), and with central greyish foul moist looking centre. This ulcer is situated in the outer aspect of the foot and ankle joints.

Right foot swollen, discolored, with thickened and nodulated integrement as in the case of the left foot. A large ulcer two inches in diameter is situated in the bottom of right foot. The edges of this ulcer are not so regular nor so elevated as in the case of the ulcers upon the legs. This difference appears to be due to pressure in walking. Surface of the ulcer like those elsewhere of a gray, foul, unhealthy hue, with a moist aspect. The discharge however, is thin and bears no resemblance to laudable pus. Another large ulcer with elevated rounded edges and dark grey surface, (one and one-quarter inches in diameter) is situated on outer aspect of leg about two inches above the ankle joint.

The nails of the toes present a discolored and diseased appearance; those of the big toes, especially appear to be diseased, the surrounding integrement being swollen and discolored. Integrement of face of bronzed color thickened and nodulated.

Sensation benumbed or destroyed over the integrements of the feet and legs, as far up as knee joints. Skin of integrements of a mottled, purplish bronzed hue; with a scaly cracked unhealthy epidermis. The nails of the toes are discolored, opaque, wrinkled and partially detached. The skin of the upper extremities is ridged, scaly and semi-opaque. The sensation in the upper extremities is impaired, but not to so great an extent as in the lower extremities. The capillaries of the face appear to be dilated. Patient says that the ulcers of the lower extremities give him pain only when he stands or walks.

Observations upon the pulse and temperature and urine have been made under my direction at various times, thus: October 16 m. temp. of axilla 98.5°; e. temp. 99°; pulse 86. October 17, m. temp. 98.8°; pulse 78; e. temp 99.5°; pulse 84. October 18, m. temp. 97.5°; pulse 80; e. temp. 99°; pulse 82. October 19, temp. 98°; pulse 81; e. temp. 99.4°; pulse 85. October 20, m. temp. 98°; pulse 76; e. temp 99°; pulse 90. October 21, e. temp. 99.5°;

PLATE 1.
LEPROSY IN LOUISIANA.

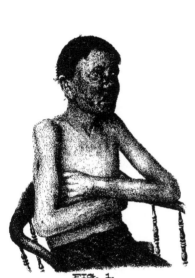

FIG. 1.
NUMA KERN.

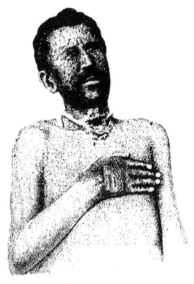

FIG 3.
DONACIEN OURBLANC.

FIG. 2.
NUMA KERN.

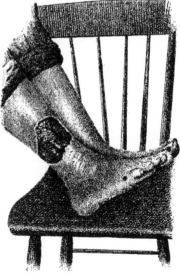

FIG 4.
DONACIEN OURBLANC.

pulse 82. October 22, e. temp. 98.8°; pulse 82. October 23, m. temp. 98.8; pulse 91. October 24, m. temp. 99.2°; pulse 94.

No distinct intermission or remission was observed in the temperature, and the oscillations were within those limits which might be regarded as normal. The pulse was, as a rule, feeble. The appetite and digestion have been good and the bowels regular. The patient, during the period which he has passed in the Charity Hospital, has been up and dressed in the day time, and walks about the hospital grounds. Always manifests a quiet and docile disposition, and readily consents to an examination of his entire person at any time that I saw fit to exhibit him to my students.

Up to the 1st of December, from time of entrance into the Charity Hospital, took pill containing ¼ grain nitrate of silver, and 1-13 grain arsenious acid, and 2½ grains subnitrate of bismuth, morning and evening. No beneficial results were observed. At the date above mentioned the stomach became irritable and the appetite failed and the medicine was discontinued, and I substituted 10 grains of the sulpho carbolate of sodium three times a day. The ulcers were, during the months of October and November, dressed with an ointment comprised as follows : R. plumbi iodidi, 1 drachm; acidi carbolici (sat. sol.), 2 fluid drachms; pulv. opii, 10 grains; cerati simplicis, 2 ounces; mix. Apply locally to ulcers and surround with soft English lint. No marked benefit was observed from the use of this ointment, and on the 1st of December I substituted the following: R. pulv. opii, 10 grains; acidi carbolici, 2 drachms; acidi tannici, 1 drachm; simple cerate, 2 ounces.

Examination of Blood, December 6, 1879.—When drawn the blood presented a thin, watery appearance; under the microscope the colored corpuscles presented the usual bi-concave figures. The colored corpuscles tended to run together and form rolleaux as in the blood of inflammation. Large pigment corpuscles and pigment granules—similar to those which I have often observed in the blood of those suffering under the prolonged action of the malarial poison—were seen. The colorless corpuscles presented a more granular appearance than usual, and many of them contained small globules, which appeared to consist of oil.

Examination of the Discharge from the Leprous Sores.—The leprous sores discharged a saneous, foetid liquid, which under the microscope was found to contain much granular matter, pus corpuscles, fibrous tissue, fragments of blood vessels (the small vessel, with its branches, was of an opaque, crimson color from the coagulated blood) and bacteria. The bacteria were most probably introduced from without, and did not appear to have any distinct relations to the leprous ulcerations. The odor of the body of this patient was most disgusting, resembling very nearly that of a mangy, unwashed, filthy dog. The breath was foul and foetid.

I have examined the urine of Kern upon several occasions, without detecting any albumen. The urine is clear, of an orange color, acid reaction, and without deposits. Albuminuria is said to be present in some grave cases of leprosy.

The appearance presented by Numa Kern, and the ulcers upon the legs, are illustrated in plate 1, figures 1 and 2, and plate 2, figure 5.

This patient died from the immediate effects of an exhausting and uncontrollable diarrhœa during the summer of 1880.

The autopsy was performed by Professor H. D. Schmidt, pathologist of the Charity Hospital, who furnished the following notes:

"*Heart* of normal size. Both the tricuspid, and mitral valves were thickened throughout by new plastic growth in the form of nodules. Corpora of the semilunar valves of the aorta greatly enlarged. Valves of the pulmonary artery healthy. Considerable portions of the lining membrane of the aorta and pulmonary artery, were of a scarlet tint. The cut muscular walls of the left ventricle of a dark red color. Lining membrane over the foramen ovale, much thickened and of a white color.

Alimentary canal—Blood-vessels, intensely congested throughout the whole alimentary canal (stomach included). Solitary glands and peyers patches swollen and many of a brownish color, lymphatic glands of the abdomen greatly swollen.

Kidneys.—One of these organs was of the natural size, but misshapen. When cut longitudinally the cortical substance of about two-thirds of the organ presented a condition of intense congestion, while the remaining third presented the yellowish tint, indicating degeneration of the parenchyma. The other kidney was below the normal size and was still more misshapen, consisting of three large and two small lobes. When divided this organ presented the yellowish tints of degeneration, with a narrow red congested border directly under the capsule.

Spleen.—Enlarged, nearly twice the normal size, and misshapen, though normal in color and consistence. When cut the trabeculæ and parenchyma exhibited a normal appearance.

Liver.—Normal size, quite soft, normal color, though in many places paler than usual and somewhat yellowish. When cut the cut surface exhibited many small white points. The gall-bladder contained a golden colored bile.

Lungs normal.

Case No. 9—Donacien Ourblanc.—Age 36 years; native of Lafayette Parish, Louisiana;

has resided in the town of Abbeville, Lafayette Parish, during the last 22 years; is a carpenter by trade: habits temperate.

Admitted to the Charity Hospital of New Orleans January 14, 1880, ward 29.

Immediately upon the completion of my examination of this case, I decided that it was undoubtedly Oriental leprosy, and transferred him to ward 13, where the preceding case (No. 8—Numa Keen) was under treatment.

He states that his mother was, during the last five years of her life, subject to an affection of the skin, which produced disfigurement and discolorations of the countenance, and more especially of the nose, and falling of the eyelashes. She died from this disease at the age of 55 years.

On inquiry, it was ascertained that a man by the name of Felix Ourblanc, who was admitted to the Charity Hospital, ward 30, with leprosy, during the early part of the summer of the year 1878, was a brother of this patient.

Donacien Ourblanc stated that he has two other brothers and a sister in good health, and without any evidence of being afflicted with leprosy. He also affirmed that he has a first cousin whom the doctors of his neighborhood pronounced had leprosy.

. The following history of his case was elicited after much questioning :

Previous to the occurrence of his present ailment, the only physical trouble with which he had ever suffered, was a gun-shot wound of the thigh, inflicted about nine years ago.

Five years ago he first noticed an erythematous eruption upon the right half of his chin, causing a furfuracious desquamation, and the loss of his beard at the situation of the eruption. This was followed by the loss of the eye-lashes and eyebrows. About the same time, the skin on those parts began to present the peculiar discoloration, which at present extends over the greater portion of the body. From these points, the disease spread gradually over the whole face, invading the mouth, tongue pharynx, larynx and ocsophargus.

About one and a half years ago, the lower and upper extremities were invaded. Occasionally, oedema of the lower extremities supervened when at his work, which disappeared at night upon assuming the recumbent posture. Patient suffered a great deal from dyspnœa and with orthopnœa, previous to, and subsequently to his admission to the Charity Hospital, which symptoms occasioned much loss of sleep.

In order to relieve the difficulty of breathing from the thickening and ulceration of the mucous membrane of the larynx, it became necessary to perform the operation of tracheotomy. This operation, without doubt, prolonged life, but was also the source of much subsequent suffering.

The patient also states that repeated epistaxis preceded the first appearance of the leprous eruption.

At the time of the admission of Donacien Ourblanc, the disease affects the whole of the face and neck, hands and forearms, and the legs up to the knees. These parts present a brownish hue, thickened nodulated skin and rigid epidermis, with entire absence of pain. Sensation does not appear to be greatly impaired about the face and neck, whilst anæsthesia is well marked in the fingers, and more especially in the last three of the left hand. The feet and legs also in the neighborhood of the ulcers have lost their normal sensation and sensibility. The skin in these parts presents a more reddish, smooth and glossy hue than elsewhere. Nodulations exist upon the fingers, which are most numerous upon those of the left hand.

The nails of the right hand present an abnormal translucent appearance; those of the middle and ring finger of the left hand are invaded by the disease; the former is nodulated and presents a small dry non-granulating ulcer on its outer edge. .

The ulcers upon the legs began to make their appearance two years ago, in the neighborhood of the ankle joints. At the time of his admission to the Charity Hospital, there are five ulcers, three on the left leg, and two on the right leg around the ankles, the largest being about 3½ inches in the long diameter and 2 inches in the short diameter.. These ulcers are deeply eroded, uncovered by scabs and of a purplish, greyish unhealthy hue, without granulations, and discharge a foul fœtid ichorous discharge.

Under the microscope the blood of the patients as well as the discharges from the ulcers presented appearances similar to those recorded in the preceding case.

The eyebrows and eyelashes have fallen; the lips are somewhat deformed, and present nodulations; nodulations were also observed in various portions of the face, and also upon those portions from whence the eyebrows have been removed. The mucous membrane of his lips and mouth presents a smooth and dry appearance.

The nose has lost portions of the bone, and is flattened and drawn towards the left side. Numerous small dilated blood vessels are seen in various portions of the face. But the ramifications of these vessels are easily detected in the nose and chin. The tongue presents bluish, smooth and elevated areas, along the middle line; the papiliae enlarged and nodulated. On the tip of the tongue; to the left of the meridian line, an excavated non-granulated and painful ulcer is found. The whole organ, as well as the mucous membrane of the mouth and fauces and pharynx, give painful sensations when used. A circumscribed arc of congestion is seen in the left anterior pillars of the fauces ; the rest of the mucous

PLATE 2.
LEPROSY IN LOUISIANA.

FIG. 5.
NUMA KERN.

FIG. 6.
DONACIEN OURBLANC.

FIG. 7.
FATHER BOGLIOLI.

membrane of the month and fauces presenting on the contrary a lighter color than usual. At the roof of the pharynx, the mucous membrane is nodulated and hyperæmic; complains of dysphagia and dyspnœa. The voice is much altered, being husky; articulation is difficult. The patient is harrassed by a croupy cough, which is worse at night, and attended with a scanty mucous expectoration.

The breath is foul, disgusting and sickening.

Appetite and digestion good; does not complain of the loss of taste, sight, audition or smell. The eyes do not appear to be affected at all by the disease.

The patient appeared to be adverse to the free expression of the past history of his disease, and was very reticent about his family. Says that he continued to work at his trade until a very recent period, when the dyspnœa, depending upon an invasion of the respiratory passages by the leprous disease, prevented the performance of labor of any kind.

The difficulty of breathing increased to such an alarming extent that, in the month of February, 1880, it was found to be necessary to perform tracheotomy, and to introduce a silver tube into the larynx, through which the patient continued to breathe for several months up to the time of his death on the 10th of December, 1880.

The nitrate of silver, red iodide of mercury, iodide of potassium and free. iodine and other remedies, were in turn employed, but without any beneficial effect.

No local application appeared to stay the march of the ulcerations.

On the first of April, when my duties at the Charity Hospital were temporarily suspended the patient although able to move around the hospital, was evidently weaker than when he had entered the hospital, and erosion of the textures were progressing.

I attributed the accelerated progress of the disease in a measure to the confinement and impure air of the hospital.

Although free ventilation was maintained in ward 13, and disinfectants were freely used the patient and Keen communicated a most foul and disgusting smell.

Upon resuming my duties at the Charity Hospital :—

Figures 3 and 4, plate 1, and fig. 6, plate 2, represent the appearance of the patient on the first of October, 1880.

I found Donacien Ourblanc in even a more pitiable condition than when I had left him in April ; he was confined to his bed ; coughed incessantly ; the ulcer of the legs had made extensive ravages, exposing the under achilles ; and the bowels were loose, the discharges being of the most offensive and foul character.

The entire ward was pervaded by heavy fœted smell, which in despite good ventilation and the free use of chloride of lime and other disinfectants, was almost unbearable.

Death happily came to the relief of this wretched man on the tenth of December, 1880.

The fatal issue appeared to have been hastened by the foul and exhausting discharges from the bowels.

It is worthy of note that although the preceding cases, Nos. 8 and 9, were treated in ward 13, which contained at all times some 20 patients suffering from paralysis of various kinds and induced by various causes, chronic articular rhumatism, epilepsy or constitutional syphilis, in no instance was the disease transmitted.

The following case presents special points of interest, and appears to sustain the generally received opinion as to the contagious nature of Oriental leprosy :

Case 10.—*Charles Boglioli, Catholic Priest.*—Charity Hospital, December 6th, 1879 Age, 66 years; height, 5 feet 11¼ inches; weight, in health, 205 pounds. Powerful, well-formed, erect, active, muscular man. Native of the Appennine Mountains, in the province of Lumbardy, about 40 miles from Genoa, Italy. Resided amongst the mountains in this portion of Italy until he attained the age of 26 years. From Italy he went to Paris, France, where he remained two months, and from thence crossed the Atlantic directly to New Orleans, which port he reached December, 1840. Remained in New Orleans three months and then went to Missouri, and remained in this State and Ohio (Perry County, Cape Giradeau and St. Louis, Mo., Brown County, Ohio,) until the month of February, 1850, when he returned to New Orleans. During the years 1847-1848, he filled the chair of geography in the Catholic College at Cape Giradeau.

In 1850 he remained only a short time in New Orleans, and went to Donaldsonville, Lonisiana. Had yellow fever in this place in 1856, and was attended by Drs. Johnson and McCormick. Was regarded as dangerously ill. Served as chaplain to the Donaldsonville Cannoniers for eleven months, 1861–1862; and then returned to Donaldsonville, where he remained until 1866, when he removed to New Orleans. I made the acquaintance of Father Boglioli in the winter of 1868. He was then in good health; erect and strong, with clear, ruddy complexion. The first symptoms of ill health were manifested during the winter of 1875. Up to this date he had enjoyed robust and uninterrupted good health, with the exception of the attack of yellow fever in 1856. During the winter of 1876, during a visit to Donaldsonville, took a "severe catarrh" in his head, which caused swelling of the mucous membrane of the nostrils, and impeded respiration. In 1877 Father Boglioli consulted me with reference to the "catarrh in his head." The mucous membrane of the nostrils were swollen and nodulated, and it was difficult for the patient to "breathe through his nose." Gradually the skin of the nose and face become nodulated, and lost their healthy hue, assuming a dirty bronzed color. The mucous membrane of the mouth and tongue also became ulcerated, and painful; both hot and cold liquids being disagreeable. A sore on the left leg appeared in 1878, and at the same time the lower extremities, especially the soles of the feet, manifested aberrations of sensation. The integumen of the lower extremities became thickened and discolored. Standing and walking felt painful, and at night the parts burned and tingled, as if they had been withdrawn from a "very *hot water bath.*" The leprous ulcer was about one-half of an inch in diameter, and appeared after the affection of the schneiderian membrane. This ulcer is now healed, and no other ulcerations have appeared upon the upper and lower extremities.

The nails became affected about one year ago. At the present time, December 6th, 1879, the nails are thin, corrugated opaque, with a scaly deposit underneath, and their extremities are lifted up from the fingers from the pressure of this scaly deposit.

Skin of hands scaly, with a densely mottled, purplish and bronzed hue.

Skin of lower extremities thickened, nodulated and discolored.

Lips and fances of paptient of an unhealthy purplish and bronzed hue. Large ulcer about one inch in the long (transverse diameter) elevated edges, depressed raw surface of a grayish yellowish coat in fauces.

Father Boglioli says that he has lost the sense of smell and, to a great extent, that of taste. Suffers greatly when cold or hot liquids are taken into the mouth.

When he sleeps at night is compelled to keep his mouth open on account of the difficulty of breathing through the thickened nodulated mucous membrane of his nostrils.

The burning sensation in the soles of the feet especially (and a painful sensation in the lower extremities, generally when walking,) was most intense during the first three months of his illness, and, for a time, greatly impeded locomotion, has almost entirely disappeared, and, with the exception of the difficulty of breathing through the nostrils and the painful sensations in the mouth and throat during the act of swallowing, Father Boglioli affirms that, at the present time, he feels strong and well, and has sufficient strength to attend to his duties amongst the sick and dying.

During the earlier and more active stages of his disease lost considerable flesh, but has been increasing in weight of late, and now weighs about 170 pounds, his weight in health being 205 pounds.

Examination of Blood, December 6, 1879. Blood presents a much richer and more concentrated appearance, than that of the preceeding case. Blood corpuseles (colored) well formed, not distorted in shape, and after abstraction adhere together, forming rolleaux as in the blood of inflammation. Colorless corpuscles appeared in the usual proportion to the colored corpuscles, and no bacteria or extraneous or abnormal bodies were observed. I did not observe the colored pigment corpuseles which existed in the preceeding case.

The sensation in the hands is impaired, and that in the lower extremities almost entirely lost. Hair has fallen from the eye-lashes and eye-brows. He has however a full suit of grey almost white hair upon his head.

During the month of August, 1879, took nitrate of silver in pill; but without any appreciable benefit ; in fact this agent administered in doses of equal strength, as were administered in the preceeding case, appeared to derange the stomach and impair the appetite. Says that coal oil was recommended as a local application, to the surface of the extremities and that he had used it with some apparent benefit, in hardening the integrement and rendering it less sensitive to pressure and to extremes of heat and cold.

During the first two years of the disease, had little or no appetite and lost flesh progressively until his weight was reduced from 205 pounds to 157 pounds. During the past six months his appetite has returned, his physical strength has increased and he now weighs 170 pounds.

With reference to the origin of the disease, Father Boglioli states that he was reared in a high, mountainous country in Italy, where such affections, as far as his information extends, were unknown. Neither his parents, nor grand parents, nor any of his relations, as far as his information extends, had ever suffered from any constitutional or cutaneous disease.

During the past fourteen years Father Boglioli has attended daily in the wards of the Charity Hospital, administering religious consolation and extreme unction to the sick and dying, in both the male and female wards. During this period he has probably come in contact with over 50,000 cases of disease in the Charity Hospital. I have myself for eleven years been witness to his faithful labors in behalf of the Catholic Church.

He says that about six years ago he attended two cases of leprosy in ward No. 7, and administered extreme unction to them, and rubbed their hands with oil during the administration of certain religious rites. Has in like manner attended the several cases of leprosy in his capacity of religious adviser and pastor, in the male and female wards.

This case has given rise to the belief that he has contracted his distressing disease, which has altered his aspect, causing a thickened and nodulated and bronzed, mottled appearance

PLATE 3.
LEPROSY IN LOUISIANA.

FIG. 8.　　　　　　　　FIG. 9.

ROSETTA FRANCISCO.

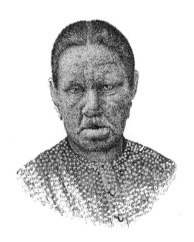
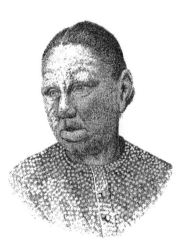

FIG. 10.　　　　　　　　FIG. 11.

FEMALE AFFLICTED WITH LEPROSY IN NEW ORLEANS.

of the entire cuticle, by contact with those suffering with leprosy in the wards of the Charity Hospital.

The appearance of Father Boglioli is represented in figure 7, plate 11.

Case 11.—*Oriental Leprosy.*—*Madame Rosetta Francisco.*—Ward 38, Charity Hospital, New Orleans, Louisiana. Age 63 years; native of Richmond, Virginia. Has resided in Algiers, Louisiana (opposite New Orleans, on the banks of the Mississippi), during the past 40 years until her admission into the Charity Hospital, April, 1874. Admitted in her 59th year.

Came to Algiers when she was 18 years of age. Gives the history of constitutional disease in her family. Her father, of Spanish descent, but born in England, died of appoplexy in Richmond, Virginia. Mother died in child-bed at her birth. Had two brothers who went to Kentucky during her infancy; has never heard of them since. Had no sisters. Both father and mother enjoyed good health up to their last illness.

Had never seen or heard of a case of leprosy until she entered the Charity Hospital in 1874, for the purpose of having her breast amputated, when she was told by the attending surgeon that she was suffering with leprosy. After the amputation of the mamma was sick only eleven days—the wound healed in this period. Has been married; has never borne children. Her husband was of intemp-rate habits, and suffered from no ailments but those caused by alcoholic drinks. Just before the recent civil war he went to France, where he died of appoplexy, supposed to have been induced by *"excessive drinking."*

Previous to the American civil war she owned a plantation and slaves and lived in comfort. During the war lost her property and was compelled to earn her living by keeping a small store.

In the winter of 1863, after a day of great fatigue and exposure, whilst crossing and recrossing the Mississippi River, the ground being covered with snow, her feet were *frost-bitten.* The toes of both feet became purple, and the skin sloughed off in different places, but the toes were not destroyed.

Mrs. Francisco, in recalling her various symptoms, fixes the date of her present disease (leprosy) at the time, or immediately after, the *"frost-bite"* of her feet.

The integuments of the toes were not only of a purple, mottled hue, but there was a tingling and aching sensation when she approached them to the fire. The feet never regained their normal sensation, and the integuments became gradually thickened, nodulated and discolored. Sensation in the lower extremities gradually diminished, and was completely lost in 1873. The discoloration of the skin of the face commenced about six years ago, and the lobes of the ears assumed a thickened, nodulated appearance. In 1874 the integument of her hands became thickened and scaly, and during this and the following year (1875) sensation was lost in the backs of her hands; and one day she discovered that a pin stuck in the back of her hand gave no pain. During the past year hard nodules have appeared upon the fingers and hands; and during the same period there has been a progressive and gradual failure of vision, hearing and taste.

There appears to have been no impairment of the intellectual faculties.

At this time, December 3, 1879, the patient is confined to her bed; complains of a numb and burning sensation in her hands and arms, which has gradually progressed from the fingers, upwards above the elbows.

The nodular swelling of the hands and face appear to lie beneath and adjacent, and attached to the discolored bronzed integument. These nodular masses are not more painful than other portions of the integument. During the past six months these nodules have at various times in different portions of the integuments of the hands and arms, ulcerated; but they have never suppurated, being bathed in a sanious fluid and emitting a disagreeable odor, presenting dark brown and grey surfaces. Breath foul and stinking. The ulcers heal and then break out again. The patient finds relief in covering the nodules and ulcers with surgeons plaster. In 1876, she suffered with catarrh of the schneiderian membrane, which has continued up to the present time. The catamenial discharge disappeared in her forty fifth year. Up to the past year had never suffered with fever but during this year has suffered with three attacks of fever, and one of dysentery.

The catamenia returned about six month ago. The patient is feeble from age and from the attacks of fever, which appear to have resembled tertian intermittent. The ears are lobulatered; the integument of the face thickened, nodulated, with a bronzed color; the eyebrows and eyelashes have disappeared; the conjunctiva is thickened, and the face has a peculiar *"frog-eyed expression."*

Appetite poor; says that she was always a moderate eater. Pulse full and strong, 92 per minute; temperature of axilla 98.5°.

The appearance presented by Madama Rosetta Francisco is represented in figures 8 and 9. The photograph of the case represented in figures No. 10 and 11, were furnished by the artist, Mr E. J. Souby.

Case of Leprosy, No. 12, *Miss Wilhelmena Boyens*, age 22; native of New Orleans; father died about 17 years ago of disease of the liver; mother died about two years ago of leprosy, father and mother natives of Germany. Has three sisters living, one in the hospital at the

28

present time (December 9, 1879,) suffering with leprosy; the others are in good health. Had one brother who died seventeen years ago of "*consumption.*" States that her mother was sick with a similar disease to that with which she and her sister are now afflicted for ten years before her death, which occurred at the age of 51 years, on the nineteenth of January, 1877. Disease appeared after she came from Germany. Miss Boyens first noticed symptoms of disease, about five years ago: "catamenia disappeared, and yellow spots appeared upon the legs; did not feel sick at this time but consulted a physician." Entered Charity Hospital, ward 21, during the latter part of November, 1879.

December 9, 1879, patient presents an aged and decrepit appearance; the surface of the face is nodulated and of a livid bronzed appearance; mouth and lips deeply eroded and partly *eaten away* by leprous sores. Nodulations of the skin greatest around the ulcerations of the lips and mouth. An irregular broken scab exists around the mouth; the purplish discoloration being greatest in the integuments bordering the leprous ulcerations. The integument of the chin below the lower lip, is the seat of two ulcers, which occasion a burning pain. There are two leprous ulcers on the right leg and four on the left. Joints of fingers swollen and purplish; leprous ulcers on hands. Eyes present an unnatural appearance with thickened conjunctiva. Palate and nares eroded by leprous ulcers; suffers with *sore throat;* voice husky and weak. Pulse weak, 88; temp. of axilla 98.0°. Speaks in a whisper, but articulation is more distinct than that of her sister. The change in her voice appears to be due to the alteration and ulcerations of the palate, fauces and larynx. Tongue smooth, and red and ulcerated; patient cannot protrude the tongue beyond the lips, and the mouth is opened with pain and difficulty. Suffers with a cough and muco; purulent, offensive expectoration. Says that her tongue gets very dry at night. Complains of disturbed and insufficient sleep. After eating suffers with pains in the abdomen. Has most generally two actions on the bowels daily. Has occasional cephalalgia in the day time, which is relieved by moving about.

Appearance of Miss Wilhelmena Boyens represented in figures 12 and 13, plate 10. This unfortunate woman died May 28, 1880.*

Case of Leprosy, Case 13. *Miss Glendena Boyens,* sister of Miss Wilhelmena Boyens, whose case has just been briefly detailed. These sisters have resided on Esplanade street; age 19 years; has had leprosy about five years, and although younger than her sister, the disease appeared in her case one year earlier. Entered the Charity Hospital, ward 21, at the same time with her sister, in November 1879. See figures 14 and 15, plate 10.

With reference to the origin of her disease, she states that at the age of 14 years she first felt a rush of blood to her head, then slight headaches followed every day; then her nose began to bleed; then headaches came on alternate days, commencing at sunrise and disappearing at sunset, subsequently yellow spots appeared upon the legs, which she states resembled "*pieces of yellow leather,*" unattended with pain. Then a node or nodule appeared upon right leg, which pained very much when the patient kneeled. The integument of the face became nodulated and changed to a bronze color. The patient has never had the catamenial discharge (menses), the disease having appeared at the time.

Two years ago her face became nodulated (fourteenth year) and disfigured, and the complexion which was originally fair has become changed to a brownish hue.

December 7, 1879 :—Has lost one toe and part of first toe from left foot; had ulcers upon right foot, but they have since healed. Has lost the nail from second toe of right foot; the nails are also partially destroyed from first and third toe of right foot. Extremities of a purplish brown appearance. Ulcers broke out upon hands about two years ago. Patient cannot breath through the nostrils. Mouth fauces, and hard palate ulcerated. Voice weak. Integument of face of a mottled and bronzed appearance, and seamed and scarred with cicatrices of healed ulcers. Mouth very much disfigured by leprous ulcerations and nodulations, and cannot be opened but to a slight extent. The eyelashes and eyebrows have disappeared; the lower eyelids are œdematous, cornea semi-opaque and eyesight much impaired. Articulation of words very indistinct and difficult. Tongue ulcerated, glazed and red, and purple with red streaks. Feels sore and painful during deglutition. Hands dis-

---

*Dr. H. D. Schmidt has furnished the following notes of the autopsy:
Lungs—Apparently healthy, but flabby, collapsing to an unusual extent when the thorax was opened.
Heart—Normal.
Alimentary Canal—The blood-vessels of the stomach and intestines were congested. The mucous membrane of the duodenum and portions of the small intestines were colored brownish yellow, as if strained by bile. A considerable number of the solitary and peyers glands were thickened and of a brownish tint. The glands of peyer in the lower portion of the ilium appeared to be more diseased than those in the upper part of the intestine. Some ulcers were observed in the mucous membrane of the ilium and ascending transverse color. Some brown and black spots were observed in the fibrous coat of the ascending colon. The mesenteric lymphatic glands were swollen, and of a blue color from congestion. The lymphatic glands generally of the abdomen and thorax were in the same condition.
Kidneys—Normal in size; cortical substance when cut presented a yellowish appearance; surface of these organs smooth, but they appeared to be rather flabby.
Spleen—Rather smaller than usual, narrow and elongated in form.
Supra Renal Capsules—Elongated in form.
Uterus and Ovaries—Quite small.
Bladder—Normal.

PLATE 4.
LEPROSY IN LOUISIANA.

FIG. 12.　　　　　　　　FIG. 13.

WILHELMENA BOYENS.

FIG. 14.　　　　　　　　FIG. 15.

GLENDENA BOYENS.

lored and scarred, as in the case of the face ; the fingers presented a mottled purplish and cerated surface. Ten deep brown scabs are evident upon the left hand ; the largest ulration, round in form with elevated edges, is situated just behind the third met:carpeolalangieal articulation. Thirteen scabs and ulcers on the right hand. The palms of both Inds present ulcerations on the lower extremities; the integument of which is thickened ; uscles of leg atrophied.

Appetite good, bowels regular, sleep disturbed, restless. Pulse 94, temperature of ax.lla ¿.75⁰. This patient although only 19 years of age looks and speaks like a decrepid old oman of at least 70 years of age.

Both sisters, Miss Glendina and Miss Wilhelmina Boyens, expresses the belief that their sease was contracted from their mother, upon whom they attended during her protracted lness.

These facts in like manner sustain the view of the contagious nature of oriental leprosy, s well as its hereditary constitution.

The appearance of Miss Glenadina Boyens is represented in figures 14 and 15.

Miss Benedina Boyens was discharged from the Charity Hospital November 6th, 1880, and eturned to her home in the city, 382 Barracks street, where she lies in a critical condition.

The following cases of leprosy have been discharged from the Charity Hospital during he past year :

Case 14.—Charity Hospital, Ward 38.—*Johann Domingo.* Admitted May 6th, 1880 , ative of Germany ; homeless ; from lower coast : in New Orleans 1 days ; married ; has een sick 13 years. Discharged June 4th, 1880.

Case 15.—Charity Hospital, Ward 13.—*Antonio Gaspaire.* Admitted June 21st, 880 ; native of France ; gardener by occupation ; residence 74 St. Phillip street ; aged 58 ears ; native of Havana ; resident of New Orleans 20 years ; widower ; sick 4 years. Discharged July 24, 1880.

Case 16.—Ward 4½.—*William Ross.* Admitted May 18th, 1880 ; native of Russia ; cook ; esidence 196 Camp street, came to New Orleans from Boston ; has resided in New Orleans 0 years. Discharged October 21st, 1880. The disease has only recently manifested itself.

At the present date, December 27th, 1880, I can learn of but one case of eprosy remaining in the Charity Hospital, namely, case 11, Madame Rosetta Francisco, Ward 38.

RESULTS OF INVESTIGATION OF LEPROSY ON THE BAYOU LAFOURCHE, LOUISIANA.

The Legislature of Louisiana, having considered the reported existence of leprosy on the Bayou Lafourche, of sufficient importance to pass a resolution requesting the Board of Health to make an investigation, and the Police Jury of Lafourche having urged the necessity of the proposed inquiry, the President of the Board of Health responded at the earliest practicable moment.

· On the second of October, 1880, the town of Thibodeaux, on the Bayou Lafourche, was selected as the starting point of the inquiry, and the following document was prepared by the President of the Police Jury :

OFFICE POLICE JURY, PARISH OF LAFOURCHE, ⎱
Thibodeaux La., October 2, 1880. ⎰

To whom it may concern :—

Dr. Joseph Jones, President of the Board of Health, of the State of Louisiana, is now at the request of the Police Jury of this parish, on a visit inquiring into the facts concerning *leprosy* said to exist on the *Lower Lafourche.*

All citizens are requested to furnish him with such facilities as are possible, to enable him to accomplish his object.   S. J. GRISAMORE, President.

Colonel Grisamore appointed Mr. John Reagan as guide, a citizen well acquainted with the section of the parish in which it was proposed to prosecute the investigation.

An excellent conveyance was also provided by the Police Jury, under the efficient management of Mr. H. Tetrau, a resident of Thibodeaux. I was also accompanied by my son, Stanhope Jones.

It having been reported that the children of lepers, and some who were suffering with this disease, were attending the public schools and mingling with healthy children, an intense feeling of anxiety and distrust had been excited in the minds of some of the citizens of Lafourche.

A consultation was held with the President of the Police Jury, Colonel S. J. Grisamore, and with Drs. Dancerau, Rogers and Fleetwood, practitioners of surgery and medicine in Thibodeaux, and it was ascertained that at this time no case of leprosy existed in this neighborhood, and only two had come within the knowledge of the physicians above named since the close of the civil war in 1865.

During this conference the belief was expressed that cases of leprosy would be found in and around Lockport, some twenty-one miles below Thibodeaux, on the Lower Lafourche.

Major Grisamore furnished a memorandum of cases which had been reported to the Police Jury.

After leaving Thibodeaux on the second of October, the inquiry was conducted along the banks of the Bayou Lafourche towards the Gulf of Mexico.

A consultation was held with Dr. Gazzo, Sr., at his office and residence, about ten miles below Thibodeaux. This old practitioner stated that no lepers would be found before the President of the Board of Health had passed beyond Lockport. Dr. Gazzo also expressed his belief as based upon an extensive practice extending over near half a century, that there were at present, fewer persons afflicted with this disease in Lafourche than formerly.

When Lockport was reached, a consultation was held with Drs. J. Caillouet, C. Melanson, Dr. J. Gazzo Jr. and Mayor Barker, and it was ascertained that nearly all the authenticated cases of leprosy were situated below Harang's canal on the Lower Lafourche.

The general results of this investigation may be thus formulated:

1· The entire region of country traversed by the Bayou Lafourche is low level alluvial land, which slopes back from the river to the cypress swamps and marshes.

The waters of Bayou Lafourche are restrained within high artificial embankments or levees, which have been annually accumulating in height.

It has been held by many that the system of artificial levees, has caused a gradual rise in the bed of this river.

The low inhabited strips of land on either side of the Bayou are elevated but a few feet above the level of the Gulf of Mexico, and are at all times several feet below the line of high water in the turbid bayou, and the entire area of habitable and cultivatable land is subject to overflow from floods and crevasses.

This region is adapted by soil and climate, to the cultivation of rice, sugarcane and the orange.

Large tracts of country below Harang's canal are devoted solely to the cultivation of rice, the fields of this grain being irrigated with water from the bayou.

Below Harang's canal along both banks of the bayou, towards the Gulf of Mexico, the narrow strips of land are thickly populated by small farmers; and in many instances the habitations arranged behind the levees are surrounded by rice fields.

I observed places where rice was cultivated up to the very doors of the houses.

It is evident, therefore, that the inhabitants of the Lower Lafourche, are subject to the constant action of a low moist malarial atmosphere. *

Another point of interest in this inquiry, is that the diet of these people consists largely of rice, fish and wild birds and animals, as the various varietes of duck, cranes, snipe, wood-cock, raccoon, opossum, squirrels and rabbits.

It is said that a fish-eating people are ill-nourished, and in Eastern countries are particularly liable to become leprous. If this be so, it must be associated with such poverty as prevents the inhabitants from obtaining a proper variety of fresh food and vegetables Certain districts on the Mediterranean Coast of Spain, are cited in illustration of these facts, where there is a fish-eating and a poverty-stricken population; and it we turn to another fish-eating community—that of part of the west coast of Norway—we find the disease, although some of the people are characterized by robustness of health and great physical strength.

It is possible that the prolongation of the leprosy in this and similar regions, whilst it appears to have gradually become extinct in the more elevated and healthier portions of Louisiana, may in a measure be due to the effects of climate, soil and food; but from the result of our investigation we are convinced that in its first origin the disease must be traced beyond the confines of this State, to the Southern States of Europe and to the coast of Africa.

In other words, the disease on the Lower Lafourche has been propagated by hereditary influences, and by personal contact, rather than engendered by climate, soil and food. The latter causes may of course form important factors in the prolongation of the disease through several generations.

It is possible that the seed of the disease imported originally from the south of Europe, and from the French settlements of Canada, would have perished in more elevated and healthy regions.

The habits of the Creoles of the Lower Lafourche, appeared to be temperate and simple; the education of many of the citizens appeared to be limited from the nature of the country, and the necessity of maintaining large families upon comparatively small areas of land. It is evident therefore, that under these circumstances, the contiguous settlements were often closely related by ties of friendship and blood.

A rumor having been circulated amongst these people, that the object of the inquiry suggested to the Board of Health by the Legislature of Louisiana, was simply to ascertain who were lepers, in order that they might be forcibly seized and carried off in ships and abandoned upon some uninhabited isolated lonely island in the sea, they were exceedingly cautious about communicating any substantial or detailed information as to the number and precise location of the unfortunate victims of leprosy.

This rumor appeared to find some confirmation in the minds of these un-

---

* To what extent the water of the Bayou Lafourche affects the health of the inhabitants. I was unable to determine. On the evening of the third of October, my son Stanhope, was suddenly seized with severe vomiting and purging, on the banks of the bayou near the cut-off. The vomited matters contained blood, and the discharges from the bowels consisted of almost pure blood.
Had not Lockport been reached about 1 o'clock at night, when the appropriate remedies were procured, his case would have terminated fatally. He had suffered with yellow fever in 1878.
I attributed this attack of "malarial hemorrhagic fever." to the combined influence of the malaria of the rice fields, and to the waters of the Bayou Lafourche. My thanks are due to Drs. Cailhouet, Melansou and Gazzo, and to Mayor Barker, for efficient and kind assistance.

fortunate beings, by the dread which their neighbors manifested to hold com-munication with them, and by the exclusion in certain localities of the chil-dren of families tainted with leprosy from the public schools.

2. Undoubted cases of Oriental Leprosy were met with on both banks of the Bayou Lafourche below Harang's canal.

No measure short of an accurate census of the entire district, can reveal the total number of cases, but after diligent inquiry and personal investiga-tion I was unable to ascertain the undoubted existence at the present time of more than twelve cases of this disease in the tenth ward, Parish of Lafourche.

Major S. J. Grisamore, President of the Police Jury, estimated the entire number at about fourteen cases.

The testimony of one of the most active and intelligent citizens living above the cut-off, was to the effect that at the present time only six families are known to present cases of this disease.

The following important information was furnished by a citizen of great activity and intelligence, who although not a graduate of a regular school of medicine, has worthily rendered aid to the citizens of the Lower Lafourche, and more especially of Cheniere Caminada. where he now resides.

It should be noted that the settlement of the Cheniere Caminada lies near the mouth of the Bayou Lafourche, the observations of this citizen, therefore who has had an extended experience from Thibodeaux to the Gulf, apply to the entire region of the parish of Lafourche, in which the leprosy has been reported.

CHENIERE CAMINADA, October 3, 1880,

Dr. Joseph Jones. Professor of Chemistry, Medical College, and President of the Board of Health, State of Louisiana, New Orleans, La :

Dear Sir—In conformity with my promise to give you all the information within my knowledge on the subject of scrofula or leprosy, in the parishes of Lafourche and Jefferson, I beg leave to represent, 1st. That I am acquainted with almost all the cases under dis-cussion, as well as with all the families either tainted or affected with the awful disease; in behalf of science and humanity, I feel I must tell the whole truth about it, so far as my knowledge extends, leaving you to judge from my statement of facts and from your own personal information, whether there is any adequate remedy for either the prevention or relief of that awful malady.

The families affected or tainted with that malady, ought to be divided into two distinct classes: 1st, those who, through inheritance, may only be tainted with *elephantiasis*; and 2nd those who are actually affected with the malady.

There are in the parish of Lafourche, 1st. tainted or subject to it by inheritance.

The * * * * family living around Raceland.

The * * family living around Crossing.

Proof.—Mme. * * * * Sen., was a * * * * by birth, and died of elephan-tiasis. Mme. * * * * was born a * * and is now lingering under the affliction, her husband * * died of it two years ago, I believe he having been affected through the close connection from his wife. We have lower down the Lafourche, at the cut-off * * * *, who is now affected with elephantiasis, and in my opinion has gone too far without medical aid to be relieved. I am unable to say whether that case has come through inheritance or through contact. Then again at the cut-off, two sons of * * * whom I believe are affected by inheritance from their grandmother, the family of * * * *, six miles below the cut-off, may be tainted with it, but to my knowledge no member of that family are presently affected; two years ago I was called upon to at-tend upon one of * * daughters, * *, aged eleven years, her whole body was covered with what seemed to be a ringworm affection, her fingers were clutched together, and since the last seven years she had lost the use of her hands, the sole of her right foot was tinged with a thick scrofulus ejection or crust a quarter of an inch thick, and she had two very bad scrofulus ulcers to the same; by the use of generous diet, and proper and judicious tonics, that girl is entirely cured, not a trace of the awful sickness being visible on her; she has recovered the use of her hands, and now that she has reached the age of puberty, I hope she will never relapse; "this cure is entirely due to prescrip-tions from you received." Lower down, * *, sister to the aforenamed * *, and her husband, * * * are affected with it, and passed human relief, further down you have * * and son, who are affected, but who I believe may be yet cured by a judicious treatment. I know of no hereditary tinge in this case, and I am certain they had it by contact with * * * and her husband. Few miles down the bayou you have the family of the late * * *, who may be set as tainted with it, although there is no actual case of sickness from the malady amongst them, * * , the head of the family, died of confirmed elephantiasis four or five years ago, he was a brother of * * , wife of * * stated above. In the case of * *, my belief is that you have been misinformed, I am well acquainted with the family, and I am free to state that the sickness now existing in that family, is due only to disorder in the function of the liver, owing to poverty and the malaria existing in their locality, their sickness is jaundice or Ieterus.

At Cheniere Caminada, we have three cases of elephantiasis, in the family of * *, a cousin to the * * from Lafourche, his wife and two children are now affected with it.

These are all the cases under my immediate knowledge doctor, and should I be able to be helpful to you in any way, shape or form, in assisting to the relief or the prevention of the sickness, you may call on me for help at any time you may elect, and I will be ready at your call. Respectfully and truly your obedient servant,

F. C. * *.

P. S. I must state something about elephantiasis in Lafourche, which I had omitted above.

The family of the * * are tainted with it. Prof. * * Sen., now diseased, joined in matrimony with one * * *. He had previously been married to one * *, out of his first marriage he had five or six children, none of which were ever affected, nor did I ever hear the * * families were ever tainted with it, but out of his second marriage with * *. Old man * * had a numerous family, two of whom died of confirmed elephantiasis, the balance of the issue being now in good health. Those must be classified as tainted from inheritance by their mother.

Respectfully yours, F. C. * *.

3. The leprosy of the Lower Lafourche, in many of the cases if not in all, can be shown to be inherited. Thus in the case of Mr. G., living on the left bank of the Bayou Lafourche about two and a half miles below Harang's canal, the following facts were ascertained by actual investigation :

Mr. G., aged about forty years ; father of ten children, six boys and four girls. Wife of Mr. G. living in good health.

The mother of Mr. G. was attacked with leprosy before the recent civil war, and suffered with the disease fourteen years, and died at the age of 60 years, in 1872, the disease therefore is supposed to have commenced about 1858.

The mother of Mr. G. had five children ; three males and two females. Up to the present time only one of her children, Madame B., living below the cut-off is afflicted with leprosy.

Madame B., has suffered with leprosy eight years, and is said to be in a most deplorable condition.

The father of Mr. G., was a native of St. John the Baptist Parish, Louisiana, and died of heart diseases in 1880. It does not appear that he contracted the disease from his wife. Grandfather and grandmother of Mr. G., born in Louisiana; could not ascertain anything further than that they were of French descent.

Of the ten children of Mr. G., only one is afflicted with leprosy ; a young lad of sixteen years of age.

Although sixteen years of age, he presents the appearance of a boy of about ten years of age.

Although the remaining nine children appear to be in good health and present clear healthy complexions, this young lad presents the sallow, bronzed, unhealthy hue, which is so common in the lepers of Louisiana.

The face presents a nodulated appearance; has lost one or more joints of the fingers off each hand ; also the joints of several toes. Has suffered with ulcers upon the legs and feet, which are swollen and discolored. Walks with a halting, uncertain gait. He is, however, cheerful and industrious, and assists in the lighter duties about the rice field (which completely surrounds the house) as the preservation of the rice from the ravages of the jackdaws and rice birds.

The leprosy is of the anæsthetica variety, as is manifest from the want of sensibility in his hands. His father and mother state that he frequently seizes the birds which are roasting upon the burning coals of fire in his hands, and can even handle the burning embers without apparent pain.

The eldest son of Mr. G., is twenty years of age ; married and the father of a fine healthy infant.

We have then the following facts :

a. Mother of Mr. G. attacked with leprosy in 1858, died 1872, from ravages of the disease.

b. The husband of Mrs. G. did not contract the disease, but died of heart disease in 1880.

c. Of the five children resulting from the preceding marriage up to the time of the investigation, October 3, 1880, only one daughter, Madame B., has manifested symptoms of leprosy, which appeared five years after the disease had been developed in her brother.

d. Of the ten children of Mr. G., only one manifests symptoms of leprosy.

. e. The eldest son of Mr. G., is the father of a fine healthy infant.

Such facts would seem to indicate that the disease may apparently skip over one or more generations, and that an apparently healthy man, although descended from a leprous mother, may engender both healthy and leprous children, without contaminating his wife.

4. Some of the cases of leprosy appear to have been contracted from contact or contagion.

Instances were cited where the disease was said to have been propagated to men by contact with leprous women.

5. The ravages of the disease were in some of the cases, of a most distressing character. Thus, in company with my son Stanhope, a case was visited and carefully examined on the right bank of the Bayou Lafourche, about three and a half miles below Harang's canal.

The patient, Mr. L., occupied a small hut, thatched with palmettoes, which he had erected with his own hands.

This leper who had lived alone and isolated from his neighbors, had lost one eye from the ravages of the disease, the face presented a nodulated, scarred appearance; several of the fingers and toes had been destroyed, and the legs were covered with large foul stinking ulcers, which the poor sufferer had wrapped in large green leaves of some succulent plant.

This man formerly owned a lugger, and peddled goods amongst those suffering with leprosy further down the bayou below the cut-off.

He attributes the disease to the effects of cold, and said that upon one occasion in digging a grave in winter his feet were frost-bitten.

I was unable to gain any accurate information as to his ancestors.

This man also had to a great extent lost the sensation in his feet and hands, and affirmed that he could handle fire (burning coals) with his hands, without experiencing any unpleasant sensation.

This man supported himself by planting a small field of rice.

Nobody associated with him, he was avoided by his relations, and was almost as completely isolated as if he had lived upon an island.

This was clearly a case of *lepra* anæsthetica, in which the disease of the nerves presented a high pathological interest.

Pathologists have shown that beginning probably with the nerves which supply the original leper spot, by degrees, the chief nerves which go to the hands and feet, become infiltrated with a peculiar deposit, which renders them of twice their natural size. It seems to invade the nerves as soon as they pierce the fascia, and they can often be felt under the skin, as rounded cords, perhaps nodulated; deeper trunks are affected later.

The consequences of this nerve disease are the same as when nerves are irritated by injury, that is to say, loss of sensation in the skin, atrophy of the skin, which losses its hair, *bullae* of *pemphigus,* which often lead to deep ulcers; atrophy of the muscles, and above all atrophy of the bones, beginning with those of the last joints of the fingers or toes.

The bones first become thin and slender, then absolutely vanish by absorption, so that the finger nails may find themselves on the ends of the metacarpal bones, through the disappearance of the parts between.

This process of mutilation is often hastened by abscess and necrosis of the bones.

Dr. Macrea has pointed out the interesting fact, that common sensation and sensation of heat and cold seem to be properties of different nervous fibres, inasmuch as either one of them may be impaired or lost without the other. (Medical Times and Gazette, July 31, 1875. A Manuel of Modern Surgery, by Robert Druett, 1878, p. 75).

PRACTICAL CONCLUSIONS.

(a). The number of cases of leprosy upon the banks of the Lower Lafourche appear to be less than has been represented. A sufficient number of cases, however have occurred, to excite the earnest attention of the public authorities charged with the educational, sanitary and legislative affairs of the people of Louisiana.

(b). Those afflicted with leprosy should be isolated. Such seclusion or isolation, may be accomplished by the construction of a leper house, ward or hospital in those districts in which the disease exists, to be placed under the direction and control of one or more local practitioners of medicine.

(c). It is manifestly the duty of the State to provide for the maintenance of the victims of leprosy.

(d). The practice of introducing patients suffering with leprosy into the crowded wards of the Charity Hospital of New Orleans, should be discontinued, and the public authorities of the City or State should provide a suitable building or ward, where the lepers may be properly isolated and ecluded.

COMPARATIVE RATES OF MORTALITY

—IN—

NEW ORLEANS DURING THE YEAR 1880, AND IN PRECEDING YEARS.

SANITARY MEASURES NECESSARY TO THE HEALTH OF NEW ORLEANS.

MORTUARY STATISTICS.

The total deaths from all causes in the city of New Orleans during the year 1880, numbered 5623, and the death rate per 1000 inhabitants was 25.98.

With the exception of two years (1827 and 1879) the death rate of 1880 was lower than that of any year since 1787, of which any records have been preserved.

In 1827, the death rate was 24.56 per 1000 and in 1879, 23.94 per 1000.

It is of the highest importance that a general view of the mortuary statistics of New Orleans should be presented, in order that the effects of sanitary and quarantine measures should be clearly defined. It should be shown by the past and present mortuary records whether the death rate per 1000 inhabitants be decreasing or increasing; whether certain diseases are increasing or diminishing in fatality, and whether differences exist in the rates of mortality amongst the different races which compose the population of New Orleans.

In order to throw light upon these important questions, the following comprehensive statement of the mortality statistics of New Orleans with the accompanying charts have been prepared:

The tabular view of the mortuary statistics of New Orleans, contains the following tables enumerated in regular order as they have been placed upon the chart:

(a). Table illustrating the relations of the population of New Orleans, to the total mortality from all causes, during a period of ninety-four years.

(b). Table illustrating deaths and death rate from all causes and from yellow fever in the city of New Orleans, during a period of sixty-four years.

(c). Table illustrating the mortality from some of the principal diseases and total mortality, together with the death rate per 1000 inhabitants of the different districts of the city of New Orleans, for the year 1880.

(d). Census of the State of Louisiana, from the tenth census of the United States, 1880.

(e). Comparative tables of mortality by months, during the twelve years. 1869 *to* 1880, *showing deaths from some of the principal diseases; total number of deaths according to race and color, and death rate per* 1000 *inhabitants per annum.*

(f). Table showing deaths from diarrhœal diseases, by months during the twelve years 1869–1880 *inclusive.*

· *(g. . Table showing deaths from phthisis pulmonalis, during twelve years* 1869-1880 *inclusive.*

(h). Table showing deaths from malarial fevers by months, during twelve years 1869–1880.

(i). Deaths in the Charity Hospital, City of New Orleans, during the year 1880.

From the preceding data, as well as from the vital statistics and meteorlogical records of this city, the accompanying *charts have been prepared, illustrating the increase of population in the city of New Orleans, during a period of ninety-four years, together with the total mortality for each year, and the death rate per* 1000 *inhabitants per annum, also deaths from yellow fever, mean maximum and minimum temperature and rain fall for a number of years.*

Without, at the present moment, entering into an exhaustive discussion of the data recorded in the accompanying tables and charts, the following points of general interest may be noted:

1. It will be observed that the maximum death-rate per 1000 inhabitants was attained in the year 1832, when 147.01 of every 1000 inhabitants of New Orleans died. In that year (1832) both cholera and yellow fever prevailed as epidemics.

The next highest death-rate was in the memorable year 1853, when the mortality per 1000 inhabitants was 102,42, and the deaths from yellow fever alone caused nearly one-half of the total mortality—namely, 7849 out of 15,-787 deaths from all causes, or 50.90 per 1000 inhabitants.

The year 1878 will ever be distinguished by the diffusion of yellow fever over a considerable area and by the wide spread alarm excited in the valley of the Mississippi by the ravages of this pestilence. The rate of mortality, however, in 1878 was less than one-half that of 1853, being 50.70 per 1000 inhabitants from all causes, and 19.20 from yellow fever; and it was only a little more than one-third that of 1832; and it was exceeded by that of 1787, 1796, 1810, 1811, 1815, 1817, 1819, 1820, 1822, 1825, 1829, 1832, 1833, 1834, 1835, 1837, 1839, 1841, 18 4, 1847, 1848, 1849, 1850, 1851, 1852, 1853, 1854, 1855, 1858 and 1867.

2. There has been an evident decline in the death-rate of New Orleans during the past 20 years—1860-1880. Of course we do not in this statement fail to note the high death-rate (55.57) of 1867, caused by cholera and yellow fever; of 1873 (40.19) and of 1878 (50.70), embraced in the period 1860-1880. The decline of the mortality rate during the period specified (1860-1880) is shown by the oscillations of the heavy black line on the chart, which represents the death-rate per 1000 inhabitants per annum from all causes.

The same fact is also illustrated by the following statement of the years, presenting the lowest death rate per 1000 inhabitants in New Orleans during the past 94 years: 1812 (32.50), 1816 (27.93), 1821 (39.57), 1826 (30.61), 1827 (24.56), 1828 (32.89), 1831 (36.71), 1838 (36.77), 1840 (39.11), 1845 (31.17), 1856 (35 24), 1857 (34.07), 1861 (33 97), 1862 (36 10), 1868 (28.96), 1869 (29.79), 1870 (36.26), 1871 (31.24), 1872 (33.54), 1874 (35.71), 1875 (32.05), 1876 (32.39), 1877 (34.32), 1879 (23.94), 1880 (25.98.)

DO NOT
SCAN

This decline in the mortality rate may be referred to several causes : (a.) The st-tionary condition of the population during the period specified (1860–1880). as shown by the line in the chart representing the increase of population in New Orleans during the past 94 years. It is cl-arly shown upon the chart that the periods characterized by the highest death-rates were precisely those periods in which the city increased most rapidly by additions from surrounding States and foreign countries; (b) the relative preponderance during these latter years of a native-born and acclimated population ; (c.) the diminution of the number of seamen entering this port, on account of the substitution of large iron steamships for wooden sailing vessels ; (d.) the institution of more rigid quarantine regulations and measures ; (e.) increased drainage of the rear portions of the city ; (f.) certain sanitary measures, as the cleansing and disinfection of privies and the removal from the city limits of night soil and garbage.

3 As far as the statistics recorded in these tables extend, they tend to sustain the view that the establishment of quarantine at the mouth of the Mississippi and at the Rigolets and on the Atchafalaya by the State of Louisiana, has tended to diminish the frequency of yellow fever epidemics ; thus from the establishment of the quarantine in 1855 to the end of 1880 (25 years) there have been but three epidemics of yellow fever of any magnitude, namely: in 1858, 1867 and 1878; whilst in the preceding 39 years (1817–1855) no less than 19 severe visitations of yellow fever have been recorded.

4. During the past seven years (that is during the period in which we have data for the calculation) the death rate has almost invariably been higher amongst the colored population than amongst the whites. This result is at variance with the popular opinion that in tropical and semi-tropical cities the black race enjoy a greater immunity from diseases, and especially from the various forms of fever than the white race. The increased rate of mortality amongst the blacks may be referred to such causes as : (a) improvidence in living ; irregular habits ; poor diet; (b) neglect of the sick ; indifference to medical aid ; neglect of vaccination; (c) crowding and imperfect ventilation ; (d) less vital power or capacity to resist the ravages of disease ; (e) ignorance of, and violation of physiological and sanitary laws. ·

Many of these causes are capable of removal or amelioration. With the advance of knowledge, and the acquisition of property by the colored race, there will be a corresponding diminution of the death-rate.

5. Phthisis pulmonalis appears to destroy as many lives in New Orleans as yellow and malarial fevers combined. Thus during the past twelve years, 1869–1880 inclusive, phthisis pulmonalis caused 9800 deaths, yellow fever 5102 and malarial or paroxysmal fevers 4854 deaths.

6. If the mortality of the past six years (1875–1880) be compared with that of the previous six years (1869–1874). it will be found that the deaths of the fi·st named period exceed but to a slight degree those of the latter, notwithstanding the epidemic yellow fever of 1878. Thus :

Total mortality for six years, 1869–1874.........................40,370
Total mortality for six years, 1875–1880.........................41,851

Excess of mortality during six years, 1875–1880................ 1,481

A portion of this difference is due to the increase of population.

This period may be characterized in the sanitary history of New Orleans, as that of the experimental use of disinfectants, and more especially of *carbolic acid.*"

Under the direction of Dr. C. B. White, President of the Board of Health

(1869–1875 inclusive), carbolic acid was more extensively used than in any other city. From the data now at hand, we find that the city of New Orleans paid the following sums for disinfectants of which carbolic acid formed the chief item.

Amount paid by the city of New Orleans for disinfectants ordered by the Board of Health: 1870, $2,851.77; 1871, $2,448.21; 1872, not recorded; 1873, $16,069.83; 1874, $2,482.35; 1875, 12,376.35; total $35,128.51.

The amount stated ($35,128.51) simply represents the amount actually paid by the city, and entered upon the records; outstanding claims are not included.

The opinion prevailed that yellow fever could be controlled and even arrested by the free use of carbolic acid : but the result of the epidemic of the year 1878, when $12,207.22 were expended for disinfectants, and more especially carbolic acid, scattered to the winds the belief that certain disinfectants, and especially carbolic acid, possessed any specific control over *epidemics* of *yellow fever.*

The signal failure of the experiments with carbolic acid disinfection, was followed by the wild panic and shot-gun quarantines of 1878.

MORTALITY OF 1880.

The accompanying charts illustrate the relations and changes of temperature—humidity and barometric pressure—to the death-rate per 1000 inhabitants during the year 1880.

The charts illustrate so fully and clearly the relations of the death-rate to meteorological conditions that any detailed explanation is unnecessary. The following points, however, are worthy of especial notice :

1. The highest mortality of 1880 occurred during the week ending the 12th of June.

2. During the six months ending June 30, 1880, the rain fall was 29.69 inches, the mean temperature 69.20°, mean barometer 30.07°; total death-rate per 1000 population, 26.84; whites 23.43, colored 36 35.

During the six months ending December 31, 1880, the rain fall was 37.68 inches; mean temperature 69.80°; mean barometer 30.09°; total death rate 25.19; whites, 22.28; colored, 33.33.

It is evident that the death rate diminished during the last six months of the year in which yellow fever most generally prevails:

3. Throughout the year 1880, the death rate of the colored race exceeded largely that of the whites.

4. If the deaths amongst the colored population be excluded from those amongst the white race, it will be seen that during 1880 the white inhabitants of New Orleans enjoyed a remarkable immunity from fatal diseases, and that this city was probably as exempt from fatal forms of disease amongst the white inhabitants as any other city of similar size in America or Europe.

RELATIVE MORTALITY IN THE SEVERAL DISTRICTS OF NEW ORLEANS.

From the table illustrating the *mortality from some of the principal diseases and total mortality together with the death rate per* 1000 *inhabitants of the different districts of New Orleans, for the year* 1880, the following important results are established :

(a). First District : Total deaths 1393; whites 884; colored 509; death

Illustrating the INCREASE of POPULATION in the CITY of NEW ORLEANS during a period of 94 years, together with the TOTAL MORTALITY for each year and the DEATH RATE per 1000 inhabitants per annum, also deaths from YELLOW FEVER. MEAN MAXIMUM, MINIMUM TEMPERATURE RAIN-FALL for a number of years, as far as obtainable. Prepared from Statistics, compiled by Prof. JOSEPH JONES, M.D. President Board of Health.

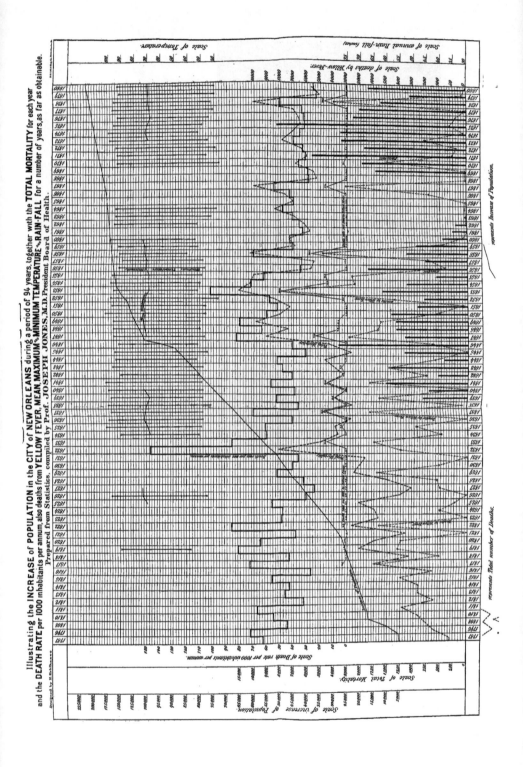

rate per 1000 inhabitants : whites 20.40 ; colored 36.10 ; death rate white and colored 24.24. In this district the death rate amongst the whites will compare favorably with that of any city in the Western or Eastern Hemisphere, whilst the death rate of the colored population, although higher than that of the whites, will compare favorably with that of the descendants of the African race in any large city in the United States. It is believed and hoped that the humane efforts of the Board of Health of the State of Louisiana will still further reduce the death rate amongst the colored population.

In the Second District total deaths 1115; whites 699, colored 416. Death rate per 1000 inhabitants, whites 22.28, colored 31.27. Total death-rate, whites and colored, 24.96. In the Second District, which lies below Canal street and embraces the first settled portions of New Orleans, or the "*city proper*," of Bienville, the death-rate was only a fraction in excess of that of the First District. This difference may be referred to the fact that there are a larger number of tenement houses in which are congregated foreigners, and especially natives of Sicily and Italy. Repeated orders were issued by the Board of Health for the cleansing and disinfection of the crowded portions of the Second District.

In the First District extending from Canal street to Felicity road, is located the new basin and canal connecting with the lake, and in the Second District extending from Canal to Esplanade street, is located the old basin and canal originally constructed by the Baron Carondelet, and communicating with the lake by the Bayou St. John.

Both the First and Second Districts, receive through the canals and basins, a considerable amount of shipping and a corresponding number of seamen.

The First District received a considerable amount of water by the flushing apparatus of the Auxiliary Sanitary Association, a portion of which found an exit in the Camp street and Melpomene canal. No case of yellow fever was reported in the Second District which had not the advantage of the flushing, whilst but three cases were reported in the First District, which have been fully detailed in the report.

In the *Third District* total deaths 1161 ; whites 774, colored 387 ; death-rate per 1000 inhabitants, whites 22.94, colored 32.62. Total death-rate 25.47.

In the Third District, extending from Esplanade street to the lower limits of the parish of Orleans, a large portion towards the swamps and lake is ill drained and subjected to the action of malaria; and the statistics show that the deaths from the various forms of malarial fever were relatively more numerous ; thus deaths from malarial fever—Fourth District, 74 ; Second District, 62 ; Third District, 82.

Without doubt, a proper system of drainage and sewerage would reduce the deaths from malarial fever to the minimum.

The cultivation of rice has been inaugurated in the rear of this district, and a portion of the sickness and mortality in this district must be referred to this the most pernicious of all forms of agriculture. The Legislature of Louisiana, the City Council of New Orleans and the Board of Health, should consider the subject of rice culture in its relations to the health of the City of New Orleans, and such ordinances should be considered and passed as will protect the inhabitants from the effects of the destructive emanations of rice fields.

In the Fourth District total mortality 720 ; whites 506, colored 214 ; death rate per 1000 inhabitants 16.52, colored 30.96. Total death rate, whites and colored, 19.18.

In the Fourth District the whites predominate greatly over the colored, and a large proportion of the inhabitants of the garden district of New Orleans, amongst whom may be mentioned its successful merchants and business men, absent themselves from the city during the hot months of Summer and Autumn, seeking health and amusement at American and European resorts of health and pleasure.

The deaths from malarial fever in 1880 in the Fourth District number 42. It should also be noted that this district offers a far less front to the woods, the swamp and the lake than the First, Second and Third Districts. This district received the benefits of the flushing system.

In the Fifth District the total mortality was 142; whites 91; colored 51; death rate per 1000 inhabitants: whites 18.12; colored 13.30; total death rate whites and colored 16.03.

The Fifth District gave the lowest mortality in 1880 of any District within the bounds of the Parish of Orleans. This district, which occupies the opposite bank of the river and may be regarded as a separate city, received none of the benefits of the flushing system or the Auxiliary Sanitary Association of New Orleans. Such facts illustrate the nature of the claim that the running of water through the gutters of the Fourth District and through a portion of the gutters of the First District, preserved the City of New Orleans from yellow fever in 1880. The Board of Health has given its countenance and support to all rational efforts to improve the health of this city, and recognizes the labors of its officers in the cleansing and disinfection of privies, the prompt removal of garbage, the disinfection and cleansing of all premises in which cases of yellow fever, typhoid fever, scarlet fever, measles and small-pox have occurred.

In the Sixth District, the total deaths numbered 329: whites, 196; colored, 123. Death rate per 1000 inhabitants: whites, 16.40; colored, 30.16. Total death rate per 1000 inhabitants, 20.52.

The colored population of the Sixth District, dominated in a measure the low death rate of the whites 16.40, which would compare favorably with the death-rate of any similar congregation of white inhabitants in any portion of the civilized world.

We have in this report recorded the relative population, white and colored, of the city of New Orleans. From this table it will be shown that the colored population is not uniformly distributed in the districts of New Orleans.

In the Sixth District malarial fever caused ten deaths and in the Fifth District 7.

In the Seventh District the total deaths numbered 128—whites 62, colored 66. Death rate per 1000 inhabitants—whites 19.92; colored 21.12; total death rate per 1000 inhabitants, 20.52. In this district the colored people, as in the Fifth District, are more comfortably situated, owning more property and being less crowded, and being also at the same time less subjected to the excitement and vices of the thickly populated portions of New Orleans, and we find a proportionately lower death rate.

As the outcome of this investigation the Board of Health has the following important results:

FIRST DISTRICT.

Death-rate per 1000 inhabitants 24.24; whites 20.40, colored 36.10.

SECOND DISRTICT.

Death-rate per 1000 inhabitants 24.96; whites 22.28, colored 31.27.

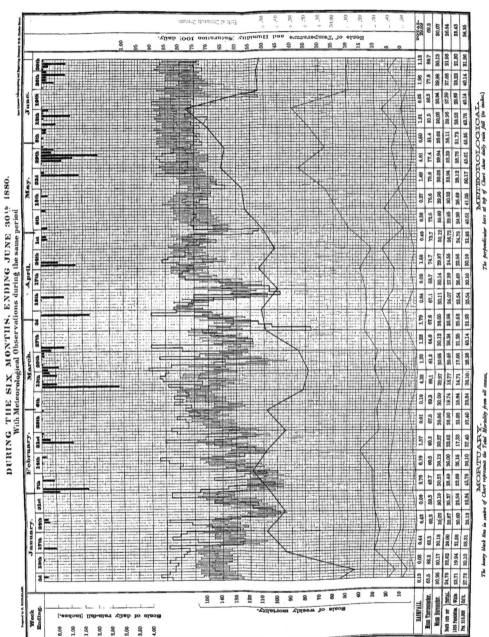

DURING THE SIX MONTHS, ENDING JUNE 30ᵗʰ 1880.
With Meteorological Observations during the same period

METEOROLOGICAL

The heavy black line in centre of Chart represents the Total Mortality from all causes.

MORTUARY

The perpendicular bars at top of Chart show daily rain-fall (in inches.)

THIRD DISTRICT.

Death-rate per 1000 inhabitants 25.47 ; whites 22.94, colored 32.62.

FOURTH DISRTICT.

Death-rate per 1000 inhabitants 19.18 ; whites 16.52, colored 30.96.

FIFTH DISTRICT.

Death-rate per 1000 inhabitants 16.03 ; whites 18.12, colored 13.30.

SIXTH DISTRICT.

Death-rate per 1000 inhabitants 20.62 ; whites 16.40, colored 30.16.

SEVENTH DISTRICT.

Death-rate per 1000 inhabitants 20.52 ; whites 19.92, colored 21.12.

From the preceding statistics it must be evident to every honest observer that this year (1880) must be regarded as a period free from any pestilential and fatal influences in New Orleans, and the earnest hope may be expressed that the Ruler of all things, will continue to vouchsafe to the people a similar exemption, in the future from epidemic diseases.

The statistics of 1880, render it evident that there is nothing in the climatic and topographical conditions of New Orleans, which precludes it from being the healthiest city in America or Europe.

With thorough sanitary regulations, with the prompt removal of all garbage and fœcal matters and with the constant destruction of the poisons of all infectious and contagious diseases, by efficient and active sanitary officers, and with a rigid but enlightened quarantine, the Board of Health may sincerely hope for continued immunity from pestilential diseases.

The absence of pestilential diseases from New Orleans, and from the valley of the Mississippi, will be followed by prosperity to all classes, and by a marked physical and moral development of all the various races congregated in the metropolis of the West.

SANITARY MEASURES AND REFORMS.

PROTECTION FROM OVERFLOW—DRAINAGE AND SEWERAGE.

The great sanitary problems of New Orleans are :

1. *Protection of the City from overflow, by substantial levees elevated at least two feet above the line of the highest waters.*

2. *Thorough surface and subsoil drainage.*

Under this head should be included the reclamation of the swamps in the rear of the city, the perfection and proper grading of gutters and surface drains, and the proper excavation, perfection, cleansing and flushing of the canals which receive the storm waters and those continually yielded by the gutters.

3. *The immediate and continuous removal of all fœcal matters.*

4. The daily removal of garbage by an efficient scavenger force.

5. *The constant repair and cleansing of the streets.*

6. *Paving the streets with the most substantial materials.*

30

Thus far the square block pavement has proved to be best adapted to the peculiar soil and location of New Orleans. The same form of gravel and small stones as those employed at the jetties by Captain Eads might be used upon many of the dirt streets. This gravel may be obtained in large quantities from an island in the Mississippi river above Baton Rouge, and might be brought down in large quantities in flat-boats and landed on the river front in any of the various districts of the city. The shells employed upon certain of the streets are, in the course of time, reduced to an impalpable powder, which forms a diffluent mud in winter, and affords an irritating dust in the dry weather.

The gravel from Profit's Island on the Mississippi river, is composed chiefly of silex and silicates of the hardest description, which have resisted the action of the elements for unknown ages.

7. Abundant supplies of river water for the use of the inhabitants and for the cleansing of private premises, and the purification of the markets, gutters and streets.

The highest interests of the citizens of New Orleans, demand the institution of a rigid scientific investigation by the most skilled engineers of the United States and Europe, of the drainage and sewerage of this city.

A properly constituted commission of civil and military engineers might devise a plan of protection from overflow, and of surface and subsoil drainage, and of sewerage, which may be capable of progressive execution and expansion during indefinite periods in the future, and in accordance with the growth of the city.

Every system of sewerage and sub-soil drainage must be adapted to the peculiar topography of the land occupied by the city.

The following facts must be considered :

(*a.*) The land on which New Orleans is built is protected from overflow of the Mississippi river by a continuous levee from the beginning of its river front to the ending of it, a distance of about twelve miles. The levee has an elevation above the natural soil of from six to ten feet.

The land upon which New Orleans is built *falls* from the river back to Claiborne street one mile, where it is twelve feet below the river.

In high water the entire area occupied by the city of New Orleans is below the level of the Mississippi river.

It is equally necessary to protect the rear of the city by a system of powerful levees, from overflows from the lake.

It frequently happens that the level of the lake is above that of a large portion of the land occupied by the city.

The basin occupied by New Orleans is further diversified by a ridge of land. On either side of the Metairie Ridge the land slopes in one direction towards the lowest depression towards the river, and in the other towards Lake Pontchartrain.

From these natural conditions, the subsoil of a large area of the city of New Orleans is perpetually saturated with water.

At the present time New Orleans is drained by large canals thirty-five miles long, which receive the surface water of over 300 miles of gutters.

At the present time these canals are more than one-half full of the foul deposits washed down through the gutters of the city.

(*b.*) According to the city map of Mr. W. H. Bell, the inclosure within the protection levees measures 26,026 acres, which, if populated with 40 persons to an acre, would give 1,041,040 persons. If the daily excrements of this population per head be estimated at three pounds, the entire amount would equal 569,970 tons in one year.

Illustrating the COURSE of the TOTAL MORTALIT'
and the CHIEF FATAL DISEA!
DURING THE SIX MONTHS
With Meteorological Obse

Prepared by H. ROBERTS

…f CHILDREN under five years of age,
EW ORLEANS
EMBER 31st. 1880.
…ume period

But if with Civil Engineers, we consider the present city to lie on the slope between the river and Claiborne street, which contains between the upper and lower protection levees, 9,319 acres, and 30 persons to an acre, it will give a population of 372,760. The daily excrements of this population would be 1,118,280 pounds, and would require to move it daily 1,118 carts, each taking half a ton at a load, or it would take 204 of the largest ships that come to New Orleans to carry a year's filth from the city, without calculating the refuse from cattle, horses and other animals.

During the present year, it has been attempted to remove a large portion of the excrements stored up in the privies of the city, by the so-called *"air-tight"* and *"odorless"* barrels and carts, to the nuisance boats, to be towed below the city limits and dumped into the Mississippi river.

If we estimate the present population of New Orleans at 220,000 inhabitants, and allow 5 inhabitants to each house, we have 44,000 houses.

It is possible that in many cases two or more dwellings are served by a single privy vault.

If the total number of privies in the city of New Orleans number about 40,000; and if the cost of emptying each of those privies be about $5 (five dollars), then it is evident that the emptying of the privies of New Orleans, annually would cost $200,000.

In ten years the cost of emptying the privies of New Orleans only once annually would reach the enormous sum of $2,000,000 (two million dollars).. And at the end of this period there would be no permanent works of sewerage or drainage and no substitute for the wretched privy system now used.

To the above estimate must be added the cost of disinfectants to destroy the foul gases, and more especially the poisonous sulphuretted hydrogen and sulphuret of ammonia perpetually generated in these foul storehouses of filth.

With all the efforts of the sanitary officers, it must be admitted that the garbage and nuisance boats and even the apparatus for emptying the privies are foul and unbearable nuisances.

(c). The streets of New Orleans, open and requiring cleaning and repairing have been classified as follows : square block pavement, 22.06 miles, cobble stone, 38.00 miles, ballast roads, 19.07 miles, shell roads, 26.54 miles, plank roads, 5.00 miles, dirt streets, 472.34. We have then nearly 500 miles of dirt streets, not including those not in general use.

There are also to be built and kept in repair, 191 canal bridges, 5,180 wooden street bridges, 459 stone crossings, 580 iron street bridges, and 3,301 wooden street crossings, together with the nine navigation bridges over the New Canal, the Carondelet Canal and Bayou St. John.

In wet weather the dirt streets become impassible quagmires, and from the failure of the garbage carts, they become the receptacle of garbage and filth of every description.

Added to this, the rear portions of the city have been overflowed upon several occasions by the waters of the lake, and incalculable suffering and hardship have been inflicted upon the inhabitants.

A thorough system of protection from overflow, combined with an effective system of sewerage and underground drainage, will practically elevate the dirt streets into dry roads and highways suitable to the purposes of transportation and commercial intercourse.

(d.) Without doubt a large number of the diseases of New Orleans are, to a certain extent, dependent upon the saturation of the atmosphere with moisture, and, under certain circumstances, with foul exhalations from privies and gutters, and ill-drained and ill-ventilated premises, and from the filthy drainage canals.

The foul exhalations may, to a great extent, be removed by a prompt removal of all fœcal matter and garbage. The moisture may be greatly diminished by thorough surface and sub-soil drainage.

In this connection the following important facts should be noted :

During the past 12 years, the average number of deaths caused by Phthisis Pulmonalis alone was 816, giving a grand total during this period 1869 to 1880, of 9,800 deaths.

One in 248 of the inhabitants of New Orleans die annually of Phthisis Pulmonalis.

It will be seen from the following table that the percentage of deaths from Phthisis Pulmonalis, varies in the different districts of New Orleans :

TABLE SHOWING NUMBER OF DEATHS BY PHTHISIS PULMONALIS IN THE DIFFERENT DISTRICTS OF THE CITY OR NEW ORLEANS, AND DEATH RATE PER 1000 INHABITANTS PER ANNUM.

DISTRICTS.	January.	February.	March.	April.	May.	June.	July.	August.	September.	October.	November.	December.	Total.	Death Rate per 1 00 per annum.
First District	21	15	27	22	21	17	22	15	6	12	25	19	222	3.86
Second District..	5	18	12	14	14	18	10	8	16	18	20	15	168	3.76
Third District...	10	7	9	11	10	14	6	12	15	11	14	16	135	2.96
Fourth District..	7	15	12	9	6	6	3	9	8	7	16	16	114	3.37
Fifth District....	1	......	3	1	1	2	......	4	3	1	5	4	25	2 82
Sixth District....	4	3	4	2	6	2	3	......	......	3	......	2	29	1.80
Seventh District	......	......	3	1	......	1	......	......	......	......	3	1	9	1.44
Total	48	52	70	60	58	60	44	48	48	52	83	73	702	3.25

The mortality is greater in the most crowded districts, being in the First 3.86 per 1000 inhabitants, Second District 3.76, Third 2.96, Fourth 3.37, Fifth 2.82, Sixth 1.80, Seventh 1.44.

During the same period, 5,144 deaths were caused by diarrhœal diseases, or on an average 428 deaths each year, are caused by these diseases.

Four thousand eight hundred and fifty-four deaths were caused during this period by malarial fevers, or 404 deaths per annum. This class of diseases appear to be directly related to defective drainage.

During the period of twelve years therefore, (1869–1880) phthisis pulmonalis, diarrhœal diseases and malarial fevers, caused in the city of New Orleans, 19,798 deaths, whilst during the same period yellow fever caused only 5102 deaths, as shown in the following table :

DEATHS BY YELLOW FEVER IN NEW ORLEANS, DURING THE TWELVE YEARS—1869–80.

Year.	June.	July.	August.	September	October.	November	December.	Total.
1869......	....	1	....	....	2	....	....	3
1870......	1	....	3	231	242	106	5	588
1871......	....	....	2	9	22	19	2	14
1872......	....	....	1	5	24	7	2	39
1873......	....	3	19	108	79	17	....	226
1874......	....	....	....	2	6	2	1	11
1875......	....	....	5	24	20	9	3	61
1876......	....	....	1	20	15	4	1	41
1877......	....	....	....	....	....	1	....	1
1878......	....	26	1025	1780	1065	147	3	4056
1879......	....	3	4	7	5	....	....	19
1880......	....	1	....	....	1	....	....	2
Total	1	34	1060	2186	1481	312	17	5102

The entire attention of the inhabitants of the Mississippi valley is concentrated upon New Orleans, to the detriment of her commerce and fair name, on account of the occasional existence of yellow fever in the epidemic form'; and her people are prone to regard this disease of far greater importance than phthisis pulmona'is, diarrœhal diseases and malarial feve.s, which perpetually claim a far greater number of victims.

It is possible by a proper system of drainage and sewerage to greatly reduce the mortality from Phthisis Pulmonalis, Diarrœhal diseases and malarial fevers.

But any philosophical and successful system must be based upon the peculiar topography of New Orleans, situated below the high water lines of the river in the front and of the lakes in the rear.

(e). Every system of sewerage and drainage adapted to New Orleans. must depend for its ultimate success upon the use of powerful pumps to lift up the liquids and project them into the Mississippi river below the limits of the city.

(f). The construction of a drainage and navigation canal circumscribing the city and connecting the waters of the Mississippi above Carrollton with those below the Barracks, promises great hygienic and commercial advantages.

To render the canal available at once to the purposes of navigation, drainage and sewerage, it should not be less than 30 feet below low-water in the river and should be not less than 300 feet in width.

Such a project could only be successfully executed by the combination of great capital, and the co-operation of the General Government.

The protection of the city from overflow, and thorough drainage and sewerage will, without doubt, render New Orleans one of the healthiest cities in the world, and do more to ward off destructive epidemics, and restore confidence in her own citizens and in those of surrounding States than even the most rigid and effective quarantine.

PROTECTION OF THE CITIZENS OF LOUISIANA FROM UNQUALIFIED PRACTITIONERS OF MEDICINE, AND THE EXTENSION OF THE REGISTRATION OF MARRIAGES, BIRTHS AND DEATHS, TO THE ENTIRE STATE.

Article 178 of the Constitution of the State of Louisiana, adopted in 1879, ordains that;

"The General Assembly shall provide for the interest of State Medicine in all its departments ; for the protection of the people from unqualified practitioners of medicine ; for protecting confidential communications made to medical men by their patients while under professional treatment, and for the purpose of such treatment; for the establishment and maintainance of a State Board of Health."

In order to diffuse a correct knowledge of all subjects relating to the important subjects, concerning the constitution and execution of quarantine, and the laws relating to sanitary and medical subjects, and to the protection of the people against the introduction and spread of contagious diseases, and to the registration of marriages, births and deaths; the Board of Health of the State of Louisiana published in the month of September, 1880, a large edition of the "*Acts of the Legislature of Louisiana establishing and regulating quarantine for the protection of the State ; organizing and defining the powers of the Board of Health and regulating the practice of medicine, midwifery, dentistry and pharmacy ; also rules and regulations of the Board of Health of the State of Louisiana, and Health Ordinances of the City of New Orleans, quarantine and sanitary.*"

These laws, ordinances and rules, collected and classified by the President

different races.

Such data would form the necessary foundation for sanitary reform and advancement.

I have the honor to remain very respectfully, your obedient servant,

JOSEPH JONES, M. D.,

President Board of Health, State of Louisiana.

New Orleans, December 31, 1880.

REPORT OF

JOSEPH HOLT, M. D.,

SANITARY INSPECTOR FIRST DISTRICT, CITY OF
NEW ORLEANS, TO THE

BOARD OF HEALTH

OF THE STATE OF LOUISIANA,

FOR THE YEAR 1880.

REPORT OF JOSEPH HOLT, M. D., SANITARY INSPECTOR, FIRST DISTRICT.

OFFICE SANITARY INSPECTOR, FIRST DISTRICT,
New Orleans, La., December 31, 1880.

Joseph Jones, M. D., President Board of Health:

Sir—I have the honor to submit the following summary report relative to sanitary affairs in the First District for the year 1880:

Concerning the general condition of health which has prevailed during the year, I will state that the amount of sickness and the mortality which have occurred, when compared with the census of the district, will indicate this period to have been remarkable in the history of the city, because of the exemption from all influences operating generally and of a kind mischievous to health and life.

An absolute exemption from zymotic fevers was not to be expected, but at no time have there prevailed any special disorders to an extent sufficient to influence materially the death rate.

ACUTE INFECTIOUS DISEASES.

Cases of scarlet fever have occurred in isolated instances, scattered here and there, during each month. The greatest number were reported in June and July. There were only nineteen deaths from this disease during the year.

In the months of March, April and May, measles prevailed. The disease was of a mild type. While the symptoms in many cases were severe, the mortality was very small.

From diphtheria thirteen deaths only have occurred; none during the months of July, August and September. The greatest number (four) were reported in November. One in December.

Two cases of yellow fever were reported; one in July, the other in October. Both were fatal.

For the first time in many years there has been an entire exemption from small-pox.

During the months of September and October, dengue prevailed as a widespread epidemic. Deaths from this disease were rare; singularly so, when we consider the violence of symptoms in many cases.

SANITARY CONDITION OF THE DISTRICT.

As set forth in the accompanying table, it will be seen that the amount of sanitary work accomplished has been very great. Even this would have been exceeded, but for the continuous rains of the summer and fall.

Vigorous sanitary work and the rains certainly succeeded in maintaining a state of cleanliness throughout the district never realized before. It is reasonable to infer that the exceptional good health was due to the exceptional cleanliness.

31

I embody here the special report touching the sanitary condition of the district presented to the Board of Health the latter part of July.

OFFICE SANITARY INSPECTOR, FIRST DISTRICT,
New Orleans, July 21, 1880.

Jos. Jones, M. D , President Board of Health:

Sir—In obedience to special instructions, I have the honor to present the following report:

1. The street gutters running from the river front, wherever in the range of the sanitary flushing main, are kept well cleaned, and even those not so flushed have been washed almost daily by copious floods of rain. As a consequence, the general condition of street gutters has been far better than has usually been the case at this season of the year.

The gutters of streets in the rear of the Camp street canal, receiving none of the water from the flushing engine, are almost wholly dependent upon the rains and the exertions of the street-cleaning force employed by the city, and are therefore particularly liable to become foul whenever the weather is dry.

The gutters of streets running parallel with the river require manual labor in cleaning, on account of the impracticability of flushing them. On this account it may be stated that all of the gutters parallel with and back of Rampart street would be intolerably filthy and offensive but for the rains.

2. The gutters flushed by the Auxiliary Sanitary Association's engine, carrying matter directly to the rear of the city, are those of Calliope, Delord, St. Joseph and Julia streets. Those streets between Felicity and Calliope, running from the river front, drain this water into the Camp street head of the Melpomene canal, rendering this formerly offensive sewer perfectly inodorous.

3 The gutters immediately surrounding the Girod-street Cemetery are well flushed, while those on the opposite sides of the boundary streets are filthy.

About the Charity Hospital and New Basin, particularly above the latter, the gutters become intensely foul as soon as the rains cease.

4. The total population of the First District, according to the census of 1879, taken by the sanitary officers, is 54,344; and occupies an area divided by streets into 503 squares having an average front of 300 feet. This embraces the whole of the First and Second Wards and the Third Ward to Galvez street.

Within this area are about 125 miles of street gutters, fully sixty-seven miles of which are usually filthy and require manual force to clean them.

The present scavenger force consists of 46 laborers, with 26 carts and drivers. There is per laborer a pro rata of about 1181 of population, and per cart about 2090.

In considering the sanitary management of the First District, it is of importance to take into special account the great obstacle offered in the natural depressions of surface, involving in some instances an area of many squares. In these low spots drainage is so imperfect that street gutters are at all times in a stagnant condition, and would require the constant exertion of a large number of laborers to prevent foul accumulations.

5. Accompanying this, I present a condensed statement of sanitary work accomplished by the sanitary officers of the Board of Health from April 15 to July 15, 1880.

6. To keep the district in good sanitary condition during the summer months would require a street cleaning force of at least 100 men.

7. From the first to the fifteenth of July, there were but forty deaths from all causes in the district. Four of these were from fevers—viz: one typho-malarial, and three congestion of brain. This does not take into account the death from yellow fever of the seaman from the Excelsior, at the Touro Infirmary.

The rate of mortality is decidedly below the general average.

In closing this report, allow me to state that every assistance has been rendered by the Department of Improvements in the sanitary work of this office; and that, according to my observation, the utmost amount of work has been accomplished by the wholly insufficient force employed on the streets. Respectfully submitted,

JOSEPH HOLT, M. D., Sanitary Inspector First District.

INSPECTION OF SHIPS AND FUMIGATION OF CARGOES.

From the first of May to the middle of October a careful inspection of all shipping was maintained; the sanitary condition of vessels in port and health of crews noted; and the cargoes of ships from infected ports, although repeatedly fumigated at quarantine, were again subjected to that process in warehouse.

PUBLIC INSTITUTIONS.

All public institutions were inspected, several of them repeatedly. A statement of their sanitary condition has been presented in a tabulated report, wherein they were shown to be generally well kept. Where exceptions to this rule were found, steps were taken to abate the trouble.

COW STABLES.

The most serious of all nuisances and the one which inflicts the greatest discomfort on the largest number of people, is the presence of cows in the densely populated portions of the district. It matters little how closely their premises are kept under observation, they are by their very nature intolerable nuisances, which can be remedied in no other way than by preventing the keeping of even one cow within certain limits. In a closely built square it is impossible to provide suitable ventilation for the proper maintenance of a cow. Besides that, the soil becomes saturated with liquid excrement which converts the entire place into a stench-emitting nidus. The emanations from the body of a closely confined stall-fed cow are peculiarly offensive. During our long-continued warm weather the annoyance is greatly aggravated. A stable containing one or two cows is by far a more grievous nuisance to the entire neighborhood than the largest livery stable, or the stables of the street car lines.

I would respectfully urge that steps be taken to secure the passage of an ordinance positively prohibiting the keeping of cows in the First District, east of Galvez canal.

This is recommended the more freely, when we consider that the benefit enjoyed by the owners, whether directly in the use of the milk or in the revenue derived from its sale, is in no measure commensurate with the inconvenience and harm inflicted upon the great majority. The harm consists in the pollution of the soil and air, and in the serious depreciation of property in the vicinity.

MORTUARY REPORT.

I present herewith a mortuary table for the district at large and one for the Charity Hospital.

TABLE ILLUSTRATING DEATHS IN THE FIRST DITRICT, CITY OF NEW ORLEANS, DURING THE YEAR 1880.

DISEASES.	January.	February.	March.	April.	May.	June.	July.	August.	September.	October.	November.	December.	Total.
Yellow Fever							1			1			2
Malarial Fevers		2	3	4	7	6	6	7	13	15	6	5	74
Typhoid Fever	1			1			1			2	2		7
Scarlet Fever	1	1	4	1		3	5	1		1	2		19
Measles				2	8	7	3						20
Small-pox													
Diphtheria		1	1	1	1	2				2	4	1	13
Diarrhœal Diseases	8	2	3	3	10	14	7	6	4	7	4	4	72
Congestion of Brain	2	3	2	3	4	3	3	3	5	6	3	3	40
Convulsions	2	3	3	5	12	6	5	5	3	5	4	2	55
Phthisis Pulmonalis	21	15	27	22	21	17	22	15	6	12	25	19	232
All other causes	94	87	64	77	86	76	63	51	58	68	83	62	869
Total number Deaths	129	114	107	119	149	134	116	88	89	110	133	96	1393
Number Deaths { White	86	71	74	74	82	84	79	52	58	78	90	56	884
Colored	43	43	33	45	67	50	37	36	31	41	43	40	509
Death rate per 1000 inhabitants per annum { Yellow Fever							0.02			0.02			0.05
Malarial Fever		0.41	0.62	0 83	1.46	1.25	1.25	1.46	2.71	3.13	1.25	1.04	1.28
Phthisis Pulmonalis	4.38	3.13	5.64	4.59	4.38	3.55	4.59	3.13	1.25	2.50	5.22	3.97	3.86
Whites	23.84	19.66	20.49	20.49	22.71	23.26	22.16	14.40	16.10	21.60	21.93	15.51	20.40
Colored	36.52	36.52	28.03	38.22	56.91	42.47	31.43	30.58	26.34	34 83	36..2	33.98	36.10
Total	26.94	23.81	22.35	24.85	31.12	27.99	24.23	18.38	18.59	24 85	27.78	20.05	24.24

Population—White, 57,445; Colored, 14,126. Total, 57,445.

In regard to the death-rate according to races it is a fact, not only interest-ing but of considerable significance, that, for the entire year, the ratio per 1000 of whites is 20.40 while that of the colored is 36.10.

This discrepancy is still more striking in a comparison of the death-rates for the month of December—whites 15.51, colored 33.98—or more than double, and this, too, in the absence of any prevailing special cause, such as small-pox.

These figures demonstrate the fact that profound influences are operating silently, but surely, to bring about a result which must eventually, and not far hence, work singular changes in our social economy.

It is evident that the great problem of the races, and also the labor ques-tion, are moving mysteriously in the direction of their own solution.

The limits of this report will not permit me to enter into an investigation of the special causes which have determined this marked difference in the mortality of the two races; I therefore simply call attention to the fact.

HOUSE TO HOUSE INSPECTION.

Premises	3,978
Premises with hydrants only	2,165
Premises with cisterns only	1,483
Premises with cisterns and hydrants	867
Premises with a well	340
Premises with no water supply	110
Houses built of wood	9,783
Houses built of brick	4,195
Houses used as dwellings only	10,476
Houses used as stores and manufactories only	1,486
Houses used as stores and dwellings	1,694
Houses vacant	322
Rooms in dwelling houses	71,585
Number of premises good	13,345
Number of premises bad	633— 13,978
Number of tenement houses	583
Number of cisterns bad	62
Number of privies without ventilators	1,970
Number of yards badly drained	204
Condition of privy, good	7,245
Condition of privy, foul	5,642
Condition of privy, defective	632
Premises with 1100 horses; 1314 mules; 265 cows and 43 hogs	1,211
Vacant lots	140
Lots not filled to grade	204
Application for building permits	10
Private complaints attended to	607

MISCELLANEOUS.

Inspections made	16,427
Re-inspections made	6,617
Nuisances requiring abatement	6,784
Nuisances abated	5,884
Notices to empty privy vaults	5,447
Notices to rebuild privy vaults	95
Notices to repair privy vaults	552
Notices to disinfect privy vaults	5,106
Notices to clean premises	1,053

Notices to repair houses.. 5
Notices to fill lots.. 105
Notices to grade lots.. 32
Notices to repair cisterns... 49
Notices to cover cisterns.. 54
Notices to clean cisterns.. 20
Notices to supply water.. 8
Notices to construct gutters....................................... 48
Notices to repair gutters.. 36
Notices to remove hogs... 9
Dangerous buildings reported....................................... 4
Premises disinfected... 1,580
Premises fumigated... 20
Cases of yellow fever.. 2
Persons reported for non-compliance................................ 5
Notices to construct ventilators................................... 1,080

Respectfully submitted,
JOSEPH HOLT, M. D.,
Sanitary Inspector First District.

REPORT OF

W. R MANDEVILLE, M. D.,

SANITARY INSPECTOR SECOND DISTRICT,
CITY OF NEW ORLEANS, TO THE

BOARD OF HEALTH

OF THE STATE OF LOUISIANA,

FOR THE YEAR 1880.

REPORT OF W. R. MANDEVILLE, M. D., SANITARY INSPECTOR SECOND DISTRICT.

NEW ORLEANS, December 31, 1880.

Joseph Jones, M. D., President Board of Health:

Sir—I have the honor to present the following condensed report of the sanitary work accomplished in the Second District during the year ending with the above date:

LOCATION.

The second municipal district of the city of New Orleans is bounded on the north and northeast by Esplanade street and Bayou St. John, and on the south and southwest by Canal street and the new canal. The district extends between these boundaries from the Mississippi river to Lake Pontchartrain, and comprises three divisions, known as the fourth, fifth and sixth wards.

TOPOGRAPHY AND DRAINAGE.

The Second District is renowned for being the most historical part of the Crescent City, since that territory bounded by the Mississippi river, Esplanade, Rampart and Canal streets constitutes the city of New Orleans as originally founded by Bienville. The streets are regularly cut in square blocks, giving to the map of that district the appearance of a chess board. Excepting most of the thoroughfares in the rear of Rampart street, the streets and banquettes of this district are narrower than those of more modern design.

Many of the houses in this part of the city were built before an abundance of light and air and free ventilation were recognized as essentials to perfect health and comfort, but, thanks to their antiquity, are now rapidly falling to ruin and decay, and in their place new ones of more recent design and architectural beauty are being erected with all the comforts now considered so necessary in this progressive age of sanitary science.

The drainage system of this district is very imperfect. Storm and waste water is drained into Lake Pontchartrain, by a number of canals known as Hagan Avenue, Broad, Galvez, Claiborne and Orleans, but these canals are too small and rapidly fill up with mud, and in summer almost completely dry up, making the air redolent with their foul miasmatic odors.

The drainage machine now in use is far from having the requisite amount of power to carry off the surplus water after heavy rains, such as visited us this year, and as a consequence the rear portion of the district after a rain resembles a miniature lake for several hours.

It is earnestly urged that these canals be thoroughly deepened and cleaned before the warm season is upon us.

WATER SUPPLY.

Water from the Mississippi river is conveyed by pipes through the district only as far as Claiborne street. Its want is felt beyond this avenue to Broad street, an area of (130) one hundred and thirty square blocks, quite densely inhabited. This supply of water is freely used in all public buildings and private residences, for cleansing purposes, bathing, etc., but its muddy condition renders it objectionable as drinking water.

32

Rain water preserved in cisterns is generally used for drinking purposes. These cisterns, especially on premises where no hydrant exists, are in the majority of cases so limited in capacity that they are soon emptied when a drouth occurs. Some are in a miserable state of decay, and it would be beneficial to have them repaired or even destroyed.

Wells are found in all parts of the district, and are used principally at dairies and stables for watering stock, and at nurseries for besprinkling plants. The water from these wells is universally considered unhealthy by the inhabitants, and is never used for drinking purposes, except in very rare instances, when no other water is obtainable.

The scarcity of water in the rear of Claiborne street is a just cause of complaint in cases of conflagration, and it would be advisable for the protection of real estate against destruction by fire, to build fire-wells at different points of that section.

The street hydrants in the more central part of the district should be allowed to flow for a couple of hours morning and evening, during the summer months, so as to thoroughly clear the gutters of their filthy accumulations.

PUBLIC BUILDINGS.

The Court-houses, Police Stations and Parish Prison are in a fair condition, and during the summer months were frequently inspected.

The authorities in charge of the Parish Prison are doing their utmost to keep the building clean, and the police regulations in regard to cells and yard are excellent. The cells are large but poorly ventilated. The p. ivy system of the prison is that known as the "Rochdale" or barrel system; they are emptied daily.

Two wells 13 feet deep, formerly used as privy vaults, should be filled as soon as possible, with river sand.

At the time of last inspection the total number of prisoners was 252; number of white males 93; number white females 29; number of colored males 84; number of colored females 46.

TREME AND FRENCH MARKETS.

The condition of these markets is tolerable. The principle cause of complaint lies in their vicinity, where banquettes are obstructed by the fruit and vegetable stands kept mostly by Sicilians. It is deplorable to verify the fact that this class of people, as a rule, seems to ignore the elements of hygiene. A glance in the interior of their abodes is sufficient to prove this assertion.

The appearance of the vegetable markets could easily be improved. The washing of the banquettes on either side from Ursulines to St. Philip would result in rendering them less slippery and dangerous to pedestrians during damp weather. The prompt removal of all garbage should not be neglected.

CEMETERIES.

There are four large cemeteries in the Second District, which are the burial grounds of some of the oldest and most respectable families of this city. The walls and many of the vaults of these cemeteries are in a dilapidated state and require immediate repair. It is especially the case with the graveyard bounded by Customhouse, Claiborne, Bienville and Robertson streets, where also the least shower renders the alleys impracticable since the water, finding no outlet, remains stagnant until evaporated by the rays of the sun. The proper authorities should find a remedy for these defects at once.

REMOVAL AND DISPOSITION OF GARBAGE.

The removal and disposition of street garbage, as actually practiced, has proven to be superior to the old system of depositing the same on vacant lots in the rear of the district.

Some complaints, however, arise about the non-hauling of garbage from the streets. This work should be attended to daily and with regularity, and consist not only in the emptying of the receptacles containing the rubbish, but also in the removal of all decaying matter from the streets.

Under this heading can be mentioned the neglectful appearance of the gutters on some of the most frequented thoroughfares of the district, such as Royal, Chartres and Rampart streets. St. Philip and Ursulines streets in the neighborhood of the French Market have a filthy and repulsive aspect.

SANITATION.

During the past year an immense amount of sanitary work has been accomplished in this district. Several thousand circulars have been distributed to the families residing in its boundaries, instructing them in domestic sanitation, and it is with no small amount of satisfaction that the statement can be made that the people were eager to receive all the knowledge possible in this line.

Disinfectants to the amount of $333\frac{1}{2}$ gallons of the copperas and carbolic acid solution, and dry copperas (17,908 ℔s.) were gratuitously distributed to all those desiring it. This was accomplished by means of a cart conveying it from house to house, accompanied by one of the sanitary officers, thus leaving nothing undone to secure health and cleanliness to the inhabitants of this district.

DAIRIES.

A thorough inspection of all dairies in this district was made during the summer months, and a detailed report presented to the Board.

Could not some means be adopted by which all milk sold in this city be first carefully tested as to its purity, etc.? . The adulteration of milk is carried on to a much greater extent than one not thoroughly acquainted with the facts would suppose, and it certainly behooves us as sanitarians and as guardians of the public health, that this important matter receive our earnest attention.

MORTALITY.

The total number of deaths in the Second Distict during the year was 1115, making an annual ratio of 24.9 per thousand population.

The annual ratio per thousand white population was 22.28. The annual ratio per thousand colored was 31.27.

The greatest number of deaths occurred in the month of June........ 116
The least number of deaths occurred in the month of January.......... 73
Mortality from January to June..................................... 555
Mortality from June to December.................................... 560
Total deaths from diseases of the respiratory organs.................. 267
Of these, consumption.. 168
Total deates from all fevers.. 96
Total deaths from congestions...................................... 22

The greatest number of deaths occurred in the Fifth Ward.

A suspicious case of yellow fever on Customhouse street, corner of Franklin, was reported, but on careful examination proved to be a case of hæmorrhagic malarial fever.

For future reference, an exact and carefully prepared table of the number of miles of gutters in the Second District is here presented, which by streets is as follows:

Street	Miles	Street	Miles
Levee	1	Canal	1½
Decatur	1	Customhouse	3
Chartres	2	Bienville	3
Royal	2	Conti	3
Bourbon	2	St. Louis	3
Dauphine	2	Carondelet Walk	2
Burgundy	2	Toulouse	1½
Rampart	4	St. P. ter	3
Basin	1	Orleans	3
St. Claude	1	St. Ann	3
Franklin	1	Dumain	3
Treme	2	St. Ph lip	3
Marais	2	Ursulines	3
Villere	2	Hospital	3
Robertson	2	Barracks	2½
Claiborne	4	Esplanade	3
Derbigny	2		
Roman	2	Total	43½
Prieur	2		
Johnson	2	Grand total of miles in the	
Galvez	2	Second District	93½
Miro	2		
Tonti	2		
Rocheblave	2		
Dorgenois	2		
Broad	1		
Total	50		

HOUSE TO HOUSE INSPECTION.

Premises 7,473
Premises with hydrants only........................... 1,858
Premises with cisterns only............................ 3,400
Premises with cisterns and hydrants................. 2,118
Premises with a well.................................... 699
Premises with no water supply........................ 97
Houses built of wood................................... 3,749
Houses built of brick.................................. 3,508
Houses used as dwellings only......................... 4,284
Houses used as stores and manufactories only......... 543
Houses used as stores and dwellings.................. 1,114
Houses vacant.. 225
Rooms in dwelling houses.............................. 36,518
Persons occupying premises, white.............31,368
Persons occupying premises, colored...........13,301— 44,669
Condition of privy, good.............................. 4,184
Condition of privy, foul.............................. 3,192
Condition of privy, defective......................... 223
Premises with animals................................. 351
Number of horses...................................... 457
Number of mules....................................... 270
Number of cows.. 671
Number of hogs.. 37
Vacant lots... 252
Lots not filled to grade.............................. 90
Private complaints attended to........................ 245

MISCELLANEOUS.

Inspections made...................................... 14,256
Re-inspections made................................... 2,432
Nuisances requiring abatement......................... 3,643
Nuisances abated...................................... 2,185
Notices to empty privy vaults......................... 2,087
Notices to rebuild privy vaults....................... 42
Notices to repair privy vaults........................ 238
Notices to disinfect privy vaults..................... 2,078
Notices to clean premises............................. 2
Notices to repair houses.............................. 0
Notices to fill lots.................................. 4
Notices to supply water............................... 6
Notices to construct gutters.......................... 34
Notices to repair gutters............................. 13
Notices to remove hogs................................ 2
Premises disinfected.................................. 2,078
Premises fumigated.................................... 17
Persons vaccinated, white................... 42
Persons vaccinated, colored................. 5— 47
Persons reported for non-compliance................... 2

In conclusion of this my report, I am pleased to place on record the able and conscientious manner in which Mr. L. C. Wiltz has performed all duties required of him as sanitary officer.

All of which is respectfully submitted,
W. R. MANDEVILLE, M. D.,
Sanitary Inspector Second District.

REPORT OF

W. H. WATKINS, M. D.,

SANITARY INSPECTOR THIRD DISTRICT,
CITY OF NEW ORLEANS, TO THE

BOARD OF HEALTH.

OF THE STATE OF LOUISIANA,

FOR THE YEAR 1880.

REPORT OF W. H. WATKINS, M. D., SANITARY INSPECTOR, THIRD DISTRICT.

NEW ORLEANS, LA., December 31, 1880.

Joseph Jones, M. D., President Board of Health, State of Louisiana:

Sir—I have the honor herewith to submit the annual report in regard to sanitation and sanitary regulations exercised in the Third District, for the year 1880.

Having been elected Sanitary Inspector of this district April 12, 1880, I at once assumed charge of the office vacated by my efficient predecessor, Dr. W. E. Schuppert.

The records for the preceding months had been carefully preserved by the sanitary officer, Mr. C. F. Gonzales, and from these, together with the reports of the former Sanitary Inspector, I have been able to fully complete the report for the year.

On the fifteenth of April, Mr. T. C. Will was assigned as sanitary officer of the district. His remarkable energy and high qualifications admirably fitted him for the position, and the methodical exactness which he has exercised reflects great credit on him.

LOCATION AND TOPOGRAPHY.

The Third District of the city of New Orleans is embraced within the following boundaries: Esplanade street, United States Barracks, the Mississippi river and Lake Pontchartrain. The District is sub-divided into the Seventh, Eighth and Ninth Wards. The inhabited portion is, however, embraced in a much more limited space, extending back from the river on an average of not more than three-quarters of a mile, and embraces about 800 square acres. Built on alluvial deposit, the whole district is almost level; highest at the river; the slope back to the lake is gradual, and, in the rear of the inhabited portion, swamps exist which are so low as to be continually covered with water.

DRAINAGE.

Surface drainage alone is the mode by which the district is cleared from storm water, and the facilities for carrying this off are inadequate. The canals and gutters in the rear require deepening, and at least another or larger draining machine is required. The only draining machine is that one located on London avenue. The result is, that after a hard rain many of the streets are inundated, though the natural grade is such that the water does not remain long.

PUBLIC BUILDINGS.

A careful inspection of the Public Schools has been made. All were found in good sanitary condition, but the number of pupils in several is so large as not to allow sufficient air-space for each. The total number of public schools in the district is twelve, but one, the McDonogh school No. 12, is yet unfinished and will not be occupied before the latter part of January,

1881. The water supply and drainage of each is good. Privy accommodations ample.

Total number of teachers					91
"	"	pupils—white			3426
"	"	"	colored		772
"	"	"	male		2226
"	"	"	female		1991
Average number of pupils to each teacher					46

The Orphan Asylums of the District are typical institutions of this kind. Care is exercised by those in charge to make each one clean and healthy. There has been little sickness in them, and no contagious disease has been reported.

The Fifth Precinct Police Station, where the Sanitary Inspector's office is located, is in a dilapidated condition ; the floors have rotted away, and the plaster is falling from the ceiling. The privy vaults need rebuilding.

There are five public markets in the district. Each is kept in good condition and regularly inspected by the sanitary officer. The private markets have been regularly inspected, and wherever nuisances have been found, they have been abated. This sanitary condition on the average is good.

CEMETERIES.

The three cemeteries located in the district are far removed from the thickly-populated areas and present no feature especially objectionable.

STREETS AND GUTTERS.

The Third District with such an extent of river front, with imperfect drainage and sloping so gradually from the levee to the swamp, presents one of the problems as yet unsolved. How shall the gutters be kept clean ? At least forty miles of streets regularly laid out are now to be looked after, and the limited means of the city caused their total neglect during the latter part of the year, where owing to heavy rains necessity demanded that they should receive attention. At the best season of the year careful inspection of street gutters was made by your orders, and in the report made at that time it was truly stated that of eighty miles of gutters quite one-half could be classed as foul or obstructed. The Eighth Ward made the best exhibit, but this was in a great measure due to the fact that in compactness and grading, it is superior to the other wards, and therefore easier to clean with a limited force. Much can be done by the proper authorities, and such work should be commenced by alignment of the gutters, improving the grade and deepening the canals so that a rapid current shall be established.

A limited number of the streets in the district are paved with ballast from ships, known as "cobble stones," and are in good repair. The streets not thus paved are in a fearful condition, and for months many of them are impassible to vehicles.

The supply of water from the "water works" of the city is so limited in the lower portion of the district, as practically to be of no service in case of drouth or fires.

DAIRIES AND STABLES.

The number of dairies is large, but in many of them only two or three cows are kept. The extensives ones are located in the extreme rear of the Seventh Ward. They have been carefully inspected and all efforts made to have them kept in good sanitary state. The milk has been frequently tested and its quality found to be excellent. The livery stables are kept clean; and the manure is frequently removed,

PRIVY SYSTEM.

: This differs in no respect from that of other districts of the city. It is defective. An inspection revealed the fact that, in numerous instances, they were not in conformi.y to law, and when cleaned soon till up with sub-soil water, causing them to be always offensive and insanitary. The inspection of 7466 premises showed that only 3743 were found in good condition, 337 required repairing or rebuilding.

The city ordinance in regard to the emptying of these vaults requires that vidangeurs shall perform this work from 6 o'clock a. m. to 6 o'clo k p. m., and for every vault to be emptied a permit shall be taken out at the office of the Board of Health. This is violated in many instances, and strict watch has been kept by the sanitary officer to prevent such an occurrence in this district. Another cause of complaint against the excavating companies, is that the barrels holding the fæcal matter are not air-tight. A careful inspection of such apparatus used by these companies convinces me that only that form of barrel having an iron top with rubber flanges is calculated to do away with all cause of complaint, on being carried to the "nuisance boat," where such matter is deposited.

The "nuisance boat" is located at a wharf built by the city at the foot of Reynes street. It is well constructed, holds about eighty loads, and since the adoption of the present system of dumping the fæcal matter, no complaints have reached this office. In the summer the boat is towed daily below the city, and its contents emptied into the middle of the Mississippi river. In the winter, owing to the small amount of work performed by the excavating companies, it is emptied but once a week.

POPULATION.

Adopting the United States census of 1880 as substantially correct, we find the Third District has a population as follows:

Wards.	White Males.	White Females.	Black Males.	Black Females.	Total by Wards.	Total in District.
Seventh Ward....................	5.989	6.451	3.373	4.317	20.130	....
Eighth Ward...................	3.925	4.274	774	905	9.878	....
Ninth Ward.................	6.190	6.903	1.197	1.290	15.580	45.588

MORTALITY.

. It is very much to be regretted that, in giving the mortuary statistics, it is impossible to classify the deaths for each Ward. The records at the Board of Health Office contain only their locality in the different districts. The accompanying table gives the total number of deaths from all causes for each month, and also the number of deaths from special diseases. It has been my good fortune to find among the records of the office the table exhibiting the number of deaths during the year 1879, carefully compiled by Dr. W. E. Schuppert, the former Sanitary Inspector, and a comparison of this with the table of deaths for the year 1880 reveals the fact that the latter year has been far more unhealthy than the former.

We note that, in 1879, not a death occurred from small-pox, measles or scarlet fever; that in the same year malarial fevers caused 55 deaths. In 1880 the number of deaths from the latter was 82. In 1880 scarlet fever caused 15 deaths and measles 35 deaths. Convulsions in 1879 caused 22 deaths, and in 1880 45 deaths. The annual death-rate per 1000 inhabitants for 1879, based upon the census of 1880, was 20.42. The death-rate for 1880 was 25.47. This large increase was due in a great measure to the prevalence of contagious diseases, such as measles, scarlet fever and diphtheria. Combined with these is an increase of malarial fevers. Convulsions and trismus nascentium caused a number of deaths, due in a great measure to the inclemencies of the weather.

MORTALITY IN THE THIRD DISTRICT FOR THE YEAR 1880.

DISEASES.	January.	February.	March.	April.	May.	June.	July.	August.	September.	October.	November.	December.	Total.
Malarial Fevers	3	4	....	4	9	12	11	9	12	6	8	4	82
Typhoid Fever	1	....	1	2	2	3	2	2	1	1	....	1	16
Scarlet Fever	....	....	....	1	....	....	2	2	1	1	2	6	15
Measles	....	....	....	12	17	6	....	....	....	....	....	....	35
Small-pox	....	....	....	....	1	....	....	....	....	....	....	....	1
Diphtheria	3	2	3	....	....	....	1	5	....	2	1	3	20
Diarrhœal Diseases	2	3	1	3	2	11	1	4	....	2	4	3	36
Congestion of Brain	2	2	1	....	2	2	2	3	2	1	....	1	18
Convulsions	7	1	3	5	6	3	....	7	2	1	3	7	45
Phthisis Pulmonalis	10	7	9	11	10	14	6	12	15	11	14	16	135
Deaths from all other causes	54	72	74	57	83	84	55	44	54	60	51	70	758
Total number of Deaths	82	91	92	95	132	135	80	88	87	85	83	111	1161
Number ⎰ White	56	60	56	79	84	87	45	61	47	59	57	83	774
Deaths. ⎱ Colored	26	31	36	16	48	48	35	27	40	26	26	28	387
Death rate per 1000 inhabitants per annum. — Whites	19.92	21.34	19.92	28.10	29.88	30.95	16.00	21.70	16.72	20.99	20.27	29.82	22.94
Colored	26.31	31.37	36.43	16.19	48.58	48.58	35.42	27.32	40.48	26.31	26.31	28.33	32.62
Total	21.58	24.95	24.21	25.00	34.74	35.53	21.05	23.16	22.90	22.37	21.84	29.21	25.47
Malarial Fever	.78	1.05	....	1.05	2.36	3.05	2.89	2.36	3.15	1.57	2.10	1.05	1.79
Phthisis Pulmonalis	2.85	1.84	2.36	2.89	2.63	3.68	1.57	3.15	3.94	2.89	3.68	4.21	2.96
Still-born Children	8	8	5	8	5	8	4	3	6	4	6	3	68

Population of District—White, 33,732; Colored, 11,856; Total, 45,588.

MORTALITY IN THE THIRD DISTRICE FOR THE YEAR 1879.

DISEASES.	January.	February.	March.	April.	May.	June.	July.	August.	September.	October.	November.	December.	Total.
Malarial Fevers	3	2	1	....	6	4	4	10	10	9	4	2	55
Typhoid Fever	1	....	2	....	....	1	1	1	2	....	1	....	9
Scarlet Fever	....	....	....	....	....	....	....	....	....	....	....	....	
Measles	....	....	....	....	....	....	....	....	....	....	....	....	
Small-pox	....	....	....	....	....	....	....	....	....	....	....	....	
Diphtheria	3	1	2	2	2	1	....	2	3	3	2	2	23
Diarrhœal Diseases	4	....	2	2	4	5	6	2	1	3	1	2	32
Congestion of Brain	2	....	....	....	....	....	....	3	2	....	1	1	9
Convulsions	1	....	....	4	2	2	1	6	....	....	2	4	22
Phthisis Pulmonalis	14	13	16	14	8	5	13	10	7	19	8	5	132
Deaths from all other causes	68	40	51	53	22	61	56	40	46	48	69	65	649
Total number of Deaths	96	56	74	75	74	79	81	74	71	82	88	81	931
White	65	36	48	46	46	51	50	46	47	56	62	56	609
Colored	31	20	26	29	28	28	31	28	24	26	26	25	322
Still-born Children	....	....	2	1	....	....	....	1	4	4	4	....	16

Population of District—White, 33,732; Colored, 11,856; Total, 45,588.
Death Rate per 1000 Inhabitants per Annum, Census of 1880—White, 18.05; Colored, 27.15; Total, 20.42.

GENERAL SANITATION.

On my appointment as Sanitary Inspector, I found that the regular house-to-house inspection had been commenced in January and prosecuted by the sanitary officer in charge of the district. Mr. Will, the sanitary officer appointed simultaneously with my election, at once proceeded with the work. The size of the district was so great that, with one sanitary officer, it was impossible to complete the work. Fortunately, on the 17th of June the New Orleans Auxiliary Sanitary Association, appreciating the necessity of thorough inspection of all the premises of the district and the abatement of all nuisances, appointed three sanitary officers to work under the supervision of the Sanitary Inspector. Work was rapidly pushed until the inhabited portion of the district was systematically and thoroughly inspected. The officers appointed by the Auxiliary Sanitary Association were Messrs. Boyer, Randolph and Carew. It affords me pleasure to testify as to their capacity and industry. The accompanying table exhibits the amount of work performed in the district during the year.

HOUSE TO HOUSE INSPECTION.

Premises..	7,466
Premises with hydrants only................................	150
Premises with cisterns only................................	6,859
Premises with cisterns and hydrants........................	337
Premises with a well.......................................	2,370
Premises with no water supply..............................	120
Houses built of wood.......................................	6,922
Houses built of brick......................................	544
Houses used as dwellings only..............................	6,264
Houses used as stores and manufactories only...............	191
Houses used as stores and dwellings........................	583
Houses vacant..	309
Rooms in dwelling houses...................................	34,272
Persons occupying premises.................................	36,817
Condition of floor, good...................................	7,240
Condition of floor, bad....................................	226
Condition of privy, good...................................	3,743
Condition of privy, foul...................................	3,707
Condition of privy, defective..............................	457
Premises with 461 horses, 736 mules, 633 cows, 231 hogs.....	526
Vacant lots..	2,187
Lots not filled to grade...................................	603
Tenement houses..	119
Private complaints attended to.............................	157

MISCELLANEOUS.

Inspections made...	9,857
Re-inspections made..	3,900
Nuisances requiring abatement..............................	5,549
Nuisances abated...	5,160
Notices to empty privy vaults..............................	3,586
Notices to rebuild privy vaults............................	137
Notices to repair privy vaults.............................	200
Notices to disinfect privy vaults..........................	3,586
Notices to clean premises..................................	148
Notices to repair houses...................................	3
Notices to fill lots.......................................	200
Notices to construct flues to privies......................	517
Notices to clean cisterns..................................	97
Notices to repair cisterns.................................	46

REPORT OF

R. A. BAYLEY, M. D.,

SANITARY INSPECTOR FOURTH DISTRICT, CITY OF
NEW ORLEANS, TO THE

BOARD OF HEALTH

OF THE STATE OF LOUISIANA,

FOR THE YEAR 1880.

REPORT OF R. A. BAYLEY, M. D., SANITARY INSPECTOR FOURTH DISTRICT.

OFFICE SANITARY INSPECTOR, FOURTH DISTRICT, }
New Orleans, January 1, 1881. }

Joseph Jones, M. D., President Board of Health:

Sir—The following report of sanitary work accomplished in the Fourth District, including health statistics, etc., during the year ending December 31, 1880, is herewith submitted.

This district is composed of the Tenth and Eleventh Wards. The population of these wards amounts in the aggregate to 30,625 whites and 6910 blacks; a sum total of 37, 535 persons. The district is thickly settled from the river as far back as Dryades street. Only two of the streets are paved, viz: Tchoupitoulas and Magazine streets. Washington street is paved, but only for a short distance.

HEALTH.

There was considerable sickness in this district from the beginning of spring to the advent of cold weather, but the rate of mortality was small. The death rate per 1000 inhabitants for that time, from February to November, averaged only 20.11. For the whole year, the death rate was 19.18; the whites being 16.52, and the blacks as high as 30.96.

The deaths from all causes, commencing with January, gradually reached its maximum in May and June, declined in a marked manner in July, and then ran up in September to a moderate figure, which was maintained with a slight increase during the last three months of the year. The majority of the deaths in the spring months was due mainly to diarrhœal and malarial diseases, which are so common at this season. The rise of mortality in September was occasioned by many cases of congestive fever proving fatal.

Measles prevailed as a mild epidemic in the months of February, March and April, but continued sporadically the whole year. The few malignant cases that occurred were attended to, and sanitary measures enforced.

Isolated cases of diphtheria and scarlet fever, usually of a malignant type, were reported throughout the year. There was no tendency to spread, except in a local manner, in the cases coming under observation. Several foci of infection of scarletina back on Jackson street were difficult of eradication. These diseases may extend to serious proportions the present winter, unless checked by energetic sanitation. Fumigation of the rooms, and disinfection of the yards and vaults of infected houses, are done whenever a death or case is reported.

The dengue fever, as a mild but yet extensive disorder, is classed among the remarkable diseases. The community groaned under this *quasi* serious visitation without any *serious* loss of life. This fever lasted about three months, and was only checked by frost in October. Nothing was attempted in the way of sanitation to arrest its rapid progress. Like influenza it swept over the entire city in a very short time. The non-malarial character of this fever is amply proven by the failure of quinine to abridge the average duration of an attack.

Malarial fevers were very common, especially in the rear of St. Charles street, during the Spring and Fall months. The conditions necessary for the generation of *miasmata* were never more strikingly present in this district, owing to the bad effects of continuous rainy weather on the unpaved mud streets and badly-constructed gutters.

Two cases and a death from hæmorrhagic malarial fever were reported in October, as having occurred in a family residing on Josephine street, between Liberty and Howard streets. These cases were declared of a purely malarial nature by competent authorities. Owing to the idea of yellow fever being associated in the minds of many persons with these cases and the *bare* possibility of danger, the sanitary measures instituted in the former disease were immediately carried out.

TABLE SHOWING THE DEATHS FROM THE PRINCIPAL DISEASES, ETC., IN THE FOURTH DISTRICT FOR THE YEAR 1880.

DISEASES.	January.	February.	March.	April.	May.	June.	July.	August.	September.	October.	November.	December.	Total.
Yellow Fever...............	....	....	....	....	....	....	....	....	....	....	....	....	....
Malarial Fevers............	1	2	....	....	1	8	2	3	13	7	3	2	42
Typhoid Fever	1	1	....	1	1	1	....	2	....	1	1	....	9
Scarlet Fever...............	....	....	....	1	1	1	....	....	....	....	....	1	4
Measles....................	....	1	2	1	3	5	1	....	....	....	....	....	13
Small-pox..................	....	....	....	....	....	....	....	....	....	....	....	....	....
Diphtheria	2	1	....	....	2	....	4	....	....	3	....	6	18
Diarrhœal Diseases........	5	....	1	6	17	13	8	6	8	3	4	2	73
Congestion of Brain	....	1	2	1	1	3	5	1	1	....	2	1	18
Convul-ions	6	....	1	1	3	2	1	4	2	6	....	2	28
Phthisis Pulmonalis	7	15	12	9	6	6	3	9	8	7	16	16	114
Deaths from all other causes..	22	28	35	28	45	44	26	31	30	43	40	29	401
Total number of Deaths	44	49	53	48	80	83	50	56	62	70	66	59	720
Deaths. { Whites	25	32	32	35	62	62	38	32	46	50	50	42	506
Colored	19	17	21	13	18	21	12	24	16	20	16	17	214
Death rate per 1000 inhabitants per annum. { Whites	9.79	12.53	12.53	13.71	24.29	24.29	14 88	12.53	18.02	19.59	19.59	16.45	16.52
Colored	32.99	29.52	36.46	22.57	31 25	36.46	20.83	41.67	27.78	34.73	27 78	29.52	30.96
Total	14.06	15.66	16.94	15.34	25.57	26.54	15.98	17.90	17.15	22 37	21 10	18.86	19.18
Malarial Fever	0.31	0 63	....	....	0.31	2.55	0 63	0 95	4.15	2.23	0 95	0.63	1 11
Phthisis Pulmonalis.	2.23	4.79	3 83	2 87	1.65	1.65	0.95	2.87	2.55	2.23	5.11	5.11	3.37

Population—Whites, 30,625; Colored, 6910; Total, 37,535.

SANITARY CONDITION.

The sanitary condition of this district may be said to be superior in some respects to that of previous years. This is improved by the constant inspection of the yards, drains and vaults of premises, which is not without good and permanent results. The people must be educated in the fundamental principles of sanitary science, as Herbert Spencer would say, before the real benefits of this work can be apparent to all.

As for the streets and gutters, the less said about them the better. To condemn their present unsanitary state in too severe language would be to cast odium on the heads of the innocent, perhaps. What could be expected, however, of a street force of only eighteen or twenty men in a district having a superficial area of two and a half or three miles? A hundred men might be able to attend to the streets with credit to the city.

A special inspection of the gutters in summer elicited a few items of interest. The parallel or cross-street gutters were the foul ones at that time, in the front and middle sections to St. Charles street; the constant stream of river water in the perpendicular ones keeping the latter washed out. The rank growth of weeds in the parallel gutters in the rear of St. Charles street, acting as nature's purifiers, keeps these drains in a comparatively clean condition. The perpendicular gutters, not so good in front, are ditches, or canals, in the rear of the district. The drainage in these latter gutters was found to admit of a uniform flow of water, gradually slowing up from the river back, when the engines of the Auxiliary Association were working at the foot of Felicity street. Above Washington street, with the exception of Toledano street, there is little drainage noticeable back of St. Charles street. The water here has to find an exit by the gutters of the above mentioned streets. The capacity of the perpendicular gutters for drainage purposes may be shown best in figures from estimates taken at the time.

Eighth street in front: Flow of water 350 feet in 5½ minutes.
Eighth street in rear: Flow of water stationary.
Second street in front: Flow of water 350 feet in 5¼ minutes.
Second street in rear: Flow of water 350 feet in 6 minutes.
St. Andrew street in front: Flow of water 350 feet in 4½ minutes.
Josephine street in rear: Flow of water 350 feet in 5 minutes.

There is not much difference, therefore, in the rapidity of the flow of water, between the extreme front and rear of the district, in the average gutters examined.

There must be some difference, however, to prevent stagnation in front, but none worth mentioning. This flatness of grade in the gutters is not calculated to facilitate drainage; it must be corrected before anything else need be attempted. If the sides and bottom of the drains were constructed of stone, the friction of the water would be less, and a more rapid flow result as a consequence.

The scavenger force in the two wards consists of ten or a dozen carts, with the accompanying drivers. This limited number of vehicles is expected (as required by law) to remove the trash, garbage, etc., from more than 7000 premises, between the hours of 7 and 10 a. m.; the undertaking is naturally a signal failure. After the streets became impassable from rains these carts stopped going around. A matter of complaint with residents is the dumping of garbage by these drivers into the bad holes on some streets. Quagmires cannot be filled with such material without the creation of public nuisances.

It is unnecessary in this report to recapitulate the sanitary evils not yet dwelt on, such as old privy vaults; low yards without drains; tenement houses; low lots, etc., etc. These nuisances come under the control of health ordinances, and are being rapidly abated with time and perseverance.

SANITARY OPERATIONS.

The limited outbreak of yellow fever in 1879 prompted and urged the completion of the inspections and abatement of nuisances at an early date the past year. Another regular officer was assigned to this District in May, and with his extra help the sanitary work was hastened considerably towards completion.

In the month of June, there were more than 5000 copies of the circular No. 3 distributed in this district. They were left at every house by the sanitary officers as far back as St. Denis street, when the supply allowed to this district gave out. This measure was followed not long afterwards by the free delivery of the copperas in the dry state. The copperas disinfectant, in quantities varying from three pounds and upwards (according to size and nature of vault), was left at every public and private building from the river to St.

Denis street; and around the markets in the rear of the district. Ample instructions were given to the occupants of the houses visited, how to dissolve and use the copperas in the vaults, sinks, drains etc., on the premises. An examination of the privy vaults was included in the above work, and notices were served immediately to abate any nuisance discovered. A saturated solution of copperas, with a strong percentage of carbolic acid added, was kept on hand in the sanitary office during the summer, for the benefit and use of persons living in this portion of the city.

These wise measures, emanating from the Board of Health, were productive of incalculable good, in a sanitary point of view. The residents of the district showed their appreciation of them by a hearty and willing co-operation at all times.

Reinspection of premises where yellow fever occurred in 1879 was repeatedly done throughout the Summer. The vaults and drains on them were subjected to thorough disinfection.

The tanks, barrels, hose, etc., belonging to the Excavating Companies located in the District were made the objects of a special examination and test in August. There was nothing found, however, of an objectionable nature, as the companies use the odorless apparatus as specified in a health ordinance. It is worth mentioning here that, in consequence of the limited number of wagons in the employ of some of these vidangeurs, the emptying of privy vaults is not as rapidly attended to as the nature of the case demands.

HOUSE TO HOUSE INSPECTION.

The regular inspections were over some time in August, but the main portions of the district had been gone over as early as July. This work had been hurried on from the beginning of the year, but not as fast as after the reorganization of the Board of Health in April.

Reinspection of premises was principally attended to during the months of July, August and September. This work is particularly necessary at this time of the year, and is the means of abating many nuisances lying over from a previous inspection.

Inspections and reinspections consist in the careful examination of the yards, drainage-gutters, alleys and privy vaults connected with any premises visited by the sanitary officer. Notices are served afterwards in the abatement of nuisances. Much trouble is often experienced in forcing parties to have their vaults cleaned. This is most likely to be the case when a notice is served within *six or eight* months subsequent to a previous one to the same effect, which is often necessary in badly constructed vaults. The average time for a vault to go uncleaned is ten months or a year. In the case of boarding-houses or asylums it is necessary at least three or four times a year, or even oftener in some instances.

The vaults in this district are usual'y faulty in construction, and, on that account, soon fill with sub-soil water after being emptied. When a vault fills in this manner a careful disinfection is all that is requisite, unless it overflows into the yard. There is a disparity then between *bad* and *foul* (water) vaults.

Ordinances are necessary to enforce, with any hope of success, the filling of low lots and the construction of drains on premises. These evils are numerous in the district, but difficult of abatement. The two ponds on Tchoupitoulas street, just above Washington street, are happily now being filled. The Board of Health, as in former years, ought to have the right to decide when a lot is properly graded for building.

Messrs. Curtis and Lussan, the regular officers, and Mr. Bobner, the detailed police officer, deserve much credit for the efficient and energetic work rendered by them during the year. Mr. Lussan was put on the force in

April and detached at the end of September, while the other officers remained on duty.

The annexed table will show the amount and kind of sanitary work done in this district in the year 1880.

HOUSE TO HOUSE INSPECTION.

Premises	7,803
Premises with hydrants only	1
Premises with cisterns only	7,506
Premises with cisterns and hydrants	272
Premises with wells	710
Premises with no water supply	25
Houses built of wood	7,290
Houses built of brick	513
Houses used as dwellings only	6,642
Houses used as stores and manufactories only	223
Houses used as stores and dwellings	545
Houses used as tenements	98
Houses vacant	303
Rooms in dwelling houses	41,203
Persons occupying premises, white	31,104
Persons occupying premises, colored	7,248
Children born and registered in 1880	242
Children born, but not registered in 1880	132
Condition of premises, good	7,448
Condition of premises, bad	355
Condition of drainage, good	6,779
Condition of drainage, bad	1,024
Condition of privy, good	3,097
Condition of privy, foul (water)	1,544
Condition of privy, bad	3,180
Condition of privy, defective	2,157
Premises with 580 horses, 953 mules, 522 cows and 141 hogs	729
Vacant lots	2,815
Lots not filled to grade	1,031
Private complaints attended to	475

MISCELLANEOUS.

Inspections	17,386
Re inspections	7,751
Nuisances requiring abatement	5,574
Nuisances abated	4,374
Notices to empty privy vaults	3,180
Notices to rebuild privy vaults	56
Notices to repair privy vaults	271
Notices to disinfect privy vaults	1,544
Notices to clean premises	355
Notices to repair houses	1
Notices to fill lots	136
Notices to register births	132
Notices to supply water	20
Notices to construct gutters	243
Notices to repair gutters	538
Notices to remove hogs	30
Dangerous buildings reported	4

Premises disinfected..   28
Premises supplied with disinfectants...........................   4,468
Premises fumigated (rooms 49)..................................   28
Cases of small-pox..
Persons vaccinated, white...   3
Persons vaccinated, colored..
Cases of yellow fever..
Persons reported for non-compliance.........................   15

DAIRIES.

There are as many as 192 premises with cows on them in this district. The total number of animals is reckoned at 522. The dairies are distributed throughout the district, but principally in the front and rear portions. There are not over twenty large dairies in all, the average number of animals kept ranging from one to five.

A personal inspection of the stables was made in the Fall, when they were at their worst in consequence of bad weather. The good, indifferent and bad ones were examined in turn, and advice was given in one instance and an order in another, as the exigencies of any particular case demanded. I was surprised to see the evidences of improvement in many places, as well as a manifest endeavor on the part of the dairymen to comply with the requirements of health and decency. The better class of,dairies had good or water-tight flooring in the stalls and drainage gutters and receptacles for the excrementitious material of the cows. There were a limited number of what might be termed filthy dairies examined, where no disposition was shown by the owners of them to keep anything clean. It is for this class of stables that a Health Ordinance. properly worded, is requisite to enforce a strict compliance with law. This is but an instance of a retrograde metamorphosis of human nature, inasmuch as these slovenly people are ignorant of what constitutes cleanliness of either person or premises. In the absence of any law to limit the number of animals to be kept within thickly-settled neighborhoods, or to define the manner of construction of the stables, the sanitary officers are able only to act as in ordinary premises. The matter of the adulteration of milk, like the food on which the animals should be fed, is still beyond the immediate control of the Board of Health.

SHIPPING.

The shipping along the river front was regularly inspected in person every day or so, from the middle of May to the end of September. The Captain, or chief officer, of the vessel was interviewed, and a written statement required of him concerning the health of the crew, ports stopped at and sailed from, kind of cargo, etc., etc. The regular printed forms were used in every inspection. Some objections were raised in the beginning, calling in question the legality of the examination, but they were easily set aside when fully explained.

No sickness was discovered on any steamship or sailing vessel visited in the Summer. The majority of the steamships had sailed from foreign ports direct, coming here for either cotton or grain. The Spanish vessels sailing between West Indian and Mexican ports and this city came here usually with water-ballast or wine and other like simple cargoes. The crews of these latter vessels are almost invariably acclimated Spaniards or Italians.

Number of steamships inspected......................................   36
Number of ships inspected...   15

Total...   51

Number of vessels sailing from infected ports......................... 13
Number of vessels touching at infected ports......................... 10
Number of so-called infected vessels................................

MARKETS.

The principal markets in this District are not in perfect sanitary condition. Complaints have been received of late concerning three out of the whole number of five.

The Saraparu market has been reported in a dangerous state, the shed at the end towards Rousseau street being shaky and liable to fall down at any time. The roof of the Magazine market leaks in several places. This has been so for the past six months. The Ninth street market is sadly in need of repair. The water-plug stationed here was reported out of order about a year ago. The Keller and Second street markets are in very good condition.

BONE-YARDS.

These establishments for the purpose of rendering and cooking the flesh of dead animals, are situated in the rear of the Claiborne canal, on Washington street. They were reported early in the summer as nuisances in the city, so long as they remained on one of the principal streets and drives in the district. A committee was appointed by the Board of Health to examine and report on them; since which time the matter continues *in statu quo*. I succeeded, with some trouble, in having a lot of hogs removed from these yards. These hogs were being fed on the flesh of dead animals, and sold to butchers at every convenient opportunity. The proprietors of two bone-yards were served with peremptory orders in September to cease further carrying on of their business, until such time as they might make application for and receive permits for so doing. Mr. Barbach, owner of bone-yard No. 1, complied with the notice served on him, and is no longer to my knowledge pursuing his business. Mr. Kolwe, owner of bone-yard No. 2, got an injunction out immediately in one of the courts and has continued working. The difference between the two establishments is decided, and in favor of the one owned by Mr. Kolwe. The latter party uses steam altogether to act on the carcasses of the animals, which are placed in cisterns for that purpose; the former party makes use of a plain iron boiler, in which the animals are imperfectly covered over during the boiling process. Mr. Barbach is willing to move off Washington street, and put up steam works in the extreme rear of the Sixth District. Mr. Kolwe, having steam works already, is now testing in the courts the question of the eligibility of the location. These cases demand the early action of your honorable body.

PUBLIC SCHOOLS.

These institutions of learning were inspected just before the holidays. There are eleven of them in the district for the children of the white and colored residents separately.

The schools were found about in the same condition as when reported on in detail a year ago. I thought proper, therefore, to omit the tables usually appended to this report. I would call attention, moreover, to the general unsanitary condition of the new Dryades street school for colored children. The yard and building are not as good as the ones in use last year.

Yours respectfully,

R. A. BAYLEY, M. D.,
Sanitary Inspector Fourth District.

REPORT OF

EUG. J. MIOTON, M. D.,

SANITARY INSPECTOR FIFTH DISTRICT,
CITY OF NEW ORLEANS, TO THE

BOARD OF HEALTH

OF THE STATE OF LOUISIANA,

FOR THE YEAR 1880.

35

REPORT OF EUG. J. MIOTON, M. D., SANITARY INSPECTOR FIFTH DISTRICT.

OFFICE SANITARY INSPECTOR FIFTH DISTRICT, {
New Orleans, La., January 1, 1881. }

Joseph Jones, M. D., President Board of Health:

Sir—The following report of sanitary operations performed in this district, including health statistics, etc., during the year ending December 31, 1880, is respectfully submitted.

Having entered on duty April 11, 1880, I make use of the records preserved in the office, and particularly the monthly reports of my worthy and able predecessor, Doctor J. H. Magruder, to complete necessary material for a full statement of the year's sanitary work.

TOPOGRAPHY.

The Fifth District, which is composed of Algiers, Tunisburg, McDonoghville, Freetown and Gretna, is situated on the right bank of the Mississippi river and extends from Harvey's canal, oppssite Carrolton, to the limits of Tunisburg opposite Chalmette Cemetery (battle grounds), and occupies an area of fourteen miles in length by half a mile in depth.

As is easily seen, the Fifth District is probably one of the largest of the city, although its population is only (14,000) fourteen thousand inhabitants.

HEALTH.

It is most gratifying to state that the amount of sickness and the mortality that have occurred, when compared with the census of the district, will show the health of the community to have been excellent. Only one hundred and forty-two (142) deaths have occurred during the past year in Algiers out of a population of eight thousand eight hundred and fifty-six (8856) inhabitants.

Not a single case of yellow fever nor of small-pox has been recorded in the district for the year 1880. The exanthemata were exceptionally mild; the malarial fevers and dengue, which prevailed throughout the summer months, were also of a mild type, there being only three deaths of malarial fevers and not a single one from dengue.

The following table shows the total mortality in Algiers from all causes for the year 1880:

TABLE ILLUSTRATING DEATHS IN THE FIFTH DISTRICT DURING THE YEAR 1880.

DISEASES.	January.	February.	March.	April.	May.	June.	July.	August.	September.	October.	November.	December.	Total.
Malarial Fevers	.....	.....	.....	.....	.....	1	.....	.....	.....	1	.....	.....	2
Measles	.....	.....	.....	.....	3	.....	.....	.....	.....	.....	.....	.....	3
Diphtheria	.....	.....	.....	1	.....	4	.....	.....	.....	1	.....	1	7
Diarrhœal Diseases	.....	.....	.....	.....	.....	1	.....	.....	.....	.....	.....	.....	1
Congestion of Brain	.....	.....	.....	.....	.....	1	.....	1	.....	1	.....	2	5
Convulsions	1	.....	.....	2	.....	1	2	1	.....	.....	1	.....	8
Phthisis Pulmonalis	1	....	3	1	1	2	....	4	3	1	5	4	25
Deaths from all other causes	7	6	8	6	16	10	11	3	7	6	6	5	91
Total number of Deaths	9	6	11	10	20	20	13	9	10	10	12	12	142
Number { White	5	3	6	8	7	16	9	6	7	6	9	6	88
Deaths. { Colored	4	3	5	2	13	4	4	3	3	4	3	6	54
Death rate per 1000 inhabitants per annum. { Malarial Fever	.....	.....	.....	.....	.....	1 04	.....	.....	.....	1.04	.....	.....	0.22
Phthisis Pulmonalis	1.04	.....	4.01	1.04	1.04	2.08	.....	5.15	4.01	1.04	6.20	6.09	2 82
Whites	12 01	7.03	14 05	19.03	16.09	38 04	21.01	14 05	16 09	14 05	21 01	14.05	17.52
Colored	10.07	9.06	15 08	6 05	40.75	12.07	12.07	9.06	9.06	12 07	9.06	18.02	14 00
Total	.....	.....	.....	.....	.....	.....	.....	.....	.....	.....	.....	.....	16.10

Population—White, 5021; Colored, 3856. Total. 8857.
Death Rate per 1000 Inhabitants per Annum –White, 9 93; Colored. 14.00. Total. 16.

TABLE SHOWING THE SANITARY CENSUS OF THE FIFTH DISTRICT (ALGIERS) DURING THE YEAR 1880.

White.

Total population	5,021
Natives of New Orleans	2,603
Born in other States or foreign countries	2,418
Male	2,993
Female	2,028
Adults	3,243
Children	1,778
Vaccinated	3,904
Unvaccinated	1,117

Black and Colored.

Total population	3,835
Natives of New Orleans	1,992
Born in other States or foreign countries	1,843
Male	1,631
Female	2,204

Total Population

White, black and colored	8,856

Table showing the number of inspections and reinspections made in the Fifth District (Algiers) during the year 1880:

HOUSE TO HOUSE INSPECTIONS.

Number of premises	2,542
Number of premises with cisterns	2,103
Number of premises with no water supply	41
Water supply, number of gallons	....
Premises with horses, 151	76
Premises with mules, 176; hogs, 374	344
Number of houses built of wood	2,526

Number of houses built of brick................................ 16
Number of houses used as dwellings........................... 2,103
Number of houses used as stores, manufactories, etc............... 301
Number of houses vacant....................................... 138
Number of rooms in dwelling houses............................. 934
Number of persons occupying premises........................... ....
Number of floors in good condition............................. 2,403
Number of floors in bad condition.............................. 139
Number of roofs in good condition.............................. 2,403
Number of roofs in bad condition............................... 139
Number of privies in good condition............................ 1,981
Number of privies in bad condition............................. 561
Number of vacant lots.. ....
Number of private complaints attended to....................... 1,365

MISCELLANEOUS.

Number of inspections made..................................... 16,322
Number of re-inspections 3,864
Number of nuisances requiring abatement........................ 8,909
Number of nuisances abated..................................... 8,909
Number of notices served to empty privy vaults................. 561
Number of notices served to rebuild privy vaults............... 33
Number of notices served to repair privy vaults................ 33
Number of notices served to disinfect privy vaults............. 2,241
Number of notices served to clean premises..................... 2,241
Number of notices served to disinfect premises................. 2,241
Number of notices served to repair houses...................... 31
Number of notices served to fill lots.......................... 129
Number of notices served to supply water....................... 91
Number of notices served to remove hogs........................ 378
Number of premises disinfected................................. 4,002
Number of premises fumigated................................... 23
Number of vessels inspected.................................... 67

SANITATION.

The almost total immunity of the Fifth District from all contagious or infectious diseases during the year which has just elapsed, can, I believe, be fairly and justly attributed to the speedy and energetic manner with which the Board of Health's instructions concerning house to house inspections, the free distribution of *disinfectants* (copperas and carbolic acid), the abatement of all nuisances, the special inspection of all the sea-faring vessels landing within the limits of the district. have been carried out. From April to the latter part of October, over 15 barrels of sulphate of iron and over 40 gallons of pure carbolic acid (Calvert's No. 5), have been freely and gratuitiously distributed to the people of the district. All the premises where cases of diphtheria and scarlatina have occurred have been thoroughly cleaned, fumigated and disinfected; the bed-clothes and the patient's wardrobe were also treated in the same manner.

PUBLIC SCHOOLS.

The public schools, two in number, McDonogh Nos. 4 and 5, were inspected several times during the past year, and their sanitary condition was made the object of careful note. Both buildings are comparatively new, having been completed in 1875; the rooms are spacious, well ventilated and kept neat and clean. Some of the rooms in these schools are quite crowded, and I presume are even more so now, the number of pupils having increased since these particulars have been obtained. The privy accomodations and play-grounds are amply sufficient, and are kept in a very commendable manner.

VACCINATION.

Although Tuesday and Thursday in each week, from 11 to 1 o'clock p. m., were set apart for gratuitous vaccination, only three applicants were vaccinated in this office during the year, showing a very deplorable indifference on the part of those who are most interested.

INSPECTION OF SHIPS.

In accordance with the sanitary rules, adopted and approved by the Board of Health of the State of Louisiana on April 22d, 1880, sixty-seven (67) ships were inspected by me from May to October. Of these vessels twenty-four (24) had sailed from Havana and Florida Keys, one (1) from Vera Cruz and forty-two (42) from healthy ports.

The sanitary condition of the vessels, crews and passengers was in all instances found excellent.

My most cordial thanks are here tendered to the officers of the Morgan line of steamers for their politeness and courtesy towards my sanitary police officers and myself.

BARK "EXCELSIOR."

On the seventeenth of August, 1880, arrived from Quarantine Station the Swedish bark "Excelsior," Captain Björkgren. The bark landed at "Wallace Wood's powder wharf," Tunisburg, Fifth District (opposite the abattoirs). I immediately repaired on board and officially took charge of her. According to the instructions I had received from the Board of Health; I placed permanently on board my detailed officer, Mr. James Nowell, with the strict order of allowing no communication from land without a written permit from the President of the State Board of Health. This rule was rigidly carried out, and during all the stay of said bark in port, there were admitted on her those only who were employed in loading the vessel, and who had been previously examined by me and found to be acclimated. I made it my duty to visit the bark twice daily, morning and evening. Two (2) cases of dengue, both ending in recovery, occurred on the bark, which cases were reported at once. The Honorable President of the Board of Health, Doctor Joseph Jones, saw both patients and confirmed my diagnosis. A light purgative and a few grains of quinine were administered, and the fever readily subsided.

The bark "Excelsior" left for Bayonne, France, on the eleventh day of September, 1880, loaded with grain.

The wise and prudent measures, rigidly enforced in this case by the State Board of Health, cannot be too highly praised, and all those who know and appreciate the delicate position of the Board at that particular moment will acknowledge the wisdom of the course pursued on this occasion.

DRAINAGE.

The drainage of this district is very defective. The portion lying between the river and Market street is well drained, but back of that street there is no sewerage at all; and, as a natural consequence, the rear of the district is overflowed after each heavy rain, and remains so for days until the water is absorbed or evaporated. This complete lack of drainage could be remedied at very little expense by opening an outlet to the swamps. The above remarks will show that the streets must be, and are, in a deplorable condition; although, in justice to the Street Commissioner, I must say that much has been done of late for their improvement.

NUISANCE BOAT.

The most urgent and pressing want of the Fifth District for the present is, most assuredly, a nuisance boat. The ground used as a place of deposit for all kinds of garbage is situated in a thickly-settled part of the district, is a source of danger and annoyance for those living in its vicinity, and a disgrace to any community. I have time and again complained of this state of affairs, but vainly so far. I earnestly hope that the Board of Health will take the necessary steps to secure a nuisance wharf and a garbage boat for the district.

MARKETS.

The markets of the district have been inspected regularly every week throughout the year, and have always been found in a clean and irreprovable condition. Not a single complaint was ever made against them during the whole year, nor has any objectionable article of food ever been seen or offered for sale.

DAIRIES.

There are from twenty to twenty-five dairies in the district, which have been regularly inspected during the year, at intervals of one and two months, and cleanliness of the premises have been carefully enforced. The condition of the dairy buildings was especially examined, and with a few exceptions—which were made the object of special remonstrance—they were found to be kept clean; the cows looked healthy and in good condition. Quite a number of persons keep from one to three cows for family use, but no complaint has ever been made against them.

SANITARY POLICE.

It is my pleasant duty to bear testimony to the perfect efficiency of Messrs. Hy. Labarre and Jas. Nowell. I must here state to their praise that they are well qualified for the position, attentive to duty, prompt in action, and that they neglect nothing that can promote the health of the district.

POLICE STATION.

The Eighth Precinct Police Station, in charge of Sergeant J. J. Pujol, is always kept clean and in the best sanitary condition.

Respectfully submitted,

EUG. J. MIOTON, M. D.,
Sanitary Inspector Fifth District.

REPORTS OF

W. H. CARSON, M. D.,

SANITARY INSPECTOR SIXTH & SEVENTH DISTRICTS,

CITY OF NEW ORLEANS, TO THE

BOARD OF HEALTH

OF THE STATE OF LOUISIANA,

FOR THE YEAR 1880.

36

REPORTS OF W. H. CARSON, M. D., SANITARY INSPECTOR SIXTH & SEVENTH DISTRICTS.

SIXTH DISTRICT.

OFFICE OF SANITARY INSPECTOR, SIXTH DISTRICT; ⎱
New Orleans, December 31; 1880. ⎰

To Joseph Jones, M. D., President Board of Health, State of Louisiana:

Sir—I have the honor to submit the following summary report of the operations of this office, and other affairs of importance, as connected with the sanitary condition of the Sixth District of this city, for the year 1880:

HEALTH.

Throughout the year this district has remained remarkably healthy. With the exception of a visit from the benign dengue fever in the later months of the year, and with but cases of contagious diseases, the health of the district has been but slightly disturbed, the death-rate falling in the month of March as low as four per cent per thousand.

This rate of mortality, with a population of over sixteen thousand, speaks unusually well for the general good health of the district.

Not even a *suspicious* case of yellow fever during the year, and the one case occurring in September of last year (1879) the premises were repeatedly disinfected and cleansed, inside and out, painted, whitewashed, water-closets emptied, and other sanitary measures incident to prevention duly attended to.

In connection with my article on the health of the Sixth District, I have prepared a tableau of mortuary statistics, showing the number and cause of death, with the per centage per thousand in the district for the past year.

I believe that the various forms of malarial fever, at times prevalent in this district, could be decidedly lessened, if not absolutely abolished, if the benefits of proper scientific drainage were in force. Many localities in the district have but little or no drainage, and it is scarcely to be wondered at that, after the rainy season, with the neighboring fields flooded with water at some localities, and saturated throughout, and with the aid of a semi-tropical sun, the powerful agents in the production of miasmatic fevers, if not of many other more pernicious diseases, that the various types of malarial fever prevail.

Still born. 13
Population—Whites 11,951; colored, 4,078. Total, 16,029.

DRAINAGE.

No efforts have been made during the past year as to the improvement of drainage in the district. That the matter requires attention, and that at an early date, is indisputable.

The continuous and heavy rains for the past four or five months have rendered the roads and highways impassable, and large drifts from the roadway have, in many instances, clogged the drainage on either side of the roadbed, in many instances resulting in the formation of quite extensive pools of water, stagnant and foul smelling.

I cannot but again refer especially to the section between Toledano and Delachaise streets. This locality and its great drainage deficiency has been repeatedly laid before the authorities, but without avail; no remedial action has been attempted. In this section referred to, heavy rains will keep the rear of the district in overflow for many weeks, and even at times many months.

WATER SUPPLY.

If the district is sadly deficient in drainage requirements, the same may be said of its artificial water supply. No extension of the water-mains has as yet been made beyond Toledano street, and its absence is made manifest in many ways, as it refers to the furtherance of sanitary measures.

Sunken wells still continue to be the main resource of the inhabitants of the district, and with the addition of their wooden cisterns furnish sufficient grounds for suspicion as to the purity and properties of their water for drinking purposes.

With not a hydrant in the district, and depending upon their supply of water from their cisterns and wells, it is almost impossible that the desired cleanliness and measures of a sanitary nature could be systematically attended to.

PUBLIC BUILDINGS.

The public buildings in the district number twenty-six (26); this includes public schools, churches, asylums, a police station and a market.

All of these buildings have been the subject of inspection during the year. The public schools, according to the usual custom, have received a most thorough sanitary investigation, and it is my pleasure to state that, without exception, they presented a most satisfactory condition.

The Jefferson market, located at the corner of Magazine and Berlin streets, is the principal and only market in the district.

No complaint can be offered as to its sanitary condition. On the contrary, cleanliness is the rule, and on one occasion have I had to take measures to prevent the sale of tainted meat.

DAIRIES.

Early in the month of September, all the dairies of the Sixth District, numbering eighty-five (85), received a most thorough inspection an inspection not only devoted to the dairy proper, stock. etc , but also the neighboring premises and outbuildings, and all was exceedingly satisfactory.

This condition is in marked contrast to that noted in my annual report of the year previous (1879), at which period but little time or attention was devoted by dairymen to many of the most simple, yet important hygenic requirements.

The inspection of the stock proved them to be in the possible condition of health; milk-pails, cans and the other attachments incident to the business were observed to be in an exceedingly clean condition.

It is with much satisfaction that I embrace the opportunity to present such a deserving and industrious class in a more enviable light than that contained in my report on this subject for the previous year (1879).

PRIVY SYSTEM.

The pernicious privy system, with its leaky, ill-constructed and foul smelling vaults, yet continue to exist and flourish ; no change, no improvement, but the same in character and build as used by generations back of the present.

In this district this unhealthy and obnoxious condition is probably not so prominent, or its unquestionable deleterious effects, to any very great degree, so noticeable, from the fact that the district occupies an extensive area in proportion to its population.

Yet in the more thickly settled and populated sections, the source of many of the so-called filth diseases, this privy system in vogue is not without just and almost positive suspicion.

· This is a subject of the utmost vital importance to every resident of this city, for the obnoxious system is not confined to any one district, and it is most sincerely predicted that ere another decade this most uncivilized and abhorrent privy sysiem, now in use, will have been abolished without even a vestige of its former residence.

SANITARY WORK.

The amount and character of the work performed is tabulated and presented herewith :

HOUSE TO HOUSE INSPECTION.

Premises 2,959
Premises with cisterns only...................................... 3,140
Premises with a well.. 81
Premises with no water supply.................................... 6

Houses built of wood... 2,891
Houses built of brick... 68
Houses used as dwellings only................................... 2,570
Houses used as stores and manufactories only................. 70
Houses used as stores and dwellings............................ 98
Houses vacant.. 143
Tenement houses... 78
Rooms in dwelling houses.. 7,570
Persons occupying premises, white............................... 7,969
Persons occupying premises, colored............................. 3,073
Condition of floor, good... 2,959
Condition of roof, good.. 2,959
Condition of privy, good... 2,047
Condition of privy, foul... 912
Condition of privy, defective.................................... 17
Premises with 193 horses, 477 mules, 516 cows. 119 hogs......... 249
Vacant lots.. 3,141
Lots not filled to grade... 1,283
No drainage.. 1,403
Applications for building permits................................ 8
Private complaints attended to 239

MISCELLANEOUS.

Inspections made... 6,015
Re-inspections made.. 3,297
Nuisances requiring abatement.................................... 3,017
Nuisances abated... 2,990
Notices to empty privy vaults 912
Notices to rebuild privy vaults.................................. 49
Notices to repair privy vaults................................... 22
Notices to disinfect privy vaults................................ 297
Notices to clean premises.. 1,006
Notices to repair houses... 1
Notices to fill lots... 7
Notices to supply water.. 6
Notices to construct gutters..................................... 757
Notices to repair gutters.. 45
Notices to remove hogs... 22
Dangerous buildings reported..................................... 1
Premises disinfected... 5
Premises fumigated, rooms.. 16
Persons reported for non-compliance.............................. 1
Capacity of cisterns in gallons.................................. 3,088,000

I take pleasure in acknowledging the ability, trustworthiness and zeal of my sanitary officer, H. F. Evans, at all times satisfactory and ever conscientious in the discharge of his duty.   Respectfully submitted,

W. H. CARSON, M. D.,
Sanitary Inspector Sixth and Seventh Districts.

SEVENTH DISTRICT.

OFFICE OF SANITARY INSPECTOR, SEVENTH DISTRICT, }
NEW ORLEANS, December 31, 1880. }

To Joseph Jones, M. D , President Board of Health State of Louisiana:

Sir—I have the honor to submit the following summary report, with its accompanying comments, of the sanitary work performed throughout the year 1880 in the Seventh District of this city.

HEALTH.

The condition of health generally has not materially differed for the past few years.

It is worthy of notice that in the population of the district, numbering in the total six thousand two hundred and thirty-seven (6237)—U. S. census, 1880—the percentage of mortality attending the colored race is in excess of that of the whites.

The two races are rather evenly divided in population, the whites numbering 3112 and the colored 3125. The deaths number in the former 62, and in the latter 66.

Notwithstanding the heavy and persistent rains of the fall season, types of malarial fever did not present an increase, though diphtheria and intestinal diseases were prevalent.

This district, in company with the neighboring and lower district, the Sixth, had each a death from yellow fever to record against them for 1879. No case or anything even suspicious appeared throughout the past year, 1880.

The premises wherein the death occurred, and above referred to, received the same careful attention in the way of disinfection and other preventive measures that its fellow in the Sixth District received.

In great part the good health of the district is to be attributed to the better drainage attending this district than that of many of the others, its mean elevation being about fourteen inches over and above that of the First and Second Districts.

PUBLIC BUILDINGS.

The public buildings in the Seventh District number in all twenty-one, subdivided as follows: Twelve churches, two fire-engine houses, one court house, a jail building, police station, market and three public schools.

These various buildings have been duly inspected during the year, and with the exception of the court house, jail and police station, were found to be in a satisfactory sanitary condition; the court house has been long in need of repair, and the neglect to attend to the same is sadly affecting the appearance and usefulness of the building. A comparative small outlay at the present time, would unquestionably save to the city a considerable outlay of money.

If the court house is in bad condition, what must be said of the jail and police station ?

The jail, a brick building of about two stories, and without the slighest pretense to sanitary requirements in its architecture, is literally falling to pieces; new joists are wanted, the floors are rotten and wanting in many places, the stair-way rickety and unsafe, many of the prison cells have had to be abandoned, no longer being habitable or secure for confinement of the prisoners, and in toto the building is but a shell, and a most decidedly unhealthy one, even admitting that its use is confined only to the criminal class.

It was estimated that over one hundred barrels of bat manure were removed last September, the accumulation of years, leaving yet in great numbers the source of the annoyance.

Various grand juries in their reports have called attention to the disgraceful condition of this building and its present unfitness for the confinement of criminals, and surely it is about time that some attention was devoted to it.

PRIVY SYSTEM.

Though the privy system in vogue in the Seventh District, and I believe confined to this one district, is rather simple in character and of primeval origin, it consisting of an excavation in the soil some four to six feet square and over which is placed a light wooden enclosure easily movable, I earnestly believe that but little of the bad unhealthy effects are produced which are assigned and now generally accepted, to the brick, and cemented and stationary vaults of the other districts.

For when their trench is no longer serviceable, the contents are disinfected, earth is thrown in covering the space in use completely, and the house is moved to another spot. The localities for erecting these temporary buildings are selected as far from the dwelling as possible, consequently the inmates are decidedly more free than those residing in the more densely populated districts of the city, where the closet is permanently built, and in the majority of cases forming part of the main building.

I do not desire to have it understood that this character of vault and the system described, applies to all of the residences in the district, for such is not the case, as there are localities in which it would be impractable and deleterious to the public health.

MARKETS.

One market centrally located, supplies the wants of the district in this respect; the meat sold is unusually good, and cleanliness is an ever present feature of the building.

DAIRIES.

The dairies are extremely numerous in this district, numbering over fifty, the majority of which are located on Carrollton avenue.

They received a careful visit and inspection in the early part of September, and but small complaint can be found against them; they are generally clean and out-buildings in good order.

MORTALITY.

The mortality of the district during the past year has not been great, the total number of deaths being one hundred and twenty-eight (128), a death-rate of 20.52 per thousand.

Since 1877 not a death from small-pox has occurred in the district.

I have prepared a tabulated statement of the mortality of the district for the year, in which is shown all the deaths from the principal diseases, showing the per centage per thousand for each of the months of the year:

STATEMENT OF MORTALITY FOR THE SEVENTH DISTRICT FOR THE YEAR 1880.

DISEASES.	January.	February.	March.	April.	May.	June.	July.	August.	September.	October.	November.	December.	Total.
Yellow Fever......................	....	....	....	....	....	....	....	....	....	....	....	....	....
Malarial Fevers..................	....	....	....	....	....	....	....	....	2	....	....	....	2
Typhoid Fever...................	....	....	....	....	....	....	....	....	....	....	....	....	....
Scarlet Fever....................	....	....	....	....	....	....	....	....	....	....	....	....	....
Measles..........................	....	....	....	....	....	....	....	....	....	....	....	....	....
Small-pox........................	....	....	....	....	....	....	....	....	....	....	....	....	....
Diphtheria.......................	1	....	....	....	....	....	....	....	....	....	1	....	2
Diarrheal Diseases...............	1	....	....	....	1	....	....	....	1	....	1	....	4
Congestion of Brain.............	....	....	....	....	....	1	....	....	....	1	....	....	2
Convulsions	....	....	....	3	....	....	....	1	....	....	....	1	5
Phthisis Pulmonalis..............	....	....	3	1	....	1	....	....	....	....	3	1	9
Deaths from all other causes......	8	11	4	12	10	8	10	9	9	8	4	8	104
Total number of Deaths........	10	14	7	16	12	9	11	9	12	9	9	10	128
Deaths. { Whites	6	6	2	8	7	4	4	3	6	8	5	3	62
{ Colored	4	8	5	8	5	5	7	6	6	1	4	7	66
Death rate per 1000 inhabitants per annum. { Whites	23.13	23.13	7.71	30.84	26.99	15.42	15.42	11.56	23.13	31.16	19.28	11.56	19.92
{ Colored	15.36	30.72	19.20	30.72	19.20	19.20	26.88	23.04	23.04	30.72	15.36	26.88	21.12
{ Total	19.27	26.93	13.47	30.78	23.08	17.31	21.16	17.31	23.08	17.31	17.31	19.27	20.52
{ Yellow Fever.......	....	....	....	....	....	....	....	....	....	....	....	....	....
{ Malarial Fever......	....	....	....	....	....	....	....	....	3.84	....	....	....	0.32
{ Phthisis Pulmonalis.	....	....	5.77	1.94	....	1.94	....	....	....	....	5.77	1.94	1.44

Still born. 5.
Population—Whites, 3125; colored, 3112.   Total 6237.

SANITARY WORK.

The amount performed during the year is tabulated and presented herewith.

The district had the benefit this year of the undivided attention of a sanitary officer, consequently the work has been the more thoroughly and satisfactorily performed. Mr. H. F. Davis served in this capacity until the 1st of September, when the force was reduced, and only one officer left on duty for the Sixth and Seventh Districts, Mr. H. F. Evans.

HOUSE TO HOUSE INSPECTION.

Premises... 1,326
Premises with cisterns only............................... 1,327
Premises with a well.. 303
Premises with no water supply............................. 68
Houses built of wood...................................... 1,301
Houses built of brick..................................... 25
Houses used as dwellings only............................. 1,103
Houses used as stores and manufactories only.............. 25
Houses used as stores and dwellings....................... 85
Houses vacant... 56
Tenement houses... 47
Rooms in dwelling houses.................................. 4,033
Persons occupying premises, white......................... 949
Persons occupying premises, colored....................... 1,716
Condition of floor, good.................................. 1,326
Condition of roof, good................................... 1,326
Condition of privy, good.................................. 896
Condition of privy, foul.................................. 430
Condition of privy, defective............................. 36

37

Premises with 126 horses, 36 mules, 600 cows, 150 hogs.............. 402
Vacant lots.. 3,636
Lots not filled to grade... 2,872
No drainage.. 2,630
Private complaints attended to...................................... 83

MISCELLANEOUS.

Special inspections... 28
Inspections made... 2,761
Reinspections made.. 1,269
Nuisances requiring abatement...................................... 902
Nuisances abated... 901
Notices to empty privy vaults....................................... 430
Notices to rebuild privy vaults..................................... 17
Notices to repair privy vaults...................................... 21
Notices to disinfect privy vaults................................... 185
Notices to clean premises... 189
Notices to repair houses.. 1
Notices to fill lots.. 1
Notices to supply water... 68
Notices to construct gutters.. 163
Notices to repair gutters... 6
Notices to remove hogs.. 1
Dangerous buildings reported....................................... 3
Capacity of cisterns in gallons.................................1,613,200

Respectfully submitted,
W. H. CARSON, M. D.,
Sanitary Inspector of the Sixth and Seventh Districts.

REPORT OF

J. C. BEARD,

CORONER CITY OF NEW ORLEANS, TO THE

BOARD OF HEALTH

OF THE STATE OF LOUISIANA,

FOR THE YEAR 1880.

REPORT OF J. C. BEARD, CORONER OF CITY OF NEW ORLEANS.

NEW ORLEANS, January 1, 1881.

To the President and Members of the Board of Health:

Gentlemen—Herewith please find Mortuary Report of Coroner's office for year ending December 31, 1880, showing, as per tables annexed, the causes of death and ages; mortality for each month, classified according to their sex and nationality; the number of suicides, their sex, color and nationality.

Respectfully submitted,

J. C. BEARD, Coroner,
per John J. Finn, Sect.

DEATHS AND THEIR CAUSES CLASSIFIED ACCORDING TO AGES.

CAUSES.	Still-born.	Premature.	Under 1 year.	1 to 5 years.	5 to 10 years.	10 to 15 years.	15 to 20 years.	20 to 25 years.	25 to 30 years.	30 to 35 years.	35 to 40 years.	40 to 45 years.	45 to 50 years.	50 to 55 years.	55 to 60 years.	60 to 65 years.	65 to 70 years.	70 to 75 years.	75 to 80 years.	80 to 85 years.	85 to 90 years.	90 to 100 years.	Over 100 years.	Not stated.	Total.
Abortion	2																								2
Abscess of spinal column						1																			2
Albuminuria									1	1		1	1	1											5
Alcoholism								2	1	1	1														5
Anæmia			3																						3
Aneurism of heart							1														1				2
Apoplexy									3		1	5	1	3		7	1								21
Ascites										1						1									2
Asphytia			1			1	1																		3
Asthma																2		2			1				5
Burns			1				1	1					1								1				4
Cancer of breast												1													1
Cancer of face														1		1		1							2
Cancer of stomach												1		1	1	1									3
Cancerous ulceration, bowels												1													1
Catarrh	3																								3
Cholera infantum	3																								3
Cirrhosis of liver										2															2
Concussion of brain										2				2										1	5
Congestion			1				1		3												1				6
Congestion of brain		2		1			2	2	4	5	2	3	1	2	2									1	27
Congestive chill	1						1		1	1	1			1	1										7
Convulsions		28	10	2					1																41
Croup	1																								1
Debility, general									1		1	1	3		3	2	1	1							13
Debility, infantile		14	3																						17
Debility, senile														1	5	4	3	7	1	3	5				29
Dentition		12	13																						25
Diarrhœa		5	1	1		1		1	2				1		1										13
Diphtheria			2																						2
Dropsy			1					1	1	1			1	1					1						7
Drowning			3	7	6	2	5	5	5	4	4	4	3	2	2	1					1			2	55
Dysentery		2	3	1							1	2	2						1						12
Dysentery, chronic											1			1					1						3
Effects of birth	1																								1
Enteritis, chronic		4	1	1					1		2		1												10
Epilepsy								2	2		1		1												6
Fever, dengue																					1				1
Fever, malarial		2	7	3			2	2		1		2							3	1					23

DEATHS AND THEIR CAUSES, CLASSIFIED ACCORDING TO AGES—Continued.

CAUSES.	Still-born	Premature	Under 1 year	1 to 5 years	5 to 10 years	10 to 15 years	15 to 20 years	20 to 25 years	25 to 30 years	30 to 35 years	35 to 40 years	40 to 45 years	45 to 50 years	50 to 55 years	55 to 60 years	60 to 65 years	65 to 70 years	70 to 75 years	75 to 80 years	80 to 85 years	85 to 90 years	90 to 100 years	Over 100 years	Not stated	Total
Fever pernicious				1																					1
Fever, puerperal								1																	1
Fever, scarlet			1																						1
Fever, typhoid			2																						2
Fracture of cranium			1		1	1	1	1	1	2	1	2	1	1				1							14
Fracture of neck																	1								1
Fracture of ribs											1														1
Fracture of spinal column				1																					1
Frozen to death																				1					1
Gangrene																1									1
Gastritis			2	1		1			1				1	1											7
Hæmoptysis							1		1	2	4		1	1											10
Hemorrhage, umbilical			3																						3
Heart disease				1	1		1	2	3	2	7	3	7	4	4	2	3	1	1						42
Hepatitis														1											1
Hernia, strangulated																					1				1
Hydrocephalus			2																						2
Imperforate anus			1																						1
Inanition			33																						33
Infanticide by drowning			1	1																					2
Infanticide by strangulation			1																						1
Infanticide by violence			1																						1
Injuries received—explosions							1	1	1	1			1												5
Injuries received—machinery							1	1	1																3
Injuries received—railroad			1	3		1	1			1	2		1		1										12
Injuries received—vehicles				1				2																	3
Kidney disease																	1								1
Marasmus			5	2																					7
Measles			5	8	3						1														17
Meningitis			2	3	1	1		1			1														9
Paralysis												1	1					1							3
Peritonitis				1							1	2		1											5
Pertussis			12	8	1																				21
Phthisis pulmonalis			1	3	2	2		4	8	10	8	7	4	5	1	5	3	1	2						66
Pleurisy															1										1
Pleuro-Pneumonia			1				1																		2
Pneumonia			19	4	1			4	1	1	2	2	1	1		2		1							39
Premature births		58																							58
Rheumatism					1									2			1	1							5
Stillborn	187																								187
Strangulation				1																					1
Suffocation			3						1																4
Suicide, drowning															1	1	1	1							4
Suicide, gunshot wound							1	1	1		1		1	2		1	1								8
Suicide, hanging						1	1		1		1		1												5
Suicide, poison								2			2		1												5
Syphilis inherited			1																						1
Tetanus			1	3						1				1											6
Trismus nascentium			43																						43
Tuberculosis			2	1			1	1	1		1														7
Tumor																1									1
Vaccinia			1																						1
Wounds, gunshot				2	2			4	1	4															13
Wounds, contused												1					1								2
Wounds, stab							1	0	1	1		1													4
Grand total	187	60	214	89	33	21	9	27	38	41	51	49	42	43	35	36	18	24	8	11	9	1		4	1050

NUMBER OF BODIES VIEWED DURING EACH MONTH, AND CLASSIFICATION OF SAME ACCORDING TO SEX, COLOR AND NATIVITY.

MONTHS.	WHITE.		COLORED.		CHINESE.		NATIVES OF				Totals.
	Male.	Female.	Male.	Female.	Male.	Female.	Louisiana.	Other states in the Union.	Foreign Counties.	Not stated.	
January	16	12	22	27	......	......	58	11	6	2	77
February	19	16	20	18	......	......	44	10	12	7	73
March	17	10	25	17	......	......	44	11	11	3	69
April	22	18	18	21	......	......	49	16	13	1	79
May	20	12	33	25	......	......	69	10	6	5	90
June	19	10	21	35	......	......	59	16	10	......	85
July	32	15	25	12	......	......	55	11	11	4	84
August	29	13	31	30	......	......	76	11	11	5	103
September	22	11	25	20	......	......	52	11	12	3	78
October	29	12	29	23	......	......	67	11	14	1	93
November	30	16	35	26	......	......	69	18	14	6	107
December	32	16	39	25	......	......	74	21	12	5	112
Total	287	161	323	279	......	......	716	157	135	42	1050

DEATHS BY SUICIDE, CLASSIFIED ACCORDING TO SEX, COLOR, NATIVITY AND METHOD OF ACT.

	White.		Colored.		Drowning.	Hanging.	Shooting.	Poison—stated.	Poison—not stated.	Totals.
	Male.	Female.	Male.	Female.						
Cuba	1	......	......	......	......	......	......	Oxalic acid 1	......	1
France	4	......	......	......	2	1	1	......	......	4
Germany	5	......	......	......	2	......	3	......	......	5
Ireland	......	1	......	......	......	1	......	......	......	1
Louisiana	4	......	1	......	......	1	3	Laudanum 1	......	5
Mexico	1	......	......	......	......	......	1	......	......	1
Poland	2	......	......	......	......	2	......	......	......	2
Switzerland	1	......	......	......	......	......	......	......	1	1
United States not Louisiana	2	......	......	......	......	......	......	Prussic acid 2	......	2
Totals	20	1	1	......	4	5	8		4	1	22

QUARANTINE.

REPORTS OF RESIDENT

QUARANTINE PHYSICIANS.

J. F. FINNEY, M. D., MISSISSIPPI QUARANTINE STATION.

DANIEL W. ADAMS, M. D., RIGOLETS QUARANTINE STATION.

N. L. SIGUR, M. D., ATCHAFALAYA STATION.

QUARANTINE CONVENTION

CALLED AT THE REQUEST OF THE BOARD OF HEALTH OF THE STATE OF LOUISIANA, HELD IN THE CITY OF NEW ORLEANS, DECEMBER 7–10, 1880, IN THE HALL OF THE HOUSE OF REPRESENTATIVES— REPORT OF COMMITTEE OF ARRANGEMENTS, DR. F. FORMENTO, CHAIRMAN.

REPORT OF J. F. FINNEY, M. D.,

RESIDENT PHSICIAN MISSISSIPPI QUARANTINE STATION.

QUARANTINE STATION, MISSISSIPPI RIVER, LA.; }
January 1, 1881. }

DR. Joseph Jones, President Louisiana State Board of Health:

Dear Sir—I have the honor to transmit to you this, the annual report of the affairs of this station for the year ending December 31, 1880, and it is with a feeling of no little pleasure, that I can say no vessels have been permitted to pass this station with sickness on board during the past seven months. notwithstanding the fact that there were 208 more vessels this year than last. It is true, sickness occurred on board the bark Excelsior after her arrival in the city, but, as you are well aware, that was due to no lack of vigilance on the part of myself or my assistant, as that vessel underwent a very rigid quarantine at this station for a period of twelve days, during which time no disease manifested itself.

I append to this report a classified list of vessels passing this station during the past year, the total number is 1271, and the aggregate tonnage of this fleet will reach nearly two millions, which is I believe the largest ever arrived at this port.

There were detained at this station during the past year, for purification, disinfection and fumigation 151 vessels, among which there were but four having any sickness on board, the patients were all transferred to the hospital for treatment, with the following results:

First. The steamer Chilian, one case intermittent fever. Discharged.

Second. The bark Excelsior, after return from the city, three cases yellow fever. Two died, one recovered.

Third. The steamer Tantalon, one case bilious remittent. Discharged.

Fourth. The steamer Wanderer, one case rubeola. Discharged.

Of the 151 vessels detained at quarantine, there were in January, 1; April, 2; May, 23; June, 21; July, 29; August, 17; September, 27; October, 29; November, 2.

NUMBER AND CLASS OF VESSELS PASSING THIS STATION DURING EACH MONTH OF 1880.

	Steamships.	Ships.	Barks.	Brigs.	Schooners.	Total.
January	47	9	47	4	11	118
February	60	16	44	5	18	143
March	43	12	31	6	20	112
April	45	7	27	3	21	103
May	48	3	23	6	20	100
June	40	2	23	1	10	76
July	45	3	22	2	7	79
August	44	4	9	0	3	60
September	64	12	6	0	7	89
October	65	14	28	1	7	115
November	55	24	40	5	10	134
December	58	15	56	6	7	142
Total	614	121	356	39	141	1271

With the hope that we may have a healthy and prosperous year before us, I remain, Very respectfully your obedient servant,

J. F. FINNEY, M. D., Resident Physician,

REPORT OF DANIEL W. ADAMS, M.D.,

QUARANTINE PHYSICIAN RIGOLETS STATION.

To the Honorable the President and Members of the Board of Health, State of Louisiana :

Gentlemen—A year of good health, yet prodigal of incident, has intervened since I had the honor to present my annual official report to your honorable body. Its events have vindicated your public policy and seem steadily pointing the way to the security which quarantine requires in order to make it acceptable to trade and commerce.

During the past season 1170 vessels in all have been inspected by me at the Rigolets Station. Of these 26 were steamers and 1144 were schooners. Of the 1144 thirty-six (36) had been acting as lighters to foreign vessels. Of the 26 steamers two (2) had been acting as lighters to foreign vessels.

: The Mexican steamer Victoria, from Frontera Tobasco, Mexico, arrived July 6, 1880. She had reported at the Jackson County Quarantine Station, Pascagoula, and had remained there seven days, was there imperfectly disinfected. I found on removing the limber boards—which I learned had not been removed for years—the bilge water offensive, and much filth from decayed lumber. President Jones was present at the inspection.

Dates of arrivals from infected ports.

· American schooner Henrietta Esch, arrived May 30, 1880, from Vera Cruz *via* Tuspan.

· Mexican schooner Norma, arrived from Tobasco, June 9, 1880.

American schooner Mary A. Rushing, from Tuspan, July 31, 1880.

American schooner Henrietta Esch, from Tuspan, Mexico, August 4, 1880.

American schoon·r Annette, from Havana, Cuba, August 9, 1880

: These schooners were detained 72 hours, and thoroughly cleansed. On the latter of these trips of the Henrietta Esch, a sick person was landed and placed in the Hospital—a case of intermittent fever yielding readily to treatment.

In the business bureau, there remained the old difficulty as to fees. Captains refused payment under advice of counsel. The neglect of Congress to provide means of enforcing payment was the cause of this, the Federal Constitution making such provision necessary in all cases of impost on tonnage.

. In the light of the foregoing figures, which denote the volume of my labors, it may not seem invidious to invite a comparison between the work done by the National, and that done by our State Board.

As an appropriate preface to my suggestions on the subject of the present National Board of Health and Quarantine, let me respectfully ask your attention to the intolerable system of county quarantine that prevails in Mississippi. It has none of the concrete elements of a system. Its health officers are practicing physicians of populous adjacent towns or cities, whose professional duties are thus divided between public and private calls, and none of whom are engrossed or recompensed singly by their public station, or devote themselves exclusively to the public service. As the system operates, the whole Mississippi coast lies unprotected—a matter in which the entire Mississippi Valley is concerned. Thus incapable of any efficient quarantine service, even of protecting its own coast, it seems ludicrous that Mississippi should yet pretend to quarantine New Orleans—but it is so. I would respectfully suggest that your honorable Board, through the executive of our sister State, or by petition to its Legislature, do make application for the abrogation of the system and the restriction of all control of quarantine matters to the Mississippi State Board of Health.

In August, 1880, the schooner Teresa G. was telegraphed to the health officer at Ship Island, from Havana, an infected port, as having left with fever aboard, and to look out for her. Notwithstanding such warning, and maugre the ill-repute of the vessel, the quarantine at Ship Island failed to intercept her. She came through Cat Island Pass, direct and unchallenged, and anchored off Bay St. Louis, a place crowded with summer residents from New Orleans and Mobile, and was boarded by the health officer there. After various delays she was brought by the National Board to Ship Island.

Schooner Annette, from Havana, had been telegraphed to the National Board as having fever on board. There had been seventy-two deaths at Havana during the week ending July 15, the day on which she left. She arrived, unintercepted and unsuspected by the National Board, at Rigolets at 3:50 p. m., August 9, 1880. She had been fumigated at Havana. By me she was twice fumigated—36 pounds sulphur to each fumigation, and solution of carbolic acid and copperas, 50 gallons I had discovered that she had been imperfectly disinfected at Havana. I found, on opening the limber boards, the limber holes stopped up, and that the disinfectant had remained in one compartment, hence leaving the work unaccomplished. I do not think the forecastle had been touched. The telegram had notified the National Board of her sailing, and by her bill of health it was learned that she came from Talapeda wharf, an infected spot in proximity with the shore, where yellow fever most prevailed. She had there been two days discharging her freight. Two of her crew were missing on her arrival at quarantine. I released her at 10:45 a. m., August 12, and she sailed for Pearlington at 2:15 o'clock p. m. of that date.

On May 30, 1880, the schooner Henrietta Esch arrived from Vera Cruz via Tuspan, Mexico. She came directly through Cat Island pass unintercepted by the Ship Island Quarantine.

And again on the 4th August, 1880, the Henrietta Esch came through Cat Island Pass from Tuspan, again running the gauntlet of the National Quarantine.

The question of efficiency as to the Ship Island Quarantine lies in its adequate protection of the Cat Island passage. Without it, it is a nameless pretense, and the National Quarantine a failure. I base these results on no other arguments than facts, which are given fully, and indicate the full measure and value of its protection. It is difficult to see that any advantage has been arrived at by its means over the fractional quarantine system of Mississippi. By both, equally, the coast is left without security, and the ultimates sought, unattained. Of both, equally, the intellectual phenomena are as eccentric as the physical. As an example of this, a particular vessel has at times, on making the passage, caused outcry, while whole fleets have at other times gone through and awakened no alarm. Nor are the usages of the Mississippi system the growth of a day or season. There are vessels that have acquired repute by the reprehensible practice, of which the Teresa G. is the most notable example.

In 1879, the Teresa G. came through Cat Island Pass, landed her crew at Lookout Bridge on Pearl river, and sent them to New Orleans on cars, without the interference of any authority.

I further cite from former annals : In 1877, the same vessel went through Cat Island Pass, up Pearl river, hailing from Havana. She was infected and was not intercepted. And again in 1874, she went directly through Cat Island Pass, up Pearl river. Some one going on board of her at that time at Pearlington contracted the disease and died.

In 1877, the schooner Leonard Daniels, Captain A. J. Moore, direct from

Havana, came through Cat Island Pass. One man had died on her three days before reaching quarantine, another was sick on arrival at quarantine, and a third was taken sick four days after—all yellow fever. It was the intention of the captain to go up Pearl river and load with lumber, in doing which he would have come in contact with other vessels in the trade, and probably have caused the disease to be taken to the city. I immediately acted on the fact that she had touched at a Louisiana port and had her brought opposite the Quarantine Station at Fort Pike, and there detained till September 23, 1877, when under safe and satisfactory conditions she sailed for Pascagoula.

In 1877 the American schooner Palma, from Vera Cruz, Mexico, via Tuspan, entered by Cat Island Pass; also the American schooner George Peabody, from Vera Cruz, Mexico, via Tuspan, entered by Cat Island Pass.

In 1879 the Mollie Emma, from Vera Cruz, came through Cat Island Pass.

In 1879 the Henrietta Esch came from Tampico; also the Anna Chase from the same port. Both came through Cat Island Pass. Also the American schooner Anna came from Tuspan. She was infected and in a most filthy condition, and had, besides, a death on board.

It is thus seen that it is Hobson's choice between the old Mississippi plan and Ship Island, and that neither can afford protection to Mississippi Sound. Cat Island lies westward of Ship Island fifteen miles, and its passage is invited by the large lumber region of Pearl River, from which there is a rapidly increasing export lumber trade, already very formidable. In the face of these temptations, and against vessels of the class of the Annette, which is more dangerous than any other, observation and demonstration alike prove that the National Quarantine at Ship Island cannot acquire efficiency, cannot protect the city, cannot protect itself against the perpetual daily breach of its laws and regulations.

Vessels from foreign ports have every inducement to avoid the river passage, provided our basin and canal are kept of ample depth, for the latter is, at once, more convenient, pleasant, and vastly more cheap.

The opportunities of the undersigned for obtaining reliable data cannot be exceeded. He is the only permanent resident official at a quarantine station, and is devoted exclusively to his public duties. I will say that, whatever a more watchful diligence on the part of the National Board might have done at Ship Island, it could not have supplied the wants of situation and relation. It might have kept the steam yacht Daydream off Cat Island rather than Biloxi, with partial benefit to the public, but not to the attainment of any lasting or substantial good.

I had the honor to notify the resident officer of the National Board, through the Secretary of our State Board, as early as July 17, 1879, of the importance, and the impossibility on the National plan, of protecting Cat Island Pass. And later, in March or April, 1880, by the advice of the late President of this Honorable Board, I gave personal notice to such officer that Ship Island was not competent to protect Cat Island Pass; and related to him the experience which bore me out in the assertion. But the warnings fell on deaf ears, and no consequences ensued. In the face of these facts a request, made *ex officio* by our President, that the National Board would make an appropriation of $2,000 to carry out the practical purposes of quarantine, was answered by the statement that Ship Island affords ample protection to the entire coast.

For opinions which an additional year's experience has strengthened and confirmed, touching the practical requirements of quarantine, I respectfully refer your honors to the closing pages of my official report for last year, contained in the annual report of the Board of Health, pp. 261, 262.

The employment of a watchman has had a beneficial effect on Quarantine discipline and in some degree supplied the wants of a collector of permits at each one of the basins.

For the ensuing season a new White hall yawl, clincher built, will be required, 16 feet long, 5 feet beam, copper fastened and riveted.

The property on hand is carefully packed and left in charge of the ordinance sergeant at Fort Pike. I have the honor to be gentlemen,

Very respectfully yours, etc.,

DANIEL W. ADAMS, M. D.,
Resident Physician, Rigolets Quarantine.

REPORT OF N. L. SIGUR, M. D.,
RESIDENT PHYSICIAN, ATCHAFALAYA QUARANTINE STATION.

MORGAN CITY, January 25, 1881.

Board of Health, of State of Louisiana:

Gentlemen—I respectfully submit the following report of the quarantine operations at the Atchafalaya Station during the year 1880:

On May 29, 1880, I inspected the steamship Gussie, of the Morgan Line, Captain Richard Hill, 998 tons, which left Havana, Cuba, in ballast, on the 26th of the same month.

On August 8th the steamship Wm. G. Hewes, also of the Morgan Line, Captain Richard Hill, 1117 tons, which left Havana, Cuba, in ballast, on the 4th of the same month.

On August 31st the schooner Adolphe Flake, Captain Edwin L. Snow, 48 tons, which left Tampico, Mexico, with a cargo of honey and dye wood.

On October 6th the steamship Gussie, above mentioned, which left Havana, Cuba, on the 2d of the same month.

All of which I have inspected, fumigated, disinfected and detained the time prescribed by the law. It affords me the greatest pleasure to state that I found them all in excellent sanitary condition and their crews in perfect health.

I feel also happy, in conclusion, to bear testimony to the officers of the Morgan Line for the many courtesies and facilities they have shown me in the discharge of my duties as a State officer. Interested as they are in the maintenance of public health throughout this section of Louisiana, they have never failed to extend to me their most strenuous support for the carrying out of all sanitary measures advocated by your honorable body.

I am, very respectfully, your obedient servant,

N. L. SIGUR, M. D.,
Quarantine Officer at the Atchafalaya Station for 1880.

QUARANTINE CONVENTION

CALLED AT THE REQUEST OF THE BOARD OF HEALTH OF THE STATE OF
LOUISIANA, HELD IN THE CITY OF NEW ORLEANS, DECEMBER 7-10, 1880,
IN THE HALL OF THE HOUSE OF REPRESENTATIVES, AT THE
STATE-HOUSE, CORNER ROYAL AND ST. LOUIS STREETS—
REPORT OF COMMITTEE OF ARRANGEMENTS.

The Board of Health of the State of Louisiana, at its meeting of August 26, 1880, adopted the following resolution :

"Whereas, the American Public Health Association will meet at New Orleans, December next, to consider sanitary matters, and knowing that nothing is more essential to the welfare of the States of Alabama, Texas, Mississippi, Tennessee, Arkansas, Kentucky, Georgia, Florida and Louisiana, than properly regulated and uniform measures ; be it

Resolved, That this Board, through its President, forward invitations to those different State and Municipal Boards of Health, requesting them to send delegates from their respective bodies to a general quarantine conference, to meet in this city at that time, to discuss those subjects so vital to sanitary and commercial welfare; be it further

Resolved, That the National Board of Health be also requested to take part in their meetings."

Invitations were accordingly issued to the Governors of all the above named States, to those of Missouri and Maryland, to the National board of Health, to the Mayors of all the larger cities and to the State and local Boards of Health of the above States, and of Illinois, to send delegates to participate in the Quarantine Convention.

These invitations were promptly answered and accepted by the different States and cities above-mentioned.

In conformity with the instruction of the Louisiana State Board of Health a Committee of Arrangements and Credentials was appointed in order to make the necessary arrangements and prepare such rules and regulations as will best promote the accomplishment of the object of said Convention.

The Committee of Arrangements has secured for the place of meeting the spacious and comfortable Hall of the House of Representatives of the State of Louisiana, the use of which was cordially granted by His Excellency, L. A. Wiltz, the Governor of the State.

The following arrangement has been adopted by the State Board of Health :

ORGANIZATION OF THE QUARANTINE CONVENTION:

The President of the Board of Health of the State of Louisiana will call the Convention to order, and request the presentation of credentials to the Chairman of the Committee of Arrangements, and invite the members to effect a permanent organization by the election of a President, Vice President and Secretary.

After the election and installation of the permanent officers, His Excellency, Gov. Wiltz, will deliver an address of welcome.

After the address of the Governor, the Chairman of the Committee will read to the Convention a series of questions whicn have been adopted by the Board of Health of the State of Louisiana, as embodying the most important subjects to be discussed by the Convention.

These questions have been prepared with the intention of facilitating the labors of the Convention by saving time, and preventing the discussion from straying away into a indefinite number of secondary questions. By following this plan it is hoped to reach practical results of great interest to public health and to the commerce and prosperity of all the States, so deeply concerned in these questions of quarantine and sanitation.

Questions to be submitted for discussion to the Quarantine Convention, at their meeting in New Orleans, December 7, 1880, in order to secure the adoption of a regular and uniform system of quarantine and of such sanitary measures and precautions as will best facilitate the interests of the public health and those of commerce and Inter-State relations:

1. In what shall quarantine consist? In detention or in disinfection, or in both? When is it to be established, and for what period of time, and by what authority?

2. Against which ports or countries? What is to be considered an infected port, or locality, or ship?

3. What diseases shall be considered as infectious or contagious, or both?

4. What shall be the period of detention for ships and their cargoes, for merchandise and passengers?

5. Establish a classification of merchandise. Name articles to be submitted to an obligatory quarantine, or to a discretionary one, and those to be exempt from quarantine.

6. How are passengers from an infected port or locality to be treated, if healthy; if diseased; if healthy, but amongst passengers who are or have been infected?

7. Shall the same quarantine regulations be enforced indiscriminately against all vessels coming from the same infected port, whether these vessels have a clean bill of health or not? Whether their sanitary condition is good or not; whether they have had cases of sickness on board whilst being in an infected port, or during their voyage, on their arrival, or not?

8. What is the best method of disinfection for ships and their cargoes to be adopted? Whether by means of cold, of heat, or chemical substances, or by the combined application of these different agents?

9. What is the value of sulphur and of sulphurous acid gas as a disinfectant and a germ destroyer?

10. What is the value of chlorine?

11. What is the value of copperas as a deodorizer and disinfectant, especially when combined with carbolic acid as a local application to the interior of ships?

12. What is the value of carbolic acid?

13. What is the best deodorizer and disinfectant for ships, houses, privies, foul drains, etc.

14. In what cases will it become necessary to discharge on lighters the cargo of vessels, and to transfer it to warehouses for more thorough fumigation and disinfection?

15. How is a uniform and general system of quarantine to be established in the different States of one section of the country, connected by a community of interest? By what action? By the combined action of the several Boards of Health of the different States having common interest, or by the separate action of a body, constituted outside of these States and not being a representative of the same?

16. Necessity for the adoption and enforcement by the different States of the Mississippi Valley of a code on quarantine and sanitary measures, which would obviate many difficulties and misunderstandings, and greatly promote Inter-State commerce and business relations.

39

17. What is the value of Ship Island Quarantine for the protection of the Mississippi Valley from the introduction of foreign pestilence?

18. Is it possible or advisable that the Ship Island Quarantine should supersede all quarantine establishments on the Gulf of Mexico, and especially those of Galveston, New Orleans, Mobile and Pensacola?

Delegates to the Quarantine Convention will please be provided with their credentials.

The State-House of Louisiana is situated on the corner of St. Louis and Royal streets.

The day and hour of the meeting of the Quarantine Convention will be announced at the first meeting of the American Health Association.

Any information cheerfully given to delegates by officers and members of the Louisiana State Board of Health.

> F. FORMENTO, M. D., Chairman.
> I. N. MARKS.
> J. C. BEARD, M. D.
> F. LOEBER, M. D.
> E. HERNANDEZ.

EXTRACT FROM THE MINUTES OF THE

QUARANTINE CONVENTION,

HELD IN THE CITY OF NEW ORLEANS, DECEMBER 7-10, 1880.

Introductory Speeches of His Excellency, Louis A. Wiltz, Governor State of Louisiana; Hon. I. W. Patton, Mayor City of New Orleans, and Prof. Joseph Jones, M. D., President Board of Health, State of Louisiana.

FIRST DAY'S PROCEEDINGS.

NEW ORLEANS, LA., December 7, 1880.

Pursuant to invitations addressed by the Board of Health of the State of Louisiana, the delegates to the Quarantine Convention assembled at the Hall of the House of Representatives, in the State Capitol, at 5 o'clock p. m.

On suggestion of Dr. Felix Formento, Chairman of the Committee of Arrangements on the part of the Board of Health of the State of Louisiana, Dr. Joseph Jones, President of the Board of Health, State of Louisiana, was called to the chair.

Dr. Jones proceeded to address the Convention as follows:

With the great commercial nations of Europe the efficiency of quarantine assumed, more than thirty years ago, a commanding position in the science of hygiene, and led to the holding of a Conference Sanitaire, in Paris, in 1851 and 1852.

The learned and accomplished Dr. Wilson Jewell, of Philadelphia, after an experience of eight years as a member of the Board of Health of that city, and after a careful examination into the character and practical workings of the laws of quarantine of his own as well as those of other States, was convinced that they were encumbered with serious defects, which weakened their influence and retarded their usefulness.

They advocated antiquated and obsolete doctrines: they embarrassed commerce, oppressed the merchants, imposed severe restrictions on the healthy, inflicted cruelties on the sick, and, when rigidly enforced, became the ready means of disseminating and entailing disease and death.

These glaring imperfections, and the inconsistency of quarantine enactments with each other in the different States, together with the frequent embarrassments arising from abortive efforts to enforce and apply quarantine regulations, led Dr. Jewell to consider whether a uniform code of regulations, operating alike in all our seaports, and offering the least hindrance to an active commerce, and with a humane regard for the health of the passengers and the crews, and for the comfort of the sick on board of vessels detained at quarantine stations, would form the only correct fundamental principle for accomplishing the necessary reform in quarantine legislation.

By an intelligent earnest and persistent course, Dr. Jewell finally received the attention, confidence and approbation of a majority of the Board of Health of Philadelphia, and, on the 10th of November, 1856, the following resolution was unanimously adopted:

" *Resolved*, That a committee of three, with the President, be appointed to correspond with the Boards of Health of New York, Boston, Baltimore and New Orleans, on the propriety of calling a convention of delegates from the various Boards of Health in the maritime cities of the United States, for the purpose of a conference in relation to the establishment of a uniform system of revised quarantine laws."

As a result of these disinterested and philanthropic labors of Dr. Jewell, the first Sanitary Congress in America was held in the Supreme Court-room in Philadelphia, May 13, 1857. Nine States on the Atlantic coast were represented by twenty-six different authorities through seventy-three delegates. These delegations were not confined to the medical profession, but were selected also from the commercial and municipal departments of five of our largest cities—Boston, New York, Philadelphia, Baltimore and New Orleans—were ably represented.

The convention remained in session during three days. Its deliberations, which were eminently harmonious, resulted in the adoption of a series of recommendations of great value to hygienic science.

It was at this first meeting that the name of the convention was changed to the "Quarantine and Sanitary Convention."

The second annual meeting was held in the Masonic Hall, Baltimore, April 29, 1858. This year twelve States were represented by eighty-six delegates, showing an increase over the first convention of three States and thirteen delegates.

The most important movement emanating from this meeting was the appointment of two committees, one on external hygiene or quarantine, and the other on internal hygiene or the sanitary arrangements of cities.

It is not our purpose to follow the valuable and exhaustive labors of the National Quarantine and Sanitary Conventions, held in the city of New York, in April, 1859, and June, 1860. Suffice it to say that—after the devastations and desolations of the great American Civil war of 1861-65, during which memorable period the labors of physicians and sanitarians were devoted to the mitigation of the sufferings and horrors of the battlefield—from the a hes of the great American Congress for Quarantine and Hygienic Reform sprang numerous State boards of health, and, in 1872, the American Public Health Association, now assembled in this city.

It would be foreign to our purpose to review the history of the terrible epidemic of 1878, and to show how the National Board of Health and the Sanitary Council of the Mississippi Valley arose from the widespread alarm of the people, which was reflected in the legislation of their national representatives.

The Board of Health of the State of Louisiana, appreciating its responsible position at the throat of this great inland sea, with its 20,000 miles of navigable streams, and at the mouth of this magnificent valley, with its area of 2,455,000 square miles, extending through thirty degrees of longitude and twenty-three degrees of latitude, with its 20,000,000 inhabitants, has respectfully, truly and earnestly asked that the health and quarantine organizations of the Southern and Western States should meet together in friendly converse for the perfection of all measures tending to exclude foreign and domestic pestilence, and for the establishment of mutual confidence upon a firm and lasting basis.

The recent American civil war demonstrated that there are no barriers—physical, ethnological or political—which can ever divide the great valley of the Mississippi.

This mighty empire must be, and shall be forever one, in political, commercial, social and sanitary interests.

Dr. Felix Formento, of Louisiana, stated that the Governor of the State of Louisiana and the Mayor of the city of New Orleans, had been invited to address the Convention, and moved that a committee of three be appointed to wait upon them and inform them that the Convention was prepared to receive them.

The motion, after having been duly seconded by Dr. J. C. Beard, of Louisiana, was carried, and the Chair appointed the following committee :

Drs. Felix Formento and J. C. Beard, and Hon. I. N. Marks, of Louisiana.

Dr. Joseph Jones introduced His Excellency L. A. Wiltz, Governor of Louisiana.

His Excellency addressed the Convention as follows :

Gentlemen of the Convention—The president and members of the Board of Health of the State of Louisiana, at whose instance this convention is called, have asked me to speak to you on their behalf, to offer their acknowledgments for the manner in which you have seen fit to respond to their request and to extend to those who represent other States and cities their kind and friendly salutation of welcome.

To me this is a real pleasure, for while I salute you in the name of our Board of Health, I can speak words of hearty welcome to you also on the part of our physicians, our scientists, our sanitarians, our legislators, our commercial men and our intelligent people of all vocations. Men of your ability, worth and standing, would be amicably received here by all these classes at any time, whatever might be the object of your visit, but coming as you now do, on business of exceeding great importance, to confer upon matters which come directly home to us, they must all join me in holding you as honored guests, in the hope that your visit may be remembered by you with pleasing impressions of the hospitality enjoyed, with satisfaction for the good results you may have been able to achieve.

If I am rightly informed your conference is to be limited to the subject of quarantine, or matters directly and necessarily connected therewith. The object of inquiry is: How shall the inhabitants of the States which you represent be thoroughly protected against the importation of dangerous forms of infectious and contagious maladies, with the least possible inconvenience to the intercourse and commercial interests of our people? What is the least amount of restraint upon the natural course of maritime trade that is consistent with safety? What shall be that system of detention and purification which, by being adopted under uniform rules, will protect all our Southern States against the deadly ravages of imported epidemics? You are doubtless of one mind as to the necessity of some system of quarantine, and as to the importance of making such quarantine conform to commercial interests as far as consistent with safety. How shall we protect our lives without destroying the means by which we live? How shall yearly visitations of pestilence be excluded from the Gulf States?—Georgia, the Carolinas, Tennessee, Kentucky, and Arkansas—without such a blockade of commerce as will paralyze business and decrease the value of lands and produce in those States, and of all forms of capital in their cities? Public health imperatively demands protection by quarantine, but public interests demand no less imperatively that such quarantine shall be wisely regulated, and be limited strictly to necessity. How then is ample protection to be harmonized with the vital interests? A wise quarantine, faithfully administered under approved rules by officers who deserve public confidence, ought to satisfy all reasonable citizens; but no quarantine can, at the same time, allay the fears of the irrationally timid on one side and satisfy the selfish greed of avarice on the other. By the aid of experience and science you may find, or approximate, the true method and least amount of restrictions which ought to satisfy all reasonable citizens, whether in, or near to, or remote from those seaport gates through which pestilence may steal, but through which the incalculable benefits of commerce must enter.

When the number of inhabitants exposed to danger by imported pestilence is fast growing, Southern and Western inter-state travel and traffic grows far more rapidly. Before the infant of to day attains his majority three-fourths of the exports of the whole republic, then to be twice as great as now, will pass out of our Southern seaports. Our intercourse with inter-tropical regions must become more and more extended from year to year. It is for you and other patriotic and thinking men to contrive the way to exclude noxious maladies without paralizing this vast commerce; to give a reasonable degree of confidence to the inhabitants of all our seaport cities, and all the people of the interior liable to suffer from imported epidemics; to give to merchants and ship-owners abroad, as well as to dealers and consumers at home, assurance that no restraint, burden or loss of time will be inflicted beyond what is clearly and strictly necessary; to give encouragement to strangers who search for homes in our Southern country; to warrant the public against all manner of ignorance, caprice or negligence in the matter of quarantine; to remove all pretext for officious external intermeddling, and to deal with the subject so as to avoid alike the incalculable damage which the country must suffer from needless restriction and the fearful dangers growing out of error in the opposite direction. The instinct of self-preservation demands an effectual quarantine, but interest and common sense also demand that such quarantine shall be regulated, limited and adopted by the lights of experience, science medical skill and sound judgement.

It may be of service to repeat here my brief recommendations respecting quarantine to our State Legislature at the opening of its session in January, as follows

"In behalf of the commercial interests of this city, and of the whole State, I invoke your special and serious attention to our existing laws and local usages upon this matter. It is conceded that some system of quarantine is necessary, but that system should be adapted to every day life, to commerce and to human interests. Its aims should be to keep foreign disease out of the State without the suspension of all intercourse with the outside world. There is no reason why New Orleans should be walled up as by an impassible barrier. Humanity and necessity call for some species of quarantine. Infected ships and diseased passengers must be kept out of our ports and harbors. No pains or reasonable expense should be spared in carrying out a well arranged preventive system. Through cleanliness and rigid sanitary regulations at home, seconded by rigid exclusion of infection and contagion, must be the chief reliance of the public for safety, but these may be secured effectually without putting an embargo upon all commerce and all intercourse with the external world. Between those measures of precaution suggested by experience and sanctioned by science and sound judgment, and the measures dictated by fear or caprice, there is a wide difference, which you cannot fail to appreciate. In behalf of our industrial and commercial interests we must find some means of adequate protection that will not paralyze the the business and blockade the ports and thoroughfares of the State."

After additional experience and free intercourse with merchants, shippers and enlightened sanitarians, I find no reasons to change my views as then expressed.

As your time is valuable I will not detain you longer from the duty you have before you. I trust that this friendly conference may have results that when you leave us to return to the personal cares and duties which interest you more directly, you may feel that your visit to this State has not been in vain.

Dr. Joseph Jones then introduced His Honor, I. W. Patton, Mayor of the city of New Orleans, who proceeded to address the Convention, and said that he was pleased to see such an active interest being taken in matters of so much importance as those about to be considered, since so far as he knew the special object of the Convention was to determine what legislation might be necessary to regulate quarantines. He said that he had no remarks to make, as the Governor had stated fully the sentiments of the people upon the subjects to be considered. He said that when science had pronounced her dictum as to what the laws should be, he as a citizen would do all in his power to carry out whatever suggestions might be made.

"I extend to you a cordial welcome and reiterate the sentiments just expressed by Governor Wiltz. When you return to your homes I trust you will recall your visit to New Orleans with pleasurable recollections and entire satisfaction. I wish you a hearty welcome to our city."

On motion of Dr. Rauch, of Illinois, permanent organization was postponed till the following day.

On motion of Dr. Thompson, of Kentucky, the Convention adjourned till Wednesday, December 8, 1880.

DR. GEO. A. KETCHUM, of Mobile, Ala., was unanimously elected President of the Convention.

DR. T. A. ATCHISON, of Tennessee, First Vice President.

DR. PINCKNEY THOMPSON, of Kentucky, Second Vice President.

DR. A. J. MILES, of Ohio, Third Vice President.

DR. R. H. L. BIBB, of Texas, Secretary.

Resolutions of Hon. Wm. R. Moore, of Tennessee:

Resolved, 1, That the chair appoint two committees, to consist of seven members each, one committee to represent the Atlantic and Gulf States here represented, and one to represent the States of the Ohio and Mississippi valleys; each committee to prepare a schedule of rules and regulations concerning those matters of quarantine and sanitation which are common to the States of each region, respectively, and which schedule shall be submitted to each of such States for ratification and adoption as the basis of action for the protection of the public health; no State to have more than one representative on either of said committees.

Resolved, 2, That it is the duty of the general government to defray the expenses of all quarantine administration of this character, that is, which extends beyond the boundaries of a single State; and said committees are hereby instructed to take the necessary steps to secure adequate appropriations by Congress for this purpose; such appropriations to be disbursed and expended in accordance with the usual treasury regulations concerning disbursements and expenditures.

Resolved, 3, That the chair be authorized to announce the members of the committees at any time within the next ten days.

Committees appointed by Dr. Geo. D. Ketchum, President of the Quarantine Convention, in accordance to the resolution of the Hon. W. R. Moore, of Memphis:

GULF AND ATLANTIC STATES.

Louisiana—*Joseph Jones, M. D , Chairman, New Orleans.*
Alabama—Jerome Cochrane, M. D.
Florida—Hon. S. C. Cobb, M. D., Pensacola.
Georgia—G. L. Freeman, M. D., Savannah.
South Carolina—H. D. Frazer, M. D., Charleston.
North Carolina—Thos. F. Wood, M. D., Wilmington.
Texas—R. M. Swearingen, M. D., Austin.
Virginia—J. G. Cabell, M. D., Richmond.
Maryland—C. W. Chancellor, M. D., Baltimore.

OHIO AND MISSISSIPPI VALLEY STATES.

Tennessee—*J. D. Plunkett, M. D , Chairman, Nashville.*
Arkansas—F. E. Pope, M. D., Little Rock.
Iowa—D. B. Hillis, M. D., Keokuk.
Illinois—John H. Rauch, M. D. Chicago.
Indiana—M. T. Runnels, M. D., Indianapolis.
Kentucky.—J. M. McCormack, M. D., Bowling Green.
Mississippi—Wirt Johnson, M. D., Jackson.
Missouri—J. Spiegelhalter, M. D., St. Louis.
Ohio—A. J. Mills, M. D., Cincinnati.

Attest: JAMES S. ZACHARIE, Assistant Secretary.

Report of the Committee of Arrangements for the Quarantine Convention:

NEW ORLEANS, December 16, 1880.

To the President and Members of the Board of Health. State of Louisiana:

Gentlemen—Your committee to which was entrusted the care of making the necessary arrangements to receive the Quarantine Convention, which has just met in our city, and of preparing a programme for the discussion of those important questions relating to quarantine, in which this Board of Health desired an expression of opinion, has the honor to report as follows:

We are sorry to have to acknowledge that the object for which this Quarantine Convention was called by us was not accomplished. No one of the questions that had been prepared by your committee with care, and which embodied in our opinion, all the points of information which might have been obtained by thorough discussion, was answered by the Convention; more than this, no question was made the subject of debate, so that we have been deprived of the information we had sought and of the light which could be reasonably expected from the debates of such an able and experienced body of men. .

This failure is greatly to be regretted; at the same time it is only just to ourselves to say that it is not to be attributed to any fault of ours, except perhaps that we were mistaken when we hoped that any practical result could be obtained from an assembly composed of elements so different and divided by antagonistic interests.

We fear that local interests and sectional pre-occupations weighed too much upon the minds of gentlemen who were invited to approach mere scientific questions. We were deceived in our expectation that our invitation would be accepted in the same spirit which prompted us in extending it; that of mutual enlightment peace and conciliation.

Whatever may be the causes, we cannot fail to acknowledge that our object was not reached. Harmony and conciliation did not reign supremo in the late Quarantine Convention. It was more a display of parliamentary tactics than of medical or sanitary science. After the experiment of the late assembly, we must also acknowledge that, if we desire any progress made in the solution of the different questions relative to sanitary interests of our State, we should solely rely on our own local efforts to obtain it.

By carefully looking over the proceedings of the Quarantine Convention, during its four days' session, we find that the only action taken relative to the solution of any of the questions submitted by our State Board of Health was the motion of Hon. W. R. Moore, of Memphis, Tenn., which was hastily adopted without discussion, just previous to the adjournment. It recommends the appointment of two committees, to consist of seven members each ; one committee to represent the Atlantic and Gulf States and another to represent the States of the Ohio and Mississippi Valleys ; each committee to prepare a schedule of rules and regulations concerning those matters of quarantine and sanitation which are common to the States of each region respectively, and which schedule shall be submitted to each of such States for ratification and adoption as the basis of action for the protection of the public health ; no State to have more than one representative. It declares that it is the duty of the General Government to defray the expenses of all quarantine administration of this character ; that is, which extends beyond the boundaries of a single State ; and said committees are hereby authorized and instructed to take the necessary steps to secure adequate appropriations by Congress for this purpose, such appropriations to be disbursed in accordance with the usual Treasury regulations concerning disbursements and expenditures.

We may charitably hope that some good results may yet come in the future from the adoption of such a measure, although, for the present, it seems to us rather problematic that committees so composed of men scattered all over the country, and who are to carry on their work without personal interview and facilities for direct and verbal discussion, which alone can modify and conciliate opinions, it seems to us hardly probable that such committee may be able to do much good.

With the exception of the resolution presented by the delegate from Tennessee, and adopted, as we have said, at the last hour, there was not a single action taken by the Convention of any importance whatever. This, at least, we can congratulate ourselves upon, that, in the haste of the assembly to adjourn, a measure, the adoption of which, it seems, was cherished by many, has not been carried, namely, the enlargement of the powers already conferred upon the National Board of Health.

Amongst the advocates of this measure, which experience has demonstrated would have been so injurious to our local interests, we are sorry to count delegates from our own midst, persons representing the interests of our own commerce, if their title be not fallacious, and if they may be truly considered, as their style imports, the representatives of the commerce of our State.

Things remain in statu quo. Experience will probably suggest to our legislative bodies the proper remedies that we have vainly sought to obtain from the deliberations and resolutions of the assembly, whose official endorsement would no doubt have had considerable weight with our State Legislature and with the Congress of the United States.

In conclusion, we must supp y an omission which is probably due to no other cause but the haste for adjournment already alluded to. Therefore, in the name of the Board of Health of the State of Louisiana, and of the Quarantine Convention assembled at its request, we beg to tender our sincere thanks to the Governor of the State, as well as to the Mayor of New Orleans, for the hearty aid and co-operation which they have vouchsafed to us, and for the cordial welcome and words of encouragement addressed by them to the Convention in the name of the people.   Respectfully submitted,

F. FORMENTO, M. D., Chairman Committee.
J. C. BEARD, M. D.,
E. HERNANDEZ,
I. N. MARKS.

REPORT OF THE

COAL OIL INSPECTORS

TO THE

BOARD OF HEALTH

OF THE STATE OF LOUISIANA,

FOR THE YEAR 1880.

40

REPORT OF COAL OIL INSPECTORS FOR 1880.

NEW ORLEANS, January 1, 1881.

To Joseph Jones, M. D., President of the Board of Health, State of Louisiana:

Sir—We have the honor to submit the following report of the gauging and inspection of Coal Oils for the year 1880:

SYNOPSIS OF WORK BY MONTHS.

No. of Barrels Received.	No. of Tanks Received.	No. of Inspections	No. of Barrels Inspected.	No. of Tin Cans Inspected.	No. of Gallons above 125° F. Inspected.	No. of Gallons below 125° F. Inspected.	Total Gallons Inspected.	Inspection Fees.	Collections.	Months.
1956	......	109	2000	1770	29,518	82,179	111,697	$281 94	$254 69	January
1970	......	107	1829	2266	21,532½	66,188½	90,721	256 95	256 32½	February.
1760	2	87	1524	2920	25,431½	71,148½	96,580	244 33½	259 88½	March.
2040	1	75	1763	1180	24,054½	70,967½	95,022	244 62	283 22	April.
1395	5	60	1226	550	25,828	56,804½	82,632½	206 82½	223 95	May.
1647	3	64	1415	490	22.442	61,691½	84,133½	212 55	199 80	June.
1016	7	55	918	472	17,796	57.618	75,414	183 98¾	196 73¾	July.
1186	2	72	1193	1044	13 207½	54,600½	67,808	162 51¼	162 51¼	August.
2240	4	86	1850	1610	27,248½	84,653½	111,902	237 98¾	287 98¾	September
2954	3	104	2889	1098	28,247½	130,181	158 428½	373 42½	331 42½	October.
4788	6	101	2468	2798	42,340	113,985½	156,325½	361 11¼	403 19¼	November
2093	......	88	1953	2142	32,126	74,412	106,538	248 00	248	December
25,045	33	1008	21 028	18,340	312.772	924.430	1,237,202	$3 064 24½	$3 107 72½	

The collections for the year, amounting to $3107.72½, include $43.48 for work done in 1879, and the expenses for the year has been as follows:

Salaries	$2400 00
Office rent	60 00
Sundries	184 30
The total expenses amount to	$2644 30

But of this last sum $26 were paid for expenses incurred in 1879, reducing the total expenses for the year 1880 to $2618.30.

By comparison with the last three years, it appears that the trade of New Orleans in illuminating oils has every year been increasing, as shown by the following comparison with previous years:

Earnings of the year 1878	$2777 20
Expenses of the year 1878	2878 70
Earnings of the year 1879	$2898 72
Expenses of the year 1879	2811 73
Earnings of the year 1880	$3064 24
Expenses of the year 1880	2618 30

As will be seen by the above comparison, the gain for the year 1880 amounts to four hundred and forty-five dollars and ninety-four cents ($445,94), and in the year 1879 it amounted to eighty-six dollars and ninety-nine cents ($86.99), while in 1878 there was a deficiency to the expenditures of one hundred and one dollars and fifty cents ($101.50).

It is also gratifying to observe that the grade of oils is improving, for the ratio of oils attaining the standard of safety (125° F. Flashing Point) was, in 1878, but 22 per cent, while in 1880 it was very near 34 per cent.

And also by comparison with the last year's receipts, we find the proportion between the standard oils and the oils below the standard has been much in favor of the former; for while the oil below the standard of safety (125° F. flashing point) has not reached 8 per cent. over the same in the year 1879, the oils above said standard has exceeded 12½ per cent., during the same period.

It has been impossible for us to obtain from the Board of Underwriters the casualities caused by the use of oils, and having no official means of obtaining the same, we think it proper to state, through the courtesy of Mr. J. Welsh, the able assistant of Captain Kalinski, of the Salvage corps, that the damages by fire to property attributable to coal oils, as taken from their record, have amounted to about $11,000.

In submitting this, our first annual report, we hope the same will be favorably received.   Respectfully yours, etc.,
LEGARDEUR AND HUMBECHT,
Gaugers and Inspectors of Coal Oils.

REPORT ON COAL OIL INSPECTION.

NEW ORLEANS, July 8, 1880.

Hon. Board of Health of Louisiana :   •

Gentlemen—Your committee, appointed to investigate the complaint made against the Coal Oil Inspectors of this Board by Mr. A. K. Shepard, agent of Chess, Carley & Co., wholesale coal oil dealers of Louisville, Ky., in his own name and in the name of several dealers in petroleum oils of this city, beg leave to report as follows:

In his communication to the Board, Mr. Shepard accuses our Inspector of Coal Oils of having branded as "explosive and dangerous" a lot of oils which, in his (Shepard's) opinion, and in that of an expert employed by him, cannot be considered as such, having been tested by them and found to come within the limit established by law.   Mr. Shepard gives the following as the result of their investigation: Flashing point 125°, fire test 145°, gravity 48; whilst the Inspector claims the tests to be: Flashing point 115°, fire test 135°, gravity 49.   Having tested said oils eight times, always with the same result, our Inspector refused to alter or correct his brand.   Hence the charge made by Mr. Shepard, involving, as you perceive, a question of ability or inability, on the part of the Inspector, to determine which, the whole subject was referred to your committee.   Fully convinced of the importance of their duties, and feeling the amount of responsibility that would justly rest upon them, in determining a question of such great interest to our community—a question which involves the lives and property of many of our citizens—your committee has spared neither time nor efforts to study the question, as it well deserves to be studied, in a spirit of impartiality and justice to all parties, in order to arrive at a true and safe conclusion.

There was such a discrepancy in the statements made by our inspector and Mr. Shepard that no good results could be reached by close interrogation and counter interrogation of both parties.   Your committee then decided that comparative tests and examinations should be made in their presence, by the interested parties, the same quality of oil to be tested by the same instrument, the Tagliabue's tester or pyrometer, as adopted by this Board. As you are well aware, there are several tests used to determine whether coal oil or any of its numerous products, used for illuminating purposes, is safe or not. There is first the flashing test, which determines the flashing point, or the lowest temperature at which it gives off an inflammable vapor; second, the burning test, which fixes the burning point of the oil, or the lowest temperature at which it takes fire. This point is always from 10° to 50° F. higher than the flashing point. It does not determine the real safety of the oil—that is, the absence of naphtha. There is also the specific gravity test. The only reliable test—the only one that the law of this State requires—is that which ascertains the exact temperature at which the oil flashes, or emits an inflammable vapor or gas, which vapor is in a great majority of cases the real cause of accidents. The operation necessary to determine the flashing point is very simple, and consists in heating the oil in a water-bath and carefully noticing the temperature at which a very small flame, flitted quickly across the surface produces a bluish flash which dies out immediately—the oil *flashes* at that point. Naturally, the oil whose flashing point is the highest is the less dangerous, as it requires the highest temperature either to explode or take fire. Animal and vegetable oils are not dangerous because they only flash at a temperature between 500° and 600° F. These have been almost entirely thrown aside since the introduction of coal oil, which possesses among other advantages that of its great cheapness. It is now used all over the world, the average daily production in the United States has now reached the enormous amount of 22,000 barrels of over 40 gallons each. When deprived of its dangers, petroleum, used also in hundreds of different industries, becomes one of the great wonders of the Nineteenth Century. Speaking of it, as an illuminating agent, the great question is to determine which is the flashing point, to be selected as a standard of safety; on this subject there is some difference of opinion, and a slight variation in the laws of different countries. In England and in a majority of our United States, the law fixes the standard of safety of petroleum at 100° F. The United States Congress has adopted the same standard in section 29 of the internal revenue act of March 2, 1867. Oils and all illuminating fluids, flashing or igniting below 110° F., are ordered to be marked "unsafe." In every State and county heavy penalties are imposed by law for selling oil below the standard, or oil which has not been inspected. In spite of these laws, shocking accidents are still very frequent, not quite so, however, as in the past. These accidents result from inferior and cheap oils. Crude oils containing naphtha sell at from three to five cents per gallon, while the refined petroleum or kerosine sells at from twenty to twenty-five cents per gallon, hence strong inducements for many of the interested parties to substitute a cheap and highly dangerous article for another; safer, but more expensive. The State Board of Health of Louisiana, in 1870, issued a circular to the public advising them as to which illuminating oils it deemed dangerous for common use, and which is considered safe, giving proper instruction as to the manner of using them, etc. In accordance with the laws of most of the States of the Union, it considered no such oil safe whose flashing point was below 110° F. By Act 37, of the Lesislature, approved April 2, 1877, the office of gaugers and inspectors of coal oils and illuminating fluids was created in the towns and cities of 2000 inhabitants. It made it their duty to test all oils sold on the market, and required them to brand all oils examined by them, marking the flashing point in degrees on the casks or cans, and to stamp as "explosive and dangerous," all such that flashed below 125°. That law is the only one now in vigor, and we should strictly carry out all its requirements. Acting under it, we shall now give you the results of the different tests that were made in our presence, and the conclusion we arrived at. The result obtained separately by our inspector, and his expert, and by

Mr. Shepard, were, with one or two degrees variation, practically the same as those mentioned in the communication before the Board, namely: The flashing point of the oils branded by our inspectors as " explosive and dangerous," was found by him to be 115°, whilst in Mr. Shepard's test the flashing point was only reached at 125°.

We noticed that during the test made by our inspector, the oil was heated rather too rapidly, whilst during Mr. Shepard's test it was heated much more slowly. This difference in the manner of conducting the experiment might to some degree explain the different results obtained by them. We therefore concluded to make a third test, under the personal direction of Dr. S. S. Herrick, whose experience and practical knowledge of all questions relating to coal oil inspection, acquired during the time he was coal oil inspector for this board, were of great value to us. This test was made with a great deal of care, and every incident noticed with precision. Particular attention was given to avoid either too rapid or too slow heating of the oil, to have a real water bath, to use an uncharred small flame for trying the oil, etc. It gave the following result:

At 1:40 p m., everything being ready, heat was applied to the water-bath, carefully filled, and containing in a vessel the same quantity of oil that was used in each previous test. At 1:43 the temperature began to rise, as shown by the thermometer attached to the tester; 2 minutes after, it marked 98°; half a minute more, 100°, rising at the rate of 4° per minute, it continued until it reached 118°, at which point it evidently flashed, 10½ minutes after heat was first applied. This experiment decided the question, and left no doubt in our mind as to the ability of our inspector to make the required test and as to his disposition to enforce the rules of our board. We can but approve his action in branding as " dangerous and unsafe," oils whose flashing point was below 125° standard of safety established by our State law. In conclusion, we will remark, as we have stated before, that we are satisfied that the least variation in the mode of conducting a physical test or experiment, is apt to change the results of said test, even with the best disposition to act fairly on the part of contending parties. We, therefore, earnestly recommend that this Board of Health, in order to make up a deficiency in legislative act No. 37, should issue as soon as possible, full and explicit directions for the guidance of coal oil inspectors of the State, enabling them to make their tests invariably alike, in all cases. Fixed and positive written rules from this board would materially facilitate the discharge of their responsible duties, and give satisfaction to the coal oil dealers.

It would at the same time make our people feel that in this important question, as well as in all questions relating to the public welfare, their interests are faithfully and zealously protected by this board.

Respectfully submitted,

F. FORMENTO, M. D., Chairman Committee, etc.,
J. P. DAVIDSON, M. D.,
E. T. SHEPARD, M. D.

REPORT OF

THE TREASURER

TO THE

BOARD OF HEALTH

OF THE STATE OF LOUISIANA,

FOR THE YEAR 1880.

TREASURER'S FINANCIAL REPORT.

OFFICE OF THE BOARD OF HEALTH,
New Orleans, December 31, 1880.

To the President and Members of the Board of Health:

Gentlemen—I have the honor to submit the accompanying financial statement for the year 1880. By reference to the statement it will be seen that
the following were the amounts of the gross receipts and the amounts of expenditures during the past year :

RECEIPTS.

Balance on hand December 31, 1879, in cash and uncollected drafts, as per Annual Report of 1879......		$4,944 01
From Mississippi Quarantine Station.................	$21,872 00	
From Rigolets Quarantine Station...................	174 75	
From Atchafalaya Quarantine Station................	00 00	
From inspection and gauging of coal oils.............	3,106 69	
From Recorder of births, deaths and marriages........	6,725 00	
From privy permits issued.....	2,610 50	
From body permits issued...........................	49 75	
From building permits issued.......................	14 00	
From interment permits issued......................	58 00	
From fines collected...............................	100 00	
Total revenue of the year...........		$34,710 69
From sundry sources, amounts refunded.............		48 00
From State of Louisiana, appropriation of 1878.......		1,181 25
Total receipts.....................................		$40,883 95

EXPENDITURES.

Mississippi Quarantine Station................................	14,388 91
Atchafalaya Quarantine Station...............................	813 83
Rigolets Quarantine Station...................................	1,720 17
Inspection and gauging of coal oil............................	2,667 30
General expenses of the Board................................	13,960 08
Sanitary expenses..	1,350 00
Quarantine Convention expenses.............................	124 75
Total expenditures of the year.............................	$35,025 04
Balance of cash and uncollected Quarantine drafts, 1877 to 1880, on hand December 31, 1880.............................	5,858 91
	$40,883 95

The revenue derived from the Mississippi Quarantine Station in 1879
amounted to $18,114 75, and in 1880, to $21,872 00, showing an increase of
$3,757 25. The revenue derived from privy permits issued shows an in-
crease of $879·30 over that of the previous year. The inspection and gaug-

41

ing of coal oils also shows an increase amounting to $234 08 more than the previous year. On the whole, the total revenue of the Board of Health for the year 1880, was $34,710 69, against $30,633 51 for the year previous, which shows an increase of $4 077 18.

In the accounts of the Board the drafts for quarantine fees are counted as cash, and the drafts on hand, as stated in the balance, are in process of collection.

On the 19th of November, 1880, the Board by resolution appropriated the sum of $5000 to repair the Mississippi Quarantine Station. This amount will, with the cost of publishing the annual report of the Board, exceed the balance on hand of December 31, 1880.

Owing to judicious management, the Board terminates the present year with no liabilities outstanding and is to be congratulated for its excellent financial condition.

In concluding this report I desire to express my high appreciation of the courtesy of Mr. I. N. Marks, Chairman, and the other members of the finance committee, as shown in their careful monthly inspection of the accounts and in valuable advice at different times, which has materially facilitated the performance of my duties; of the politeness and promptitude of the State Auditor, Honorable Allen Jumel. in the quarterly examination of the books, and of the competency and fidelity of Mr. James S. Zacharie, clerk and book-keeper of the Board.

Respectfully submitted,
S. S. HERRICK, M. D.,
Treasurer of the Board of Health.

DETAILED STATEMENT.

THE TREASURER OF THE BOARD OF HEALTH,
In account with
STATE OF LOUISIANA.
DR.

To cash and uncollected drafts on hand January 1, 1880...........$ 4,479 01
Uncollected drafts of 1877 and 1878 on hand, as per suspended drafts account .... 465 00— $4,944 01
To Mississippi Station:
To amount fees on vessels, via the station, from January 1 to December 31, 1880.............. 21,872 00
To Rigolets Station:
To amount fees collected from vessels via the Station..................................... 174 75
To Atchafalaya Station:
To amount fees collected from vessels via the Station.................................... 00 00
To Inspection of Coal Oils:
To amount fees collected during the year for inspection and gauging of coal oils.............. 3,106 69

To Recorder of Births, Deaths and Marriages :
　To amount fees received during the year from reg-
　　is'ration of births, deaths and marriages....... 6,725 00
To Secretary's Office :
　To amount fees received for privy permits issued
　　during the year............................... 2,610 50
　To amount fees received for body permits issued
　　during the year............................... 49 75
　To amount fees received for building permits is-
　　sued during the year.......................... 14 00
　To amount fees received for interment permits is-
　　sued during the year 58 00
　To amount fines received during the year 100 00

Total revenue for the year...................... 34,710 09

　To amount received from Dr. Carrington, Resident
　　Physician, Mississippi Station, in May, for half.
　　barrel of oil used by him..................... 8 00
　To amount received from National Board of Health
　　on account of wages advanced, in 1879, to West
　　Wade, for services as boatman at Carrollton.... 40 00
　To amount received from State of Louisiana,
　　under Act No. 3 of 1878, for repairs of
　　Mississippi Quarantine Station—State war-
　　rants................................ $3000
　Less amount of $500 of warrants collected
　　cash and deposited in the New Orleans
　　Savings Institution, "Deposit Book No.
　　26,761, Mississippi Quarantine Funds,"... 500

　　　　　　　　　　　　　　　　　　　$2500
　Discount on $2500 State warrants, sold
　　at 40 cents............................ 1500

　　　　　　　　　　　　　　　　　　　$1000
　First and second dividends collected of
　　New Orleans Savings Institution in liquida-
　　tion, on account of deposit of $500 as
　　above stated......................... 181 25
　Total amount realized from appropriation
　　to date.............................. 1,181 25

　　　　　　　　　　　　　　　　　　$ 40,883 95

CR.

By Mississippi Station :
　Paid balance of salary of resident physician for
　　the year 1879............................... 1,203 11
　Paid balance of salary of assistant resident physi-
　　cian for the year 1879...................... 166 74
　Paid balance of wages of boatmen for the year
　　1879 .... 410 00
　Paid Samuel Jamison for lime furnished Station
　　in 1879.................................... 48 00

Paid St. Bernard Coal Company for coal furnished Station in 1879............................... 15 00
Remitted fees on sundry vessels via Station during 1879.................................... 391 00
Accepted discount on sundry drafts for fees on vessels, via the Station in 1879................ 22 00

Paid salary of the resident physician for the year 1880 .... 4,999 92
Paid salary of the assistant resident physician for the year 1880................................. 1,099 92
Paid wages of the Station boatmen for the year 1880.. 2,810 30
Paid I. L. Lyons for disinfectants................ 16 71
Paid G. R. Finlay & Co. for disinfectants furnished in 1880.. 651 11
Paid John Hennesey & Bro. for making disinfecting apparatus for Station..................... 252 75
Paid Woodward & Wight for hospital supplies... 21 30
Paid Rice, Born & Co. for disinfecting pots....... 27 54
Paid Insurance Oil Tank Company for illuminating oil and sundries for Station........ .... 75 15
Paid Woodward & Wight for ship chandlery and hardware for Station 106 28
Paid G. R. Finlay & Co. for hospital drugs and medicines.................................... 77 37
Paid E. Vinet, sundry supplies for Station........ 47 35
Paid Rice, Born & Co., sundry articles for Station, 91 34
Paid J. S. Rivers for printing vessel permits and record books for Station..................... 44 25
Paid F. F. Hansell for stationery furnished....... 9 95
Paid D. H. Holmes, sundry supplies for Station... 67 63
Paid J. B. Hubbard, sundry articles for Station... 75 50
Paid L. Frigerio for a marine glass 18 00
Paid A. W. Moffett for lumber to repair wharf at Station... 42 00
Paid Folger & Co. for hardware and paints supplied....................................... 85 18
Paid W. E. Perry for a stove for Station......... 13 00
Paid Overton & Conrad for coal furnished Station, 24 00
Paid Mercier Sons for boatmen's uniforms........ 61 50
Paid H. Ellersly and others for labor at Station... 56 15
Paid for telegrams and postage 25 35
Paid freight on sundry articles for Station........ 77 05
Paid for boarding patient...................... 7 50
Paid for sundries furnished Station.............. 57 46
Remitted fees of French man-of-war Chateau Renaud 20 00
Remitted fees of sundry vessels via the Station during the year................................ 104 50
Accepted discounts on sundry drafts for fees on vessels via the Station during the year........ 167 00— 14,388 91

By Atchafalaya Station:

Paid balance of salary due the late Dr. J. A. Smith,
as resident physician for the year 1879......... 158 33

Paid salary of the resident physician for the year
1880 (May 10th to November 1st).............. 427 50
Paid wages of boatmen of Station for the year
1880 (May 10th to November 1st).............. 228 00— 813 83

By Rigolets Station:

Paid salary of the resident physician for the year
1880 (May 10th to November 1st).............. 712 49
Paid wages of bargemen of the Station for the
year 1880 (May 10th to November 1st)......... 643 61
Paid Insurance Oil Tank Company for illuminating
oil furnished Station.................... 16 82
Paid John Mahony for repairing Station boat..... 22 60
Paid J. S. Rivers for printing vessel permits...... 4 00
Paid Rice, Born & Co. for hardware and sundry
supplies for Station.......................... 14 35
Paid H. Cassidy for bunting and rope............ 3 05
Paid L. Henry for a lantern stand.............. 2 50
Paid Woodward & Wight for sundry supplies for
Station....................................... 61 75
Paid G. R. Finlay & Co. for disinfectants......... 42 38
Paid G. R. Finlay & Co. for hospital medicines.... 32 10
Paid J. B. Hubbard for bedding supplied Station, 39 15
Paid E. Riley, extra services.................... 13 50
Paid sundry freight bills and passage of boatmen
to city....................................... 33 40
Paid Dr. Adams, resident physician, amounts ad-
vanced by him for telegrams, etc.............. 78 47— 1,720 17

By Coal Oil Inspection:

Paid salaries of Inspectors for 1880.............. 2,400 00
Paid office rent of Inspectors of 1880............. 60 00
Paid W. P. Converse, Jr., & Co., for glue fur-
nished 27 10
Paid George Schaeffer for bungs furnished....... 26 75
Paid J. C. Morris for bungs furnished............ 22 40
Paid sundry parties for bungs furnished.......... 12 85
Paid J. S. Rivers for printing certificates........ 11 00
Paid Seymour & Stevens for stationery furnished. 27 55
Paid I. L. Lyons for an oil metre................ 75
Paid S. M. Todd for alcohol furnished............ 2 75
Paid E. Smith for stencils...................... 6 00
Paid L. Gugenheim for stencils.................. 6 00
Paid incidental expenses during the year......... 18 15
Paid office rent of December, 1879.............. 5 00
Paid W. P. Converse, Jr., & Co , for glue furnished
in 1879.. 21 00

Paid C. Duhamel for a pyrometer purchased in 1879   20 00— 2,667 30

By General Expense Account:

Paid I. L. Lyons balance of account for
disinfectants supplied the Board and
Quarantine Stations during 1879.... $437 44
Less amount paid by the National Board
of Health......................... 8 80 —   428 64

Paid Seymour & Stevens balance of account for
stationery furnished the Board and Quarantine
Stations during 1879......................   480 01
Paid Rice, Born & Co., for pots furnished in 1879.   19 10
Paid L. Graham for printing 800 copies of Annual
Report of 1879.................................   590 80
Paid H. Wehrmann for lithographing charts for
Annual Report of 1879.........................   315 00
Paid New Orleans Gaslight Company for gas bill
of December, 1879.............................   3 80

Paid salary of President Samuel Chop-
pin, M. D., January 1 to April 8, 1880. $653 33
Paid salary of President Joseph Jones,
M. D., April 9 to December 31, 1880. 1,746 67—   2,400 00
Paid salary of Secretary and Treasury for 1880....   1,999 92
Paid salary of clerk and book-keeper for 1880.....   825 00
Paid salary of Registration Clerk.................   1,200 00
Paid salary of Assistant Registration Clerk for 1880   813 32
Paid salary of messenger for 1880...............   330 00
Paid salary of attorney for 1880.................   600 00
Paid salary of porter............................   30 00
Paid salary of Dr. B. F. Taylor, Inspector at Port
Eads..   236 66
Paid salary special sanitary officer and inspector of
vessels for one month.......................   100 00
Paid Dr. Lemonnier salary as Secretary of the
Board, May 1st to 18th, 1877.................   27 75
Paid Seymour & Stevens for printing and for sta-
tionery furnished offices......................   301 43
Paid J S. Rivers for printing Compendium of Laws
and Ordinances..............................   171 20
Paid F. F. Hansell for stationery furnished.......   80 13
Paid L. Soards & Co. for copy of Directory of 1880   5 00
Paid subscription to city papers. 35 00
Paid New Orleans Gas Light Company for gas con-
sumed in the office during year...............   32 35
Paid Vandenbroncke for ice supplied office during
year...   19 25
Paid Montgomery & Co. for an office armoire.....   12 00
Paid subscription to "Ame ican Journal of Medi-
cine" 2 50
Paid D. Boatson for map.........................   2 00
Paid George Ellis for "Lippincott's Gazetteer"....   10 00
Paid F. F. Hansell for Acts of 1879 and 1880.....   2 75

Paid Hunter & Genslinger for official stamp......	9 00	
Pa'd Overton & Conrad for office coal...,........	9 50	
Paid J. S. Rivers for printing weekly mortality sta'ements, blanks, etc., and furnishing record books, blank books, stationery during the year for the office, Recorder births, deaths and marriages office, and District Sanitary offices.;.....	403 60	
Paid George Ellis, printing letter heads.,........	11 00	
Pa'd Fitzwilliam & Co. for a hektograph........	9 50	
Paid for clerical services.......................	40 00	
Paid Dr. Taylor for transportation.............	15 00	
Paid Goodwin for use of pump.................	3 50	
Paid expenses of President and clerk inspecting Mississippi, Rigolets. and Atchafalaya Quarantine Stations..............................	62 00	
Paid G. R. Finlay & Co. for disinfectants supplied during year, for distribution	334 92	
Paid Rice, Born & Co. for disinfecting pans......	8 00	
Paid expenses attending removal of infected bark Excelsior from city to Quarantine Station—		
Civil Sheriff fees.................... $63 50		
Tug Wilmot, towage bill............ 150 00		
Eager, Ellerman & Co., for ballast... 15 00		
Dr. Mioton, special services......... 25 00—	253 50	
Paid expenses of Texas Health Committee by special boat to inspect Mississippi Quarantine.....	139 00	
Paid L. Graham for printing circulars and shipping regulations................................	146 00	
Paid A. W. Hyatt printing brief for attorney.....	2 00	
Paid Court costs, sundry cases..................	24 75	
Paid H. Lewis lithographing maps for Compendium of Laws and Ordinances.................	250 00	
Paid J. S Rivers for printing advanced portion of Annual Report of 1880......................	468 20	
Paid New Orleans " Democrat," printing Bruns' report......	21 00	
Paid storage of Fifth District disinfectants.......	28 00	
Paid C. Springer three months' rent Sixth District Sanitary Office..............................	24 00	
Paid for ferriage and car fare of messenger and others during the year....	73 00	
Paid for postage during the year...............	227 85	
Paid for telegraphing during the year............	75 95	
Paid ferriage of Fifth District Sanitary officer....	32 50	
Paid for vaccine virus........................	5 00	
Paid other incidental expenses during the year....	138 50	
Paid for telegrams..............................	14 90	
Paid for sundries during the year................	56 30—	13,960 08

Sanitary Expenses :

Paid salaries of City Sanitary Inspectors and other officers for the months of November and December.........	1,350 00

Quarantine Convention :
Paid expenses of Quarantine Convention called by
the Board and held in the State-house in Decem-
ber, 1880.. 124 75

Total amount expended...................... 35,025 04
Unpaid drafts of 1877 and 1878 on hand........... 465 00
By cash and uncollected drafts of 1879 and 1880 on
hand.. 5,393 91— 5,858 91

$40,883 95

OFFICE OF STATE AUDITIOR, }
New Orleans, La , January 13, 1881. }

I have this day examined the books, vouchers and papers of the Board of
Health of the State of Louisiana, for the year ending December 31, 1880, and
have found the same correct in every detail.

ALLEN JUMEL,
Auditor of Public Accounts of the State of Louisiana.

METEOROLOGICAL REPORT

TO THE

BOARD OF HEALTH

OF THE STATE OF LOUISIANA,

FOR THE YEAR 1880.

METEOROLOGICAL REPORT.

NEW ORLEANS, December 31, 1880.

To the President and Members of the Board of Health of the State of Louisiana:

Gentlemen—I have the honor to submit the meterological report for the year 1880 and to present, in connection therewith, the following tables of meteorological observations, made by the United States Signal Service Station of this city.

Tables Nos. 1 to 12. The daily meteorological record of the year 1880, tabulated according to months.

Table No. 13. The meteorological summary of the year 1880, with a record of the velocity of the wind, number of rainy days, total rain-fall and monthly observations.

Table No. 14. A comparative meteorological summary of the annual means, etc., from 1873 to 1880 inclusive.

Table No. 15. A comparative table showing the means of the hottest and coldest days and the dates of the first and last frosts of each year from 1873 to 1880, together with the number of thunder storms, and days on which lightning was observed during the last three years.

Table No. 16. A table showing the direction of the winds least likely ,and most likely to be followed by rain for each month of the year, prepared from observations made at the United States Signal Service Station of the city during the last eight years.

METEOROLOGICAL OBSERVATIONS.

The record of meteorological observations is furnished weekly to the Board of Health by the United States Signal Service Station, located in this city. This Signal Service Station was organized in 1870, and the first observation recorded November 1, 1870. From that date regular observations have been daily taken, and on January 1, 1873, the number of observations were increased, and tabulated forms were prepared. At present three local observations are daily taken, viz: at 7 a. m., 2 p. m. and 9 p. m. (New Orleans time), and a record of the same is sent to the Board every week for publication in our weekly mortality statement. Besides these, four other observations, called telegraphic observations, are daily taken at 7 a. m., 11 a. m., 3 p. m. and 11 p. m. (Washington time), and telegraphed to the Chief Signal Office at Washington. The station is located in a room on the northwest corner of the third floor of the Custom-House, at an elevation of 44 feet above the side, walk. The Custom-House, the exact location of the flag-staff of the building being latitude 29° 58', longitude 90° 07' west of Greenwich, is a large building of stone and brick, situated on a square surrounded by four streets, and is distant about eight hundred feet from the Mississippi river.

The instruments used are of the most approved kind and were all tested at the Chief Signal Service Station, Washington. The barometers in which were made by Green of New York, are placed in the room about two feet from the window and are hung at an elevation of 56 feet above sea level. The room faces north northeast, and outside of the window, in an open shelter of wooden lattice work and blinds, the Fahrenheit thermometers and the

hygrometers are exposed. The hemispherical cup anemometer in use is the one invented by Robinson, is placed on the roof of the Custom-House at an elevation of 90 feet above the ground, and is connected with an automatic self-registering electric instrument placed in the office. The rain-guage is of the simple pattern used at all the United States Signal Service Stations, and is placed on the roof of the Custom-House at an elevation of 77 feet above the ground. During the past year the Station was in charge of Dr. Geo. H. Rohe until the 19th of May, when Dr. Rohe was assigned to duty as meteorologist of the Polar expedition. Since that date the office has been in charge of Sergeant L. Dunne and his assistant, Mr. C. H. Schaap. To these three gentlemen are due the thanks of the Board, for the weekly data furnished, and to the latter for the interesting summary and comparative tables accompanying this report.

Ozone observations were formerly taken by officers of the Board at two Stations in different parts of the city, but were discontinued in the month of June, and their absence from this annual report is thus accounted for. No ozone observations are made by the United States Signal Service, as the Chief Signal Officer has not heretofore deemed them of sufficient importance.

TEMPERATURE.

The annual mean temperature of 1880, was 69.5° F. against 69.9° F. in 1879. The hottest day of the past year was the 5th July. when the mean temperature was 85.7° F. The last frost appeared on January 24, and the first on November 16. The first ice of the season formed on November 19, three-days after the first frost. The weather during the last week of December was extremely cold, the mean temperature of the coldest day, December 29, being as low as 26.2° F. In the meteorological tables (Nos. 1 to 12 inclusive) is given a complete record of the daily temperature, the maximum and minimum, with the mean of these two observations. During the month of June numerous thunder storms occurred, and the latter part of the month was cool and pleasant.

RAIN-FALL.

During the year 1880 the total rainfall was 69.86 inches, against 51.27 inches in 1879 and 66 16 inches in the yellow-fever epidemic year of 1878. Thunder storms during the past year were frequent, and thunder and lightning were observed on eighty-two days. In 1879 thunder was noted on forty-one days, and in 1878, the epidemic yellow-fever year. only on thirteen days. The number of days on which rain fell in 1880 was 185, against 134 in 1879 and 122 in 1878. As to what constitutes a *rainy day* is not settled., but the fall of .01 inch of rain, as suggested by Mr. G. J. Symons, the well known English observer, is generally adopted. The Signal Service, however, calls those days *rainy days* only on which the fall of rain can be measured. Owing to the proximity of New Orleans to the Gulf of Mexico, the annual rainfall is generally heavy, but it never equals the famous rainfall recorded in meteorological works to have taken place on the Khasia Hills of the Bay of Bengal, where one year the annual rainfall was 600 inches, about 500 inches of which fell in seven months, during the southwest monsoons. .According to Buchan, the United States are chiefly dependent for their rain, not on the Pacific Ocean, but on the Gulf of Mexico. In his work on meteorology, he says that "the high range of the Rocky Mountains in Central America [North America] plays an important part in the rainfall. In the northern parts they drain westerly winds of their moisture, as they cross them. Further south they present a barrier to the passage of the easterly winds which blow across the Gulf of Mexico, which are partly on account of the heated plains of the States,₀ turned or drawn to the northward, and spread themselves over the States, especially over the low basin of the Mississippi. Thus, then, the greatest part of the moisture will be drawn into the valleys where the heat is greatest, and the least part into the high mountainous regions, where respectively it will be disengaged and fall in rain. If this be the case, then the greatest quantity will fall in the valleys, and the least on the higher grounds—a mode of distribution the opposite of what obtains in Europe. That such is the case, the following remarks by Blodget on the rainfall of America, given in the Army Meteorological Register, will show: 'for much the larger area of the United States, and for all portions east of the Rocky Mountains, the distinguishing feature of the distribution of the rainfall *is its symmetry and uniformity* in amount over large areas. The quantity has rarely or never any positive relation to the configuration of the surface, which would identify it with Europe and the North Pacific coasts; and in contrast with these it has a diminishd quantity at greater altitudes generally; and the largest amounts in the districts near the sea-level. It also differs from these districts, and from large land arears generally, in having a larger amount in the interior than on the coast, for the same latitude, at least as far north !as latitude 42°.' The rainiest districts are Florida, the low flats of the Mississippi, then along the course of its valley, then in Iowa, that remarkable depression at the head of the river; and the least quantities on the Alleghanies, especially their higher parts, and the high grounds of the Missouri district."

The heaviest rainfall during the year 1880 occurred on the 8th of March, when 2.81 inches of rain fell. The next heaviest rainfalls were on May 27th, of 2.06 inches, and on December 27th, of 2.00 inches. Owing to the favorable spring and summer, the crops of cotton and sugar throughout the State promised to be abundant until the month of November, when a series of storms visited many portions of the State and caused great damage. During the thirty days of this month rain fell on twenty-two, on nineteen of which the rainfall measured 6.04 inches.

HUMIDITY.

By reference to table No. 14, it will be seen that the annual mean relative humidity of 1880 was 73 per cent., against 70 of 1879 and 74 of 1878. Relative humidity, or, as it is also called, the humidity of the air, means the degree of its approach to complete saturation, dry air being assumed as 0 and saturation as 100, and should not be confounded with absolute humidity. The Signal Service report for 1880 is not yet published, and, for the sake of comparison, the following table from the report of 1879 of the annual mean relative humidity and the annual mean temperature of several points in the Uni ed States, is annexed:

YEAR 1879.

	New Orleans.	Mobile.	Galveston.	Shreveport.	Vicksburg.	Memphis.	Nashville.	St. Louis.	Pike's Peak.	Chicago.	Savannah.	Charleston.	Washington.	Philadelphia.	New York.
Annual mean relative humidity	73.0	73.2	75.7	70 2	68.8	6¹.7	65 8	62 6	50.5	70.3	70 0	70 0	68 4	68 9	70 0
Annual mean temperature	69 5	66 8	69 4	66 3	65 8	61 3	59 7	55.8	21 3	49 5	67 0	66.5	51 8	53.5	51 5

WINDS.

The annual mean maximum velocity of the wind was thirty-six miles per hour, and the general direction of the wind was from the southeast. The

I have the honor to be, gentlemen, your obedient servant.

JAMES S. ZACHARIE, Clerk.

(Table No. 1). METEOROLOGICAL TABLE. JANUARY, 1880.

Day.	BAROMETER.				TEMPERATURE.				HUMIDITY.				Rain fall.
	7 a. m.	2 p. m.	9 p. m.	Mean.	Max.	Min.	Range.	Mean.	7 a. m.	2 p. m.	9 p. m.	Mean.	
1	30.33	30.27	30.30	30.30	70	58	12	64.0	94	71	83	83	.00
2	30.27	30.24	30.25	30.25	72	59	13	65.5	94	84	84	87	.13
3	30.23	30.21	30.27	30.25	73	61	12	67.0	94	67	90	84	.00
4	30.26	30.25	30.28	30.27	73	63	10	68.0	84	71	90	82	.00
5	30.24	30.20	30.26	30.24	75	63	12	69.0	94	69	84	82	.00
6	30.26	30.22	30.24	30.24	75	64	11	69.5	90	69	84	81	.06
7	30.26	30.23	30.25	30.24	74	62	12	68.0	83	85	84	84	.00
8	30 17	30.07	30.07	20.09	73	62	11	67.5	83	79	84	82	.03
9	30.05	30.03	30.09	30.06	72	62	10	67.0	94	67	75	79	.00
10	30.13	30.07	30.10	30.10	74	63	11	68.5	88	67	79	78	.00
11	30.13	30.11	30.15	30.14	75	62	13	68.5	83	63	84	77	.00
12	30.20	30.20	30.27	30.23	72	66	6	69.0	90	79	84	84	.44
13	30.38	30.31	30.30	30.30	66	52	14	59.0	73	48	53	58	.00
14	30.24	30.16	30.19	30.19	65	49	16	57.0	71	68	83	74	.00
15	30.20	30.14	30.19	30.18	68	58	10	63.0	87	75	88	83	.00
16	30.16	30.13	30.13	30.14	68	57	11	62.5	94	73	73	80	.00
17	30.12	30.08	30.11	30.11	72	57	15	64.5	88	67	78	78	.00
18	30.20	30.17	30.21	30.20	68	58	10	63.0	76	35	66	59	.00
19	30.21	30.13	30.11	30.14	71	56	15	63.5	74	64	68	69	.00
20	30.07	30.00	30.05	30.04	70	59	11	64.5	82	67	84	76	.00
21	29.88	29.80	29.80	29.82	69	63	6	66.0	89	79	84	84	.25
22	29.78	29.85	29.93	29.87	68	59	9	63.5	77	33	76	62	.17
23	30.05	30.03	30.04	30.04	59	46	13	52.5	55	43	48	49	.00
24	30.10	30.07	30.08	30.08	56	42	14	49.0	59	34	38	44	.00
25	30.02	29.95	29.95	29.97	52	46	6	49.0	51	42	48	47	.00
26	29.84	29.79	29.84	29.83	62	46	16	54.0	57	53	53	54	.00
27	29.93	29.96	30.00	29.97	65	49	16	57.0	54	45	57	52	.00
28	30.09	30.10	30.14	30.12	68	51	17	59.5	73	60	70	68	.00
29	30.14	30.09	30.11	30.11	71	53	18	62.0	79	49	68	65	.00
30	30.12	30.11	30.17	30.14	74	61	13	67.5	88	71	90	83	.00
31	30.17	30.15	30.18	30.17	72	61	11	66.5	88	84	78	83	.00
Mean	30.14	30.10	30.13	30.12	69.0	57.0	12 0	63.0	80	60	76	72	1.02

(Table No. 2). METEOROLOGICAL TABLE. FFBRUARY, 1880.

Day.	BAROMETER				TEMPERATURE.				HUMIDITY.				Rain fall.
	7 a. m.	2 p. m	9 p. m.	Mean.	Max.	Min.	Range.	Mean.	7 a. m.	2 p. m.	9 p. m.	Mean.	
1	30.15	30.08	30.07	30.09	57	46	11	51.5	80	62	77	73	.62
2	29.60	29.68	29.94	29.79	56	43	13	49 5	93	53	42	63	1.69
3	30.12	30.09	30.17	30.13	56	43	13	49.5	52	38	48	46	.00
4	30.28	30.21	30 28	30.26	56	43	13	49.5	56	48	48	51	.00
5	30.32	30.32	30.39	30.35	55	45	10	50.0	63	71	71	68	.43
6	30.43	30.43	30.44	30.44	54	43	11	48.5	75	43	53	57	.02
7	30.49	30.46	30.46	30.47	55	45	10	50.0	55	43	48	49	.00
8	30.40	30.32	30.33	30.35	60	48	12	54.0	52	53	76	60	.00
9	30.31	30.24	30.28	30.28	64	50	14	57.0	86	73	81	80	.00
10	30.28	30.25	30.25	30.26	70	51	19	60.5	80	74	83	79	.00
11	30.20	30.10	30.05	30.11	71	57	14	64.0	87	75	90	84	.03
12	29.98	29.86	29.81	29.87	73	65	8	69.0	94	76	90	87	.00
13	29.92	29.85	29.98	29.91	69	59	10	64.0	70	48	53	57	.16
14	30.08	30.07	30.13	30.11	63	48	15	55.5	66	36	44	49	.00
15	30.28	30.32	30.36	30.33	65	53	12	56.0	53	48	57	53	.00
16	30.37	30.32	30.32	30.33	66	53	13	59.5	61	48	70	60	.00
17	30.27	30.22	30.28	30.26	71	56	15	63.5	70	56	78	68	.00
18	30.18	30.17	30.24	30.21	74	62	12	68.0	88	76	90	85	1.15
19	30.37	30.37	30.39	30.38	64	56	8	60.0	82	70	62	71	.31
20	30.37	30.29	30.25	30.29	58	48	10	53.0	48	70	70	63	.03
21	30.12	30.08	30.11	30.10	69	56	13	62.5	76	90	76	81	.08
22	30.13	30.08	80.08	30.09	65	53	12	59.0	87	78	83	83	.00
23	30.12	30.00	39.11	30.11	71	60	11	66.5	83	71	78	77	.00
24	30.12	30.06	30.06	30.08	72	60	12	66.0	82	71	78	77	.00
25	29.98	29.96	30.06	30.01	76	61	15	68.5	88	63	84	78	.00
26	29.98	29.99	30.05	30.02	76	67	9	71.5	90	69	84	81	.01
27	30.09	30.07	30.07	30.07	77	63	14	70.0	84	59	75	73	.00
28	30.04	30.02	30.10	30.06	77	66	11	71.5	84	56	81	71	.00
29	30.08	30.04	30.12	30.09	76	61	15	68.5	84	72	78	78	.09
Mean	30.17	30.14	30 18	30.17	65.9	53.7	12.2	59.8	75	62	71	69	4.62

Day.	7 a. m.	2 p. m.	9 p. m.	Mean.	Max.	Min.	Range.	Mean.	7 a. m.	2 p. m.	9 p. m.	Mean.	Rainfall.
1	30.13	30.15	30.22	30.18	68	57	11	62.5	78	68	83	76	.00
2	30.26	30.23	30.19	30.22	68	58	10	63.0	82	79	84	82	.00
3	30.13	30.08	30.08	30.09	78	64	14	71.0	90	56	90	79	.01
4	30.05	29 99	30.00	31.01	78	64	14	71.0	100	61	85	82	.00
5	30.02	30.03	30.06	30.04	81	68	13	74.5	84	61	85	77	.00
6	30.08	30.04	30.06	30.06	81	69	12	75.0	90	58	85	78	.00
7	30.06	29.98	30.02	30 02	80	66	14	73.0	94	61	81	79	.00
8	29.98	29.90	29.89	29.91	75	64	11	69.5	89	69	94	84	2.81
9	29.96	29.99	30.05	30.01	70	61	9	65.5	78	60	78	72	.55
10	30 03	30.05	29.90	29.97	70	58	12	64.0	76	88	95	86	.03
11	29.91	29.88	29.89	29.89	80	67	13	73 5	94	78	90	87	....
12	29.93	29.92	30 03	29.98	79	67	12	73 0	90	74	90	85	.74
13	30.08	30.04	30.06	30.06	71	60	11	65.5	88	75	90	84	.30
14	30.11	30.06	30.05	30.06	68	63	5	65.5	94	90	90	91	.24
15	29.92	29.81	29.88	29.87	77	64	13	70 5	94	76	78	83	.62
16	30.04	30.05	30.18	30.11	64	49	15	56.5	78	62	64	68	.06
17	30.23	30.19	30.14	30.18	55	42	13	48.5	67	53	73	64	.00
18	30.03	29 84	29.82	29.83	75	51	24	63.0	81	84	95	87	.02
19	29.99	30 02	30.10	30.05	71	58	13	64.5	82	68	70	73	.13
20	30.20	30.17	30.26	30.22	66	56	10	61.0	64	41	70	58	.13
21	30.27	30.26	30.24	30.35	63	56	7	59.5	81	70	87	79	.38
22	30.14	30.17	30.20	30 18	63	54	9	58.5	94	88	87	90	.84
23	30.18	30.16	30.17	30.17	68	54	14	61.0	81	52	61	65	.00
24	30.20	30.17	30.17	30.17	72	57	15	64.5	82	24	57	54	.00
25	30.18	30.14	30.15	30.16	73	56	17	64.5	65	36	78	60	.00
26	30 11	30 03	29.96	30.01	77	59	18	68.0	77	52	79	69	.00
27	29.95	29 91	29.97	29.95	77	67	10	72.0	90	56	48	65	.00
28	30.07	29.99	30.01	30.0	76	58	18	67.0	49	20	29	33	.00
29	30 09	30.10	30.11	30.10	69	55	14	62.0	51	38	52	47	.00
30	30.18	30.19	30.16	30.17	67	53	14	61.0	51	38	66	52	.00
31	30.14	30.12	30.11	30 12	73	55	18	64.0	69	42	73	61	.00
Mean	30.08	30.05	30 07	30.07	72 0	59.0	13 0	65.5	80	61	77	72	6.66

(Table No. 4). METEOROLOGICAL TABLE. APRIL, 1880.

Day.	BAROMETER.				TEMPERATURE.				HUMIDITY.				Rain fall.
	7 a. m.	2 p. m.	9 p. m.	Mean.	Max.	Min.	Range.	Mean.	7 a. m.	2 p. m.	9 p. m.	Mean.	
1	30.11	30.08	30.03	30.06	75	57	18	66.0	82	56	78	70	.00
2	29.96	29.96	29.95	29.95	72	65	7	68.5	90	90	90	90	1.78
3	29.99	29.96	30.00	49 99	81	69	12	75.0	90	67	85	81	.01
4	30.04	30.02	30.04	30 04	81	72	9	76.5	90	70	85	82	.00
5	30.06	30.05	30.05	30.05	81	70	11	75.5	85	65	81	77	.00
6	30.05	30.01	30 02	30.02	82	70	12	76.0	76	58	90	75	.00
7	30.02	30.01	30.10	30.06	79	61	18	70 0	90	56	57	68	.02
8	30.11	30.16	30.22	30 18	61	49	12	55.0	81	79	66	75	.82
9	30 28	30.25	30.29	30.28	62	49	13	55.5	64	30	38	44	.00
10	30.26	30.17	30.15	30.18	70	53	17	61.5	62	31	51	48	.00
11	30.17	30.12	30 23	30.19	75	56	19	65.5	76	33	36	48	.00
12	30.37	30.38	30.39	30.38	64	51	13	57.5	73	38	62	58	.00
13	30.35	30.27	30 22	30 27	73	51	22	62.0	74	46	78	66	.00
14	30.16	30.13	30.14	30 14	80	58	22	69.0	88	61	85	78	.02

(Table No. 5). METEOROLOGICAL TABLE. MAY, 1880.

Day,	BAROMETER.				TEMPERATURE.				HUMIDITY.				Rain fall.
	7 a. m.	2 p. m.	9 p. m.	Mean.	Max.	Min.	Range.	Mean.	7 a. m.	2 p. m.	9 p. m.	Mean.	
1	30.30	30.23	30.21	30.24	68	63	5	65.5	50	45	60	52	.00
2	30.14	30.08	30.03	30.07	68	63	5	65.5	68	73	78	75	.21
3	30.02	30.00	30 00	30 00	77	63	14	70.0	80	60	80	76	.00
4	30.02	29.98	30.00	30.00	80	66	14	70.3	90	58	79	76	.00
5	30.01	29.97	30.00	29.99	82	67	15	74.5	90	58	76	.75	.00
6	30.02	30.00	30 01	30.01	81	68	13	74.5	85	55	81	74	.00
7	30.00	30.00	30.00	30 00	82	69	13	75 5	81	62	81	75	.00
8	29.98	29.92	29.91	29.93	82	69	13	75.5	81	58	85	72	.17
9	29.93	29.89	29.90	29.93	83	70	13	76.5	81	60	81	74	.00
10	29.98	29.97	30.02	30.00	86	70	16	78.0	83	61	82	75	.00
11	30.03	30.02	30 02	30.02	84	74	10	79.0	82	63	73	73	.00
12	30.01	29.94	29.93	29.95	83	72	11	77.5	76	52	81	70	.00
13	29.86	29.79	29.84	29 83	82	69	13	75.5	85	55	85	75	.24
14	29.84	29.87	29.94	29 90	81	69	12	75.0	81	55	72	69	.02
15	30.01	30.09	30.14	30.09	77	73	4	75.0	81	63	71	72	.01
16	30.21	30.22	30.22	30.22	77	69	8	73 0	68	56	67	64	.00
17	30.18	30.14	30.12	30.14	80	67	13	73.5	71	59	71	67	.00
18	30.19	30.05	30.02	30.05	80	67	13	73.5	71	55	81	69	.00
19	30.03	29.99	29.97	29.99	81	69	12	75 0	72	55	76	68	.00
20	29.91	29.87	29.87	29.88	76	71	5	73.5	85	90	90	88	.93
21	29.88	29.85	29.89	29.88	85	71	14	78.0	90	61	82	78	.11
22	29.97	29.94	29.97	29.96	86	72	14	79.0	86	55	82	74	.00
23	30 01	29.86	30.01	29.90	87	73	14	80.0	83	61	82	77	.00
24	30.01	29.99	29.99	29.99	85	73	12	79 0	78	70	82	77	.03
25	29.97	29.99	29.97	29.97	81	70	11	75.5	86	85	90	87	.75
26	29.93	29.96	29.94	29.94	81	70	11	75.5	90	85	90	88	1.13
27	29.92	29.90	29.93	29.92	81	70	11	75.5	90	82	86	86	2.06
28	29.92	29.89	29.91	29.90	83	73	10	78.0	90	70	86	82	.39
29	29.91	29.87	29 93	29.91	83	74	9	78.5	82	79	86	82	.45
30	29.98	29.94	30.00	29.98	87	75	12	81.0	82	65	82	76	.05
31	30.05	30.02	30.02	30.03	88	75	13	81.5	82	55	78	72	.00
Mean	30.01	29.98	29.99	29.99	81.2	69.8	11.4	75.5	81	63	80	75	6 58

(Table No. 6). METEOROLOGICAL TABLE—JUNE, 1880.

Day.	BAROMETER.				TEMPERATURE.				HUMIDITY.				Rain-fall.
	7 a. m.	2 p. m.	9 p. m.	Mean.	Max.	Min.	Range.	Mean.	7 a. m.	2 p. m.	9 p. m.	Mean.	
1	30.08	30.03	30.02	30.04	88	74	14	81.0	78	62	78	73	.00
2	30.08	30.00	30.04	30.04	88	78	10	83.0	82	62	82	75	.03
3	30.09	30.07	30.06	30.07	86	74	12	80.0	82	55	82	73	.00
4	30.08	30.06	30.04	30.05	88	75	13	81.5	74	74	78	75	.18
5	30.03	29.99	30.00	30.01	89	75	14	82.0	86	74	78	79	.19
6	30 00	29.99	29.99	29.99	86	75	11	80.5	78	64	78	73	.00
7	30.04	29 98	29.99	30.00	86	76	10	81.0	82	64	82	76	.52
8	30.03	30.00	29.98	30.00	88	76	12	82 0	73	58	78	71	.00
9	30.03	29.99	30.02	30.02	89	74	15	81.5	74	59	78	70	.00
10	30.02	30.03	30.05	30.04	88	76	12	82.0	78	71	86	78	1.08
11	30.08	30.09	30.08	30.08	87	75	12	81.0	78	67	82	76	.03
12	30.11	30.09	30.07	30.08	89	76	13	82.5	78	71	82	77	.25
13	30 09	30.07	30.04	30.06	87	76	11	81.5	82	71	74	76	.02
14	30.07	30.01	30.00	30.02	90	76	14	83 0	82	52	74	69	.00
15	30.04	29.96	29.98	29.99	90	76	14	83.0	74	49	79	67	.00
16	29.99	29.98	30.02	30.01	87	75	12	81.0	78	61	60	67	.00
17	30.07	30.04	30.05	30.05	83	69	14	76 0	59	44	54	52	.00
18	30 11	30.10	30.10	30.10	85	71	14	78.0	59	49	65	58	.00
19	30 14	30.10	30 08	30.10	88	72	16	80.0	53	41	65	53	.00
20	30.08	30.04	30.02	30 04	85	73	12	79.0	58	62	81	64	.05
21	30.00	29.96	29.90	29.90	81	69	12	75.0	67	54	72	64	.00
22	29.86	29.85	29.89	29.89	79	70	9	74.5	90	69	81	80	.46
23	29.93	29.90	29.92	29 92	85	71	14	78.0	72	73	82	76	.24
24	29.96	29.96	29.98	29 98	85	73	12	79.0	78	57	82	72	.24
25	30.02	30 02	30.04	30.04	85	74	11	79.5	78	82	81	80	1.84
26	30.10	30.08	30.12	30.12	87	73	14	80.0	90	62	86	79	.13
27	30.13	30.12	30 13	30 13	89	75	14	82.0	78	61	78	72	.04
28	30 13	30.09	30.07	30.09	88	75	13	81.5	82	65	78	75	.23
29	30.09	30.13	30 09	30 10	87	73	14	80 0	82	77	81	80	.82
30	30.10	30.13	30 12	30.12	86	73	13	79 5	78	63	82	74	.03
Mean	30.05	30.03	30 03	80 03	86	73	12	80 3	76	62	77	72	6.43

(Table No. 7). METEOROLOGICAL TABLE. JULY, 1880.

Day.	BAROMETER.				TEMPERATURE.				HUMIDITY.				Rain fall.
	7 a. m.	2 p. m.	9 p. m.	Mean.	Max.	Min.	Range.	Mean.	7 a. m.	2 p. m.	9 p. m.	Mean.	
1	30.14	30.13	30.08	30.11	89	74	15	81.5	82	79	78	80	1.
2	30.13	30.05	30.05	30.07	89	76	13	82.5	78	56	79	71	.
3	30.08	30.05	30.08	30.07	90	77	13	83.5	74	44	71	63	.
4	30.10	30.06	30.08	30.08	91	77	14	84.0	74	43	68	62	.
5	30.10	30.06	30.07	30.07	92	78	14	85.0	71	48	68	63	
6	30.09	30 07	30.08	30.08	89	79	10	84.0	71	67	82	73	1.
7	30.10	30.12	30.12	30.11	89	76	13	82.5	71	82	83	79	.
8	30.16	30 13	30.15	30.15	89	75	14	82.0	78	70	86	78	1.
9	30.18	30 13	30.11	30.13	89	76	13	82.5	78	75	78	77	.
10	30.13	30 08	30 07	30.09	90	76	14	83.0	78	56	79	71	.
11	30.10	30.08	30.08	30.09	89	78	11	83.5	78	56	75	70	
12	30.13	30.08	30.12	30.11	91	78	13	84.5	79	53	78	70	
13	30.11	30.02	30.03	30.05	89	75	14	82.0	82	53	82	72	.
14	30.05	30.00	30.01	30.02	88	73	15	80.5	78	56	78	71	.
15	30.04	29.99	30.01	30.01	89	76	13	82.5	78	71	75	75	.
16	30 02	29.99	30 02	30.02	89	76	13	82.5	74	53	75	67	.
17	30.04	30.01	30.04	30.03	89	75	14	82.0	78	62	75	72	.
18	30.06	30.03	30 02	30.03	90	78	12	84.0	74	47	64	62	.
19	30 02	29.99	29.98	29.99	91	77	14	84 0	74	45	64	61	.
20	30.03	30.05	30.07	30.06	90	78	12	84.0	78	72	74	75	.
21	30.06	30.04	30.07	30.06	89	77	12	83 0	74	71	79	75	.
22	30.06	30 05	30.06	30.06	84	75	9	79 5	83	82	82	82	1.
23	30.04	30.04	30.05	30.04	83	71	12	77.0	85	63	77	75	.
24	30 06	30 04	30.07	30 06	84	72	12	78.0	68	64	72	70	.
25	30.10	30 07	30.06	30.07	88	74	14	81.0	82	87	81	72	.
26	30.03	30.07	30.05	30.06	87	77	10	82.0	78	74	78	77	.
27	30.08	30 09	30.05	30.08	88	75	13	81.5	78	91	82	84	.
28	30.08	30.04	30.01	30.04	87	75	12	81.0	87	78	82	82	.
29	30.02	29.97	29.98	29.99	84	74	10	79.0	91	70	91	84	1.
30	29.99	29.98	30.01	30 00	85	74	11	79.5	86	67	87	80	.
31	30.06	30.05	30.09	30.07	86	75	11	80.5	82	61	78	74	.
Mean	30.08	30.05	30.06	30.06	88.3	75.7	12.6	82.6	77	64	77	73	11.

(Table No. 8). METEOROLOGICAL TABLE—AUGUST, 1880.

Day.	BAROMETER.				TEMPERATURE.				HUMIDITY.				Rain-fall.
	7 a. m.	2 p. m.	9 p. m.	Mean.	Max.	Min.	Range.	Mean.	7 a. m.	2 p. m.	9 p. m.	Mean.	
1	30.10	30.06	30.05	30 06	86	74	12	80.0	78	68	82	76	.
2	30.01	29.92	29.92	29.94	88	77	11	92 5	78	56	87	74	.
3	29.86	29.82	29.88	29.86	88	75	13	81.5	82	55	82	73	1.
4	29.93	29.94	30.00	29.96	79	73	6	76.0	95	74	82	84	1.
5	30.02	30.01	30.04	30.03	84	71	13	77.5	76	50	74	67	.
6	30.04	30.02	30.03	30.03	86	74	12	80.0	73	51	73	66	.
7	30.06	30.05	30.07	30.07	88	76	12	82.0	78	49	74	67	.
8	30.29	30.07	30.05	30.07	86	75	11	80.5	87	64	87	79	0.
9	30.03	29.97	29.99	30.00	87	75	12	81.0	82	71	82	78	.
10	29.97	29.99	30.02	30.00	87	75	12	81.0	82	74	82	79	.
11	30.03	30.08	30.08	30.07	82	72	10	77.0	95	95	95	95	.
12	30.07	30.09	30.07	30 07	86	73	13	78.5	86	79	87	84	.
13	30 05	29.02	30.03	30.03	87	76	11	81.5	91	65	83	80	.
14	30.00	30.98	29.99	29.99	88	77	11	82.5	82	71	83	79	.
15	30.00	30.00	30.03	30.02	89	77	12	83.0	78	68	79	75	.
16	30.09	30.13	30.17	30.14	88	77	11	82.5	83	62	75	73	.
17	30.19	30.17	30.18	30.18	89	78	11	83.5	74	56	79	70	.
18	30.17	30.10	30.12	30.13	88	78	11	83.5	78	56	79	71	.
19	30.07	30.03	29 99	30.02	89	78	10	84.0	70	57	75	67	.
20	29.98	29.93	29.90	29.93	89	77	12	83.0	74	52	71	66	.
21	29.93	29.92	29.92	29.92	87	76	11	81.5	74	67	74	72	.
22	.....	29.95	29.97	.....	89	77	12	83 0	.....	55	74	.....	
23	30.01	30.01	30.02	30 02	90	77	13	83.5	78	56	75	70	

(Table No. 9). METEOROLOGICAL TABLE. SEPTEMBER, 1880

Day.	BAROMETER.				TEMPERATURE.				HUMIDITY.				Rain fall.
	7 a. m.	2 p. m.	9 p. m.	Mean.	Max.	Min.	Range.	Mean.	7 a. m.	2 p. m.	9 p. m.	Mean.	
1	29.81	29.83	29.90	29.86	90	76	14	83.0	74	53	75	67	.00
2	29.99	29.96	30.00	29.99	80	78	11	83.5	82	68	60	70	1.30
3	30.01	29.96	29.96	29.97	85	76	9	80.5	82	67	64	71	.30
4	29.95	29.95	29.97	29.96	86	75	11	80.5	86	61	86	78	.30
5	29.99	30.02	30.02	30 01	88	75	13	81.5	82	61	67	70	.41
6	30.03	29.90	29.99	29.98	87	76	11	81.5	82	78	68	76	.18
7	29.95	29.88	29.88	29 90	85	75	10	80.0	86	91	90	89	1.65
8	29.90	29.90	29.97	29.94	80	70	10	75.0	90	62	95	82	.16
9	30.05	30.02	30 08	30.06	76	64	12	70.0	89	52	70	70	.00
10	30.08	30.10	30.09	30.06	74	64	10	69.0	94	81	90	88	.08
11	30.12	30.12	30.17	30.14	80	71	9	75.5	95	78	95	89	.19
12	30.17	30.11	30.11	30.12	86	75	11	80.5	91	64	82	79	.00
13	30.08	30.00	30.05	30.04	87	74	13	80 5	95	83	86	88	.00
14	30.04	30.01	30.01	30.02	81	71	10	76.0	81	59	61	67	.00
15	30.06	30.02	30.05	30.04	81	67	14	74.0	80	63	75	73	.00
16	30.05	30.05	30 05	30.05	79	68	11	73.5	95	61	76	77	.00
17	30.06	30.06	30.07	30.06	82	70	12	76.0	86	60	82	76	.00
18	30.08	30.07	30.12	30.05	85	73	12	79.0	72	54	86	71	.00
19	30.12	30.12	30.12	30.12	84	73	11	78.5	86	61	77	74	.10
20	30.15	30.10	30.12	30.12	84	71	13	77.5	81	57	60	66	.00
21	30.11	30.08	30.09	30.09	82	73	9	77.5	86	74	86	82	.00
22	30.11	30.04	30 08	30.08	85	74	11	79.5	91	67	86	81	.19
23	30.05	30 03	30.06	30.05	86	72	14	79.0	82	74	90	82	.66
24	30 05	30.02	30.04	30.04	80	73	7	76.5	95	86	90	90	1.03
25	30 04	29 99	30.01	30.01	81	72	9	76.5	95	82	86	88	.26
26	30.03	29.93	30.03	30.01	84	72	12	78.0	78	78	87	81	.31
27	30 01	30.00	30.01	30.01	85	74	11	79.5	86	82	91	86	.43
28	30.09	30 07	30.13	30.10	75	64	11	69.5	47	47	53	58	.03
29	30.16	30.14	30.15	30.15	79	64	15	71.5	43	43	68	60	.00
30	30.23	30.18	30.21	30.21	75	63	12	69.0	68	36	61	55	.00
Mean	30 05	30 02	30.05	30.04	82	71	11	77.0	84	66	78	76	7.48

(Table No. 10). METEOROLOGICAL TABLE. OCTOBER, 1880.

Day.	BAROMETER.				TEMPERATURE.				HUMIDITY.				Rain fall.
	7 p m.	2 p. m.	9 p. m.	Mean.	Max.	Min.	Range.	Mean.	7 p m.	2 p m.	9 p m.	Mean.	
1	30.21	30.18	30.20	30 20	78	61	17	69.5	67	46	66	60	.00
2	30.17	30.11	30.11	30.13	80	65	15	72.5	74	66	90	77	.02
3	30.07	30.04	30.05	30.05	80	71	9	75.5	81	71	81	79	.18
4	29.98	29.94	29.97	29.96	79	70	9	74.5	90	66	81	79	.00
5	29.99	29.98	30.01	29.99	72	65	7	68.5	95	71	79	82	.00
6	30.01	29.98	29.97	29.99	77	66	11	71.5	90	69	81	80	.00
7	29.96	29.90	29.92	29 93	81	67	14	74.0	70	70	85	75	.00
8	29.92	29.90	29.95	29 92	77	70	7	73.5	85	73	76	78	.00
9	29.99	30.01	30.05	30.02	72	67	5	69.5	75	71	80	79	.00
10	30.05	30.00	30.04	30.03	74	66	8	70.0	90	95	95	93	.31
11	30.07	30-06	30.15	30.09	83	69	14	76.0	95	67	90	84	.04
12	30.20	30.14	30.15	30.16	83	72	11	77.5	86	67	91	81	.07
13	30.15	30.09	30.13	30.12	84	72	12	78.0	95	67	86	83	.00
14	30.15	30.08	30.09	30 11	84	71	13	77.5	86	60	86	77	.00
15	30.05	29.97	30.00	30.00	84	70	14	77.0	86	60	86	77	.00
16	29.94	30.04	30.18	30.05	76	58	18	67.0	86	72	59	72	.25
17	30.24	30.26	30.33	30.29	66	54	12	60.0	47	31	46	41	.00
18	30.40	30.36	30.38	30.38	69	53	16	61.0	55	35	49	46	.00
19	30.36	30.26	30.27	30.29	67	55	12	61.0	63	60	62	62	.00
20	30.21	30.16	30.16	30.17	69	59	10	64.0	66	74	74	71	.00
21	30.11	30.05	30.07	30.08	72	61	11	66.5	89	62	73	75	.00
22	30.07	30 03	30.14	30.09	73	58	15	65.5	83	39	65	62	.00
23	30.24	30.20	30.28	30.25	65	53	12	59.0	68	30	65	54	.00
24	30.38	30.44	30.35	30.38	66	55	11	60.5	69	36	65	57	.00
25	30.35	30.25	30.22	30 26	70	56	14	63.0	70	53	83	69	.00
26	30.15	30.03	30.04	30.05	75	59	16	67.0	77	52	84	71	.00
27	29.94	29.84	29.86	29.87	75	63	12	69.0	95	63	90	83	.03
28	29.82	29.76	29.80	29.80	74	56	16	65.0	94	85	88	89	.98
29	29.80	29.77	29.85	29.82	61	56	5	58.5	75	71	82	76	.00
30	29.89	29.91	30.00	29.95	63	56	7	59.5	81	78	88	82	.00
31	30 08	30.07	30 16	30.12	65	52	13	58.5	78	68	74	77	.00
Mean	30.09	30.06	30.09	30.08	74.0	62 1	11.9	68 0	79	62	77	73	1.88

(Table No. 11). METEOROLOGICAL TABLE. NOVEMBER, 1880.

Day.	BAROMETER.				TEMPERATURE				HUMIDITY.				Rain-fall.
	7 a. m.	2 p. m.	9 p. m.	Mean.	Max.	Min.	Range.	Mean.	7 a. m.	2 p. m.	9 p. m.	Mean.	
1	30 18	30.13	30.15	30.16	62	49	13	55.5	65	36	71	57	.00
2	30.10	30.03	30 02	30.04	62	57	5	59 5	76	71	88	78	.08
3	29.95	29.85	29.91	29.91	68	59	9	63.5	94	95	95	91	.28
4	29.91	29.90	29.98	29.94	74	65	9	69.5	95	76	95	89	.35
5	30 03	30 02	29.93	29.97	68	64	4	66.0	100	79	90	90	1.18
6	30 03	30 14	30 24	30.10	68	49	19	58.5	80	54	51	62	.30
7	30.28	30 20	30.18	30.22	53	43	10	48.0	68	42	65	58	.00
8	30.13	30 03	30.00	30.04	59	47	12	53.0	71	64	87	74	.00
9	29.98	29 90	29 90	29.92	72	55	17	63.5	94	85	95	91	.26
10	29.93	30 01	30.12	30.05	73	62	11	67.5	79	39	72	61	.09
11	30.21	30.21	30.22	30.18	67	54	13	60.5	74	50	77	67	.00
12	30.24	30 25	30.26	30.19	66	57	9	61.5	66	57	83	68	.00
13	30.22	30 14	30 26	30 15	63	53	10	58.0	88	94	87	89	1.38
14	30.24	30.26	30 29	30.28	55	43	12	49.0	86	85	76	82	.33
15	30.29	30.13	30.12	30.17	58	43	15	50.5	61	36	54	50	.00
16	30.21	30 13	30.22	30.19	61	45	16	53.0	70	40	69	60	.02
17	30 23	30.17	30.17	30.18	63	54	9	58.5	87	85	88	88	.97
18	30.34	30.26	30.40	30 37	60	36	24	48.0	83	65	63	70	.15
19	30 32	30 16	30.13	30.18	56	34	22	45.0	61	65	78	68	.00
20	30.45	30.15	30.24	30.19	60	47	13	53.5	86	80	73	80	.01
21	30 29	30 31	30.37	30.34	51	43	8	47.0	76	76	49	67	.03
22	30.38	30 42	30.47	30 43	48	44	4	46.0	46	48	41	45	.00
23	30 49	30.40	30.40	30.42	54	37	17	45.5	46	36	44	42	.00
24	30 30	30 23	30.18	30.22	50	47	3	48.5	85	85	93	88	.25
25	30.15	30.13	30.16	30.15	60	48	12	54.0	100	84	94	93	.12
26	30 21	30.25	30 24	30.23	61	54	7	57 5	94	87	87	89	.00
27	30 22	30.11	30.12	30.14	57	56	7	53 5	93	87	94	91	.15
28	30 08	30.05	30.10	30 09	75	56	19	65.5	100	81	100	94	.00
29	30 19	30.22	30.25	30.23	69	53	16	61.0	94	82	87	88	.07
30	30.17	30.04	30.00	30.05	68	55	13	61.5	100	100	100	100	.02
Mean	30 19	30 14	30 16	30 16	62.0	50 1	11.9	56.0	80	60	78	70	6 04

[Table No. 13.]

METEOROLOGICAL SUMMARY OF 1880.

DATE. 1880.	BAROMETER							THERMOMETER								Mean Relative Humidity Local Observations (Per cent.)	WIND			Amount of Rain or Melted Snow (Inches and hundredths)	Number of Days on which Rain or Snow Fell.
	MEAN OF—				RANGE.			Local Observations	MEAN OF— Telegraphic Observations			RANGE.					Prevailing Direction.	Total Number of Miles.	Maximum Velocity during Month.		
	Local Observations	Telegraphic Observations																		
		Corrected for temperature, instrumental error, and elevation.			Highest.	Lowest.	Difference.		A.M.	P.M.	Mid-night.	Maximum.	Minimum.	Difference.							
		A.M.	P.M.	Mid-night.																	
January	30.126	30.133	30.102	30.141	30.403	29.774	629	63	58.7	67.6	62.4	75	42	33	73	N.E.	4,954	21	1.02	5
February	30.168	30.169	30.140	30.185	30.547	29.600	947	02	56.1	64.6	59.8	77	43	34	69	N.E.	5,499	32	4.62	12
March	30.069	30.081	30.053	30.072	30.311	29.811	500	65.7	61.5	70.4	64.7	84	49	39	71	N.	6,222	21	6.66	16
April	30.075	30.078	30.066	30.083	30.412	29.862	580	71.2	67.5	76.3	69.9	84	49	35	73	N.E.	6,259	28	6.47	10
May	29.982	30.001	29.979	29.995	30.308	29.792	516	76.6	75.1	79.9	73.9	90	58	30	71	N.E.	6,304	36	6.54	14
June	30.036	30.048	30.029	30.037	30.163	29.834	309	80.1	77.7	83.9	78.4	88	71	21	73	S.E.	5,274	29	6.43	20
July	30.062	30.074	30.051	30.063	30.175	29.973	205	81.7	78.6	86.1	80.5	92	63	21	73	S.E.	3,382	24	11.42	21
August	30.001	30.011	29.991	29.999	30.223	29.617	481	3	78.1	86.6	79.9	92	64	27	73	E.	3,961	27	4.60	15
September	30.044	30.047	30.023	30.057	30.361	29.789	472	76.8	73.1	80.7	75.9	84	57	32	73	E.	5,131	21	7.45	19
October	30.026	30.002	30.051	30.097	30.441	29.752	663	68.0	64.6	72.7	66.3	76	34	41	73	N.	5,417	19	1.37	10
November	30.167	30.177	30.141	30.168	30.517	29.832	665	56.4	53.5	61.3	56.4	75	34	41	70	N.	6,404	31	4.22	21
December	30.118	30.162	30.127	30.156	30.595	29.795	800	53.0	49.8	56.5	53.2	78	30	58		N.	6,305	26	6.45	12
Annual means	30.076	30.089	30.063	30.088	30.366	29.790	576	69.5	66.2	73.5	68	83	51	32	73	N.E.	65,162	36	69.86	153

GENERAL REMARKS.

1880.

January—Precipitation below the average.

February—High barometer; temperature about normal.

March—Precipitation about normal.

April—Precipitation about normal, and mild weather.

May—Precipitation about normal, and temperature about the average.

June—Latter part cool and pleasant; numerous thunder-storms.

July—Numerous thunder-storms.

August—Deficiency in rainfall.

September—No storm.

October—Precipitation about normal.

November—Unusually wet month; considerable damage to cotton and sugar crops; first frost on the 16th, first ice on the 19th.

December—Very cold in last week.

UNITED STATES SIGNAL SERVICE STATION, NEW ORLEANS.

L. DUNNE, Sergeant Signal Service, U. S. A.

(Table No. 14)—COMPARATIVE METEOROLOGICAL SUMMARY OF ANNUAL MEANS, ETC., FROM 1873 TO 1880; NEW ORLEANS, LA.

YEAR	BAROMETER ANNUAL MEAN				THERMOMETER ANNUAL MEAN									MAXIMUM AND MINIMUM					Relative Humidity	WIND			Number of days on which rain fell	Total amount of rainfall
	Local Observations	A.M.	P.M.	Night	Local Observations	A.M.	P.M.	Night	Maximum	Minimum	Maximum	Minimum	Difference	Maximum	Minimum	Date of Maximum	Minimum	Date of Min.		Prevailing Direction	Highest Veloc'y	Total number of miles		
1873	30.07	30.09	30.04	30.08	68.3	64.7	72.8	66.8	82.8	52.5	61	30.77		93	30	July 7 and 8	30	Dec. 28	72	SE	27	60,543	146	66.58
1874	30.08	30.09	30.04	30.08	70.5	66.7	74.3	68.6	83.4	54.0	68.3	30.80		96	35	August 15	35	Jan. 7	71	SE	32	63,270	140	62.74
1875	30.07	30.08	30.04	30.09	68.6	65.6	73.1	67.1	81.7	51.7	68.9	30.75		92	28	July 16	28	Jan. 10	76	SE	29	65,563	135	85.73
1876	30.07	30.09	30.04	30.08	68.6	64.9	73.1	67.1	83.9	50.9	58.8	30.71		93	28	June 24	28	Dec. 30	74	SE	34	64,518	142	67.25
1877	30.05	30.06	30.01	30.06	68.6	64.9	73.2	66.7	84.0	51.4	65.8	30.82		96	36	July 6	36	Jan. 9	69	SE	39	68,594	130	63.09
1878	30.01	30.02	29.97	30.01	69.2	65.7	74.1	68.1	83.4	52.2	65.9	30.70		94	27	August 22	27	Dec. 28	74	SE	40	62,146	122	66.16
1879	30.07	30.08	30.04	30.08	69.5	65.7	74.5	69.5	84.6	49.9	63.9	30.34		91	20	July 11,13,14,15	20	Jan. 6	70	E	40	66,260	134	51.27
1880	30.08	30.09	30.06	30.09	69.5	66.2	73.5	68.4	83.8	51.2	69.5	30.37	29.79	92	20	July 5	20	Dec. 30	73	SE	36	65,162	185	69.86

Barometer corrected for Temperature and Elevation.

(Table No. 15.)—COMPARATIVE TABLE SHOWING THE MEANS OF THE HOTTEST AND COLDEST DAYS AND THE DATE OF FIRST AND LAST FROSTS IN EACH YEAR FROM 1873 TO 1880; NEW ORLEANS, LA.

YEAR	HOTTEST AND COLDEST DAY				DATES OF FROST		NO. OF DAYS IN EACH IN WHICH THUNDER OR LIGHTNING WAS OBSERVED													REMARKS
	Mean ther-mometer	Date	Mean ther.	Date	First	Last	January	February	March	April	May	June	July	August	September	October	November	December	Total	
1873	90.0	July 7	33.5	January 7	Novem'r 29	January 20							1	2					13	Thunder
1874	89.0	August 13	38.0	January 16	Novem'r 26	February 10	2	1	2	2	2	4	9	9	2				41	Thunder
1875	86.5	July 16	34.0	January 10	Decemb'r 18	February 8						1	1	1					3	Thunder and lightning
1876	86.7	August 29	32.7	Decemb'r 30	Novem'r 30	February 5			4	7	7	7	10	15	15	3	2	1	82	
1877	89.2	July 31	35.0	January 9	Novem'r 11	January 25		2	7	1		1	6	3		1				
1878	87.7	July 24	35.0	Decemb'r 27	Novem'r 1	February 1	1			1	7	1	9	1	1					
1879	86.5	July 15	29.2	January 6	Novem'r 20	February 27			2	1	1	1	10	1						
1880	85.7	July 5	26.2	Decemb'r 29	Novem'r 16	January 24	1	1	1			2	16	15	3		3			

MORTUARY REPORT

OF THE

BOARD OF HEALTH

OF THE STATE OF LOUISIANA,

FOR THE YEAR 1880.

ber 31, 1880, inclusive, and the births and marriages reported during the year.

Very Respectfully,
H. PERALTA,
P. HENRY LANAUZE,
Registration Clerks.

Table No. 1, GIVING THE MORTALITY FROM ALL CAUSES, BY MONTHS, CLASSIFIED ACCORDING TO COLOR, FOR THE YEAR 1880.

DISEASES.	JAN. From January 1 to 31, inclusive.		FEB. From Feb. 1 to Feb. 28, inclusive.		MAR. From February 29 to April 3, inclusive.		APRIL From April 4 to May 1, inclusive.		MAY From May 2 to May 29, inclusive.		JUNE From May 30 to July 3, inclusive.		JULY From July 4 to July 31, inclusive.		AUG. From Aug. 1 to Aug 28, inclusive.		SEPT. From Aug. 29 to Oct. 2, inclusive.		OCT. From Oct 3 to Oct. 30, inclusive.		NOV. From Oct. 1 to Nov 27, inclusive.		DEC. From Nov. 28 to Dec. 31, inclusive.		TOTAL	
	W.	C.	W.	C.	W.	C.	W.	C.	W.	C.	W.	C.	W.	C.	W.	C.	W.	C.	W.	C.	W.	C.	W.	C.	W.	C.
General Diseases.																										
Small-pox																							1	
Measles			1		3	1	15	5	19	20	15	10	3	4	1				2			2	57	40
Scarlatina			1		4	2	3		5		6		9	2	4		1		1		4		49	7
Dengue																							1	2
Typhus Fever			1				4		1						1	2			2				1	
Cerebro-Spinal Fever	4								1		5		2				1	1	2	3	3		3	2
Enteric or Typhoid Fever	1	1	3					1	3	1	1	1	4	3	1	1	3	1	3	2	1	1	3	20
Simple Continued Fever	1	1					6		10	5	2	1		3	3		3		1		1		1	7
Yellow Fever																					1	1	2	
Malarial Fevers—																								
Intermittent			5	2	2	1	2	1	3	1	1	2			1	1	2	2	3	2	1	1	12	7
Remittent	1	1	2		10		1		10		17	2	4		3	3	11	3		3	1	1	33	17
Congestive	1	1	4				6	1	3		3	2	5		6	5	23	5	13		1		115	36
Typho-Malarial							1		1		3		2			1	12	14	10		1	1	18	5
Malarial (unclassified)	5	1	2	1	3		6	2	2	2	2				1		5				7		56	37
Simple Cholera (chol. mor.)	7		4		10		6		13	1	4	1			1		3	2	2	2	2		8	6
Malignant Cholera																								
Cholera Infantum									4	4	14	11	8		5	2		2		1			65	24
Diphtheria	1		1		1	1	2		1		4	1	1	3		1	3	3	12	10	10	7	75	6
Whooping Cough		1	2	2			6	6	6		4	6	6		1	1	3	3				1	33	37
Influenza																								
Congenital Cachexia	1				1																		1	
Phacelana														1							1		1	1
Hospital Gangrene		1	1	2	1		2					2							1				10	
Erysipelas (variety stated)	2		1		1		2	2	1	1				3	1	1	1	1		2	2	1	15	1
Addison's disease									1														1	
Pyæmia					1																			
Scrofula	1				2				1				1		1		1		1		1		9	4
Puerperal Fever					1				1		2				1				1		1		5	3
Acute Rheumatism			2		2		2		1				1				1		1		2		5	2
Chronic Rheumatism			1		1				1								1	1					6	5
Acute Gout																							3	2
Syphilis (congenital)					1																		3	2
Syphilis					3		3		1				1				1		1				9	2
Cancer of the Abdomen	1	1			1		1								1	1							7	1
Cancer of the Breast																								
Cancer of the Face							1		1															
Cancer of the Liver																								
Cancer of the Rectum	2						1		1		1		1				1		1				4	2

44

Table No. 1 (CONTINUED), GIVING THE MORTALITY FROM ALL CAUSES BY MONTHS, CLASSIFIED ACCORDING TO COLOR, FOR THE YEAR 1880.

DISEASES.	JAN. W	JAN. C	FEB. W	FEB. C	MAR. W	MAR. C	APRIL W	APRIL C	MAY W	MAY C	JUNE W	JUNE C	JULY W	JULY C	AUG. W	AUG. C	SEP. W	SEP. C	OCT. W	OCT. C	NOV. W	NOV. C	DEC. W	DEC. C	TOTAL W	TOTAL C
Cancer of the Stomach	3	1	4			3	1	2	3	3	1	1	1	1	3		2	1	3	2		1		2	22	5
Cancer of the Womb	3		1			3	5		2	3	5		4		2		3		6		3		2		38	17
Cancer of the Month	1		1		2		1										1								4	2
Cancer of the Bladder					1												1								3	
Cancer, Unclassified	1				1			1																	1	
Cancer of the Testicle																									1	
Cancer of the Lungs	2																1								1	
Cancer of the Eye	1						1												1						2	
Cancer of the Bowels							1				1						2				2		1		5	8
Scrofula											1			1			2			1		2		1		
Tubercular Meningitis	24	1	36	1	46	30	47	21	36	33	49	31	37	20	25	29	37	25	40	20	63	31	54	37	517	346
Phthisis Pulmonalis	10	2	4	2	2	8	12	1	15	6	16	4	6	4	6	4	8	3	7	4	5	4	6	2	97	47
Tabes-Mesenterica					2	1						1												1		
Rickets					1		1				1	1		1			1		1							3
Diabetes	1				1							2		2				2				1		1		1
Purpura																										
Scurvy																								3		
Anæmia		2	2	2		1		1	2		4		2		1		1		1	1	4	1	6		13	5
General Dropsy (Anasarca)	2		3	4	1	1	1				4		2				2		1			1		3	24	23

Local Diseases.

Diseases of the Nervous System.

DISEASES.	JAN. W	JAN. C	FEB. W	FEB. C	MAR. W	MAR. C	APRIL W	APRIL C	MAY W	MAY C	JUNE W	JUNE C	JULY W	JULY C	AUG. W	AUG. C	SEP. W	SEP. C	OCT. W	OCT. C	NOV. W	NOV. C	DEC. W	DEC. C	TOTAL W	TOTAL C
Congestion of Brain	3	3	5	2	6	1	4	3	10	2	14	2	8	2	8	7	14	5	10	2	5	6	11	5	98	34
Encephalitis (Inflammation of the Brain)	5		5		1		2	2	3		1	1	1				1	1		2		2	1	1	11	3
Meningitis	3		2		3		2	1	4	3	4	2	3	4	3		3	3	6		1		6	1	53	20
Softening of the Brain			5		5	1	5		1		3		4		1		1		1				5	1	32	5
White Softening of the Brain											1														1	1
Abscess of the Brain											2														3	1
Apoplexy	5		7	1		1	5		2	1	2	1	9	3	7	1	8	3	3	2	6	3	8	2	75	33
Sunstroke											1										1				3	
Chronic Hydrocephalus			2		1						1										1	1			9	2

Diseases of the Cerebral Arteries—

DISEASES.	JAN. W	JAN. C	FEB. W	FEB. C	MAR. W	MAR. C	APRIL W	APRIL C	MAY W	MAY C	JUNE W	JUNE C	JULY W	JULY C	AUG. W	AUG. C	SEP. W	SEP. C	OCT. W	OCT. C	NOV. W	NOV. C	DEC. W	DEC. C	TOTAL W	TOTAL C
Atheroma																										
Ossification																		1								
Aneurism											1														4	2
Thrombosis					1													2							4	
Embolism			2		1																			2	2	2

Spinal Meningitis
Spinal Haemorrhage
Myelitis
Paralysis—
  Hemiplegia
  Paraplegia
Paralysis (general)
Locomotor ataxia
Tetanus—
  Traumatic
  Trismus-Nascentium
Hydrophobia
Convulsions, Infantile
Convulsions
Epilepsy
Hysteria
Delirium Tremens
Mania
Paralysis of the Insane
Inflammation of Middle Ear

Diseases of the Circulatory System.

Pericarditis
Dropsy of Pericardium
Endo-carditis
Valve Disease of the Heart—
  Aortic
  Mitral
Hypertrophy of the Heart
Dilatation of the Heart
Paralysis of Heart
As ripa al
Fatty Degeneration of Heart
Rupture of the Heart
Degeneration of the—
  Fatty
  Calcareous
Embolism (locality stated)
Thrombosis
Aneurism of Heart
Aneurism of Aorta
Phlebitis
Phlegmasia Dolens
Heart Disease (unclassified)

Diseases of the Respiratory System.

Croup (Membranous)
Laryngitis
Œdema of Glottis
Bronchitis—
  Acute
  Chronic

Table No. 1 (CONTINUED), GIVING THE MORTALITY FROM ALL CAUSES, BY MONTHS, CLASSIFIED ACCORDING TO COLOR, FOR THE YEAR 1880.

DISEASES.	JAN. From January 1st to January 31 inclusive		FEB. From Feb. 1 to February 28, inclusive.		MAR. From February 29 to April 3, inclusive.		APRIL From April 4, to May 1, inclusive.		MAY. From May 2nd to May 29 inclusive.		JUNE. From May 30 to July 3 inclusive		JULY. From July 4 to July 31st inclusive.		AUG. From Aug 1 to Aug. 28th inclusive.		SEPT. From Aug. 29 to October 2 inclusive.		OCT. From Oct. 3 to October 30, inclusive.		NOV. From Oct. 31 to November 27, inclusive.		DEC. From Nov. 28 to December 31, inclusive.		TOTAL.	
	W.	C.	W.	C.	W.	C.	W.	C.	W.	C.	W.	C.	W.	C.	W.	C.	W.	C.	W.	C.	W.	C.	W.	C.	W.	C.
Asthma	1		3	1			1														3				12	3
Pneumonia	18	19	24	18	21	20	14	8	14	12	14	17	5	10	5	5	12	8	10	9	7	5	19	13	163	144
Abscess of Lungs				1			1											1					1		2	1
Gangrene of Lungs													1	1		1	1	1								1
Emphysema of Lungs			1		3			2	1	1	1	1	1		1			2							3	3
Atelectasis. (Pulmonary also)	1																1								3	2
Pneumonic Phthisis—																										
Acute														1		2		2		1				2		
Chronic		1	1				1		1		1			1			1	1	1	1		1		2	9	14
Hemoptysis				2												2									15	
Œdema of Lungs																									5	3
Pleurisy											1														2	3
Empyema					3							1													2	
Diseases of the Digestive System.																										
Hæmatemesis		1																				1				1
Stomatitis—																										
Ulcerative	1											1		1				1				1			3	1
Aphthous																										
Parasitic				2		2		2		1		1		2		3		2		1		3		2		14
Teething											1					1									1	3
Ulcerative Sore Throat	6				5	2			11		13	13	4			3			3		6				29	29
Thrush			2										1		3		2		1				2		4	
Sloughing Sore Throat		3			1																			2	1	
Goitre																1									2	
Tonsillitis							1						1	1			4	1			1	1			3	1
Abscess of Pharynx																									1	1
Stricture of the Esophagus																										1
Gastritis				2	4			1		2	3	3	2	1	3		2		3		1		2	2	3	1
Ulcer of the Stomach	8		6	2			10		25	10	35		7	4	10	9	13	7	12	4	11	4	7	2	27	12
Dyspepsia	7	1	2		3		3		6	4	8	3	4	2	2	3	4		6	3	2	1	2	2	148	55
Enteritis						3						3	1												46	38
Dysentery	1	1			1	1		2	3		10	1	2	2	1	1		1		4	11	4			1	1
Ulceration of the Bowels					1	2	2						1	1							2	1			4	1
Hemorrhage of the Bowels			3		1	1	2		3		10			1								2		2	5	2
Intussusception of Bowels								2																		1
Obstruction of Bowels																									9	
Diarrhœa	10				4		4		3		10	19	2	3	10	2	3	8	7		13	2	8		83	61
Colic	1		3		1	2	2						1		1										3	
Constipation					1		4																			

Gastralgia
Hernia (Class stated)
Fistula of Anus
Tuberculosis of Liver
Hepatitis
Abscess of the Liver
Cirrhosis of the Liver
Atrophy of Liver

Degeneration of the Liver—
Fatty
Fibroid
Amyloid
Jaundice
Splenitis
Leucocythæmia
Peritonitis
Ascites

Diseases of the Urinary and Generative Organs.

Bright's Disease—
Acute
Chronic
Suppression of Urine
Cystitis
Rupture of the Bladder
Enlargement of Prostate
Stricture of the Urethra
Ovarian Dropsy
Extravasation of Urine
Cystic Tumor of Ovary
Pelvic Cellulitis (Non-Puerperal)
Pyelitis

Affections Connected with Parturition.

Abortion or Premature Labor
Difficult Labor (cause stated)
Hæmorrhage
Puerperal Mania
Metroperitonitis
Puerperal Convulsions
Purulent Ophthalmia
Puerperal Septicæmia

Diseases of the Organs of Locomotion.

Caries—Vertebral
Ostitis

Table No. 1 (Continued), GIVING THE MORTALITY FROM ALL CAUSES, BY MONTHS, CLASSIFIED ACCORDING TO COLOR, FOR THE YEAR 1880.

DISEASES.	JAN.		FEB.		MAR.		APRIL.		MAY.		JUNE.		JULY.		AUG.		SEPT.		OCT.		NOV.		DEC.		TOTAL.	
	W.	C.	W.	C.	W.	C.	W.	C.	W.	C.	W.	C.	W.	C.	W.	C.	W.	C.	W.	C.	W.	C.	W.	C.	W.	C.
Necrosis																			1	1					1	1
Osteo-Sarcoma																									1	
Amputation of leg																									1	
Psoas Abscess															1										2	2
Diseases of the Cellular and Cutaneous																										
Scald Head	2										1	1														1
Carbuncle (Anthrax)												1							1			1			3	
Phlegmonous Abscess					1								2					1			1		3		7	
Senile Gangrene									1		1								1		1	1	1	3	7	10
Elephantiasis of Leg								2								1									1	
Eczema																	1				1				1	
Bedsore	1						1							1											1	
Abscess of Rectum																									1	
Psoriasis																									1	
Frost Bite																					1		1		1	
Leprosy									1										1						3	
Conditions not necessarily associated with General or Local Diseases.																										
Premature Birth	2				4		1		2	1	4	1	1		2	2	4	2	5		5	1	1	1	31	12
Difficult Birth	7	1	7	1	3	3	2	5	4	2	2	2	3		2	2	4	4	5		3	8	1	5	43	99
Old Age																	1			1					1	
Syncope																										
Debility—																										
Infantile	6		6	8	7	1	6	2	13	6	12	8	7	1	8	8	11	5	6	5	8	8	6	6	98	63
Senile	5		8	11	10	4	6	6	6	4	10	5	6	8	12	3	12	9	6	5	15	13	8	13	107	87
Accidental Poisoning—																										
Mercurial Salivation																					1				1	
Carbonic Acid																										
Chloroform																										
Lead																			1	1					1	
Uræmic Poisoning									1														1		1	

General Injuries.

Burns.
Scalds.
Burns by Coal Oil.
Lightning Stroke.
Traumatic Hæmorrhage.
From Surgical Operations. { Shock. Hæmorrhage.
Multiple Injury.
Asphyxia from—
Drowning.
Strangling.
Obstruction of air passages.
Overlying.
Starvation.
Exposure to Cold.
Infant Exposure.
Neglect.

Local Injuries.

Concussion of the Brain.
Compression of the Brain.
Fracture of Neck.
Fracture of Skull.
Fracture of Spine.
Fracture of Leg.
Fracture of Femur.
Gunshot wound of neck.
Head.
Abdomen.
(Unclassified).
Incised or Penetrating Wound of—
Neck.
Chest.
Abdomen.
Heart.

Human Parasites.

Intestinal Worms.
Echinococcus.
Trichinosis.

Tumors Non-Malignant.

Of Abdomen.
Of Brain.
Of Leg.
Of Neck.
Of Ovary.
Of Womb.

Table No. 1 (CONTINUED), GIVING THE MORTALITY FROM ALL CAUSES, BY MONTHS, CLASSIFIED ACCORDING TO COLOR, FOR THE YEAR 1880.

DISEASES.	JAN. From Jan. 1 to Jan. 31, inclusive.		FEB. From Feb. 1 to Feb. 28, inclusive.		MAR. From Feb. 29 to April 3, inclusive.		APRIL From April 4 to May 1, inclusive.		MAY. From May 2 to May 29, inclusive.		JUNE. From May 30 to July 3, inclusive.		JULY. From July 4 to July 31, inclusive.		AUG. From Aug. 1 to Aug. 28, inclusive.		SEPT. From Aug. 29 to Oct. 2, inclusive.		OCT. From Oct. 3, to Oct. 30, inclusive.		NOV. From Oct. 31 to Nov. 27, inclusive.		DEC. From Nov. 28 to Dec. 31, inclusive.		TOTAL.	
	W.	C.	W.	C.	W.	C.	W.	C.	W.	C.	W.	C.	W.	C.	W.	C.	W.	C.	W.	C.	W.	C.	W.	C.	W.	C.
Congenital Malformations																										
Imperforate Anus													1											1
Open Foramen Ovale (Cyanosis)	1		2				1					1			1		3		2				13	
Spina Bifida					2														1					
Umbilical Hemorrhage					1				1				1								1		1	4
Malformation of Head							1																1	1
Malformation of Heart																						1	1	
Suicide—																								
Drowning				1						1											2		4	
Hanging							1				2												5	
Shooting							2						1		1		2			1	2		2	1
Cutting or Stabbing							1				2		1								1		4	
Opium																								
Killed or Murdered.																								
Shooting															1								1	
Stabbing																								
Poisoning					1						1													1
Beating																				1				
Infanticide (mode stated)									1			1											2	
Total Deaths																								

(Table No. 2)—GIVING THE WEEKLY MORTALITY FOR THE YEAR 1880, CLASSIFIED ACCORDING TO COLOR AND SEX.

WEEK ENDING	WHITE.			COLORED.			TOTAL.		GRAND TOTAL.
	Male	Female.	Total.	Male.	Female.	Total.	Male.	Female.	
January 3	18	13	31	9	4	13	27	17	44
January 10	35	26	61	22	11	33	57	37	94
January 17	33	33	66	21	21	42	54	54	108
January 24	37	26	63	17	15	32	54	41	95
January 31	46	23	69	20	16	36	66	39	105
February 7	42	28	70	31	17	48	73	45	118
February 14	37	38	75	12	21	33	49	59	108
February 21	32	21	53	15	26	41	47	47	94
February 28	34	33	67	20	21	41	54	54	108
March 6	22	24	46	17	19	36	39	43	82
March 13	26	19	45	14	19	33	40	38	78
March 20	31	23	54	12	19	31	43	42	85
March 27	36	29	65	21	23	44	57	52	109
April 3	44	33	77	17	18	35	61	51	112
April 10	41	31	72	12	16	38	53	47	100
April 17	51	30	81	18	15	33	69	45	114
April 24	35	34	69	15	18	33	50	52	102
May 1	41	35	76	21	14	35	62	49	111
May 8	41	33	74	23	27	50	64	60	124
May 15	46	35	81	23	22	45	69	57	126
May 22	50	36	86	28	27	55	78	63	141
May 29	42	46	88	22	28	50	64	74	138
June 5	61	36	97	25	28	53	86	64	150
June 12	66	52	118	23	25	48	89	77	166
June 19	36	34	70	21	23	44	57	57	114
June 26	35	36	71	25	19	44	60	55	115
July 3	47	26	73	20	19	39	67	45	112
July 10	33	33	66	17	16	33	50	49	99
July 17	39	29	68	21	11	32	60	40	100
July 24	40	20	60	16	17	33	56	37	93
July 31	26	21	47	17	12	29	43	33	76
August 7	24	17	41	30	18	48	54	35	89
August 14	29	18	47	13	12	25	42	30	72
August 21	40	31	71	19	17	36	59	48	107
August 28	40	25	65	19	18	37	59	43	102
September 4	35	27	62	20	20	40	55	47	102
September 11	30	27	57	19	14	33	49	41	90
September 18	47	29	76	27	24	51	74	53	127
September 25	42	30	72	16	16	32	58	46	104
October 2	42	29	71	17	15	32	59	44	103
October 9	26	39	65	20	22	42	46	61	107
October 16	39	29	68	16	12	28	55	41	96
October 23	47	26	73	15	16	31	62	42	104
October 30	52	37	89	9	17	26	61	54	115
November 6	58	29	87	16	18	34	74	47	121
November 13	45	41	86	24	13	37	69	54	123
November 20	35	31	66	17	29	46	52	60	112
November 27	41	43	84	18	29	47	59	72	131
December 4	41	30	71	9	18	27	50	48	98
December 11	27	22	49	20	16	36	47	38	85
December 18	47	32	79	13	15	28	60	47	107
December 25	26	27	53	26	19	45	52	46	98
December 31	34	32	66	25	18	43	59	50	109
Total	2050	1587	3637	1003	873	1986	3053	2570	5623

45

(Table No. 3.)—GIVING THE WEEKLY MORTALITY FOR THE YEAR 1880, CLASSIFIED ACCORDING TO DIVISIONS OF AGE AND COLOR.

WEEK ENDING.	Under 1 year W	Under 1 year C	1 to 2 years W	1 to 2 years C	2 to 5 years W	2 to 5 years C	5 to 10 years W	5 to 10 years C	10 to 15 years W	10 to 15 years C	15 to 20 years W	15 to 20 years C	20 to 25 years W	20 to 25 years C	25 to 30 years W	25 to 30 years C	30 to 40 years W	30 to 40 years C	40 to 50 years W	40 to 50 years C	50 to 60 years W	50 to 60 years C	60 to 70 years W	60 to 70 years C	70 to 80 years W	70 to 80 years C	80 to 90 years W	80 to 90 years C	Above 90 years W	Above 90 years C	Age Unknown W	Age Unknown C	Color Unk'wn W	Color Unk'wn C	Total by Weeks W	Total by Weeks C
Total	774	473	240	133	244	144	142	69	64	51	82	47	176	103	159	108	373	207	430	171	391	143	305	144	153	81	69	62	21	42	14	6			3637	1986

(Table No. 4.) GIVING MORTALITY FROM SOME OF THE PRINCIPAL DISEASES, CLASSIFIED ACCORDING TO AGE AND COLOR.

DISEASES.	Under 1 Year.		1 to 2 Years.		2 to 5 Years.		5 to 10 Years.		10 to 15 Years.		15 to 20 Years.		20 to 30 Years.		30 to 40 Years.		40 to 50 Years.		50 to 60 Years.		60 to 70 Years.		70 to 80 Years.		80 to 90 Years.		Above 90 Years.		Age not stated, but Color stated.		TOTAL of COLOR.		TOTAL of BOTH COLORS.
	w	c	w	c	w	c	w	c	w	c	w	c	w	c	w	c	w	c	w	c	w	c	w	c	w	c	w	c	w	c	w	c	
Yellow Fever	26		17	7	19	19	6	6	2	2				15		9		6		8		2	1	4		1		1			2		234	102	336
Malarial Fevers			12	1	1	1	11	3	5	5	3	6	32	4	21	2	38	6	24	5	12	2		4	3		1	3					32	20	52
Typhoid Fever	2	2	1		26	1	9	1	5	3	8		3	1	2		1	1	2		2	1	1		1								49	7	56
Scarlet Fever	6		21	14	19	8	1	2	1			1	1		1																		57	40	97
Measles	1																																1		1
Small Pox	4			13	4	20	6	4	5	2	2	1	9	8	1	5																	75	6	81
Diphtheria	73	35	13	14	13	13	11	6	2	1			1																		2		201	130	331
Diarrhœal Diseases	9	14	4	4	4	9	3	4	1	2		2	9	6	19	5	21	15	22	15	18	12	6	6	3	3	2						98	34	132
Consumption of Brain	9	2	4	6	13	13	2	4	2	3		20	4	96	19	136	40	11	53	36	8	4	1					1			2		517	346	863
Congestion of Brain	41	17	17	22	9	14	4	4	2	2		2	14	20	13	13	6	13	22	5	5	10	5	4	1	1	1				2	1	164	143	307
Pneumonia	2		1	1	1		1	1				3	3	2	17	4	17	3	21	8	22	5	1	1	2		1				1		102	27	129
Bright's Disease			1																																
Cancerous Diseases																																			
Suicides																																			20
Total	166	116	90	68	138	73	75	40	34	25	26	33	215	158	245	124	241	85	196	83	111	49	42	21	13	8	7	1	7		4,1619	895	2214

TABLE NO. 5. GIVING THE MORTALITY FROM SOME OF THE PRINCIPAL DISEASES, CLASSIFIED ACCORDING TO NATIVITY.

	Yellow fever.	Malarial fever.	Typhoid fever.	Scarlet fever.	Measles.	Diphtheria.	Diarrhœal diseases.	Phthisis Pulmonalis	Pneumonia.	Congestion of Brain.	Bright's Disease.	Cancerous Diseases.	Suicide.	Small-pox.
Africa								2	2	1				
Austria and Hungary												1		
Belgium														
British America			1											
China													1	
Denmark														
France		1	9	4				18	6	15	6	7	7	
Germany		1	18	1	1			16	3	18	12	12	25	
Great Britain and Ireland	1		38					28	2	17	17	1	29	
Greece														
Holland				1						2				
Italy	1		3	1	53		78	206	3	208	67	44	36	
Louisiana			219	41						2				
Mexico			2					2		2	2	1		
Norway and Sweden										3				
Portugal										2	1			
Russia										1				
At Sea														
South America		2					2	1	4	4	5	1	3	
Spain			40	6	1	1	2	61	181	45	23	27	20	3
Switzerland									3	1			2	
Turkey														
United States not Louisiana														
West Indies		1											1	
Not Stated														1
Total	2	336	52	56	97	81	331	863	307	132	107	129	18	1

(Table No 6) GIVING THE NUMBER OF STILL BORN ACCORDING TO SEX AND COLOR.

MONTH.	WHITE. Male	WHITE. Female	Total white	COLORED. Male	COLORED. Female	Total colored	Total of both colors, by months.	Total for the year.
January	11	10	21	5	9	14	35	....
February	10	5	15	5	5	10	25	....
March	10	6	16	7	6	13	29	....
April	5	8	13	9	3	12	25	....
May	6	7	13	3	5	8	21	....
June	5	9	14	3	10	13	27	....
July	7	5	12	4	1	5	17	....
August	7	7	14	8	11	19	33	....
September	18	6	24	11	7	18	42	....
October	8	4	12	4	8	12	24	....
November	9	9	18	12	4	16	34	....
December	14	7	21	7	10	17	38	....
Total	110	83	193	78	79	157	350	350

(Table No. 7,) GIVING THE BIRTHS BY MONTHS. CLASSIFIED ACCORDING TO COLOR, SEX, AND NATIVITY OF PARENTS.

MONTH.	COLOR. Whites.	COLOR. Colored.	SEX. Males.	SEX. Females.	NATIVITY OF PARENTS. Both United States	NATIVITY OF PARENTS. Both Foreign.	NATIVITY OF PARENTS. Father alone Native.	NATIVITY OF PARENTS. Father alone Foreign.	Total Births by Months.
January	243	29	144	128	145	55	15	57	272
February	265	41	160	146	190	68	10	48	306
March	256	35	137	154	173	58	10	50	291
April	196	29	115	110	137	32	8	48	225
May	194	25	116	103	132	36	1	47	219
June	164	16	84	96	108	40	7	25	180
July	234	19	146	107	126	47	16	52	253
August	221	31	137	115	154	36	19	43	252
September	185	25	125	85	118	47	16	39	210
October	172	17	91	98	114	28	7	40	189
November	207	18	119	106	125	35	35	25	225
December	105	11	51	65	68	19	8	21	116
Total	2442	296	1425	1313	1590	501	152	495	2738

(Table No. 8,) GIVING THE MARRIAGES BY MONTHS CLASSIFIED ACCORDING TO COLOR AND NATIVITY.

MONTHS.	Both Whites.	Both Colored.	Husband alone White.	Husband alone Colored.	Both United States.	Both Foreign.	Husband alone United States.	Husband alone Foreign.	Total.
January	119	36	......	......	120	12	6	17	155
February	92	32	1	......	101	6	1	17	125
March	79	24	......	......	83	9	....	11	103
April	80	14	......	1	73	12	3	7	95
May	89	10	......	......	60	19	7	13	99
June	99	14	......	1	95	5	1	13	114
July	75	10	1	......	61	7	2	16	86
August	57	25	1	......	59	3	2	19	83
September	80	25	......	......	69	19	2	15	105
October	93	13	......	......	79	8	2	17	106
November	90	20	......	......	96	3	1	10	110
December	96	20	1	......	102	2	3	10	117
Total	1049	243	4	2	998	105	30	165	1298